D0152351

A History of the Conservative Party

A History of the Conservative Party

This series, originally to have been published in four volumes, will now be appearing in five, of which those asterisked have already been published. The series was established by an editorial board consisting of: John Barnes, Lord Blake, Lord Boyle of Handsworth and Chris Cook.

* The Foundation of the Conservative Party 1830–1867
Robert Stewart

* The Age of Disraeli, 1868–1881: the Rise of Tory Democracy
Richard Shannon

The Age of Salisbury, 1881–1902
Richard Shannon

* The Age of Balfour and Baldwin 1902–1940
John Ramsden

The Conservative Party since 1940
John Ramsden

The Age of Disraeli, 1868–1881: the Rise of Tory Democracy

Richard Shannon

Longman
London and New York

Longman Group UK Limited,

Longman House, Burnt Mill, Harlow,
Essex CM20 2JE, England
and Associated Companies throughout the world.

Published in the United States of America
by Longman Inc., New York

First published 1992

British Library Cataloguing in Publication Data
A catalogue record is available from the British Library

Library of Congress Cataloging in Publication Data
Shannon, Richard.
The Age of Disraeli, 1868–1881: the Rise of Tory Democracy / Richard Shannon
p. cm. — (A history of the conservative party)
Includes bibliographical references and index.
ISBN 0–582–50713–8 (csd).
1. Great Britain—Politics and government—1837–1901.
2. Conservative Party (Great Britain)—History—19th century.
3. Disraeli, Benjamin, Earl of Beaconsfield, 1804–1881. I. Title.
II. Series.
DA560.S44 1992
324.2414'09'034—dc20 91–37163
CIP

Set by 5EE in 10/12½ Bembo

Produced by Longman Singapore Publishers (Pte) Ltd.
Printed in Singapore

Contents

Part III Disraeli's High Years, 1874–8

Part IV The Undoing of Disraelian Conservatism, 1878–81

Abbreviations used in footnotes

Note: Throughout the footnotes the place of publication is London unless otherwise specified.

AR	*Annual Register*
BL	British Library
Buckle	W.F. Monypenny and G.E. Buckle, *The Life of Benjamin Disraeli, Earl of Beaconsfield*, 2 vols (1929)
CCO	Conservative Central Office
Cecil, *Salisbury*	Lady Gwendolyn Cecil, *Life of Robert, Marquis of Salisbury*(1921)
Clayden	P.W. Clayden, *England under Lord Beaconsfield* (1880)
Derby Diary	The diaries of the 15th earl of Derby, Liverpool Record Office
Hardy, *Diary*	Nancy E. Johnson (ed.), *The Diary of Gathorne Hardy, later Lord Cranbrook, 1866–1892* (Oxford 1981)
Hanham	H.J. Hanham, *Elections and Party Management, Politics in the time of Disraeli and Gladstone* (1959)
HP	Hughenden papers, Bodleian Library, Oxford
Kebbel, *Speeches*	T.E. Kebbel (ed.), *Selected Speeches of the late Earl of Beaconsfield* (1882)
Morley	J. Morley, *The Life of William Ewart Gladstone* (1905)
NUCCA	National Union of Conservative and Constitutional Associations: Conference Minutes, Bodleian Library Oxford
PD	*Hansard's Parliamentary Debates, Third Series*
PRO	Public Record Office
QR	*Quarterly Review*

Acknowledgements

My first duty, and pleasure, must be to thank those bodies who generously granted me the inestimable boons of time, space, and money to prepare this book. The Research Awards Advisory Committee of the Leverhulme Trust elected me to a research fellowship, the tenure of which they kindly extended from one to two years. The Council of the University College of Swansea, University of Wales, did not stint the necessary sabbatical leave. The Research Fund Committee of the British Academy likewise from time to time extended its beneficence. The master and fellows of Peterhouse, Cambridge, by electing me to a visiting fellowship, allowed me to enjoy a compound of Cambridge's vast scholarly resources with its finest collegiate amenities.

I am grateful to the owners or custodians of copyright material for permission to publish extracts within the conventions of scholarship and research. In particular I must thank the earl of Derby, Mr Christopher Wall of the National Trust, Hughenden Manor, and Mr A.B. Cooke of the Research Department, Conservative Central Office. Dr Jonathan Parry's assistance I gratefully acknowledge. Lord Blake and Dr Chris Cook have been most encouraging editors. I am much in the debt of Mrs Brenda Rees, Mrs Beryl Claybrooke, and Mrs June Morgan for their technical expertise.

Swansea R.T.S.
1991

'No doubt the history of recent times as it will be written is a very strange history.'

The marquess of Salisbury addressing the National Union of Conservative and Constitutional Associations, St James's Hall, London, 16 November 1897.

Prologue: The name and nature of Tory Democracy

There are difficulties about terms which must at once be encountered. 'Tory Democracy', as one of its most scholarly connoisseurs has observed, is an idea at once potent and elastic.[1] It is also doctrinally notoriously problematic. At a certain long and broad level of historical interpretation its explanatory potency is sufficiently if crudely attested by the fact that since the opening of the democratic epoch of British politics the Conservative party has either monopolised or shared power for 83 of the 124 years since the second Reform Act of 1867 or for 75 of the 107 years since the third Reform Act of 1884. Robert McKenzie and Allan Silver, authors of a standard text on the phenomenon of working-class Conservatism, pointed out that since 1885 the Conservatives have enjoyed a record of electoral success almost unrivalled among political parties in parliamentary systems. They calculate, for instance, that between 1885 and 1918 Conservatives captured or held 47 per cent of parliamentary seats compared with 37.4 per cent for Liberals and 15.4 per cent for other parties. And Conservativism has in the twentieth century distinctly improved upon this impressive performance. Between 1885 and 1918, again, Conservatives polled 48.7 per cent of total votes cast in parliamentary elections, with Liberals polling 38.2 per cent and Irish and Labour sharing the meagre remainder. They conclude: 'From whatever perspective the Conservative electoral record is examined, it remains one of the most striking political achievements in the history of modern politics.'[2] The salient implication of this achievement is that it depended absolutely on the electoral loyalty of a certain mass of 'the great democracy', the artisan and labouring 'occupier' voters successively enfranchised in 1867 and 1884. This critical and necessary mass allowed the Conservative party to remain electorally buoyant and to be the only party politically great throughout both the nineteenth and twentieth centuries.

As to elasticity: if Tory Democracy has not quite meant all things to all men, it has often meant different things to different men. Lord Derby startled the Lords by using the phrase 'Conservative Democracy' during the Reform debates. He was quite familiar with arguments such as had been earlier put to him by Lord Malmesbury that the Tories ought to 'go on to universal suffrage', since the 'labourers', once they had the vote, would very likely vote Conservative.[3] Indeed, ever since the French elections in

1848 Liberals and Radicals had cause to be nervous on this point. At the same time, Conservatives in Britain had to take care not to alienate nervous middle-class voters. Disraeli stressed his abhorrence of unmitigated or 'American' democracy often in the Commons' debates to this end. In the earliest days of its currency as a concept many sceptical Conservatives such as Lord Salisbury dismissed Tory Democracy as a mere 'phantom' and predicted that an electorate with a working-class majority guaranteed the exclusion of Conservatism from control of the House of Commons. This dismal prediction seemed amply confirmed by the general election of 1868. By the time the concept became less phantasmal in the 1880s it remained no less doctrinally elusive. Lord George Hamilton remarked of the years 1881–85 that '"Tory Democracy" just then became a popular cry with some of our stalwart go-aheads, but what it meant was never clear.'[4] The politician most famously associated with the phrase in that period, Lord Randolph Churchill, 'playing the part of the honest rogue', confessed in conversation in April 1885 with the maverick Radical Wilfred Scawen Blunt:

> You ask me to tell you in two words what it is. That is a question I am always in a fright lest someone should put it to me publicly. To tell the truth, I don't know myself what Tory Democracy is, but I believe it is principally opportunism. Say you are a Tory Democrat and that will do.[5]

For public consumption Lord Randolph would offer more demure definitions along such lines as 'Tory Democracy means ancient permanent institutions becoming the instruments of far-reaching reform'.[6]

Other Conservatives of that time, celebrating the existence of what the journalist and writer T.E. Kebbel described as 'the powerful and popular Conservative party of the present day', deprecated the label as a 'contradiction in terms, a solecism'. Kebbel's complaint was about confusion of categories. Properly, he held, it meant a form of government, not a class in the community. 'It would be rash to assert that it was never used in the latter sense by Lord Beaconsfield himself; but it is, nevertheless, a very misleading use of the term.' Disraeli was pre-eminently the Conservative statesman whose genius led him, in the words of *The Times*, to discern in the inarticulate mass of the English populace 'the Conservative working man as the sculptor perceives the angel prisoned in the block of marble'.[7] But Disraeli, as Kebbel pointed out, always carefully drew a distinction between 'popular privileges and democratic rights'. The former was consistent with 'great inequalities of condition'; the latter not. He certainly never intended to establish democracy as the form of government. As the keeper of Disraeli's historical reputation Kebbel insisted that he used the term 'only under protest'.[8]

Kebbel's protest illustrates the abiding power of solecism. And to solecism add bad faith. Many less sympathetic definers have alleged that the 'contradiction in terms' is one of dishonesty as much as logic. Tory Democracy, they accuse, is a fictional device whereby Conservatism conceals behind a mask of mythic working-class privilege its real visage, which is one of middle-class advantage. The original *locus classicus* of the Tory *embourgeoisement* theory is the Positivist Frederic Harrison's 'The Conservative reaction' in the *Fortnightly Review* of March 1874. Shocked by the unexpected Conservative electoral success of the previous month, Harrison explained what other astounded and dismayed Liberals could account for only as an 'untoward event' by interpreting it as a matter of middle-class aberration. But he saw the consequences and implications as nonetheless profound. 'There is nothing now exclusive about the Conservative party. It is, in the old sense of the words, just as popular and democratic as the Liberal party.'

Then there have always been true believers willing to use 'popular' and 'democratic' without any sense of constraint or reserve. Harold Gorst, the son of Churchill's Fourth Party henchman John Eldon Gorst, offered what can be called the Authorised Version. Disraeli's great achievement, he argued, was to have 'organized and educated the Conservative party'.

> When he entered Parliament the Tories were a party of privilege. He saw the democratic tendencies of the age, and grasped the fact that the people would not remain satisfied with the Reform Act of 1832. The Tories, as he found them, were a party doomed to failure. He took them in hand and educated them. He formed out of them a great national and popular party, and taught the people of this country that the Conservative was their true friend. He created that generous and almost forgotten doctrine called Tory democracy.[9]

The process by which that generous doctrine was reanimated after Disraeli's death and then, goes the argument, ultimately betrayed by the Old Identity leadership under Salisbury and Balfour, was recounted by Harold Gorst in *The Fourth Party* of 1906. It was indeed in that year that his disillusioned and disaffected father finally abandoned the Conservative party as a lost cause and stood (unsuccessfully) as a Liberal candidate in the next general election on free trade principles. Sir John Gorst defined the elixir he alleged he could never get his old party to swallow: 'It is democratic because the welfare of the people is its supreme end; it is Tory because the institutions of the country are the means by which the end is to be obtained.'[10] And it was as a converted Liberal MP that Randolph Churchill's son Winston in 1906 winningly offered the world the biography of his father in which Lord Randolph's public flourishes of the 'excellence and soundness of true Tory principles' as 'animated by lofty and liberal ideals',[11] were wrapped in a warm glow of solemn filial piety and persistent political myth.

But what in the hands of the Gorsts and the younger Churchill was the occasion of bitter indictment or polemical regret in an epoch of deserved political retribution, became in the hands of others in more spacious times and better fortunes for the party an eirenic of reconciliation and a formula for recalling the Conservative party, 'in an age of threatening plutocracy', to a 'true sense of its inheritance and duties'. Thus Lord Henry Bentinck in his *Tory Democracy* of 1918:

> Under the leadership of Disraeli, the influence of Randolph Churchill, and the guidance of Salisbury, the Tory party realised its true destiny; it rose above the mere interests of a class, and became a great national party; standing for great principles, it identified itself with the welfare and happiness of the people.

By the 1950s, with the younger Churchill leader of a peacetime Conservative party, the wheel of semantic history had turned full circle. Iain McLeod proclaimed in 1954 that 'Disraeli started the idea of the Tory Democracy and Lord Randolph proclaimed it; Lord Randolph's son today is at the head of a team of ministers that is trying to put it into practice'.[12]

Such difficulties about terms will never be reconciled to universal contentment, even among Conservatives – perhaps especially among Conservatives. Summary expedience must at a certain point be imposed. For present purposes it is expedient to assert that while Tory Democracy was a famous crux of doctrinal dispute, that very fame allows it to transcend the polemic level of contraverted doctrine and to attain to a status of blandly descriptive historical category. *Habent sua fata libelli.* That ironic fate would greatly appeal to the ghost of the elder Churchill's sardonic and cynical turn; it would outrage the ghost of the priggish and prefectorial elder Gorst.

Thus: 'a great national and popular party'; 'the powerful and popular Conservative party of the present day': these are held to be the descriptive consequences of 'the rise of Tory Democracy'. This book's purpose therefore is to attempt to explain how and why the Conservative party became and remained, in the first epoch of our democratic politics, great, national, powerful, and popular.

It was certainly not all of these things in the 1860s. It possessed certain historical claims to greatness founded upon appeals to the memory of the Younger Pitt as mediated mainly through Canningite propaganda; and to appeals to carefully selective memories of Peel. Plausible claims about its national character could also be asserted, though with waning conviction as failed general election followed failed general election. Popular and powerful the Conservative party decidedly was not. Lord Derby, its leader since the calamitous split of 1846, had held office briefly as prime minister of minority governments on occasions when the hegemonic Liberals chose to quarrel among themselves. He had come to office for the third time in 1866 on just such an occasion. A group of anti-reform Liberals in the Commons was led by Robert Lowe into what John Bright denounced as the 'Cave of Adullam' to join the Conservatives to block the Reform Bill proposed by Gladstone on behalf of Russell's ministry. Russell resigned forthwith. It was a jubilant matter of exchanged congratulations with Disraeli, the party's leader in the House of Commons, when in June 1867 Derby could celebrate while still in office the anniversary of that accession. There had been times in the early 1860s when Disraeli himself was hard put to keep the faith. He said to his whip, Jolliffe: 'We must trust to providence which always guards over the Conservative Party.'[13] Sir George Grey was a characteristic Whig when, at a

Grillion's Club dinner in February 1871, he remarked affably on the 'constant predominance of his party', which, as the embattled Tory Gathorne Hardy had to admit, 'is certainly curious'.[14]

By 1900 all was changed. Indeed, it was 'a very strange history', in the bemused words of Lord Salisbury, who had the most reason of any man to say them. Yet the theme of Conservative success in the later nineteenth century has curiously been little attended to. Dr. Martin Pugh, an eminent Liberal scholar, writing in 1985, remarked that 'the Conservative half of society is still largely awaiting its historians'. He commented further: 'Historians of socialism, often suspicious of political leadership, tend to exaggerate the significance of the rank and file. Consequently a tiny organisation such as the I.L.P. has attracted a disproportionate share of the attention of researchers.' He added a devastating point to that comment: 'It is a sobering thought that the total paid membership of the ILP in 1900 has been put at 6,000, a figure equivalent to the paid membership of the Primrose League in Bolton at that time!'[15] Neglect of the Conservative side of politics, he continued, has led to a 'somewhat unbalanced impression of historical development', with the march of mind and the march of time being seen in Liberal or Labour colours. Dr. Pugh has himself helped impressively to redress that imbalance with a fine study of the Primrose League. Others, as the pages following will acknowledge, have helped towards redress no less impressively. But still the resistance of the clerisy and the academy to Conservatism – especially to a Conservatism now of the market – remains the given cultural constant. Salisbury in wonderment celebrated in 1897 the deliverance of the Conservative party from the demolition he had himself mordantly predicted in 1867. The later enemies of Conservatism have equal cause to wonder at the 'very strange history' of that deliverance.

Perhaps this neglect is explained in Dr. Pugh's conclusion that 'ultimately Conservatism has proved comparatively elusive'[16] as a system of ideas. Conservatism is undoubtedly either much more or much less than a system of ideas. Liberalism and socialism are both heirs of the Enlightenment science of ideology, the foundation of what Disraeli always used to define contemptuously as 'philosophic politics'. And it was a very characteristic Tory of the present century who denounced 'intelligentsia' as 'an ugly name for an ugly thing'.[17] A socialist scholar, Dr. Brian Harrison, has contended that Conservatism's 'real strength often lies in silence. The historian is therefore less likely to be able to depict Conservatism satisfactorily either as doctrine or as party programme, but is obliged to look into the informal, underlying conservatism which reveals itself in ill-defined but widespread phenomena such as patriotism, monarchism, and imperialism.'[18] Both these historians find it easy to believe that 'the popular sentiments characteristic of the era of Lord Salisbury remain only just beneath the surface of British society'. That may well be so.

Certainly, this present study will not attempt to depict Conservatism, satisfactorily or otherwise, either as doctrine or as party programme. It will attend to matters of doctrine and programme when it is necessary that they be attended to. The Conservative party has often been in possession of something roughly describable as a doctrine, and it used occasionally to be (*pace* Disraeli), and latterly invariably is, in possession of something describable as a programme. But it could exist, and flourish, without the second, and perhaps even without either. What it has never been, however, is silent. The following pages will, it is to be feared, testify only too faithfully to that fact.

Notes and References

1 R.F. Foster, 'Tory democracy and political elitism: provincial conservatism and parliamentary tories in the early 1880s', in A. Cosgrove and J.I. McGuire (eds), *Parliament and Community* (Belfast, 1983), 148–9. See also W.J. Wilkinson, *Tory Democracy* (1925), 14, on its 'very spacious significance'.

2 R. McKenzie and A. Silver, *Angels in Marble. Working Class Conservatives in Urban England* (1968), 11–12.

3 *Ibid.*, 36.

4 Lord G. Hamilton, *Parliamentary Reminiscences and Reflections, 1868 to 1885* (1917), 200.

5 W.S. Blunt, 'Randolph Churchill. A personal recollection', *Nineteenth Century* (1906), 407.

6 T.E. Kebbel, *Lord Beaconsfield and Other Tory Memories*, (1907), 254.

7 McKenzie and Silver, *Angels in Marble*, ii.

8 Kebbel, *Lord Beaconsfield and Other Tory Memories*, 256, 259.

9 H. Gorst, *The Earl of Beaconsfield* (1900), 225–6.

10 Buckle, ii, 709.

11 W.S. Churchill, *Lord Randolph Churchill* (1906), i, 240.

12 Conservative Political Centre, *Tradition and Change* (1954), 65.

13 P. Cohen, *Disraeli's Child. A History of the Conservative and Unionist Party Organisation* (unpublished, CCO, 1964), i, 18.

14 Hardy, *Diary*, 126.

15 M. Pugh, *The Tories and the People, 1880–1935* (1985), 2.

16 *Ibid.*, 3.

17 Lord Cobham, while governor-general of New Zealand, used this phrase in the aftermath of the Suez crisis.

18 B. Harrison, *Separate Spheres* (1978), 241.

Part I

From Derby to Disraeli, 1868

Chapter 1

'Re-establishing Toryism on a national foundation'

Challenging the Liberal borough monopoly

Benjamin Disraeli, chancellor of the Exchequer and leader of the House of Commons in Lord Derby's third ministry, wrote to Lord Beauchamp in April 1867: 'There are, no doubt, breakers yet ahead, but I feel great hope of overcoming them, and of realising the dream of my life and re-establishing Toryism on a national foundation.'[1] Disraeli hoped on the strength of the new broader electorate he planned to create by the Reform Bill he had lately introduced to an amazed House of Commons.

From the Reform Act he eventually saw through parliament in 1867 – 'the happy opportunity' as he later called it, 'to enlarge the privileges of the people of England'[2] – Disraeli got rather more of an extended electorate than he had bargained for in April. His and Derby's strategy at that time had been to produce at some conveniently distant date in 1868 a carefully balanced borough electorate wide enough to outflank the existing 'sleek, narrow-minded, dissenting rulers of the boroughs'[3] who embodied the Liberal hegemony, but not so wide as to make a disturbingly unpredictable 'democratic' preponderance. As it turned out Disraeli found himself throwing these carefully contrived distances and balances to the winds and ended up in 1867 adding nearly 1 million new voters to the existing electorate of just over 1 million. Theoretically the borough electorate was increased by 138 per cent. But in fact complexities of registration meant that the immediate increases were often not so dramatic as many hoped or feared.

Derby and Disraeli sowed a wind and reaped a whirlwind. The essence of the affair had been that the Conservative minority in the Commons could get a majority for a Reform Bill only by a tacit compact with a sufficient number of Liberals who were both willing to defy their leader, Gladstone, and eager to squeeze Disraeli to see how far they could sell their support to a point beyond what Gladstone would have given them and at which Disraeli could still deliver his own, rather nervous, party. Left to themselves, the Conservatives in the Commons would have preferred either to continue blocking the Liberal reform policy in alliance with Whigs and resistant Liberals as had happened in 1866, or to make a deal with Gladstone to ensure the most anodyne possible degree of franchise extension. Disraeli, with Derby's backing, insisted on the bolder manoeuvre of discovering the point at which a substantially united Conservative party could be persuaded to meet the advanced party of radical Liberals and pay their blackmail. That point was found to be 'household suffrage' in the boroughs. Disraeli audaciously allowed himself to be hustled and blackmailed into conceding what amounted to an 'occupier' franchise of adult urban males founded on the principle of residence in rateable premises. This was dramatically stretched to include the very large class (estimated at half a million) of ratepayers who 'compounded' with their landlord to include rate charges within the rent. The one concession to caution within this frenzy of electoral adventure was acceptance of Cairns's amendment in the Lords which provided that in eight of the largest English borough constituencies voters would have two votes when electing three MPs (and in the case of the City of London three votes when electing four MPs). Cairns's purpose in this 'cumulative' system was to ensure that minorities in the great cities who possessed the 'greatest amount of property and intelligence' could secure a degree of representation.[4]

Apart from this finicking 'cumulative' amendment (which, by stimulating Radical electioneering counter-measures, failed almost entirely in its Conservative purpose), Disraeli's Reform Bill left the spirit of the ancient constitution unbreached. As with the act of 1832 the medieval tradition of two-member borough and county constituencies remained largely intact. Aside from a little judicious redistribution to add more county divisions and tidy away encroaching urban infections the counties were left very much as they were. A new £12 county rating franchise was introduced, adding to the already arcane complexities of county registration. The Conservative party was already strong in the counties. There would be no advantage in tampering with them. The new £12 voters were calculated to top up Conservative strength.

The substantial purpose of franchise reform in 1867 from the point of view of the government of Derby and Disraeli was to make a big enough change in the borough franchise to put into question the political future of the borough constituencies. These were much more numerous than the county seats. More to the point, they had hitherto been the chief source of Liberal electoral strength. The Conservative party had failed consistently in all elections since it lost its majority in 1846 to penetrate and demolish the Liberal borough hegemony. What would now come of the huge increase of the overall borough electorate? Lord Derby himself, a famous horseman, had candidly described his government's reform gambit as 'taking a leap in the dark'. He rallied his doubting fellow peers by insisting 'Don't you see how we have dished the Whigs?'[5] But many Conservatives could not see this 'great experiment' in so breezily sporting a light. To them Derby was bluffing: making a virtue of a cynical gamble he had weakly and unnecessarily allowed Disraeli to foist upon him. Their poetic voice was Coventry Patmore's bitter evocation of 1867:

> The year of the great crime,
> When the false English Nobles, and their Jew,
> By God demented, slew
> The Trust they stood twice pledged to keep from wrong.[6]

This kind of thing, like Carlyle's equally hysterical fulmination in 'Shooting Niagara', could to a great extent be discounted as beyond the bounds of sober public discourse. But no public discourse was more sober than that of Sir Michael Hicks Beach, MP for East Gloucestershire, who avowed that 'very many, including myself, felt that this was something like a repetition of Sir R. Peel's betrayal'.[7] Lord Carnarvon wrote to the duke of Richmond: 'Household suffrage will produce a state of things in many boroughs the result of which I defy anyone to predict.'[8]

There was no convincing answer to that proposition, which is why Carnarvon, along with Lord Cranborne (soon to be 3rd marquess of Salisbury) and General Peel, resigned from the cabinet as being unwilling to share responsibility for so reckless a gamble. Cranborne's philippic in the October *Quarterly Review*, 'The Conservative surrender', commented so pungently on Disraeli's political honour as to make personal and social intercourse between them impossible for more than six years. Carnarvon's electoral calculations, however, were more to the immediate point. They suggested to him in the case of Leeds, for example, that an existing electorate of some 8,500 would burgeon to something like 35,000. 'Is there anyone who dares to say', asked the dismayed Carnarvon, 'what will be the character and tendency of that constituency? It may be good or bad: but it is a revolution.' Carnarvon's calculation proved in fact to be quite accurate. And while many of the smaller boroughs were relatively unaffected, the large industrial centres such as Leeds would unquestionably reflect the same kind of electoral revolution. It was not possible to calculate accurately the overall numbers involved. Stanley remarked in January 1869 that it was 'singular that we cannot ascertain with any approach to certainty the numbers of the enlarged constituency. According to an estimate in one of the magazines, it is probably between 1,700,000 and 2,000,000, or about equal to one-fourth of the total adult males of the country.'[9]

Conservatives could, of course, hope that it would be a revolution to their advantage. There was much canvassing of the idea of the 'Conservative working man', the artisan who might well feel no compelling sense of political identity with Liberal employers of labour or Radical or Nonconformist shopkeepers. Working men's Conservative clubs or associations had existed since at least the 1830s. Something might be done to enliven the tradition. But it was far from being strong enough in 1867 to reassure anxious Conservatives like Carnarvon that the monarchy, the aristocracy, the territorial constitution, and the established Church stood in no danger if from out of electoral revolution were to come political democracy.

Yet Disraeli's pragmatic counter-argument convinced most Conservatives that the prize was worth the risk. The only chance of loosening the Liberal grip on the boroughs would be by an enfranchisement larger than that proposed by the Liberal government in 1866. That was to have been a genteel Liberal topping-up exercise. By upsetting it Disraeli created two possibilities. The first was that he had merely aggravated the existing Liberal borough ascendancy. In that case little was lost to Conservatives who were already hopelessly disadvantaged. The second was that somewhere beneath the social stratum of reliably Liberal support there might be hitherto untapped resources of popular Toryism. Most Conservatives accepted, with varying degrees of trepidation, Lord Derby's sporting view of the game. As they had little joy of the boroughs as things were there was nothing to lose by going for a big change and hoping for the best. Disraeli put the matter on to a more formal basis in his Mansion House speech at the end of the session. His theme was to contrast the 'national' principles of Conservatism with the 'cosmopolitan' principles and jargon of Liberalism. He deprecated fears of democracy by insisting that what the Conservative government and party had summoned into being was the reality of a truly national politics.

> I have seen in my time several monopolies terminated, and recently I have seen the termination of the monopoly of Liberalism . . . the Tory party has resumed its natural functions in the government of the country. For what is the Tory party unless it represents national feeling?[10]

Having thus launched their great gamble in the boroughs it was now up to the Conservatives to make the most of it and get the artisan vote into deliverable condition. Markham Spofforth, principal agent of the party and representative of the Conservative managerial legal firm of Baxter, Rose, Norton & Company, presented Disraeli in August 1867 with an American axe and an English saw, 'both I am told of the finest temper'. 'Should you flatter me by using them in the woods of Hughenden I trust the effect will be as benign to your timber as your eloquence and policy have been to the monopoly of the Liberal Party!'

> We have commenced organizing the new Boroughs. Good local candidates are already cropping up for some of them. We must get the newly enfranchised into good training – by management. But this requires funds.[11]

Management and funds were not in themselves sufficient to break the Liberal borough monopoly, but they were supremely necessary. They were also supremely present and available in the Conservative party. The central problem confronting Derby and Disraeli at the end of 1867 was by no means that the party lacked money. What was lacking was rather a resolute will to match the parliamentary achievement of the Reform Act with a corresponding organisational response. It has been established that the most 'pernicious' effect on the long-term prospects of the Conservative party after 1846 was that the counties and boroughs consistently returned a 'large enough Conservative bloc to Westminster for the party to avoid looking elsewhere for new support'.[12] The party's fortunes after 1867 still depended on overcoming, one way or another, this structural impasse. What becomes evident is that Disraeli was a great deal more nervous about getting the 'newly enfranchised into good training' than he had been about getting them into being. Disraeli had brilliantly put into question the political future of the borough constituencies. But he proved to be much less brilliant in returning his answer.

Since Disraeli's reforms from 1853 the Conservative party had become, by the standards of the time, something of a model of management. Those standards imposed severe limits on any degree of centralised organisational effectiveness. The nineteenth century may not have been quite the golden age of the independent member of the House of Commons, but it was decidedly the golden age of independent local or constituency political management. The disciplines provided by lavish Crown patronage and honest bribery in the eighteenth-century style or stricter central party control in the twentieth-century manner were not available for party managers in the days of Peel or Derby or Disraeli or Salisbury. It is also true that since the first Reform Act and electoral disaster in 1832, Conservative attention to party organisation clearly mirrored Conservative apprehension of structural disadvantage in the new electorate. But sharper and more intensive methods of garnering votes were in themselves insufficient to create the critical mass necessary for a structural breakthrough. Disraeli's 'immense interest' in organisation was well known. Kebbel recalled that 'he often referred to his own success as a party leader, and I have known him contrast his own reconstruction of the party after 1846 with Peel's reconstruction after 1832'.[13] Disraeli was always punctilious and assiduous in providing morale-building sessional dinners for his Commons followers; and he would extend this amenity as leader of the party. By the 1860s and 1870s the serried ranks of busy clerks in the Victoria Street chambers of the party's management firm were a notably impressive sight. Cranborne in 1867 testified to the Conservative party's becoming 'famous for its organization and prompt discipline'; 'elaborate and successful electioneering became one of the attributes of the party'.[14] All that elaborate electioneering could achieve had been achieved in 1859 and 1865; which, in the nature of the electorate, could not as yet be success in carrying a general election.

As party chief in the Commons Disraeli was fortunate in his aides. On taking the Exchequer in 1866 he engaged as official private secretary Montagu Corry, the 28-year-old son of H.T. Lowry Corry, Disraeli's colleague as first lord of the Admiralty in Derby's cabinet and brother of the 3rd earl of Belmore. Adroit and winning, Corry promised Disraeli he would give 'all my time and energies to the Conservative cause'.[15] Disraeli ever after had cause to bless the moment they met, at Raby in 1865. Corry as smooth factotum quickly gained and deserved Disraeli's entire confidence, and proved especially to be his perfect *alter ego* among the party managers. The greatest of these was William, Lord Nevill, from 1868 5th earl of Abergavenny.

A Conservative zealot, Nevill became the prime money-gatherer of the party and the most influential of its back-room eminences. It was Nevill who presided along with the chief whip, Colonel T.E. Taylor, over the disbursement of party funds. It was Nevill who plucked his own 'confidential agent' Spofforth from the party's management firm of Baxter, Rose and Norton and recommended him in 1859 as principal agent in place of Philip Rose, whose position had been compromised by charges of corruptly tampering with petitions on electoral bribery. Nevill was an active member of the committee which in 1866 set up the *Yorkshire Post* in Leeds. In that year also he took over superintendence of the National Conservative Registration Association, established originally in 1863 at the instance of Lord Shrewsbury, to systematise the already fine arts of county party agents' procedures in their most important responsibility, the registration of electors. From the first Nevill took a keen interest in the foundation of the Junior Carlton Club in 1864, designed precisely, as Colonel Taylor explained to Disraeli, 'as a central point for county solicitors, land agents, etc. – who are winning and are to win our elections'.[16] Spofforth was able to assure Disraeli by the end of 1867 that it had 'been the greatest success and of material benefit to the Party'.[17] Nevill's cousin by marriage, the hostess and raconteuse Lady Dorothy Nevill, dubbed him 'the Tory bloodhound' for his indefatigable zeal in the Conservative cause. Disraeli had cause to tell Spofforth amid the disappointments of the 1865 elections:

> I am sure what I have seen of Lord Nevill throughout these affairs has made me often wish that I had such a man by my right hand in public life. I have never known an instance of such fiery energy and perfect self control united with all those personal qualities which make exertion with such an inspiring comrade a labour of love.[18]

Nevill, later dubbed also 'the Great Panjandrum of the Tories' and the 'great electioneering Warwick',[19] was no doubt also flattered by Disraeli's hyperbole: 'What, my supporter! Why, he is my leader, my head, my chief.'[20] Yet when Nevill undertook the initiative in fulfilling the organisational logic of the new borough electorate what becomes most evident is an absence of inspired comradeship amid a political labour of love.

Precariously founding the National Union

1

Following on from the precedent of the National Registration Association for the counties, Nevill conceived the project of gathering together existing Conservative borough associations, societies, constitutional clubs, working-men's clubs, instituting such where none existed, and forming them into a national association or union in England and Wales. 'The National Union', as its first secretary later explained,

> has for its object the forming of a Centre from which while repudiating any appearance of dictation will endeavour to give unity of idea & of action to the Constitutional Associations which are in course of formation throughout the country. It has been established by Viscount Nevill and is guided by his advice and direction and has met with the hearty support and concurrence of very many influential members of the Constitutional Party.[21]

The term 'Constitutional' was often preferred to 'Conservative' at this time and in this area of activity as being less likely to be compromised in the view of working men with the kind of social and political taint some might hold against the formal party name, or for that matter the informal name of 'Tory.'

Nevill and the allegedly very many influential members of the party cherished no high directive ambitions for the National Union. The essential work of mobilising a Conservative vote in the constituencies would always, it was assumed, be a local matter. Nor was local suspicion of, and resistance to, any hint of central authority or direction ever to be underestimated. Nevill's plan was to provide a central focus which would offer assistance, guidance, and general stimulus for local activity where it was needed and requested. Many new local borough associations had sprung up during the Reform excitement, and it was highly expedient for the party to encourage them to continue in existence. It was equally expedient to encourage the formation of local borough constituency bodies where none existed. Above all it was desirable, in the new era of borough household suffrage, to stimulate consistency and persistency in electoral work. The prevailing habit was that organisation, like the flowers of the desert, bloomed only during the rain of money at times of electoral contests. At such grateful times agents and canvassers were hired in profusion; otherwise the electioneering land lay dead and untilled. There were, moreover, strict limits on the National Union's range of reference. It was to have no competence outside England and Wales. Since 1853 Irish party affairs were in the hands of the Central Conservative Society of Ireland. Taylor, the chief whip, was an MP for Dublin County, and so provided a strong connection with headquarters. Scotland remained virtually a Conservative wasteland. The counties also were strictly out of bounds. Counties had always looked down upon boroughs as vulgar and inferior; an attitude decidedly enhanced among county Conservatives by the new artisanal borough electorate. As Randolph Churchill was to complain in 1884 on behalf of the Council of the National Union, 'the counties have fought very shy of us'.[22] The counties of England and Wales were in 1867 in the aristocratic hands of Major the Hon. Charles Keith-Falconer, secretary of the County Conservative Registration Association, lodged next to Messrs Baxter, Rose, & Norton, of Victoria Chambers, Westminster.[23] Keith-Falconer also attended to any Scottish business in London. This demarcation was to last until the comprehensive reforms of Akers Douglas and Middleton in 1886–7, after the counties had swallowed an even more drastic dose of democracy than the boroughs gulped in 1867.

As his borough organising demiurge Nevill selected a young barrister and promising politician, Henry Cecil Raikes. Defeated by Willy Gladstone for his hometown Chester seat in 1865 and then in a by-election at Portsmouth in 1866, Raikes took eagerly to the work as a way of building a reputation in the party. He started with the immense boon of having already been denounced at Chester by Willy Gladstone's father as 'the most impudent young man in England'.[24] He welcomed the opportunity to foster a popular 'Constitutionalism' (being of that Tory stripe which deprecated 'Conservative'). Raikes impressed Nevill as 'a man of remarkable genius, a splendid speaker', and most likely to become 'some day . . . *leader* of the Commons House'.[25] Nevill had one of the Lewes seats in view for him in the great East Sussex Nevill domain centred on Eridge Castle. This intended patronage was actually frustrated by the redistribution aspect of the 1867 Reform; Raikes eventually won a Chester seat in 1868. He worked very hard in the mid and late months of 1867, helped by young friends, mainly barristers like himself: A.G. Marten, William Charley, and W.C. Harvey, vetted by Spofforth as 'zealous and respectable'.[26] Another young recruit was Edward Clarke, later famous as solicitor-general. To Clarke, the son of a City silversmith, Raikes appeared as 'one of the ablest of the younger followers of Disraeli', 'tall and thin, with kindly smiling eyes, and soft deliberate voice, a poet and a scholar'.[27] Raikes had already engaged himself with various journalistic ventures (very much a follower of the young Disraeli). He cherished ideas in 1865 of a 'new Conservative paper on really sound principles'. He managed, with Spofforth's encouragement, to get the London evening *Globe* for the party in 1866.[28] In the following year he started the weekly *Imperial Review*, 'in conjunction with Mr. Luckie (afterwards owner of *John Bull*, part proprietor and editor)'. This 'ill-fated' paper, though 'patronized to some extent by the party, and supported by some of the cleverest writers of the day, failed to gain much hold upon the affections of the public', and foundered 'after about a year and a half'.[29]

The same fate seemed likely to hang over the nascent National Union. With 'much labour and travelling' Raikes and his helpers fought to overcome hostility, indifference, and inertia. Clarke recalled the daring, unprecedented, and downright dangerous provocation of speaking at an open meeting at Swansea. Hostility of a different kind came mainly from the already well-established associations, especially in Lancashire and London. The 'enlightened manufacturing centres of Lancashire, where intelligent operatives had organized themselves into working-men's political associations',[30] saw little benefit to be had from Raikes or remote Nevill, but consented reluctantly to send representatives to preliminary conferences in the north convened to urge the gospel of union. In London the Westminster Association financed by the newsvending magnate W.H. Smith could be prodded into acquiescence by its patron. Much more problematical was the Metropolitan London and Westminster Conservative Association, the largest of all, already itself with a considerable connection with associations throughout the country, probably hoping 'to rise to a position of supreme authority', at some not too distant date, and planning to hold a grand banquet at the Crystal Palace, Sydenham, in November 1867 to celebrate the government's Reform Act. Raikes observed glumly that its 'moving spirits . . . regarded the new venture, in spite of its official character, with suspicion as likely to interfere with their operations and lessen their importance'.[31] Among these 'moving spirits' was another young barrister, soon to be its secretary, John Eldon Gorst, MP for Cambridge borough since 1866. Gorst was a budding politician with very much the same ideas and ideals as Raikes. Thus began the uneasy connection between the two ambitious rival exponents of popular Toryism, whose jockeyings would provide the subplot to the affairs of the National Union for many years to come.

For his labours Raikes deserved well of the party. Spofforth in August 1867 was sure the Conservative party would never be out of Raikes's debt for his 'continuous and unremitting exertions'. He hoped, along with Raikes, that the party would have 'Conservative Working-men's Associations established in every borough in England, those to be in communication with the Conservative Union'.[32] The secretary of the projected union was to be 'a *protégé* of Lord Nevill's' and a fellow Yorkshireman of Spofforth's, Leonard Sedgwick. Disraeli was informed through Corry that

> Leonard Sedgwick a Yorkshire gentleman has undertaken at Lord Nevill's desire to organise the various working-men's Conservative Associations throughout the country – and Mr. Colleton Rennie, son of Sir John Rennie and a barrister, is helping him. They want one or two questions as to the constitution of their Union decided, the chief of which at present is whether members of the government will countenance the scheme. I think it would be well if you saw Mr. Sedgwick.[33]

At that time the plan was to inaugurate the union with a flourish, by exploiting the opportunity provided by the London and Westminster Association's Crystal Palace project. However, Raikes was to find to his dismay that, on top of the suspicion directed at his own venture by the London and Westminster Association, the party leaders were far from enthusiastic about any large manifestation of working-class Conservatism. Countenance from the official chiefs of the party for such an occasion would be the *sine qua non*. There were clearly grounds for anxiety on that point. Raikes himself wrote to Corry the following day inquiring specifically 'what part, if any, members of the Government are likely to take with regard to the proposed Conservative demonstration at the Crystal Palace'. He stressed that Sedgwick was 'acting in the matter for Lord Nevill'. 'I am sure Ministers will not fail to recognize the importance of making such a demonstration successful, and I need scarcely add how important an element of success would be supplied by the presence of any, even subordinate, member of the Government.'[34]

Disraeli had already been alerted by his chief whip, Taylor, who hoped that he would soon be able to report that 'our "Working Men's Constitutional Association", is established'. Taylor had circularised Conservative MPs a few days earlier after the prorogation 'and the answers are very generally satisfactory'. Colville, the Lords' whip, would do the same shortly. Taylor had 'advanced for present purposes money sufficient to carry on with & propose placing its expenditure at the joint discretion of Nevill & Gerard Noel', Taylor's assistant whip. Taylor would confer immediately with Nevill and Spofforth about latest developments.[35] Meanwhile, the guardian of the counties, Keith-Falconer, commiserated with Nevill about the impending obligations assuredly about to descend upon him. 'All this must be a great bore for you, but it is the result of your popularity and the great confidence they have in you.' Keith-Falconer reported that Mr. Bennett of the London and Westminster Association, hard at work canvassing for the coming election of Poor Law guardians in the parishes of Westminster, 'invariably winds up by saying "if Lord Nevill is only good enough to help us our success is a certainty"'. Keith-Falconer continued in a less touchingly anecdotal vein:

> It is quite wonderful the way these working men devote their time and energy to politics. I trust however that we shall not be like Frankenstein, & have raised a spirit that we cannot control! – it is a dangerous power to give them, but they are so determined to have it, and all we can do is to keep them on the right road.

Keith-Falconer hoped that Nevill would be willing to come up from Eridge to lend his presence to the inauguration, which would do more for its success than all the others put together.[36]

Images of the monstrous problem Dr. Frankenstein created for himself in Mary Shelley's novel no doubt obtruded on many another anxious Conservative mind with a turn for literature. The obstacles which began to obtrude upon the union's inaugural plans had to do originally, however, with more mundane considerations. Taylor declared to Disraeli on 20 September that he found himself in a difficulty: 'our good and zealous friend Nevill, with some of his A.D.C.'s, holds a different opinion from me on a rather important point.' Disraeli may have heard of a proposed working-men's banquet at the Crystal Palace. The promoters were anxious that members of the government 'and even of the cabinet' should attend. But Taylor feared a repetition of what had happened earlier in the summer at St. James's Hall when a Conservative working-men's demonstration in support of the government's Reform policy became an embarrassment; 'and Spofforth, who has reliable information entertains a similar apprehension.' A 'fiasco, if the Government were ostensibly identified with the demonstration, would of course be very damaging'. Taylor took issue with Nevill over what should be done:

He thinks that we should openly encourage it, & make ourselves responsible for its success. I on the contrary advise that the dinner, having been advertised, should go on, but the promoters should privately be allowed to understand that we approve but that no members of the Government should attend.

Help with expenses would be given; but recalling that the expenses of the sorry St. James's Hall affair still caused trouble, Taylor urged the importance of the party's not falling into a 'second scrape of that kind'.[37]

It appears that Disraeli needed little urging in that way. He disliked the class separatism embodied in the associations and their projected union. There is little doubt also that he was concerned about the negative impression such a working-class emphasis would have on nervous middle-class opinion.[38] He was in any case engrossed at this time with preparations for the great Edinburgh banquet in his honour planned for the end of October and the opening of the brief autumn session due to commence on 19 November. By contrast, Derby seems to have been much more relaxed about the affair. When Nevill wrote to Spofforth early in November about Raikes's proposal to circularise all Conservative MPs and peers soliciting support for the 'Constitutional Union', he indicated that it had been prepared by 'Col. Taylor Mr. Noel Lord Colville & yr humble servant', and approved by 'Lord Derby and others of the cabinet'. Nevill remembered showing it to Derby's son and heir, the foreign secretary, Lord Stanley, 'who thought it excellent'.[39] The Stanleys were, after all, familiar enough and easy with Lancashire working-class Toryism. The point here was that Spofforth had been instructed by Disraeli through Corry to suppress the circular and to make sure that no members of the government were named in it as indicating official endorsement. Given this dampening response it is little wonder that Nevill wished 'to heaven this Crystal Palace business was well over'. He was, he assured Spofforth, indeed 'bored', and had refused 'point blank' to preside. 'I quite approve of it but too much is expected of me.'[40] It was left to Noel to pacify Disraeli about Raikes's circulars. 'You can tell the Chancellor of the Exchequer', he assured Corry, 'that I have issued some, but only to Officials of the Govt. The circular was concocted by Taylor, Colville and myself, and I was told had been seen and approved by Lord Derby or I should not have sent them out.'[41]

All this left Raikes flailing away to little purpose. In all matters concerning the Conservative party it was necessary to have Lord Derby's approval. But in matters particularly concerning the Conservative party in the House of Commons it was essential to have Disraeli's countenance as well. As between the rival versions of popular Toryism represented by the actual London and Westminster Association and Raikes's projected national Union, the party leaders decided to back the former. The Crystal Palace affair would be countenanced; Raikes and his Union would be left to fend for themselves. There is more than a touch of pathos in Raikes's letter to Corry from 'The Conservative Union', 19 Henrietta Street, Covent Garden, enclosing a letter from Lord Dartmouth 'whom Lord Nevill wished me to secure as Chairman of the Committee of the Union. You will see that he declines to act.' Failing Dartmouth Raikes lowered his sights and was 'very desirous to secure Mr. Russell Gurney in that capacity'. Would Corry kindly give Sedgwick an introduction to Gurney (MP for Southampton and recorder of London) 'which may lead him to consider the proposal favourably?' 'The arrangements', Raikes pointed out, 'require speedy completion.'[42] Evidently Gurney was as little forthcoming as Dartmouth. The Conservative National Union would come into the world unbaptised and unblessed by the Conservative hierarchy.

Meanwhile, the Crystal Palace demonstration went splendidly ahead. Two thousand members of metropolitan and provincial constitutional associations dined on 11 November to celebrate Reform and to consecrate the happy union of 'Altar, Throne and Cottage'. Derby and Disraeli wrote encouraging letters and regretted their inability to attend. The government was represented by Lord John Manners, flanked by a decent assortment of conservative MP's. Raikes's union venture was thus hopelessly upstaged. All he could do was tag along pathetically at the Crystal Palace and make a rather desperate response and late toast to 'success at the Conservative Conference.' That bedraggled conference, snubbed, perforce took place the following day (12th November) humbly at the South London Freemason's Tavern. *The Times* woundingly noticed the Crystal Palace event as an 'agreeable introduction to a tedious conference' held at the Freemason's Tavern.[43] There was no lustre, no ministerial presence. The conspicuous absence of official countenance was underlined by the doubly ironic circumstance that the chair was filled, *faute de mieux*, by the obscure young MP, John Gorst, who was probably attending as a hostile observer from the triumphantly rival London and Westminster Association.

2

Gorst's almost comically false position in the chair at the inaugural National Union conference set the seal on the anomalous and ambiguous relationship thereafter between the union and the party leadership. The National Union had come into being in spite of the leadership and almost in spite of its original instigator, Nevill. Although a few notables eventually allowed their names to be used as honorific officers, even Gorst's embarrassment was patent in the apologies for the absence of the few hoped for grandees, Lords Holmesdale and Dartmouth, and Gathorne Hardy, the home secretary. Apart from Raikes, the only 'name' present was Spofforth. The 97 pages of the minutes of proceedings record delegates from 65 associations and branches. It was, Gorst explained rather desperately, a 'business meeting', not a meeting to discuss Conservative principles, which all were agreed upon. The great task was to fix upon a method of organisation 'which may make those Conservative principles effective among the masses'.

Declaration of general intent was made by the honorary secretary, Raikes's associate Harvey. The working classes of England 'sometime back' commenced forming themselves into associations to support the present government upon the question of Reform, 'and to maintain the fundamental principles of our ancient constitution'. It was felt that 'their position would be strengthened and their influence augmented' by the formation of a central union. Conferences had been convened, Harvey explained, in 1867 to consider the question, which were 'numerously attended by representatives, especially from the northern districts.' This new union would afford a centre of communication and action between local associations. There was, 'of course, no intention to interfere in any way with local action'; the object of the union was to strengthen the hands of local associations where existing and to encourage establishment of associations in districts where they were wanting; 'and further, to organize associations by the holding of meetings for the general expression and diffusion of constitutional principles, and the dissemination of sound information upon topics of general public interest, and to secure the combined action of all constitutional associations'.[44]

The conference adopted a set of rules for procedure, membership, and affiliation and voted down ('Hisses and confusion') a proposal that the word 'Conservative' be left out of the union's title as calculated to deter working men from supporting it. Several delegates resisted election to the union's ruling council on the grounds that working men, quite apart from the difficulties they would have in finding the time and meeting the expenses of regular attendance, were inappropriate to such offices. One delegate proposed that the council 'should be of a mixed character, comprising both the upper and the working classes'. 'What could working men do there?' asked Mr. Smith of Rotherhithe. 'They required men of influence and men of money. . . . He was a working man and would stick up for the working men, but still he had no business at that board. His business was in his own locality.' Another delegate insisted that the council 'was not the place for a working man, but should be composed of the best men they could possibly obtain'.[45] And, indeed, one of the first promotional circulars issued by the union, *Suggestions for the Formation of Conservative and Constitutional Associations*, placed at the head of its practical advice the adjuration to secure persons 'of position and influence' to take the leading part.[46]

Disraeli would no doubt have been gratified to hear such impeccably deferential accents of working-class Toryism. There was little sign of any threat of 'dangerous power' in the list of the elected officers: Dartmouth as president, Holmesdale as chairman of council, flanked by an assortment of peers and MPs (including Nevill) as vice-presidents. Raikes became vice-chairman. The one augury of possible resistance existed in Gorst's place as a member of the council. But at that time Gorst was much more of a dangerous threat to the National Union itself than he was to the party leadership. Sedgwick thought it well to make sure Disraeli was kept reassuringly abreast of developments and intentions. He wrote to Corry a long justificatory letter on the objects and working mode of the union, covering himself with the caveat that 'in our infancy, as we are at present, it is difficult to define anything strictly'.

> We think the local associations strong as they are in themselves will be improved by central organization, that more uniformity of action will be secured & that much of local diffidence and difficulty will be removed by an extended action & the consequent reliance that individuals will have that they are acting under the well-considered advice of those who are best competent to judge the actual or probable working of a particular course of action. We propose that in every large town there shall be an association in each parish or ward, that each such association numbering not less than 100 members shall send to a central committee one representative, that the secretary of this comm^{ee} shall be a person in whom we have confidence who shall be the channel of communication between the National Union and every parish or district of the Town.

Hence there would be 'a machinery' acting throughout the country by which ideas at headquarters might be rapidly conveyed. 'We think we can do no harm, we hope we may do much good.'

> The failures of the opposition . . . have resulted we think from having to work on uncongenial material. We believe there is a strong constitutional feeling in the people at large requiring only to be guided & directed by energy & example. . . . We believe we are not too sanguine in the matter but are prepared at all events if the plan meets with approval to work it with steady perseverance.[47]

Immersed now in the autumn session and distracted by his wife's sudden and serious illness, Disraeli could hardly in decency have done other than approve, though he continued to convey through Spofforth his objection to members of the government being involved. Soon Sedgwick was dispatching circulars from Henrietta Street bearing a handsome National Union device, a garter surmounted by crown and sceptres, asking associations to provide him with all relevant particulars of their circumstances and plans. Raikes confirmed with Corry that while members of the government might not be officers of the Union there was no objection to the present list of notabilities remaining. After all, as Raikes emphasised, 'we wish to be as obedient as possible'.[48]

That was not exactly the humour in which Gorst envisaged the union's role or his own role in the union. Indeed, he continued to work for the London and Westminster Association to such effect that Raikes feared for the life of his fragile new-born creature. 'Gorst's immense capacity for organization was of the greatest value' to the London Association, 'which began seriously to threaten the position and independence of the Union'.[49] The danger indeed became serious and eventually it was resolved only by Gorst's being appointed principal agent of the party in place of Spofforth in 1870 and by his subsequent encompassing the union within the framework and premises of the new Conservative Central Office which he set up.

3

Since proclaiming the end of the Liberal monopoly in August Disraeli had himself lived in interesting times. Great demonstrations were arranged to honour the party leaders. Lancashire feted Derby at Manchester in October, where he paid generous tribute to Disraeli's tact, temper, and judgement in seeing the great Reform matter to its triumphant conclusion. Disraeli was invited to a banquet at Edinburgh, where the keener Scottish Conservatives were intent on striking a blow against the Liberal monopoly at its most monopolising. Disraeli was initially reluctant. It was enemy country. Scotland held unhappy memories for him personally. His health troubled him. The duke of Buccleuch and other Scottish Tory grandees were lukewarm. The queen pressed with untimely hospitality that he must take in Balmoral on his way – which meant far out of his way. This was the kind of occasion when Corry came into his own. Corry reflected the inner party view that a grand Scottish manifestation was both desirable and necessary. Corry set about keeping his chief straight and getting him up there despite himself. 'Evidently a great and valuable demonstration and expression of good-will is in store for you', he pressed upon Disraeli; 'and I earnestly hope nothing will intervene to prevent your seizing the occasion.'[50] Corry made sure that nothing did prevent and shepherded Disraeli up to speak on 29 October. Nevertheless, Disraeli attended 'against much advice'.[51]

At Edinburgh, amid tremendous pomp, Disraeli defended the honesty and consistency of his seizing the 'happy opportunity' of doing more in the way of Reform in 1867 than he had prevented Gladstone from doing in 1866. He mocked Cranborne ('a very clever man who has made a very great mistake'). He enrolled himself in a reformist Tory filiation from Bolingbroke through Wyndham and the Younger Pitt and asserted that he 'had to prepare the mind of the country, and to educate – if it be not arrogant to use such a phrase – to educate our party'. This phrase, or variants of it, has since echoed down the years. Disraeli's claim related to larger issues of principles of comprehensiveness and residential rating as the basis of suffrage. He did not specifically insist or admit that his allowing himself to be squeezed by radical Liberals was part of his educating his party by example. But his larger point holds good. Given that the alternatives – junior partnership with the Liberals and Whigs in an agreed limited reform along the lines of 1866, or Cranbornian anti-Reform resistance – were either inexpedient or impolitic, or both, the party had to be cajoled and jostled into adventure. Moving in bold courses was in itself the best political education. If the Conservative party were in truth to prove itself the national party of England (Disraeli never condescended to Scottish sensibilities by using what he held to be the artificial formalism 'British'), it must avoid above all any character of narrowness or oligarchy. In a progressive country, he pronounced, change is constant. The great question is not whether to resist change which is inevitable, but how to manage change in deference to historic customs, laws, and traditions; not on the basis of abstract principle or 'philosophic system'.

> Whenever the Tory party degenerates into an oligarchy it becomes unpopular; whenever the national institutions do not fulfil their original intention, the Tory party becomes odious; but when the people are led by their natural leaders, and when, by their united influence, the national institutions fulfil their original intention, the Tory party is triumphant, and then under Providence will secure the prosperity and power of the country.[52]

Disraeli enjoyed, and perhaps deserved, his well-managed Edinburgh triumph; and then proceeded to an evening meeting of working men at the Music Hall, where an 'enthusiastic reception' and deputations awaited him.[53] He proceeded on the day following to take his degree at the university and to appear at an 'entirely new experiment' in Scotland, an open Conservative party meeting, which successfully established a precedent for so daring a thing. Disraeli had every cause to feel satisfied with the effect of the Edinburgh demonstrations. Possibly the event that most touched him was a note by an anonymous hand which he received on the day following the banquet, quoting prophetically from the second volume of *Contarini Fleming*:

> That beneficent demon who will not desert those who struggle to be wise and good – tore back the curtain of the future and I beheld, seated upon a glorious throne on a proud Acropolis, one to whom a surrounding and enthusiastic people offered a laurel wreath.[54]

Being offered a laurel wreath amid popular acclaim in Edinburgh was for Disraeli a supremely gratifying experience. It was an experience, however, within a largely conventional political mode. The Conservative working men at the Music Hall added a novel twist but did not alter the well-understood shape of things. The triumphant Edinburgh affair sets the snubbing of the National Union in a singularly telling perspective. Disraeli was by no means as yet a new politician to match the new borough electorate, for all that it was there that he needed to obtain new results. The next general election could not be far off. Derby's government would have, in decency, to be allowed time and space in which to get its complementary Reform bills for Scotland and Ireland through parliament. But the life of that 1865 parliament thereafter would depend on decisions made among the majority Liberals in the House of Commons. It was probable they would sooner rather than later break Derby's government. Spofforth would not have many months more to organise and train the boroughs of England. How were Conservative principles to be made effective among the masses? It was by no means apparent that the working men of the National Union were up to it. Gathorne Hardy, deputising for Disraeli in February 1868 in receiving a 'great deputation of the National Union of W.M. Associations' who congratulated the government on its Reform Act, was decidedly unimpressed by the political calibre of the working men. 'I must say it was ill-managed and the speakers of the worst order. I said little. . . .'[55]

The angle of vision of the Conservative party chiefs at this juncture was focussed much too narrowly to take in the scope and implications of so large a question as that of the calibre of its grassroots support. The extra and late parliamentary session had to be coped with, and Disraeli contended with vexing difficulties. Derby was too ill to bear his share of the sessional burdens. Both Disraelis collapsed also at a time when pressing affairs – Abyssinian vote of credit, Fenian outrages, naval scare, education matters, the proposed Corrupt Practices Bill which outraged the judges by handing over to them the invidious onus of deciding between partisan claims, patronage problems – demanded the closest attention of the leader of the Commons during that 'hectic winter'.[56] There were schemes afoot to create a minister of education and a minister of health: projects which Stanley had been pressing upon Disraeli, and which Disraeli was willing to entertain.[57] The larger, strategic question lying beneath the political surface grimly persisted. Re-establishing Toryism on a national foundation looked to be a more problematic venture at the beginning of 1868 than it had in the middle of 1867.

Notes and References

1 Buckle, ii, 262
2 *Ibid.*, 287. See also the previous volume in this series, R. Stewart, *The Foundation of the Conservative Party, 1830–1867* (1978), ch. 17.
3 F.B. Smith, *The Making of the Second Reform Bill* (Cambridge, 1966), 90.
4 *Ibid.*, 212.
5 Buckle, ii, 285.
6 '1867.' Circulated for private distribution 1868. Later published in *The Unknown Eros* 1877, bk i, xiii. B. Champneys, *Coventry Patmore* (1900), 244.
7 Smith, *Second Reform Bill*, 93.
8 Stewart, *Foundation*, 362
9 Derby Diary, 2 Jan. 1869.
10 Buckle, ii, 287.
11 Spofforth to Disraeli, 19 Aug. 1867; HP, B/XXI/s/421
12 Stewart, *Foundation*, 369.
13 T.E. Kebbel, *Lord Beaconsfield and Other Tory Memories* (1907), 21.
14 *QR*, Oct. 1867, 559.
15 Corry to Disraeli, 29 June 1866; HP, B/XX/Co/1. This was endorsed by Corry (cr. Lord Rowton 1880). 'The first letter I ever wrote to Mr D. R. Aug. 23/94!' Corry in the letter reminded Disraeli that they had met 'three years ago'. Possibly Corry misremembered; or possibly Disraeli failed to recall an earlier meeting.
16 Kebbel, *Lord Beaconsfield and other Tory Memories*, 213, 228–9.
17 Spofforth to Disraeli, 30 Dec. 1867; HP, B/XXI/S/442. See also A.W.P. Fawcett, *Conservative Agent* (1967), 53.
18 Lady D. Nevill, ed. R. Nevill, *Reminiscences of Lady Dorothy Nevill* (1906), 71–2.
19 T.H.W. Escott, *Randolph Spencer-Churchill as a Product of his Age, being a Personal and Political Monograph* (1895), 126; P. Cohen, *Disraeli's Child. A History of the Conservative and Unionist Party Organisation* (1964), i, 21.
20 Cohen, *Ibid.*
21 Sedgwick circular, December 1867; HP, B/IX/D.32K.
22 NUCCA, minutes of 18th conference, Sheffield, 23 July 1884, 109.
23 See Keith-Falconer to Corry, 15 June 1868; HP, B/X/B 45.
24 E.G. Clarke, *The Story of My Life* (1918), 95.
25 H. St. J. Raikes, *Life and Letters of H.C. Raikes* (1898), 53–4.
26 *Ibid.*, 60.

27 Clarke, *My Life*, 95.
28 Raikes, *Raikes*, 56–7.
29 *Ibid.*; Clarke, *My Life*, 97.
30 H. Gorst, *The Earl of Beaconsfield* (1900), 123.
31 Raikes, *Raikes*, 59–60.
32 *Ibid.*, 61.
33 J. Ferguson to Corry, 24 Oct. 1867; HP, B/X/8/20a.
34 Raikes to Corry, 25 Oct. 1867; *ibid.*, 206.
35 Taylor to Disraeli, 7 Sept. 1867; HP, B/XX/T/95.
36 Keith-Falconer to Nevill, 1 Sept. 1867; P. Smith, *Disraelian Conservatism and Social Reform* (1967), 117–18.
37 Taylor to Disraeli, 20 Sept. (1867); HP, B/XX/T/99.
38 See Smith's comments, 99–100. See also E.J. Feuchtwanger, *Disraeli, Democracy and the Tory Party* (Oxford 1968), 124.
39 Nevill to Spofforth, 6 Nov. 1867; HP, B/IX/D 32d.
40 Nevill to Spofforth, 6 Nov. 1867.
41 Noel to Corry, 7 Nov. 1867; HP, B/IX/D/32c.
42 Raikes to Corry, 7 Nov. 1867; HP, B/IX/D/32e.
43 *Times*, 13 November 1867, 5. For the Crystal Palace banquet, *Times*, 7 Sept. 1867, 6, and 12 November 1867, 12. Feuchtwanger, 124, incorrectly states that 'the Crystal Palace demonstration never took place', by conflating the rival projects on the London and Westminister Association and the National Union.
44 Minutes of proceedings of the first conference of the National Union of Conservative and Constitutional Associations, 1867, 5–6.
45 *Ibid.*, 92–3.
46 HP, B/IX/D/32a.
47 Sedgwick to Corry, 25 Nov. 1867; HP, B/IX/D/32g.
48 Raikes to Corry, 11 Dec. 1867; HP, B/IX/D/32j.
49 Raikes, *Raikes*, 63.
50 Corry to Disraeli, 14 Sept. 1867; HP, B/XX/Co/25.
51 J.T. Ward, *The First Century. A History of Scottish Tory Organisation 1882–1982* (Edinburgh 1982).
52 R. Blake, *Disraeli* (1966), 482.
53 Buckle, ii. 292.
54 HP, B/X/A/42 (30 Oct. 1867).
55 Hardy, *Diary*, 64.
56 Blake, *Disraeli*, 485.
57 J. Vincent (ed.), *Disraeli, Derby and the Conservative Party, Journals and Memoirs of Edward Henry, Lord Stanley. 1849–1869* (Hassocks, 1978), 327.

Chapter 2

Conducting government on sufferance

Smuggling Disraeli into the leadership

1

One of the most heartfelt reasons Disraeli gave in 1873 for refusing to accept office on Gladstone's resignation was the memory of bitter experiences at the head of a minority government in the 1868 session; 'no wholesale censure, but retail humiliation.'[1] Recalling in 1889 that unhappy time, Gathorne Hardy commented that it was

> not easy to abbreviate the history of our miserable session in 1868, but it was humiliating to be the butt of the mean and the envious, and to be over-ruled as we were. Looking back, I doubt if we could have done otherwise than we did. Disraeli challenged a vote of censure which Gladstone would not move.[2]

Hardy would certainly have welcomed a 'speedier release' than he received eventually from the session at the end of July and from office at the beginning of December, when Disraeli created a precedent by resigning immediately after the results of the general election had become decisive.

It was a bad augury for the session when in January 1868 Derby's health collapsed. He prepared the queen for the impossibility of his carrying on. This raised two problems. A minority government stood all the more in need of a leader of prowess and renown. Derby had been a first-rank politician since 1830. He had been leader of the Conservative party since 1846. He first became prime minister in 1852. Derby's expectation and desire was to carry on the government through 1868 and lead it in the elections as soon as the Scottish and Irish Reform Bills were through and the new registers ready. The ambition he candidly avowed was to crown his public career by breaking the Liberal grip on the constituencies. He had every reasonable ground to count on the necessary time to lead such an offensive and put the new electorate to the test in 1868 or 1869. He was not yet 70 years old. Russell had been 73 when he took office as prime minister in 1865. Palmerston had been 75 when he formed his government in 1859.

The party was as much dismayed by Derby's collapse as the queen. The question of his successor was by no means as straightforward as in the case of Gladstone's succeeding Russell in 1867. This was the other problem. Disraeli was beyond question the second man of the administration, presiding over cabinets in Derby's absence, unchallenged as leader of the Commons. Few grudged him that place. But that very absence of grudge to a great extent depended on the reassuring presence of Derby. Disraeli's origins were so exotic and his career so eccentric as to make his leadership of the party questionable to a degree which only later memorable events caused to fade out of sight. Barrington, Derby's private secretary, discussed the matter with Stanley, who recorded: 'He expects that Ld. D. will shortly wish to retire, that Disraeli will take up the reins, but will not be able to manage the concern: after that, all is uncertainty.'[3] There was the consideration also as to whether his leadership might be a drawback to the party in the country. Disraeli had gained great credit for his bold performance over the Reform issue in 1867. But he had also made many and great enemies, chiefly the remorselessly bitter and formidable Cranborne. And many Conservatives who had applauded his leadership of the Commons in 1867 blanched at the prospect of his becoming leader of the party. Their problem was that they had no candidate both able and willing to interpose. Stanley and Richmond were often enough mentioned, though without conviction. Stanley in any case felt himself bound by many years of special friendship with his father's lieutenant. Cranborne had made himself impossible. The question of Derby's successor as party leader had never been seriously attended to. Prognostication earlier had invariably been about a realignment of parties, based on the presumption of Conservatism's ineradicably minority destiny. When Russell and Gladstone were defeated in June 1866 there was much talk of a new 'moderate party' fusion of Conservatives and right-wing Whigs to be led perhaps by Lansdowne, with Derby supporting out of office and Disraeli exiled to the Lords, to be succeeded by Stanley as leader of the Commons.[4] These ingenious notions withered in the light of Derby's and Disraeli's determination to preserve the integrity of the Conservative party and to bid to fulfil another kind of destiny. It is also material that the question of his succeeding as leader of the party had never seriously exercised Disraeli.

When in February 1868 the immediate contingency of his succeeding first came upon Disraeli, he wrote to Derby that he had 'never contemplated nor desired it'.

> I was entirely content with my position, and all that I aspired to was that, after a Government of tolerable length, and, at least, fair repute, my retirement from public affairs should have accompanied your own; satisfied that I had enjoyed my opportunity in life, and proud that I had been long confidentially connected with one of the most eminent men of my time, and for whom I entertain profound respect and affection.[5]

There is no need to suppose these words disingenuous. Disraeli was but five years younger than Derby and, if anything, seemingly in less robust health. He had no grounds for projecting for himself any significant lease of political life beyond the span prudently allotable to Derby at the end of 1867. Every year that Derby survived after 1867 would have exponentially diminished Disraeli's claims and chances. The most important and least attended to facts about Disraeli as leader of the Conservative party are that his great personal triumph, the leadership itself, and his great political triumph, the general election victory of 1874, came to him as brilliantly unexpected surprises.

Disraeli became prime minister and thereby leader of the Conservative party in February 1868 as a consequence of a benign conspiracy between Derby and the queen. This conspiracy was calculated to present the party with a *fait accompli* and thus preclude any possibility of anti-Disraeli sentiment being allowed vent and scope for articulation. Derby, after all, was well aware that to many resentful Conservatives he was tarred with the same brush as his lieutenant. Cranborne had pointedly referred in his 'Conservative surrender' diatribe to Derby himself as 'one whose Conservative connections were an accident of his career'.[6] Derby was in no doubt that Disraeli had fairly earned the prize and was the best man available; and the queen was of the same mind. Still, this constituted a very odd precedent. Both Peel and Derby had been freely acknowledged as party leaders by a party out of office. The case now was that the party was to have its leader chosen for it by the Crown. The nearest, and from the party's viewpoint, not very reassuring analogies, were George IV's appointments of Canning, Goderich and Wellington. Alerted by Derby that his retirement was unavoidable and imminent, the queen collusively invited Disraeli to Osborne for a couple of days in January. He reported in guarded terms to his wife: 'The most successful visit I ever had: all that I could wish and hope. . . . She spoke of everything without reserve or formality.' Corry, present on business, was informed by the queen's secretary, General Grey, that the queen intended to ask Disraeli to be first minister on Derby's resignation. Derby asked Stanley to 'prepare' Disraeli for the event. Stanley took the opportunity to promise Disraeli 'cordial co-operation and support'.[7] With highly doubtful constitutional propriety, Derby himself sealed the conspiracy in writing to the queen on 21 February:

> if he may be permitted to offer any suggestion to your Majesty as to his successor, he would venture to submit that, as there is no question of any political change, your Majesty should apply to the Chancellor of the Exchequer, who has held the most important, and next to his own, the most prominent post in the present Government. Lord Derby believes that, although with a deep sense of the responsibility attaching to it, he would not shrink from undertaking the duty; and that he, and he only, could command the cordial support, *en masse*, of his present colleagues.[8]

Having thus been privily smuggled into the Conservative leadership, Disraeli kissed hands at Osborne on 27 February. The queen's comments to her daughter, the crown princess of Prussia, were highly indicative of Disraeli's ambivalent situation: 'Mr. Disraeli is Prime Minister! A proud thing for a man "risen from the people" to have obtained! And I must say – really so loyally; it is his real talent, his good temper and the way in wh. he managed the

Reform Bill last year – wh. have brought this about'.[9] For all that Disraeli was indeed the first untitled prime minister Queen Victoria appointed, the phrase 'risen from the people' was hardly apt. Disraeli regarded himself as a person of profoundly innate aristocratic temper and fibre. This was of a piece with his exotic romanticism and his early 'society' novels (which had provoked his father to ask: 'What does Ben know of dukes?' Still, Ben had come to know quite a lot about dukes.) Much more apt was the phrase Disraeli himself is said to have used at the celebratory reception he and Mary Anne gave at the Foreign Office: 'I have climbed to the top of the greasy pole.'[10]

2

Disraeli set about reconstructing the ministry. He took care to confer particularly with Stanley and to keep Derby courteously informed. Northcote advised on the undesirability of Disraeli's attempting to combine the offices of first lord and chancellor of the Exchequer, 'unless it were a temporary arrangement with a view to coalition of some kind; of which I see no prospect'. (So pervasive were such notions still.) Northcote, who had often crossed swords on financial affairs with Gladstone himself, was prepared to take the Exchequer, but felt it necessary for the present to stay at the India Office in times of Abyssinian crisis; and suggested Walpole or, failing that former collapsed home secretary, Disraeli's financial secretary at the Treasury, Hunt. Northcote had a way of suggesting Hunt to Disraeli always as the second man in prospect (as in January: 'Cave and Hunt on our side' were the only men in the Commons of the right stature as 'parliamentary financiers').[11] But for Disraeli the 6 foot, 4 inches, over 21 stones Ward Hunt was the first prospect, 'and I have prepared the Queen for it', he told Derby. In this matter he was also able to please Delane of *The Times*, always a point of high concern. Delane's 'clear and sagacious judgement came to my aid opportunely', Disraeli blandly assured the mouthpiece of Jupiter the Thunderer.[12]

There was no stint of advice from others. Gerard Noel reported from the whips' office to Corry that, having gathered 'all the information I could' within the party, he heard a 'general wish expressed that Peel should be brought back into the Cabinet. It would be done as I suggested by sending P. up to the Lords.' Disraeli was not likely to have viewed the recapturing of the late Sir Robert's son as a great prize. Stanley was hostile. The general had always been a greater man on the turf than in the War Office. Of more moment was Noel's further advice: 'I am also sure it would be advisable to make overtures to Cranborne. He would not accept but it would please the party.'[13] Philip Rose urged the case a little more positively: 'I have seen Montagu Corry and I cannot help hoping that you may see your way to make an offer to Cranborne tho' I cannot hazard even an opinion as to the result. All I can say is that I have observed a change of tone of late both on his part & that of a relation of his.'[14] This was asking much of Disraeli. But on any calculation the advantage to the party of bringing Cranborne back into harness was worth the risk of extreme incivility; almost as great as the disadvantage of his roaming unharnessed among the back benches. There was no question of an invitation being addressed directly; Northcote was deputed to make the delicate overture, which duly met with a decisive snub.

Cranborne's refusal of office at least left room for fewer rearrangements. Stanley's appointment to the Foreign Office in 1866 had been widely thought a mistake; but there was no moving him now. Disraeli was too much in debt to the house of Stanley. Disraeli kept Hardy at the Home Office ('You, who are my sword-arm'),[15] Lowry Corry at the Admiralty, Pakington at the War Office, and Lord John Manners (an old Young England comrade) at the Office of Works. Lord Mayo also continued as chief secretary at the Irish Office. One cabinet colleague Disraeli determined to be rid of was Lord Chancellor Chelmsford. Disraeli's animus against Peel's former attorney-general had less to do with formal disqualifications alleged ('feeble in council, useless in debate') than with Chelmsford's remissness in laying out his 'prodigious' patronage candidly for the service of the party. He found a more robust partisan in the Ulsterman Hugh Cairns, former attorney-general and now lord of appeal; whose advancement was also stipulated for by his friend and fellow churchman, Hardy. Disraeli also wanted to drop the veteran Malmesbury as Lords' leader. A strong team would be necessary there, he felt, if only because of Cranborne's imminent elevation (he succeeded as 3rd marquess of Salisbury in April). But his preferred choice, Marlborough, was unavailable, and Malmesbury agreed to stay on to see the 1868 session through. Richmond kept the Board of Trade and Buckingham kept the Colonial Office. The only basis upon which Disraeli would have welcomed Carnarvon back there would have been as part of a deal with a reconciled Cranborne.

Thus Disraeli had the gratification of presiding over a cabinet including three dukes of decently adequate ability (Buckingham, Richmond, and Marlborough as lord president) and a ducal younger son (Manners). The strong 'new men' were Cairns and Hunt. Disraeli soon came to look to Cairns as the clearest brain and weightiest adviser among his colleagues. Of the veterans of 1859 vintage only Stanley remained a front-rank force, as much through dynastic connection as innate talent. His ex-Whig father's retirement from the leadership exacerbated his own fundamental dilemma: was he really a Liberal falsely positioned? Most prominent among the 1866 vintage was Stafford Northcote, who first made a reputation as Gladstone's assistant; a Peelite who entered the Commons too late to follow Peel. As much as with Stanley, his natural political habitat was that ground upon which coalitions with Whigs and moderate Liberals were congenially projected. Of the generation that came to the front in 1867 Gathorne Hardy was the foremost, combatively Tory and churchly, very different in temper from both Stanley and Northcote.

3

Reconstructing the Conservative government at the beginning of 1868 was a much easier matter than deploying it for Conservative purposes. Its first purpose was simply to stay in office. There would be advantages from the point of view of eventually dissolving the House of Commons. The disadvantages of not being in government for general elections had been brought home in 1865. Government wielded the inducive weapons of patronage. More to the point, the patronage secretary of the Treasury (as the Commons' chief whip was designated when in office) disposed annually of £10,000 from the Secret Service Fund. It was a recurrent theme of these times that Liberal monopoly of office and therefore of patronage had allowed Liberalism to cement its hegemony with the inducements of places, perquisites, and honours. The Conservative party and the Conservative cause had been starved and debilitated. Time was needed to make opportunities for this kind of healing political balm. Disraeli had, furthermore, his own personal motives for office. He wanted to make his mark and his name as prime minister. He had no taste for flitting across the political stage (to use his own phrase from *Endymion*) 'a transient and embarrassed phantom'. He no longer suffered acutely from the financial embarrassment which had earlier compromised his honourable ambition for office.[16] All the more did Disraeli enjoy the power and circumstance of the queen's first minister. Especially did he enjoy his new relationship with the queen. 'He can only offer devotion', he wrote to her on 26 February; which, as Buckle commented, 'set the tone'.[17] Disraeli's notorious zest for gallant blandishment and flattery of his widowed royal mistress expressed a genuine romanticism within himself. But always behind it were practical, even cynical, motives. Often nerve-stricken and wilful in matters small and great, the queen had to be carefully and cleverly managed. Gladstone was hopeless at it; and Disraeli would later avow to Stanley that 'to keep in good humour the Queen is in itself an occupation'.[18] To an embattled minority government it could matter crucially whether prerogative smiled or frowned. This might – as indeed it did – apply particularly to questions of the survival of the government and the timing of the dissolution of parliament. There was guile as well as glee in Disraeli's message to Corry from Osborne on 28 February: 'All is sunshine here: moral & material.'[19]

The urgency of the case of Ireland

1

The new session at Westminster promised little in the way of sunshine. The vulnerable Conservative government could expect accommodation of sorts to get necessary and acknowledged public business through, but little mercy otherwise. Gladstone took defeat badly and was casting about for some great stroke to restore the unity of the Liberal party and nullify the humiliation of the turn of events in 1867. Disraeli's unexpected succession to the premiership added insult to injury. But quite apart from Gladstone's volcanic personal frustration Derby's departure and Disraeli's coming to the front made a decisive difference. Derby commanded respect and forbearance among Whigs and Liberals which Disraeli simply did not. This circumstance bore important implications. It became increasingly clear through 1867 that the problem of Ireland would come soon to the political forefront. A series of incidents of 'Fenian' inspiration in Canada, in Ireland itself, in Chester, and in Manchester (where a policeman was killed) were in themselves abortive and politically inconsequential. But a greater public stir was caused in December 1867 when an attempt to engineer a break-out at Clerkenwell gaol in the City of London by means of explosives led to much loss of life and many injuries. Gladstone converted this public stir into political ammunition by interpreting terrorist outrages as Ireland's cry of distress. At Southport he declared that Irish Catholic grievances in the matter of the Protestant Church establishment ministering to a small minority of the people of Ireland, tenure of land, and education ought to receive sympathetic attention. This resonant declaration reverberated with memories of Gladstone's definition in 1865 of his view of the future status of the Irish disestablishment question: 'perhaps five years, perhaps ten years.' The pace of political movement since then exceeded Gladstone's expectations. The great issue of Reform was now resolved. What should the great new reformed electorate be asked fittingly to address itself to? The government was thus confronted with a veiled but formidable menace.

Derby had been a battle-hardened warrior in the Irish political wars since the 1830s, when he defended Whig reform policies against resistant young Tories such as Gladstone. Derby would not in 1868 have been the target of any enthusiastically united Liberal assault on Irish ground. But Disraeli was quite a different matter. He had no standing in Irish affairs. He inherited from Derby a flimsy Irish policy. This consisted of a Royal Commission on the Irish Church establishment designed to recommend concessions sufficient to pre-empt radical demands for disestablishment and disendowment and an initiative to offer a charter to a Roman Catholic university to relieve pressure on the Anglicanism of Trinity College, Dublin. These manoeuvres were modestly calculated to attain the optimum balance where Irish and Roman Catholic demands were decently appeased and British and Protestant susceptibilities not dangerously strained. Gladstone's intervention signalled the need for less leisurely tactics. At the same time, in cabinet 'the church question was approached with great caution, Cairns being known to have strong opinions upon it'. Cairns, indeed, was convinced that 'if the Irish Church goes, which he sees to be probable, the English will follow within twenty years'.[20] The government responded in a pre-sessional speech at Bristol by Stanley. The foreign secretary, flanked by other members of the cabinet, declared that the condition of Ireland was indeed 'the question of the hour'; and enlarged on the 'painful, the dangerous, and, to us, the discreditable state of things which unhappily continues to exist in Ireland'. These matters would shortly demand the intervention of the legislature. However, on the main point at issue, the question of the Protestant Church establishment, Stanley reserved from immediate attention as being 'inexpedient'. It 'ought not to be the work of a dying Parliament, returned by a constituency which is itself about to be considerably modified'.[21]

Stanley's highlighting 'the urgency of the case of Ireland' served, among other things, to bring home the extreme precariousness of the government's parliamentary situation. Solicitor-general Baggallay had to be denied the vice-chancellorship, simply, as Cairns insisted, because his Hereford seat was 'not *trustworthy*'. Taylor the whip must 'smooth him over.'[22] Disraeli concurred: 'Now we must not lose another seat, or we really shall tempt the enemy to action.'[23] 'Tempting the enemy to action' was code for an eruption by Gladstone on Irish Church disestablishment. This dramatic recourse was much in Gladstone's mind. But it was treacherous political ground that had to be trod warily. Gladstone never forgot the trouble Whigs and Liberals had got themselves into in the 1830s over Irish ecclesiastical matters. He warned John Bright, an eager disestablishmentarian, that to take up the cause of Irish disestablishment 'may again lead the Liberal party to Martyrdom'.[24] As against that, Gladstone was very ready to insist that the government's strategy of leaving the matter over to the new parliament was unacceptable.

As long as Gladstone lay thus circumspectly low Conservative ministers could indulge themselves in ingenious Irish plans. There were in fact considerably differences of opinion among them about the Irish Church. Pakington and Stanley were the most prone to be critical of it and to lean towards a more or less radical approach to it; Cairns and Hardy were its sturdiest defenders. Disraeli himself was widely rumoured to be pragmatically ready to 'dish the Whigs' on the Irish Church question as he had done on Reform.[25] At this stage the government's position was one of fairly latitudinarian compromise. 'I was anything but displeased with the tone of the cabinet today on the crucial question', Disraeli told Cairns on 2 March; 'I think you and I may not only steer the ship thro' all the difficulties – but in time – which is wanted – tranquillize a chronic irritation.'[26] The tranquilliser in view was a revival of old and never very convincing schemes from the days of Pitt and Castlereagh and the ministry of 1858–9 for concurrent endowment in Ireland of Roman Catholicism and Presbyterianism, between them the confessions of the overwhelming majority of the people of Ireland. Lord Russell for the Whigs and Archbishop Manning for the Catholics both seemed friendly. Although as an Ulster churchman personally opposed to concurrence, Cairns was sure the cabinet 'came to the only resolution *possible* for a Conservative Government'. Much would depend on the way words were used in the Commons. 'I think it would be desirable,' he advised Disraeli, 'even in hinting at a scheme which wd ameliorate the position of R.C. & Presbyt^{n} ministers, to put it that this was for the new Parlt.'

> If Gladstone & his friends go for anything *like* Ld. Russell's proposition they will fail signally. If they throw it over, & go for complete disendowment of every body, they may catch voluntaries, radicals, & anti-popery men, & make a formidable phalanx.[27]

Meanwhile something more solid would be offered parliament in the way of an Irish Land Bill to deal with aspects likely to attract general 'concurrence of opinion' and to provide for a further commission to inquire into remaining issues of controversy; and the Irish Chief Secretary Mayo would also prepare the ground by launching the government's project for a charter and even some finance for a Roman Catholic university in Dublin. There was 'great difference of opinion in the Cabinet on the merits of the question', Disraeli reported to Derby, 'but there was unanimity that it ought not to be treated except in a new Parliament; and also that no pledge should be given of maintaining absolutely unchanged the present state of ecclesiastical affairs.'[28] Derby's blunt but unseasonable advice was to 'abstain from making any proposition whatever' on the Church issue; 'your safety is to sit still, and instead of shewing your hand, to compel your adversaries to exhibit theirs, with all their discrepancies and contradictions.'[29]

Early in March Disraeli made his first public appearances as leader of the party. They were not overwhelmingly reassuring. His ministerial statement for the Commons on 5 March slithered uneasily between eagerness to please and too characteristic rodomontade.

> With reference to domestic policy, I say at once that the present administration will pursue a liberal policy. [Cries of 'Hear!'] I mean a truly liberal policy – a policy that will not shrink from any changes which are required by the wants of the age we live in, while, at the same time, we will never forget that it is our happy lot to dwell in an ancient and historic country, rich in traditionary influences that are the best security for order and liberty and which form the most valuable element of our national character and our national strength.[30]

At a 'well-attended' party meeting at the Home Office the following day the new leader, as Hardy recorded, 'spoke well but told nothing as was the case in the House itself'. Hardy foresaw 'storms & doubt if the ship will not founder'.[31] Disraeli was not in a position to adopt Derby's sturdily negative line that no likely Catholic gratitude would make it worth while disturbing traditional Conservative Protestant loyalties. Admitting the urgency of the case of Ireland, Disraeli was bound to attempt a positive lead calculated to pre-empt or spoil any Liberal initiative. Even with a majority behind him in the Commons such a lead would have been an awkward manoeuvre. As the head of a minority government Disraeli's predicament was that his lead more than anything else, *nolens volens*, provided a focus against which the Liberals could begin to unite.

By the end of the debate on the address Gladstone nerved himself to strike. Desperate Liberal party illness called for desperate Irish remedy. Nothing else offered itself readily. The autumn session in 1867 had left the Liberals as disunited as ever. There was an urgent need to outbid the government's Catholic university bribe. As Argyll candidly avowed when asked to explain the sudden convergence of Liberals upon disestablishment of the Church of Ireland, 'there really was no other way of getting Dizzy out of office'.[32] Gladstone's announcement on 16 March of his conviction that the Anglican establishment in Ireland should be swept away altogether as grossly unrepresentative of the religious beliefs of the Irish people and of his intention to bring before the Commons resolutions to that effect was a carefully calculated risk.[33] Hardy recorded that his speech was 'extravagantly violent', and that Disraeli replied 'skilfully & with much humour in parts'.[34] Cairns congratulated Disraeli on his 'great achievement.' 'The issue on which you have placed our Policy with Gladstone is excellent.'[35] As Kebbel often pointed out, Disraeli was always at his ecclesiastical best on the general ground of the efficacy of establishments of religion.

Gladstone's sweeping proposal, Disraeli told Cairns, 'has come upon us like a thief in the night'. Conservatives felt they had a right to be indignant that, in the midst of their efforts to wind up the session and the parliament, Gladstone had chosen, at a few days' notice, to propose to disestablish the Church of Ireland. Disraeli conveyed to Cairns his 'present impressions as to the critical position at which not only the Cabinet, but the country, has now arrived'. Disraeli's view was that the Conservative government 'ought to hold, that the whole question of national establishments is now raised; that the Irish Ch. is but a small portion of that question; & that those who wish to demolish it must be held to desire the abolition of national establishments in the three kingdoms'. His strategy was to 'detach the Irish Ch. as much as possible from the prominent position of the subject, for, there is no doubt, it is not popular.' He hoped that 'if the principle, that the State should adopt & uphold religion as an essential portion of the Constitution, be broadly raised, a great number of members from the North of England & Scotland, called Liberals', would be obliged 'to leave the philosophic standard'. Disraeli wanted Cairns to draw an amendment in such high and broad tones which could then be introduced to 'one or two leading spirits' and then imposed upon their colleagues rather than having an 'unprepared cabinet' resolve on the ground of the lowest common denominator. 'There ought to be no faltering on my part in that case', Disraeli explained, speaking as a tyro in Irish Church affairs. This recessive tactic on Disraeli's part of leading indirectly through Cairns contradicted his bold assertion: 'We are on the eve of great events, & we ought to show ourselves equal to them.'[36]

Disraeli's public response in reply to a memorial from Lord Dartmouth on behalf of the National Union expressing confidence in his leadership was in the same strategy of detachment and in the same exalted tone. It was, he insisted, really a 'crisis in England' rather than Ireland, for the purpose was now avowed to destroy that 'sacred union between Church and State' which had hitherto been 'the chief means of our civilization and is the only security of our religious liberty'.[37] This was sound strategy given Disraeli's manifest weakness on Irish ground. Gladstone tabled his three harsh and peremptory resolutions on 23 March proposing disestablishment and disendowment of the Church of Ireland. The government's response on 27 March, however, was an amendment in far less bold terms from the one which Disraeli had intended that he and Cairns impose; and it was to be moved by Stanley, notoriously second only to Pakington in his coolness to the cause of the Irish Church. It was to be a case of discretion rather than valour. Perhaps the very brutality of Gladstone's stroke stunned and unnerved the cabinet. At all events the high tone diminished. The amendment admitted baldly that 'modifications of temporalities might be expedient', but that disestablishment 'ought to be reserved for the decision of a new parliament'. Hardy glumly described it as merely a 'dilatory move'.[38]

Even so the very baldness of Stanley's speech leading the government's case against Gladstone caused a sensation. John Bright long savoured the pleasurable spectacle of gentlemen opposite sitting 'almost aghast'[39] as Stanley feebly affirmed the proposition that 'some modification, be it what it may, in the *status* of the Irish Church establishment is to all appearance inevitable'.[40] Hardy had an equally long but extremely painful memory of the occasion. 'Our champion was Stanley! Anything so disheartening as his speech was never heard. The cry of a whipped hound! The party was dismayed and Cranborne's taunts were felt because deserved.'[41] Why was so 'ill-chosen' a champion selected? The long and short of it was undoubtedly Disraeli's 'faltering' on being bereft of Cairns's guiding brief. This left him adrift. The queen advised Disraeli *'carefully to avoid'* anything likely to encourage a spirit of retaliation among Protestants and to show 'moderation and forbearance' despite all provocation.[42] Stanley was the rational choice for such a role. He was *prima facie* also the best choice for enticing moderate Liberals to leave the 'philosophic standard'. Stanley himself saw the case he had to argue as one of 'extreme delicacy', for it was 'impossible not to see that even on our own side, the feeling is all but universal that some great change must take place in the status of the Irish Church'.[43] Unfortunately for the government, Cairns's prediction about the 'formidable phalanx' of 'voluntaries, radicals, & anti-popery men' which Gladstone might catch with 'complete disendowment of every body' proved to be nearer the mark. Disraeli tried to repair the damage by getting Hardy to intervene and rally the shaken Conservative ranks. Hardy found 'all the symptoms of disorganisation, aggravated by an attack from Cranborne, sneering as regards us all; venomous and remorseless against Disraeli'.[44] After Hardy's gallant counter-attack the party 'seemed to rally again'; and Gladstone looked 'stern and black'. But Gladstone looked set now to have what Disraeli defined as the best repartee, a majority.

By the end of March Conservative prospects had deteriorated markedly. Northcote proposed that the cabinet consider their course in the event of being beaten on Gladstone's motion, 'as we pretty certainly shall be'. Northcote wanted a new counter-resolution 'indicating to some extent our own policy', since, by defeating Stanley's dilatory plea, 'Gladstone will have forced our hand, and we ought, at whatever risk, to be prepared to play it.' Northcote envisaged a bid to rescue some last vestiges of the concurrent endowment principle.[45] But Cairns, hostile to any endowment for Roman Catholicism, recognised that Gladstone's comprehensive offer had killed utterly any last lingering interest among Catholics and Nonconformists in concurrence; and preferred a direct negative as 'our only straight & safe course' as asserting 'a principle on which we should not hesitate to speak clearly and distinctly'.[46] It mattered little by now what despairing Conservative ministers on the run proposed. Gladstone disposed in the end of a handsome majority of 56. Hardy was in no doubt that the decisiveness of the defeat reflected accurately the extent of the 'failure on our part'. Disraeli, he thought, did not rise to the occasion, and was 'obscure, flippant, and imprudent'.[47] Cairns, on the other hand, thought it possible to congratulate Disraeli on a 'magnificent speech'; but the only comfort he could take from the surprisingly large majority was that the very magnitude of the defeat would during the Easter recess 'make the country awake to the gravity of the position'.[48] No gloss would disguise the fact that the Conservative leaders had failed signally to show themselves equal to great events.

2

What the Conservative leaders now did show themselves equal to was evading the consequences of great events. They decided not to resign; and held on bravely to that decision for the remaining four months of the parliamentary session and for nearly four more months beyond that. They did so in full knowledge of the pains and penalties involved. 'The Opposition has tasted blood', observed Hardy, 'and will bully and endeavour to control us, so as to place us in minorities constantly.' Hardy did not like his own position in such a government at all, and mused hopefully on the prospect that if Stanley 'would but strike and break us up it would be for the best'.[49] Pakington reviewed the situation to Northcote:

> I don't think we could have resigned after the late division – we should not have been justified and the Q would not have accepted – but I confess I think our position is become very difficult, and I suspect Mayo and Hunt are right that we shall be exposed to vexatious opposition and defeat on all sorts of questions, in the hope of driving us out.

Pakington was sure that recent divisions on army disciplinary matters 'have been the first steps in this course'; and he had heard that Gladstone was planning further attacks in that quarter. The government's 'time of difficulty' would come when Gladstone's resolutions were carried in committee.

> If between this day and that, there is neither rally in the country, nor repentance among the Whigs, I think we must either yield to the completion of their preliminary scheme, and then wait for the dissol^{n}, or, submit to a vote of want of confidence, for which I suspect they would then be able to get their Party together![50]

Ministers justified their remaining in office on the grounds that they had essential parliamentary business to complete, and that a dissolution on the old electoral registers would be highly impolitic while a dissolution on the new registers being assembled would not be possible until after the normal term of the session. It remained to be seen how effectively that resolution could be sustained after the imminent Easter recess. Disraeli reported the queen 'excited' at the present state of affairs 'wh she looks on as very grave, tho' sanguine, that the county will rally to sound views'.[51] The queen visited Derby at St. James's Square on 3 April speaking 'in most unreserved terms of condemnation of Gladstone's motion and conduct'. Derby reported to Disraeli: 'I took it upon myself to say that I had strongly urged you in the event of defeat, not to think of resigning, to which H.M. answered "Quite right".'[52] Derby marked this letter 'most confidential' with good reason: for it heralded the beginning of the queen's vehement policy of doing everything in her power to keep Disraeli in office. Hardy remarked to Disraeli that he had been 'greatly struck by the dread which the Queen expresses of Gladstone and his scheme'. 'The Queen is, as you say, extraordinarily friendly, and anxious not to have a change.'[53]

The respite of the Easter recess was now at hand to allow the country to awake to the gravity of the position and to rally to sound views. Spofforth assured Disraeli that there were promising signs of repentance among the Whigs. 'In London today & at the Clubs there is a very confident expression of opinion that Mr. Gladstone's move will fail & I think the vacation so admirably arranged will be productive of good effect.'[54] Spofforth was already in touch with the 'head of the Wesleyans', hoping to work with his 'Central Board' and use his organisation 'for the purpose of influencing Members to stay away from the next division'.[55] Spofforth was also deep in plans to rally the country. He and Colonel Taylor busied themselves in a campaign to agitate the Protestant political conscience. Disraeli had given an ecclesiastical lead in a letter to a High Church clergyman (dated 'Maundy Thursday', to general public merriment) denying any intention to cast a slur upon the High Church party, but insisting that there was an 'extreme faction in the Church, of very modern date, that does not conceal its ambition to destroy the connection between Church and State'.[56] Disraeli identified a sinister conspiracy of Irish Romanists (with reservations in an effort to keep on terms with Archbishop Manning), the Nonconformist Liberation Society ('shallow and short-sighted fanaticism'), and the Ritualists. Disraeli appealed to his diocesan bishop, Samuel Wilberforce of Oxford, to give a lead to the clergy. The fate of the established Church 'will depend on the opinion of the country as it is directd, formed, and organised during the next eight months'; and it would be very unwise of the High Church to let their imperfect sympathy with the Irish Church – 'a Calvinist branch of the establishment' – neutralise their action.[57]

The principal agent reported to the chief whip on preparations for a Protestant rally at St. James's Hall on 17 April. He found 'already at work' a group of associations 'united for the purpose of the preservation of the Protestant Institutions and Endowments in Ireland': the Church Institution, the Ulster Protestant Defence Association, the Central Protestant Defence Association, the United Protestant Defence Committee, and the 'Federal Union of Conservative & Constitutional Associations'.

> The principal objects of the association will be to organise petitions and meetings in the Boroughs represented by M.P.s returned as Protestants & bring every legitimate power to bear on them so as to induce them to vote against Mr. Gladstone's resolutions or at least to stay away.
> The questions will be continued unremittingly until this object is accomplished – & the Committee will continue to work till the next Genl Election.[58]

The chief whip's side of the operation was to issue a circular:

> Are there any of the leading Liberals in your Borough likely to have been annoyed at the vote of Mr. — and who are well affected towards Church and State? If so send us by return the names of three of four of them.
> Please also send the names of such of your Clergy as are against the proposed spoliation of the Irish Church.[59]

Spofforth reported to Disraeli of the rallying of the Irish bishops and Irish peers through the action of the United Protestant Defence Committee. Letters had been sent to all lay patrons in Ireland and to every beneficed clergyman and curate in England and Wales to sign an address to the queen. Failing the archbishop, the bishop of London would be asked to rouse the English bishops to the danger of the crisis.[60] Corry contributed intelligence to the effect that the 'Protestant cry' would 'land Ministers with a triumphant majority' at the general election – '*if* we can shake off' the Roman Catholic university plan. 'There can be little doubt that Members will return from their Constituencies less keen for immediate action than they were on the 4th inst.' Corry also found much to cheer him in the 'tone of the Press'.[61] Taylor confirmed the point about the Catholic university. 'The more I consider it, the more convinced I am that you should let the Catholic College go, if you possibly can – it is the only drawback to the Protestant feeling in our party.'[62] Spofforth reported to Disraeli further that satisfactory replies were being received as to petitions and the address, 'but we cannot report favourably as to meetings'. 'The North is stirring more than any other quarter. The Clergy are slowly awakening to the crisis. Your letter will do good with the High Church people. The Ritualists have small voting power.'[63] Next day: 'Reports very favourable this morning – the alarm is spreading & I have confidence in your ultimate triumph.'[64] Spofforth indefatigably canvassed the wife of the archbishop of Canterbury, Mrs. Longley, 'who stated the Archbishop was thoroughly alive to the danger and anxious to meet it in the most forcible yet prudent way'. The bishop of Ripon, it appeared, undertook 'to get the Archbishop of York', despite that prelate's distressingly Gladstonian leanings. Placards were 'doing good in small boroughs'. Lecturers and speakers were being sent forth; meetings being organised. 'Upwards of 33,000 circulars have been sent off since last Friday.' Spofforth added slyly apropos of the Protestant rally scheduled for 17 April: 'A riot is likely to take place at St. James's Hall tonight. It will do no harm – probably good. Measures are taken.'[65] Under the chairmanship of Mr. Campbell Colquhoun the existing connections between religion and the state, the ecclesiastical supremacy of the Crown, and the principles of the Reformation were all fittingly celebrated; and a riot did indeed fittingly take place.[66]

A more sedate manifestation of Church opinion was to follow at St. James's Hall in May, presided over by an episcopal galaxy of Canterbury, York, Armagh, Dublin, London, Oxford, Dean Stanley of Westminster, and others.[67] Spofforth assured Disraeli that 'at last we can boast of a successful "Church & State" gathering'. The meeting was, in his view, an 'unmeasured success, and will rouse the Protestant feeling throughout the country'. Canterbury assented to the idea of a United Protestant League, and 'a committee of this League should sit daily until the crisis, or the General Election is past'.[68] But whether riotous or sedate, these Protestant Church rallies made little mark on general opinion. Disraeli had no publicly and persuasively identifiable fellow feeling for the Church and certainly no sure touch in his dealings with it. He was the first leader of the Conservative party whose Anglicanism was not of the cradle, the school, and the college. His handling of the Irish Church question up to this point had been distinctly unimpressive. His notorious earlier (1844) dismissal of 'an alien Church' had not been forgotten. The Church, reciprocally, could never quite take him seriously. It has been authoritatively estimated that defenders of the Irish Church comprised perhaps two thirds of the English clergy, 'but they were weaker than their numbers'. High churchmen especially distrusted Disraeli; and they, together with most moderate churchmen in the Conservative party, disliked his proneness to the primitive 'no popery' cry.[69] What Taylor, Spofforth and Corry presented as deep insights into 'the Protestant feeling of the country' were in fact misapprehensions of essentially superficial phenomena lacking in material political impact.

Parliament reassembled after the Easter recess on 20 April. On that day Cairns remarked to Disraeli on 'these horrid resolutions'.[70] The queen's opinion was that Gladstone's resolutions were 'unseasonably raised', and could not be resolved without an appeal to the constituencies. Her view as to that appeal coincided entirely with Disraeli's. His advice was that her ministers should not resign but should advise a dissolution of parliament as soon as practicable. The queen desired to be advised by Disraeli when such a dissolution would best be made; she particularly did not wish Disraeli to ask the 'opinion of the House'. Disraeli conveyed to a cabinet on 22 April his views as to Her Majesty's 'special desire & command' and to their duty 'as regards themselves & their party'.[71] He asked for confirmation as to the accuracy of his record of Her Majesty's special desire and command from his 'principal colleague', the embarrassed and uneasy Cairns. It was a delicate and problematic situation. Some members of the cabinet – Stanley, Hardy, Richmond, and Marlborough as well as Cairns – were unhappy at staying on, and even more unhappy at the appearance that would be presented of staying on by means of a special desire and command of the Crown, possibly at odds with the desire of the House of Commons. Disraeli set about soothing these tender political consciences. He assured Hardy that he possessed the most reliable information that Gladstone, 'instead of wishing to upset us, has no Cabinet ready, & though sanguine as to his future, is at present greatly embarrassed'. Gladstone wished, alleged Disraeli, to 'build us a golden bridge, and if we announce a bona fide attempt to wind up, he would suggest Bills to extend the time of registration, which would be necessitated by the passing of the Scotch and Irish Bills'. It was true, Disraeli admitted, that Bright and Ayrton and others among the more irreconcilable Radicals disagreed with Gladstone and were demanding 'violent and instant action'. But the 'commercial Liberals' looked with the greatest alarm to Lord Russell's return to the Foreign Office, or even Lord Clarendon's. Disraeli professed himself entirely assured that 'there never was a moment in which a want of confidence vote had a worse chance', and that 'all the intentions of humiliating the Government' were 'quite superficial'. Disraeli's informant predicted they would 'disappear before a firm announcement of our intention to wind up, & that any attempt to precipitate the dissolution would be quite unnecessary, and perhaps unpopular in the House itself'.[72]

Hardy and the others remained for the time substantially unsoothed. The first and most material of the 'horrid resolutions' came unsoothingly to a division on 30 April. Despite Disraeli's urging that the 'principle of property' would be shaken and the royal supremacy compromised, Gladstone carried the day with an improved majority of 65. The lull of an adjournment supervened to allow the government to collect itself before formally confronting the Commons with its decision. Taylor, enclosing an analysis of the Irish Church division, advised Disraeli that there was 'but one expression of feeling' in the party, that the government 'ought *not* to resign with a dissolution on either the new or the old constituencies'. Spofforth had given assurances that he had 'returns *today* for South Lancashire saying Gladstone can be easily defeated there – from West Yorkshire that we can return two – and the same from

Wolverhampton'.[73] On the strength of what he chose to interpret as a general consent of the in fact rather inconclusive cabinet of 22 April, Disraeli advised the queen on 1 May that the parliament should be dissolved 'as soon as the public interests will permit, and that an earnest endeavour should be made by the Government that such an appeal should be made to the new constituency'.[74]

Disraeli returned from Osborne on 2 May and attempted to square his two most formidable doubters, Cairns and Hardy. He had Derby once more behind him. He determined to brazen it through. He carefully avoided holding another cabinet. That would have given too much scope for scruples. Back at Osborne on 3 May Disraeli, in what even Buckle admitted to be a 'somewhat high-handed departure from precedent' in not consulting the cabinet,[75] committed his colleagues to remaining in office. The queen accepted his advice, seeing no necessity to accept (what Disraeli had also offered) an immediate resignation, but sanctioning a 'dissolution of parliament, under the circumstances stated by him'. Those circumstances, as Disraeli informed indignant Liberals in the Commons on 4 May who demanded to know whether the queen had been advised to dissolve on the old or the new constituencies, did not exclude a 'penal' dissolution on the old registers.[76] Disraeli thus armed himself with a formidable weapon of political blackmail. He was in a position to wither his old enemy Robert Lowe with the superb challenge: 'If you wish to pass a vote of Want of Confidence, propose a vote of Want of Confidence.'[77] Gladstone consequently was in 'a white heat with an almost diabolical expression of countenance'.[78] John Bright's 'rabid rage' at the continuation of the 'ambrosial provender which is set before those who hold high Office in this country' was preliminary to the great outburst against Disraeli which ended their personal relationship.[79] Liberals widely accused Disraeli of using 'servile' language to the queen and of dragging Her Majesty into politics. Disraeli's language was merely idiosyncratic and characteristic; the queen was perfectly willing to accept the risks of being so dragged.

It was Disraeli's cabinet colleagues who had the greatest cause to complain. His deliberate non-communication with them they thought 'strange'. As Hardy noted: 'A cabinet before Osborne would have altered everything, but now?'[80] Before Osborne Hardy was inclined to resignation as the only way out. Dissolution with the present constituencies would not gain assent but the new registers might well not be ready until 1869; 'and we cannot live through a session baited and overpowered for a dissolution next year.' If the Conservative government were to meet parliament in 1869 Hardy foresaw the embarrassing problem 'that we should not be agreed on the Irish Ch. question. I cannot but think our reign draws to a close . . .'.[81] Now, after Osborne, Disraeli had much ado soothing the scruples of colleagues about getting the new registers and the election expedited. He was in a position to inform the Commons that a November dissolution would be feasible.[82] In spite of this it remained clear that many of Disraeli's intimate colleagues were uncomfortable with his unabashedness. It was certainly in marked contrast to his earlier recessive faltering on the Irish question. Disraeli next had to smooth down the fretful Cairns and Hardy with assurances that in expediting the dissolution no suspicions would be allowed to 'enter the mind of the new Constituency that there is any design to neutralise the large franchise with wh they have been wisely invested by hurrying and hustling them in the establishment of their electoral privileges'.[83] Hardy was put in charge of a Registration Bill to secure this end. Cairns, pressed by Hardy, put candidly to Disraeli the danger that if the government appeared to 'hang back' in urging a dissolution, the general public would accuse it of acting in bad faith, and of using the present anomalous position of affairs as a means of delaying the great appeal to the Country'. The government's honour was 'greatly concerned with avoiding such a suspicion'.[84]

3

The 1868 session was not otherwise heavily controversial. Gladstone prudently did not take up the challenge Disraeli delivered to Lowe. The Scottish and Irish Reform Bills were harassed on their way through the Commons by Radical attentions similar to those which had pressed upon the 1867 bill. Hardy was indignant at the way in which Disraeli was fecklessly and without consultation ready to give things away. Hardy, Northcote, and Hunt managed to block a move whereby the 'Small Boroughs of England' would have fallen 'victim to Scotch necessities'.[85] Of more moment was the circumstance that the government's minority situation meant that it could not recast Irish constituencies in the way of reducing them overall for the benefit of Scotland and of giving Ulster greater weight. Ireland was overrepresented generally within the United Kingdom; Ulster was underrepresented within Ireland itself. These anomalies, disadvantageous to the Conservative interest, as it happened persisted until 1918: a fact which later National Union conferences regularly pointed to indignantly but unavailingly.

Nor were 'arguments about religion'[86] stilled in 1868 by Gladstone's triumph over the Irish Church resolutions. Ministers had no choice but to swallow in the Commons a bill introduced by Gladstone to suspend Irish Church appointments. But they had the satisfaction of seeing Cairns dispose of it in short order in the Lords at Derby's almost exhilarated instigation. The electorate would decide. Getting rid of Russell's Ecclesiastical Titles Act of 1851 pleased the anti-clerical queen, as Disraeli recounted to Cairns, 'because . . . she would now be able to control, if necessary, the Scottish Bishops, whose assumption of titles, she seemed to deem quite as offensive, as those of the Papists.'[87] Above all there was the famous matter of the old and vexed church rates question, the resolution of which illuminates better than anything else the curious relations between the reunited Liberal opposition majority and the governmental Conservative minority. Ostensibly, this was a case of Gladstone's masterfully seizing the initiative to impose a policy of abolishing compulsory payment of church rates, expressive of a new Liberal dynamism fuelled by Nonconformist energy which a Conservative government was helpless to stem or stay.[88] The reality of the matter was that Gladstone resumed a bill he had inherited in 1866 but which had been trampled underfoot in the Reform stampede. Conservative ministers in 1868 granted it sessional accommodation partly, of course, because they had to, but partly also because they wanted to. There had been earlier Conservative attempts to meet legitimate Dissenting grievances and get rid of exacerbations between Church and Chapel. It was the Lords, however, who settled the matter in a struggle not between Church and Dissent but between different schools of churchmanship. The Orange Protestant Cairns with a majority of the Low Church bench of bishops altered Gladstone's bill in a way which, ironically, pleased Dissenters, who got more than Gladstone had offered them. The existing rating system was preserved, less its compulsory aspect, which was politically important in rural areas. Payment of rates in urban areas was in any case virtually defunct. Back in the Commons Gladstone was confronted with an amended bill which in fact represented a sharp personal defeat. Conservative ministers indicated that their accommodation would not apply to a new bill. Gladstone grudgingly accepted defeat. It was only in a later, clouded, political mythology that what Anderson points out would better be termed a 'Church Rates Regulation Act' was confused with the general surge of Gladstone's aggressive reforms in his second administration.

Conservative sessional buoyancy was given a further fortuitous lift by the successful outcome of Napier's Abyssinian expedition, brilliantly exemplary of the Palmerstonian tradition of *civis Romanus sum*. The great news of victory and the release of British captives came to Northcote at the India Office on 26 April, at a time when glad tidings were especially appreciated. Northcote's son found Disraeli 'gorgeously arrayed in a dressing gown and in imposing headgear', 'opulent in compliments'.[89] Disraeli was able to gratify himself with rodomontade about the standard of St. George being hoisted on the mountains of Rasselas. Hunt was left to pay the bills, which were nearly double the amounts initially estimated. Disraeli brushed aside financial carping. He told his confidante Lady Bradford: 'It certainly cost double what was contemplated, and that is likely to be the case in all wars for wh. I may be responsible. Money is not to be considered in such matters: success alone is to be thought of.'[90] Northcote, who had stayed at the India Office when Disraeli left the Exchequer in February, now indicated that he would quite like India itself, the reversion of which was at hand.[91] Disraeli, however, had already promised it to Mayo. Hypothetical reflections are at this point irresistible, not least because of Mayo's tragic assassination in 1872, but principally on the consideration that had Northcote gone for a tour in Calcutta he would not have been, as a peer, in a position to succeed

Disraeli as leader of the Commons in 1876, and to have gone therefrom to his own tragic fate. Comical fate, in 1868, was reserved for the chancellor of the duchy of Lancaster, the Lancashire MP Wilson Patten, who was thrust, most unwillingly, into Mayo's place at the Irish Office, where he flitted, a transient and most embarrassed phantom, across the political stage for the remaining few months of the government's life.

Notes and References

1 Kebbel, *Lord Beaconsfield and Other Tory Memories* 50. *Speeches*, ii, 547.
2 A.E. Gathorne-Hardy, *Gathorne Hardy, First Earl of Cranbrook* (1910), i, 273.
3 J. Vincent (ed.), *Disraeli, Derby and the Conservative Party, Journals and Memoirs of Edward Henry, Lord Stanley, 1849–1869* (Hassocks 1978), 328.
4 Hardy, *Diary*, 187.
5 Buckle, ii, 319.
6 *QR*, Oct. 1867, 559.
7 Buckle, ii, 320–1; Vincent, *Disraeli, Derby and the Conservative Party*, 329.
8 *Ibid.*
9 R. Blake, *Disraeli* (1966), 487.
10 *Ibid.*
11 Northcote to Disraeli, 16 Jan. 1868; BL, Iddesleigh 50016, 1. Stephen Cave stayed on as paymaster general.
12 Buckle, ii, 330.
13 Noel to Corry, [Feb. 1868]; HP, B/IX/F/69.
14 Rose to Disraeli, 25 Feb. 1868; HP, B/IX/F/170.
15 Gathorne-Hardy, *Cranbrook*, i, 280.
16 In 1862–3 Andrew Montagu, a wealthy bachelor and eccentric Yorkshire and Nottinghamshire landowner, advised by Rose and Lionel de Rothschild, bought up Disraeli's debts and, in return for a mortgage on Hughenden Manor, charged Disraeli 3 per cent instead of the ruinous 10 per cent he had been paying. In addition Disraeli received some £30,000 as the residuary legatee in 1866 of Mrs. Brydges Willyams. Buckle, ii, 418–19; Blake, *Disraeli*, 421, 424.
17 Buckle, ii, 325.
18 Derby Diary, 21 Jan. 1877.
19 HP, B/IX/F/34.
20 Vincent, *Disraeli, Derby and the Conservative Party*, 331, 328.
21 *AR*, 1868, 2–3.
22 Cairns to Disraeli, 1 and 2 March 1868; HP, B/XX/Ca/15,17.
23 Disraeli to Cairns, 2 March 1868; PRO, Cairns 30/51/1.
24 P.M.H. Bell, *Disestablishment in Ireland and Wales* (1969), 75.
25 *Ibid.*, 88.
26 Disraeli to Cairns, 2 March 1868; PRO, Cairns 30/51/1.
27 Cairns to Disraeli, 2 March 1868; HP, B/XX/Ca/17.
28 Buckle, ii, 353–4.
29 *Ibid.*, 353.

30 *PD*, cxc, 1118–19.
31 Hardy, *Diary*, 65.
32 J.P. Parry, *Democracy and Religion. Gladstone and the Liberal Party 1867–1875* (Cambridge 1986), 269.
33 Bell, *Disestablishment*, 75.
34 Hardy, *Diary*, 66.
35 Cairns to Disraeli, 17 March 1868; HP, B/XX/Ca/20.
36 Disraeli to Cairns, 19 March 1868; PRO, Cairns 30/51/1. Buckle, ii, 358–9.
37 *Ibid.*, 360.
38 Gathorne-Hardy, *Cranbrook*, i, 265.
39 *PD*, cxci, 1735.
40 *Ibid.*, 506.
41 Gathorne-Hardy, *Cranbrook*, i, 265–6.
42 Buckle, ii, 360–1.
43 Vincent, *Disraeli, Derby and the Conservative Party*, 332.
44 Hardy, *Diary*, 68.
45 Northcote to Cairns, 31 March 1868; PRO, Cairns 30/51/5.
46 Cairns to Northcote, 1 April 1868; BL, Iddesleigh 50021, 107.
47 Gathorne-Hardy, *Cranbrook*, i, 273. Pakington, baffled, commented to Northcote on Disraeli's speech: 'the startling passage is that announcing Gladstone as "the Representative of a combination of Roman Catholics & Ritualists to seize upon the supreme authority of this Realm"! Such a statement must be either most important – or most serious – what does it really mean?' (Pakington to Northcote, 5 April 1868. BL, Iddesleigh 50022, 267).
48 Buckle, ii, 364.
49 Gathorne-Hardy, *Cranbrook*, i, 273.
50 Pakington to Northcote, 6 April 1868; BL, Iddesleigh 50022, 269.
51 Disraeli to Cairns, 8 April 1868; PRO, Cairns 30/51/1.
52 Buckle, ii, 367.
53 *Ibid.*, 368.
54 Spofforth to Disraeli, 11 April 1868; HP, B/XXI/S/427.
55 Spofforth to Disraeli, 8 April 1868; HP, B/XXI/S/424.
56 Buckle, ii, 365.
57 *Ibid.*
58 Spofforth to Taylor [1868]; HP, B/XXI/S/423.
59 Taylor to Disraeli, 9 April [1868]; HP, B/XX/T/108.
60 Spofforth to Disraeli [April 1868]. HP. B/XXI/S/428.
61 Corry to Disraeli, 14 April 1868; HP, B/XX/Co/37.
62 Taylor to Disraeli, 19 April [1868]; HP, B/XX/T/112.
63 Spofforth to Disraeli, 14 April 1868; HP, B/XXI/S/431.
64 Spofforth to Disraeli, 15 April 1868; HP, B/XXI/S/432.
65 Spofforth to Disraeli, 17 April 1868; HP, B/XXI/S/433.
66 *AR*, 1868, 75.
67 *Ibid.*
68 Spofforth to Disraeli, 6 May 1868; HP, B/XXI/S/429.
69 W.O. Chadwick, *The Victorian Church* (1970), ii, 429.
70 HP, B/XX/Ca/27.
71 Buckle, ii, 368.

72 Gathorne-Hardy, *Cranbrook*, i, 275–6.
73 Taylor to Disraeli, 1 May 1868; HP, B/XX/T/113.
74 Buckle, ii, 370–2.
75 *Ibid.*, 373.
76 *PD*, cxci, 1742.
77 *Ibid.*, 1744.
78 Hardy, *Diary*, 72.
79 *PD*, cxc, 1740, 1943.
80 Hardy, *Diary*, 73.
81 *Ibid.*, 71.
82 *PD*, cxci, 1706, 1742.
83 Disraeli to Cairns, 29 May 1868; PRO, Cairns 30/51/1.
84 Disraeli to Cairns, 30 May 1868; HP, B/XX/Ca/32.
85 Hardy, *Diary*, 74.
86 A memorable keynote phrase employed in Parry, *Democracy and Religion*, 3.
87 Disraeli to Cairns, 13 March 1868; PRO, Cairns 30/51/1.
88 The episode is dealt with brilliantly by Olive Anderson, 'Gladstone's abolition of compulsory Church rates: a minor political myth and its historical career', *Journal of Ecclesiastical History* (1974).
89 Buckle, ii, 383.
90 *Ibid.*, 385. See also F. Harcourt, 'Disraeli's imperialism, a question of timing, 1866–68', *Historical Journal* (1980).
91 Northcote to Disraeli, 7 June 1868; BL, Iddesleigh 50016, 30.

Chapter 3

The election of 1868

A great Protestant struggle

1

The election campaign had in reality commenced as early as the parliamentary conflict over the Irish Church. It thus took on the character of a contest centred on a single great issue, rather in the manner of the Reform election of 1832, the free trade elections of 1847 and 1852, and the Palmerstonian foreign policy election of 1857. As Lord Clinton put it to Northcote apropos of arrangements in Devonshire, Conservatives should take their canvass 'on constitutional v Radical, principles & appeal to the constituency as supporters of the Irish Church & of Church establishments generally'.[1]

Having been outbidden by Gladstone for Irish Roman Catholic support Disraeli felt no further need to placate that interest. He told the queen that he had no doubt 'from all that he observes and all that reaches him' that it would be 'a great Protestant struggle – and that if the Government of the country temperately but firmly and unequivocally enlist the Protestant feeling on the side of existing authority the institutions of this country will be greatly strengthened and the means of governing proportionately facilitated'.[2] Moreover, Disraeli allowed himself to be drawn into rather a narrow and impolitic definition of 'Protestant feeling'.

This ill-judged definition of Protestantism was partly the result of his personal predispositions. Given his oft-declared antipathy to English Dissent or Nonconformity, there was little chance that he would sway that traditionally Liberal interest away from its commitment to the principle of religious disestablishment by the argument that its threatened current application would be largely to the benefit of Rome. His impolicy lay rather in the crudity of his handling of the English Church. Kebbel lamented Disraeli's allowing himself to be drawn 'into the arms of the Orange party'. This put him out of touch with the 'great body of Tory High churchmen, who were his natural allies'. The Church of England, its history, its claims, were not indeed 'Mr. Disraeli's strong point'. This led him to deceive himself about the general election of 1868. He grossly overestimated 'the strength of the purely Protestant feeling to which he had appealed'.[3] Disraeli was obsessed with the conviction that 'there is no sort of doubt that the great feature of national opinion is an utter repudiation by all classes of the High Church party'.[4] But as the queen's ecclesiastical adviser Dean Wellesley of Windsor pointed out, though the people would not tolerate 'Ritualism' they would even less tolerate its suppression by the 'Puritanical party'.[5] Disraeli tended to listen too much to Cairns and too little to Hardy and Manners. Had the new marquess of Salisbury been still a colleague Disraeli's rashness might have been tempered into discretion. Another colleague to whom he would not listen was Stanley, at the other end of the cabinet spectrum. Stanley continued to press for compromise rather than resistance on the Irish Church. Disraeli insisted that the days of compromise were over. He worried that Stanley's address to his Lynn constituents might expose fundamental differences in the governing party nakedly to public view. He pleaded: 'Pray don't stab me in the back after all the incredible exertions I am making for the good cause.'[6] Stanley proved mercifully discreet.

Disraeli's crudity in his handling of the Church revealed itself early and often in his ecclesiastical patronage. It happened that during his short tenure of office many sees and other major benefices fell vacant. 'Another Deanery!' as he exulted to Corry. 'The Lord of Hosts is with us!'[7] The Lord of Hosts, in fact, tempted Disraeli into trouble. Disraeli almost certainly did himself more harm than good in his Church preferments. The queen, wiser and more experienced in these affairs, did her best to deflect her prime minister away from trouble, but could not always prevail. And Disraeli, it must be said, also rather enjoyed playing it as a game. 'Send me down tomorrow the Clergy list', he wrote to Corry from Hughenden. 'I don't know the names and descriptions of the persons I am recommending for deaneries & mitres!'[8] From Balmoral: 'Ecclesiastical affairs rage here. Send me Crockford's Directory. I must be armed.'[9] He liked to set off the 'Rits' (Anglo-Catholic 'Ritualists') and the 'Rats' (Broad Church 'Rationalist' Liberals) against what he conceived to be the doctrinally sound and patriotically 'national' body of the clergy.

The first telling specimen of Disraeli's clumsy ecclesiastical patronage was to prefer the rabidly anti-papist Canon McNeile of Liverpool to the deanery of Ripon. The queen attempted to resist on the grounds that old sectarian feuds would be reignited. Disraeli insisted on the basis of reports from Corry of Sir Walter Farquhar's opinion: 'nothing can be stronger than his recommendation of McNeile for the Deanery. Though not of his school, he speaks with great confidence of the appointment as *the* one which is most likely to unite *all* branches of the Low Church Party in your support.'[10] Certainly, the appointment pleased Orange Toryism in Lancashire. But, as Dean Wellesley advised the queen, Disraeli thereby would 'not gain by it more votes than he will lose, mainly from the moderate party'.[11] Disraeli did from time to time prefer High Church clergy – Mansel, Leighton, Gregory, Bright – but always unwillingly and with citations of 'moans & lamentations over High Ch. appointments' from within the Conservative party.[12] He was warned that the 'selection of Liddon for any Government appointment [would] be most injurious – as he is a mere satellite of Pusey's'.[13] In the case of a 'Rat' he was happy to follow Nevill's advice that 'altho he is a good Conservative he is slightly *Broad* so he will not do'.[14] When it came to sees the queen made special efforts to outpoint her prime minister. She manoeuvred adroitly to get the 'Rat' Tait from London to Canterbury and Magee from the deanery of Cork to Peterborough. Disraeli was taken aback to find Magee being urged by Manners, on the ground that promotion from Ireland would assert the unity of the Church, and 'wd satisfy all parties'. Disraeli's objection, that Magee's appointment 'would give us nothing', failed to block one of the most brilliant episcopates of the Victorian Church.[15] Hardy was nervous about Magee but found his Oxford friends content. Tait for Canterbury, however, he thought 'most unfortunate'. It had 'told against us already & alarms many'.[16] Disraeli could only console himself by blocking the indignant High Church Wilberforce from London.

Alienation of 'moderate men' by the stridency of Disraeli's 'Orange' approach to the Irish Church issue was one aspect of his electoral weakness. Another was that there were Conservatives who, rather in the mould of Stanley, were unable in conscience to defend the Irish Church as it stood. One such was the MP for Barnstaple, Sir George Stucley, of Moreton, Bideford, a Devonshire magnate, who told Disraeli in late September:

> Up to this time I have in no way exerted my influence in Devon and Cornwall, except for the safety of Sir S. Northcote. My best return for your obliging consideration to me for my Father's and my own service with the Conservative Party extending over many years and at heavy cost to ourselves, is frankly . . . to confess that I believe in the necessity for great Ecclesiastical change in Ireland, and although I would not vote against the Government on Mr. Gladstone's motion I was then strongly of the same opinion.[17]

Stucley withdrew from the Barnstaple nomination (he had headed the poll in 1865, with a Liberal as second member). His Conservative replacement managed to hold the second seat in November 1868. Cases such as Stucley's were not numerous in 1868. Yet the fact was notorious that the Conservative party was far from the monolithic Protestant entity which Disraeli's campaign made it out to be. In the end this more than anything else made it inexpedient for the Conservative government to meet the new parliament elected in 1868.

2

The Conservative party, now near 300 strong in the Commons, needed to win something between 30 and 40 seats to have a working majority. There were grounds for not regarding this as hopeless. 'I hear that Election prospects are fair', Hardy wrote to Northcote in September. He was thinking of gains which would destroy the Liberal majority without giving the same to his own party. 'If we could but get 320 Members what a power we might be. Stronger probably than with 15 more.'[18] Recent by-elections were cheering.[19] Disraeli talked over the situation generally with Stanley on 9 October: 'he is sanguine as usual, talks of 300 seats as secure, and allowing the same number to the other side, reckons on one half or more of the odd 58.' Stanley was more cautious; but still thought it 'likely that the new voters will be more favourable than we could have ventured to expect, and that we shall at least be a strong opposition'.[20]

One problem was a feeling growing in the party that Spofforth was 'not the most suitable man to inspire popular constituencies'. He was thought to be 'over-optimistic, heavy-handed and tactless'.[21] Rose was prone not to see in him an entirely adequate replacement. As the session ended Disraeli decided to take the preparations for the elections out of Spofforth's hands. Corry was critical of Spofforth's judgement and reliability in matters of constituency negotiations. 'I have opened Spofforth's letters today, & judge that his correspondents know that he has what he calls a "manor".'[22] There was a sense also in which the older breed of party managers, of which Spofforth was a type, was becoming obsolete. Spofforth's great service to the party had been to reconstruct the system of local agents wrecked when Bonham, Peel's party manager, followed his chief out of the party in 1846. At that time, as Spofforth was studious to record in his *Who's Who* entry, only a small minority of agents remained loyal to the Carlton Club. Since then the tendency of legislative efforts to suppress electoral corruption had been to accentuate the role of constituency agents.[23] This tendency was given a strong impulse in the 1868 session by the Election Practices and Corrupt Practices at Elections Act, which removed adjudication of electoral petitions from a committee of the Commons to a panel of judges. Constituency agents were given a more important responsibility for declaring election expenses. The rise of a new kind of professional agent designed to prevent corruption matched the decline of the old species of electoral solicitor whose practice thrived on the consequences of corruption. There would yet, for the next three general elections, be great scope for thriving electioneering solicitors; and a modern style of professional Conservative constituency and divisional agents would not be forthcoming until the later 1880s and the early 1890s. But even in 1868 there was a sense that the great new electorate which was in the process of registration demanded an appropriately new response to constituency management.

Taylor as chief whip was also being complained of. Ward Hunt was at feud with him about management, and Spofforth was further blamed for exacerbating their friction.[24] Taylor's reputation was as the undisputed 'manager in Ireland'; and he was very much Derby's man.[25] Taylor was in any case not in good health and quite ready to go. 'Elections are not to my taste', as he admitted, '& they do not prosper when I interfere.'[26] Wilson Patten's promotion to the Irish Office gave Disraeli the opportunity to accede to Taylor's plea for the reversion of the duchy of Lancaster, where he would continue to be useful without being in the way.[27] He would always, of course, be the link between the central and Irish managements, especially after Mayo's departure for India. Gerard Noel succeeded as chief whip, though not without some anxious hesitation on grounds of fitness for the task. After interviewing Noel as Taylor's intended successor, Disraeli recounted to Corry being frightened out of his wits. 'He must consider the situation immediately, & decide whether, or no, he can undertake it. . . . If he have not sufficient self-reliance, however painful, he had better resolve to remain as he is.'[28] Noel nerved himself to be sufficiently self-reliant. The party's electoral management, as Disraeli reported to Derby, was now to be in the hands of a 'limited but influential Committee of gentlemen', comprising Nevill, Noel, Corry, and Taylor.[29]

Spofforth for the time being retained the style and emoluments (£300 per annum and expenses)[30] of principal agent and kept his interest in such specialities as the Junior Carlton. As Disraeli put it to Cairns in 1875, 'Spofforth served us for years, and years of adversity, if not always with perfect judgment, with great talent, honour, and devotion. He was not well used by us, but he has never murmured.'[31] In fact, Spofforth's fall was eased by his original sponsor, Nevill, in whose retinue he continued to subsist, wrapped in the Inverness cloak that was his trademark, as a regular guest at Eridge Castle. He eventually received his material reward in 1877 as a taxing master in Chancery. Spofforth's last service to the party as principal agent for the 1868 election campaign was to prepare his *Hints on County Registration*. As he explained to Disraeli, it had been 'prepared with great care', and its advantage was that 'a county Agent under these instructions would be able to conduct the new Registration as altered by the Reform Act of 1867 without reference to Law Books or to the act itself'. Copies had been sent to each principal county agent who would pass as many copies on to district agents as required. Spofforth's elaborate machinery provided for central and district committees and central and district agents, with precise instructions on the handling of procedures, forms, 'Visits to Parish and Township', and 'Practical Hints as to Claims and Objections'.[32]

Revision of registers was a crucial matter in 1868. Spofforth's attention might have been more appropriately directed at the boroughs, where Conservative effort was mostly needed, and, to all appearances, mostly wanting. In the case of Blackburn, as an instance, the Revision court in 1863 completed its business in three hours. In 1868 it took seven days, hearing 2,800 claims and 2,000 objections. Blackburn had 1,865 voters in 1865; 9,700 in 1868. This time and money-consuming procedure became a standard feature of rival party manoeuvring.[33] Taylor advised Disraeli on 28 September that 'another ten days will have disposed of the greater part of the revision of the registers, and we shall then be able to calculate with some accuracy what the result of the General Election will be – at present I have no reason to be disheartened'.[34] As for money, Disraeli determined on a drive for unprecedented quantities of it. 'The impending General Election', he told Beauchamp, 'is the most important thing since 1832, and will, probably, decide the political situation for a long period.' It was highly characteristic of Disraeli to insist that 'the party that is best organised will be successful'. No seat where there was a 'fair prospect' should go unchallenged.

> To effect this, and to operate on a class of seats hitherto unassailed, it is necessary that a fund to aid the legitimate expenses of candidates, should be raised, and that upon a scale not inferior to the range which democratic associations, on more than one occasion, realised in order to advance their views.[35]

What reliable knowledge Disraeli had of the finances of 'democratic associations' is not clear; very probably, in any case, a picturesquely exaggerated notion of such things. His notion of a Conservative election war chest was much in the same extravagant vein. He aimed for £100,000. Expert opinion doubts if he achieved more than half of this.[36] Colville would press the peers (the Lords' chief whip was traditionally the main parliamentary money-gatherer) and Gerard Noel the Commoners. Disraeli in fact pressed his colleagues hard. He told Beauchamp by way of encouragement that he had induced the cabinet to subscribe a minimum of £10,000.[37] Stanley contributed £1,000. Hardy recorded on 14 June: 'I have been with Disraeli about the Elections & certain reports are not unpromising. I fear we shall have to subscribe largely . . . Still the coming Election may turn events for a quarter of a Century & we ought to fight vigorously.'[38] Hardy provided £1,000. This was, apparently, more than certain of his grandly wealthy ducal colleagues. 'Spite of the "Dukes"', he noted, 'the cabinet raised the £10,000 for Elections.' Hardy was under particular pressure because his son was to contest (successfully as it happened) the Liberal borough of Rye.[39]

The special circumstances in 1868 of the way in which the Irish Church issue exploded early in the session, combined with the unavoidable delays in completing the new electoral registers, meant that the election campaign was, in the heartfelt words of Trehawke Kekewich, one of the Devon Conservatives, 'this long contest';[40] and it was, therefore, inordinately expensive. Disraeli's ambition to fight every seat 'with a fair prospect' further added to costs. In 1865, 159 Liberal seats had been uncontested, while 143 Conservatives were allowed a free return. Disraeli and his managers reduced the tally of unchallenged Liberals in 1868 to 122; but, in response, Liberals allowed only 100 Conservative members to escape contest. The Conservative party ended up, thus, marginally worse off in 1868 than it had been in 1865 to the tune of half a dozen seats.[41] Uncontested Liberals reflected Conservative structural weaknesses. More than 60 per cent of such Liberals were in Scotland (22), Wales (10), and Ireland (44). As against this, whereas Liberals left only 10 English borough seats uncontested, they allowed no less than 49 English county seats to return Conservatives unchallenged. These were traditional patterns. The novel feature of the 1868 elections was that Conservatives left only 27 English boroughs uncontested, compared with 56 such seats in 1865.

3

The managers, as Taylor put it, saw no reason to be disheartened. Disraeli himself was cheered when, meeting Lord Clinton on Aberdeen station, he found the former Devon MP speaking 'with confidence of returning the six members for Devon!'[42] He reported further that Sir James Fergusson, a former Ayrshire member, 'assures me we shall gain a little' in Scotland. 'He suggests it would be politic to ask *Lord Bute* to move or second the address.' (Taylor conveyed also that Fergusson himself would 'greatly appreciate being made a Privy Councillor'.)[43] Corry expanded on this congenial Scottish theme. 'Fergusson is confident we shall not lose in Scotland', he told Disraeli. 'He even talks of the possibility of gaining one or two seats.' After all, the Conservative situation in Scotland was so bad that it was perfectly reasonable to assume it could only get better. Corry reinforced the advantages of cultivating the immensely wealthy and influential Bute, who had extensive interests in south Wales as well as Scotland: 'a *zealous Conservative*, & has so arranged matters that no reasonable doubt exists of the right man being returned in Cardiff, Bute, & the two Ayrshires.' (The young marquess, it so happened, was on the point, embarrassingly, of submitting to the Church of Rome, and so providing Disraeli with much of the material for *Lothair*.)

> Our time was chiefly spent in 'posting up' Taylor in what has passed. As much depends on the impression conveyed to his mind, I felt it very important that I should remain, to check – and occasionally contradict – the Spofforthian version of past transactions. . . . Thursday is to be the great day, when Noel and Nevill will join us. . . . All I can say at present is that *we* have increasing hopes of the new electors: that I have every hope in your address.[44]

Disraeli took pains after the August lull in framing his election address for Buckinghamshire (where he was uncontested), which would, in the conventions of the time, be in effect the party manifesto. 'I propose to send my address, in due course printed, to each member of the cabinet', he told Northcote, '& to invite their remarks.' This would be 'a more convenient & I think, advantageous way of settling the affair, than holding a premature cabinet on ye matter'.[45] There is no doubt that the convenience and advantageousness of this arrangement from Disraeli's point of view was that he would be less inhibited by the carpers and compromisers among his colleagues. As Hardy put it to Northcote apropos of the Irish Church, 'between ourselves I by no means see my way to union. We shall see & must do our best.'[46] The best that Disraeli could do was judged widely not to rise to the occasion. He had invited Cairns to rewrite it if he so wished. But there is no indication that Cairns or any other of the cabinet felt it worth while to attempt to patch up or gloss Disraeli's Protestant text. Corry tried loyally to make the best of it:

> Nothing has ever equalled the pithiness and power with which you advocate the maintenance of the Establishment. Years hence, when all of us are dead, and the Church too, (perhaps), men will quote what you have just written.
>
> Not that I think the Church is moribund yet, for I believe that thousands of waverers, when they see that banner unfurled, will enlist in your ranks.[47]

The banner unfurled by Disraeli blazoned an 'uncompromising resistance' to the dissolution of the union between Church and state in Ireland. The connection of religion with the exercise of political authority was 'one of the main safeguards of the civilisation of man'. Disestablishment in Ireland was a contagion which would spread, threatening the religious integrity of the community. Confiscation also was contagious. The fall of the Church would involve the fall of the Crown. The 'ultimate triumph' would be to the Church of Rome, and the 'supremacy of a foreign prince'.[48]

The integrity of the Church of Ireland simply was not a large, convincing cause upon which a great political party could frame its plan or direct its course. The threatened triumph of the pope was widely thought to be a bad joke in embarrassing taste. This was flogging the Protestant horse nigh to death. Conservatives who expected that the first general election on what could be termed a popular franchise would evoke an appropriately positive and popular response from a Conservative government were disappointed. This was a view strongly expressed in Lancashire. Blackburn Tories were reported to feel 'left in the lurch by Disraeli's negative election address' and dismayed by Disraeli's weak leadership.[49] There were pamphlets put out by the National Union directly addressed to working men on the boon conferred on them by the Conservative Reform Act; they had such themes as *Practical Suggestions to the Loyal Working Men of Great Britain on Points of Policy and Duty at the Present Crisis* and *Who are the Real Friends of the Working Class?* evoking Shaftesbury's Factory Acts. But these were forlornly marginal gestures. It was later to be a great feature of Raikes's *Imperial Review* that the Conservative party crucially failed to 'put its case across to working men'.[50]

The Times, never friendly to Disraeli, chimed in with deadly effectiveness, lamenting that Disraeli's address 'contains many promises to resist the policy of others, but no signs of any policy for the great Conservative party itself'.[51] After so many fruitless endeavours to ingratiate himself with Delane, Disraeli wavered feebly between exasperated counter-attack and timid discretion. 'Give a hint to the "Standard"', he instructed Corry, 'to castigate the insolence of the "Times" article of this morning: that is to say, if it be wise to do so?'[52] Indeed, Delane was an ugly enemy, whose influence at that time matched his truly bloated arrogance. Hamilton speaks of Delane as being 'on the warpath against Disraeli. . . . His conversation was a diatribe against Disraeli and the conduct and management of the Conservative Party.'[53] Delane made his reputation and that of *The Times* by 'being strong on the stronger side'. The events of 1868 were prime examples of the efficacy of that policy.

'Unfortunately there is no chivalrous feeling among the middle classes with regard to the Irish Church'

1

Notwithstanding Delane and *The Times*, the Conservative management committee advised Disraeli that they had reason to expect enough Conservative gains to furnish 330 Conservatives in the new House of Commons of 658 members. They estimated 266 English and Welsh seats, 51 Irish, and 13 Scottish.[54] The counties were never likely to be a great problem. There were of course local difficulties. 'Noel has been with us today', reported Corry to Disraeli. 'Under Nevill's advice, he and I are trying to bring about a readjustment of the candidates in the West Riding, without which they say we shall fail to get more than one man in out of the six.' [55] In the event Conservatives carried the two seats in the eastern division in what was generally enemy territory. Similar 'readjustments' were in train in Hampshire. Here it was a case of going for both seats in the southern division instead of the politely uncontested share-out of the three previous elections. In spite of opposition from the Sloane-Stanleys of Paultons, Romsey, to this bold manoeuvre, as Corry wrote to Disraeli, 'we do not resign all hope of south Hants'. Corry intrigued to induce the sitting Conservative, Colonel H.H. Fane, to retire with the bribe of a peerage ('Taylor is for promising the Peerage') and to replace him with Lord Henry Scott and 'a nominee of Lord N[evill]'. 'Fane would not stand in the way, as he tells Taylor he does not care for his seat. I think also that the Party, in the County, might rally, if the two men were really out.'[56] Lord Henry as it happened won the second seat, behind a Liberal, in an extremely close four-way contest.

Cairns, likewise, troubled himself with complications in Berkshire and Northamptonshire, and wrote to Disraeli from Bournemouth:

> You will probably in London see the men who are working as to the Elections. Can anything be done to get Col. Lloyd Lindsay to go to Northamptonsh: in place of Knightley, & leave Berks for Sir C. Russell? I believe L.L. would be safe in Northamptn and the idea is that Lord Overstone wd. like it: and Sir C.R. (who is here) tells me he (Sir C.R.) wd probably head the poll in Berks. But *he* cannot move in the matter. If anything be done, it must be done ab extra.[57]

Corry reported: 'Noel is staying in Northamptonshire, and attempting to mend matters there.'[58] In spite of the desire of Lord Overstone, the eminent banker and Northamptonshire grandee, Knightley held on in South Northamptonshire at the top of the poll; Lindsay had to stay in Berkshire, where he retained his seat; and Sir Charles Russell, VC, formerly a Berkshire member, had to wait for a Westminster seat in 1874.

Lincolnshire offered more substantial electoral matters for attention. Two new seats had been created in a midland division, which caused perturbations among the members already sitting for the county. The nub of the matter was put to Taylor by Christopher Nisbet-Hamilton of Archerfield. 'Unfortunately there is no chivalrous feeling among the middle classes with regard to the Irish Church.' 'The Wesleyan Dissenters are neutral, and all the other Non-Conformists are in favour of Gladstone's scheme. The Dissenting interest is very powerful through the whole County of Lincoln.' One fortunate circumstance was that Colonel Packe, a Liberal landowner of the county, proved on the Irish Church issue to be an 'old Whig', and refused to allow his son Hussey Packe to be nominated by the North Lincolnshire Radicals. (Packe was in fact eventually defeated for the southern division.) 'With respect to the Northern division of the county,' Nisbet-Hamilton advised Taylor, 'I still hold that any attempt to set up an opposition to Lord Yarborough's interest would utterly fail.' In the new midland division, however, the Conservative interest was much stronger; and in young Henry Chaplin, of Blankney Hall, Sleaford, they had a generous candidate whose horse, Hermit, had sensationally won the Derby in 1867. 'Chaplin's progress through the district has been very successful,' as Nisbet-Hamilton reported. Rumour had it that Colonel Amcotts, the likely Liberal candidate, was disappointed with his canvass; which invited consideration of the feasibility of a second Conservative entry. 'If any move is made in that direction it must proceed from the Yeomanry and Tenant Farmers, and if they show much enthusiasm I think it possible that a candidate may be found.' No such enthusiasm manifested itself and the uncontested constituency was peaceably shared. In the northern division no Conservative challenge was offered to Lord Yarborough's interest and the Conservative candidate, Rowland Winn, also shared an uncontested election. It was only in the southern division that the Conservatives determined to challenge and force a contest, despite Nisbet-Hamilton's pessimistic reports that Lord Kesteven and Mr. Everett from Holland advised it would be 'more prudent not to attempt it'. The attempt, however, came off, and Conservatives took both seats handsomely.[59]

A Liberal county challenge could be viewed as an act in bad taste. Gathorne Hardy was shocked that a 'contest threatened & Sir B. Phillips assured me real in Mid Kent', a new division created in 1867. Two Liberal candidates were positively to show their faces in Maidstone, 'absolute strangers to the County no doubt sent by the Reform Club, a new thing in a County'.[60] These interlopers (one was Lord John Hervey) were, however, briskly seen off at the elections in November by Sir William Hart Dyke and Lord Holmesdale, and Hardy breathed freely again at Cranbrook. In Shropshire, on the other hand, the problem demanding most managerial attention was the relationship between candidate and money. Corry received intelligence from the southern division that Colonel Corbett was 'keen to stand' as a Conservative challenger to Lord Powis's interest, and that '*by miles he is the strongest candidate in the county* and a great personal friend' of the sitting Conservative member, General the Hon. Percy Herbert, 'to whom he would be a help, though I dare say the Powis's would like a compromise'. Corry's informant was '*convinced the seat can be won* for both'. 'Now you know our magnates, Forester, Boyne, Bradford, etc. Can't you get the division redeemed?' (The Liberal, Jasper Moore, had topped the poll in 1865.) 'The working men are ready, parsons keen and only £.s.d. lacking'.[61] Another Conservative Shropshire manager informed Corry that Corbett was 'undoubtedly the best man we could have – but how about the money?' Corbett would not come cheap at £5,000. 'I do not think the S[outh] S[hropshire] Squires could find more than a fifth of that sum.' 'We must see if we can see our way to the money and then see if the General [Herbert] would coalesce.' 'I write to Lord Bradford by this post. Lord Boyne ought to give largely because the proper candidate was his son – and then he would have had to have paid all. He must be managed from London – with say *two thousand.*' Eventually it was settled: 'I have written today to Colonel Corbett to have it in writing that he will stand if met with £5,000. . . .'[62] Corbett's challenge did the trick, and the Liberal Moore was duly ousted and the division redeemed.

Devon was a county which in 1868 exhibited many characteristic features and traits of electoral significance. Again, a new (eastern) division had been carved out in 1867 which caused perturbations in the existing party orbits. C. Lupton of Brixham wrote to Northcote, one of the members for the northern division, in January apropos of arranging meetings of the Registration Committee and Quarter Sessions.

> I am very much obliged to you for letting me know what is likely to be done in regard to the representation of the County & to the preparation for the next Election. In regard to the management of the Registration, I think, it would be best managed by a principal agent, resident in Exeter, acting under the guidance & control of a small Committee, and that he with the sanction of the Committee should find a sub-agent for each Division of the County. On entering upon an Election the sub-agent, if approved by the Candidates could act as Chief agent for his Division, or the Candidates might appoint separate agents if they feared to encounter the Cry of 'Coalition'. The difficulties to be encountered in bringing into operation this system . . . would not be great, & would chiefly consist in smoothing down petty jealousies, & inducing the selected agents to work harmoniously together. The selection of Candidates is a serious & difficult question. Kekewich as the former member for the Southern Division should, as I infer from your letter he already has been, be offered either the East or South Division & requested without delay to make his selection. For his not doing so hampers the party and prevents further arrangements being made. I think he would come in for the South or East. But the state of his affairs which are very publicly talked about, would invite a contest, & therefore might be prejudicial to providing him with a good Colleague. Bastard would be a good man for the South if he will exert himself but he is so shy & so retiring that he is thoroughly unknown, & young Walter Carew is almost as bad. Garnier is lively & much liked & if he could consent to come forward I feel nearly sure that he & Lopes could secure the South. I am sorry to write what follows, but Courtenay would be a bad candidate for either Division, hardly any body would exert themselves

for him & many of our good Conservatives would vote against him. If you can get Kekewich to declare himself & you wish any communication to be made to either Bastard or young Carew I can undertake to do that – and if anything else suggests itself to you. . . .[63]

Samuel Kekewich of Peamore selected the southern division and carried it with Massey Lopes against Lord Amberley. (John Carpenter-Garnier succeeded when Kekewich died in 1873.) Despite Lupton's prognostications Lord Courtenay (heir of the earl of Devon) would not be denied the eastern division, which he carried in the company of Sir Lawrence Palk of Torquay.

Northcote's own special problem was that he had little money and could not afford contested elections. He had allowed himself unwisely to be tempted to transfer from the Cecil borough of Stamford (where Cranborne was his colleague) to his native county when the Hon. C.H.R. Trefusis succeeded in 1866 to the Clinton peerage. Now he confronted a formidable challenge from Thomas Dyke Acland of Killerton in a situation where the county Conservative management insisted on running a second Conservative, J.W. Walrond, as Northcote's colleague. Clinton consoled the dismayed Northcote with rather cold comfort:

I can quite understand that the impending contest will be an unpleasant one for you, & it is only as a matter of duty & because I believe we have a chance at this moment we ought not to neglect that I have come to the conclusion that we ought to engage in it.

He assured Northcote that he would not be asked to put down anything like £2,000, but 'no doubt a successful contest may entail trouble at future elections'.[64] Colonel Fane of Clovelly Court, Bideford (he who was being bribed with a peerage to retire in Hampshire), helpfully declared himself 'prepared and willing to pay down £2,000 to defray your expenses in this contest'. Fane calculated that 'a contested election in the North of Devon would not cost less than £5,000, probably more for the two candidates'. 'Representing the property I do in the Division, I feel bound, having declined to come forward myself, to help materially in any contest . . . determined upon by the Party.' Fane doubted the expediency of putting Walrond up for North Devon. Some gentlemen had refused to sign a requisition on the grounds that he was not well known (the Walronds were of Bradfield, Collumpton). Fane himself, as with his own Hampshire seat, was opposed to a second Conservative candidate in any case,

though of course if one were brought forward any influence I might have should be used to forward the views of 'the party'. But I hold and am strongly of opinion that with the great influence of Fortescue, Portsmouth, Poltimore F. Davie & others, not to mention the Aclands that, the success of any such attempt was to say the least of it doubtful, and might end in our losing.[65]

But the county managers, no doubt prodded from on high, were relentless against proponents of a quiet electoral life and cosy sharing of constituencies. Clinton did his best to stiffen Northcote's resolve.

> I believe the party in N. Devon is thoroughly in earnest & I feel very confident. Stucley's tenants must be well looked after, they will all vote right if not interfered with by Mr. Brown and it would be very useful if you could get a letter from Sir G. Stucley promising his support to yourself & Walrond & giving you his permission to canvass his tenants. If you can get this & let us have it we will 'get at' his tenants & keep them right.[66]
>
> Brown is also agent for Sir Arthur Chichester & Mr. Yeo of Fremington; these two will be hearty supporters.[67]

Other managers were getting out forms of requisition for Walrond. Expenses had been talked about and Bremridge, the Conservative agent for North Devon, reported to Northcote that Walrond 'would not put down more than £1000 and that you ought not to be asked for more than £2000 and I suggested that before the requisition is presented it should be ascertained that the funds (say £6000) are forthcoming'. Money promised was 'very different' from money assured; and 'Mr. Walrond will of course see that he is guaranteed before accepting the requisition.' The rumour in Exeter was that Lord Fortescue was 'very angry at the thought of our opposing Mr. Acland who will in the event of a contest withdraw and Mr. Dudley Fortescue will be brought in'.[68] Acland, however, stayed in; and Northcote reported to Disraeli that he thought 'we shall carry North Devon, but it will be a tough battle. Lopes seems to be in good heart about the South. There will be a fight in the East, and some of our friends say that Palk is not safe.'[69]

Clinton had cheered Disraeli with the prospect of all six Devon seats. In the end Conservatives won a creditable five, with Acland the only successful Liberal. From the south Trehawke Kekewich wrote of his father's success to Northcote:

> You will have rejoiced at our triumph of yesterday: South Devon, always supposed to be the weaker division, has eclipsed East Devon, and if they will adopt a plan I have suggested the Conservatives may return two members in the South for many parliaments. You will have observed the loyalty of Lopes and my father not to be shaken by the falsehoods which the Radicals did their utmost to circulate. The combination was certainly the only one which could ensure the return of the two C members while it gave a certain seat to Ld Courtenay. This was your opinion in the summer, & your utmost hopes have been realised. If we had lost one seat both must ere long have been in great jeopardy. As it is, we have rejected the philosophical Lordling [Amberley] who will never trouble us again. The victory will raise up a strong Conservative Association, and utterly dishearten our opponents.[70]

If Devon thus exhibited county electoral politics in traditional forms and manners, the county of Middlesex offered salient glimpses in 1868 of a new political order potentially extremely advantageous to the Conservative party. Since Reform in 1832 Middlesex had been notable for returning only two Conservative members: one in 1837 and one in 1841. Otherwise it reflected faithfully the Liberal hegemony of London and its region. There was no Conservative challenge in 1865; nor was there a Conservative challenge at a by-election in 1867 when Henry Labouchere was returned. The Conservative decision to contest Middlesex in 1868 was part of Disraeli's policy of 'operating on a class of seats hitherto unassailed'. Even so, only one Conservative candidate could be found. With his penchant for young sprigs of the aristocracy, Disraeli encouraged Lord George Hamilton, a younger son of the viceroy of Ireland, Lord Abercorn, and a junior ensign in a guards regiment, to stand. When Hamilton (who was 22 but looked more like 18) received a requisition at the Guards Club from a group of householders he treated the matter as a practical joke until visited by the whip Taylor, who told Hamilton the offer was serious and that Disraeli wished him to fight the seat. Disraeli personally confirmed his interest and desire at an interview, when he exuded sympathy and encouragement. (Hamilton recalled that Delane was 'particularly severe upon the absurdity of putting up ignorant young aristocrats for popular constituencies'.) Hamilton was assured that he was 'sure to get a big Protestant vote, there being in Middlesex a strong Low Church element'. Lord Abercorn was willing to put up the money. Hamilton expended about £10,000, big county elections in those days being 'ridiculously expensive'. 'All kinds of abuses prevailed; a vast number of solicitors was engaged at high fees as district agents; all the flies, buses, and carriages available were hired on the pretext of conveying voters to the poll, and travelling expenses from all parts of the kingdom were allowed.'[71]

Hamilton triumphed at the head of the Middlesex poll. He ascribed that dramatic upset to two new factors in politics. The first was the emergence of a new type of party agent. Among the Conservative agents for the Middlesex election in 1868 was Wollaston Pym, heir of Hazells Hall in Bedfordshire and descendant of the great seventeenth-century parliamentarian. 'He showed', as Hamilton reminisced, 'such aptitude in this election that he became the prominent agent for the Conservative Party in the whole of Middlesex. The appointment was a novelty, as up to that date solicitors had had a monopoly of that work.' Solicitors were in general not actively motivated in politics, were too sedentary in habit, and above all too expensive. Pym, on the other hand, 'showed what could be done by daily attention to the ins-and-outs of life in a big constituency. He was ubiquitous, a born fighter either with tongue or fists, and a thorough gentleman.' He was 'trusted and liked by all, and he gave the whole-hearted service which can come from conviction alone'.

> Our example was followed by many other constituencies, and thus arose the modern class of whole-time political agents whose work has been so invaluable to our party, being far less costly and much more efficient than the work of the class whom they superseded. Pym never lost an election, and when Middlesex was

> cut up in 1885 into eight divisions we won every seat by very large majorities. Statesmen may formulate grandiloquent policies on the platform, but efficient machinery to drive home the ideas of that policy into the apathetic masses is as essential to success as the conception of the policy itself.

Hamilton emphasised that Pym's lasting legacy was to have founded 'a school of political agents, and amongst these who were there trained was Captain Middleton, afterwards the well-known and very successful general manager of the Conservative Party'.[72]

The second factor in Middlesex was the formation of a new kind of electorate. Long after the event, Hamilton was able to look back and discern the beginning of a social transformation which was to have a profound impact upon politics.

> My electoral success was due to the strange chance of my being selected for a constituency which, unknown to the wire-pullers, had during the past ten years been converted from Radicalism to Conservatism. Rapid extension of suburban railroads and the outpouring of professional men, tradesmen, and clerical employees into the rural outskirts of London had steadily changed the tone and politics of the constituency. I was merely the mouthpiece of that transformation, but I got the whole credit of the victory.

As member for Middlesex, Hamilton was to gain 'a pretty wide knowledge of the views, ideas, aspirations, and prejudices of the well-to-do middle class'.[73] The parallel victory of W.H. Smith at Westminster (at the expense of John Stuart Mill) signalled something of the same beginnings of a social transformation of metropolitan politics.

2

Middlesex was a particular case of Conservatism's benefiting from the suburbanisation of a county. Lancashire, another area of marked Conservative advantage in 1868, exhibited somewhat of the same kind of blending of county and borough characteristics. Lancashire comprised eight county seats, of which three had been created in 1867. In the old truly county northern division Conservatives held their one seat and gained the second (at the expense of Lord Hartington); in the new north-eastern division they carried both seats. In the two southern divisions they took all four seats (seeing off Gladstone in the south-west). Thus, compared with 1865, when Lancashire returned three Conservatives and two Liberals, in 1868 Conservatives took all eight seats. This was Conservative county hegemony with a special Lancashire vengeance.

But it was in the boroughs that Lancashire Conservatism established its fame and reputation in 1868. In the industrial Lancashire region, including the then contiguous Cheshire manufacturing boroughs of Birkenhead and Stockport and omitting Lancaster (which in any case was disfranchised for corruption in 1867), 15 Liberal members were returned in 1865 compared with 13 Conservatives. From a Liberal point of view this represented already an anomalously strong Conservative borough presence in a region which had once been famously Liberal. In 1868 12 Liberals were returned compared with 24 Conservatives. This was startling. A Conservative came top of the poll in Manchester, hitherto a purely Liberal fief. Two Conservatives topped the poll at Salford, another former Liberal monopoly. Salford, the twelfth most populous borough in the country, was the largest capture by Conservatives: its electorate had increased by 250 per cent; and it had been the subject of particularly confident Liberal prognostications by such as Thorold Rogers.[74] Bolton, Ashton-under-Lyne, Clitheroe, and Stockport were further scenes of unwonted Conservative gain. They carried also the newly created borough of Stalybridge. Conservatives held their existing advantage in Birkenhead, Preston, Blackburn, and, of course, Tory Liverpool. Liberals carried newly created Burnley, held their own in Rochdale, Oldham, and Bury, held two of their Manchester seats, but made gains only in Wigan, Warrington, and Macclesfield.

Lancashire had been the subject of close pre-election attention by W.A. Abram in the Radical *Fortnightly Review*. Abram reflected Liberal disquiet at the singular fact that the Lancashire boroughs constituted a region which by 1865 had so unaccountably strayed from the Liberal fold: a 'source of much surprise'. This made the part to be played by the new 1867 constituency a matter of exceptional interest.

> The manufacturing boroughs of Lancashire, which a generation ago were decisively radical, are represented by ten Liberal and ten Conservative members in the parliament that is now awaiting its dissolution . . . Whence this retrogression – what is its cause, and how far is it likely to proceed?[75]

Abram explained the strange 'wave of reaction' by a combination of new prosperity dulling the old radical temper, a 'sluggishness of operative's reason' leading to a 'sheer inability to construe events', and of influence of employers ambitious to advance themselves socially, to be '*en rapport* with the territorial gentry'. 'It is an axiom with election managers in Lancashire boroughs', Abram commented, 'that the politics of a town are determined solely by the relative number of spindles and looms driven by Tory and Liberal employers.' In Abram's view, however, this was a superficial and unconvincing explanation of anomalous Conservative strength in the Lancashire manufacturing boroughs. He predicted that the sluggishness of reason and inability to construe events so lamentably apparent in the old operative constituency would be swept away by the fresh winds of the second Reform Act and that Lancashire would in November 1868 renew its loyalty to its true Liberal cause.[76]

The full horror of the Lancashire borough results coming upon the Liberal world provoked the editor of the *Fortnightly Review*, John Morley, into some bitter reflections. In his December piece on 'The chamber of mediocrity', he pointed to Lancashire as an ominous portent. 'Manchester, thriving home of mean ambitions, has just filled three out of five seats with Conservatives, whilst her largest neighbours have thrown their entire weight into the same scale.' It was the same portent as the defeat of John Stuart Mill in Westminster: the one standard bearer of intellect and high principle felled by a 'coalition of true patricians, stuccoed patricians, and shopkeepers'. It was 'as significant as the fall and disgrace of the great Turgot'. Morley detected a 'new feudalism' at large, which was 'only just beginning to organise itself . . . the Lancashire towns are turning to what they consider the politer faith'. In a larger but not less daunting perspective Morley, in an analysis which prefigured much of his *On Compromise* of 1874, argued that while in the overall election results the Conservative party had been, ostensibly, handsomely defeated, yet Conservatism 'as a social principle' had suffered no defeat, 'nor had Radicalism, as a social principle, won any victory'. Morley discerned already the 'germs of a perilous alliance between genuine Tories and sham Liberals'. Had not Lord Salisbury made a signal appearance in the Lancashire heartland? 'The able territorial prince of Hatfield and the merchant princes of the Manchester Exchange only the other day exchanged their first salutation – omen of a closer union to come, which it will tax all the skill and foresight of good citizens to bring to nought.'[77]

Morley's analysis at the time was substantially in agreement with Hamilton's in retrospect, *mutatis mutandis*. But special circumstances in Lancashire gave a special edge to its Conservatism, one which doctrinally and temperamentally both Abram and Morley preferred not to contemplate. Lancashire was pre-eminently a place where some degree of 'chivalrous feeling among the middle classes with regard to the Irish Church' obtained. However interpreted – and 'chivalrous' is perhaps not the most appropriate definition of much vociferous anti-Irish and Orange anti-Roman Catholic populism – the religious dimension of politics must be allowed its full value as a fuel of Lancashire Tory energies. Modern investigation points to the way the 'Irish issue' provided a substitute vote-catcher for Conservative candidates to 'compensate for Disraeli's rather feeble leadership in the election campaign'.[78] There are indications also that the Conservative working-men's associations in Lancashire were effective participants in the campaign; enough, at any rate, to give the National Union a specious ground for claims to a part of the credit for the Lancashire victories.[79] Employers of labour, moreover, were certainly important. 'The dynamic element in Blackburn's Toryism was provided by the millowners, especially the Hornby family, reinforced by the drink trade and buttressed by militant Anglicanism.' 'Hornbyism' could be defined as a 'compound of enlightened paternalism with a swashbucking approach to politics'.[80] This compound was to become an abiding tradition in Conservative Lancashire, particularly as embodied in later years by the exemplary local political boss, Alderman Archibald Salvidge of Liverpool. And there was ever the great presence of the Stanleys of Knowsley. Stanley conferred with Hornby and understood that the South Lancashire election would cost 'about

£8,500'. Stanley did not know how much his father, Derby, was contributing. He knew that Derby and Stanley's brother, Frederick, standing for North Lancashire, agreed that the cost there would be 'exactly double, £17,000: of which £10,000 is Ld. D's share'.[81]

Clearly, the case of the borough of Westminster, cited so readily as a kind of connecting link between the phenomena on display in both Lancashire and Middlesex, demands attention. W.H. Smith, converter of a newsagent's business into a famous newsvending retail chain, had challenged the Liberals, the Hon. Richard Grosvenor and J.S. Mill, unavailingly in 1865. An exemplary embodiment of certain social and political signifiers, Smith was by origin a tradesman, a Methodist and a Liberal who gradually transmuted these classic qualifications to become a brilliantly successful newsvending entrepreneur by way of solidly bourgeois Palmerstonian and Anglican loyalties. By 1866 Corry could remark to Disraeli that 'Smith has both money and manners. He is much too good a fellow to be a Radical, I should have thought.'[82] Smith set out to replace the pre-eminent philosophic Liberal in 1868 in a constituency nearly doubled in numbers. Corry reported on 18 September that 'George Cubitt tells me that he is growing pretty sure that Smith will beat Mill'.[83] Smith and his friends starting working hard in the winter of 1867/8.[84] Smith's campaign set new standards in assiduity of organisation and conspicuous expenditure, especially as it was waged against Mill, who ostentatiously made a virtue of not spending money. It became a particular complaint against Smith that he owed his election to the unscrupulous activities of the Hon. Robert Grimston, a famous sportsman and rider to hounds, a country neighbour of Smith's and a business associate in a telegraph company.[85] Grimston was chairman of the St. George's, Hanover Square, ward, where he played a crucial role in delivering the vote of the aristocratic elements otherwise aloof from the 'newsvendor'.[86] Grimston's ruthless resourcefulness in such matters as canvassing shopkeepers to display placards at a shilling a board a day led to Smith's being cited before the judicial tribunal under the new provisions of the Election Petitions and Corrupt Practices at Elections Act of 1868. These hearings disclosed that the London and Westminster Working Men's Constitutional Association had spent 'substantial sums', and that Smith himself and his business partners had put over £9,000 into the contest, mainly on hiring of cabs. (The two Liberals returned a little over £2,000.) However, the judge, Baron Martin, ruled that the association was an 'independent agency', and that a candidate could not be held responsible for the action of agents. This judgement has been held to show 'how imperfectly the new party institutions were understood'; reflecting also a judicial coyness at a strange world of political rough-and-tumble into which judges had been unwillingly thrust.[87]

Smith came head of the poll at Westminster, leaving Mill ousted in third place. The shock expressed by such as John Morley helped to establish Smith unassailably as a totem of anti-'philosophical' bourgeois politics. Under

Disraeli's careful patronage, Smith became exposed deliberately as a model specimen of a new style of middle-class slippage across into Conservatism as the implications of Gladstone's succession to the Liberal leadership began to make themselves explicit. And there was promise, for Conservatism, of further benign contagion in the neighbouring City of London constituency. Since 1832, the City, with four members, had elected Liberals on 38 occasions (not counting re-elections on acceptance of office), and Conservatives on eight occasions. No Conservative had been elected in the City in fact since 1852. That a Conservative, Charles Bell, should be returned, even if in fourth place, in 1868, can be seen as a portent of what soon enough revealed itself to be nothing less than a metropolitan political revolution.

3

But this metropolitan revolution was not yet. Otherwise, there was little enough cheer for the Conservative party in the boroughs. What is most evident about the borough campaign other than isolated instances, mainly in Lancashire, is the entire absence of any concerted or comprehensive effort to cater for and comprehend the new popular electorate in any manner for which the National Union was purportedly designed. The testimony on this point by Joseph Gould of Exeter, a volunteer party worker in 1868 and later three times chairman of the Western Division of Conservative Agents, is highly cogent. Conservative candidates were defeated in boroughs in 1868, Gould later recorded, simply because they relied on 'old-fashioned methods, utterly unsuited to cope with the requirements under the extension of the Franchise in the Boroughs by the Act of 1867'.[88] Far from giving a lead, Disraeli had done his utmost to dampen any prospect of the National Union's being effectively or even usefully in place for the 1868 elections. What is most apparent among the records of the Conservative borough campaign in 1868 is either a haplessly unaware optimism or a shiftless defeatism. The likes of Wollaston Pym and Joseph Gould (or for that matter of Robert Grimston) were few and far between in 1868.

In the category of hapless optimism J.L. Wharton, candidate for Durham City, offers himself as a prime specimen: 'The *new* (Durham) Electors do well for me, it makes one see the wisdom of Dizzy.'[89] Dizzy's wisdom notwithstanding, Wharton ended up at the bottom of the poll. Sheffield provides another characteristic case. Corry informed Disraeli:

> Jno. Price Q.C. – a clever and sensible man – has been to Sheffield on the invitation of a Protestant League, which has been got up during the summer by the working men there. He returns with a marvellous report.
>
> He is informed by the council of the League and by men of position in the town – the clergy and some large employers – that they have *13,000* men on their books who will support a Protestant Candidate. The only stipulation they make is that the candidate must promise legalization of T. Union funds. I told

> him *certainly* not to stick at that; and he has done so. He has brought us the whole thing in black and white. Expense 3,500.
>
> We have considered this very carefully today & yesterday, as not only in itself, but as an example to the working men of the whole country, it is of great importance.
>
> What a coup to have Jn Price Q.C. the popular candidate for Sheffield, and that he might soon be as he is *just* the sort of man 'the people' like. We think of giving 1,000, he finding 2000.[90]

All this was fantasy. Out of nearly 42,000 Sheffield votes, Price collected 5,272, at the bottom of the poll, behind three Liberals.

Helston, likewise touted as 'a certainty' for the Hon. T.A. Bruce by its former member, the judge, Baliol Brett,[91] disappointed in the event. Greenwich, reserved by the Liberals as a resort for Gladstone in the likely event of his defeat in Lancashire, naturally became a Conservative target. 'What do you intend to do in Greenwich as to opposing the *future Premier*?!! of England', Corry was somewhat tactlessly asked. 'He surely is not going to be allowed to walk the course?!'[92] Viscount Mahon, selected as one of the Conservative challengers, thought there was 'every reason to be sanguine of success at Greenwich'; though it was worrying that 'distress among the poor is so great that if Salomons spends money he will succeed'.[93] Alderman Salomons did succeed at the head of the poll for the Liberals (Gladstone won the second seat). One Conservative problem here was that the vital necessity of gaining 'control of the D[ock] Yard artisans' at Deptford was compromised by the fact that Admiral Robinson was *'not eaten up with zeal'*.[94]

In the category of shiftless defeatism the case of Frome is illustrative. 'Frome is pronounced quite hopeless for us,' Corry told Disraeli, 'so our man – Haig – has given it up.'[95] 'With regard to the City of Lincoln', reported Nisbet-Hamilton to Taylor,

> Henry Chaplin had almost made up his mind . . . to allow his brother to stand provided he saw a reasonable chance of success. The new Constituency in that place will be very much under the influence of Clayton and Shuttleworth the steam engine manufacturers. They are great Radicals and very possibly H. Chaplin after circulating his friends may have found the prospect of a Conservative candidate's success, hopeless.[96]

In the end there was no Conservative challenge in Lincoln and the two Liberals were returned unmolested. There was a scheme afoot at one time to promote a last-minute bogus 'Independent Liberal Candidate' to try to split the Liberal vote;[97] but this too came to nothing. It is true that candidates were sometimes hard to come by. 'I expect to have a Mr. Pott, a vinegar merchant, soon out for Southwark', Corry informed Disraeli on 'a quiet day at Victoria Chambers'. 'A good man I am told.'[98] But Pott did not materialise to contest what had been uncontested in 1865. Eventually Alderman Cotton was drafted unsuccessfully. Derby, observing closely from retirement, felt obliged to comment severely on the apparent 'lamentable apathy' on the part of Conservatives in abandoning seats 'which might fairly be contested', or failing to avail themselves of the 'rival pretensions of Liberal candidates for a single seat'.[99]

The case of Weymouth illustrates a revealing degree of timidity. Unlike Frome or Lincoln it had a fair record of Conservative success: two Conservatives were elected in 1859, and one in 1865. 'Charles Hambro has gone to Weymouth', Corry told Disraeli, 'to make up his mind. I think it will end in his starting. A "one and one" compact has existed there, but the other day the Liberals broke it – to our advantage, we think. Hambro will be a good candidate, and his wife the best canvasser in England.'[100] The Conservatives did not risk responding to the Liberal challenge, and ran only one candidate. Hambro topped the poll. At Marylebone there was something of the same lack of resource. Corry had information from the borough on the understanding that the government was anxious that a Conservative candidate should be started. There must be a chance, for three if not four Liberals would go to the poll. Mr. Stanford had declined, despite an offer if he would put down £500 to find another £500 toward his expenses.

> Now I do not suppose the Society will be able to guarantee anything, but if the Government could find a candidate and support him with funds, we would do what we could. Ld. Thomas Clinton I have no doubt would come forward if funds were found and would doubtless poll a considerable number of votes, tho' at the eleventh hour we can not confidently predict success.
>
> I am very sorry we should be in these straits but I understand from Mr. Stanford that Mr. Spofforth had entirely declined giving any money, and this is the principal cause of our present difficulty.[101]

It is hardly surprising that the Conservative candidate eventually pressed to stand for Marylebone finished fifth after four Liberals.

No doubt Spofforth had reasons founded on long and disappointing experience for not throwing good money after bad. Nor were all his calls wrong. Disraeli wrote to Corry on a sardonic note: 'I don't like what Rose says about Marlow, for which I was not unprepared. But this, of course, is one of Spofforth's certain seats.'[102] And so indeed it proved to be. Disraeli accused Lord Hylton, the former chief whip Jolliffe, of default at his old Petersfield seat: in Stanley's words, of not giving more help 'than from local reasons he was able or willing to give'.[103] Little could have been done by anyone to mend the case at Nottingham, where Sir Robert Clifton, deaf to Protestant pleas, 'has broken off negotiations with us, & declares for Gladstone';[104] and came top of the poll as a 'Liberal Conservative'. And for that matter nor was expertise in the arts of making Conservative principles effective among the masses any guarantee of success with the new popular constituency: Gorst came bottom of the poll in Cambridge borough. As against that, his rival Raikes contrived to win the second seat at Chester, but in a manner ironically far removed from the spirit of democracy and the masses. Lord Grosvenor, heir to the marquess of Westminster, was a Liberal candidate, and a certainty for a seat. The critical situation arose that Raikes was drawing too near the earl when the second Conservative withdrew so as not to split votes.

> Towards the close of the day some of Mr. Raikes's supporters grew frightened at the situation. The possibility of Earl Grosvenor occupying any place but the first had never occurred to their minds; and the position of their man, gratifying though it was, was also alarming, for the Grosvenor influence was a very real factor in the life of the citizens, and if 'the Earl' were to be deprived of the place of pride, no man could tell what the consequences might be. A little judicious splitting of votes was therefore indulged in . . . and . . . Earl Grosvenor headed the poll by seventy-two votes.[105]

'Our men seem to be running away'

1

The Conservative failure to challenge comprehensively and effectively in the English boroughs was reflected in a net loss of 33 English borough seats. As it happened, this was largely compensated by county successes. Conservatives thus won 223 English seats as against 240 Liberal. But the results from Scotland and Ireland put the issue beyond doubt. As Hardy noted, 'County & large towns in England do well but Scotland and Ireland! eheu!'[106] Scotland returned a mere eight Conservatives out of 60 seats: a net loss of four and a decisive comment on Sir James Fergusson's talk of one or two gains. There is more than a touch of pathos in the appeal to Corry from Richard Nugent, secretary of the National Protestant Union.

> Pray tell Mr. Disraeli with my best respects that he must not be discouraged about Scotland. . . . The movement has spread & is spreading. The Conservative Agents now ask for our Lecturers. The *People* ask for them. Their meetings are crowded. I have had to send two more gentlemen, and yet the demand is for *more*. . . . I believe in my heart we shall do great things in Scotland.[107]

There was no hint in Scotland of any popular responsiveness in support of a beleaguered Anglican establishment of religion. Lord Bute's zealous Conservatism failed to do great things in the two Ayrshires, where two Liberals were duly returned. Lord Elcho's return for Haddingtonshire was considered by expert Conservative opinion to be 'safe' ; but even so, 'he cannot be too vigilant for the opposite side are still very persevering in their efforts'.[108] Elcho survived as a 'Liberal Conservative'.

Taylor's prediction as to Conservatives holding their own in Ireland was likewise proved false. Ireland returned 40 Conservative members from 105 seats: a net loss of ten. This was the heaviest Conservative loss in Irish seats since the first Reformed parliament in 1832. The borough of Bandon was a case in point. A traditional Protestant outpost in County Cork, it had been held by Conservatives, largely unopposed, in eleven elections since 1832. It was lost in 1868, narrowly, by three votes out of 275. Such voting numbers are in themselves eloquent of the fact that, outside the Dublin Pale and Ulster, such Conservative seats as survived (14 only) depended largely on their having small electorates. Up to this election Conservative support in Ireland had been spread over all types of constituency. Even so it was by no means obvious in 1868 that 'ultimate withdrawal into the northern laager' was decisively in train.[109] It was as recently as 1865, after all, that the Conservative party had been the largest Irish parliamentary party. Yet the fact that so expert and experienced a veteran of Irish politics as Taylor could misjudge the Irish situation in 1868 was in itself a significant indicator of the passing of an order in which, after the collapse of 1832, extraordinary Conservative exertions in Ireland had produced impressive results. In 1868 Taylor 'poured the balm of patronage over warring Conservative factions' in quite the old style, but without any of the old results.[110] Disraeli desperately grasped at straws when he adjured Corry on 26 October: 'We must exert ourselves more than ever. Spare nothing for Ireland: it's a rich mine, I can't help thinking.'[111] Disraeli's Protestant delusions were never more delusory than in Ireland.

Although Wales (and Monmouthshire), by returning ten Conservatives, thus registered ostensibly a net Conservative loss of only one seat, the underlying psephological trend promised to be as damaging as in Ireland. A borough such as Brecon could still be gained through the influence of the former Liberal member, since succeeded as Lord Camden, and moving across to the Conservative party. 'I hear Camden is *quite* neutral at Brecon', Corry had reported in 1866, 'it is even whispered that he shows signs of coming our way before long. It is too soon after his father's death, to expect it just yet.'[112] By 1868 Camden was in a position to deliver Brecon (the second title of the Camden marquessate was in fact earl of Brecknock; Brecon Priory was one of the Pratt residences). But it could only be delivered in such manner as led to the Conservative's being unseated on petition in 1869 (a Conservative was eventually returned again in 1870).

However, it was the famous Merthyr election of 1868, when the Radical Nonconformist Henry Richard won a stunning victory over the Whig-Liberal Anglican grandee H.A. Bruce, that signalled the beginning of the end in Wales of such politely traditional electioneering. The difference was at bottom simply a difference in mass: the Brecon electorate, which had never been near 300 in the few contested elections before 1868, totalled 729; in Merthyr nearly 25,000 votes were cast.[113] The only two contested elections in Merthyr before 1868 had yielded 444 votes (1837) and 906 votes (1859). A critical mass of electors began a transmutation of political quality. As in Ireland, Welsh Conservatism survived largely in a political environment of small constituencies. Even more telling for the future was the collision caused by the new electorate between insurgent Welsh Radical Nonconformity and English and Anglican conventions about the electoral decencies to be observed by tenant voters. In Cardiganshire 43 instances of punitive evictions were proved and 26 in Carmarthenshire, where there was a contest for the first election since 1837, and where a Liberal had not won a seat since 1835; but where in 1868 a Liberal came top of the poll. In north Wales 80 quarrymen were dismissed by Lord Penrhyn. These evictions created a Welsh popular martyrology, making the aftermath of the 1868 elections more important than the elections themselves.[114] Hardy noted in 1869 'unpleasant Welsh evidence' at the elections committee about landlord intimidation. 'There is a case there wh. will tell on the ballot.' It availed little that Hardy could appeal to the undoubted fact that there was Welsh Nonconformist 'spiritual terrorism' in the Irish Catholic manner on the other side of the case.[115]

2

Disraeli wrote to Corry on 21 September:

> H.M. is very anxious about news of the elections: she frequently recurs to the hope, that, at all events I shall have a material accretion of strength. I told her what I believe is the truth: that the new Constituency in the counties appears to be safe & conservative: that the bulk of the new Constituency in the towns, without any enmity to us, are holding back, & will not commit themselves to either side; & that victory will probably be to the party wh. is wealthiest & best organised.[116]

Again: 'H.M. is most anxious about the Elections; *scrutinising*: she hears, of course, by different accounts from the other side: & always concludes 'But, I think, you must get an accession of strength'.[117] The queen's wish was father to her thought. Disraeli was in much the same case. He was still, in early November, trying to persuade himself of the 'difficulty – perhaps the fallacy' in forecasts of Conservative defeat. He advised Stanley not to 'believe newspapers, and newspaper writers, too much. The result of the General Election, rest assured, will surprise all the students of that literature.'[118] Hardy dined at the Carlton with his fellow member for Oxford University, Mowbray, on 30 October. 'His auguries as to the Election generally are far less favourable than I expected & it is clear that freedom is at hand.'[119] Soon Disraeli himself began to abandon his illusions. 'Send me a line of news', was his stricken plea to Corry on 10 November. 'Our men seem to be running away.'[120] In remarking to Cairns on 18 November that Conservative returns were 'but poor in appearance today', Hardy commented that Disraeli appeared to be in a state of stunned distractedness: 'He seems in a strange way. . . .'[121]

On 19 November Hardy voted for Smith in Westminster (he had seven votes in various constituencies); 'Mill out to my great joy . . .' But he was disappointed by the City results: one Conservative only out of the four seats. 'Manchester, Blackburn, Bolton, Ashton, Staly[bridge], Southampton & other large places speak for us. In small boroughs we are unlucky.' Instances of such were Exeter, Hereford, Cardiff, Canterbury.[122] Ministers now had to confront decisive defeat. Derby underlined to Disraeli the fact on 22

November: 'our numbers will not only disappoint your sanguine hopes, but will fall considerably below even my more modest anticipations.'[123] Gladstone was heading towards improving his 1865 majority of 60 to a round hundred. The great Conservative efforts in 1859 and 1865 now seemed set at nought. The question now arose as to the government's response. Disraeli had never considered any alternative to the conventional procedure of meeting the new parliament and putting matters to the test in the House of Commons. Stanley, who had already practically perjured himself to his Lynn electorate on the Irish Church issue in order to placate Disraeli, wanted to avoid any further necessity of that political perjury at the opening of the new parliament. He broached the unprecedented expedient of an immediate resignation to Cairns and Hardy, at the other end of the cabinet spectrum on the Irish Church. They responded positively. A breach in constitutional convention was well worth escaping further embarrassment and humiliation. The queen was perfectly complaisant. 'The Queen talked of the Elections' Hardy recorded; 'she wd clearly like what I had talked over with Stanley & Cairns, resignations without a struggle. There are difficulties but it would be wise if possible.'[124]

There were plausible arguments for it; in the normal course of procedures, after all, the government would have resigned in April after defeat on Gladstone's Irish Church resolutions. The 'difficulties' had to do not only with the breach of precedent with its implication that the voice of the electorate 'out of doors' counted more than the voice of the Commons; they had to do with the turn taken in Cairns's mind as to 'scruples'. Cairns had come round to 'observing what seems to be the temper in places where we have gained'. He told Disraeli: 'I greatly fear that it might dishearten & displease our friends, & be treated by others as a step taken to shrink from discussion & embarrass the ordinary course of Parliamt.' As he explained, he attached more weight to his fears, as they pressed counter to his wishes; but was quite open to further discussion.[125] As the Liberal majority increased with every post, further discussion in cabinet on 28 November resulted in a decision to resign forthwith, without meeting parliament. 'Never was a Cabinet more unanimous in opinion & action than this has been.' Disraeli made a farewell speech. Ministers composed a circular to the party to explain the decision and head off any alienation or offence. The government stood by its policy of resistance to disestablishment and disendowment of the Church of Ireland. But, given the patent circumstance that it could not hope to command the confidence of the new House of Commons, ministers held it due to their own honour and their policy not to retain office unnecessarily for a single day. The convenience of the public business as well as the just influence of the Conservative party both pointed to resignation.[126]

The drastic breach of constitutional convention inevitably caused a stir. There was applause on the ground that facts are better guides than theories. Hardy was amused during the 'nine days wonder' to see Disraeli getting all the credit. 'Whereas, I believe Stanley first suggested it & Cairns & I backed him.'[127] The irony of the event was that Disraeli's bowing to the will of the new electorate he had created was the only serious relationship he forged with it since the 1867 Reform Act. Constitutional (and anti-democratic) purists deplored the 'first open recognition that the House of Commons itself was of less importance than the electors who formed it', and that members of parliament would more and more be reduced to mere 'delegate' status.[128] Raikes, now MP for Chester, was one of those Conservatives who would have preferred the 'bolder policy' of confronting parliament. Spofforth robustly responded to his complaints as to Disraeli's timidity.

> A debate on the Irish Church, which might have occurred had we continued in, would have enlightened Mr. Gladstone as to the likeliest measure to pass; as it is, he must introduce a crude and ill-digested measure, which will in all probability leave the Irish Establishment where it is. The move appears to have met with universal satisfaction. I have only heard of another dissentient besides yourself, and you will see it will turn out all right.[129]

Disraeli caused a final stir in his resignation honours in December by indulging himself in promoting the viceroy of Ireland, Lord Abercorn, to a dukedom, and by prevailing upon the embarrassed queen to create his wife a viscountess in her own right (with the Burkean title of Beaconsfield). There was a good deal of snobbish laughter at the odd elevation of Mary Anne. But there was a great deal more Conservative regret expressed that Disraeli had made such a point of not making Mary Anne a countess by accepting for himself the earldom which by convention he was entitled to as a retiring prime minister, thereby conveniently leaving the defeated party freedom to find itself a more effective leader.

Notes and References

1 Clinton to Northcote, 28 Aug. 1868; Bl, Iddesleigh 50037, 115.
2 R. Blake, *Disraeli* (1966), 508.
3 T.E. Kebbel, *Lord Beaconsfield and Other Tory Memories* (1907), 41–2.
4 Blake, *Disraeli*.
5 Buckle, ii, 412–13.
6 *Ibid.*, 431.
7 Disraeli to Corry, 9 Oct. 1868; HP, B/XX/D/105.
8 Disraeli to Corry, 14 Aug. [1868]; HP, B/XX/D/80.
9 Disraeli to Corry, 19 Sept. [1868]; HP, B/XX/D/92.
10 Corry to Disraeli, 14 Aug. [1868]; HP, B/XX/D/80.
11 Buckle, ii, 412–13.
12 Disraeli to Corry, 22 Aug. 1868; HP, B/XX/D/86.
13 W.H. Corke to Corry, 12 Oct. 1868; HP, B/IX/G/20.
14 Nevill to Disraeli, 18 Aug. 1868; HP, B/XXI/A/46.
15 Hardy, *Diary*, 83.
16 Disraeli to Corry, 21 Sept. 1868; HP, B/XX/D/93.
17 Stucley to Disraeli, 27 Sept. 1868; HP, B/IX/D/31.
18 Hardy to Northcote, 10 Sept. 1868. BL, Iddesleigh 50037, 153.
19 Hardy, *Diary*, 70.
20 J. Vincent (ed.) *Disraeli, Derby and the Conservative Party. Journals and Memoirs of Edward Henry, Lord Stanley, 1849–1869 Hassocks* (1978) 336.
21 P. Cohen, *Disraeli's Child. A History of the Conservative and Unionist Party Organisation* (1964), ii, 6.
22 *Ibid.* Corry to Disraeli, 1 Sept. 1868; HP, B/XX/Co/43.
23 See R. Stewart, *The Foundation of the Conservative Party, 1830–1867* (1978), 330.
24 E.J. Feuchtwanger, *Disraeli, Democracy and the Tory Party* (Oxford 1968) 54, 111–12; Vincent, *Disraeli, Derby and the Conservative Party*, 334.
25 For Taylor see T.K. Hoppen, *Elections, Politics, and Society in Ireland 1832–1885* (Oxford, 1984), 293–9.
26 Stewart, *Foundation*, 328.
27 Taylor to Disraeli, 23 Sept. [1868]; HP, B/XX/T/114.
28 Disraeli to Corry, 9 Oct. 1868; HP, B/XX/D/105.
29 Buckle, ii, 414.
30 Stewart, *Foundation*, 280.
31 Cohen, *Disraeli's Child*, 6.
32 Spofforth to Disraeli, 7 March 1868; HP, B/IX/N/2a; B/XI/N/5.

33 J.C. Lowe, 'The Tory triumph of 1868 in Blackburn and in Lancashire', *Historical Journal* (1973), 736.
34 HP, B/XX/T/114.
35 Buckle, ii, 396–7.
36 H.J. Hanham, 371–2; Stewart, *Foundation*, 331. The Liberal Fund in 1868 was a mere £15,000.
37 Buckle, ii, 396–7.
38 Hardy, *Diary*, 77.
39 *Ibid.*, 83.
40 Kekewich to Northcote, 28 Nov. 1868; BL, Iddesleigh 50016, 68.
41 See T. Lloyd, 'Uncontested seats in British general elections, 1852–1910', *Historical Journal* (1965). Many contests ended up being purely nominal, as candidates abandoned expensive and hopeless electioneering before the poll.
42 Disraeli to Corry, 19 Sept. [1868]; HP, B/XX/D/92.
43 Taylor to Disraeli, 28 Sept. [1868]; HP, B/XX/T/114. Fergusson was duly elevated to the Privy Council in November 1868.
44 Corry to Disraeli, 22 Sept. 1868; HP, B/XX/Co/45.
45 Disraeli to Northcote, 8 Sept. 1868. BL, Iddesleigh 50016, 46.
46 Hardy to Northcote, 10 Sept. 1868; BL, Iddesleigh 50037, 153.
47 Corry to Disraeli, 22 Sept. 1868; HP; B/XX/Co/45.
48 Buckle, ii, 427–8.
49 Lowe, 'The Tory triumph of 1868', 737–8.
50 Feuchtwanger, *Disraeli, Democracy and the Tory Party*, 129; H. St. J. Raikes, *Life and Letters of H.C. Raikes* (1898), 56.
51 *The History of 'The Times'*, III: *The Tradition Established* (1939), 407. See also S. Koss, *The Rise and Fall of the Political Press in Britain* I: *The Nineteenth Century* (1981), 175.
52 Disraeli to Corry, 26 Oct. 1868; HP, B/XX/D/106.
53 Lord G. Hamilton, *Parliamentary Reminiscences and Reflections, 1868 to 1885* (1917), 27, 68–85.
54 Buckle, ii, 427.
55 Corry to Disraeli, 14 Aug. 1868; HP, B/XX/Co/39.
56 Corry to Disraeli, 23 Sept. 1868; HP, B/XX/Co/46. Fane, of Clovelly Court, Bideford, Devon, died in 1868 before any promised peerage was forthcoming.
57 Cairns to Disraeli, 11 Sept. 1868; HP, B/XX/D/90.
58 Corry to Disraeli, 21 Aug. 1868; HP, B/XX/Co/41.
59 Nisbet-Hamilton to Taylor, 20 Oct. [1867]; HP,B/XX/T/102.
60 Hardy, *Diary*, 84.
61 R.A.B. to Corry, 20 Oct [1868]; HP, B/IX/G/25.
62 W.L. Lowndes to Corry, 21 and 26 Oct. 1868; HP, B/IX/G/26, 34.
63 Lupton to Northcote, 7 Jan. 1868; BL, Iddesleigh 50037, 67. B.J.P. Bastard of Kitley, Yealhampton; Walter Carew was of Haccombe, Buckfastleigh, and Tiverton Castle, son of Sir Walter, 8th baronet.
64 Clinton to Northcote, 28 Aug. 1868; BL, Iddesleigh 50037, 115.
65 Fane to Northcote, 25 Aug. 1868; BL, Iddesleigh 50037, 115.
66 See above, 54.
67 Clinton to Northcote, 17 Aug. 1868; BL, Iddesleigh 50037, 108.
68 Bremridge to Northcote, 21 Aug. 1868; BL, Iddesleigh 50037, 109.

69 Northcote to Disraeli, 24 Sept. 1868; BL, Iddesleigh 50016, 54.
70 Kekewich to Northcote, 28 Nov. 1868; BL, Iddesleigh 50016, 68. Courtenay did not last long; he took the Chiltern Hundreds in 1870. See Derby Diary, 26 June 1869, on the scandal of Courtenay's £200,000 debts.
71 Hamilton, *Parliamentary Reminiscences*, 1–3.
72 *Ibid.*, 9–10.
73 *Ibid.*, 10–11.
74 R.L. Greenall, 'Popular Conservatism in Salford, 1868–1886', *Northern History* (1974), 122–6.
75 'Social condition and political prospects of the Lancashire working men', *Fortnightly Review*, October 1868, 426–7. Abram refers to strictly Lancashire boroughs.
76 *Ibid.*, 437–41.
77 *Fortnightly Review*, December 1868, 682–92.
78 Lowe, 'The Tory triumph of 1868', 738–41. See also Greenall, 'Popular Conservatism in Salford', 131. For insights into Liverpool's popular Conservatism see P. J. Waller, *Democracy and Sectarianism* (Liverpool 1981), 21.
79 National Union annual conference minutes (1869).
80 Lowe, 'The Tory triumph of 1868', 741.
81 Vincent, *Disraeli, Derby and the Conservative Party*, 338.
82 Corry to Disraeli, 5 Oct. 1866; HP, B/XX/Co/12.
83 Corry to Disraeli, 18 Sept. 1868; HP, B/XX/Co/44.
84 Lord Chilston, *W.H. Smith* (1965), 56.
85 See F. Gale, *The Life of the Hon. Robert Grimston* (1885), 203.
86 Chilston, *W.H. Smith*, 57.
87 C. O'Leary, *The Elimination of Corrupt Practices in British Elections, 1868–1911* (Oxford 1962), 50–1.
88 *The Tory*, May 1895, quoted in A.W.P. Fawcett, *Conservative Agent* (1967), 12–13.
89 Wharton to Mowbray, 8 Nov. [1868]; HP, B/IX/G/66.
90 Corry to Disraeli, 23 Sept. 1868; HP, B/XX/Co/46.
91 Corry to Disraeli, 21 Aug. 1868; HP, B/XX/Co/41.
92 Hamman to Corry, 23 July 1668; HP, IX/G/10.
93 Mahon to Corry, [? Nov. 68]; HP, IX/G/67.
94 Hamman to Corry, 23 July 1868; HP, IX/G/10.
95 Corry to Disraeli, 18 Sept. 1868; HP, B/XX/Co/44.
96 Nisbet-Hamilton to Taylor, 20 Oct. [? 1867]; HP, B/XX/T/102.
97 HP, B/IX/G/58 (12 Nov. 1868).
98 Corry to Disraeli, 18 Sept. 1868; HP, B/XX/Co/44.
99 Buckle, ii, 429.
100 *Ibid.*
101 A. Ross to Corry [? Nov. 1868]; HP, B/IX/G/62c.
102 Disraeli to Corry, 10 Oct. 1868; HP, B/XX/D/112.
103 Derby Diary, 18 July 71.
104 Corry to Disraeli, 18 Sept. 1868; HP, B/XX/Co/44.
105 Raikes, *Raikes*, 70–1.
106 Hardy, *Diary*, 85–6. For Scotland see also Hanham, *Elections and Party Management*, 160–161: especially the lugubrious analysis of the Scottish whip, Sir G. Graham Montgomery.

107 Nugent to Corry 6 Oct. 1868; HP, B/X/A/28. See also Hanham, 214–15.
108 Nisbet-Hamilton to Taylor, 20 Oct. [1867]; HP, B/XX/102.
109 See Hoppen, *Elections, Politics, and Society in Ireland*, 289–90.
110 *Ibid.*, 269.
111 HP, B/XX/D/106.
112 Corry to Disraeli, 3 Sept. 1866; HP, B/XX/Co/5.
113 Merthyr was in 1868 the only considerable Welsh borough. The contemporary Cardiff electorate was 4,556.
114 K.O. Morgan, *Wales in British Politics, 1868–1922* (Cardiff, 1963), 25.
115 Hardy, *Diary*, 97, 100.
116 Disraeli to Corry, 21 Sept. 1868; HP, B/XX/D/93.
117 Disraeli to Corry [Sept. 1868]; HP, B/XX/D/98.
118 Buckle, ii, 429, 431.
119 Hardy, *Diary*, 84.
120 Disraeli to Corry, 10 Nov. 1868; HP, B/XX/D/112.
121 Hardy to Cairns, 18 Nov. 1868. PRO, Cairns 30/51/7.
122 Hardy, *Diary*, 85–6.
123 Buckle, ii, 432.
124 Hardy, *Diary*, 86.
125 Cairns to Disraeli, 27 Nov. 1868; HP, B/XX/Ca/58.
126 Buckle, ii, 435–6.
127 Hardy, *Diary*, 86–7.
128 See, for example, Spencer Walpole, *The History of Twenty-five Years* (1904), ii, 347–8.
129 Raikes, *Raikes*, 71–2.

Part II

The Making of Disraelian Conservatism, 1869–74

Chapter 4

Disraeli's uncertain leadership, 1869–72

'The utmost reserve and quietness'

1

Lord Derby failed consistently as leader of the Conservative party to win Commons' majorities in general elections in 1847, 1852, 1857, 1859, and 1865. As a traditional grandee his reputation did not suffer; only his temper. For a parvenu such as Disraeli it was a very different matter. Severe defeat in 1868 seemed to bear out the complaints made against him when he took over the leadership: that he had made his career in Derby's shadow; that he was an exotic, with no 'bottom' in the country or in the party; that he had been perfectly suited as Derby's subaltern, but was not adequate to the first place. No one could claim that he had cut an impressive figure in the country. There were many, like Hardy, who wondered whether the Conservative party would benefit by Disraeli's eccentric decision to honour his wife and himself stay on in the Commons.[1] It seemed such a good opportunity for Disraeli to withdraw gracefully. He had advanced much farther than he or any one else could ever have dreamed possible. There were many rumours in December 1868 that he would retire. Edward Levy of the *Daily Telegraph* approached Disraeli on this question and indicated that one of his senior journalists, Thornton Hunt, was standing by to receive any communication.[2]

There were to be many passages during the next few years when Disraeli gave indications of weariness with his task and of likely retirement to valetudinarian pleasures, literature, and above all to nursing his devoted and ailing Mary Anne. He admitted to Stanley (by then Derby) in December 1869 that 'though still willing to exert himself for the benefit of the party if necessary, his interest in it was diminished, he had obtained his object, and if he never held office again, he should not feel that his life had been a failure'. He often doubted whether he should go on with the leadership in the Commons: 'the fatigue was considerable: but he saw no one in whose hands he could leave it, and that circumstance had decided him.'[3] The 'two years apathy'[4] of 1870 and 1871 were a particularly testing period for Disraeli's leadership. As Cairns remarked to Richmond in January 1872, 'You know that last year, and in 1870, he was down in the mouth and rather repelling meetings to concert plans etc.'[5] Everybody now remembered abiding doubts about Disraeli. Salisbury's highly articulate and vehement doubts about Disraeli seemed all the more apropos. Salisbury's predictions about the new electorate had come to pass. General resentment in the party against Disraeli tended to look for relief to the Conservative who most particularly and famously resented Disraeli.

This instinct for relief emerged immediately after the election defeat in a crisis over the Conservative leadership in the Lords. When Derby retired Malmesbury had taken over but now declined to continue. Many Conservative peers now looked to Salisbury who since his elevation to the Lords in April 1868 had maintained a political deportment gloweringly consistent with his curt dismissal of Disraeli's oblique offer of office in February. His election would have been for Disraeli an intolerable humiliation and a virtual invitation to abdicate. Disraeli wrote to Cairns:

> The Leader in the Lords must be one, who shares my entire confidence, and must act in complete concert with myself. I do not know, whether Lord Salisbury & myself are even on speaking terms. You contemplate making a man leader of a party, of wh. he is not even a member.
>
> If we show a strength in parliament & the country it is probable, in due time of course, he will join us. If we try to force the result, we shall only subject ourselves to humiliation.[6]

Disraeli was quite clear that Cairns must lead in the Lords. He thought he had already settled this,[7] but Cairns was trying to wriggle out; and, indeed, to Disraeli's consternation, eventually stipulated that he would replace Malmesbury for the 1869 session only. As he later explained to Disraeli,

> I thought – and I continue to think – that there were obvious reasons why this post would have been more fittingly assigned to some member of the House of traditional & material weight in the Country & of great social position: & that any service I could render would be given more effectively in the way of assistance and support to a person selected on those considerations.

Also, Cairns pointed out, as an ex-lord chancellor he had judicial obligations. Moreover, if the Conservative party were called to office again, with Cairns back on the woolsack, he would not be able to continue as leader.[8] In any case, there was going to be a mood among the Conservative peers less deferential to the party leadership. Beauchamp, for one, welcomed the end of Derby's active participation in the Lords 'of which he made use to stifle debate and to destroy the vitality of the Upper House'.[9]

Cairns in fact long hankered himself after the resolution he had propounded back in the 'fusion' time of 1866 when Russell resigned: that Stanley would be the man to fuse with the Whigs and moderate Liberals, with Disraeli exiled to the Lords. He was to be talking much of Stanley (by then Derby) still as leader in early 1872. In February 1874, when Disraeli's fortunes had risen and were cresting, Disraeli was 'quite touching in his expressions of gratitude' to Hardy for the way Hardy 'had understood him in the days of dissension five years ago'.[10] That dissension was provoked by Derby's death in October

1869 and Stanley's accession as 15th earl. This event exposed Disraeli more than ever as Derby's legatee: a disposition not to be challenged in Derby's lifetime, but challengeable thereafter. At Highclere, Carnarvon's Hampshire house, Hardy heard Carnarvon 'very anxious for entire reunion in the party & looking for Salisbury as leader when & if the impediment [Disraeli] can be removed'.[11] The circumstance that Salisbury succeeded Derby as chancellor of Oxford University seemed very suggestively to underline Salisbury's larger succession claims. It ratified his senior Tory grandee status. It was Disraeli's fate to live through the next few sessions an 'impediment' in the eyes of many of his party; all the 'dear "old lot"', as Corry later described them; 'frondeurs' and 'cynics'[12] as things indeed turned out, but sensible, worried Conservatives in the depressed aftermath of 1868.

Why did Disraeli persist? There was the practical consideration of who could fittingly take the lead in the Commons in his place, with Stanley departed to the Lords. Hardy? Northcote? There were to be serious doubts about both of them seven years hence. Beyond that inhibition there was the abiding hope of yet realising the dream his life, of re-establishing Toryism on a national foundation. And he 'loved the great game'.[13] But more than love now was pride. Disraeli wanted above all else to prove himself right about 1867, to vindicate his purpose and justify his policy. To abdicate with Salisbury's gibes and flouts and jeers ringing in his ears was impossible. If he chose not to go, there was little chance of his being ousted. There were no relevant precedents. Peel's case offered no useful guidance. If Disraeli could be likened to Addington, there was no equivalent to Pitt available. Disraeli's severest critics could not plausibly cite the case of Goderich as being in point. As long as he remained in the Commons no alternative in that House was feasible. As Hardy remarked to Cairns in February 1870, Disraeli's position in the Commons must be 'in the lead or nowhere'. While there 'he must lead, and his own view as you know was and probably is that by his lead the best hope of securing the future of the party exists'.[14] That last point was always in the end decisive. No conceivable alternative leader could convincingly inspire confidence so long as Disraeli retained confidence in himself.

At the opening of the session in February 1869 Hardy dined with Disraeli and a cabinet party. 'All in good spirits but waiting for events to come to definite decisions.' The speech from the throne disclosed nothing of Gladstone's plans. It was comforting to reflect that Salisbury would support Cairns in the Lords 'in every way I doubt not'. The appearance of the Commons was, to Hardy's eye, 'much changed'. There were 'some very strange people among its members'.[15] No doubt Hardy had particularly in mind the large contingent of Nonconformist Radicals who made their presence felt for the first time in the Commons that session. Disraeli's attention to affairs was of a somewhat detached kind. He had already secretly commenced his first novel since 1847, *Lothair*, inspired by Bute's conversion to Rome. He would indulge himself in it with hits at Archbishop Manning, Bishop Wilberforce, and the

Radical Professor Goldwin Smith. Disraeli otherwise often desponded. 'D. acknowledged to me that he did not at all see his way', Stanley recorded on 3 March. 'He thought that after this success the violent party would give Gladstone a great deal of trouble: e.g., by raising the land question, that of the church in England, &c.' Dining with Disraeli a few days later Stanley noted, 'he is out of spirits, says he thinks the monarchy in danger, which he never did before: not from immediate causes, nor from any feeling against it of a strongly hostile character, but from gradual loss of *prestige*'. The Queen, Disraeli morosely suspected, had 'thrown away her chances'. Stanley added: 'Nothing as to party prospects, which are obviously hopeless.'[16] As for immediate business, Disraeli made clear to Stanley, in the course of declining an invitation to a public dinner in Lancashire, his view as to the Conservative party's appropriate posture in the current political state of affairs: 'I think on our part there should be, at the present, the utmost reserve and quietness.'[17]

2

For Disraeli the doctrine of 'utmost reserve and quietness' was the necessary and logical consequence of his government's not meeting the new parliament. The same reasons which led to immediate resignation in December made resistance on the Irish Church issue pointless in March. Disraeli's own inclination was against even contesting the second reading,[18] but to leave all serious obstruction and negotiation to the Lords. Hardy was the only Conservative eminence in the Commons to show fight. 'Disraeli was sparkling and brilliant but far from earnest,' was Hardy's comment on 20 March. 'He gave no reality to his objections.'[19] Hardy insisted that the second reading be challenged. 'We have a difficult task before us,' he told Cairns, 'but I do not despair of obtaining better terms than are now offered.'[20] Gladstone, exalted in his tribunicial status as the nemesis of Ascendancy privilege, was indomitable and irresistible. Spofforth's prognostications as to the difficulties he would be in were entirely groundless. Gladstone set the value of the Irish Church's endowment at £16 million, half of which he proposed to expend in buying out the Church, and the other half in putting to ameliorative uses in Ireland. Gladstone's plans included also proposals consistently to end the existing 'concurrent' endowment procedures with respect to aiding Presbyterian ministers and (to the pleasure of many anti-Roman Catholic Liberals) to the grant to the Roman Catholic seminary of St. Patrick's, Maynooth.

Conservative notions of holding out for better terms for the Irish Church tended to look to defence of these endowments as a cover for deeper Anglican purposes. Northcote's advice to Disraeli was that the party must avoid an anti-Catholic line. It had been a mistake to raise the anti-popery cry. Conservatives should stand on different ground from anti-Catholic Liberals.

> If we can hope for anything, it is the rescue of the surplus from the great fund with which Mr. Gladstone means to corrupt the people of Ireland, and its appropriation to the disestablished Church; and I think we shall be taking a step in the wrong direction if we disendow Maynooth, and add to the bribery fund.

Soundings recently had led Northcote to the feeling that there would be a reaction in favour of the Irish Church if it were seen not to help to immolate itself. 'Moderate Liberals' in Devonshire admitted that Gladstone's measure was a 'very strong one'. Northcote's own opinion was that Conservatives ought to oppose the anti-Catholic Liberal line 'and to propose the appropriation of the bulk of the surplus to the Church body, – giving a part, if you please, for the purchase of houses and glebes for the Roman Catholics, and Presbyterians'.

> We should not carry it, but we should show a disposition to do something positive, which might be of use hereafter. Of course we should give offence to our Protestant friends; but I do not think we shall save the Church by merely crying No Popery.[21]

It was rather late for the Conservative party to regroup for this strategy. Nor was Gladstone in a humour to be deflected. He gained his second reading handsomely. 'Such a House!' Hardy exclaimed. 'Bright spoke as a dictator, ably but arrogantly.[22] Northcote had a scheme ready for concerted action by the Conservatives in both houses. In the Commons they would lead up to the third reading with ideas which would become the basis of Lords' amendments after passing their own second reading 'under protest'. 'We could also put our friends in the Press on the right track.' If Gladstone refused the amendments it would be a question of whether the Conservative peers would have 'nerve enough' to decline taking the original bill back into consideration. If their nerve held, the government would prorogue and meet parliament again in the autumn with its bill intact. 'But the resistance of the Lords, especially upon some well-defined point might have raised a new spirit in the country, and the battle might be then less unequal than at present.' Northcote on the whole feared the consequences in the country of a final collision, although he thought 'anything is better than an absolute surrender'. The difficulty would be to keep the peers united and present in the autumn.[23]

The difficulty was rather to keep the Conservative peers united in the spring. Disraeli conferred with Archbishop Tait with a view to rallying them. Tait, however, had already been squared by Gladstone, and was being urged by the Queen to avoid any degree of defiance likely to provoke confrontation between Lords and Commons. Tait firmly proposed letting the second reading through with a view to amendments in committee. A few Conservative peers, including Salisbury, approved this tactic. Most were ready to follow Derby in uncompromising rejection, let the constitutional consequences be what they may. The Conservative chiefs had to consider the likelihood thereby of 'raising a new spirit in the country'. Northcote was not all that sanguine.

Even Hardy, their most resolute churchman, confessed that the feeling in the country was 'not easily ascertained', but it looked 'as if there were no strong current either way'.

> The question however which will follow rejection, 'What next', is one the solution of which I do not yet see. After all however the Bill is hateful & contrary to justice & principle: good grounds for getting rid of it though expediency may have a word to say in the matter.[24]

Expediency indeed had the last word. The well-worn subtleties of concurrent endowment would not raise the spirit of the country when 'No popery' had failed. Cairns was in any case as personally hostile as ever to any endowment of Roman Catholic clergy. Disraeli would not challenge Tait with the Queen behind him. None of them was willing to challenge Gladstone with the country behind him.

With prudent expediency thus rampant behind the scenes, the dramatic opening of the Lords' debates on 14 June was more an occasion of political theatre than of reality. 'Much and free talk about the effect on the Lords', Stanley had noted on 6 June; 'can they exist as they are? Can they work along with a H. of C. composed as ours now is? If not, what modification can be made in their constitution?' Some Conservative peers avowed 'that they may as well be abolished as live under a perpetual threat of extinction, and vote for what they object to under a moral coercion which leaves them no choice'.[25] The second reading passed on 18 June despite Derby's defiant fulminations. Cairns, Carnarvon, Salisbury, and Tait between them transformed Gladstone's bill of disestablishment and disendowment into a measure of 'partial disestablishment, of actual re-endowment, and of absolute exemption from all future control'.[26] Salisbury made himself prominent with such combative remarks as that the Lords must not bow meekly to the Commons, and need not be afraid of 'possible extreme measures'; that 'the opinion of the constituencies has been over-rated'; but that in any case it was not for the Lords to be frightened by electioneering calculations. 'If no one raised the standard none would follow; and it at all times became the duty of some one to "bell the cat".'[27] This gasconade did Salisbury's reputation no harm in the party and, as with Derby, was useful in ventilating Tory spirit and diverting attention from surrender. The cat Disraeli intended to bell was, precisely, Salisbury. He put it to Cairns that the Conservative party in the Lords faced the alarming threat of being 'put into a situation of supporting the Government with a fraction of yr followers, & that not the most influential, & dividing against the bulk of your friends. This would be serious.'[28] Back in the Commons Gladstone responded stiffly. Stanley was amused to observe Malmesbury 'rather excited, and likens the present to the worst days of the French Revolution'.[29] Tait mediated, and Cairns duly compromised with Granville, the Liberal leader in the Lords. Conservative stipulations for concurrent endowment were dropped. Gladstone conceded certain points as to disposing of the surplus and the terms for clergy commutation. The bill for disestablishing and disendowing the Church of Ireland on 1 January 1871 was accorded the Royal Assent on 26 July 1869.

3

It was all very prudent and statesmanlike, but the effect was undeniably ignominious. The Conservative party and the House of Lords had been overawed and overborne. The Irish ecclesiastical Ascendancy was humiliated. It was all a dire and ominous precedent. Would Gladstone now make a like target of the Irish territorial Ascendancy? Stanley's reflections as he took leave of the Commons at the end of the session expressed a new sense of personal difficulty:

> But with the settlement of the Irish church question a new scene in politics opens: and I am henceforth more free to act independently of party than was ever possible while Lord Derby remained a political leader. The chief difficulty which I feel, and long have felt, in deciding questions of policy, is that on many of them my reason tells me that the party of innovation must succeed, and that resistance is foolish: while at the same time I have not the slightest sympathy with the movement or its authors. E.g. the ballot which in some shape I regard as inevitable, and may perhaps acquiesce in rather than oppose it, but which is avowedly pushed forward with the view of lessening the power of the upper and middle over the lower classes. To questions of land, and the distribution of property, the same argument applies still more forcibly. It is hard to choose between what you feel to be distasteful, and what you know to be impracticable; and for a moderate man, of aristocratic sympathies, and detesting political enthusiasts, this is often the only alternative.[30]

Amid these tribulations Derby's death in October had the effect of reopening wounds as to the leadership in the Lords, with wider implications for the party leadership. The new earl of Derby commented on *The Times* giving him 'very sensible advice to refuse the Conservative leadership in the Lords (which has never been offered) and assume a neutral position for the time, watching events. This is what I shall most likely do.'[31] Already Cairns had made it clear he would not go on as leader. His experiences in the session aggravated his initial reluctance. He repeated to Disraeli his points of February about the need for a peer of traditional and material weight in the country, and of great social position, and of the impossibility of the post continuing to be filled by a 'legal member of the House'.[32] In February Cairns presumably had the new marquess of Salisbury in mind as the possessor of relevant qualifications. Now he had the new earl of Derby very much in mind. Moreover, Salisbury produced another of his embittered diatribes in the October *Quarterly Review*, 'The past and future of Conservative policy', which took over abuse of Disraeli pretty much where he had left off with his 'Conservative surrender' piece of 1867. Hardy reported having talked to Cairns at the Carlton, 'who reported unsatisfactorily of the future'. Cairns's account of Salisbury's 'mood' was discouraging. On the other hand, Hardy was even less happy with Cairns's view that the new Derby 'might lead as Church questions need not affect the party'. Hardy indignantly wanted to know what, were that the case, would be 'left to bind the party at all'.[33]

It was a good question. Malmesbury's account to Cairns in November of having seen Derby and telling him how the land lay as to the leadership in the Lords being 'in abeyance' constitutes a curious and revealing comment on a man widely touted as the best prospect for leader of the party as well as the party's leader in the Lords. 'My impression is that he intends to follow a Conservative line in politics but thinks he is not sufficiently of an obstructive character to be pleasing to the Lords. I think that if you speak to him as you did to Salisbury that he wd. have no objection to sit on our bench.'[34] Removal of a heavy paternal weight had left the former Lord Stanley almost free-floating. He recorded in his diary on New Year's Day 1870: 'In regard to politics my present position is that of a neutral, singularly free from pledges or ties. My inclination is rather to support than to oppose the government of the day, be it which it may, provided that those who compose it abstain from violent or extreme measures.' He had, equally illuminatingly, commented a few days previously: 'Very little passed between D[israeli]. & myself as to present politics. We both rather avoided the subject.' Again: 'Nothing passed between D. and myself as to current events. . . . I can see that he wishes me to be Conservative leader in the H. of Lds, but recognises the impossibility of my assuming that post at once, even if on other grounds I desired it.'[35] Cairns reported to Disraeli that he had talked to both Salisbury and Derby as to the Lords' leadership, but both declined. Salisbury wanted his 'freedom & liberty of action to be unimpaired'. Derby had 'no idea of pursuing a course otherwise than Conservatism', and would not be disagreeable to leading the party in the Lords; but he anticipated 'the possibility of his differing from them (as he has done before) on isolated questions, & that sections of the party would divide between him & Salisbury etc.', especially on 'Ecclesiastical questions'.[36] This left Cairns no less resolved to quit. 'A little anarchy may set it right, & I see at present nothing else for it.' Clearly, Cairns saw Derby as the likelier hope. 'As far as I can learn, *he* is the man the party wd. like.'[37] Disraeli himself conferred with Derby. 'Nothing cd. be more cordial or more satisfactory, than the expression of his relations towards myself,' Disraeli reported back to Cairns, 'but I could not expect any man to walk into a House of Parliament for the first time, & at once offer to take the conduct of affairs.' Certainly, Disraeli added, such a course could not be expected 'from a man of the cautious & usually reserved habit of the present Ld. Derby'.[38] Derby himself, in the course of returning his late father's Garter insignia to the queen at Windsor, informed her that the Conservative leadership in the Lords 'would probably fall to Ld Salisbury.'[39]

The problem of the Conservative leadership in the Lords was still unresolved at the beginning of the new session in February 1870. At least Taylor was able to inform Disraeli that Salisbury had accepted Cairns's invitation to a peers' dinner. Colville (the Lords' whip) attached great importance to Cairns's consenting to lead until Derby was ready to take over. 'He is of opinion that the interregnum of a *duke*, could split up the party in the Lords.'[40] This referred to Richmond, an amiable mediocrity. Carnarvon, for himself and on behalf of Salisbury, insisted to Cairns that 'no one is better fitted for the place than Stanley', since the difficulty in carrying on the necessary communication with the party in the Commons 'under its present leadership there appeared insurmountable' with Salisbury leading the Lords. Carnarvon wanted a meeting of Conservative peers to place matters on a definite footing.[41] Richmond also backed Derby. 'I am very glad to hear there is a chance of Salisbury and Carnarvon being present, and hope all will go smoothly.'[42] Malmesbury was unable to attend, but would vote for Derby. He hoped that Salisbury and Carnarvon would support Derby openly. 'The former won't run & the latter can't.'[43] The meeting was attended by peers. Richmond proposed Derby, who was not present. Derby delayed replying, though Chelmsford 'does not doubt his accepting', as Corry reported to Disraeli. Corry reported also that Granville, on hearing that Derby had been elected as his opposite number, 'expresses himself much pleased, "as he and Lord Derby, agree on nearly all points"'.[44]

Disraeli would hardly have been surprised thus to find Derby the Liberal party's favourite as his first colleague in the Lords. But in any event, after 24 hours' deliberation, Derby declined. 'My habit of mind is not that of a partisan', he explained to himself. 'By accepting the leadership of one political party, I lose all hold over members of the other, many of whom now look to me.' The Conservative party, moreover, in Derby's view was 'in a minority which seems likely to be permanent'. Derby thus calculated that the benefits of 'a larger degree of personal independence' prospectively in politics outweighed the 'position of being the mouth-piece of a party'.[45] This put Colville in despair, reluctant to publish what he was sure 'must be fatal to the hopes of the whole Conservative Party'.[46] Hardy wrote to Cairns in dismay:

> What a mess Lord Derby has led his friends into & yet I really believe he only made up his mind at the very last moment as it were with a pistol to his head. His private note to Colville reveals more of the man than the published one and I cannot help thinking that in many points he is right in disqualifying himself for leadership. What is to be done? I write to tell you of a long interview I have had with Carnarvon at his request. He has been strongly urging Salisbury the last two days to accept the position on the understanding that [it would be] a leadership *in & for the Lords* & that he need not and will not hold any confidential communication with our leader here. He thinks that he has made much impression but as Salisbury has gone to Hatfield this evening I dread the influences there. Failing him he has tried hard with the Duke of Richmond and does not despair . . . in case of real difficulty of persuading him to accept.

> Carnarvon is really hearty and most anxious to prevent anything of deception or disruption & has promised Richmond that he in any case would sit by him and would do his best to bring Salisbury with him. He asked me if I thought that Disraeli wd. take any step to make Salisbury's acceptance easy. I replied as I strongly feel that D's position in this House must be in the lead or nowhere. While here he must lead, & his own view as you know was & probably is that by his lead the best hope of securing the future of the party exists. I thought you would like to know something of my talk with Carnarvon. I suppose his leading would not do. Indeed [I] think [neither] health or nerve would allow of his taking it. Disraeli looks ill & the Speaker pleasantly told him last night on his appearance that he had never seen such a change in a fortnight. The frost having returned very sharply he is not down tonight.[47]

The possibility of Salisbury's leading after all in the Lords on a basis of not being required to be in confidential communication with the leader of the party would have made Disraeli look very sick indeed. Notwithstanding, a 'small meeting' of peers 'deputed Carnarvon to try Salisbury' again. He, however, refused also, as Richmond reported to Cairns. 'We were therefore without a leader. Malmesbury urged me very much to take it, as did Carnarvon.' Thus Richmond emerged *faute de mieux*. 'I must do my best,' he told Cairns, 'but I do not feel equal to the task. However I fancy it was a case of me or no one.'[48] The one advantageous by-product of the affair was that Salisbury and Carnarvon now consented to leave their seats below the gangway and take their places on the front bench – though Salisbury took 'occasion to say in a rather pointed way, that he was not to be reckoned as a follower of Disraeli'.[49] Richmond, who made no bones about assessing field sports as more important as well as more interesting than politics, adopted a simple but effective method of leading the Conservative peers: he looked to Cairns ('my best friend') as his mentor and keeper, and did what Cairns bade him do.

Looking forward to Gladstone becoming useless to the Radicals

1

Triumph over the Irish Church fuelled Gladstone's huge appetite for strenuous politics. Within two years he drove his government relentlessly into the ground. But now he was at optimum point of potentiality. His overaweing of the Lords in 1869 opened vistas never before contemplated. Neither Gladstone nor his government was committed to the electorate for Irish land reform on a scale equivalent to Irish Church reform. Yet, given Gladstone's deep personal sense of 'mission' to 'pacify Ireland' and his extraordinary personal and political ascendancy at this juncture, and given that land was in the conventional wisdom yoked to Church as the twin evils of Ireland, there was every prospect that the demoralised Conservative party and the intimidated House of Lords would now, in 1870, be confronted with a second grand stroke of legislation. This was intended to do justice to Ireland in the form of a measure to resolve the vexed questions at odds between Irish landlords and Irish tenants. There was much propensity among the Irish to keep up the pressure on Gladstone and the Liberals. They had them on the run. Stanley had reports from Tipperary of the 'peasantry full of vague hopes, which perhaps they hardly define to themselves'.[50] And, as with the case of the Irish Church, Disraeli was not the best qualified of Conservatives to lead a stout and telling resistance. In his notorious and unforgiven exposé in 1844 of what the Irish question was, Disraeli had done more than any other public man in Britain to link to the evil of an alleged 'alien Church' the evil of an alleged 'absentee aristocracy'.[51] The leadership of the old Lord Derby would never be more painfully missed.

Rumours of something big on Irish land were rife before the end of 1869. Corry recorded in December that he had heard nothing worth reporting 'as to the details of the Land Bill', other than that Spofforth claimed to have privy information ('This *is* Spofforth!').[52] By January, from Crichel, Wimborne, in the company of Henry Percy and Henry Somerset ('who, when he is of age is to be our candidate for W. Gloucestershire, and is keen for the battle'), Corry relayed the rumours that Bright had revealed that the government's course on the land question was 'not settled, and that, in fact, the matter had never been seriously considered till the last cabinet!'[53] There would be more heavy business besides: education, university tests, the ballot, reform of armed services and civil service establishments. Disraeli in this session was often ill, often absent, depending heavily on Hardy (Northcote was away in Canada on Hudson Bay Company business). Derby reported 'much talk' in the Commons 'about Disraeli's retiring from the lead of his party'. Derby himself judged it 'possible that he may do so formally, as from want of health he has virtually abdicated during the present session'. Derby did not believe there was any other reason; 'though in the actual state of affairs, there being no prospect of political success, and probably none for him at any time of return to office, he may naturally grow indifferent: the more so as he has won the great prize, and nothing can deprive him of the honor of having once been Prime Minister.'[54]

Disraeli's one signal achievement in 1870 was his novel *Lothair*, a surprise event (even Corry was not in on the secret), which caused a stir as a bizarre occupation for an active political leader and former prime minister to engage himself in. Though it sold well it did nothing to stem the slump in Disraeli's political stock. It seemed sensational and frivolous and was not received in the party with anything like the relish of the general public. Granville relayed the news to Northcote in Canada that 'Dizzy's novel though criticised in Society, is a success'.[55] Disraeli's publishers opportunely issued a collected edition prudently revised by the author; but this again tended to remind sober Conservatives of the immense amount of Disraeli's earlier stuff and nonsense. More telling as a cheering note for the party was success in February in a by-election at Southwark. Corry wrote from the Carlton that the result had 'much inspirited our men here'. He added: 'The Club is crowded, and there is a Babel of talk on the Land Bill, which I, now, hear denounced by nearly all; Redesdale and Lucan (who is positively yelling on the hearth rug) having set the tone.'[56]

Denunciation of the Irish Land Bill in that particular yelling Carlton tone had mainly to do with the fact that, on the ground of circumstances allegedly peculiar to Ireland, Gladstone was prepared to compromise the conventional notion of property rights of landlords for the assumed benefit of tenants. As became clear, Gladstone, under the impact in 1868 of a gathering swell of Irish expectations of a radical land measure to twin with his Church measure, aggravated by notorious instances of attempted and resisted eviction, had plumped for a version of the programme long urged by the Irish tenant-right agitation. Gladstone became convinced that the only way of achieving a healthy 'English' style of landlord – tenant relationship would be, paradoxically, to abandon 'English' notions of absolute rights in property. Through the key principle of compensating tenants for improvements when giving up short-term tenancies and of free sale of tenancies where such had already been the custom, Irish tenants in effect were to be given a share in the property of Irish landlords. A hint to that effect had been given in a Liberal proposal on Irish land reform in 1866. But in those days the House of Lords was an unintimidated body.

The Irish Land Bill of 1870 was a daring bid on Gladstone's part to create such a landlord – tenant relationship as would exert a benign social and moral influence throughout Ireland. He was not at all in favour of provisions to encourage tenants to purchase tenancies from amenable landlords; though under pressure he reluctantly included such provision in his bill.[57] Having behind him in his party little of the broad supportive consensus which had sustained him over the Irish Church issue, Gladstone's party or his government at various points in the preparation of the measure might well have broken up. Whig and moderate Liberal views as to its impolicy with respect to the actual conditions of Irish agriculture and to its profoundly dangerous implications with respect to property rights elsewhere in the United Kingdom were widely and effectively canvassed. Debate on this central question of high principle tended to be within the Liberal party rather than between the Liberal and Conservative parties. The politician who caused Gladstone the greatest trouble and came nearest to upsetting him was Roundell Palmer, formerly Russell's attorney-general. The Conservative party in 1870 found itself marginalised on Irish land in particular and therefore on the rights of property in general.

Why was this so? Partly it was inhibited weakness at the top. There was absolutely no way in which Disraeli could confront Gladstone's imperious public and parliamentary masterfulness with any conviction. All he could do was to put the best face on retreat. On top of that cardinal fact, Disraeli could not project authority on the Irish land question any more than on the Irish Church question, in the way the late Lord Derby could. Partly it was because the Conservative government in 1867 in the person of the Irish secretary, Naas (later Mayo), had itself made a bid in the direction of statesmanlike comprehensiveness on the question. Irish landlords did not have a universally sweet reputation, even in the Conservative party. Naas had forthrightly condemned the Liberal bill of 1866 as 'entirely repugnant to all principles of British law and . . . fatal to the rights of property'. Yet in 1867 Naas proposed to compensate Irish tenants for improvements made without their landlords' consent as a measure appropriate to 'a free country, and in an age of rapid change'. He added inducive hints to the Irish to the effect that this would be only the beginning of a larger settlement.[58] It was this kind of adventurous disposition that made Salisbury in 1869 much more suspicious of Disraelian plots to repeat the Reform trick of 1867 applied to Irish land than of Liberal and Radical subversiveness on property rights.[59] Disraeli was indeed thinking throughout the Irish land affair much more about the possibility of Gladstone's coming to grief than of resisting Gladstone's measure. Disraeli promised 'candid consideration'[60] for it, and offered no obstacle to the second reading. For his own part, Gladstone had made a special point of cultivating Disraeli's last Irish secretary, Wilson Patten.

More important was the fact that though Irish landlords like Lord Lucan might yell on Carlton hearth rugs, they adopted as a class a much less fierce aspect among their Irish tenants. Conservative Irish landlord temporising was most tellingly signalled by Lord George Hamilton, son of the former viceroy, the newly promoted duke of Abercorn. Hamilton allowed the beneficial advantage in principle of extending customary Ulster tenant right.[61] The Irish territorial Ascendancy, terrified at the prospect of a peasants' war, would settle in the end on Gladstone's terms: which amounted in effect to giving away something like one third of their property. Cairns's plans for Richmond's stout resistance in the Lords foundered on Irish landlords' lack of stomach for a fight. Richmond himself, with 'appalling frankness', confessed that if the Lords dismissed the present bill they would have to deal with something worse in the next year.[62] Salisbury, in his 'wild elephant' mood, asserted the competence and prerogatives of the Lords to little avail. Salisbury learned in 1870 the bitter lesson he took to heart for the rest of his long career as a Conservative statesman: the Irish landlords were beaten and finished; 'they are not capable of holding their own in the open fight of politics.' This awareness led Salisbury to welcome the clauses tacked on to the bill at John Bright's urging providing for loans to tenants to buy out their landlords.[63] This strategy would be at the heart of his own government's policy on Irish land in 1885 and thereafter.

Irish landlord hopelessness was responded to accordingly by a good deal of cool detachment on the part of Disraeli's chief colleagues. Derby, himself a considerable Irish landlord, willingly sacrificed 'undoubted rights' in order to establish in British public opinion that the limit of concession had been reached;

the better to confront the emerging Home Rule movement with 'immovable firmness'.[64] Before leaving for Canada, Northcote drew Disraeli's attention to the views of a County Cork landlord, Bence Jones, with these comments:

> I cannot divest myself of the idea that by this sort of legislation we are going to act the part of 'Dî faciles', and to inflict a blow on the agricultural prosperity of the Irish; but then it is 'optantibus ipsis'; and there is a good deal to be said under existing circumstances for letting them go to the devil their own way.

Like Salisbury, Northcote took the residual point about the logical cogency of buying out the landlords (though he could not resist a pointless flourish of legalistic equity):

> It certainly strikes me that there may be advantage in providing means for the extraction of the tenant right by purchase; but surely the same facilities for buying up should be given to the landlord as to the tenant.[65]

Other rather distanced Conservative country members gave the Liberal *Times* great encouragement that their 'assistance' would be of benefit in resisting 'any really dangerous interference with the rights of property'.[66] As was becoming the pattern, it was left to the honestly indignant Gathorne Hardy to articulate the necessary but irrelevant conventional back bench Conservative sense of outrage (Gladstone 'used such dangerous language that I protested amidst tremendous applause against it').[67]

2

Gladstone expended such tremendous quantities of his public and parliamentary credit in ramming through his Irish Land Bill that neither he, nor his ministry, was ever anything like as formidable thereafter. Gladstone himself put it with uncanny prescience when he told Clarendon that he felt about the imperativeness of his bill 'as a bee might feel if it knew that it would die upon its sting'.[68] This was the great gain for the Conservative party. Gladstone had wounded his government mortally, though it would yet live on for two more years, and limp, stricken, through a third. With every year that passed it became more apparent that disestablishment and land reform were not having the pacifying effects on Ireland Gladstone had postulated for them. Disraeli, for his part, revealed something of a like prescience when he told Hardy, in May 1870, that, though desponding for the present, he 'looks forward to Gladstone becoming useless to the Radicals & a disruption. Gives two years or more.'[69]

Gladstone duly became useless to the Radicals with disruptive effects over the education question in the 1870 session. Provision of public money to assist the widest possible diffusion of elementary education in England and Wales had long been a topic of urgent public concern. The state's only contribution to the better education of the people was to provide modest grants to independently funded or voluntary schools which submitted to its inspectorate. Gladstone had been doing his best for years to cut these grants as extravagant and debilitating to true voluntaryism. But the public mood was now changed. Modern industrial society needed a modern scale of educational provision. The Liberal government of 1868 regarded such provision as an imperative calling. It got itself, however, into a bind with the sectarian religious interests which had always regarded themselves as having particular duties with respect to the education of the people. The Conservative party's position in this matter was relatively straightforward. It was the party of the Church, and stood for the support and extension whenever feasible of voluntary or independent schools conforming to the doctrines of the Church of England, which already, one way or another, provided the vast majority of the schools of England and Wales.

Within this general principle of denominational education, the Conservative party could ally with interests more or less congruous: Roman Catholicism and certain sections of Wesleyanism. The Liberal party was not so conveniently placed. One of its most powerful *corps d'armée* now were the political Dissenters or Nonconformists. They were determined to unshackle the education of the people from the grip of the Church. All Nonconformists were (pretty well) Liberal; but not all Liberals were Nonconformists. Gladstone himself was a firm believer in voluntary Anglican or at any rate denominational popular education. Roman Catholics, and especially Irish Roman Catholics, were zealous voluntaryists. But Gladstone's mind was on Ireland and his only serious interest in the education of the people was still to restrict the amount of public money allocated to it.

The most formidable sectional pressure group bearing upon the Liberal government was the National Education League, founded in Birmingham in 1869 under the directional impetus of the rising young Radical Joseph Chamberlain, soon to make his name as a new kind of urban reforming mayor of Birmingham. The militant energies fuelling the league were predominantly Nonconformist; and though not strictly a movement urging purely secular democratic education, it was decidedly a movement urging democratic non-Anglican education; which in the circumstances of 1870 came to near enough the same thing in practice. Circumstances were curiously exacerbated by the fact that the Liberal minister given charge of the Education Bill, W.E. Forster, was a renegade Nonconformist turned Anglican.

The National Education League ideal was for a national, compulsory, free, non-denominational publicly funded system of education fit to produce progressive citizens in an urban, democratic age. What Forster in the end offered on behalf of the Liberal government was reinforcement of existing provision by an increase in state grants to voluntary schools, together with a new system of rate-funded local schools of a non-denominational character designed merely to fill any gaps left in the existing voluntary system; which was, in effect, being invited to fill such gaps if it could within a fixed period of grace. The Liberal government, its nature, and particularly by its unwillingness to expend large sums of public money which the Education League ideal would entail, could not come to other than such a compromise of recognising two parallel systems of elementary education: one voluntary Church-aided, the other rate-based, practically secular, school board administered. Moreover, a certain Clause 25 of the bill, while forbidding rate aid to voluntary schools directly, allowed rate money to be provided to fund scholarships for such schools. Elections by ratepayers to the new school boards largely became battles between rival sectional groups to help or hinder such provision.

The Education League militants were naturally outraged by Forster's bill, which they construed as an educational charter for squire and parson and denounced as treachery and set about trying to upset and repeal. Clause 25 was anathematised as the heart of iniquity. Conservatives could look upon these internecine Liberal squabbles with a certain relaxed detachment. The Church of England, as the largest existing provider of elementary education, had in effect been accorded recognition by the state in that capacity. The new school boards established in gap areas were worth capturing in order to garner rate money for voluntary pupils. Disraeli was careful throughout the 1870 session to say nothing calculated to reconcile the warring Liberal factions, and took considerable pleasure in leading the Conservative party in the House of Commons into the voting lobby to help save Forster's bill from its Liberal enemies.

This educational episode was excellent for Conservative morale amid the tribulations of Irish land. The Church had been served; secularism had been held at bay. There were acceptable incidental bonuses. Roman Catholicism cleaved to the anti-secularist cause. Corry reported gleefully Gladstone's difficulties over convent inspection. 'Out-of-the-way Shropshire is already alive on the question.' The foremost Roman Catholic layman, the duke of Norfolk, was to lead an indignant deputation. The Roman Catholic party threatened to withdraw support from the government.[70] Within a year one of the Roman Catholic MPs, Lord Robert Montagu, was telling Disraeli: 'I meet all the Catholic MPs at the Archbishop's, & have been surprised at how much they are alive to your friendly policy. They hope for a better system of denominational education than they are likely to obtain from the Radical party.'[71] It would take some time for it to become clear that two rival parallel systems of denominational and secular elementary education were a nonsense in a modern state. It would also take time to become clear that the board school system would develop into something much bigger and more important than merely a filler of gaps in the voluntary system. Above all, it would take a little time before the Church became uncomfortably aware that, in an age of developing educational sophistication, it would need far greater doses of public money to keep its voluntary system going than could be provided under the 1870 act. Within a generation the seemingly triumphant voluntary system of 1870 was to become the poor relation of the rate-funded board school system; and thereby one of the chronic political ulcers of Conservatism.

The imaginary ulcers Conservatives thought they were suffering from in 1870, as opposed to the real ones in store for them, were such things as abolishing purchase of commissions in the army, replacing patronage with merit as the guiding principle of reform of the Civil Service (along the lines of the Northcote-Trevelyan recommendations of 1853), releasing Oxford and Cambridge from the grip of the Church of England, and provision of a secret ballot for parliamentary elections. All these measures were promoted by Liberals with a view to damaging the interests of their political enemies. Conservatives responded accordingly. The Liberals gained all their points, either in 1870 or soon after, but benefited in the end but little from them. Reform of the Civil Service was locked into reform of the public schools and the two ancient universities in such a way as to reinforce rather than dilute the socially restricted catchment of its candidates. Oxford and Cambridge were reformed in such a way as to temper the old clerical monasticism with a new secular monasticism. Giving Nonconformists equality amid the Anglican grandeurs of their courts and quadrangles did no harm to the Church and much harm to Nonconformity.

Disraeli, as Kebbel assures us, 'hated the ballot'.[72] It bothered him that many of the new Lancashire Tories were in favour of it, 'and say at this moment we should carry every great town of the North, were it adopted'. But Disraeli apprehended 'the great body of our friends would not like to see it applied to counties; and then there are Ireland and Scotland and Wales also to be remembered'.[73] These latter anxieties were quite rational; but it is doubtful whether open voting would have made any material difference to Conservative fortunes in what was becoming known as 'the Celtic fringe'. Open voting was naturally a shibboleth of territorial influence. 'I feel grave doubts as to the Ballot', as Richmond told Cairns in 1872; 'I dislike it as much as ever, but will it be prudent to reject altogether, if sent up by a large majority?'[74] The Lords duly gave way. The ballot was to give the Conservative party one great fright in the counties, in 1885. But no more than that. There is no doubt whatever, on the other hand, that the ballot would be a crucial aid to the passage into Conservatism of masses of suburban Liberals. On balance, this was the most important possible advantage to be had from it.

Because of the way in which great issues of foreign policy came to the forefront in 1870 and 1871 questions of army reform took on an enhanced interest. They illustrate appositely many of the problems inherent in the political debates of the early 1870s whose ramifications and implications were not readily apparent. The one which was famously an occasion of dramatic Gladstonian shock politics can be easiest disposed of. Gladstone caused an immense amount of stir and constitutional fuss in 1871 by by-passing obstruction in the Lords to abolition of purchase of commissions by advising the queen to issue a royal warrant to that effect. Abolition of purchase made no difference whatever to the social composition or professional competence of the army officer corps. This was not because the queen's cousin, the reactionary duke of Cambridge, remained limpet-like as commander-in-chief until dislodged in 1895. Rather, it was because Cardwell's comprehensive army reforms at the War Office created a military system explicitly geared on the one hand to Gladstonian Liberal notions of public economy and of Britain's post-Palmerstonian pacific international role, and on the other implicitly to post-Crimean military realities which meant effectively Britain's ceasing to be a seriously interventionist European military great power. The post-1870 British army, in short, would have no need of a new kind of professionally expert officer corps on the much-canvassed Prussian model because it was in practice being relegated from its traditional Marlburian and Wellingtonian role to that of – in effect – an imperial police force. This policy had behind it the unchallengeably decisive argument posed by the drastic European facts of 1870–1. No party or interest in Britain was willing to undertake the accordingly drastic political or military requirements of a Marlburian or Wellingtonian capacity to intervene decisively in the European states system.

3

Domestic political fall-out from the resounding collapse of France and the new European hegemony of Bismarckian Germany tended to the benefit of the Conservative party. It was the early French disasters as much as the education imbroglio which put Disraeli in good spirits at the end of the 1870 session. Hardy reported to Cairns, having fallen in with Disraeli on his road to see Derby at Knowsley, 'looking very well & expressing himself as feeling so. Corry too was at the Club looking revived from Carlsbad.'[75] Gladstone was no longer in command of the agenda of politics. Spofforth could offer his meed of end-of-the-year encouragements: 'Altogether affairs do not look prosperous for the Government & it is a "sign" when one hears in the street a general opinion that Mr. Gladstone will be out before Easter.'[76] Certainly, Disraeli sniffed new possibilities in the air of politics. He wrote to Corry four days after the proclamation of the king of Prussia as German emperor at Versailles: 'Affairs, I hear, are very critical with the Govt. There never was a Ministry & a party in such difficulties & such disunion: but Cardwell says "it does not signify, as there is nobody to take their place".'[77] Cardwell's jibe was well found, for the time being. But a ministry's losing its way is a more significant event than an opposition's finding theirs.

Disraeli accurately expressed this emerging sense of advantage when he told Derby in January 1871 that he was not sorry 'to see the country fairly frightened about foreign affairs'.

> 1st, because it is well, that the mind of the nation should be diverted from that morbid spirit of domestic change and criticism, which has ruled us too much for the last forty years, and that the reign of priggism should terminate. It has done

its work, and in its generation very well, but there is another spirit now, and it is time that there shd. be.

2nd, because I am persuaded that any reconstruction of our naval and military systems, that is practicable, will, on the whole, be favourable to the aristocracy, by wh. I mean particularly the proprietors of land: and 3rdly because I do not think the present party in power are well qualified to deal with the external difficulties wh. await them.[78]

Disraeli was equally prescient in his diagnosis of the nature of those external difficulties. He told the Commons at the opening of the 1871 session that the Franco-Prussian war was 'no common war' on the pattern of the Crimea, Italy in 1859, or Germany in 1866. 'This war represents the German revolution, a greater political event than the French revolution of the last century.' That had been a great social revolution. What had happened now, however, was that 'not a single principle in the management of our foreign affairs, accepted by all statesmen for guidance up to six months ago, any longer exists'.

We used to have discussions in this House about the balance of power. Lord Palmerston, eminently a practical man, trimmed the ship of state and shaped its policy with a view to preserve an equilibrium in Europe. . . . But what has really come to pass? The balance of power has been entirely destroyed, and the country which suffers most, and feels the effects of this great change most, is England.[79]

It was indeed a 'new world'.

The particular item of fall-out expressive of this new world which caused Gladstone's government most diplomatic embarrassment and domestic hurt was repudiation by the Russians in November 1870 (after collusion with Bismarck) of the Black Sea clauses of the Treaty of Paris of 1856. These clauses, designed to hobble Russia permanently by forbidding a Russian naval fleet in the Black Sea, had been the jewel in the crown of Palmerstonian foreign policy: the only jewel left, it might be said, in what was by now a decidedly tarnished crown; but no doubt all the more precious for that. It was a particularly cruel blow to Gladstone, who had outspokenly denounced Palmerston's Black Sea policy in 1856 as counter-productively humiliating to Russia. It was also true that Disraeli's own opinion at that time was very much the same as Gladstone's; but Disraeli kept prudently silent on that point in 1870 and thereafter. 'National' public opinion, stunned at what was happening to France, responded with 'Crimean' belligerence to what it saw as provocative insolence on the part of the Russians; and accused Gladstone of being what he was not (a Cobdenite 'Little Englander') and blamed him for failing to reimpose a policy he had originally and consistently deprecated as mischievous nonsense. Gladstone and Granville patched over the Black Sea issue by getting the Russians to go through the motions of seeking Europe's ratification; to much public and Conservative heckling. But the seeds of future trouble within the Conservative party were sown also. Derby, destined to be the next Conservative foreign secretary, was in no doubt that the moral of this tale was that 'the Black Sea arrangement has undone the main result of the Crimean war, and made it clear that we shall not again fight for Turkey'.[80] For the time being, however, it was all grist to Conservative mills.

More grist was provided for Conservative mills by the new public sentiment reacting against what it interpreted as Cobdenite Liberal withdrawal from empire. Cardwell had recalled British regiments from the colonies. This policy reflected Gladstone's insistence on cutting back public expenditure, not any repudiation of imperial connections or obligations. But colonial governments, dismayed and indignant at being told to pay for their own native wars, especially as they insisted on their right to raise their own protective tariffs against imports from Britain, raised a clamour in British opinion. Imperial federation notions became much in vogue. Sentiment about the grandeur and power of the British Empire, which had not much obtruded before in British print and on public platforms, chimed in very appositely with the concurrent dismay in British opinion at Britain's manifest impotence, for the first time in the modern European states system, to make its opinions count in Europe. Empire became, and long remained, a very important source of 'national' compensation. Disraeli, himself by no means hitherto distinguished for any notable degree of imperial consciousness,[81] would make a resonant reputation out of exploiting that simple (and purely mythical) connection. For the present it was yet another matter of embarrassment for the Liberal government. Disraeli's talk on February 1871 reflected this hurt to Gladstone's prestige: 'he does not wish to turn out the ministry, especially by the help of the ultra-Liberals'; but 'it may not be easy to keep them where they are.' Disraeli insisted that he 'had had enough of being a minister without a majority: and did not intend to try that position again'.[82]

It happened also that Gladstone's own bid to offer the British public countervailing compensation of a quite different kind, the settlement of the rancid *Alabama* dispute with the United States, threatened to come badly unstuck. Disraeli was quite *au fait* with the inwardness of the matter because, with his blessing, Northcote (after Derby's refusal) had accepted Granville's invitation to become one of the British commissioners negotiating in Washington. Since the end of the Civil War in America, the United States government had alleged British responsibility for the immense depredations of the confederate privateer against the US merchant marine. There was no doubt as to British liability; it was a question of whether to seek arbitration, and of whether US claims for indirect as well as direct liabilities should be admitted. Northcote explained to Disraeli when setting off for Washington at the beginning of 1871 the thinking behind Gladstone's policy. Gladstone's idea was to subsume the *Alabama* question in a much larger international agreement on the rights and duties of neutrals; to get big general questions agreed as between Britain and the United States as a model for a general international convention on arbitration; and to treat the *Alabama* issue secondarily on the basis of an avowed compromise, by which the Americans would renounce indirect claims.[83] Gladstone's notion of turning the *Alabama* legal dispute into a model of high-minded internationalism was susceptible to the danger that the American commissioners were extremely acute and not necessarily very gentlemanly and were determined, amid the fuzziness of moralism, to keep their indirect claims in contention. Northcote, very much Gladstone's kind of man, was now floundering. 'I wish', he ruefully told Disraeli in March, 'I had some of your power of reading characters just now.'[84] Disraeli insisted that 'he had warned Northcote against giving up everything "which he always used to do in debate"'.[85] The US government had recently shown itself, in Granville's plaintive phrase, 'very unfriendly to say the least'.[86] It was quite possible that instead of offering a triumphantly countervailing model against Bismarck, Gladstone would end up like Louis Napoleon, confronted with a choice between humiliation or war. Knowing Northcote, Disraeli had ground, meanwhile, for fearing the worst.

The irony was that Cardwell's recalling his legions evoked the imperial police-force vocation of the army, which itself reflected, more profoundly, British impotence in Europe. Either way, the Liberals lost ground and Conservatives gained. All this contributed decisively to Disraeli's so-called 'waking up' in the early days of the 1871 session. Kebbel's version has it that, provoked by a motion from the Whig Lord Hartington, now Irish chief secretary, on the state of lawlessness in parts of Ireland, Disraeli 'sprang to his feet' and delivered a 'very telling speech'. He taunted the government by pointing out mordantly that Gladstone's 'heroic' legislative exploits, for all their condoning sacrilege and confiscation and shaking property to its foundations, had manifestly failed to pacify Ireland. The word went round the Press Gallery that he was 'waking up'. A little later, on the Black Sea issue, Disraeli 'rose to his full height, and it was felt that "Dizzy" was a man again'. This latter speech Kebbel recalled as having a 'marvellous effect'.[87] Disraeli was observed dining at the Stanhopes' 'in high spirits' about the problems and blunders of ministers, and especially the success of his own recent Black Sea speeches, which exasperated Gladstone 'so much that some unparliamentary violence was feared'.[88] Indeed, it looked for a moment quite likely that the government might be defeated on the Irish vote. Disraeli recounted to the absent Northcote that the Conservative leaders in the Commons felt obliged to leave the house with 'between 50 and 60 of our friends to prevent a catastrophe, or something approaching one'. Affairs soon calmed down; but Disraeli could with reason assert that the government's unpopularity daily increased. 'If we only had fifty more votes, I could and would turn them out, but in the present state of affairs, they must remain'.[89] Northcote responded: 'You seem to be going through some curious scenes.' Would the English Liberals, he wondered, or the American Republicans, be the first to go out? 'A question easier to ask than to answer.'[90] Still, the point was that the question could now be asked.

Further curious scenes bedevilled Gladstone's luckless ministers. Lowe bungled his budget in April with his notorious match tax and increased succession duties which greatly offended the Whigs. Gladstone was forced to intervene and shift all the necessary extra revenue on to the income tax. Financial expertise was the highest vaunt of Gladstonian Liberalism: now a spell was broken. On top of this discredit two major policy bills had to be withdrawn: Bruce's licensing plans for public houses were much objected to by the powerful trade lobby; and Goschen's local government proposals provoked vehement hostility from the country gentlemen. It was in this rather heady atmosphere that the Conservative 'colonels' got out of hand in the purchase of commissions matter, which Disraeli did not think merited any serious obstinacy. This gave Gladstone the opportunity to hit back hard at the Lords with his royal warrant stroke. Conservative plans to rally public opinion on the 'shameful affront' to the Lords on the grounds that, as Northcote put it, the purchase issue in itself was 'wholly eclipsed by the Constitutional question',[91] were sadly compromised by Richmond's insistence on priority for the Goodwood Races ('This would enable all our sporting friends to get away on Saturday or Monday', as he explained to the somewhat dashed Cairns).[92] It was little consolation for Cairns to be congratulated by Disraeli: 'Your speech was equal to the occasion, & the occasion was a great one. It will be something for the country to rally round.'[93] It would, in sober fact, be nothing of the kind; of which Disraeli was no doubt perfectly aware. This was the point of Cardwell's jibe as to the Conservative opposition's not projecting itself convincingly as a serious alternative government: a point well taken by Disraeli. Gladstone's ruthless stroke cowed the Whigs and moderate Liberals in the Lords, as Richmond pointed out to Cairns.[94] Disraeli himself soberly deprecated efforts to pursue the 'Constitutional question'. 'From all that reaches me,' he told Northcote, 'I am convinced, that it would be unwise to pursue, certainly at present, the object we contemplated; and that our policy should be the utmost reserve.'[95]

This reversion to the doctrine of 1869 dismayed many Conservatives. It made good sense then. But why apply it to a political situation as in 1871 or 1872 upon which the judgement of the electorate in 1868 had no bearing? Even the Liberal-leaning *Annual Register* drew the moral from 'the unlucky session' for the Liberal government in 1871 that it was 'impossible to avoid the conviction that Liberalism, for the time at all events, was on the decline'.[96] By-election gains, especially a famous win in East Surrey, where a brewer, Watney, saw off one of the Whig Leveson Gower clan, seemed to confirm Conservatism's rising fortunes. 'Is this', asked Derby, 'a beginning of the middle-class reaction against Gladstone?' Derby was inspired to some characteristic ruminations. 'I am convinced that the opportunity is either come, or near at hand, for a ministry like that of Sir R. Peel. But who is there to take advantage of it? Disraeli is disliked by many, and not much trusted by those who like him best.' Hardy was 'honest, sincere, and has a kind of ability', but Derby did not consider he had 'sufficient range or breadth of mind 'to manage the Commons'. 'And there is no one else.'[97]

Mercifully, there was no excoriation in the usual style from Salisbury in that autumn's *Quarterly Review*. Salisbury was too much engaged in Francophile attacks on Bismarck and the new Reich (attacks much deplored by Disraeli). *The Times* anxiously debated the strange conceivability of a Conservative government, but reassured itself that 'anything like a permanent tenure of office' for Conservatives was 'impossible'. The leaders of the party, *The Times* was sure, did not believe in it. The country gave them no confidence. The majority was against them. 'All the forces of the time are strained in an opposite direction.'[98] There is no reason to suppose that Disraeli was other than in substantial agreement with this diagnosis. About the most sanguine length he would go to was his remark to Hardy in December that the Conservative party was 'in a tolerably robust state at present.'[99]

The most telling indicator of Disraeli's prudent reserve at this time is his marked reluctance to respond to a renewed invitation by Lancashire Conservatives led by Algernon Egerton, MP for South-East Lancashire, that he be the central feature of a grand demonstration in Conservatism's new northern heartland. This had first been projected in 1870. Disraeli's initial positive response was soon clouded by doubts as to the ripeness of the time. Lancashire pressed its invitation anew in 1871. Another by-election gain at Truro would set the scene. Corry did his best (from a cure at Schlangenbad) to coax Disraeli into a more receptive frame of mind.

> I anxiously, and in vain, look daily in the Papers for some notice of a visit on your part to the North. I sincerely hope it has not fallen through. Gladstone's cant about 'the people' will be no where so well refuted as in Lancashire. It is a matter very constantly in my thoughts, now, and I feel more convinced than ever that the opportunity is made for you, and you for the opportunity.[100]

Disraeli replied languidly from the shades of Hughenden:

> Lancashire hangs fire. They themselves only propose the end of Jany or the first week of Feb: I wd not, under any circs, involve myself in such distant engagements, & am still very doubtful, whether affairs are yet ripe enough for the move: in spite of Truro. I have answered Lancashire in your name, not extinguishing hope.[101]

It would take long to budge Disraeli from that assessment of the ripeness of the times. The 'waking up' of February appeared now as a mere evanescent flash. When he wrote to Cairns in October describing his heroic battle against gout ('I have entirely cured mine by giving up sugar, Burgundy, & Champaigne; almost as great a surrender as Sedan'), and his agreeable seclusion ('We have been here two months, & scarcely out of our own grounds'),[102] this was the kind of evidence contributing to the severity of Cairns's strictures shortly afterwards on Disraeli's 'two years apathy'. Corry, aware of the growing underswell of dissatisfaction in the party at Disraeli's insouciance, warned his chief in December: 'I am beginning to think that you will find it difficult, consistently with good policy, to avoid a public appearance before the Session.'[103] Disraeli's response seems to have amounted to nothing beyond a rather more authoritative and hectoring assertion of his prerogatives as leader, mainly at the expense of the inoffensive and aggrieved Richmond. ('He spoke kindly of the D. of Richmond but said that his total want of political training made it difficult to discuss matters with him in a satisfactory way.')[104]

The New Social Alliance

In a curious way, however, Disraeli's reluctance to engage in pre-sessional autumn and winter campaigning paid extra dividends when he did eventually emerge to give battle out of doors in the spring of 1872. Northcote, now returned, wrote in October 1871 proposing himself and Pakington for a visit to Hughenden 'that we may be able to talk over many things'.[105] One of the things they talked over was the phenomenon which gained considerable public attention that autumn, generally referred to as the 'New Social Alliance'. As Disraeli told Corry on 22 October, Pakington and Northcote were coming on the following day 'to consult about the "secret treaty" – & perhaps Sandon'.[106] Sandon did indeed join them at Hughenden. The originator of the project for a 'secret treaty' was the engineer and ship designer John Scott Russell, who, in the autumn of 1871, 'came prominently before the public' as the author of a scheme with the object of effecting 'a union between some of the leading Conservative members of the legislature and certain self-styled representatives of the working classes, with a view to the amelioration, through the intervention of the state, of the condition of the working men'.[107] Events in Paris leading to the bloody suppression of the Commune left a deep impression. The leading Conservatives with whom Russell initially had links were Northcote, who had been joint secretary with Russell of the Great Exhibition of 1851, and Pakington, who gave the project its initial public boost in his opening address on the theme of the condition of the working class to the Social Science Congress at Leeds early in October.

It was in July that Pakington arranged to visit Derby at Holwood, in Kent, to press upon him the advantages of 'creating a committee or commission of Conservative peers & landowners' to consider sympathetically the case put to them by 'the artisan class, as stated by their leaders' on such matters as limitation of hours of labour, compulsory purchase of land for workmen's dwellings, and the setting up of technical schools. Derby recorded his interpretation of the project:

> The idea of the men . . . is to work on the feelings or party interests of the landed class, as against the mercantile and manufacturing employers: an ingeniously-conceived scheme, which appears to have succeeded to some extent, for J. Manners takes it up warmly. Carnarvon rather approves, Pakington is hot for it, and Disraeli sees in it a new method of outbidding the Whigs, or rather Gladstone.

Pakington explained the several objects of the social charter to Derby 'at length and seemed to approve'. Astonished, Derby

> tried to point out to him that the compulsory limitation of hours of labor for adults involved in principle something like an economical revolution, and that the whole scheme pointed in one direction – to the suppression of the capitalist, which would be followed by that of the landowner and fundholder: though these latter parts of the Socialist programme are, for prudential reasons, kept in the background at present. In fact the plan, as he laid it before me, is that of the Socialists. . . . I endeavoured to impress on P. the gravity of the questions with which he is playing: but not . . . with much success. He is intoxicated with the prospect of being one of the regenerators of society, and reconciling the people with the aristocracy.

A letter the following day from Carnarvon begged Derby not to reject Pakington's scheme. Derby, accordingly, responded to Pakington with a politely evasive expression of regret at not being able to join his committee, 'saying nothing as to the merits of the scheme in itself'.[108]

Russell had been preparing the ground since the beginning of the year. The stimulus was the new and disturbing prevalence of industrial disputes: strikes by Newcastle engineers, Northumberland and Gloucestershire colliers, North Staffordshire iron workers, Bradford dyers, Leeds quarrymen, and pottery workers were the subject of much anxious comment. Derby remarked on 'something like a panic' spreading among the upper and middle classes in May 1871. Opinion among the masses was feared to be revolutionary. There was anxiety about the rights of property being increasingly challenged; and a sense of a general unsettlement of all opinions, social, political, and religious.[109] Later, at Osborne, the queen put Derby on the spot: 'she asked especially why, with such enormous growth of wealth, there is so much distress as ever among a certain class of the poor?' Derby confessed to giving 'no very satisfactory answer'. All he could suggest was that 'drink, improvidence, misdirected charity, and the tendency of all who failed or came to grief in any way to migrate to London, seemed the most probable solutions'.[110]

After making approaches to the Council of Skilled Workmen of which George Potter was secretary, Russell became president of a 'Council of Representative Working Men'. In this capacity Russell approached a number of Conservative peers and members of parliament, including, as well as Northcote and Pakington, Salisbury, Carnarvon, Manners, Hardy, Lichfield, and the two Lancastrian notabilities, Derby and Sandon. Russell presented himself as a 'fit ambassador' between intelligent artisans and the 'natural leaders of the people'. His central and urgent proposition was the pressing need to bring social classes together through legislative cooperation and thereby to achieve the great ideal of the 'advantages of a cultivated and self-respecting working class'.[111]

The 'seven points' of the New Social Movement' specifically urged by

Russell were: a garden city ideal of housing; local self-government and common land provision; an eight-hour day; availability of elementary and technical education (Russell was especially strong on the latter); public recreation, knowledge, and refinement to be available to workers; public markets regulated for quality and cheapness; and a 'great extension of the organization of the public service, on the model of the Post Office, for the common good'.[112] None of the Conservative eminences approached is known to have endorsed the programme as a whole. Salisbury, for example, approved of some of the proposals, disapproved of others. Derby denied giving his assent *en bloc*, as also did Hardy and Carnarvon. 'Of the persons mentioned', commented the *Spectator*, which took a keen interest in the matter from a rather anxious Liberal viewpoint, 'only Lord John Manners and Sir John Pakington have . . . made as yet no sort of disclaimer. But Mr. Disraeli, who was said to be "privy" to the negotiations, has also been silent.'[113]

It was Pakington's address to the Social Science Congress at Leeds that made most public impact. He held, according to the *Spectator*'s report, that the government might to do much more than they did 'to secure to the working classes decent house and wholesome food at a fair price'; and, in short, delivering 'an address inclining almost too strongly to that beneficent view of Government which but a few years ago political economy was never weary of denying'. Pakington's specific theme was that the working classes did not want the ballot but they wanted social reform.[114] The *Spectator* made much of the significance of this in relation to the story of the 'New Social Alliance': 'We can scarcely doubt that this address was really intended to strike the first note of an aristocratic and Tory movement on behalf of the working man, – which should outflank Mr. Gladstone's political justice by a liberal offer of social generosity.'[115] Within a week the *Spectator* was in full flight on this 'curious treaty with the artisan class'. It pointed out that Raikes's Conservative *Globe* was supportive of this truly Conservative *métier* of helping the working classes to discover the 'sound principles of action and policy which go to make up Constitutional Conservatism'; 'and of course they come to Mr. Disraeli.' The *Spectator* rather nervously looked forward to 'healthy party competition' in this field of social amelioration.[116] In its main leader, entitled 'Mr. Disraeli's Flank March', the *Spectator* exposed the 'great political revelation' of Disraeli's proposing to outflank the Liberals by carrying out some of the less visionary suggestions of *Coningsby* and *Sybil*, with reminiscences of Disraeli's support for the Ten Hours' Agitation as part of his ideal for 'filling the chasm between "the two nations"'. 'Might not', continued the *Spectator*, warming to its work, 'he outflank Mr. Gladstone by spontaneously offering to the dazzled eyes of the working-men – and offering it as a free gift of the aristocracy – something which they would prize far more than either secret voting or, for that matter, every point of Fergus O'Connor's old Charter . . .?' 'Such were the thoughts which we may suppose to have possessed Mr. Disraeli during the Sessions of 1869 and 1870, and which seem to have ripened during the latter year into a practical scheme.'[117]

There is no evidence that Disraeli took anything more than a politely benign general interest in the scheme. Derby's pointing to its 'socialist' character and its anti-mercantile and manufacturing implications would have been a restraining influence. He was certainly not amenable to any notions of challenging orthodox political economy. On the other hand, as became abundantly clear, he was very amenable indeed to the line of political argument which stressed that working men cared little for traditional institutional reforms such as the ballot and cared much for prospects of social betterment. He seems to have kept a wary distance from Russell personally; and there is no record extant of any correspondence between them. He seems not to have been in possession of much first-hand information about the affair. Barrington, the late Lord Derby's former private secretary, reported to him having asked one of the Liberal whips, Glyn, 'what was said about the so-called "Social Movement", & he declared that, notwithstanding the disclaimers that had been published by certain noble lords and others, said to be connected with the "movement", it was, to say the least of it, odd that no contradiction has been given by Pakington, John Manners, or Lichfield.'[118] Corry of course had earlier kept Disraeli posted: 'I suppose Lord Salisbury's letter will *quite* convince the Spectator that the "Alliance" is a flank march of yours!' Corry had seen 'no big fish' lately, 'but, with the minnows, I find the "New Alliance" popular in principle, tho' the seven resolutions are "un peu trop forts".'[119] Gladstone's reaction in a speech at Greenwich on 28 October was satirical. He announced himself as sceptical of the 'mysterious and mystical part of that transaction', adding remarks on 'quackery' together with some comical touches. His main thrust was to warn of 'vast dangers' and deprecate the 'introduction of new principles'.[120]

'Popular in principle', though the seven points were 'un peu trop forts', probably sums up tolerably accurately the broad tone of Conservative party response. The Conservative *Standard* defended Disraeli against the *Spectator*'s censures of 'intrigues'.[121] There seems to have been no disposition to treat the matter with Gladstone's kind of disdain, though Russell's assumption of ambassadorial offices on behalf of the earnest artisans was vulnerable to mockery. Derby recorded the 'just' strictures of *The Times* as to 'encouragement to wild theories', and concluded apropos of Pakington that 'the explanation of the matter is that P. with some activity and public spirit has much vanity and not a very clear head, and thus he enunciates principles which he has not cared to work out to their results'.[122] Though Russell's New Social Alliance faded quickly from the scene, it left a ghostly mark. Corry confided to Disraeli: 'There is one point, with regard to the "Secret Treaty" wh. I am right glad of: – and that is that your name is not mentioned in the matter. It seems to have been a most unbusinesslike transaction.'[123] Unbusinesslike it undoubtedly was; but Disraeli's name and reputation became, and remain, indelibly identified with its central argument as the vital element of what was later mythologised into Disraelian Conservatism and Tory Democracy.

The Burghley House gathering

It was not unusual for Conservative leaders to gather at Burghley House, near Stamford, seat of the marquess of Exeter, as they did at the end of January 1872. Burghley was one of the great houses occasionally used for such periodic pre-sessional gatherings. Again, as often, there were important absentees. Disraeli had been a guest at Burghley a few days earlier. Derby was conveniently absent, detained as a guest of the queen at Osborne. Richmond and Malmesbury likewise could not attend. Pakington, Lowry Corry, Ward Hunt, Manners, Hardy, Marlborough, were present. Hay, the MP for Stamford, attended. So did Annesley, an Irish representative peer. Eustace Cecil, MP for West Essex, represented, it may be assumed, the interests of his elder brother, Salisbury. Samuel Graves, one of the Liverpool MPs, represented the Lancastrian and possibly, the Derby, interest. Noel, the chief whip, was the expert on Commons party sentiment. Northcote and Cairns arrived a little later. Perhaps the knowledge that Disraeli would not be repeating his earlier visit gave the occasion a special flavour of possibilities.

What was unusual about the Burghley gathering was that discontent with Disraeli's performance as party leader had now reached a pitch of articulation within the party's leading circles so as to impose itself as the agendum of any such gathering. The point of it was not a sense that the party was in deep trouble: quite the contrary. What was exercising several of the party chiefs was the worry that Disraeli as leader would not be adequate to the prospective consequences of the rising curve of Conservative fortunes. It did not happen adventitiously, simply because of Disraeli's absence. It was privily provided for, though Hardy later denied that there were 'secret intrigues'.[124] There were simply intrigues. Richmond, explaining his absence to Cairns, hoped that 'nothing rash will be decided on, and as you and Hardy are to be of the party, I have no fears'.[125]

These words could be interpreted as evidence that Richmond had but dim inklings of the inwardness of things. They could equally well be interpreted as evidence of Richmond's uneasiness at Cairns's well-known hankerings after a Derby lead, and as a bid to hold Cairns steady. It was precisely Cairns who 'boldly broached the subject of Lord Derby's lead and the importance of Disraeli's knowing the general feeling'. Both Cairns and Hardy interpreted Disraeli's recent picking a quarrel with Richmond as evidence of Disraeli's problems rather than of remissness on Richmond's part. Richmond complained then that he could 'not help fancying that there is some influence at work of which I am ignorant'. Cairns's sardonic explanation was that 'after two years apathy he is beginning to wake up and fancies all beside are asleep.'[126] Hardy's diary tells the story:

> John Manners alone professed ignorance of the feeling in or out of doors. I expressed my view that D[israeli] had been loyal to his friends & that personally I wd not say I preferred Lord D[erby] but it was idle to ignore the general opinion. Noel said that from his own knowledge he cd say that the name of Derby as leader wd affect 40 or 50 seats. It seemed conceded that the old government could not stand again. What then must follow? Disraeli could not combine a new one. Wd it not be better that he should not try & fail. Why not serve under Derby for wh there is abundant precedent. Corry sd he knew that Dis. hd no such intention now. Such were some of the incidents of the talk. For my own part I do not look forward with hope to Derby but I cannot but admit that Disraeli has not so far as appears the position in House & country to enable him to do what the other might. It is not a bad thing to have conversed on so difficult a matter & to have seen the views of others.[127]

'Nothing rash' was done. There were too many doubts about Derby, a man who had recently declined the Conservative lead in the Lords mainly on the grounds that he was uncertain of his own Conservatism. The implications of a Derby leadership would have been decisively 'fusionist', looking to Conservatism's future in some kind of conjunction with Whigs and the Liberal right. Nothing in Derby's diaries gives any hint that he was aware of what passed.

Ironically, considering his own predilections in that direction, it was Northcote who seems to have interposed most effectively on Disraeli's behalf. He did this because of his opinion as to Derby's wider, personal unfitness for the responsibility. In his diary in 1880 Northcote commented: 'I wonder whether the Chief ever heard of the gathering at Burghley, years ago, when Manners & I were the only two who stood up against the absurd notion of deposing him from the head of the party & putting up Stanley in his place.'[128] Richmond, who of all his colleagues had most reason to feel nettled about Disraeli, nonetheless 'seemed hurt at the ideas about Lord Derby'.[129] Richmond nursed his own ambitions. What was possible for the Lords was by no means impossible for the party. Buckle's opinion was that it could be 'taken for granted that none of Disraeli's colleagues informed him of the opinions expressed at Burghley'.[130] Considering, however, that one of the participants, Lowry Corry, was the father of Disraeli's confidential factotum, Disraeli was very likely to have had more than an inkling of the occasion. It is certainly clear that the elder Corry had privy information about Disraeli's intentions. In any event, it seems that 'some representation of the discontent of a section of his followers in the House of Commons was conveyed to him'; to which he responded that he would readily abdicate at the party's desire in favour of Derby, but that he would not retire to the Lords. Who in that case could convincingly lead the Conservatives in the Commons? Disraeli still in the Commons 'below the gangway' would make an alternative Conservative leadership there impossible, as Disraeli well appreciated.[131] The fitting epitaph to the untoward event at Burghley in January and February 1872 was provided by Hardy, looking back in 1891 on his diary entry for 1 February 1872:

> Looking back on the Burghley discussion on leadership, how futile it seems! Time did the work, and showed what the position really was. Fancy our having begun 1874 with Derby for our leader! How impossible! and what a fiasco would have ensued![132]

Notes and References

1 Hardy, *Diary*, 86.
2 Levy to Disraeli, 2 Dec. 1868; HP, B/XX/A/38.
3 Derby Diary, 23 Dec. 1869.
4 Hardy, *Diary*, 150.
5 E.J. Feuchtwanger, *Disraeli, Democracy and the Tory Party* (Oxford, 1968) 11.
6 Disraeli to Cairns, 14 Dec. 1868; PRO, Cairns 30/51/1.
7 Beauchamp to Cairns, 11 Dec. 1868; PRO, Cairns 30/51/1a.
8 Cairns to Disraeli, 27 Sept. 1869; HP, B/XX/Ca/78.
9 Beauchamp to Cairns, 11 Dec. 1868; PRO, Cairns 30/51/19.
10 Hardy, *Diary*, 103.
11 *Ibid.*
12 See below, 178.
13 R. Blake, *Disraeli* (1966) 515.
14 Hardy to Cairns, 22 Feb. 1870; PRO, Cairns 30/51/7. See above, 93.
15 Hardy, *Diary*, 88–90.
16 Derby Diary, 3 and 15 March 1869.
17 Buckle, ii, 443; Derby Diary, 13 Jan. 1869.
18 *AR*, 1869, 10, 29–30.
19 Hardy, *Diary*, 92.
20 Hardy to Cairns, 25 March 1869; PRO, Cairns 30/51/7.
21 Northcote to Disraeli, 7 April 69; BL, Iddesleigh 50016, 71.
22 Hardy, *Diary*, 94.
23 Northcote to Disraeli, 14 May 1869; BL, Iddesleigh 50016, 74.
24 Hardy, *Diary*, 96–7.
25 Derby Diary, 6 June 1869.
26 *AR*, 1869, 106.
27 *Ibid.*, 86, 98.
28 Disraeli to Cairns, 27 June 69; PRO, Cairns 30/51/1.
29 Derby Diary, 21 July 1869.
30 *Ibid.*, 30 July 1869.
31 *Ibid.*, 26 Oct. 1869.
32 Cairns to Disraeli, 27 Sept. 1869; HP, B/XX/Ca/78.
33 Hardy, *Diary*, 103.
34 Malmesbury to Cairns, 15 Nov. 1869; PRO, Cairns 30/51/20.
35 Derby Diary, 23 Dec. 1869; 24 Dec. 1869.
36 Cairns to Disraeli, 19 Nov. 1869; HP, B/XX/Ca/79.
37 Cairns to Disraeli, 11 Dec. 1869; HP, B/XX/Ca/80; Derby Diary, 13 Feb. 1870.

38 Disraeli to Cairns, 12 Dec. 1869; PRO, Cairns 30/51/1.
39 Derby Diary, 10 Dec. 1869.
40 Taylor to Disraeli, 24 Jan. 1870; HP, B/XX/T/119.
41 Carnarvon to Cairns, 16 Feb. 1870; PRO, Cairns 30/51/8.
42 Richmond to Cairns, 17 Feb. 1870; PRO, Cairns 30/51/2.
43 Malmesbury to Cairns, 17 Feb. 1870; PRO, Cairns 30/51/20.
44 Corry to Disraeli, 19 and 20 Feb. 1870; HP, B/XX/Co/56, 57.
45 Derby Diary, 20 Feb. 1870.
46 Corry to Disraeli, 20 Feb. 1870; HP, B/XX/Co/57.
47 Hardy to Cairns, 22 Feb. 1870; PRO, Cairns 30/51/7.
48 Richmond to Cairns, 27 Feb. 1870; PRO, Cairns 30/51/2.
49 Derby Diary, 26 Feb. 1870.
50 *Ibid.*, 24 Feb. 1869, 6 May 1869, 18 Sept. 1869.
51 Buckle, i, 589–90.
52 Corry to Disraeli, 22 Dec. 1869; HP, B/XX/Co/51.
53 Corry to Disraeli, 2 Jan. 1870; HP, B/XX/Co/52.
54 Derby Diary, 30 May 1870.
55 Granville to Northcote, 17 May 1870; BL, Iddesleigh 50022, 14.
56 Corry to Disraeli, 16 Feb. 1870; HP, B/XX/Co/56.
57 For the bill generally see E.D. Steele, *Irish Land and British Politics. Tenant-right and Nationality, 1865–1870* (Cambridge 1974); and for a convenient overview, M.J. Winstanley, *Ireland and the Land Question, 1800–1922* (1984).
58 Steele, *Irish Land*, 58.
59 *Ibid.*, 167.
60 Buckle, ii, 456.
61 Steele, *Irish Land*, 171.
62 *Ibid.*, 307.
63 *Ibid.*, 312. The provision was that tenants might borrow two-thirds of the cost at 5 per cent over 30 years.
64 *Ibid.*, 309. Derby promptly and prudently sold up his Irish estates in 1871. He encouraged his tenants to purchase through the Landed Estates Court. 'My intention of selling was well known, and had produced an uncomfortable feeling in Ireland, as indicating my opinion that the state was one of political insecurity. (I cannot say that those who reason so are wrong.)' Derby Diary, 21 Jan. 1871.
65 Northcote to Disraeli, 5 March 1870; BL, Iddesliegh 500166, 76.
66 Steele, *Irish Land*, 172.
67 Hardy, *Diary*, 111.
68 Steele, *Irish Land*, 305.
69 Hardy, *Diary*, 115.
70 Corry to Disraeli, 21 April. 1870; HP. B/XX/Co/59.
71 Montagu to Disraeli, 17 March 1871.
72 T.E. Kebbel, *Lord Beaconsfield and Other Tory Memories* (1907), 47.
73 Buckle, ii, 463.
74 Richmond to Cairns, 21 Jan. [1872]; PRO, Cairns 30/51/2.
75 Hardy to Cairns, 16 Aug. 1870; PRO, Cairns 30/5/T.
76 Spofforth to Disraeli, 31 Dec. 1870; HP, B/XXI/5/438.
77 Disraeli to Corry, 22 Jan. 1871; HP, B/XX/D/152.
78 Buckle, ii, 472.

79 *Ibid.*, 473–4; M. Swartz, *The Politics of British Foreign Policy in the Era of Disraeli and Gladstone* (1985), 28–9.
80 Derby Diary, 22 Aug. 71.
81 But see F. Harcourt, 'Disraeli's imperialism, 1866–68: a question of timing', *Historical Journal* (1980), 108–9.
82 Derby Diary, 5 Feb. 1871.
83 Northcote to Disraeli, 19 Feb. 1871; BL, Iddesleigh 50016, 82.
84 Northcote to Disraeli, 14 March 1871; BL, Iddesleigh 50016, 86.
85 Derby Diary, 13 May 1871.
86 Granville to Northcote, 29 Jan. 1870; BL, Iddesleigh 50022, 8.
87 Kebbel, *Lord Beaconsfield and Other Tory Memories*, 46–7.
88 Derby Diary, 1 March 1871.
89 Disraeli to Northcote, 10 March 1871; Buckle, ii, 478–9.
90 Northcote to Disraeli, 29 March 1871; BL, Iddesleigh 50016, 90.
91 Northcote to Disraeli, 22 July 71; BL, Iddesleigh 50016, 98.
92 Richmond to Cairns, 3 Aug. 1871; PRO, Cairns 30/51/2.
93 Disraeli to Cairns, 1 Aug. 1871; PRO, Cairns 30/51/1.
94 Richmond to Cairns, 24 July 1871; PRO, Cairns 30/51/2.
95 Disraeli to Northcote, 22 July 1871; BL, Iddesleigh 50016, 101. See also Derby Diary, 24 July 1871.
96 *AR*, 1871, 101.
97 Derby Diary, 24 Aug. 1871.
98 *The Times*, 20 Nov. 1871; Buckle, ii, 511.
99 *Ibid.*, 487.
100 Corry to Disraeli, 15 Sept. 1871; HP, B/XX/Co/78.
101 Disraeli to Corry, 17 Sept. 1871; HP, B/XX/D/154.
102 Disraeli to Cairns, 9 Oct. 1871; PRO, Cairns 30/50/1.
103 Corry to Disraeli, 5 Dec. 1871; HP, B/XX/Co/82.
104 Buckle, ii, 514–17; Derby Diary, 5 Feb. 1871.
105 Northcote to Disraeli, 22 Oct. 1871; BL, Iddesleigh 50016, 109.
106 Disraeli to Corry, 22 Oct. 1871; HP, B/XX/D/157.
107 *Men of the Time* (1879), 864. Russell's dates were 1808–82.
108 Derby Diary, 26, 27, 29 July 1871.
109 *Ibid.*, 6 May 1871.
110 *Ibid.*, 30 Jan. 1872.
111 *AR*, 1871, 120.
112 *Ibid.*, 116–20.
113 *Spectator*, 21 Oct. 1871, 1257.
114 *Ibid.*, 7 Oct. 1871, 1195.
115 *Ibid.*
116 *Ibid.*, 14 Oct. 1871, 1225–6.
117 *Ibid.*, 1228.
118 Barrington to Disraeli, 23 Oct. 1871; HP, B/XX/Na/12.
119 Corry to Disraeli, 16 Oct. 71; HP, B/XX/Co/80.
120 *AR*, 1871, 108, 114, 115–20.
121 *Spectator*, 21 Oct. 1871, 1263.
122 Derby Diary, 6 Oct. 1871.
123 Corry to Disraeli, 28 Oct. 1871; HP, B/XX/Co/81.
124 Hardy, *Diary*, 150.
125 Richmond to Cairns, 21 Jan. [1872]; PRO, Cairns 30/51/2.

126 *Ibid.*; Hardy, *Diary*, 150.
127 *Ibid.*, 148–9.
128 Copy in M. Corry's hand, HP, B/XX/Ce/ between 175 and 176.
129 Hardy, *Diary*, 150.
130 Buckle, ii, 513.
131 *Ibid.*, 513–14.
132 A.E. Gathorne-Hardy, *Gathorne Hardy, First Earl of Cranbrook* (1910), i, 304.

Chapter 5

Arts of management 1869–73

Gorst replaces Spofforth

1

Spofforth finally bowed out in June 1869 with a new and augmented edition of his *Hints on County Registration.* The original 1868 edition was so much in demand, he informed Disraeli, that Dudley Baxter (a junior member of Messrs Baxter, Rose, Norton & Company) had taken the trouble 'of putting them in an amended form and correcting them according to the decision of the Court of Common Pleas and Registration Courts up to the present time; and has also added a separate short summary for canvassers'. The particular interest of Spofforth's new edition was twofold. He warned all party central agents in counties: 'As a dissolution may at any time take place Mr. Noel hopes that you will call immediately together your Central Committee' to make appropriate arrangements, and report also to Spofforth for Noel the state of the county organisation.[1] This sense of urgency reflected Spofforth's notorious over-optimism. The second point of interest is a negative one. Spofforth seems not to have considered the desirability of providing the party with a parallel edition on borough registration machinery. This in itself is a curiously apt comment on the general insensibility the party leadership had so far revealed in its approach to the matter of garnering artisan votes. Fixation on preserving the party's comfortable county heartland seemed to inhibit any disposition to adventure into strange and exotic reaches of the boroughs.

Perhaps the chief whip had this inhibitedness in mind when he wrote to Disraeli in April 1870 that it was important that Spofforth's place as principal agent 'should be filled up with as little delay as possible'; and Noel would be much obliged if Disraeli would kindly let him know his opinion 'about Mr. Gorst as his successor'.[2] Gorst had made a reputation out of his work for the London and Westminster Conservative Association, later known as the Metropolitan Conservative Alliance, and for his role in the National Union. The latter body had played scant discernible part in the 1868 elections; and indeed looked set to expire when its second national conference, called in 1868 at Birmingham on the unseasonable date of 29 December, produced a derisory six delegates presided over by a nonplussed earl of Dartmouth.

The organisational heart-beat was barely detectable. However, Raikes, the new MP for Chester, was present, as a faint token of serious purpose and possible survival. Gorst, unsuccessful in retaining his seat for Cambridge, was absent. In any case, he was secretary of the Metropolitan Conservative Alliance, which no doubt he regarded as a much more serious affair. But the point was that, to Noel, Gorst's absence from the Commons meant that he was available for employment. Possibly Disraeli was not immediately very responsive, for Noel followed up a little later:

> I have been trying to find someone to fill the place, and it seemed to me that we could not find a better successor than Mr. *Gorst*, the late Member for Cambridge, provided he could be induced to undertake the duties . . . I think Mr. Gorst combines the necessary qualities, he is a Gentleman, with a good manner, an excellent temper, has had a legal education, and is also very energetic in all he undertakes.[3]

By 22 April Noel could report that he had seen Gorst and thought he would agree to take Spofforth's place. 'The only thing that makes him hesitate is the idea of giving up the House of Commons for some time.'[4] There was no impressive list of alternative candidates. It seems Noel had next in line Carnarvon's former private secretary, Cyril Graham. But Gorst accepted. He took on the job as a stop-gap until he could win a seat in the next elections. With a place again in the Commons he could reasonably expect, when political opportunity offered, some signal benefits of patronage to mark the party's favour to him. Thus the threads which were to entangle Gorst's Commons ambitions, his legal ambitions, his political ambitions, his organisational ambitions, his Tory Democratic ambitions, with the Conservative party's Central Office, its National Union, its 'Old Gang', its Fourth Party, and sundry unworthy offices of state over the next 30 years, were given their initial twist.

Gorst underlined his gentlemanly status and the implied interim nature of his tenure by remaining, unlike Spofforth, unsalaried. His arrival at the principal agentship has been held to mark an epoch, if only because his first (and only) general election, in 1874, resulted, stunningly, in the first Conservative Commons majority since 1841. To accredit Gorst exclusively for this feat (which Gorst himself did not dare to predict) would no doubt be unfair to the battling Spofforth, who, in the later palmy days, could remark unabashedly to Taylor on his 'long and I may say, successful servitude under Lord Hylton and yourself'.[5] Still, Gorst's arrival at Victoria Street Chambers did mark significant points of departure. First, symbolically, was his actual departure from the chambers of the party's old firm and his setting up in a new 'Central Office'. Second, was his crucial and indispensable concern with the boroughs. The other point of departure which marked Gorst out decisively from Spofforth was his robust demeanour before Abergavenny, whose feudally heavy-handed attentions to the party tend during the next few years to fade away.[6]

Gorst made quite clear to Noel what he thought the central purpose of the party's organisation needed to be. 'We are generally strong in the counties & weak in boroughs, & we shall never attain stable political power till the boroughs are conquered.'[7] For this great task Noel was never very effective as chief whip.[8] In any case, he worked himself conscientiously into forced retirement through ill-health in 1873, when Hart Dyke helped out and Taylor was asked to return. On the other hand, in Keith-Falconer, the county manager, Gorst had an able and quite sympathetic colleague. This was important in a situation where the line of demarcation between the whips and the principal agent still remained unclear. It was important also that the 'new man' Gorst could work easily with at least one of the aristocratic hierarchs at the centre of the party's inner managerial circle. Certainly, the whips kept close control of the money. Certainly, Gorst was not invited to pay much attention to the counties. But this did not trouble him because he had confidence in Keith-Falconer (who also kept up his Scottish connections) and because he wanted to concentrate his work primarily in the big boroughs. The smaller boroughs would be more problematic because of the high incidence there of jealous local influence. And Noel, meanwhile, was having his successes. Southwark, in February 1870, was one. Even though he felt 'very nervous' later about East Suffolk ('we have no good candidate'), Lord Mahon nevertheless held the seat creditably against Sir Shafto Adair.[9]

The now pointless duplication and rivalry between Sedgwick's National Union and Gorst's Metropolitan Conservative Alliance led to a sensible amalgamation, with Sedgwick retiring and Gorst becoming honorary secretary of the National Union in March 1871. Gorst's next step was to set up in 1872 a new office for himself as principal agent at 53 Parliament Street, thus becoming independent of the old haunt of Rose and Spofforth. Into 'Central Office', as his headquarters came to be known, Gorst also removed the machinery of the National Union, from Henrietta Street. Keith-Falconer agreed to add to this party agglomeration his county Conservative Registration Association, until then next-door to Baxter, Rose, Norton & Co. in Victoria Street. His move was doubtless encouraged by the party chiefs, who looked to Keith-Falconer to provide reliable steadying ballast for the new dispensation. Gorst thus gave the Conservative party a potentially formidable hub for its machine. Keith-Falconer became Gorst's chief assistant, looking after the counties and liaising with Scotland and much beside, including supervision of the secretarial work of the National Union as joint secretary. Gorst in 1874 praised Keith-Falconer to Disraeli as doing 'all the work' of the National Union and as having arranged the great Crystal Palace demonstration in 1872. 'The Conservative Registration Assn has been under his management for 7 years: it has been admirably conducted and both in 1868 and 1874, & at many by-elections, has proved of the greatest service in contested county elections.'[10] One of the first major productions of the new order was the Central Office's Report on the General Election, 1868, presented to Disraeli on

3 August 1871 by Keith-Falconer. This 34-page document provided analyses of returns, majorities, voting, and divisions of population. There were also appendices on the results of the elections in the new constituencies and in London, Birmingham, Leeds, Liverpool, and Manchester. The document was based on figures supplied by Dudley Baxter.[11] What this report did not attempt to answer, however, was the simple question asked by the puzzled queen in 1872: 'why the Conservatives always lost votes at a general election?'[12] What had become a kind of psephological folk-lore constituted the Conservative party's gravest difficulty.

Under the new dispensation the National Union became simply and frankly 'the Central Office in its capacity as a propaganda agency'.[13] This suited both the party hierarchy and their principal agent. For the leadership it guaranteed that a spirit had not been raised which they could not control; and with Keith-Falconer in effective charge they could rest content that no Frankenstein was at work and that the working men would be kept on the 'right road.'[14] For Gorst it offered a guarantee that the National Union would be subservient to his organisational needs, and that above all it would not get in his way in delicate dealings with suspicious local associations and awkward local party notables.

Efforts had already been made in 1869 to breathe life into what appeared to be a corpse. A General Consultative Committee was set up, loaded with grandees including Abergavenny, Taylor, Keith-Falconer, Sandon, Noel, and Lord Henry Scott, one of the members for Hampshire, together with provision for attracting notables through a roster of honorary officers and patrons, including the old Lord Derby himself.[15] Hardy noted a National Union meeting at the Carlton 'wh. was ill attended'.[16] The third annual conference at the Adelphi Hotel in Liverpool in June 1869 was certainly better attended than the 1868 fiasco, with the Lancashire magnate Lord Skelmersdale presiding and Raikes very much to the fore. The fourth conference at York in April 1870 is notable as being the first occasion at which there was important debate on organisational method. Barland of Liverpool complained that want of funds had prevented a plan for 'travelling agents'. Organising associations was 'quite a science', needing tact and judgement. Sedgwick expounded on the problems caused by local jealousies and obstruction. The prevailing theme was lack of money. 'Repeatedly the Council had been grieved in having to give up their plans from this cause – and their operations had been comparatively crippled.'[17]

The fifth conference at the Conservative Registration Society's rooms, Queen's Square, Bristol, in June 1871 was a quiet affair; but it was the sixth conference at the Westminster Palace Hotel, London, on 24 June 1872, Lord George Hamilton presiding, which first showed the stamp of the new regime. This was the most impressive line-up of peers, notables, and delegates so far. Hamilton, hero of the 1868 Middlesex election, spoke on the theme of the circulation of opinion between the party leadership and the provincial associations. The new arrangements with Central Office were explained, stressing the advantages of closer contact between the union and the leaders of the party, and the financial savings. The total of associations now affiliated was now 151. Upwards of 42,000 pamphlets had been published in the past year, mostly the new Lord Derby's recent speech at Liverpool extolling (on Social Alliance lines) measures of sanitary reform and regulation of mines as welcome substitutes for constitutional changes, and Disraeli's recent speech at Manchester, in April. That Manchester speech was the centrepiece of the great Lancashire demonstration to which, eventually, Disraeli nerved himself. But the most glorious moment for the emerging National Union was Disraeli's second great speech out of doors on 24 June 1872, when the Conservative Associations repaired to the Crystal Palace, to fete Disraeli, and be addressed by him. The National Union was now really on the political map.

2

The practical nub of Gorst's work in the constituencies was to encourage the adoption of a new system of placing Conservative candidates. The prevailing notion was to send candidates drawn from a central pool to the constituencies, at short notice, rather randomly, and primarily on the basis of financial eligibility. The new procedure, which Disraeli had himself been urging for many years, was to encourage constituencies to build up their own pools of possible candidates 'from carefully vetted and selected specimens' provided in the register carefully maintained by Central Office with a view to their suitability to special local requirements, and to have an approved choice ready in place well before any likely dissolution. Candidates would thus, it was to be hoped, be less a matter of chance and more a matter of design. The concomitant feature of this new strategy was to encourage local notables and people of influence to build up adequate constituency committees and to collaborate with working men's associations where these existed.[18] Central Office, however efficient it might be made in itself, would always, in the circumstances of nineteenth-century politics, be a remote body of strictly limited effectiveness. It followed that the key to organised electoral effectiveness had to be found in the constituencies themselves. The twin barriers against effective local participation in the political process by the general body of the 'respectable classes' had for long been the heavy expenditures involved, with inordinate incidence of open or covert bribery, together with the parasitic technical monopoly of electioneering solicitors. One of the most consistent aspects of Gorst's concept of Tory Democracy was the need to break this old system. His departure from Victoria Street Chambers signalled this determination. Ironically, it was Liberal legislation from 1872 onwards designed to suppress excessive electoral expediture and bribery which provided Gorst with the indispensable means of doing this.

By freeing constituencies from the thrall of money and its attorneys, local politics became open to 'an enormous amount of dormant influence, which had hitherto been lost to the party'.[19]

Such changes took time. Disraeli could not, in general, complain of Gorst that he partook of Spofforth's sin of too ready optimism. Gorst's explanation to his chief why the Conservative candidate had failed to mount a respectable challenge in the Rochester by-election of July 1870 lacked nothing in pungent analysis. 'The Register has not been attended to for years; no Conservative agent appears at the Revision Court.' Fox, the recent Conservative candidate, had announced himself as an independent. He was adopted by the Conservatives only on the evening of the polling day; 'he had been proposed by a discharged attorney's clerk and seconded by a common labourer: there was no time to bring the strength of the party to bear in his favour.' The mayor, the entire town council, the registration overseers and assistant overseers and rate collectors were all Liberals (or 'radicals', as official Conservative usage always prescribed); 'both register and burgess-roll are no doubt affected by this circumstance.' The chief employers of Labour were of the same party. Those Conservatives who took an interest in Kent county politics took little in borough concerns. The cathedral chapter clerk who used to exert great influence was now agent to the Admiralty and private solicitor to one of the Liberal employers, a large government contractor; '& so remains quiet.' The cathedral chapter itself was 'antediluvian', and exercised no influence at all. The one gleam of hope Gorst could point to was that 'an association of working men is about to be formed to advocate what is called "Reciprocity"' – an early manifestation of protectionist sentiment. 'It is hoped by this means to get a hold upon the lower class of voters. The ballot is looked forward to rather as an advantage than otherwise.' And with a 'fairly prepared burgess-roll' Gorst hoped that 'with the help of the woman voters who are Conservative a change will be effected in the Town Council'.[20]

Rochester would be a tough nut to crack. Yet, for reasons which may well have had to do with the ballot, protectionist sentiment, and the growing political participation of Conservative women, Rochester elected one Conservative member in 1880. By the middle of 1880s and through the 1890s, Rochester was, as a single-member constituency, solidly Conservative, apart from a lone Liberal by-election success in 1889. Coventry was another borough in which anti-free trade opinion was helpful to the Conservative interest.[21] Gorst's indefatigable travellings, visitings, and urgings also undoubtedly contributed to the improvement in Conservative borough fortunes. Corry remarked to Disraeli that 'Gorst seems to be doing his work admirably. If we should win Truro . . . it *appears* it will be entirely due to this fact.'[22] Truro was indeed duly won, and Gorst was the gratified recipient of Disraeli's personal acknowledgements. There had been earlier gains. 'Colchester, following up Shrewsbury', as Disraeli exulted, 'ought to raise the confidence of our men in their measure.'[23] Failure at Newport Gorst accounted for by bribery. Had he been consulted he would have recommended a petition 'at the expense of the party fund'.[24] By late 1870 Gorst could assure Disraeli that the 'results of the Revision in England have been most favourable'. Success in the Registration Courts showed 'a healthy state of activity'.[25]

That 'healthy state of activity' in the registration procedures had no doubt contributed decisively to the epochal East Surrey victory in August 1871. Gorst pressed on with a policy of contesting all vacancies. A gain in North West Riding was hailed by Hardy in February 1872 as 'a sign of the times'. Lowe admitted to Derby that it was 'significant', and that other constituencies would follow suit. Derby himself thought it important, 'because when the old West Riding was divided in 1867–68 it was assumed that the district now contested would be a Liberal constituency, being full of great towns and manufacturing villages: and indeed the Liberal party claimed a majority of 1800 on the register'.[26]

Disraeli was systematically kept abreast: 'after every borough election, an expert visits the scene of action, and prepares a confidential dispatch for me, that, so far as possible, I may be thoroughly acquainted with the facts.'[27] The ballot held no terrors for Gorst. It was a pity at its electoral debut that Childers would not be unseated at Pontefract in August 1872 on his re-entry into Gladstone's cabinet. But at the first large-scale election under the ballot, at Preston in September, it was noted that 'Conservatives appeared to be infinitely more active with their agents at the various polling booths than the Liberals',[28] and defended successfully. By 1873 the party was equipped with *Hints for Candidates*.[29] Gorst was assiduous also in the arena of municipal elections. He later celebrated Conservative municipal successes in 1872 and 1873 as a 'fore-shadowing' of future parliamentary successes in the boroughs.[30] Gorst treated them as a testing ground and 'barometer' in the 'great burst of municipal electioneering in Lancashire which resulted in severe Liberal defeats'.[31] In these contests in 1873 Conservatives won 112 seats and lost 83. Later experience was to indicate that municipal elections were not invariably accurate barometers of general electoral pressures; but for the present it was well that Gorst be spurred on by such illusions. For good measure, Gorst could also, by February 1873, inform Disraeli that during the past year, 'no less than 69 new Conservative Associations, exclusive of branches,' had been formed in England and Wales. Two associations had died out, leaving in existence 420 associations, 'the great majority of which are in good working order, and most of which have largely increased their numbers of members since last year'.[32] A healthy tone in Manchester was attested in 1872 when Derby was invited to take shares in a Conservative Club Society, which planned to build a new clubhouse. After careful inquiries, Derby concluded that it would be a sound investment, and took, on his estate account, 40 shares of £25 each.[33]

Scotland, on the other hand, remained stubbornly a problem area. As Gorst reported to Disraeli in 1870,

> Keith-Falconer, on his return from Scotland, was asked by us to visit Edinburgh. He had a long interview with Pitman and Winchester, the heads of our Scottish National Association, and also with E.S. Gordon. They discussed the prospects of the party in Scotland generally, and in each constituency particularly. Falconer has given me a detailed report in each Constituency: this I am sorry to say does not show much prospect of an improvement in our position in Scotland at the next General Election.[34]

No doubt this assessment reflected accurately the Conservative situation in Scotland in 1870. But, as events were to reveal by the beginning of 1874, Gorst was being unduly pessimistic about Scottish prospects. The next three years would in fact see something of a rebuilding of Scottish Conservatism towards the kind of respectable minority status characteristic of its solid electoral plateau of 20 or so seats from the elections of 1837 to 1852.

3

Scepticism about prospects in Scotland reflected Gorst's generally cautious assessment of party prospects prior to the entirely unexpected denouement of 1874. This did not, of course, inhibit Gorst later from constructing a plausible and persistent personal and political myth out of his role as the principal agent of victory. His own notions about the possibilities of a truly popular Conservatism and the role of the National Union as the designated embodiment of its principles and purposes also became an important part of that myth. But the realities of the politics of the early 1870s meant that the National Union and its local associations played but a marginal part in the resurgence of Conservative fortunes. In fact, the tendency was for the union to be at odds with Central Office agents in the smaller local borough associations. This was partly because local bodies were jealous of their independence and resented central pretensions, especially when such pretensions were unaccompanied by the great needful thing, money. Central party funds were kept carefully in the hands of a small group of trustees, Abergavenny presiding. It was partly also because agents developed their own expertise, their own professional identity, and their own esprit, which they related to their kin at Central Office, and decidedly not to the people at the 'talking shop', which is how they came to see the National Union. These tendencies only took clear shape later in the century, when the National Union, taken out of the hands of such as Gorst and rendered harmless, became the all too congenial home of the grand old backbench hacks of the party.

Agents saw themselves as fighters in the front line. From the beginning of the new constituency associations, especially in Lancashire and the north generally, there were stirrings of mutually supportive agents' societies, gathering benefits in cooperation, sharing a sense of the endemic absence of serious resources available from the centre and of identity as an emerging profession, a new kind of Conservative political subculture. Wollaston Pym in Middlesex, though as an idiosyncratic and aristocratic figure *sui generis* and not a type of this new breed, was still a portent of the beginnings of a new borough constituency order which would eventually realise itself in a National Society of Conservative Agents, complete with its journal. What is certainly to be stressed at this point is that much the greatest part of the new Conservative borough constituency organisational strength engendered itself from the localities and owed little to the centre, whether Central Office or National Union, for all the undoubtedly devoted services of Gorst and his team.

The new subculture is illustrated in the case of Joseph Gould of Exeter, earlier noted for his contempt for the party's feeble performance in that borough in 1868. As the greatest man in the Western Division of Conservative Agents and one of the later founders in 1891 of the Conservative Agents' Society, he came to be accorded heroic status among his peers. Arthur Fawcett, the historian of the Conservative agents, celebrated Gould's deeds accordingly. 'When the National Society came into existence there was little or no organisation in the constituencies, and agents had to build it up entirely by their own efforts with no past experience to guide them.' In January 1872 Gould became secretary to the reconstituted Exeter Conservative Association, managed by a representation committee chosen by each ward and district. 'In 1873, the Conservative Working Men of Exeter formed a Union in which Gould ultimately became secretary, and "The Tory" records that the Exeter Conservative Association and the Working Men's Conservative Unions worked harmoniously together.' Gould's first conspicuous feat was to organise in 1872 a demonstration at Powderham Park attended by 25,000 people, 'which was considered to be party management of a high order, "when the art of conducting such affairs was in its infancy"'.[35] Northcote reported this manifestation to Disraeli as 'highly successful', with hopes that it had done good not only at Exeter but in several western constituencies also.[36] A by-election at Exeter in December 1873 consequent on Coleridge being promoted to lord chief justice had Winn worrying to Taylor that 'it will be a terrible business if we fail'.[37] Fail Gould did not. The Liberal seat was handsomely captured, a prelude to the capture of the second seat a few weeks later.

Gould's later exploits included being instrumental in founding a Conservative Club and in equipping the party in Devon with two newspapers, one a half-penny paper 'designed to give the working classes a newspaper at a cost within their means to read during their evening's leisure'.

> Individuals such as Gould were giants who founded the National Society and moulded its early days. There were no area agents to lean upon, no Central Office services to advise, supply and inform them. They were on their own, and it was their rugged individualism which influenced the National Society in its development.[38]

Gould's practical legacy to Devon Conservatism was the fact that between 1874 and 1906 Exeter elected but one Liberal member for one parliament.

Ramifications: the press; Lancashire

1

The question of the relationship between the Conservative party and the political press at this juncture was vexed. As with borough constituencies, Liberalism tended toward a monopoly. The power, influence, and prestige of the established commercial press made it a political factor of capital importance. Conservatism undoubtedly suffered from the hostility of both *The Times* and the *Daily Telegraph* and of the great mass of the provincial press engendered by the abolition of the newspaper stamp tax in 1855 and paper duties in 1861. It had proved in this commercial climate very difficult to establish successful papers in the Conservative interest. Disraeli, an old and disillusioned hand in this quest, had every ground for complaint in 1868 that the party was 'over-papered' with unconvincing ventures. Disraeli had not been convinced by Spofforth's assurance in 1866 that Raikes's acquiring the London evening *Globe* would, if unknown to the public, be of material advantage to the party. As Hart Dyke explained to Disraeli in December 1869, he had been much involved in keeping the paper 'on its legs' by subscriptions from the party, and proposed to keep it going until the next meeting of parliament. Hart Dyke sketched a possible scheme for the funding of a limited company directed by the party leaders.[39] By January 1870 Corry remarked to Disraeli that the increase of the *Pall Mall Gazette* to two pence would give that paper 'a hard fight of it. The change must materially assist the Globe – in the future of which I have some confidence – now.'[40] The *Globe* established itself for the time as the leading evening metropolitan organ of the Conservative party, 'and Mr. Montagu Corry was the *interpres* who brought the news from Olympus.'[41]

In 1871 a concern in the London Strand called the Central Press Board was purchased on behalf of the party with a view to converting it into an agency to feed the provincial Conservative press with telegrams, articles, and stereotypes. Gorst told Disraeli that Rowland Winn was asking for Disraeli's advice on the appointment of an 'editor for our Conservative Central Press Association'. A 'good practical Board of Directors' had been appointed of which Winn was chairman. As to possible editors, it was thought initially that a member of parliament might be best placed. E.G. Eastwick, MP for Penrhyn, was thought of.[42] Corry reported soon after that he had attended a meeting of the Central Press Company Board, 'with satisfactory results'.

> After much discussion we agreed to offer the Editorship to Eastwick. . . . Today, the concern is handed over to us, and Gorst and Falconer take the control until his arrival. Kebbel was a candidate for the post, and attended the Board. I think

the general prospects of the concern are encouraging, and that greater results than we contemplate may ensue.[43]

Keith Falconer remained as Central Office's guiding representative on the board, liaising especially with Winn and Corry.[44] In 1874 Eastwick was succeeded by Keith-Falconer's successor as honorary secretary of the National Union, Lt Col. Edward Neville.

Thus the Conservative provincial press was catered for. The metropolitan clubs and news rooms also enjoyed the benefits of the parliamentary reports in large type and special reports which were dispatched by the association at half-hourly intervals during sittings of parliament. In the metropolis the *Standard* was the Conservative morning paper. From the appointment in 1873 of W.H. Mudford as manager and then editor in 1876 the *Standard* began to establish itself as the pre-eminent cheap Conservative press organ. With Noel's blessing, Gorst established a connection with the *Standard* as an authoritative source of political intelligence.[45]

Like the *Globe* it was a penny paper. What the party lacked as yet was the prestige of a heavyweight three-penny morning paper. Ever and anon there were hopes of *The Times*. As Corry remarked to Disraeli of its assistant editor in 1869, 'Dasent is noisy, vulgar & pretentious; but not ill-disposed, & may be of use, some day.'[46] Alas, Dasent left to become a Civil Service commissioner for Gladstone. There was always more to be hoped of from the *Morning Post*. Algernon Borthwick, who succeeded his father as editor in 1852, had been Palmerston's grand commis of the press. His turning in Disraeli's direction in 1873 was one of the more telling signs of the times. Spofforth had so advised Taylor: 'When you write to Mr. Disraeli suggest to him that it would be of great value if the Morning Post could be propitiated from now till the General Election. It has of late taken a very favourable turn.'[47] Taylor did indeed impress upon his chief that the *Morning Post* was 'friendly & I have told Borthwick that I will endeavour to get him a suitable seat at the dissolution'.[48] Corry engaged himself very much in the business of propitiating Borthwick henceforth. Although by 1875 the *Morning Post* was still listed as Whig and Palmerstonian as well as High Church, its Conservative loyalties were no longer in doubt.[49]

2

Into the difficult business of prodding Disraeli up to Lancashire Gorst entered with gusto as an ally of Corry and Noel and Keith-Falconer at the metropolitan end and of Egerton and Callender and Edge '(one of our best electioneers in Lancashire)' at the Manchester end. For Gorst (himself a Preston man in origin) a grand Lancashire manifestation would above all else celebrate the new borough power of Conservatism. Gorst set about marginalising the county element led by Egerton. He preferred to deal with

W.R. Callender, president of the Workingmen's Conservative Association and of several election committees in Manchester who had first written to Gorst in September 1870 urging the expediency of a visit by Disraeli. 'Recognition of our efforts would be most gratefully appreciated – it would give an *enormous* stimulus to the efforts of the working men & its benefit could not be overrated.' No county had 'so completely responded to the appeal of the Conservative Govt as Lancashire & our gain was far beyond our anticipations.'[50] Gorst passed the message on Noel. 'I know that it is generally my duty to protect Mr. Disraeli from importunities of this kind, but . . . I know there is a very wide spread desire throughout Lancashire of long standing for a visit from the leader of the Conservative Party.' That desire, Gorst advised, was attributable to two causes:

> (1) The people of Lancashire are a very loyal people. They like to have a personal acquaintance with the leader they follow. The late Lord Derby was personally known throughout the County, & you will remember the pains Mr. Gladstone took to make himself equally well known at the time of the general election.
>
> (2) Lancashire is the stronghold of our party. We are generally strong in counties and weak in boroughs, & we shall never attain stable political power till the boroughs are conquered. The only boroughs where we are really the stronger party are the Lancashire boroughs. Where the artisans practise small trades ministering to the wants of the rich as in Birmingham London & so many of the minor boroughs, it is easy to see the influences which make them dissenters & radicals. It is among the employés of large staple trades like the cotton trade or ship-building trade that we must look in the first instance for Conservative workmen. Some special causes were no doubt at work in Lancashire at the last election, but from my own knowledge of the county I have no hesitation in saying that the operatives of Lancashire are to a large extent bona fide Conservatives.
>
> If Mr. Disraeli would attend some properly organised demonstrations in Lancashire, he would meet with the most enthusiastic reception to himself personally: he would meet an intelligent appreciative audience, interested in public affairs & especially in foreign policy, beyond the mere sphere of their own physical wants: & I think he would give a great impetus to the party which would assist – what I live in hopes of seeing – a revulsion of feeling in the great towns of the West Riding.[51]

Noel was loyally supportive and assured Disraeli that 'it would be of the greatest service to the Party if you would consent to attend a public meeting in Lancashire'.[52] But there was no encouragement from Derby: 'Talk with D. as to a Conservative meeting, which I deprecate, partly because there is nothing to be said or done, partly because the Catholics are so much annoyed at certain passages in D.'s late novel that they would not join in any reception to be given to its author. . . .'[53] Gorst himself bombarded Disraeli with a barrage of inducements. It is quite probable, however, that he overplayed his borough hand.

> Among the working classes of Preston, Bolton, Blackburn, Accrington, Clitheroe, Darwen, Burnley, etc – the men by whom the Lancashire borough elections were

> carried – there is a very strong desire that a working man's meeting should take place either at Blackburn or Preston. They want to see & hear you and they want you to see the newly enfranchised electors of your own creation. Amongst them at least you would receive genuine thanks for the Reform Bill of 1867 – & in their quaint old-fashioned way, with guilds and strange customs & medieval ceremonies, they would give you a reception that would I think please you.[54]

This was characteristic Gorst tactlessness. Manchester was one thing. Blackburn or Preston quite another. (Gathorne Hardy responded to an invitation to a Rochdale banquet with the comment: 'of all places.')[55] Above all, the notion of an exclusively working-class manifestation was not likely to find favour with Disraeli. By April 1871 a chastened Gorst was regretting on behalf of the Lancashire invitation committee that Disraeli declined 'for the present'; and did not wish to offer an opinion as to the 'wisdom of the decision', but trusted earnestly that an opportunity would be afforded 'ere long'.[56]

There were other difficulties. Lancashire was Stanley territory. A visit by Disraeli would be awkward at a time when the new Lord Derby's qualifications to replace Disraeli as leader of the party were being widely canvassed. Derby remained persistently discouraging. By March 1871 he accepted that Disraeli might find it difficult not to attend, but himself kept his distance:

> partly because I see no use and some inconvenience in these electioneering appeals made at a time when no election is in prospect: partly because the only articulate expression of opinion that has come from the Conservative side of late is in favor of a policy of war, increased armaments, and the retention of purchase in the army: three things to all of which I am opposed.[57]

Moreover, neither Sandon nor Cross registered anything better than lukewarmness. A visit would be of no use without a definite policy to proclaim.[58] In south west Lancashire there was jealousy of Manchester's pretensions.[59] Derby confided to Cross his worries 'because Disraeli must be invited to make the principal speech, and no one knows, or can guess, what he is likely to say'. If Disraeli laid down a programme for the future, 'we do not know what we may find ourselves pledged to'. As he told Cross, Derby suspected that Disraeli 'was inclining to the semi-socialist ideas of "Young England"' of which Pakington had just given a sample in his 'New Social Alliance' address at the Leeds Social Science Congress. 'Still,' concluded Derby grudgingly, '. . . if the local leaders insisted upon it, the thing must be, and I could not refuse to attend, unless absolutely aware that the language to be held was contrary to my views.' Cross concurred in Derby's suspicions of Disraeli's likely temptation into semi-socialist Young England excesses. ('Every conversation I have had with Cross raises my opinion of his good judgment and good sense.')[60]

Clearly, Disraeli had to be the judge of the timing. There was the state of the party to consider; even more, the state of the government. The optimum point of impact would be a nice calculation. Gorst went ahead with his Conservative working men project independently. He reported to Disraeli in December 1871:

> I have just come from Manchester & I think you may like to have a line to tell you the present temper of Lancashire.
>
> The people are as eager as ever for your promised visit, but they thoroughly understand your position as leader of the party, and they will wait confidently & patiently until you yourself give the signal for such a demonstration as they contemplate.
>
> There is to be a large meeting on the 29th of Jan of working men from all the Lancashire Towns in the Free Trade Hall: it is to be a demonstration in favour of social legislation; and they are going to ask Ld. John Manners to attend.
>
> I believe that the people in every part of the country are thoroughly disgusted with Gladstone, and I expect before many months elapse a new man will be chosen as the popular leader. Dilke has been most useful to us.[61]

Notes and References

1 Spofforth to Disraeli, 18 June 1869; HP, B/XI/N/2 B.
2 Noel to Disraeli, 2 April [1870]; HP, B/XXI/N/118.
3 Noel to Disraeli, 14 April [1870]; HP, B/XXI/N/114.
4 Noel to Disraeli, 22 April [1870]; HP, B/XXI/N/115.
5 Spofforth to Taylor, 12 March 1875; HP, B/XXI/S/441a. See also R. Stewart's comments deprecating the exaggeration of Gorst's role in remaking the party: *The Foundation of the Conservative Party, 1830–1867* (1978), 338–9.
6 E.J. Feuchtwanger, *Disraeli, Democracy and the Tory Party* (Oxford, 1968), 121.
7 Gorst to Noel, 22 Sept. 1870; HP, B/XXI/N/120a.
8 Feuchtwanger, *Disraeli, Democracy and the Tory Party*, 54.
9 HP, B/XXI/N/113.
10 Gorst to Disraeli, 26 Feb. 1874; HP/XXI/G/250.
11 HP, B/IX/G/69.
12 Derby Diary, 29 Jan. 1872.
13 Feuchtwanger, *Disraeli, Democracy and the Tory Party*, 128.
14 See above, 19.
15 Feuchtwanger, *Disraeli, Democracy and The Tory Party*, 126.
16 Hardy, *Diary*, 101.
17 NUCCA, minutes of proceedings, 4th conference, York, 20 April 1870.
18 See H. Gorst, *The Earl of Beaconsfield* (1900), 123–4.
19 *Ibid.*, 129–30.
20 Gorst to Disraeli, 25 July 1870; HP, B/XXI/G/234.
21 Hanham, 115–16.
22 Corry to Disraeli, 15 Sept. 1871; HP, B/XX/Co/78.
23 Disraeli to Corry, 11 Nov. 1870; HP, B/XX/D/145.
24 Gorst to Disraeli, 22 Dec. 1870; HP, B/XXI/G/236.
25 Gorst to Disraeli, 19 Nov. 1870; HP, B/XXI/G/235.
26 Hardy, *Diary*, 150; Derby Diary, 7 and 8 Feb. 1872. The seat was, in fact, lost in 1874.
27 Buckle, ii, 525–6.
28 *AR*, 1872, 75.
29 Hardy, *Diary*, 188.
30 Gorst to Disraeli, 2 Dec. 1874; HP, B/XXI/D/463a.
31 Hanham, 388.
32 Gorst to Disraeli, 12 Feb. 1873; HP, B/XXI/G/240.
33 Derby Diary, 3 Sept. 1872.

34 Gorst to Disraeli, 19 Nov. 1870; HP, B/XXI/G/235.
35 A.W.P. Fawcett, *Conservative Agent* (1967), 12–13.
36 Northcote to Disraeli, 23 Sept. 1872; BL, Iddesleigh 50016, 135.
37 Winn to Taylor, 5 Dec. 1873; HP, B/XX/T/126.
38 Fawcett, *Conservative Agent, ibid.*
39 Hart Dyke to Disraeli, [12 Dec. 1869]; HP, B/XXI/D/451.
40 Corry to Disraeli, 2 Jan. 1870; HP, B/XXI/Co/52.
41 H. StJ. Raikes, *Life and Letters of H.C. Raikes* (1898), 229.
42 Gorst to Disraeli, 23 Sept. 1871; HP, B/XXI/G/238.
43 Corry to Disraeli, 28 Oct. 1871; HP, B/XX/Co/81.
44 Gorst to Disraeli, 26 Feb. 1874; HP, B/XXI/G/250.
45 Feuchtwanger, *Disraeli, Democracy and the Tory Party*, 120. For *The Standard* see D. Griffiths, 'The early management of *The Standard*,' in L. Brake, A. Jones, and C. Madden, *Investigating Victorian Journalism* (1990) 120–132.
46 Corry to Disraeli, 22 Jan. 1869; HP, B/XXI/Co/49.
47 Spofforth to Taylor, 21 Aug. 1873; HP, B/XX/T/128a.
48 Taylor to Disraeli, 22 Aug. 1873; HP, B/XX/T/128. There was no seat available in 1874. Borthwick contested his father's former seat at Evesham unsuccessfully in 1880. He was MP for South Kensington 1885–95.
49 See R. Lucas, *Lord Glenesk and the 'Morning Post'* (1910), 250.
50 Callender to Gorst, 21 Sept. 1870; HP, B/XXI/N/121a.
51 Gorst to Noel, 22 Sept. 1870; HP, B/XXI/N/120a.
52 Noel to Disraeli, 24 Sept. 1870; HP, B/XXI/N/120.
53 Derby Diary, 19 Oct. 1870.
54 Gorst to Disraeli, 22 Dec. 1870; HP, B/XX/G/23b.
55 Hardy, *Diary*, 143.
56 Gorst to Disraeli, 4 April 1871; HP, B/XXI/G/237.
57 Derby Diary, 14 March 1871.
58 Feuchtwanger, *Disraeli, Democracy and the Tory Party*, 10.
59 Gorst to Disraeli, 22 Dec. 1870; HP, B/XXI/G/236.
60 Derby Diary, 7 Oct. 1871.
61 Gorst to Disraeli, 8 Dec. 1871; HP, B/XXI/G/239.

Chapter 6

Better times, 1872–3

Manchester and Crystal Palace

1

Gorst's reference to Sir Charles Dilke's utility pointed to the republican agitation led by that Radical politician in protest at the queen's stubborn widowed seclusion. Gladstone had innocently contributed to this critical sentiment by what was widely called a 'gaffe' at his recent pre-sessional speech at Blackheath when he quoted from a secularist and republican handbook.[1] The republican campaign rebounded on its authors when the prince of Wales's recovery from desperate illness provoked a surge of emotional support for the monarchy. The opportunity was not disdained in the Conservative party. Gathorne Hardy eagerly proposed to improve the shining hour. He wrote to Cairns that the prince's recovery 'will be a great blessing to the country if properly used'. The suspense of the last few weeks had roused a wonderful feeling of loyalty and affection; sincere prayers had been answered.

> I wish some intimation were given from high quarters that a public recognition say at St. Paul's would take place when the Prince was fit for it. I should like quietly to suggest it but hardly know with whom to communicate. Such a step would I believe be appreciated by the best of the people and confirm the feeling that has been roused. Don't you agree?[2]

The duke of Cambridge was fixed on as the channel to Gladstone; and eventually a service of public thanksgiving at St. Paul's was arranged for 27 February.[3]

Hardy's immediate motives were monarchical and religious; he could hardly have foreseen the strictly political consequences of the event, when, in the returning carriage procession, Disraeli received a striking popular ovation while Gladstone was the target of dull silence or hoots. This was the first occasion out of doors since Derby's resignation of the leadership on which Disraeli enjoyed signal public applause. He was observed back at the Carlton later that day being talked to by the MP for North Hampshire, Sclater-Booth. Disraeli's countenance was 'that of a man who looks into another world'. Sclater-Booth, aware that his Hampshire concerns were not being intently attended to, was quite clear what Disraeli was thinking about: 'he was thinking that he will be Prime Minister again!'[4] Already Disraeli had given his promised undertaking to Lancashire, for the Easter recess. He had reason now to feel confirmed in his judgement that the time was ripe. The Burghley intrigues at the beginning of February were not only too little in terms of the plausibility of their intended beneficiary, Derby; they were too late in terms of Disraeli's vulnerability.

Even before the opening of the 1872 session Disraeli could sense the pregnancy of events. He was helped, as ever, by Northcote.

> There is a good deal to consider with reference to our position. I saw Matt. Arnold (Forster's brother-in-law) at the Athenaeum yesterday, and he told me he had heard from a well-informed dissenter that there was a real desire on the part of a good many of them to get the Govt out, with a view to reorganise themselves in opposition.[5]

A few days later the queen made it 'evident' to Derby at Osborne that she was 'expecting a political crisis', which gave Derby the 'opportunity of saying that we . . . could not think of taking office while in a minority of 100, but that while remaining as we were, we would do what was possible to prevent embarrassment and help in working the machine'.[6] Already, addressing the Conservative Working Men's Constitutional Association at Liverpool, Derby had made a point of deprecating taking office without a majority. He found Disraeli concurring 'emphatically'. Disraeli took the view that after 1866–8 the party was in no immediate need of the patronage of office. 'He seemed well, eager, animated, altogether different from what he was twelve months ago.'[7]

Over Gladstone's government hung a pall of discredit. Disraeli's worry was that there might be too much ripeness in its time. He remarked to Corry on 27 January on the 'curious' article in the *Spectator* of that day, on the political situation: 'a wail of agony. I fear we are on the eve of critical events to wh., from circumstances, we shall scarcely be equal.' Disraeli could list a series of 'scrapes' and scandals which Gladstone and his colleagues had inflicted on themselves, from Gladstone's perverse obstinacy in matters of patronage to 'anarchy' in the Admiralty, persistent Nonconformist disaffection on education, 'moral prostration' in the licensing question, embarrassment over the income tax; but above all, the lowering presence of the *Alabama* issue.[8] That question assumed 'portentous proportions', he wrote to Cairns, '& the public mind is getting very excited about it'; all else was 'absorbed' in it.[9] The point was that through a combination of Foreign Office carelessness and what Northcote ruefully described as Yankee cuteness, Gladstone's dismayed government found itself confronted by the fact that, after all, the American indirect claims would go forward to the proposed international tribunal at Geneva. Disraeli conveyed to Northcote rumours that 'unless the Cabinet withdraw from the arbitration, they must break up. God grant they may withdraw. It would take a load off my mind.'[10] Cairns, however, was in no doubt that the Washington treaty justified the American demand. 'He holds withdrawal from the arbitration, a clear casus belli.'[11]

Given so grave a consideration relating to the national interest, quite apart from his own party's implication in the affair through Northcote, Disraeli was far from rejoicing at the Liberal government's discomfiture. Even less was he rejoicing at the contingency of taking office over the debris of a broken Gladstone cabinet. The circumstances which in his view would make the Conservative party unequal to such a challenge obtained in force, and would apply still when the actual contingency presented itself a year hence. What Cross and Sandon had urged against a Lancashire visit in the previous year persisted at the heart of the difficulty. The great want was a 'definite policy to proclaim'. The great task for Disraeli in Lancashire in a few weeks' time was to proclaim something that might begin to take the shape and colour of a definite policy in the public mind. One element in that forming shape and colour would be the legacy of Scott Russell's abortive New Social Alliance initiative, as mediated by Pakington. Already Derby had launched his own version of the initiative in his speech at Liverpool Conservative Working Men's Association in January. 'Lord Derby approved measures of sanitary reform and the regulation of mines as a welcome substitute for constitutional changes.'[12] Much could be read into this in the febrile atmosphere of the Burghley intrigues. Hardy recorded in his diary on 5 February that another Lancashire MP, Wilson Patten, had spoken to him 'strongly' of the effect of Derby's speech, '& said that there was an opinion which he found it difficult to combat that Disraeli was coming to counteract that effect. Absurd!'[13]

Absurd or not, Derby, as Tory chief of Lancashire, was bound to see the affair from his own special angle. There was 'much discussion' in March as to the 'advantages or otherwise' of his attending 'the meeting at Manchester at wh. Disraeli is to deliver a manifesto'. To stay away 'might look either like jealousy of D. (which I should be sorry were supposed to exist) or indifference to politics altogether'. Derby was quite clear that if he did go it could not be 'as a listener only'. He must speak; 'and then the meeting is not exclusively in honor of D. – besides which if our language is different, or can be made to appear so, comments to that effect are sure to be abundant.' Derby added his own gloss on the Burghley conclave: 'The question is complicated by the existence of a section of the party who would follow me, but who will not follow D. What their number may be I have no means of guessing.' Consultations with two of his Lancashire protégés, Richard Cross and Patten, led Derby to conclude that he could not avoid attending, but would confine himself to a 'short speech of a complimentary kind'.[14] When Derby discussed the matter with Disraeli at the end of March, he found Disraeli 'very nervous, more so than I have known him to be on any occasion of late years'. Disraeli insisted that he 'did not like his visit to Manchester, it had been forced upon him by importunity continued ever since the last general election (this I know to be true) and at last he was obliged to give way'. No doubt Disraeli made these protestations partly in deference to Derby's susceptibilities; but there was also no doubt of Disraeli's misgivings and uneasiness as to what to say and how to say it. He rehearsed his proposed speech with Derby, admitting that he was 'anxious about the chance of any ill-considered phrase escaping him in so long a speech'.

> He talked of the Reform bill of 1867, which he intended to vindicate: would contend that it only restored to the working classes the electoral privileges which they had before 1832 in the boroughs where scot-and-lot vote existed: which Ld Grey's bill took away, and the loss of which he said had caused the chartist movement. He said he had gone carefully into the figures with Lambert: the gross total of registered electors in the U.K. . . . is 2,500,000: but deductions have to be made for double returns, deaths etc. which he is told reduce the effective total to 2,250,000 or thereabouts: in other words of the adult males throughout the country not much more than 1/4th have votes – and this is the system which by opponents on both sides is said to be a near approach to universal suffrage![15]

2

Disraeli came up at last for his 'wondrous week' at Manchester at the beginning of April, 'to meet the county and all the Boroughs of Lancashire'. Gorst, his impresario, briefed him amid the rounds of receptions and parades on the inwardness of Lancashire Conservatism, regional and local, with emphasis on the identities of strategically important employers of labour.[16] Disraeli consented also to receive a deputation of Conservative operatives agitating for shorter hours of factory labour. He responded sympathetically, promising that the question would be inquired into whenever he was in a position to arrange it.[17] The grand centrepiece was Disraeli's oration on the evening of 3 April in the Free Trade Hall, Callender presiding. Derby was at his side, who, it was noted, 'distinctly and maybe designedly, referred to Disraeli as his "chief"'.[18] Hardy noted Disraeli's 'reception in Manchester extraordinary.' His speech 'very long & in parts very good. No programme, as how could there be? His reception Wilson Patten says was beyond anything he ever saw.'[19] Unlike the previous grand out-of-doors excursion at Edinburgh, Disraeli was in friendly territory. Derby was perhaps a candid friend. Disraeli spoke to a crowd of 6,000 from 7.30 p.m. to near 11 p.m. in 'oppressive heat'. The 'constitutional essay' with which he started was, in Derby's view, 'ingenious, but to my mind somewhat unreal'. The best parts of Disraeli's speech were the passages on the 'condition of the laboring classes and on current affairs' 'but it was delivered to an audience already exhausted, and in a weaker voice, not heard through the entire room'. Derby felt that on the whole, 'though a remarkable intellectual feat, being admirable in point of style, and delivered without reference to a note', the oration 'fell flat'. Disraeli was not at home on the platform. As against that, Derby was in no doubt as to the success of the occasion, if not the speech. 'The enthusiasm shown by those who came to receive and to see him has surprised all parties – Conservatives not less than Liberals. There has been nothing like it in my recollection.'[20] Cairns congratulated Disraeli on his 'splendid oration at Manchester':

> It was a great occasion, & the speech was as great as the occasion. As regards the present crisis there was everything in it that ought to have been in it, & nothing that ought not. But as regards the future, it will live & be read not only for its sparkling vigour, but also for the deep strata of constitutional thought & reasoning wh pervade it.[21]

Disraeli's strategic purpose was to reassert convincingly a consistent Conservative party policy at the critical moment of perceived Liberal exhaustion. To the accusation that the Conservative party had no programme to offer to the country he responded with his opening sally: 'The programme of the Conservative party is to maintain the Constitution of the country.'[22] On the ground of his proposition that 'in political institutions are the embodied experiences of a race', Disraeli defended the role of the throne as the foundation of that 'continuous order which is the only parent of personal liberty and political right' and of the Lords who, as the guardians of 'territorial property', were thereby 'representative', and whose sense of the responsibility inherent in hereditary landowning gave them 'every inducement to study public opinion', and to yield to it when convinced of its justice. He insisted that 'no addition to the elements of the popular constituency' had 'placed the House of Commons in a different position with regard to the Throne and the House of Lords from that it has always constitutionally occupied.' He extolled the wisdom which connected authority and religion, pointing out that there was 'the same assault against the Church of England and the union between the State and the Church as there is against the Monarchy and against the House of Lords'.[23]

Disraeli's second theme was the 'condition of the great body of the people', with a special excursus on the conditions of agricultural labour. Here he inserted a positive element, with a certain political novelty, possessing two considerable advantages. The first was the currency recently engendered by the debate stemming from the New Social Alliance; the second was that it presented a distinctively Conservative line of approach to social questions as against prevalent Liberal and Gladstonian orthodoxy. Disraeli pointed to the great progress made in the condition of the mass of the people over the past 40 years (a standard Liberal theme), but insisted that this was not an argument 'that there is nothing to be done to increase the wellbeing of the working classes of the country'. Much would depend upon the 'sympathy between classes' which was now such a distinctive feature of public life. But to Disraeli it was clear that 'no inconsiderable results may be obtained by judicious and prudent legislation'. Such legislation should be predominantly sanitary in direction: 'pure air, pure water, the inspection of unhealthy habitations, the adulteration of food, these and many kindred matters may be legitimately dealt with'. Disraeli enhanced his assertion that it was 'impossible to overrate the importance of the subject' with the quip which gave his initiative instant and gratifying notoriety: '*Sanitas sanitatum, omnia sanitas.*'[24]

Having thus asserted a distinctive Conservative identity in practical policy, Disraeli turned on the Liberals. He denounced what he termed the 'principle of violence' at the base of the policies of Gladstone's government. In Ireland especially 'you witnessed the incubation of a portentous birth': a policy purporting to bring content to Ireland at the price of 'sacrilege and confiscation' had resulted in 'sedition rampant, treason thinly veiled', with a vast encouragement to the Home Rule agitation. In Britain 'every institution and every interest, every class and calling in the country' had been under Liberal attack and harassment. But now the point of debility had been reached. Disraeli's passage on the spectacle of the jaded Liberal cabinet well deserved Morley's tribute to 'one of the few classic pieces of oratory of the century':

> The unnatural stimulus was subsiding. Their paroxysms ended in prostration. Some took refuge in melancholy, and their eminent chief alternated between a menace and a sigh. As I sat opposite the Treasury Bench the ministers reminded me of one of those marine landscapes not very unusual on the coasts of South America. You behold a range of exhausted volcanoes. Not a flame flickers on a single pallid crest. But the situation is still dangerous. There are occasional earthquakes, and ever and anon the dark rumbling of the sea.[25]

This superb mockery was a prelude to Disraeli's ending on a high note of foreign and imperial policy. He taunted Liberal ministers with having subjected themselves as well as the country to humiliation over the Black Sea and *Alabama* issues. This was an appeal by Disraeli to the Palmerstonian 'national' public. But, as with his earlier stress on the judiciousness and prudence which would govern any ventures into social legislation, Disraeli was careful to stipulate that he was no advocate of a 'turbulent and aggressive diplomacy'. England was in a new situation *vis-à-vis* Europe. Moreover, the queen of England was now sovereign of the most powerful of oriental states and there were colonies belonging to her 'teeming with wealth and population'. There was also the new power and presence of the United States. 'These are vast and novel elements in the distribution of power.' As for English policy towards Europe, this 'should be a policy of reserve, but proud reserve'. England had not decayed in power or resources. And there was the unbroken spirit of her people, 'never prouder of the imperial country to which they belong'. Disraeli closed his peroration with a toast to the 'cause of the Tory party, the English Constitution, and of the British Empire'.[26]

There is no doubt that Disraeli had judged both the time and the tone well. His image of exhausted volcanoes caught the political moment memorably. His implicit undertaking was that Conservative policy would substitute repose and stability for Gladstone's strenuousness. His speech was far too long, and was marred by patches of characteristic humbug, as in his denials that the past 40 years had seen any change in the balance between the Commons as against the Crown and the Lords, or in indignant accusations that the Liberals were conspiring to set up a large standing army contrary to all the traditions of the constitution, to be officered by 'a class of men eminently scientific, but with no relations necessarily with society'. But Disraeli's substantial achievement at Manchester was to blend advantageously the old doctrines of constitutional Conservatism with new emphases on social reform and empire. With these two themes he manoeuvred the Conservative party into a position where it could benefit from the infiltration of two important emanations of the public mood. First, there was a significant body of opinion ready to welcome the end of the Liberal era of institutional or apparatus reform, and to see an era of social reform as a plausible, or necessary, or even desirable alternative. Disraeli could balance fears about the possible shape of the latter with relief at the ending of the threats of the former. Second, there was an even more significant body of opinion bewildered and resentful at the eclipse of Britain as a European power and very much in need of comfort and reassurance. Without actually using words as revealing as 'consolation' or 'compensation', Disraeli went as near as made no difference to offering empire to the 'national' public for precisely such a purpose.

3

From Disraeli's point of view the Manchester triumph vindicated and ratified his leadership of the party. He made a special point of thanking Derby 'warmly for having come to the Manchester meeting'.[27] Certain postures in the party became subject to readjustment. Derby found himself approached by Carnarvon, 'who volunteers to express satisfaction at the political condition of affairs, saying it was very different from what he and others had expected: and praises Disraeli's late speech in very high terms. So that quarrel is ended.'[28] Disraeli could indulge himself in relaxed political postures. He is recorded as having said shortly afterwards to Wilson Patten, apropos of the likely defeat and resignation of the government over Fawcett's bill to abolish religious tests at Trinity College, Dublin, that 'his objects in life were attained & that though for personal objects the immediate assault might be best', for the party, on the other hand, 'he rather thought time desirable'.[29] This was perhaps a little careless, for Wilson Patten was prone to be linked with people who looked to Derby as a preferable leader. From the point of view of Gorst and Keith-Falconer at Central Office the expediency of introducing the newly laurelled leader of the party and the newly revived National Union to one another at such a time of ministerial troubles suggested itself with compelling cogency. For Disraeli, his address to the National Union at the Sydenham Crystal Palace on 24 June, as the climax of its sixth conference, would be a valuable opportunity to press home his advantage and his directives for Conservative policy in a metropolitan setting. Keith-Falconer was the impresario for Disraeli's second sortie.

The Crystal Palace speech was a much more terse and considered text than the Manchester oration. It was also more deliberately apt for what must be called its strategic Palmerstonian purposes. Disraeli started out with a Tory interpretation of nineteenth-century party politics. This had it that the party's 'great overthrow' of 1832 had been 'deserved', because instead of pursuing the national principles of Pitt and Grenville it had allowed itself to degenerate into exclusiveness and restriction. Thus bereft of its natural and national leadership, the country was vulnerable to the introduction of a 'new system' into its political life, an endeavour to 'substitute cosmopolitan for national principles', under the plausible name of 'Liberalism'. Liberalism attacked the institutions of the country 'under the name of Reform', and made war on the manners and customs of the people 'under the pretext of Progress'. During the 40 years since the commencement of this new system the 'real state of affairs has been this: the attempt of one party to establish in this country cosmopolitan ideas, and the efforts of another – unconscious efforts, sometimes, but always continued – to recur to and resume those national principles to which they attribute the greatness and glory of the country.'[30] Disraeli thus offered the notion of a disinherited party at the point of beginning to retrieve its inheritance. There were implicit subplots within this drama: the role of Peel and Aberdeen and their disciple Gladstone in betraying the party's unconscious efforts to recur to and resume national principles; and, correspondingly, the way in which the national political inheritance had been fortuitously available to be appropriated by the Canningite Whig, Palmerston. The crucial, but unavowable, point implicit in Disraeli's argument was that the Conservative party was now claiming back as rightful possessor both the Palmerstonian national vocation and the Palmerstonian national public.

This point became clear as Disraeli proceeded to analyse the 'three great objects' of 'the Tory party, or as I will venture to call it, the National party'. These were to maintain the institutions of the country, to uphold the empire, and to elevate the condition of the people. The first he dealt with perfunctorily: it was old and familiar matter. The last he expounded in even more characteristically Scott Russell terms than he had at Manchester, rebutting cosmopolitan Liberal sneers at a 'policy of sewage'. But one new point of significance was Disraeli's evident sense that it would be well to cover himself from possible dangers of exaggerated expectations. He inserted some, as it were, small print: the 'great problem' was how to elevate the condition of the people 'without violating those principles of economic truth upon which the prosperity of all states depends'. The Palmerstonian bourgeoisie need not fret that he might try to dilute orthodox political economy with any 'Young England' extravagances.

But the pith and moment of Disraeli's Crystal Palace message was identification of the old national idea with the new imperial idea. He was, in fact, as cautious in his commitments in this area as he was in the area of social reform. The polemical thrust of his evocation of empire was to accuse Liberalism of a cosmopolitan conspiracy: 'there has been no effort so continuous, so subtle, supported by so much ability and acumen, as the attempt of Liberalism to effect the disintegration of the Empire of England.' This effort had failed because of 'the sympathy of the Colonies for the Mother Country'. Disraeli was evoking a mood rather than proposing a policy. He made it quite clear that the terms upon which Liberalism had granted colonial self-government in fact meant that the crucial historical opportunity for a 'great policy of imperial consolidation' had been allowed to pass by default. Derby recorded in 1870 that Sir George Grey, the great colonial governor, had approached Disraeli with plans for imperial consolidation and systematic colonisation: but Disraeli 'thinks it too late to do anything that will unite the colonies more closely with England'.[31] All that he could undertake in the aftermath was to pledge that 'no Minister in this country will do his duty who neglects any opportunity of reconstructing as much as possible our Colonial Empire, and of responding to those distant sympathies which may become the source of incalculable strength and happiness to this land.'

This was perfectly safe and perfectly consistent with what historians have come to describe as the Palmerstonian 'imperialism of free trade'. It was a formula promising maximum political benefits from sentiment and minimum political obligations in practice. The crux was the painless means whereby a 'great country, an Imperial country' would 'command the respect of the world'.

When, however, Disraeli descended in his peroration to address directly the 'representative assembly' of National Union activists his sureness of touch evaporated. He urged them to rally their 'classes and powerful societies' in the great contest between national and cosmopolitan principles; but he almost ruined the effect in assuring them that in their struggle against the Liberal borough ascendancy they had nothing to trust to but 'their own energy and the sublime instinct of an ancient people'.[32] This unlucky touch of Disraelian extravagance exposed his speech to much ridicule. However, there is no ground for assuming that this bathos disturbed his audience. Judging from the records of the conference in the Westminster Palace Hotel from which they had just repaired they were well capable of indulging their own forms of bizarre activism. Their view of the possible passing of the Ballot or Secret Voting Bill had to do mostly with its likely promoting of 'secret political societies' of 'revolutionary opinions'.[33] Derby's judgement that Disraeli 'performance not reckoned a success' was accurate enough on the ground that he had nothing to say either new or important.[34] It was, however, new and important in itself that Disraeli addressed the National Union in the setting which had been, in effect, the scene of his snubbing it in 1867. It was also new and important that that party be equipped with a convenient version of its historical credentials which became before long in itself historic.

New and unaccustomed political prosperity

1

Getting his Ballot Bill through parliament was indeed one of Gladstone's few substantial successes in the largely barren 1872 session. It also got through a Corrupt Practices Act, after threatening a dissolution, aimed at stemming the flow of electoral largesse. There was, naturally, a good deal of Conservative perturbation on these issues.[35] In the case of the ballot, this was less from immediate electoral concern than from prospective anxiety at its likely efforts in consequence of an extension of the borough occupiers' franchise to the counties. This was bound to be the next big push by the Radicals. This prospective threat to the Conservative county ascendancy was no doubt much in Stafford Northcote's mind when he expressed the 'well-founded and consistent objection of his party to a system which, whatever may be its bearing on corruption, tends to diminish the legitimate influence of character and station'.[36] Disraeli's line was to attempt to restrict the ballot as a 'penal statute' to be imposed upon corrupt constituencies. In the Lords Richmond had schemes to amend it into a measure 'compelling all dependent persons to vote openly', together with notions about 'optional secrecy'.[37] All these manoeuvres came to nought. Some Conservatives such as Hardy were nervous that too stout a resistance might give Gladstone a handle for a rally. 'Ballot ought to be out of the way as the last "liberal" cry for it might turn elections which on general principles would go with us.'[38] Likewise, the Liberal government got its Licensing Bill through with much cooperation from Conservative members led by Selwin-Ibbetson: but was rewarded for its pains by the declaration of *Licensed Victuallers' Guardian* that 'we shall hail with delight the advent of a Conservative Ministry'.[39]

Serious politics in 1872 was much more a matter of events out of doors than within parliament. Disraeli's two great excursions aptly symbolised this fact. The *Alabama* issue would be decided at Geneva. The Conservative opposition in both Houses during the session treated the question with deliberate forbearance. Gladstone acknowledged the 'caution and moderation' which generally marked Disraeli's conduct; and conceded that occasional 'inflammatory expressions' were 'warmly cheered', but by a 'portion, and a portion only, of the opposition'.[40] At Geneva at the last moment the American commissioners gave way on the dispute as to their indirect claims, and an arbitration was achieved in September which, though punitive for Britain, was a welcome relief for both parties in Britain in view of the possible alternative catastrophe.

Closer to home, Conservatives could observe with satisfaction that the Liberal majority of 1868 was haemorrhaging away in by-elections. In 1872 Conservatives captured seven seats and lost none. By early 1873 Disraeli could claim to have reduced the Liberal majority by 30 seats. An Oldham

Liberal seat was handsomely picked up in June 1872. The Liberal candidate, Lyulph Stanley, was advised by his agent 'that the miners as a body have been accustomed to vote for the Conservative party, but with the ballot, if they see who understands their questions, and speaks favourably of them, they will when the election comes round give their votes for those parties'.[41] As it happened, Stanley was defeated without the ballot; but the second Liberal seat was lost with the ballot in 1874. There was much Conservative relief that Preston was successfully defended with the ballot later in 1872. 'You will be interested in the Preston election', as Hardy pointed out to Cairns, 'which appears to be very satisfactory as indicating that the Lancashire fire has not gone out.'[42] The Liverpool by-election in February 1873 seemed to confirm, in Derby's words, that 'the ballot does not seem to have made any difference'.[43] Disraeli declared himself dismayed that 'the Conservatives, excited by success in recent elections, are growing eager: they want us to take office, and dissolve immediately: he dissuades them to the best of his powers, but finds them no longer willing to listen to moderate counsels.' Disraeli calculated that a dissolution would give the Conservative party large gains but not a majority: 30 to 40 seats most likely; good but not enough. 'He is not afraid of what some friends say "that he is missing the opportunity by not dissolving now." The same thing was said in 1839, but it did not prevent Peel from coming in with a vast majority in 1841.'[44]

By late 1872 it was clear that the situation of the Conservative party was quite transformed from its sorry state at the beginning of the 1868 parliament. Now that he was ever more secure in his seat as leader, Disraeli indulged further symptoms of doubt about his future. Already he had been noted as insisting that his 'objects in life were attained'. Hardy was alarmed in September to receive a 'very cordial letter' from Disraeli 'throwing future responsibility on *me* as he speaks of holding his position transitionally in a period of difficulty!' Hardy hoped that Disraeli might long 'hold on' as he had no faith in his fitness to take his place – 'though it would be absurd not to look the thing in the face when so many people speak openly to me of it'.[45] Did Disraeli doubt that a solid Conservative Commons' majority would come in his time? Did he view himself as Moses seeing far off a promised land in which he would never himself set foot? His wife's deteriorating health was undoubtedly a great distraction. Hardy reported to Cairns of their chief's 'great disquietude by the state of Lady B.':

> He said next to nothing on politics but gave the idea that he rather wishes himself out of them. This no doubt results from the present state of his home. I do not think he cd. bear withdrawal.[46]

Lady Beaconsfield died in December 1872. Though sorely afflicted, Disraeli let it be known through Corry and Taylor that he intended to be in his place at the beginning of the 1873 session. Derby reported early in

February: 'Disraeli has been seen: said to be in good spirits: Monty Corry is to live with him, and take care of him which he greatly wants, for no one is more helpless in private life.' Derby himself met Disraeli a few days later. Disraeli declared a wish to retire, 'but did not see who was to do the work. Hardy would not hear of taking the place of leader, and who else was possible?'[47] There is no evidence that Disraeli expected, or predicted, the kind of political sea-change which in fact occurred at the beginning of 1874. It was a commonplace that, to quote Salisbury, 'a considerable accession of force to the Conservative cause cannot be far distant'.[48] But it was equally a commonplace for Salisbury to assume that the consequence reasonably to be hoped for from this would be the action of a strengthened Conservative opposition.

Not that there was any dearth of new possibilities in the air. One of the most significant straws in the winds of later 1872 was an encounter at the great Powderham Castle demonstration between Northcote and Carnarvon. 'I had a short cruise with Carnarvon after it', reported Northcote to Disraeli, 'and found him very friendly in tone, very much alarmed at the possibility of a great attack on the land, suspicious of Gladstone and of an attempt to set tenants against landlords etc.'

> Speaking of the Reform bill he said he must admit that he had been overmuch frightened about it, and that it had worked out better than he expected. He said nothing about yourself, but told me he had felt Lord Derby's conduct to him at the time of the rupture very keenly, though they had made it up personally before Lord Derby's death. He praised your Manchester speech warmly and said he could not recall an expression with which he did not agree. Lowe seems quite to have lost the influence he at one time had over him.[49]

As with the case of Carnarvon's earlier conciliatory approach to Derby, the point of this was not Carnarvon himself so much as Carnarvon the pilot fish to Salisbury's shark.

Salisbury's regular piece in the *Quarterly Review* for October 1872, 'The position of parties', was also a highly significant straw in the wind. Since 1867 Salisbury had not printed a civil word about Disraeli. The year 1871 had seen a gap in his series of autumn polemics, since he was diverted by foreign affairs. Resumption of the series in 1872 would, in consistency, mean resumption of abuse of Disraeli. Such abuse was conspicuously absent from 'The position of parties'. It was not that Salisbury was now civil to Disraeli. That would have been too much to hope for. Disraeli was simply not mentioned. That was the tremendous thing.

Many other things were mentioned. Salisbury was sharply observant of Liberal debility. He pointed particularly to the significance of Lowe's failed budget of 1871 as 'breaking the spell'.[50] He was sardonically acute on Liberal insensibility on foreign policy, in the best manner of his famous critiques of Palmerston and Russell in the 1860s. On Ireland he was grimly without illusions:

> The optimistic view of politics assumes that there must be some remedy for every political ill. . . . But is not the other view barely possible? Is it not just conceivable that there is no remedy that we can apply for the Irish hatred of ourselves?[51]

But the nub of Salisbury's concern was to advise the Conservative party as to its best course in the context of better times and promising prospects. The Conservative party needed to be educated in its handling of new and unaccustomed political prosperity. 'Many circumstances combine to indicate a gradual drift of the well-to-do classes towards Conservative opinions.'[52] A surge of strength to the Conservative cause could not be long in coming. But that had its dangers and temptations as well as its advantages. There might well be a marked change of political tune in the boroughs, but what the Conservative party realistically needed to prepare itself for was 'incomplete victory'. That would expose Conservatives to seductions known of old: impatience with exclusion from power, the promptings of short cuts, above all the siren calls of Whig fusionists. This opened up painful memories of the unhappy series of 1829, 1846, and 1867.

At this point Salisbury shifted gear: another in such a series of unwholesome alliances, he held, was not now possible. It would be 'regarded by Conservatives of every shade as the heaviest disaster their party could undergo'. Then the crux: 'Be our judgement of the past what it may, no difference of policy can exist as to the future.'[53] This was the nearest Salisbury could or would come towards conceding a material point. He went on to urge that the Conservative leaders could only escape from 'adding another to the sinister successes of which their last half-century's annals are made up' by 'resolutely refusing to avail themselves of any chance of office' which might be opened to them by 'allies of whose general support they are not assured'.[54] No doubt this was a 'superfluous precaution'. Still, it was necessary to insist that should such a contingency arise premature acceptance of office would be 'servitude in disguise'. The Conservative party's most valuable contribution to the political wellbeing of the nation would be its action as a strong opposition. 'We are promised an era of "social" legislation – for which, doubtless, there is an ample field. In helping good work from whatever quarter . . . the strength of the Conservative party will be usefully employed.'[55] But the 'special duties to the Constitution' owed by the Conservative party must not become entangled with provision of further doses of reforming legislation. When the 'present mania' for that shall be 'worn out', the 'time for the Conservative party to accept office will have arrived; but as long as such legislation is demanded, they cannot propose it'.[56]

Two marginal glosses need to be attached to Salisbury's text. The first is that given the nature of his case against Disraeli, he would be rather more prone than most Conservatives to discount prospects of anything beyond 'incomplete' victory. That having been said, however, it remains to be stressed that Salisbury was not at all out of line with prevalent party opinion. The second gloss is that, for all the studied absence of the old public animus against Disraeli, it is not possible to interpret Salisbury's angle of approach as indicative of a willingness to resume official political relations with the party leader. There was no question of Salisbury's owning, as Carnarvon had done, that Reform in 1867 had worked out better than he expected. It was always the lot of 'Twitters' to have to say such things. It is much more likely that, just as Salisbury saw his party's most valuable role as a strong opposition, so he saw his own contribution to Conservatism in something of the same independently formative influence. Still, gears had shifted. The two surrogate performers, Northcote and Carnarvon, set busily to acting out their respective chiefs' parts in a little comedy of new political manners. Northcote attended gravely to Carnarvon's current obsession on the agricultural labourers question and the dangers presented, in Carnarvon's view, by 'agitators & unionists'. Northcote proposed a 'series of tracts' which Carnarvon welcomed as a 'valuable' suggestion; but, as he concluded despairingly, who had time to write them?[57]

2

As things turned out in 1873, Salisbury's minatory advice about the dangers of premature acceptance of office soon became very apposite. The Conservative leaders planned to launch their sessional campaign with an offensive on the *Alabama* arbitration. It was a great relief that this could now be translated down into low politics. Cairns had earlier fulminated that the 'hypocrisy of the view wh. the Govt. are taking of the Geneva Award is disgusting';[58] Hardy avowed that he felt 'very sore' about the *Alabama* arbitration '& think the Government view as expressed by Lowe & Forster mean & disgraceful'.[59] Disraeli doubted that ministers would 'get out of the Award as easily as they think. . . . The subject will not die. It will be alive on the address.'[60] In planning their attack the Conservatives, in Derby's words, thought their line 'should be, not an attack on the principle of arbitration, but a complaint that the principle has been discredited by using the form of arbitration when the object was, not to obtain a decision, but to make a surrender'.[61] The great worry exercising the Conservative chiefs was that of the 'danger of any unsure move' which would give the government an opportunity to resign and pass the problem over to the Conservatives. Refusal of office in such a circumstance would make a very sorry appearance.

However, news of ominous import suggested that, after all, an inquest on the *Alabama* affair might not take top billing for the 1873 session. Gladstone had plans of his own. Corry reported to Disraeli: 'Horsman told me . . . that there's no doubt whatever that Gladstone had prevailed, after much contention, and that the cabinet have determined "to run their heads against the wall" (as he expresses himself) by dealing with Irish education.'[62] Gladstone was determined to launch a mighty bid to reimpose his political mastery. He would equip Ireland with a university in Dublin transcending religious sectarianism. It would nurture intellectually an Irish ruling class with a vocation shaped within the great works Gladstone had already laid shown for the regeneration of Ireland, religious equality and justice as between landlord and tenant. Gladstone knew perfectly well that he would have in his favour neither the general consensus over the Irish Church question nor the landlord funk of the land question. There was no chance whatever of persuading the parties concerned to arrive at a compromise. His plan was simply to impose a compromise upon them by sheer force of political will. His great difficulty would be that whereas over the issues of church and land he was going with the grain of Irish Roman Catholic interest and sentiment, over higher education he was asking the Irish hierarchy to concede the principle of a university outside clerical control for other than certain reserved areas of study. He was also asking British Liberalism as well as Conservatism to accept that those 'gagged' areas of study should include not only theology, but also modern history and moral and mental philosophy. And Cardinal Cullen soon made it clear that there would be grave objection to a university which might appoint professors dangerous to Catholic eyes who might teach English literature, geology, or zoology.[63] Nonetheless, when he introduced his bill on 13 February Gladstone hoped that the support of Archbishop Manning, together with Irish Catholic gratitude for past boons, would be sufficient to get his scheme around these obstacles.

Liberal ministers' initial confidence soon began to fade. Disraeli observed by 17 February that there seemed 'much discontent about sundry portions of the Ir. Ed. Bill among the Liberal sections. We must have a council on it. . . .'[64] On the merits of the case, the Conservative party was in various minds. They had sore memories of their own bid to give the Irish a university based on concurrent endowment, which Gladstone trumped in 1868 with his disestablishment proposal. They had sore memories also of Manning's eager collaboration.[65] There was traditional Protestant resentment at the subjection of Trinity College, Dublin, to the proposed new order. On the other hand they rejoiced at one of the main Catholic grievances, that there would be no endowment of Catholic education from public money. The Conservative party had no objection to the principle of education infused by religion, even in Catholic Ireland. It had greater objections to the kind of Liberal educational secularism currently being espoused by Fawcett. But, confronted by Gladstone's gagging clauses and further provisions for the dismissal of professors deemed to be objectionable on religious grounds, Conservatism had to agree with Liberal secularism that the bill was a nonsense. As Disraeli put it, 'it is all humbug.'[66]

Gladstone attempted to shore up his crumbling position by declaring the bill to be a matter of confidence. Disraeli denounced this as 'an unwise and rather arrogant declaration.'[67] There were dismaying implications. Disraeli, already in turmoil following his wife's death, was now looking in the face of the contingency of government defeat and resignation which Salisbury had canvassed 6 months earlier. Disraeli, Cairns, and Derby had in fact consulted in anticipation of such 'a possible and not improbable contingency' (in Derby's words) 6 weeks before.[68] Now they could see victory looming ominously before them. There was genuine pathos in Disraeli's protestation to the house that 'No one wishes to disturb the right hon. gentleman in his place.'[69] He was reduced to declaring defiantly that he would vote against the second reading even though it was a vote of confidence. By the beginning of March there were rumours that Gladstone would withdraw his bill. 'So Ld Stanhope told me this morning at Brit. Mus.', Disraeli relayed to Corry, 'but I doubt it. He will not lose the opporty of self-vindication in many speeches.'[70] On 2 March Hardy observed that parliament was 'very quiet but storms brewing upon the Irish U. Bill. I never remember so growing an opposition from all quarters.'[71] On 4 March: 'I cannot imagine their forcing the Bill through.' It grew hourly more unpopular. Hardy called on Disraeli: '*We agreed that taking office before a dissolution was a delusion & a snare.*' Disraeli said 'that was Lord Derby's view & finding it mine also he should in any event act upon it.'[72] Richmond could still 'fancy the 2nd Reading will be carried by a very small majority', allowing the bill to go to committee to be dismembered.[73] But on 12 March the very small majority was against the second reading, owing largely to Irish desertions. After thus duly running his head against the wall, and after denouncing a malignant and factious combination of Toryism and Romanism who would now have to sort out the mess they had created, Gladstone thereupon offered his resignation to the queen.

Derby heard of the event while vacationing in Switzerland. 'I do not suppose that a Conservative government is either possible or desirable.' He hurried back to London and conferred with Disraeli, who stood firm despite clear indications from the queen of her desire to be rid of Gladstone. Derby drafted a memorandum which formed the basis of Disraeli's reply to Gladstone's argument that the Conservatives were bound constitutionally to assume responsibility.[74]

The Conservative party, especially in its lower echelons, was not entirely united behind the policy of refusing office. Both the *Standard* and the *Globe* had expressed great disappointment at the tame ending of the 1872 session, convinced that a great opportunity had then been lost. Now there was a strong presumption that a second opportunity must not be missed. Cairns was prone to waver somewhat, much as in November 1868. Taylor reported conflicting opinions, citing a letter from 'a young member', Major Arbuthnot, who had won the Hereford by election in 1871, who quoted Cross and W. H. Smith as sharing his view that the call to office ought not to be shirked. Taylor felt 'bound however to say that the preponderance of opinion is the other way – but there is no question that if there were a dissolution now, we should gain largely, probably near a majority of 100, certain *English* returns – to be *reduced* however considerably by the Irish & Scotch.' As to the Irish, however, Taylor was assured by Kavanagh, MP for Carlow County, 'with a *mixed* constituency', that 'at this moment we should have the *Catholic* vote'; and Ball, one of the Dublin University members, was 'also of that opinion'.[75] The *Standard*, misled by Gorst, jumped the gun by eagerly backing what it assumed would be the party's policy of taking office. This probably reflected grassroots Conservative activist sentiment.

The crisis also had the seismic effect of opening the leadership fault-line once more. Taylor had this additionally to report to Disraeli on the morrow of Disraeli's having being received by the queen and asked to undertake the government:

> I think it right to mention *all* I hear – and there are several influential men both in and out of Parliament, who believe we should be strengthened, if Lord *Derby* were nominally premier, *you* continuing to lead the house of Commons – they say that their conviction is that such an arrangement should widen our basis considerably and give us therefore greater power.[76]

Hardy recorded on the same day that Henry Lennox came to report the wishes of the Whigs Horsman, Bouverie, and others 'for a *Derby* ministry'. Hardy responded unpropitiously to this fusionist Whig manoeuvre. He found Pakington 'evidently much annoyed' at his support for Disraeli's stand. Then Lennox returned to the attack, stressing how much the Whigs wanted to be considered in the new arrangement. Hardy dismissed this: 'Combination useless & impossible at present.'[77] Derby continued to be under pressure from anti-Gladstone Liberals who hoped for such a 'combination'. One of them (Pender, Liberal MP for Wick) assured Derby that 'the reaction against Gladstone and in favor of a policy of repose is exceedingly strong'; many Liberals were 'changing their views'. They were alarmed at the 'attitude of the working men, and at the power acquired by the trades unions'. But while they disliked Gladstone and feared his ambition and 'sentimental sympathy' for the democracy,

> they are equally suspicious and afraid of Disraeli: they think him the enemy of the capitalist class, and remember his writings of 30 years ago, of which one leading idea seemed to them to be the union of the aristocracy and peasantry in an attack on manufacturers and merchants.

Pender 'went on to say that D. was not trusted': and thought that if Derby were leader 'the party would gain a great accession of strength'. Others made similar representations to Derby: to all of whom he replied 'that D. was a personal friend and an old colleague, and that I was therefore the last person who could entertain the idea of superseding him. Besides, who is to manage the H. of C. if he retires?'[78]

It was Northcote who stood centrally at the junction of the crossed lines of refusal of office and fusionism. He advised Disraeli most emphatically against accepting the queen's commission. It would not be possible, in the state of public business, to dissolve parliament before early May.

> You would moreover go to the country at a great disadvantage, from having been obliged on the one hand to huddle up a good deal of important work which ought to be done deliberately, and on the other hand not having had time to mature with your Colleagues a scheme of policy. . . . I cannot say how strongly I feel against the idea of your taking office just now.

It was clear that Gladstone was going to try to force Disraeli to assume office on the grounds of taking responsibility for having ousted him. Northcote denounced it as a 'monstrous' doctrine to link the Conservative vote with the Roman Catholic vote as if they formed a consistent block rather than being, in fact, two groups with entirely unrelated motives and intentions.

> But looking at the matter broadly, and in the interest of the Conservative cause as distinct from that of the present representatives of the Conservative party, I am strongly convinced that time is required to mature the fast-ripening Conservatism of the country, and to dispel the hallucinations which have attached a great mass of moderate men to the Liberal cause. I believe that the disintegration of Gladstone's party has begun and that nothing but precipitancy on our part can arrest it. He has expended the impetuous force which brought him into office, and now is brought face to face with new, or rather old, difficulties which he can hardly surmount without alienating one or other wing of his party. If he goes on with the Extreme section, a large body of his moderate supporters will rank themselves with the Conservatives: If he quarrels with the Extreme section, they will become the opposition, while the conduct of affairs will fall to the acknowledged Conservatives, who will obtain the support of the moderate Liberals. But if we appeal to the country before the breach in the Liberal ranks is fully made, and before the policy of the Extreme men is fully developed, we shall consolidate them; the Extreme men will hold back a little, the moderates advance a little, and there will be more confusion and confiscation.[79]

Here Northcote outlined, in effect, the analysis at the basis of the strategy which, as leader of the Conservatives in the Commons after 1880, led him to political destruction. He was supremely right about the tactic of response to the immediate crisis for profoundly the wrong strategic reason.

Lennox's brother Richmond was quite in accord with Disraeli's resolve to refuse. He reported to his minder, Cairns:

> Hardy and I had a long talk with him on Wednesday and agreed with him that we could not take office now, in the face of a decided majority agst us. Disraeli quite concurred and sd that this was also the opinion of you and Derby.
>
> Hunt Malmesbury and Wilson Patten also concur, and so I imagine the Queen will be compelled to send again to Gladstone, and insist on his going on with the Gov.
>
> I have not seen Disraeli since his interview but I conclude he acted as he said he wd. when we saw him on Wednesday.[80]

In stark contrast to his behaviour in staying in office in May 1868, Disraeli could afford elaborate consultations with a view to staying out of office in 1873.

At Buckingham Palace on 13 March Disraeli told the queen that he had not expected the government's defeat. The queen recorded his determined attitude: 'I decline to form a Government in the present parliament, and I do not ask for a dissolution.' Disraeli, by way of a preliminary, insisted that the Conservative party 'never was more compact or more united'. There was the 'most perfect understanding' between him and all those who served with him, naming especially Derby, Cairns, Hardy, and Northcote. He was 'perfectly able to form a Government at once, perfectly fit to carry on the administration of the country' to the queen's entire satisfaction. He could command 280 votes, for since he had left her '*immediate* service' the party had gained about 30 seats against the government. He had laboured to keep the party 'as much together and in as efficient a state as possible'. But it would be useless to attempt to carry on the government with a minority in the House of Commons.[81] Given the queen's manifest willingness to keep Disraeli on in 1868 and her manifest readiness to be rid of Gladstone at this moment, it was not the time to dilate upon painful memories of the 1868 minority government; but those memories were clearly vivid in the minds of Disraeli and his colleagues.

There was a general chorus of approval, as opinion tended to move strongly towards the stronger side in the Conservative argument. Derby recorded on 16 March: 'Saw Corry & Barrington: who agree that the party in general are satisfied with our refusal of office under present circumstances.' Henry Lennox now unctuously assured Disraeli that the great Delane approved his 'judgement and spirit'. Abergavenny endorsed Disraeli's having 'acted most wisely'.[82] Salisbury, primed by Hardy, Hunt, and Richmond, 'tho' characteristically doubting Disraeli's consistency of opinion', quite thought 'they were right not to take office'.[83] Salisbury could hardly have done other: it was almost as if the party leaders had taken his October *Quarterly Review* piece as their text. The one notably sour note came from Gorst, who felt he had been ill-used as the party's liaison with the *Standard*. He had written to Corry on the 14th that the 'Standard people were much disturbed last night by a rumour . . . that D. had positively declined to form a ministry'. Gorst told the *Standard* to give no further lead unless they heard directly from Corry.[84] This unfortunate little mishap was concluded by Gorst's very curt avowal that he was 'very sorry if the *Standard* has through me made mistakes during the late crisis', but 'being however entirely in the dark as to the opinion & wishes of the Leader, I was obliged to take the general sentiment of the Party as my guide'.[85] This was not the last occasion on which Gorst would feel that he represented the 'general sentiment of the Party' against its leaders.

The question also abided even yet as to whether the 'general sentiment of the party' remained quite content with Disraeli's leadership. Cross told Derby 'at some length that I ought to take Disraeli's place, inasmuch as the constituences have more confidence in me than in D. – which may or may not be the fact, but what he proposes is impossible.' Delane, the wish no doubt father to the thought, wrote to Derby on the following day inquiring whether it was true that Derby was 'engaged in forming a government'. 'A question easily ansd.' Instead, Derby consoled himself by drawing out with Disraeli a list of the future Conservative cabinet: Derby himself was to return to the Foreign Office and Cairns to the lord chancellorship. Hardy was to return to the Home Office and Northcote was to go on to the Exchequer. Richmond would be lord president. Hunt would have the War Office. Carnarvon was to be offered India. Thereafter it was more conjectural. Either Buckingham or Manners might have the Colonial Office; Pakington perhaps the Admiralty. Possibly Manners might have the Board of Trade, with Stanhope as privy seal and Malmesbury a virtual sinecure at the Post Office. 'Besides these', noted Derby, 'there are Cross, Patten, & H. Lennox who have a claim to moderately high office.' Stanhope might be satisfied with something done for his son; and Malmesbury might well not care to serve again. In any case Derby was sure that 'Cross & Patten would be more useful in cabinet'.[86]

Gladstone fought tenaciously to stay out. But Disraeli foiled him. In Kebbel's admiring words, Disraeli confuted 'the doctrine that no leader of opposition should ever give a vote liable to defeat the minister unless he is prepared to take his place'. Such a doctrine, if acted upon, 'would make all effective criticism impossible; since a statesman strong enough to take the minister's place could not long remain in opposition; and one not strong enough to succeed him would not be entitled to oppose him.'[87] The affair did not end, however, without Disraeli's tripping over his own foot. In his vindication to the Commons of his refusal of office Disraeli cited a formidable series of considerations: the government's still large majority; the rank unsuitability of the Irish University Bill for an appeal for confidence; the contingent and fortuitous nature of the resulting majority; the miseries and humiliations attendant upon a minority government under pressures of necessary public business. In the middle of all this he lapsed badly by appealing to the house: 'is it not clear that we could not appeal to the country without having a policy?'[88] This was greeted by a roar of Liberal laughter, and squirmings on the Conservative front bench. Hardy remarked that 'dangerously minute language as to our want of policy etc. etc. will be laid hold of & worked against us every day.' Hardy was only too correct in this; as also in his opinion that it was 'singularly invidious & unnecessary for explaining his difficulty'.[89]

In his peroration, however, Disraeli recovered himself in a performance which the *Annual Register* of the time cited as a 'political manifesto',[90] and which Kebbel later celebrated as being redolent with prophetic power.[91] Disraeli offered a general interpretation of the future scope of politics. The 'fiscal period' in which almost all the public men of the present generation were brought up was coming to an end. The great questions of trade and taxation and political economy were settled. But new issues, 'not less important, and of deeper and higher reach and range' would soon come forward, and become 'burning' questions. Should the constitutional monarchy be preserved? What of the 'aristocratic principle' of the constitution? Shall the national Church be maintained? The 'function of corporations, the sacredness of endowments, the tenure of landed property, the free disposal and even the existence of any kind of property – all those institutions and all those principles' which had made the country 'free and famous, and conspicuous for its union of order with liberty', were now impugned; and would soon need defending.

> I think it is of the utmost importance that when that time – which may be nearer at hand than we imagine – arrives there shall be in this country a great constitutional party, distinguished for its intelligence as well as for its organisation, which shall be competent to lead the people and direct the public mind. And, Sir, when that time arrives, and when they enter upon a career which must be noble, and which I hope and believe will be triumphant, I think they may perhaps remember, and not perhaps with unkindness, that I at least prevented one obstacle from being placed in their way, when as the trustee of their honour and their interest, I declined to form a weak and discredited Administration.[92]

Notes and References

1 See Buckle, ii, 486, n.1.
2 Hardy to Cairns, 20 Dec. 1871. PRO, Cairns 31/51/7.
3 A.E. Gathorne-Hardy, *Gathorne Hardy First Earl of Cranbrook* (1910), i, 302.
4 Buckle, ii, 522–3.
5 Northcote to Disraeli, 24 Jan. 1872; BL, Iddesleigh 50016, 110.
6 Derby Diary, 29 Jan. 1872.
7 *Ibid.*, 9 and 13 Jan. 1872.
8 Disraeli to Corry, 27 Jan. 1872; HP. B/XX/D/165. *Spectator*, 27 Jan. 1872, 100–1, 'The Prospects of the government'.
9 Disraeli to Cairns, 24 and 27 Jan. 1872; PRO, Cairns 30/51/1.
10 Disraeli to Northcote, 27 Jan. 1872; BL, Iddesleigh 50016, 114.
11 Disraeli to Northcote, 30 Jan. 1872; BL, Iddesleigh 50016, 125.
12 *AR*, 1872, 25.
13 Hardy, *Diary*, 149.
14 Derby Diary, 13, 14 March 1872.
15 *Ibid.*, 30 March 1872.
16 E.J. Feuchtwanger, *Disraeli, Democracy and The Tory Party* (Oxford, 1968), 119. On Disraeli's 'American' departure in shaking hands with 124 presenters of addresses, see F. Harcourt, 'Gladstone, monarchism and the "New Imperialism", 1868–74', *Journal of Imperial and Commonwealth History* (1985), 32.
17 H. Gorst, *The Earl of Beaconsfield* (1900), 133–4.
18 *Ibid.*, 135.
19 Hardy, *Diary*, 154.
20 Derby Diary, 3, 6 April 1872.
21 Cairns to Disraeli, 6 April, 1872; HP, B/XX/Ca/89.
22 Kebbel, *Speeches*, ii, 491.
23 *Ibid.*, 493–502.
24 *Ibid.*, 507–12. See Buckle, ii, 530.
25 Kebbel, *Speeches*, ii, 516; Morley, ii, 1024.
26 Kebbel, *Speeches*, ii, 518–22.
27 Derby Diary, 28 April 72.
28 *Ibid*, 16 April 72.
29 Hardy, *Diary*, 156.
30 Kebbel, *Speeches*, ii, 523–4.
31 Derby Diary, 26 April 1870.
32 Kebbel, *Speeches*, ii, 535.
33 NUCCA, minutes of 6th conference, 24 June 1872.

34 Derby Diary, 4 July 72.
35 C. O'Leary, *The Elimination of Corrupt Practices in British Elections, 1868–1911* (1962) 84–5.
36 *AR*, 1872, 64. PD, CCXI, 873. For its general irrelevance in Ireland see M. Hurst, 'Ireland and the Ballot Act of 1872', *Historical Journal* (1965).
37 *AR*, 1872, 68–9.
38 Hardy, *Diary*, 156.
39 P. Smith, *Disraelian Conservatism and Social Reform* (1967), 169.
40 Morley, ii, 15–16.
41 J. Vincent, 'The effect of the second Reform Act in Lancashire', *Historical Journal* (1968), 88.
42 Hardy to Cairns, 20 Sept. 1872; PRO, Cairns 30/51/7.
43 Derby Diary, 8 Feb. 1873;
44 *Ibid.*, 2 March, 28 April 1872.
45 Hardy, *Diary*, 165.
46 Hardy to Cairns, 20 Sept. 1872; PRO, Cairns 30/51/7.
47 Derby Diary, 2, 4 Feb. 1873.
48 *QR*, Oct. 1872, 592.
49 Northcote to Disraeli, 23 Sept. 1872; BL, Iddesleigh 50016, 135.
50 *QR*, Oct. 1872, 560.
51 *Ibid.*, 569.
52 *Ibid.*, 570.
53 *Ibid.*, 575.
54 *Ibid.*, 580.
55 *Ibid.*, 593.
56 *Ibid.*, 582.
57 Carnarvon to Northcote, 21 Dec. 1872; BL, Iddesleigh 50022, 195.
58 Cairns to Disraeli, 1 Oct. 1872; HP, B/XX/Ca/92.
59 Hardy to Cairns, 3 Oct. 1872; PRO, Cairns 30/51/7.
60 Disraeli to Cairns, 8 Oct. 1872; PRO, Cairns 30/51/1.
61 Derby to Cairns, 25 Dec. 1872; PRO, Cairns 30/51/8.
62 Corry to Disraeli, 22 Nov. 1872; HP, B/XX/Co/87.
63 Morley, ii, 43.
64 Disraeli to Corry, 17 Feb. 1873; HP, B/XX/D/195.
65 Buckle, ii, 542: 'Once again Manning was deep in the counsels of a British premier hopeful of finding a solution; and he was to mislead Gladstone as he had misled Disraeli.'
66 *Ibid.*, 543.
67 *AR*, 1873, 28; PD, ccxiv, 1828.
68 Buckle, ii, 547.
69 *AR*, 1873, 29.
70 Disraeli to Corry, 1 March 1873; HP, B/XX/D/202.
71 Hardy, *Diary*, 172.
72 *Ibid.*, 173.
73 Richmond to Cairns, 8 March 1873; PRO, Cairns 30/51/2.
74 Derby Diary, 12, 14 March 1873.
75 Taylor to Disraeli, 14 March [1873]; HP, B/XX/T/124.
76 *Ibid.*
77 Hardy, *Diary*, 174–5.
78 Derby Diary, 18 Sept. 1873.

79 Northcote to Disraeli, 14 March 1873; BL, Iddesleigh 50016, 144.
80 Richmond to Cairns, 14 March 1873; PRO, Cairns 30/51/2.
81 Buckle, ii, 548–9.
82 *Ibid.*, 558.
83 Cecil, ii, 41.
84 Gorst to Corry [14 March 1873]; HP, B/XXI/G/246.
85 Gorst to Corry, 17 March 1873; HP, B/XXI/G/241.
86 Derby Diary, 16, 17, 25 March 1873.
87 Kebbel, *Speeches*, ii, 536.
88 This is the version stood by in the *Annual Register*, 1873, 36. Disraeli's edited version in *Hansard* comes out as: 'is it not quite clear that we could not appeal to the country without having a matured and complete policy? [*Laughter*].' *PD*, ccxiv, 1933.
89 Hardy, *Diary*, 176–7.
90 *AR*, 1873, 39.
91 T.E. Kebbel, 'Party obligations to-day', *Nineteenth Century*, March 1883, 427.
92 Kebbel, *Speeches*, ii, 551–2; *PD*, ccxiv, 1943–4.

Chapter 7

Toryism re-established, 1873–4

In sight of the promised land

1

Forced reluctantly back into office, but not power, Gladstone dragged his stricken ministry through its last barren session. Lyon Playfair, a Scottish Liberal MP, assured Northcote that 'the Govt. will be driven to a dissolution this year, and added, "I think you would gain 40 seats"'.[1] This was probably an accurate estimate. Since Gladstone had still a majority of near 90, the Liberals would in such a case have been left with a sufficient margin to deny the Conservatives but not enough to permit them full freedom of parliamentary action. Salisbury's prescription for the benign action of a strong Conservative Opposition would have come to pass. Luckily for the Conservative party, Gladstone decided to limp on into 1874 to gain time and to try his luck with some bold stroke to repair matters.

The crisis had not left the Conservative party unscathed. Disraeli's picture of it for the queen as monolithically compact was, like all his pictures for the queen's benefit, a rather hazily romantic vision. Certain irritations abided. Cairns and Hardy among the party chiefs exchanged reservations after the event: Cairns about the event, Hardy about its management. 'The explanations are over,' wrote Hardy, 'but not quite to my mind.'

> I think Disraeli was wrong in dwelling so much on the necessity of our making up our policy on many questions after we are in office. That assures almost perpetual exclusion. With regard to the course which he has pursued there is a thorough & general agreement among the best of our men. I admit your view has force but the present House would be so hostile & the Election so uncertain that I think three month's office might be followed by great discomfiture. I felt so sharply that I could not have taken office and Hunt at least was of the same mind, but it was needless to consider this matter as Disraeli adopted the view more strongly than he generally does. . . . There is a dispersion after the crisis and general disinclination to take up new questions.[2]

At the other end of the party the perturbations were if anything more persistent. Gorst was a man easily offended. He took the point that Disraeli's speech of 20 March was virtually an election manifesto and proposed to print and circulate it 'as widely as possible . . . among the Conservative

Associations'.[3] Those associations gathered at Leeds in April for their annual conference. On the face of things, it should have exuded an atmosphere of good cheer and heightened expectations. Raikes in the chair expatiated on the 'flourishing condition' of the National Union. But evident also was an undercurrent of disappointment, no doubt representative of what Gorst had defiantly insisted to Corry was the 'general sentiment of the Party'. If 1872 was the conference that first set the National Union seriously on the political stage, the 1873 conference was the first to give rise to the faintest *frisson* of recalling Dr. Frankenstein. Raikes, in his earnest way, made the mistake of telling the delegates only too precisely what they wanted to hear. Raikes told them that 'we had outlived the time of great family influences, and also that period which succeeded the first Reform Bill, which might be called the period of middle class influence in the boroughs'. The implications of this were left hanging eloquently in the air of Leeds Town Hall. When they were duly taken up by delegates complaining that the union was not doing in the Conservative party all it ought to be doing, Raikes retreated in some disorder. No doubt mindful of his earlier assurances to Keith-Falconer (now the union's effective secretary) about obedience, he offered the lame response that the union 'had been organized rather as what might be called a handmaid to the party, than to usurp the functions of party leadership'.[4]

And though there was indeed a dispersion after the crisis and a general disinclination to take up new questions, there was the rump of a session to be got through. Apart from the legal reforms of the great Judicature Bill, which much exercised Cairns, every occasion tended to take on an electoral aspect. Northcote – now 'evidently aware', as Derby noted, 'that he is to be C. of Ex. if we come in'[5] – thought something to advantage might be made of the long-standing grievances of country gentlemen about the unfair burdens on land of local taxation. The argument was that with the ending of fiscal privilege for land in 1846 its burdens of financing such things as the judiciary, the police, and lunatic asylums ought in equity to have been shifted on to the general community. Goschen had exacerbated the problem and there was a danger that Gladstone might try something to placate his Whigs. Northcote proposed to take an issue which was making 'our local taxation friends unhappy' and to convert the occasion 'as a great one for laying down, broadly and cautiously, the framework of a system of Conservative financial policy'. In thus talking of means of avoiding 'discontent in our own ranks' and of the need for a thorough investigation of direct taxation and relations between direct and indirect taxation, Northcote of course was also signalling his expectation of the Exchequer, in the event of office.[6]

There were such opportunities, but there were also lurking embarrassments. Forster's bill to amend the 1870 Education Act was one such. Its aim was to provide places for children of out-door paupers and to make other encouragements in like vein. But Forster also proposed to transfer the right of school boards to provide places in voluntary schools to the Poor

Law guardians. This he urged on grounds of economy and efficiency.[7] But he was also striking a blow against the provisions of the famous Clause 25 of the 1870 Act which in effect gave Church of England schools money from the rates. The bill opened Conservative fault-lines. Disraeli found himself confronted with the following advice from his party's principal agent:

> I ought to communicate to you my fear that a Party Opposition to the Education Bill will alienate an important section of our supporters.
>
> With country gentlemen & farmers in the agricultural counties such a policy might be popular: they really dislike education & school boards altogether. But in the Boroughs and populous counties, our party embraces zealous and active promoters of education, and Forster's Bill is founded on the very principle for which they have as they think so successfully contended. They look upon it as a great triumph of Conservative principles that the Govt. have felt compelled to turn their backs on the Education League & bring in such a bill as the present; and they desire to give the measure an active support and claim it as the expression of their own views. I confess that the idea of defeating the government and having an appeal to the country on this question fills me with dismay. We cannot carry the English majority we hope to without the active help of those, who on this question will be opposed to our policy.[8]

This was, in its way, the kind of unspoken implication left in the air at the Leeds conference put into concrete, and unwelcome, form. This impinged far beyond Gorst's mere presumption.

Then on top of borough presumption came borough mutiny. There were Conservatives who sympathised with Forster's larger aims, and who agreed with him that costs had to be kept under control, and that guardians would do this better than boards when it came to voluntary places. Forster, after all, was altering the method of Clause 25 rather than abolishing it altogether, as the Education League was furiously demanding. W.H. Smith of Westminster and the London School Board gave a lead in this direction. Disraeli, who tended to a straightforward simplicity of view in such matters, was outraged. He wrote in exasperation to Cairns:

> I find it difficult to guide affairs at this critical juncture. Mr. Smith of Westminster has only just been stopped from putting a notice on the paper for the Abolition of the 25th Clause of the Education act; the shibboleth of our party, wh. will be one of the symbols in the impending County election,[9] & at a dissolution might dispose of thirty or forty votes. Mr. Smith decides on the abstract merits of the case obtained in his experience of the London Board with[t] the slightest reference to the general political situation.[10]

Dyke administered the official rebuke to Smith for his 'simply suicidal' proceedings, which Mr. Disraeli desired him (Dyke) to state would meet with Mr. Disraeli's 'most strenuous opposition'; and that Mr. Disraeli could 'no longer consider any member who brings forward such a proposition as belonging to the Party of which he is the Leader. This much Mr. Disraeli bids me say & for myself I can not but think the position of his Party most perilous if such a Motion be made.'[11] Thus flattened, Smith played no part in the debate on the second reading.

Things got to the point where Taylor forwarded to Disraeli a report by Winn 'on the troublesome men of the Party – or at least some of them' on the education question. These included, as well as Smith, E.S. Powell (Yorkshire West Riding, North), Lord Mahon (East Suffolk), Raikes (Chester), Thomas Salt (Stafford), Sir George Jenkinson (Wiltshire North), and the Lancashire trio of Cross, Lord Sandon, and Hugh Birley. Marked against Smith was: 'doubts policy of opposing the Govt. Bill'; against Birley: 'doubts policy of doing anything to throw Forster into the hands of the Birmingham party'.[12] They might also have added Adderley (North Staffordshire), another Forster sympathiser, and a senior privy councillor to boot.[13]

A further lurking embarrassment was the Household Franchise (Counties) Bill, a mere Radical *ballon d'essai*, but one which nevertheless had to be encountered. Gladstone allowed the issue to be an 'open question'. Disraeli was too much discomposed by the drama of March and too much in retreat at Hughenden to exert himself. Conservative resistance was left in the hands of the lesser men, with only John Manners to lend some front-bench authority. The essence of the Conservative problem was to project a perfect confidence that the extension of the 1867 borough occupier franchise to the counties offered no threat to Conservatism, even as coupled now with the ballot; yet at the same time to convey genially that such extension was neither wanted nor needed. What was needed rather was plenty of time for the country to digest its great franchise ingestion of 1867. The traditional distinctions between counties and boroughs ought to be preserved. The agricultural labourers did not want new-fangled votes and ballots but decent conditions of life. In any case the franchise was a privilege not a right. These were well-worn Conservative themes. The new emphasis was on the revolutionary implications for the redistribution of seats and the inevitable consequence of the disappearance of masses of small borough constituencies.[14] Salisbury in fact took the view that this in itself would be enough to deter the Liberals from ever taking up the county occupier franchise seriously.[15]

An exchange between the Conservative whips is sufficiently indicative of Disraeli's Fabian strategy on the county occupier franchise question. Winn wrote to Taylor in July 1873:

> I am going to work on Disraeli's proposed 'Borough Defence Alliance'. . . . Under any circumstances it must be made to appear as *proceeding* from . . . the smaller Boro's & certainly no County M.P. must appear in it at all. I am working now at some statistics to show the effect of Household suffrage [in the counties], & the result of Electoral districts which must be a part of it. I have got so far as to find that at the least 137 Boroughs in England and Wales must go, leaving

> only 53 Boros . . . of these at least 22 (including London City) will have only one member.[16]

Considering the elixir of political life given to the Conservative party by the revolutionary redistribution of constituencies in 1885 consequent on the county occupier franchise extension of 1884, it is supremely ironic to find the Conservatives constructing ramparts of small boroughs, mostly Liberal, to protect the political innocence of the agricultural labourers. Disraeli went so far as to argue, to Northcote, that while the disenfranchisement of towns in the 10,000–30,000 population bracket might not be 'immediately unfavourable to the Cons. cause', it was still not desirable, 'without deep consideration and clear necessity', to diminish 'the influence of urban populations in our system of Govt., being one favourable to public liberty and enlightenment'.[17] Gorst would have blinked at that.

Then again, as Disraeli further complained to Cairns, having arranged for the Rating Bill to be defeated in the Lords, he found Richmond half inclined to recede from this policy after talking to Hardy. They ought not to do this without due consultation.

> It is of great importance, that the impotence of the government should be demonstrated to the country. This is the high political course wh. ought to absorb all petty considerations of the merits, or demerits, of their measures . . . the degradation of the government, not the character of petty measures, shd be the consideration that influences us at this juncture.[18]

A bout of administrative scandals, centring upon financial irregularities at the Post Office, afflicted Gladstone's hapless ministry as the 1873 session drew to its weary end. 'Another damaging day for Government', as Taylor reported; but there were 'not above 50 of our men left in London'.[19] The house, indeed, as Hardy put it, was 'past work'.[20] Disraeli himself was past work: 'I cannot stand any longer the provisional state of affairs, wh. destroys me';[21] 'I am so harassed & worn out with all this changing of scene.'[22] How and when would the great political change of scene reveal itself? 'The government really seems on its last legs', Disraeli told Corry. 'They will probably, also, lose every election, that occurs before the reassembling of Parliament.'[23] Political horizons were scanned, as ever, for signs of Whig defectors coming across. Disraeli was in hopes that Vernon Harcourt 'might be secured'.[24] As to by-elections, Derby noted that 'Conservative candidates succeed where three or four years ago they would not even have made an attempt'. An unexpected win at Dover in September 1873 had Derby rejoicing: 'This really looks like winning at the next general election, if we make no blunder.' He set down his analysis of the shape of the situation.

> The causes which have led to the existing reaction – for its reality cannot be doubted – are mainly as, I think, the following. (1) Employers are alarmed by the growing strength of the trades unions, and ballot enables them to conceal their change of vote. (2) Dissenters stand apart, supporting no candidates except those

who will pledge themselves against the principle of establishment. (3) The whole of the liquor-traffic has thrown its weight into the Conservative scale: alarmed at the growing power of the 'U.K. Alliance.' (4) People have got tired of Gladstone – not the less so because one or two newspapers devoted to his cause show their zeal by continuous and rather fulsome flattery of him personally. (5) Movements abroad such as that of the Paris Commune, and of the insurrection in Spain, give some ground for the belief that modern Liberalism runs easily into revolution. The Catholics especially oppose it on that ground, and in Ireland they have no inducement to do otherwise, having got out of the Liberal party all that they well can get. (6) There is in politics a natural ebb and flow: the progressive or democratic tendency has been dominant since 1865, and for the time has become relatively weak: people have had enough of change, and want rest: an inclination strengthened by the great material prosperity of the last five years.[25]

Gladstone's reconstruction of his government in the recess provoked much derision. Disraeli's initial reaction was that it was 'merely a diversion to escape dissol^{n}. which was inevitable had they done nothing'. And: 'the idea of their being saved by the return of that hysterical old spouter, Bright, is absurd.'[26] The crucial ministerial change was that Gladstone shunted Lowe out of the Exchequer across to the Home Office, and took charge directly of financial policy. Gladstone himself would have preferred giving it to Goschen, but his colleagues calculated that only Gladstone's return to the office he had made the most powerful and famous fount of policy could rescue them in their extremity. Conservatives were puzzled. Was this merely a holding operation in view of impending dissolution of parliament? Surely Gladstone could not pile the burden of the Exchequer on top of that of first lordship on any other basis? Northcote soon had news that gave pause. He had it from Cardwell that dissolution was not in contemplation and that Gladstone's resumption of the Exchequer was 'quite *bonā fide*'. Northcote's own impression was that 'they mean to try to win back the Nonconformists, but have not quite made up their minds how far they will go, and are therefore keeping back Bright's speech for the present – till they see their way'.[27] The way that Gladstone was seeing, however, back at the Exchequer for the first time since 1866, was how a great redeeming stroke might be struck in finance.

2

Taylor asked Disraeli on 19 August: 'Do you believe in the possibility of a dissolution this year? . . . Meanwhile we are becoming prepared everywhere'.[28] Recent by-elections confirmed the strong swing to the Conservatives. Dyke commented:

> The results at Greenwich & in Staffordshire exceed anything we had hoped for and show a state of things *most* encouraging for the future. I attribute much of the feeling in the Constituencies to your refusal of office: at Greenwich I was perfectly astonished at the Tory complexion assumed by the rough mob elements: should Gladstone vacate his seat as I believe he will be obliged to do . . . we shall use

every effort to get a good man against him, but even after the recent Election I fear it will be most difficult: we tried for so many weeks to get a better candidate than Boord and failed.

The change to the Government cannot surely mean anything more than a temporary patchwork, and a popular Budget next Spring with Dissolution to follow. Lowe will produce nothing less than Civil War at the Home Office . . . We must fight every vacancy as it occurs, and I have used your name with regard to the NW Riding so far as to say that you consider it *most* important in the present position of affairs that the seat should be contested.[29]

The North West Riding by-election was a consequence of Lord Frederick Cavendish's appointment as a lord of the Treasury. Despite Disraeli's express desire, and despite the earlier by-election victory in that division in 1872, the seat was not contested; which is indicative of the limits set to central party authority in great and proud county constituencies.

Disraeli in fact had been on this particular warpath for some time. He was particularly anxious to suppress the cosy gentlemen's compacts whereby county seats were shared out between the parties, so avoiding expensive contests. As far back as April, in the immediate aftermath of the crisis, he insisted to Corry:

It will be impossible to get a Tory majority, if lukewarmness, or selfishness of those who have a safe seat, prevent contests. There are more than 30 seats in this predicament, & I have appointed a small commēe of men of social influence to take them in hand.

Ld. J. Manners
Barrington
Chaplin & Mahon[30]

It was essential, of course, to keep Gorst's sticky fingers out of county pies. This sharp rap of leadership had been provoked by a complaint from Lord Lonsdale about the eastern division of Cumberland. Sir Richard Musgrave, having been primed to stand as the second Conservative candidate (his recently deceased father having forbidden him hitherto), now declined, explaining that he did not wish to 'annoy' the sitting Liberal member; nor, just as likely, the sitting Conservative member as well. No doubt Disraeli set his committee of men of social influence on to Musgrave; who in any case was brought to heel and contested in 1874 (as it happened, to no avail). In general, judging by the events of February 1874 in the relevant counties where compacts existed, the committee did not have an easy time of it. They failed to disturb compacts in five English county seats (including no less than Northcote's own North Devonshire division). A new truce in South Staffordshire was perhaps excused on the ground of gaining an inexpensive Conservative seat. Seats were left uncontested in a further ten English county divisions: with disgrace abounding particularly in North Norfolk, where two existing Conservative seats were surrendered without contest. As against these failures, however, new Conservative candidacies were promoted in fourteen county divisions, mostly with better results than Musgrave in Cumberland. In Wales an attempt to find a second Conservative candidate for Denbighshire was frustrated by Sir Watkin Williams Wynn. 'I am sorry to hear Watkin has made such a mess in Denbighshire,' Disraeli commented to Corry, 'but he is very obstinate and his wife has a great objection to his spending money in Election matters.'[31]

An autumn dissolution, *contra* Cardwell, was by no means ruled out. Disraeli had 'much talk' with Derby in October 'as to possible appointments'. Derby found him in a 'quite natural and collected state of mind, not excited, nor confident of immediate success,' but aware of the need to be ready for any eventuality.[32] Elaborate plans for the Irish county constituencies were afoot, under Taylor's eye. Along the lines of Spofforth's model each county was divided into polling districts. Election committees were to be found for each district with subcommittees and a 'competent legal agent' for each 'Barony'. There was to be more efficient registration with full registers both of names and property. There were to be booth inspectors and tally papers.[33] Hardy recorded on 22 August: 'Disraeli approves our suggestion of "Hints for Candidates" & will try to find a fit compositor.'[34] Dyke reported to Disraeli that he had talked to Gorst about Hardy's letter and his idea of getting someone to put together something about the 'many blunders & enormities of the past 3 years'.[35] Gorst did see Hart Dyke at the Carlton where Disraeli's suggestion for a National Union pamphlet on those lines was passed on. Gorst duly sent to Disraeli a series of pamphlets for advice about additions and changes. Gorst would also have ready a paper on 'The wasted session of 1873' whenever the dissolution was announced. It would be composed in such a form 'as to make it a kind of handbook for Conservative candidates at the election'.[36]

In his own peculiar way, Northcote reassured Disraeli about the West Country. 'Things look healthy down here, but I hope we shall not be led into a contest in North Devon.' Northcote, with painful memories of the expense he was put to in 1868, elaborated ingenious reasons why this should be so (a 'contest provoked by us in the North Division might probably lead to an attack on Palk's seat in the East'). Northcote eventually got his way. The only cosy compact was in the north, while two Conservatives remained uncontested both in the south and the east; which might be considered a reasonable bargain. Northcote's comments on Exeter, however, betrayed a haughty county sensibility as yet unaware of a new dispensation at work in the boroughs: 'Exeter is most uncertain. Any two of the four candidates seem to me to have as fair a chance as any other two.'[37] But the fact was that Joseph Gould had Exeter wrapped up. It was a world of politics in which Northcote was increasingly out of his depth.

Northcote at this point exhibits other traits worthy of notice. He was, as he explained to Disraeli, grandly on his way to visit the likes of Beauchamp, Pakington, Cave, and Gore-Langton; but mostly he was concerned that he was soon due to attend a Conservative demonstration in Devonshire and wanted Disraeli's advice about 'lines to take'. The question arose, as he pointed out with exquisite tactlessness to Disraeli, 'out of the use which people are making down here of what you said at the time of the Crisis, and which they twist into a declaration that the Conservatives have no policy'. Northcote proposed to respond to the effect that there were many questions pressing for immediate settlement 'which it would be necessary for an incoming Ministry to study by the light of official information' before they could frame a policy;

> but I would add that the policy of the Conservative party was in its essence, and its outlines what it has always been, and that if it was difficult to define it very strictly that was because it was necessarily to some extent a policy of defence and must therefore depend upon the line of attack chosen by our opponents.
>
> Do you think this sort of thing desirable?[38]

No one but Northcote could have written such a letter with a straight face. Disraeli assumed one in reply, insisting that such hapless defensiveness was not at all desirable, as playing into the enemy's hand.[39]

Disraeli soon offered a model specimen of his aggressive style in his letter to Lord Grey de Wilton apropos of the Bath by-election. Fired off from Weston Park in Shropshire (where he was dallying with his new romantic attachment, Selina, countess of Bradford), it accused Gladstone's government of waging a kind of 'civil warfare', in the course of which they had 'harassed every trade, worried every profession, and assailed or menaced every class, institution, and species of property in the country', varied at intervals by the perpetration of jobbery. This career of 'plundering and blundering', Disraeli asserted, would soon be closed.[40] Hardy thought the letter 'pungent & terse'.[41] It provoked an outcry, however, as being unseemly and demagogic; and it may have contributed to Bath's standing out against the electoral trend by electing the Liberal. Disraeli was probably correct, on the other hand, in his unapologetic prediction that his jingling phrases would go down quite well in the country at large. 'Lord Salisbury, and the Hull election', he assured Lady Chesterfield (another elderly *innamorata)*, 'will effectively silence my critics.'[42] The Hull by-election at the end of October indeed resumed the Liberal haemorrhage. The reference to Salisbury denoted Disraeli's interest in Salisbury's latest *Quarterly Review* piece. This, 'The programme of the Radicals', repeated the 1872 formula of conspicuous avoidance of abuse of Disraeli. Apart from denouncing the 'superstition' of party and asserting that a 'more independent bearing is required by the dangers of the time',[43] Salisbury was quietly congruous with the Conservative line. Was the shark showing signs of following the pilot fish?

3

An opportunity presented itself to Disraeli in November to give what he defiantly called his 'Weston manifesto'[44] more resonant and decorous expression. He was to be installed as lord rector of Glasgow University.

A programme was arranged for him to be received also by the city and by the Glasgow Conservatives. Glasgow marked a public sense that Conservative fortunes were on a rising curve. As Disraeli later assured Philip Rose, 'Glasgow, without exaggeration, was the greatest reception ever offered to a public man: far beyond Lancashire even!'[45] There was a sense too that times were waxing late. Disraeli by now was calculating that there must be a dissolution by March.[46] He framed his Glasgow declarations on the assumption that there would be at least a token last session of the 1868 parliament. His leading theme was to point to a future epoch of political tranquillity after the storms and stresses of Gladstone's time. A Conservative government would govern responsibly and uncontroversially, attending to good administration and social questions. There would be no more heroic adventures or organic changes. Ireland would be governed in the same spirit of administrative firmness without concessions to Home Rulers or the priests who manipulated them. Irish priests gave Disraeli his cue to offer a vision of Europe convulsed by a coming grand conflict between atheism and ultramontane sacerdotal usurpation. If a 'national' party were allowed to govern Britain it would play a 'noble part' in such a struggle, 'taking a firm stand upon the principles of the Reformation which for 300 years had been 'the source of our greatness and our glory'. No doubt this Protestant bombast went down well in the land of Knox. And as was not the case in 1868, Disraeli now had Bismarck and his *Kulturkampf* as bearings of political alignment. On a more homely level Disraeli advised the Scots to 'leave off mumbling the dry bones of political economy, and munching the remainder biscuit of an effete Liberalism'.[47]

On more strictly Conservative party business Disraeli took occasion to make two points. The first was to pay the National Union back for its stirrings of mutiny at Leeds in April. He told the Glasgow Conservatives: 'I have never been myself at all favourable to a system which could induce Conservatives who are working men to form societies confined merely to their class.'[48] It is most likely that Keith-Falconer had requested this rap on the knuckles to strengthen his hand as organising secretary of the union. The second was to bring into the open the party leadership issue in such a manner as to establish once and for all that it was closed. Disraeli confided to the civic dignitaries of Glasgow that he could not help smiling sometimes when he heard the 'constant intimations that are given, by those who know all the secrets of the political world', of the 'extreme anxiety' of the Conservative party to get rid of his services. The fact was the Conservative party could be rid of his services whenever they gave him an intimation that they wished it. He had led the party in the Commons for a record period of 25 years, 'under some circumstances of difficulty and discouragement.' The reason why he was still leader was that the Conservative party was 'the most generous and most indulgent party that ever existed.' 'Whenever I have desired to leave the leadership . . . they have too kindly requested me to remain where I was; and if I make a mistake the only difference in their conduct to me is that they are more indulgent and more kind.'[49]

This was outrageous teasing. Even Buckle felt constrained to comment that it gave 'perhaps a somewhat idealised version of the relationship between leader and party.'[50] But Disraeli now felt himself in a secure enough position to so mistreat the matter in public. Corry reported Richmond's heavily enthusiastic response to Disraeli's remarks on the leadership, which the duke thought 'well-timed and in excellent taste'.

> He hopes the mouths may now be shut of those who, 'whenever Lord Derby goes about starring at Mechanics Institutes etc' cry out
> 'He is *the* man!'
> With such the Duke does not agree, nor seems to deem the Earl better qualified to lead in his own Chamber![51]

Derby himself remained blandly discreet. Corry again: 'Lord Cairns has just come from Lord Derby, who pronounces the political Glasgow Speech to be "the best thing" you "ever did" – "the most concise, and the best sustained"'.[52] Hardy likewise confined himself to thinking that Disraeli's speech to the Conservatives was 'in his best style'.[53] There were Conservatives, however, who were reportedly less than satisfied. They had hoped for a 'more positive attitude' as to policy; they felt disappointed that Disraeli's stance at Glasgow had no 'meaning as a bid for power.'[54] These were the words of a Liberal enemy, Clayden; but they probably reflected accurately enough that Conservative constituency which had complained of feeble leadership in 1868 and whose appetite for more 'positive attitudes' had been whetted in Manchester in 1872.

The annual conclave of Conservative chiefs to plan for the new session gathered in December 1873 at Hardy's place, Hemsted, in Kent. Hardy records Disraeli as being 'in good spirits & we had much talk before dressing.'[55] What was conspicuously absent from this conclave was indeed any lead from Disraeli in the sense of making a 'bid for power.' Disraeli's game was purely one of waiting on events. Evidently, Gladstone, having decided against an autumn dissolution, was going to present some sort of programme at the new session. Hardy's judgement on the Hemsted gathering was: 'Nothing serious concluded.' Disraeli pottered agreeably. 'Corry & Northcote were the only shooters . . . we graver ones walked about talking.' The only animation was provided by the absent Richmond, fretful about current tensions between landlords and tenants. Shock-waves from Gladstone's Irish Land Act had begun to make palpable impact in Britain. Wilson Patten was disquieted by the formation of a tenant farmers' club in Lancashire in 1872. Should the gentry ignore it, thus incurring unpopularity? Or should they join to keep it out of 'bad hands'? In the event, they joined.[56] But 'bad hands' were not easily kept off. 'I hope', Richmond told Cairns, 'you will impress upon our Chief the necessity of doing nothing rashly in reference to Tenant Right. I think he went further than was quite prudent last session.'[57] Disraeli cared, probably, as little for Richmond's frets as he did about National Union sulks. His mind was on other things. Hardy gives the clue: 'Jane drove D. & Corry to Bedgebury.'[58]

Bedgebury Park, Cranbrook, was the seat of Beresford Hope, MP for Cambridge University. Hope was Salisbury's brother-in-law; and he hated Disraeli quite as much as did Salisbury. Disraeli's target was Hope's wife, Lady Mildred, Salisbury's sister. Salisbury himself at this time was abroad, shivering in Sorrento. The text at the background of this encounter was Salisbury's recent *Quartely Review* piece attacking the 'programme of the Radicals', particularly their menacing new champion, the Birmingham Nonconformist screw manufacturer Joseph Chamberlain. The thrust of Salisbury's analysis was the working out of the class war implications of 1848: the political position of the middle classes was fundamentally changed by the arrival of a new power of democracy, spearheaded by trade unions. Confronted with the threat of confiscatory and socialist measures from this 'labour movement', the 'bourgeoisie' were detaching themselves from the Liberal party and rallying to defence of the throne, property, and established religion. It is true that Salisbury would not go so far as to recommend that they simply attach themselves to the existing Conservative party under its existing leadership: he speculated rather on the break up of the inherited party system as being outmoded in new circumstances. But that Salisbury should celebrate the forming political alliance of the hitherto inimical interests of bourgeoisie and gentry was as salient a sign of the times as the concurrent realignment of Borthwick and his Palmerstonian *Morning Post*.

There were other Conservatives who observed relevant and concordant phenomena. 'One Arch, the chief promotor of unionism among the agricultural labourers', was giving landlords and tenant farmers much cause to think less of their quarrels and more of their common interests. Also noted was the formation of 'a new association of employers; united in resistance to trades unions, and intended to include all departments of industry'.[59]

What profit Disraeli and Corry had from their courtesy call on Lady Mildred is not readily evident. Signals no doubt were relayed and pondered. Salisbury himself had lately been taking pains to ease his 29-year-old nephew Arthur James Balfour into the nomination for the borough of Hertford. He feared there might be a contest. Two possible Liberal contenders were spoken of. 'I doubt if either of them have much chance', Salisbury reassured his nephew, 'but under the Ballot all is uncertain.'[60] As it happened, Balfour had an unobstructed run. But what was also becoming apparent as the extraordinary series of Conservative by-election successes gathered pace was that, in Salisbury's own words in the *Quarterly Review*, 'the Ballot has evidently covered a large number of Liberal desertions'.[61]

In this buoyant atmosphere talk of a possible Conservative majority began to arise. Derby recorded on 29 June: 'Cross called: he thinks a crisis probable . . . he wants to know whether I think the time favourable for dissolving? I say yes, the ministry are weak & discredited, they have just renewed their quarrel with the Nonconformists. They may gain by delay, and can hardly lose.' Personally Derby would not have liked a dissolution 'just now, but it is clearly in the interests of the party'. Nonconformist resentment on the education question flared anew. It remained to be seen, in Derby's view, whether this split would be general: 'if so, a Conservative majority in the next elections is certain: a thing of which I have never as yet seen much appearance, though it is commonly predicted.'[62] Dyke reported that Lord Ebury, the Grosvenor Whig, '& all his friends consider our majority assured at the next Dissolution. Gladstone's Church appointments, have outraged the low Church party, & Lord E. was violent against him.' On the other hand, Dyke was having 'a deal of trouble with our Kent Boroughs':

> they have all been left for years in the hands of local attorneys, who have only cared for the filthy lucre, & been content to lose any seat, as long as the victim they brought forward paid the bill. Now, a spirit of energy has sprung up at Greenwich & Rochester & other places, which disturbs the 'attorney element' – and will prove most valuable in the end, but at present I have my hands full, between contending parties.
>
> I hear we have a good majority of promises at Shaftesbury, but I hear the other side are working very hard & pulling some votes out of the fire.[63]

Shaftesbury was duly captured. Gorst, who had something to do with the 'spirit of energy' now manifest, was notable for restraint. Renfrewshire might have been a 'great victory', but Gorst could not be sanguine about Dover – 'influenced much by private and corrupt motives, and little by public spirit', as he informed Disraeli.[64] Even success there left Gorst with reservations: 'The victory at Dover is great & for the moment most successful.'[65]

The larger context of Gorst's restraint is probably best conveyed in a message to Taylor about the Staffordshire East victory from Dyott, the MP for Lichfield.

> Thank you for your exertions to obtain a frontbencher to join in the celebration of Allsopp's victory. If the leaders look for a full triumph at the approaching contest, there should be no hanging back at the present time, there is much work to be done around Birmingham. . . . If D'Israeli could but be convinced of the effect which his presence would have amongst the working man in the Black Country at this time, I think he would strain a point. I would not ask for, & do not desire a Manifesto, let them feel that their leader cared for them, was ready to come amongst them.[66]

What it can be reasonably assumed was depressingly clear from Gorst's point of view is that Disraeli was not going to strain a point in any manner indicated by Dyott. There was indeed going to be no 'Manifesto', as Glasgow was to demonstrate; and Glasgow further demonstrated a quite deliberate deprecation on Disraeli's part of specifically working-class manifestations of Conservatism. And for that matter, Taylor did not succeed in getting a frontbencher to mark the leadership's notice of popular Black Country Conservatism. It is correspondingly reasonable to assume that Disraeli's strategic thinking was congruent rather with the kind of analysis recently provided by Salisbury.

4

By the end of 1873 the whip's office was in crisis. Noel's health finally collapsed. Taylor offered to return as a temporary substitute. Dyke advised Corry that the very best thing to be done was to accept Taylor's offer at once.

> He can be spared a great deal of night work if I have an assistant. Winn would do well enough if Taylor helped also but of course a difficulty might arise if Noel did not come back, as by his assisting again this Session he [Winn] might think he had a quasi-right for a permanent appointment. I saw Noel in the street again today; he has fairly improved . . . & I do not at all give up the idea of his return in good health.[67]

Corry felt able to assure Disraeli that 'Taylor Dyke and Co. will hit it off well together'. But Dyke's own report to Disraeli confessed that the position was one of 'anxiety' to him, 'as I have had just enough of the work to know that you *must* have a strong staff, to keep the Party well in hand'.[68] Noel did not return: 'it is very hard after the uphill fight we have had together,' he told Dyke, 'to be separated just now.'[69] 'Taylor Dyke and Co.' did in fact hit it off well enough to be an efficient team until Dyke formally took over as chief whip in 1874.

At all events Dyke could console himself in Noel's absence that 'our prospects seem to grow brighter every day and I look forward to the gradual dislocation of our opponents with much interest'. He assured Disraeli that the 'Glasgow campaign pleased me more than any of our victories, however, and even the "traditional grumbler" is obliged to acknowledge it as a triumphant success'.[70] He felt able to advise Disraeli in the new year that 'there is a fair chance at Stroud: my informant Reginald Yorke attended a large meeting there' – and left 'confident'.[71] The Conservative capture of Stroud on 8 January with a sweeping majority stunned the world of politics. Disraeli noted the role of a 'very able and rising young man', Sir Michael Hicks Beach. He agreed with Sir Michael that, 'after Stroud, nothing ought to astonish us'. He observed further that 'even the *Spectator* acknowledges that to deny the "reaction" now is impossible and absurd'.[72] One element of the 'reaction' evident in Stroud which would have gratified Disraeli especially was the intensity of Low Church hostility to Ritualism.

One congenial problem the Conservative managers had in view for the forthcoming 1874 session was how best to exploit Gladstone's predicament as to whether he was legally obliged to resign and recontest his seat at Greenwich in consequence of his taking over the Exchequer from Lowe.[73] The legal experts differed, with a distinct propensity to do so along party lines. Dyke looked forward to 'more sport this session', as he told Disraeli, 'as Gladstone is the last man after his defeat, to allow his Government to assume a worn-out or moribund aspect for many weeks and we shall hear of some startling proposition before long.' Dyke felt sure that a 'blank session' would damage the government, coupled with their defeat, more than anything which could befall them. He was nervous, much as was the case with Richmond, about the possibility that there might be a Liberal stroke on the landlord–tenant issue.[74]

Conservative reaction: crossing over Jordan

1

Dyke was at least accurate on the matter of a 'startling proposition before long'. Gladstone astounded the political world by announcing abruptly a dissolution of parliament for 25 January, with an immediate general election. His motives had to do mainly with his being blocked from reductions in government expenditure by Childers and Goschen in the service ministries. It was a dramatically bold bid to retrieve the situation; and it took the Conservative leadership entirely by surprise. In his address to his Greenwich constituents Gladstone piled upon the Ossa of stunningly abrupt dissolution the Pelion of an undertaking to use the existing financial surplus to abolish the income tax. This – something Gladstone had been frustrated from achieving earlier by the Crimean War – was assessed generally and immediately as a master stroke. Frederic Harrison was in no doubt at the time that Gladstone had pulled off 'a dextrous party move'.[75] Conservatives feared that indeed it would prove only too much so.

Hardy was on his way up to town to see Disraeli when he learned from the newspapers of Gladstone's 'extraordinary proceeding' in dissolving the parliament which was just then preparing to meet. Like all Conservatives, Hardy was staggered by the 'huge bribe' of the proposed repeal of the income tax. Disraeli himself had been 'by accident for a night in London and was aroused by his servant in the morning with the news which at first he hardly believed'.[76] Hardy found the Carlton Club 'full and excited', with 'great writing of addresses, telegraph sending etc.' Money started to flow as the electoral sluice-gates opened. Derby gave his £1,000 to the Carlton Fund. He guaranteed £500 towards the South-West Lancashire election. Charles Turner was ready to pay on his own account up to £4,000. 'Cross being a poor man is to be brought in for nothing if possible'.[77] As it turned out, there was to be no contest in the south-west division. Derby's generosity was more needed by Egerton and Hardcastle in the south-east. Disraeli had given Cairns his 'only rough copy of address and begged me to stay all night so as to see it yesterday morning which I did'.[78]

Thus hastily cobbled together, Disraeli's address to his Buckinghamshire constituency betrayed a shocked discomposure. On the income tax he merely alleged a Conservative wish to do likewise. He had always been in favour, in or out of office, of measures for the improvement of the condition of the people. He deprecated the 'incessant and harassing legislation' of the past five years and pointed to the advantages there would have been if that period had been characterised by 'a little more energy in our foreign policy and a little less in our domestic legislation'. He made much of footling matters concerning the Straits of Malacca and the Ashanti war. He concluded by absolving Gladstone personally of being, at least at present, hostile to the national institutions or to the maintenance of the integrity of the empire (though noting 'ominous suggestions' about Irish local government). But Disraeli pointed to the hostility within Liberalism to the monarchy, the Lords, the Church, and the union with Ireland. After a final flourish about the Reformation and the importance to the cause of civil and religious liberty in Europe of the strength and stability of England, he asked the electors of Buckinghamshire to return him to the Commons 'to resist every proposal which may impair that strength and to support by every means her imperial sway'.[79]

Buckle apologetically described this address as bearing rather a 'negative character'.[80] It would be more aptly described as a document betraying a failure of nerve. It was as if Gladstone's bold manoeuvre had magically restored the old intimidating spell of the 'constant predominance' of the Liberal party; as if at a stroke he had exorcised the spirit of the 'Conservative reaction' with its phenomenal run of by-election portents. It was indeed extraordinary that neither Cairns nor Hardy, the two of Disraeli's senior colleagues who read his draft, thought it appropriate that their party's leader ought to have matched Gladstone's boldness with a correspondingly bold claim to office. The partisan Liberal Clayden afterwards summed up with brutal shrewdness this nerveless trepidation of merely undertaking to resist future Liberal initiatives: 'He did not even ask for power.'[81]

Cairns's savagery on Gladstone's address certainly betrayed a dismal foreboding that Gladstone had indeed pulled off a master stroke.

> The Dissol^{n} is chargeable to us, because we wd not take office without it.
>
> The charge is not the Dissol^{n}, but the suddenness & treachery of it, & the mockery of asking Boros to make a deliberate choice in six days. He does not touch the question, why not dissolve six weeks ago, & with fair notice?[82]

Northcote's advice was more calculatedly defeatist:

> But we must bear in mind that, if he gets a narrow majority, and if, when he comes to propose his new schemes, involving as they will a good amount of new taxation, they prove to be unacceptable, he will find himself in an awkward

position in the new parliament, while we, having a dissolution in hand, shall occupy a position of advantage.

Northcote was sardonic on the financial logic of Gladstone's proposal to abolish the income tax. He conceded, however, that it was likely to commend itself to the constituencies, because of the way it was linked to rebates of taxes on articles of popular consumption: a contradictory policy, but calculated to be popular.[83] Derby assumed that the £7 million or £8 million that Gladstone was prospectively giving away would be covered by readjustments to other taxes: 'which rightly or wrongly will be construed to mean, by increased burdens on realised property'. However, Derby was much more shrewd and much less panicky in his assessment of the likely fortunes of Gladstone's coup. 'To the Conservatives, I see no loss in this sudden summons: they are confident, well-organised, and have been long preparing. It is too early to judge, but on the whole I incline to think that Gladstone has made a mistake.'[84]

Once recovered from their initial shock, the party managers rallied with braver estimates. They could report to Disraeli that every constituency in which there was a chance of victory was provided with a Conservative candidate (which was not in fact strictly true),

and he was furnished with an estimate of the majority which the Central Office expected to gain at the elections. This estimate, which gave all doubtful seats to the Radicals, promised a majority of twenty-five; but the management expressed the private opinion that the Conservatives would come into power with a majority of fifty.[85]

Gorst, who knew the boroughs best, was not so sanguine. He predicted a majority of 82 English seats and a deficit in Scotland, Ireland, and Wales of 79 seats: thus giving Disraeli a nugatory overall majority of 3. Gorst allowed that 'Taylor says we have underestimated. We have been rather hard on the boroughs, but we have taken a sanguine view of the counties.'[86] All the indications are that Disraeli's own view corresponded with Gorst's rather than Taylor's. He dined alone with the Derbys on 26 January: 'D. did not seem either sanguine or eager, as to the result: he seems to think the majority either way will be narrow, but not to expect that we shall win. Still he is turning over, in his mind the appointments which must be made if we come in.'[87] He later told the queen that he thought there might have been 'a very small majority' for the Conservatives. He 'expressed great surprise at the result of the elections', for 'nothing like this had been anticipated'. Disraeli's shrewdest comment on the majority of over 50 which he eventually commanded was that 'no party organisation could have caused this result'.[88]

On paper there was now in place a formidable Conservative organisational order of battle. The party could boast a 186-page prospectus of agents, associations, clubs, registration societies, and their secretaries.[89] Hardy remarked to Cairns amid a 'whole world' astir '& contests everywhere in boroughs' in optimally fine weather for canvassers, that George Cubitt, the uncontested MP for Surrey West, was to preside at a 'great meeting at Exeter Hall for the Conservative Candidates'.[90] There is no doubt that Conservative candidates were better supplied with political munitions than they had ever been before. They had their *Hints for Candidates* and their handbooks. Gorst had done his best to give to the boroughs the level of solicitous care which the party managers had hitherto reserved almost entirely to the counties. Comment has been made that the Conservative campaign in 1874 was 'remarkably well-orchestrated, at least in southern England'. Front- and backbenchers adopted very similar arguments.[91] But behind the façade of organisational apparatus there were dire gaps and deficiencies. Conservative organisations in the 49 boroughs with a population over 50,000 'varied enormously' in quality and efficiency. Two were still without any kind of Conservative agent; some were still in the hands of solicitors and without committees; many were still run by old-fashioned registration associations. In the 34 boroughs with populations between 30,000 and 50,000, the position was often much worse. No less than 9 were still in the hands of solicitors, and 5 were run by registration societies.[92]

To the credit of the managers in 1874, however, there was nothing of the vacuous optimism of 1868 about Scotland and Ireland. For many months Richmond had been the source of dusty news about the Scottish constituencies.[93] Nor did his tune change when the elections came on: 'I consider Aberdeenshire to have been completely mismanaged.'[94] The Conservative party nonetheless ended up in 1874 with 20 Scottish seats, a net gain of 12. There were impressive gains in the Border counties.

Ireland was another story. Cairns told Disraeli on 3 February that the 'news wh. Taylor has today from Ireland as to Derry & Down is disquieting, but I hope for the best'.[95] Cairns hoped in vain: 2 seats were lost in Derry County and 1 in Down. Richmond was sorry to see that Cairns's advice had not been followed in Tyrone by Corry's cousin, Lord Belmore. 'I conclude Belmore must have been obstinate and stupid.'[96] Whatever the case, it cost Lord Claud Hamilton his seat, who had been a member for the county since 1835.[97] At least Cairns had the satisfaction of reporting to Disraeli that 'his arrangements at Belfast' had 'turned out' as he expected.[98] Not counting the eccentric Lord Robert Montagu, elected as a Home Ruler for Westmeath, 33 Conservatives were returned for Irish seats; a net loss of 7. This was partly compensated for by a Conservative rally in Wales, with a net gain of 3: thus, outside England, the Conservative party marginally but usefully lessened its deficit. Scotland had always been deficit country; but not Ireland or Wales. What was established in 1874, however, was that both Ireland and Wales would henceforth definitely join Scotland as deficit territories. In 1874 only 12 Conservatives were returned for Irish constituencies outside Ulster: the slippage which had commenced in 1868 continued.

Yet the fact that Irish Conservatism could now clearly be seen to be retreating to its Ulster laager and its lesser Dublin redoubts paled into insignificance beside the fate of Irish Liberalism in 1874. An eruption of Catholic and nationalist Home Rule sentiment destroyed Liberalism as an Irish electoral power. The near 70 Liberal seats of 1868 collapsed to a mere 10 in 1874. Over the corpse of Irish Liberalism in 1874 60 Home Rule members marched to Westminster.[99] This Liberal catastrophe was far from being something at which Conservatives could rejoice. It exploded one of Gladstone's last arguments for disestablishment in 1869 and tenant right in 1870: that on no other basis could Home Rule for Ireland be held at bay. That argument had routed the Irish landlords in 1870; Derby had recommended acceptance of the Land Act of 1870 precisely on that basis. It was Derby (lately the disposer of his Irish properties) who, in June 1871 at the time of the Westmeath by-election, observed the 'throwing over' of the Liberal candidate by the priests, who gave their support to a 'nationalist' Home-Ruler, 'which means a repealer'. Derby correctly judged the future significance of this event: 'The priests cannot control their movement, and therefore put themselves at its head. If this precedent is to be followed (and that it will be, appears probable) a new Irish difficulty has arisen, more serious than any we have yet dealt with.'[100] That new and serious Irish difficulty was now in place. The Conservative party now had to confront the uncomfortable fact that it was in the exposed position of being the only effective unionist interest in Ireland.

2

Any such sombre considerations were hardly to be thought of amid the dazzling electoral events taking place in England. Cairns, who presided over the 'Managing Committee' at Central Office, wrote to Disraeli on 3 February: 'Winn says that on the whole of the elections as yet our gain is only 1 short of what they had reckoned on. The prospects of Westm^{r} & Middsx are Excellent.'[101] The reckoning Winn referred to was for a 25 majority. The prospects first opened in 1868 in Westminster and Middlesex of suburban middle-class desertions from Liberalism now enlarged to the status of a national psephological phenomenon. Cairns exulted: 'I lose my breath at Manchester, Brighton, Nottingham, Marylebone, & Westminster! & I may have some further shocks of an agreeable kind from the City & other Metrop^{ln}. Boros for wh. we are waiting.'[102] The shock City of London result proved indeed to be of an agreeable kind: the three conservatives headed the poll, with Goschen managing to scramble in a very poor fourth, and the two other Liberals (one a Rothschild) nowhere. This in itself constituted an electoral revolution. It was true that the eminent banker and City merchant J.G. Hubbard, former MP for Buckingham, could only be induced by Noel and Taylor to enter the contest by the bribe of a privy-councillorship (duly honoured by Disraeli).[103] But it was a good investment, especially as Hubbard's son, thereby encouraged, revenged his father's defeat in 1868 and 'ousted Sir H. Verney from the borough of Buckingham'. Smith headed the Westminster poll as he had in 1868; but the second Liberal seat was captured, handsomely. The voting figures spoke volumes: 18,052 Conservative votes; 7,184 Liberal. The *Spectator* commented aptly: 'This is Conservative reaction with a vengeance!'[104]

'Three cheers for Marylebone!' cried Malmesbury to Cairns on 5 February.[105] Capturing this suburban London seat symbolised for Conservatism in 1874 what Middlesex had done in 1868. The taking of the second Middlesex seat, as with the case of Westminster, seemed more in the category of occupying enemy territory already strategically conquered. Even before the end of January Disraeli was aware of the stirrings of something big in the metropolitan constituencies. This 'enthusiasm among the great constituencies', as he explained to Lady Bradford, was 'never known before'. Westminster and the City more than fulfilled his rising hopes. 'Chelsea even looks promising, and there are absolutely spontaneous fights in Finsbury and Hackney. Nothing like this ever occurred before.'[106] Finsbury and Hackney both escaped; but a seat captured in Chelsea was as important and significant as a seat in Marylebone. Seats in Greenwich, Southwark, and Tower Hamlets underlined the point. Derby was struck by the captures in the City, Westminster, Tower Hamlets, and Chelsea. 'These victories in a quarter where success of late years has not been even hoped for, show the strength of the popular reaction, and make a change of government inevitable.'[107] Disraeli himself was incommoded by the vexation and expense of a 'mock contest' in Buckinghamshire which prevented his dining with Cairns in London to celebrate the telegrams of the early victories – Guildford, Andover, Kidderminster, even Eye and Lymington. 'I must dine at Newport Pagnell,' he apologised, '& address the lieges.'[108] It was on 5 February that Disraeli was informed by the managing committee that 'they now absolutely contemplate obtaining a majority'.[109] Gorst reported on the 6th: 'If all the elections were to go as we estimated at the time when we made out a majority of 3, we should have a majority of 27.'[110]

Other Conservative chiefs reeled in a state of astonished delight. Hardy: 'So much seems to have passed in the busy exciting days in London that instead of two & a half I seem to have been there many days.' He witnessed half in disbelief the metropolitan victories 'which are indeed extraordinary'; and presided at Exeter Hall over celebrations for Westminster.[111] Richmond also: 'How wonderfully the elections seem to have gone in our favour. I am astonished at Brighton. Sussex will have distinguished itself on this occasion.'[112] For Conservatives with long memories there was an extra relish in the occasion. Richmond again: 'Our success is quite wonderful. I do believe I shall at last find myself in a party which has a majority in the Country. A position I do not think I have been in since 1841!'[113] Corry wrote to Disraeli from the Carlton on 6 February with emotions which may be imagined.

Gorst, I know, wrote to you on facts by this evening's post – and I saw no advantage in dilating on our speculations, or adding my comments.

Till the cup is at your lips I say nothing of what is in my heart.

There is panic, I am told at Brook's: there *was*, I should say, for all is now bitterness and despair. Wolverton [the Liberal whip] has fled from town in horror, and the cry is 'They are in for years.' Gladstone is prostrate and astounded, and his colleagues (in two cases at least which have come to my knowledge). announce in their offices that the next is their last week of power.

Wolverton's advice has caused the whole catastrophe, which has caught a Cabinet in a fool's paradise.

The Carlton is crowded till midnight: all the dear 'old lot' whom we know so well – all the 'frondeurs' and the cynics – professors, *now*, of a common faith, cry for 'The Chief' as young hounds bay for the huntsman the day after the frost has broken up . . . I hear on every side, that the Newport Pagnell speech has immeasurably influenced the events of the last 48 hours . . . P.S. I can't help adding that I think Gorst's estimate of our chances too severe.[114]

By this time something like 30 English boroughs had been captured. The Home Countries were virtually cleared of Liberals. Lancashire was as solid as in 1868. All the county divisions were returned, with contests only in half of them. In the manufacturing boroughs losses in Blackburn, Bolton, and Liverpool were handsomely more than offset by gains in Manchester, Oldham, Stalybridge, Warrington, and Wigan.

Spofforth wrote from Eridge Castle, whence his patron Abergavenny (no longer the kingpin of the election managers) kept watch over his Sussex and Kent constituencies:

As I have never been reproached for exercising my privilege of writing to you in times of adversity, I venture to do so now that success has crowned your efforts – placed your party in the proud position, which you once told me it was the object of your life to see – viz 'the greatest power of the state'. . . .

When the dissolution was announced it was only by a few, that your majority was guessed at ten: – Lord Abergavenny has just shown me figures giving you a solid majority of twenty-two (without counting one Home Ruler) and you may safely calculate on at least five more seats.

Borthwick of the Morning Post told me yesterday that if you adopt a Palmerstonian policy you will be Prime Minister for life – and that seems to be the general impression . . . I need not tell you what rejoicing there is in this castle, and I am privileged to convey to you its owner's *kindest regards & best wishes.*[115]

Disraeli's initial expectation was that Gladstone would meet the new parliament, 'if only not to imitate me'.[116] Richmond called on Disraeli on his return to London and reported to Cairns: 'He is in high force and spirits. He imagines that Gladstone will meet parliament, and that in all probability we shall move an amendment to the Address.'[117] But it soon became clear that Gladstone, pressed by his colleagues, would follow Disraeli's precedent of 1868 and resign forthwith. This he did on 17 February. The queen summoned Disraeli to Windsor on the 18th. He who had 'not even asked for power' was about to have power thrust upon him.

3

What had happened? Not, as even Disraeli himself was aware, a triumph of improved organisation. 'Elections are never won by organisation', as a historian has sagely observed; 'but the history of party organisation is dominated by the rhythm of elections.'[118] It is important to assert this here, because future vicissitudes, both of the party and of personalities, will have the effect of putting the 1874 victory in a different, mythical, light. Gorst, as was proper, was duly congratulated and thanked for his services. He responded to Disraeli's acknowledgements by insisting scrupulously that 'Keith-Falconer shares equally with Mr. Noel & myself any credit due for the organisation of the constituencies previous to the late election, of which you have so kindly spoken in terms of commendation'.[119] And it was only to be expected, when the National Union gathered in the Westminster Palace Hotel for its conference in July 1874 that appropriate claims would be made. 'The council wish to direct especial attention to a remarkable fact connected with the signal victory gained by the Conservative cause at the General Election, which appears to them to prove, in an unanswerable manner, the great value, even for electoral purposes, possessed by political associations.' That 'remarkable fact' was that 'among the 74 English and Welsh constituencies which were wholly or partially wrested from the Radical party, in no less than 65 cases were Associations of this nature in active operation'.[120] This unanswerably proved nothing. It suggested the more likely deduction that actively operating political associations are just as, if not more, likely to be consequences as causes of effective electoral action.

The explanatory power attributable to specific interests likewise lacks convincing sufficiency. It is true that the Nonconformist activists, caught on the hop by the suddenness of the dissolution, had difficulty changing the front of their attack away from the government and towards the Conservatives. It is true also that in the drink trade the government had a good enemy. The *Annual Register* could point to the 'incongruous alliance' of publicans and 'sticklers for religious education in the Board Schools', 'Bible and Beer' being the real Conservative programme at the hustings.[121] The trade was indeed vociferously Anglican. As if in gratitude for Bishop Magee's famous aphorism on the licensing question in 1872, 'better England free than England compulsorily sober',[122] publicans reciprocated in 1874 with: 'stand by your National Religion and your National Beverage.'[123] But close investigation suggests that these were subsidiary and contributory components of a much larger and wider and less conveniently identifiable electoral shift.[124]

Application of swing of opinion psephological analysis to the voting figures in 1874 suggests that there was a 5 per cent movement of voters away from Liberalism towards Conservatism: Liberals polled only 36.24 per cent of registered voters as opposed to 42.09 per cent in 1868; the Conservative proportion rose from 31.56 per cent in 1868 to 36.53 per cent in 1874.[125] Liberal weakness was marginally more apparent than Conservative strength. Analysis of Conservative gains as a percentage of 1868 Liberal seats indicates that the best execution was done in the counties and the southern boroughs. It was in fact in 1874 rather than in 1868 that the Conservative party 'made unambiguous major gains in the counties: the result of a disaffection among the Liberal magnates and Anglican voters of a far greater order than that of 1868'.[126]

There is no doubt that Salisbury was correct to detect the ballot as cover for large numbers of Liberal desertions. There is also no doubt that embattled Anglicanism, resentful at Nonconformist disestablishmentarian and educational aggression, and disillusioned with the fruitlessness of disestablishment in Ireland, was the energy that fuelled many such desertions. The dismayed Sheffield Radical Mundella noted that the 'middle classes are everywhere becoming more and more Ecclesiastical and Conservative'.[127] Undoubtedly, the term which has most explanatory resonance for this moment is Borthwick's word to Spofforth, 'Palmerstonian'. This word was also at the centre of Salisbury's evocation of a middle-class yearning to return to 'the golden age of the moderate Liberals'.[128] The great difficulty of course for Salisbury was that whereas he had celebrated the Palmerstonian era as one of loose party allegiances, collusive party arrangements, and healthily negative government, he was now confronted with the horrid prospect that his middle-class deserters from Liberalism had fortuitously provided Disraeli with a decisive Conservative majority for what Disraeli himself was gleefully describing as 'the strongest Government since Pitt'.[129]

Of all the contemporary essays in determining the inwardness of 1874, perhaps the most acute was Frederic Harrison's piece on the 'Conservative reaction' in John Morley's Radical *Fortnightly Review*. His general interpretation is very similar to Salisbury's, with the same mixture of shrewd objective observation and subjective special pleading. In Harrison's case the latter had to do with the need for Liberalism to renew its vocation. There is more than a reminiscence also of Morley's own dismayed auguries of 1868: 'As compared with six years ago, there is very real change in the country as a whole. The change is perhaps not very deep in political convictions; but it is a very real change in political temper.' The 'backbone of the Conservative reaction', Harrison declared, was 'the change of front of the great composite middle-class'.

> The real truth is that the middle-class, or its effective strength, has swung round to Conservatism . . . When we look at the poll in the City of London, in Westminster, in Middlesex, in Surrey, in Liverpool, Manchester, Leeds and Sheffield, in the metropolitan boroughs and in the home counties, in all the centres of middle-class industry, wealth and cultivation, we see one unmistakable fact, that the rich trading class, and the comfortable middle class has grown distinctly Conservative.[130]

There were, Harrison insisted, no special or accidental causes; and Gladstone's income tax bonus was simply ignored. The 'inference' was 'unmistakable'. The great merchants of London, the great spinners of Manchester, were Tories of Tories; 'and the small merchant and tradesman has begun to follow the fashion.'

> The brewer, the distiller, the soap-boiler, the cotton broker, and the drysalter, have strong constitutional principles. The sleek citizens, who pour forth daily from thousands and thousands of smug villas round London, Manchester and Liverpool, read their *Standard* and believe the country will do very well as it is.[131]

Harrison, as a Positivist friend of trade unionism and enemy of Liberal 'economic sophisms', added a warning to his fellow Liberals that these owners of smug villas, moreover, were flanked by incongruous auxiliaries: there was now an artisanal Toryism which counted. The Liberal party man 'has been wont to smile at the vision of the Conservative working man. Perhaps he smiles no longer. He has had a good deal to do with the making of the Conservative working man.' At this point special pleading overwhelmed Harrison's objectivity. No doubt the great bulk of the skilled artisans would continue 'on broad grounds on the side of Progress'; but in the cotton and textile trades, 'where political intelligence is not very broad, where trade questions are very absorbing, and where factory system stimulates a local and domestic partisanship the Conservative working man may be found in masses'. Especially among the unskilled artisans, where the 'influences of clergyman, publican, wealth and mere ostentation, are almost paramount', a 'little demagogism can easily win for the Conservative side'. This, in Harrison's view, was the 'body which the genius of Mr. Disraeli secured for the British constitution': the 'stratum of casual employment, low education, and habitual dependence', where 'political action is dormant'.[132] Harrison is here inventing a Liberal version of a Tory lumpenproletariat: a myth which has proved highly resilient and long-lived. His valuable contribution is to draw attention to the phenomenon of working-class deference. But there was, and is, no reliable evidence for linking that with his politically depraved 'stratum'. What a 'perfectly astonished' Conservative whip had described at Greenwich in 1873 as 'the rough mob elements' was not exclusive to either party, as Dyke's astonishment at the 'Tory complexion' of those elements suggests. The working-class aspect of Harrison's analysis of 1874 could also be objected to as being too flattering to Disraeli's powers of political divination. In any case, the critical value of Harrison's analysis remains rather his vision – if unadmiring – of the sleek citizens commuting to their smug villas. 'This, then, appears to be the great lesson of 1874, that, the middle-classes have gone over to the enemy bag and baggage.'[133]

Notes and References

1 Northcote to Disraeli, 19 March 1873; BL, Iddesleigh 50016, 148.
2 Hardy to Cairns, 30 March 1873; PRO, Cairns 30/51/7.
3 Gorst to Disraeli, 21 March 1873; HP, B/XXI/G/42.
4 NUCCA, minutes of the 7th annual conference, Leeds, 16 April 1873.
5 Derby Diary, 14 May 1873.
6 Northcote to Disraeli, 30 April [1873]; BL, Iddesleigh 50016, 150.
7 *PD*, ccxvii, 502ff (17 July).
8 Gorst to Disraeli, 21 June 1873; HP, B/XXI/G/243.
9 Devonshire South – Kekewich deceased. Conservative hold (17 June).
10 Disraeli to Cairns [1873]; PRO, Cairns 30/51/1.
11 Dyke encl. HP, B/XXI/D439a.
12 Taylor to Disraeli [1873]; HP, B/XX/T/165, 166. E.J. Feuchtwanger, *Disraeli, Democracy and the Tory Party* (Oxford 1968), 45. Birmingham party' = Education League. Derby in 1869 described Jenkinson as 'an energetic High Tory who means to be a Conservative leader' (Derby Diary, 16 Feb. 1869). Jenkinson retired from the Commons in 1880, not contesting his seat, having held no office.
13 *PD*, ccxvii, 549ff.
14 *Ibid.*, 806ff. (23 July).
15 P. Smith, *Lord Salisbury on Politics* (Cambridge 1972), 317–8.
16 Winn to Taylor, 29 July 1873; HP, B/XX/T/125.
17 Disraeli to Northcote, 11 Sept. 1873; Buckle, ii, 599.
18 Disraeli to Cairns, 11 Sept. 1873; Buckle, ii 599.
19 Taylor to Disraeli, 30 July [1873]; HP, B/XX/T/125a.
20 Hardy, *Diary*, 179.
21 Disraeli to Corry, [26 July 1873]; HP, B/XX/D/211.
22 Disraeli to Corry, [27 July 1873]; HP, B/XX/D/212.
23 Disraeli to Corry, 1 Aug. 1873; HP, B/XX/D/214.
24 Derby Diary, 1 April 1873. Gladstone instead secured him as solicitor-general in November, 1873.
25 *Ibid.*, 6 Aug. and 23 Sept. 1873.
26 Disraeli to Corry, 10 Aug. 1873; HP, B/XX/D/216.
27 Northcote to Disraeli, 10 Sept. 1873; BL, Iddesleigh 50016, 152.
28 Taylor to Disraeli, 19 Aug. 1873; HP, B/XX/T/126.
29 Dyke to Disraeli, [9 Aug. 1873]; HP, B/XXI/D/455. T.W. Boord was a distiller who topped Gladstone in the Greenwich poll in 1874, and went on to represent Greenwich until retirement (knighted) in 1895.
30 Disraeli to Corry, 5 April [1873]; HP, B/XX/D/206.

31 Disraeli to Corry, 4 April [1873]; HP, B/XX/D/206a.
32 Derby Diary, 12 Oct. 1873.
33 HP, B/XXI/A/186b.
34 Hardy, *Diary*, 188.
35 Dyke to Disraeli [23 Aug. 1873]; HP, B/XXI/D/456.
36 Feuchtwanger, *Disraeli, Democracy and the Tory Party*, 128.
37 Northcote to Disraeli, 10 Sept. 1873; BL, Iddesleigh 50016, 152.
38 *Ibid.*
39 Buckle, ii, 599.
40 Buckle, ii, 602. Buckle is incorrect in stating that Grey was the Conservative candidate. Grey had won a seat in a previous by-election, in June 1873. The Conservative candidate in October was W. Forsyth, QC.
41 Hardy, *Diary*, 189.
42 Buckle, ii, 603.
43 *QR*, Oct. 1873, 572.
44 Buckle, ii, 608.
45 *Ibid.*, 607.
46 *Ibid.*, 689.
47 J.P. Parry, *Democracy and Religion, Gladstone and the Liberal Party 1867–1875* (Cambridge 1986), 383–4; Buckle, ii, 607–8.
48 M. Pugh, *The Tories and the People 1880–1935* (1985), 140.
49 Buckle, ii, 607.
50 *Ibid.*
51 Corry to Disraeli, 28 Nov. 1873; HP, B/XX/Co/91; Buckle, ii, 608.
52 Corry to Disraeli, 4 Dec. 1873; HP, B/XX/Co/92.
53 Hardy, *Diary*, 190.
54 Clayden, 5–6.
55 Hardy, *Diary*, 191.
56 Derby Diary, 29 April, 5 Oct. 1872.
57 Richmond to Cairns, 12 Dec. 1873; PRO, Cairns 30/51/2.
58 Hardy, *Diary*, 191.
59 Derby Diary, 10 and 16 Dec. 1873.
60 Salisbury to Balfour, 18 July 1873; BL, Balfour 49688, 5.
61 *QR*, Oct. 1873, 548.
62 Derby Diary, 29 June, 6 July 1873.
63 Dyke to Disraeli [23 Aug. 1873]; HP, B/XXI/D/456.
64 Gorst to Disraeli, 11 Sept. 1873; HP, B/XX/G/244.
65 Gorst to Disraeli, 23 Sept. 1873; HP, B/XX/G245.
66 Dyott to Taylor, 19 Sept. 1873; HP, B/XX/T/130a.
67 Dyke to Corry, n.d. HP, B/XXI/D/509.
68 Dyke to Disraeli, 24 Dec. 1873; HP, B/XXI/D/457.
69 Dyke to Disraeli [1 Jan. 1873]; HP, B/XXI/D/459. See also Feuchtwanger, *Disraeli, Democracy and the Tory Party*, 54.
70 Dyke to Disraeli, 24 Dec. [1873]; HP, B/XXI/D/457.
71 Dyke to Disraeli, n.d. HP, B/XXI/D/459.
72 Buckle, ii, 611.
73 Taylor to Disraeli, 22 Jan. [1874]; HP, B/XX/T/133.
74 Dyke to Disraeli, n.d. HP, B/XXI/D/458.
75 'The Conservative reaction', *Fortnightly Review*, March 1874, 296.

76 Hardy, *Diary*, 193.
77 Derby Diary, 27 Jan. 1873.
78 Hardy, *Diary*, 193–4.
79 *AR*, 1874, 5–6.
80 Buckle, ii, 614.
81 Clayden, 21.
82 Cairns to Disraeli, 29 Jan. 1874; HP, B/XX/Ca/108.
83 Northcote to Disraeli, 25 Jan. 1874; BL, Iddesleigh 50016, 156.
84 Derby Diary, 24 Jan. 1874.
85 H. Gorst, *The Earl of Beaconsfield* (1900), 151–2.
86 Buckle, ii, 617.
87 Derby Diary, 26 Jan. 1874.
88 Buckle, ii, 626.
89 Feuchtwanger, *Disraeli, Democracy and the Tory Party* 122.
90 Hardy to Cairns, 31 Jan. 1874; PRO, Cairns 30/51/7.
91 Parry, *Democracy and Religion*, 389.
92 Hanham, 115.
93 See, for example, Richmond to Cairns, 16 Nov. 1873; PRO, Cairns 30/51/2.
94 Richmond to Cairns, 8 Feb. 1874; PRO, Cairns 30/51/3.
95 Cairns to Disraeli, 3 Feb. 1874; HP, BXX/Ca/109.
96 Richmond to Cairns, 13 Feb. 1874; PRO, Cairns 30/51/3. Belmore was, after all, Gladstone's nephew-in-law as well as Corry's uncle.
97 With one brief interval, 1837–9.
98 Cairns to Disraeli, 6 Feb. 1874; HP, B/XX/Ca/110.
99 See T.K. Hoppen, *Elections, Politics, and Society in Ireland 1832–1885* (Oxford, 1984) 274–6. Many of the Home Rulers were at this stage Liberals in disguise; a few even claimed to be Conservatives in the tradition of Isaac Butt; but the point was that they had to adopt the disguise in order to survive.
100 Derby Diary, 14 June 1871.
101 Cairns to Disraeli, 3 Feb. 1874; HP, B/XX/Ca/109.
102 Cairns to Disraeli, 6 Feb. 1874; HP, B/XX/Ca/110.
103 Hay to Disraeli, 23 March 1874; HP, C/VI/81. Hubbard eventually received a peerage in 1887 as Lord Addington.
104 7 Feb. 1874.
105 Malmesbury to Cairns, 5 Feb. 1874; PRO, Cairns 30/51/20.
106 Buckle, ii, 618
107 Derby Diary, 6 Feb. 1874.
108 Disraeli to Cairns, 1 Feb. 1874; PRO Cairns 30/51/1.
109 Buckle, ii, 618.
110 *Ibid.*, 619.
111 Hardy, *Diary*, 195.
112 Richmond to Cairns, 6 Feb. 1874; PRO, Cairns 30/51/3.
113 Richmond to Cairns, 8 Feb. 1874; PRO, Cairns 30/51/3.
114 Corry to Disraeli, 6 Feb. 1874; HP, B/XX/Co/96aa. The last reference is to Gorst's revised estimate of a 27 majority. Buckle, ii, 619–20.
115 Spofforth to Disraeli, 8 Feb. 1874; HP, B/XXI/S/440.
116 Buckle, ii, 623.
117 Richmond to Cairns, 11 Feb. 1874; PRO, Cairns 30/51/3.

118 Feuchtwanger, *Disraeli, Democracy and the Tory Party*, 132.
119 Gorst to Disraeli, 26 Feb. 1874; HP, B/XXI/G/250.
120 NUCCA, minutes of 8th annual conference, 1 July 1874.
121 *AR*, 1874, 44.
122 N. Longmate, *The Waterdrinkers. A History of Temperance* (1968), 219.
123 Parry, *Democracy and Religion*, 396.
124 Hanham, 225; Parry, *Democracy and Religion*.
125 J.P.D. Dunbabin, 'Parliamentary elections in Great Britain, 1868–1900: a psephological note', *English Historical Review* (1966), 86.
126 Parry, *Democracy and Religion*, 393.
127 *Ibid.*, 383.
128 *QR*, Oct. 1873, 55.
129 Buckle, ii, 623.
130 *Fortnightly Review*, March 1874, 298, 304.
131 *Ibid.*, 305.
132 *Ibid.*, 303–4.
133 *Ibid.*, 305.

Part III

Disraeli's High Years, 1874–8

Chapter 8

Resuming where Lord Palmerston left off

Attachment to aristocratic government

1

When Disraeli formed his administration in February 1874 he made signal acknowledgement to the forces of middle-class Conservatism by preferring to office three of his colleagues in the Commons most cited as aligned with it. He advanced Richard Cross to his cabinet at the Home Office. Cross's fellow Lancastrian Sandon he put in charge of the education department as vice-president of the Privy Council. He made W.H. Smith financial secretary to the Treasury. Cross had held no previous ministerial office. It was thus a dramatic gesture on Disraeli's part to make him a secretary of state. This was much pressed for by Derby. When in 1877 and 1878 Smith and Sandon were both promoted to the cabinet, Sandon recorded in his cabinet journal that when he and Smith arrived for Sandon's first council 'Cross joined us, & said most cordially "here we are all 3 once more together" (alluding to our sitting & working together in opposition since 1868) – "we are the people in fact who brought the Govt. into power".'[1]

Smith was the first man directly connected with trade to enter a Conservative cabinet; as he was also the first and only borough member to sit in Disraeli's second cabinet. By the standards of the Conservative party of that day, Disraeli's acknowledgement was ample. It was a question essentially of gestures, not substance. Smith's promotion to the Admiralty in 1877 caused an even greater sensation than Cross's to the Home Office in 1874. Derby had doubted that Disraeli would be likely 'to agree to give high promotion to a man like Smith, who is one of the middle-classes, & in business'.[2] Derby, a great traditional aristocrat, consistently advocated the cause of the 'middle-class men who are the strength of our party'; it was perhaps rather unperspicacious of him to find Disraeli's dislike of them 'odd'. The Queen fretted at the offence she feared Smith's appointment would give to the aristocratic temper of the navy.[3] Disraeli's own aristocratic temper would lead him often enough to make satirical remarks about his awkwardly bourgeois colleagues. But it was a price he was willing to pay; and he purchased the desired political effect at a cheap enough rate. The great point about Disraeli as a politician and as leader of the Conservative party was what Lady Dorothy Nevill defined as his 'attachment to aristocratic government'.[4] This could take the form of intense hostility to the idea of life peerages. It was evident in his often ambivalent relationship with even so proclaimedly weighty a counsellor as Cairns. It was one of the 'peculiarities' of Disraeli's mind, as Derby observed of Disraeli's being out of humour with his lord chancellor, 'to dislike lawyers, and men of the middle classes: and he is a little jealous of colleagues who are not closely tied to him by personal influences.'[5] But even Derby, for that matter, never doubted the justness of Henry Reeves's ascription of the political misfortunes of France 'to the absence of local self-government and an aristocratic class. The dead level of society produces no natural leaders: and all power passes to officials, merely because there is no one else to take the initiative.'[6] Besides the sheer consistency of this attachment, all Disraeli's fleeting adventures with Tory Democracy and wry-faced gestures to middle-class Conservatism fade into insignificance.

Kebbel, who knew his man well,[7] called attention to the same clue. He drew this portrait of Disraeli in 1888:

> He was an aristocrat of aristocrats. He had no notion of allowing political power to be divorced from the principle of birth and property. He always spoke of the country gentlemen of England as the natural leaders of the rural population. Both in his speeches and in his writings he loved to dwell on the advantages of what he called 'a territorial constitution.' . . . He believed himself to possess a pedigree compared with which the pedigrees of the oldest families in Christendom were as things of yesterday.[8]

Kebbel drew attention also to Disraeli's admiration for the Whigs, his great opponents, politically and historically: their courage, consistency, and discipline; though they had the people against them, they held their own by 'management', 'generalship'.[9]

The spirit in which Disraeli formed his government in 1874 and conducted it thereafter could not be more accurately expressed than in these terms. Through management and generalship he would retain political power for the class of birth and property in an era of extended political privilege for the popular constituencies. He never wavered from the doctrine he had put to Derby in 1848: that the office of the Conservative leader was 'to uphold the aristocratic settlement of this country', and that that was the 'only question at stake however manifold may be the forms which it assumes in public discussion, and however various the knowledge and labour which it requires'.[10] Disraeli's greatness consisted in the courage and consistency with which he addressed himself to this office.

2

Of the manifold forms and variety of knowledge and labour exercising Disraeli in February 1874 none was more consequential to him than the question of Lord Salisbury. Retrieving Salisbury for the party would be both a personal triumph and a capital political advantage. Certain of his cabinet places filled themselves: Derby would return to the Foreign Office; Cairns ('my most faithful & ablest Counsellor, one often tried & never found wanting')[11] would return to the Woolsack; Northcote's claim to the Exchequer was now secure. All dispositions otherwise depended on Salisbury and his henchman Carnarvon. Lowry Corry's death in 1873 and Pakington's failure to be re-elected ('Providence had disposed' of him, as the queen recorded Disraeli's having 'amusingly' remarked)[12] left the two service places conveniently vacant. Disraeli would have considered Carnarvon as supremely dispensable as Pakington, but knew well that his overtures through Lady Mildred and Lady Derby would be to no avail unless he treated with Hatfield and Highclere as a partnership.

Salisbury returned from Sorrento on 7 February, by which time Disraeli's majority was substantially in shape. All Salisbury's wishful calculations about a Conservative party materially strengthened to a point at which it could restrain Liberal initiatives without allowing Disraeli to claim justification for his 1867 adventure had fallen apart. The unexpected Conservative majority exploded all those comforting predictions of a crumbling of traditional party lines and the return of a harmless kind of Palmerston – Derby epoch. The Conservative party, as Disraeli had stipulated to Cairns apropos of Salisbury in 1869, had manifestly 'shown strength in Parliament & the country'. The 'humiliation' of the prospect of Salisbury's having to renounce his determination 'never again to work with this particular man'[13] plunged him into what his daughter described as 'a torment of doubt whose decision was probably the most painful, and was certainly the most critical in his life'.

Carnarvon turned up at Hatfield and nobly played the part he had implicitly sketched for Northcote's benefit at Powderham. Salisbury reported to Lady Salisbury: 'We had a very long talk. He decidedly leans towards taking office.' Salisbury's line was that they were not 'in the same boat'. Carnarvon could perfectly well take office independently of Salisbury. Carnarvon countered by pressing upon Salisbury that if he remained outside he would be 'a perfect cypher'; which Salisbury allowed as 'entirely true; but slavery might be a worse evil than suicide.' That evening Salisbury dined with the Derbys (Derby had recently married Salisbury's widowed step-mother). 'He hinted much,' Salisbury reported, 'but said nothing directly. I gathered that they had not quite given up the idea of his having the first place. As far as I could, I encouraged it – for it would undoubtedly solve many difficulties.'[14] Perhaps Derby was hoping that Salisbury might stipulate a Derby premiership as the price of adhesion. Salisbury's agony was exacerbated by urgings from the veteran Oxford University MP, Heathcote ('who hates D. as much as I do'), Northumberland, and above all, Beresford Hope, to submit. Salisbury's 'earnest hope' was that Disraeli's 'arrogance may be my friend, and that he will not offer it'. But, as Salisbury had to admit to Heathcote, 'except intense personal dislike, I have no justification for refusing'.[15]

This ultimately was the decisive consideration. Behind it lay calculations about the hopelessness of any prospect of a satisfying public role outside the new government. Salisbury had quite enjoyed his term as chairman of the Great Eastern Railway, 1868–72; but in the circumstances of 1874 the tide of larger fortunes offered itself undeniably. Lady Derby was agreed on as the intermediary. In all essentials a 'treaty of reconciliation' was settled at Derby House. Salisbury's one cavil as to policy was that he was unhappy about notions of possible legislation to put down Ritualism in the Church. He dined with the Derbys on the 18th: 'in good humour, seemingly quite indifferent about politics, and chiefly concerned to know what sort of bishops D. is likely to make.' After calling unavailingly on the absent Disraeli at Whitehall Gardens Salisbury retreated to Bedgebury for succour and stiffening from the Beresford Hopes. It was there that he received Disraeli's letter of 16 February conveying his understanding through Lady Derby that Salisbury would 'not altogether disagree' with her view that it was very desirable that Salisbury should have conversation on the state of public affairs with the leader of the Conservative party; which Disraeli himself considered likely to be 'not disadvantageous to either of us, or to the public interests'. Salisbury responded that it would be 'satisfactory' from his point of view to hear Disraeli's opinions, especially since 'I do not anticipate they would be materially in disaccord with my own'.[16] So the great personal rift of more than 6 years was quietly closed. Salisbury would return to the India Office.

Once that was settled Disraeli was free to dispose elsewhere. As a corollary Carnarvon returned to the Colonial Office. This meant that Buckingham had to be dispensed with; but he was consoled eventually with Madras. Hunt would very conveniently be moved over to Corry's former Admiralty slot. Other dispositions were more problematic. When Disraeli called on Derby on 9 February the dispositions then provisionally settled on were still very much as they had been in March 1873, except that Pakington's then slot at the Admiralty could be made available for Salisbury, and Manners was thought of for the Colonial Office decidedly as against the Board of Trade. The crucial point on 9 February was that Hardy was still destined for the Home Office. At some point thereafter, presumably owing to Derby's instigation, Hardy's standing slipped. Derby recorded advising 'some reference to old Lord Russell, who is very friendly, and might encourage young Whigs to come over: and pressed for the admission of Cross to the Cabinet, to which D. seemed averse.' Derby also advised against Manners being given a secretaryship of state. Disraeli dined alone with the Derbys on 11 February. Things were going well as far as Derby was concerned: 'I never saw him [Disraeli] in a mood which promised better for the conduct of affairs: not excited nor elated, but calmly hopeful, and busy in forming his ministry.' There was more talk about Cross for the cabinet; on the 'question of the offer to Salisbury, which must be made', Derby professed to 'see plainly that D. does not expect it to be accepted, nor greatly desires that it should be'.[17]

Derby's pressure on behalf of Cross made things very awkward. Disraeli would have preferred Hicks Beach, the impressive Gloucestershire MP, at the Home Office; and then thought of Beach for Local Government (outside the cabinet) before deciding on Sclater-Booth.[18] Beach he eventually placed at the Irish Office; and to underscore his determination to 'keep Ireland in the background', Disraeli kept Beach as chief secretary out of the cabinet, which had not been the case in the previous three administrations. Cross remarked that 'in 1874 Scottish and Irish affairs were both supposed to be under the Home Secretary'.[19] Disraeli wanted his cabinet as small and tight as possible, with six members in either house. He sacrificed rather too much in the way of efficiency to this exclusive end. Cross he had, very sensibly, first thought of for the Board of Trade; and that eventually, and unfortunately, went to Adderley, without a cabinet place. John Manners was loyally brought in, this time at the Post Office. Malmesbury was to assist in the Lords as privy seal. Richmond wanted the War Office, but was put off with the presidency of the Privy Council. This allowed for Disraeli's most bizarre appointment: that of Gathorne Hardy to the War Office. Hardy was Derby's victim. He was in a strong position to have insisted on returning to the Home Office. But, having been flattered by Disraeli that he was his chief's 'right hand', who had 'always stood by him & c.', and being begged 'to select what office I would'[20] naively allowed himself to be side-tracked to the War Office on the ground that it would be particularly pleasing to the queen. Hardy should have stipulated for his former office with Cross accommodated less dramatically but no less effectively at Trade or Local Government. He haplessly let himself be exiled in a political backwater at the same time as his obvious rival for future influence in the party, Northcote, took over the Exchequer. 'If this stands.' Derby noted on 18 February, 'the promotion of Cross will be my doing, and I don't regret it.'

No doubt Disraeli made a mistake in allowing Derby to have his way with Cross at the Home Office. His debts to the house of Stanley were to prove very onerous in more ways than one. This meant not only the beginning of Hardy's virtual eclipse, but also allowed the disastrous appointment of Adderley to the Board of Trade. Cross proved a great success as home secretary, but he would have been just as great a success elsewhere; and it was most important in the party's interest to keep Hardy on his toes in a first-rank business department. Hardy's fate was indeed something of a political black comedy: he became so much a favourite of the queen in a department close to her heart that she put every obstacle in the way of any future suggestion of his being transferred; and it was a serious fault on Disraeli's part as leader of his party and government that for reasons of courtly complaisance as well as mere convenience he allowed the queen for so long to get her way.

Most of the great Tory interests were represented in the new cabinet. Various altitudes of the High Church had Salisbury, Carnarvon, and Hardy. Low Protestantism had Cairns, as did Ulster. Land and the old families had

Richmond. Lancashire and the middle classes had Derby and Cross. Manners stood, as ever, for the long-lost cause of Young England. The glaring gaps were the new boroughs and the metropolis. But for these Smith could stand as a kind of promise in reserve. There were relics to be discarded: despite Derby's efforts on his behalf, Wilson Patten was paid off with a peerage (Winmarleigh) and the chairmanship of the National Union. There were *novi homines* to be taught a hard lesson. Raikes, that eager ornament of the National Union and prophet of the new epoch of post middle-class borough influence, who expected great things, found himself chairman of committees: in which dim post he was imprisoned relentlessly until the fall of the ministry in 1880. Thus were the 'troublesome men in the party' and the National Union once again put in their places. It was in his distribution of ministerial loaves and fishes that Disraeli most blatantly signalled his attachment for aristocratic government. Abercorn's return to Ireland as viceroy was entirely in order. Derby's younger brother Frederick Stanley made a respectable financial secretary at the War Office. But, in Buckle's words, Disraeli 'astonished his colleagues in the Cabinet by the high position in the public service for which he thought Henry Lennox was suitable'.[21] Lennox, Richmond's brother, was self-deludedly bitter at not getting into the cabinet; and caused infinite trouble until he had to be dumped from the Board of Works in 1875. Lennox had first been thought of for Ireland; but Disraeli concluded that he 'cannot be trusted to go to Ireland': 'he is too much mixed up in companies not of the best sort.'[22] Likewise, 'little George Bentinck' was a flop at the Board of Trade, likened rather to something out of operetta and resented by Lancashire borough Tories as representing, with Adderley, an inappropriately aristocratic ethos. Equally unconvincing was the 24-year-old earl of Pembroke as undersecretary at the War Office, whose taste of office was mercifully brief. Derby, primed no doubt by his brother, told Disraeli of Pembroke that he 'never goes to his office, partly from ill-health, partly from indolence – has ability, but habits of work seem wanting'. Derby urged Cadogan's cause.[23] While such flimsy lordling careers crashed in ruins about him, Disraeli would make slighting remarks about Cross. Derby wondered at Disraeli's 'odd dislike of middle-class men, though they are the strength of our party'.[24]

Disraeli wanted to put his favourite aristocratic sprig, Lord George Hamilton, into the Foreign Office, as undersecretary; but Hamilton's deficiency in French meant that he had to go to the India Office. To the Foreign Office, in exchange, as a gesture of piety for the murdered Mayo, Disraeli sent Mayo's brother, Robert Bourke, of whom few had a high opinion; and who himself had a low opinion of his chief, Derby. In the Household appointments Disraeli could indulge himself harmlessly in a vision of a 'generous aristocracy round a real throne' (though the queen made difficulties about Beauchamp and Bath as 'Ritualists')[25]; and Marlborough was a respectable replacement for Abercorn in Ireland in 1876. But undoubtedly the most grossly symptomatic and damaging case of Disraeli's weakness for the territorial feudality was his appointment of the duke of Northumberland to the cabinet in 1878. Derby scouted rumours of this ducal preferment as being too absurd to be credited.[26] It is probable that even the duke, whose previous political responsibility had been as vice-president of the Board of Trade in 1859, was astonished. The only plausible explanation offered is that Disraeli simply cherished a 'romantic penchant for the great noble houses'.[27]

Northumberland's appointment, at a time when Disraeli's government was under dangerous pressure and in serious need of stiffening, carried political insouciance almost to the point of frivolity. Disraeli's reputation subsequently suffered curiously little from this; mainly because it was needed, ironically, to boost the Tory Democratic cause. Even so, Kebbel felt constrained to comment that perhaps Disraeli 'did not always make sufficient allowance for the inroads which had been made' in the territorial constitution 'during the fifty years that followed the first Reform Bill'.[28] And again: 'I cannot help thinking that he must have sometimes shut his eyes to the effect of recent changes in our political and social system, which have certainly weakened, though they may not have finally destroyed, the foundations of the ancient *regime*.'[29] Kebbel drew a distinction between Disraeli 'in his library, giving rein to his imagination, and tracing all kinds of analogies between the past and present state of politics', and Disraeli 'in the House of Commons, dealing with the actual circumstances and educating his party upon questions calling for immediate settlement'. In the latter capacity 'the popular Toryism with which he is associated was founded on an acute perception of the character of his own times, and of the only means by which Conservatism could become a real power in the country.'[30] The tensions which developed in the party during the time of Disraeli's leadership had to do centrally with the fact that Disraeli's 'acute perception', and the management and generalship he deployed, had for their purpose the frustration of the logical consequence of Derby's proposition about the middle classes being the 'strength of our party', or Cross's insistence that they were the people who in fact brought the government into power. Kebbel observed this side of Disraeli quite accurately:

> In one respect, and in one only, does he seem to have been always the same, and that was in his distrust of the middle classes as an element of political stability. . . . He believed that permanent and powerful governments might be founded on either monarchy, oligarchy, or democracy. But he had no faith in a *bourgeois* constitution.[31]

Frustration would in due course articulate itself. 'Two Conservatives' in 1882 looked back sternly on 1874. 'A Ministry was formed composed almost exclusively of peers and county members. . . . The distinction between county and borough members was revived.'

> It was unfortunately the custom of Lord Beaconsfield to appoint to offices of importance either men of aristocratic antecedents or men of a humbler stamp

who were content to receive and execute his orders. At one time six dukes were serving under him, and among the secondary members of his Government there were not wanting representatives of the blue blood which supported him.[32]

One of the 'Two Conservatives' of 1882 was Gorst, pre-eminent among those claiming to have in fact brought the government into power. There were others who deplored the party leadership's neglect of the new borough interest, and especially its great metropolitan manifestation. Derby was ready to concede that the 'only reasonable fault that I have heard found with us is that we have not done enough for the borough-members'.[33] George Hamilton in 1878 recommended unavailingly to Corry that C.T. Ritchie, one of the new members for Tower Hamlets, should second the address at the opening of the session. He reported Ritchie's complaint that no metropolitan MP had ever been asked.

It was the case of Gorst himself which in 1874 most appositely highlighted the grudged claims of 'the strength of our party'. His position was that his 'official engagement' to the party as interim replacement for Spofforth ended with the election. The awkwardness of his situation was that he had taken on the principal agentship to fill the gap between losing his Commons' seat in 1868 and winning another. But the work of the principal agentship was incompatible with parliamentary ambitions. Being without a seat in 1874 made Gorst ineligible for the first fruits of parliamentary patronage. He expected Central Office to slot him into the first likely vacancy. But such were not strewn thickly upon the ground; and Gorst of all people would have known of the limits to Central Office's capacity to make local associations 'tremble and obey'. Dyke had little alternative but to request Gorst to stay on at Central Office in 'a sort of undefined position', increasingly without power or influence.[34] Dyke assured Disraeli that he felt 'bound to say' that Gorst was 'of great use to me with all his crotchets', and was 'much disposed to keep Gorst in hand crotchets and all'.[35] The end of Gorst's principal-agentship was marked symbolically in 1874 by the removal of Central Office to new premises in St. Stephen's Chambers, Westminster Bridge.[36]

According to his son's later testimony, Gorst made the mistake, with truly proud middle-class diffidence, of not pressing his claims directly on Disraeli in 1874 in the unabashed aristocratic manner with which Disraeli was familiar.[37] Moreover, not only did Gorst fail to beg: he compounded this error by presuming to recommend on behalf of others. After pressing on Disraeli the claims of Keith-Falconer for a vacancy on the Board of Works he added: 'I hope you will not think I am taking too great a liberty in writing to express my opinion on his merits.'[38] There is every ground for supposing Disraeli would think precisely that. Meanwhile, as Gorst waited for his seat, the old managers were sharing the spoils: the baronetcy for Rose, the privy councillorship for Noel, the Inland Revenue place for Keith-Falconer. It was noticeable, however, that Spofforth had to wait much longer. And when Gorst did eventually, in February 1875, get a seat at Chatham, he returned to the House of Commons in a cloud of unappeased grievance. Later he denied having reproached Disraeli personally for responsibility or even awareness 'of the way in which the party managers have since 1874 behaved towards me: and I have received *their* hostility as the natural consequence of my steadfast adherence to those popular principles in politics, which you taught me, which won the boroughs in 1874'.[39] This exemption of Disraeli, profoundly unmerited, was to become the greatest of all Gorst's 'crotchets'.

For the moment, however, Gorst had quite enough other crotchets to be going on with. His particular frustration in February 1874 was the way he was being treated as 'political representative' of the *Standard*. He put it to Corry: 'I have never been so thoroughly 'en rapport' with the leader of the Party as I expected to be when at Noel's request I reluctantly occupied the position.' Memories of his and therefore the *Standard's* gaffe at the time of Gladstone's thwarted resignation in 1873 were still painful. 'At the present time I cannot help seeing that the Times has information denied to me. Such an announcement as that of Lord Salisbury's adhesion to the Party & willingness to take office should I think have been made by the Standard.' With heavily patient reasonableness, Gorst inquired: 'Am I now & on occasions like this to have more information given to me than is given to other papers – or am I at least to have as much as is given to the Times?' Gorst wanted to be able to act to Johnstone, proprietor of the *Standard*, 'in a manner consistent with my own honour'.[40] As between the exigencies of Gorst's honour and the expediency of cultivating Delane, the Conservative managers could never be in doubt. As Dyke was to report later to Disraeli: 'The Standard people are always at him & they will never forgive me.'[41]

3

The grievances of Gorst and his ilk were of small consequence to the Conservative party as it addressed itself to the unwonted responsibilities of majority government. The Conservative party had had power thrust upon it. What to do with it? Unlike the Liberal government in 1869, there was no great or obvious work in hand. Disraeli himself had nothing specific in mind nor much in the way of guidance to offer. After all, the whole point and purpose of Conservatism in 1874 was to establish that the Gladstonian epoch of heroic legislation was an aberration in the otherwise calm flow of government: Conservatism in 1874 would resume where Lord Palmerston left off in 1865. Normality would reassert itself. The problem was that the old normality had been characterised by loose and tangled party lines and collusive front-bench arrangements, whereas the new normality was ushered in by as dramatically decisive an election majority as had been produced in 1868. Conservatism and the Conservative government were to that extent in something of a false position in 1874. They wanted Palmerstonian ends but they held in their hands Gladstonian means.

The business of the session would necessarily be a matter of improvising. There was very little ground for Cross's being famously 'disappointed' at the 'want of originality' and the absence of 'legislative schemes' shown by the prime minister when the cabinet met to discuss the Queen's Speech.[42] The programme of 1872 was an outline without substance. The conditions which obtained in March 1873, when Disraeli protested that he could not go to the constituencies without a policy, still obtained in the circumstances of Gladstone's precipitate dissolution in January 1874. Something like a sessional programme was cobbled together out of any legislative bits and pieces ready to hand. Cross was given the Licensing Act to amend as a sop to the trade. He also took the opportunity to fit in a Factory Act, which, by reducing the statutory hours worked by women and children, had the practical effect of satisfying the general 9 hours movement for all factory workers, particularly strong in Lancashire. Callender made clear to Corry that the election in Lancashire had 'hinged upon 2 questions – the 9 Hours Bill and the demands of the trade unionists'. The 9 hours was the more pressing question, and every Conservative borough candidate in Lancashire was pledged to it. It would be 'in accordance with the previous vote of Mr. Disraeli, Lord John Manners and other leading members of the Cabinet . . . it would strengthen all we have said as to the policy of the Conservative party attending to the health and comfort of the nation rather than wretched political agitation.'[43] Gorst also had his finger firmly in this pie. He warned Disraeli before the dissolution in January that there was grave danger of the Liberal government's striking a deal with the leaders of the 9 hours movement; and that Mundella had a bill ready for the purpose; and that William Fison, W.E. Forster's partner 'and one of our most active supporters in the West Riding', together with Callender wanted to consult with Disraeli for advice as to how best to exert their own influence with the 9 hours leadership.[44] As things turned out, Cross was in a position to trump Mundella. The thing looked very well as an earnest of the government's good faith on the larger question of social reform.

Northcote would also do his best to make something out of the budget. Despite a surplus in hand of £5 million there was no notion of out-doing Gladstone by abolishing the income tax. Northcote, indeed, wanted to keep it where Lowe had left it, at 3d in the pound, to allow for a mass of remissions on brewers' licences, sugar, horses, railways, police subsidy, and relief for lower incomes. 'The Brewers then, being disposed of, and the rate-payers presumed to be satisfied, there are no other complainants of whom I am afraid,' Northcote assured Disraeli, 'provided we can face the anti-Income Tax agitators.'[45] Disraeli, however, deemed it 'indispensable' that a penny be taken off the income tax; with a separate rating bill to relieve taxpayers of police and lunacy burdens. Salisbury was more concerned about the exemption levels. He wanted the level to be raised from £100 to Peel's original figure of £150. 'My fear is that whatever we do on these distinctly class issues', he told Northcote, 'will be the starting point for concessions to the democratic party on the part of our adversaries hereafter: & will moreover give cause to the enemy to blaspheme at present.' Do not, he urged Northcote, 'let them have any reason for saying that we are bidding for Fred. Harrison: & don't promote graduated income tax to a place in the list of possible policies'.[46] Northcote, at all events, achieved in 1874–6 the distinction of having reduced the income tax to its lowest rate in the history of the British revenue. Northcote's business went smoothly. As Derby remarked, 'You seem to be getting well through your budget troubles: to which Gladstone certainly is not disposed to add.'[47]

Gladstone in truth had virtually renounced active leadership of the Liberal opposition. This greatly eased the government's way. The county franchise issue, raised with dog-like persistence yet again by the Radicals, was faced down, with much flourishing of Winn's researches about the fate of borough seats. He now offered calculations that the effect of equal electoral districts would mean the extinction of 147 English borough seats, 13 Scottish, and 27 Irish, with a vast excess of county over borough electors.[48] Gladstone kept away. Lowe supported the government. Hartington led the Whigs out of the chamber without voting. Butt's motion on Irish Home Rule was likewise confidently faced down. It was, however, slightly disturbing that though Beach was rearmed with coercive powers, he seemed to be pursuing a distinctly conciliatory line. Irish Conservatives grew restless; after so many defeats and humiliations they looked to the new government for reassurance and unbendingly unionist orthodoxy. Lord Arthur Hill, MP for Down, passed on through Northcote the warning that Beach should understand the 'importance of treating our Irish friends with more confidence etc.' 'As it is, they are taking it into their heads that he ignores them and takes counsel of the Home Rulers, and this idea may do harm.' It would be worth while, Northcote added for Disraeli's benefit, if something could be done to keep them in a good humour. 'The sort of talk in which they indulge is calculated to injure us with some of the English friends among whom they sit, and I think a little time could be well spent, or even well wasted, in talking over questions with them before they come on.'[49]

Still, there seemed little reason to doubt that a salient feature of the restored political normality would be successful in keeping Ireland largely out of sight and out of mind. As Salisbury had put it in 1873 when outlining the general lineaments of a post-Gladstone political order, 'Parliament seems at last to have parted from the maxim that everything is to be given to those who bluster for it.' The days of 'pulpy statesmanship' were past.[50] One token of a sterner Toryism was Sandon's Endowed Schools Act Amendment Bill, much applauded by Salisbury, which aimed at restoring to Church of England schools upon which their founders had impressed a distinct church character certain powers removed in the previous parliament. This was, specifically, 'reaction'; and it cost Disraeli some trouble to steer a conciliatory course between Liberal outrage and Salisbury, 'alone, but very unmanageable'. It was more important, on the whole, that the Conservative party's educational shibboleth, Clause 25 of the 1870 act, should be successfully defended.[51]

Putting down Ritualism

1

All these things added up to a perfectly creditable parliamentary performance by the new Conservative government; and the 1874 session, on the strength of it, could have been justified on grounds of restoring a desirably unhectic politics. Much of ministers' time was innocently taken up by such problems as whether, and how much, to contribute to the funeral expenses of the late African missionary, David Livingstone, whose alleged corpse lay embarrassingly unattended. Derby was inclined to urge Northcote to give way to the 'Livingstone enthusiasm', arguing that it would be 'a popular move generally, but especially in Scotland'. Disraeli 'half-believed' the affair was a 'swindling transaction got up by young Bennett of the New York Herald & Stanley'.[52] Disraeli's noticeable torpidity seemed appropriate to this new style of politics. He disguised it by cultivating an image of an impassive hieratic mask of sphinx-like Sidonian statesmanship.

The latter end of the 1874 session, however, was marked by an ecclesiastical storm provoked by the Public Worship Regulation Bill.[53] This, originally introduced as a private measure by Archbishop Tait in the Lords, aimed at tightening the disciplinary powers exercised by diocesan bishops over their clergy. The archbishop's initiative was the result of a long train of consultations arising from the public scandal caused by the 'ritualistic' practices of certain High Church 'Anglo-Catholic' clergy, held to savour of popery. The recent case of the Rev. Mr Purchas in Brighton indicated deficiencies in the existing state of the law. Gladstone had announced that something needed to be done, but did nothing. The church authorities decided that they would have to take action on their own behalf. It so happened that Tait's initiative coincided, quite undesignedly, with the coming into office of the Conservative government. Already the bishop of Gloucester and Bristol, in dilating to Disraeli on the '*most* critical' state of the Church at the time of Gladstone's dissolution of the old parliament, had put his view of the nub of the matter in candidly Gladstonophobe terms:

> This Romanism, fostered by the evil genius and I fear inward predilection of one man, has now penetrated the whole body of the *Clergy* (not easily) to an extent that can hardly be conceived, – and this one man, ere he is hurled from office, may yet do more mischief in the same evil direction.[54]

As events proved, it was going to be easy for the Ellicotts of the Church to draw out Disraeli's inveterate dislike of High Church sacerdotalism with the bait of Gladstone's 'ecclesiastical unsoundness'.[55]

As with all ecclesiastical causes of that era, the technicalities of an ostensibly minor item of projected legislation carried, like electrical conductors, enormous charges of religious energy. The climate of religion was at high pressure. The acts of the Vatican Council reverberated throughout Europe. In 1872, as the Prussian government launched a drive against Roman Catholic influence in schools, made civil marriage compulsory, and banished the Jesuits, Bismarck defiantly announced that he would 'never go to Canossa'. In 1873 the Prussian authorities sharpened their assault with the May Laws. It was to these events that Disraeli alluded in his Glasgow speech, when he referred to a Europe convulsed in a grand conflict involving the two deleterious forces of infidelity and ultramontane sacerdotal usurpation; and when he sketched the 'noble part' Britain could play in such a struggle, taking a firm stand on the principles of the Reformation, if only a 'national party' were allowed to govern.[56]

Now the national party governed. And, somewhat as with 1841, the Conservative reaction of 1874 was itself intensely charged with religion of a distinctly churchly and Protestant cast: that 'steady infiltration of Church principles' which the bishop of Gloucester and Bristol had not scrupled to impress upon Disraeli had 'much to do with the victory at Stroud'.[57] Tait and his friends in the Church now found themselves in a fortuitously promising situation: not only was the High Church Gladstone, likely only to be an obstacle, out of the way, but they had Disraeli, standing firmly on the principles of the Reformation, to all appearances at their service. Tait lost no time in impressing upon the prime minister the view of himself and his right revered brethren, heartily concurred in by the queen, that unless the Church found 'some simple, summary, and inexpensive process, for securing obedience to the law', it would 'go on the breakers'. Tait concluded: 'I think you may be able and willing to help us.'[58]

Disraeli was indeed willing and, eventually, only too able. Here at last was the prospect of a Protestant militancy which, unlike 1868 and the Irish Church, was a truly popular cause. While it could not be positively asserted that Disraeli was spoiling for a fight with the 'Rits', there is no question but that he had convinced himself that they were planning an imminent aggression. He told Derby in October 1873 that he was quite prepared to go against the Ritualists if necessary. He thought they were about 7,000 strong among the clergy, and would 'before long make some decisive move to test the strength of their position'.[59] Another very important difference was that in 1874 the queen chose conspicuously not to exert the cautious and restraining influence she had exercised in 1868. From the party point of view there were inhibiting considerations to give pause. Whatever line the government took, it could not fail to give some degree of offence to one or other of the ecclesiastical parties. Would the damage done by resisting the Protestant tide be less than by going with it? The latter could be justified as, in Gorst's phrase, the 'least disadvantageous course open to us'.[60] But there would be obstacles to this in the very seat of government.

Salisbury had remarked ominously at the time of his adhesion to the government of his anxieties about possible legislation against scandalous

Ritualists. Carnarvon and Hardy would also be offended at any ecclesiastical policy which seemed to mark out the High Church for special pains and penalties. Derby advised Disraeli that there was no doubt that Tait's proposal would be popular in the country, but that that in itself might not be enough to keep Salisbury and his other High Church friends under restraint.

> I don't imagine that Salisbury is exactly a 'Ritualist': in fact he makes no secret of his opinion that that party are bringing the cause into contempt by their follies: but he sympathises with a great deal of what they teach, and (like Gladstone) he attaches more importance, personally, to that class of questions than to all political or national considerations. His feeling in that respect seems to me exactly what it was when he left Oxford.[61]

Cairns made it clear that, though in his own way a militantly Orange Low Churchman, he considered it likely to be 'a very embarrassing question'; and warned of his 'strong opinion' that if it were to be attempted to carry or support such a bill as Public Worship Regulation '*as a Government*, it wd lead to a secession of several members of the Cabinet'.[62]

Thus for the time being Disraeli held his hand. The archbishop of Canterbury's bill, much amended and patched up by Cairns, passed through the Lords under the eyes of a neutral government. But though the government remained neutral, the bill did not. It was now manifestly a partisanly Protestant bill; the queen herself avowing it as such, indiscreetly. Salisbury warned Disraeli that the queen must be 'calmed'. 'If the notion that she was personally pressing a one-sided legislation got abroad, it would produce really disastrous events.' Salisbury pressed upon Disraeli his view about the need for a mutually tolerant forbearance within the Church and the need for that forbearance to be reflected in the government's ecclesiastical policy. 'I can't help feeling that a principle which all sides might fairly accept is that we should recognise and frankly tolerate the three great schools in the Church' – which he dubbed the 'sacramental', the 'emotional', and the 'philosophical' – 'but that all individual eccentricities should be repressed. If that principle were accepted there would be little difficulty in coming to an agreement.'[63] Salisbury was willing to see an amended and more workable version along such lines through the Lords on the basis of continued government neutrality. Cairns was careful to reiterate his insistence that 'it wd be really safer & easier that in the further stages of the Bill, it shd be considered an open question'.[64]

Had Tait's bill then been allowed to proceed into the Commons under the guidance of the recorder of London, Russell Gurney, for what it was, an ecclesiastical curiosity, little more would have been heard of it. Salisbury had already pointed accurately to the nub of the archbishop's legislative difficulty: he was 'asking for an impossibility – that it shall be made as easy to apply a much disputed law, as if it were undisputed.'[65]

Why did Disraeli abandon prudent neutrality and commit himself and his government to 'afford facilities' for making sure that the bill would not fail? His speech of 15 July resonated with notorious phrases: it was candidly a bill to 'put down Ritualism'; to suppress the 'Mass in masquerade'.[66] Kebbel later shudderingly recorded that these catchphrases 'did him an infinity of harm'. Such expressions 'rather jarred on the *ethos* . . . of a highly cultivated class, always shrinking from epigram on sacred subjects'.[67] Disraeli, however, calculated that he need not be too worried by this highly cultivated class. Information from Dyke told him that he had little to fear from the High Church and that he could safely be stronger on the stronger side.[68] There was no doubt, at least in the short term, about the strength of popular Protestant opinion. The perhaps less cultivated but certainly less shrinking and more numerous classes of Orange Lancashire were reported as adamant that if the government gave way to Ritualist agitation the 'consequences would be most serious and that in fact no member should be returned for any division of the county or any borough on our side of the House who voted against the bill'. And if the bill were delayed to a future session there might be serious divisions in the party. Cross had been informed that he might 'assure Mr. Disraeli that no member of this part of the country who votes against the bill can hope to be returned'.[69]

Menaces of this kind are generally easily discountable by politicians. They are also readily available to reinforce a prevailing disposition. There were other reinforcements at that time of formidable weight. Tait wrote to Disraeli on 8 July that the queen had desired him to state the reasons which made it 'highly inexpedient' that the Public Worship Regulation Bill should fail to pass that session. Agitation for a further year would be dangerous to the Church. Violent Dissenters and Romanising High churchmen would have time to coalesce. Bishops might be intimidated in convocation. Postponement would be regarded as a triumph for the 'violent party'.[70] Then on 9 July Gladstone intervened with a passionate attack on the bill and six voluminous resolutions. This provoked a rift in the Liberal ranks, which Disraeli studiously observed. The combination of incitements was irresistible for Disraeli. Whatever doubts there might be about opinion in the country, there no doubt that the bill had the overwhelming support of parliament. The queen bombarded Disraeli with demands for an assertion of Protestant faith, and insisted that he should state to the cabinet how strongly she grieved at their want of 'Protestant feeling'. By 11 July she could thank Disraeli for his reassurances and remark that 'Mr. Disraeli must have managed his refractory Cabinet most skilfully'.[71] Derby noted how urgently the 'Bishops' Bill' impinged. 'Northcote says majority for in Commons wd be nearer 300 than 200. Disraeli told us plainly that the question was not now whether we should let the bill pass or not, but whether the House would not take matters into its own hands.' There was general agreement among Cairns, Cross, and Derby that ministers should put themselves at the head of the movement 'if only to be able to control it better'. Hardy, Hunt, Salisbury, and to a lesser degree Northcote opposed, but gave way before thc obvious necessities of the case. Derby observed with satisfaction a 'marked desire to keep together', Salisbury especially having 'an inclination to conciliate: which is not his nature, and particularly not where ecclesiastical questions are concerned'.[72] The obvious necessities of the case rather than skill freed Disraeli to announce his message to the Commons and the country: that the world was watching a great struggle between temporal and spiritual power, and that Britain could set an example by rallying around 'the broad platform of the Reformation', and the 'institutions of the Church of England, based on those principles of the Reformation which the Church was called into being to represent'.[73]

It need not, however, be supposed that the queen's bombardment was decisive in pushing Disraeli towards his crucial intervention of 15 July. Disraeli was perfectly capable of generating his own inner-directed ecclesiastical motivations. Quite what his Protestantism precisely consisted of was never very clear; but whatever it was, it was an urgent, genuine, and consistent sentiment. When Pakington wrote in puzzlement to Northcote in April 1868 about Disraeli's 'startling passage' denouncing Gladstone as 'the Representative of a combination of Roman Catholics & Ritualists to seize upon the supreme authority of this Realm!', remarking that such a statement must be most important, or most serious, he despairingly concluded: 'what does it really mean?'[74] What must be supposed is that it really meant, in Disraeli's own formula, that he half-believed what he said. It is also material to point out that while in 1868 Disraeli's talk of the 'ultimate triumph of the Church of Rome' and the 'supremacy of a foreign prince' was dismissible as a bad joke in embarrassing taste, by 1874 that was no longer quite the case. The new *Zeitgeist* and the backbench pressure which embodied it no doubt greatly aided Disraeli's handling of his refractory cabinet. Certainly, Gladstone thought it worth while later in 1874 to acknowledge the force of that *Zeitgeist* by producing his own 'political expostulation' against the machinations of a foreign prince in *The Vatican Decrees in their Bearing on Civil Allegiance*.

The bill, with virulently Protestant amendments, passed triumphantly in the Commons without a division. Gladstone and those Conservatives led by Hardy who supported him were routed. Back in the Lords, resistance to the amendments was led by Salisbury and Carnarvon. This caused a dangerous brush between Disraeli and Salisbury. Salisbury's forthright defiance of Commons' 'bluster' led Disraeli to characterise the secretary of state for India as a 'great master of gibes, and flouts, and jeers'.[75] This, of course, was quite accurate; but, as Hardy remarked, inexpedient: 'too strong in his terms & dangerously so.'[76] Salisbury and Disraeli both took immediate steps to defuse the potential explosion. Another personal breach after the break of 1867–74 would have been too absurd. Having swallowed the camel of Disraeli, Salisbury would not strain at even so distasteful a gnat as the Public Worship Bill, particularly as he could discern its practical unworkability. Tait, alarmed particularly by Gladstone's talk of abandoning the establishment, set about circumventing the difficulties. High Church Conservatives nursed their bruises and resentments. Carnarvon was so annoyed that 'it sent me down to the country very much indisposed'. He thought Disraeli's speech 'most offensive'.[77] Hardy recorded his heartfelt hopes that 'no such sundering measure will be blundered over by the Archbishop again'.[78]

2

The Public Worship Regulation Act did not put down Ritualism. It persecuted Ritualists. Its judicial enforcer, Lord Penzance, created a series of clerical martyrs whose martyrdoms kept the Church in feverish distemper over the coming years. Dean Wellesley's advice in 1868 was as true in 1874 as then: the public would not tolerate popishness, but it would equally not tolerate its suppression by the 'Puritanical party'.[79] Disraeli would have been well advised to have kept as healthy a distance as feasible from Archbishop Tait's plans. There is no doubt that Disraeli's going so far beyond the 'necessities of the case' and blatantly identifying his government with the Public Worship policy lost the Conservative party more from High Church alienation than it gained from Protestant gratitude. Nothing, for example, was gained from the 'profound admiration of your conduct of the Public Worship Bill' which the senior curate of St. Paul's, Shotford, conveyed to Disraeli. He fully supported the 'importance of something being done to stamp out Ritualism'; 'and I never felt so proud of having voted for your supporters (Mr. Baring & Col^{n} Makins).'[80] As against that, many Conservative MPs were worried about High Church defection. Henry Drummond Wolff, MP for Christchurch, wrote to Disraeli enclosing a letter from a clerical constituent known to be a 'strong Conservative exercising considerable influence' informing him that if the bill were to pass 'not a few of us will be forced to change our political coats & go in for disestablishment'.[81] Wolff returned to the point later, vainly urging the great importance of 'making the question as little as possible irritating to the Constituencies & embarrassing to their representatives'.[82]

Gorst reported much the same kind of reaction via a former Conservative agent in Derby. It had been difficult enough persuading many Conservative High churchmen to vote against Gladstone; and now 'nearly a score of influential electors' in south Derbyshire 'will certainly not *again* vote for any supporter of the ministry. This is serious, for it cuts only *one* way.' Liberal Low churchmen would never vote against the Liberal party in gratitude; many Whig Low churchmen who detested Gladstone's ecclesiastical appointments were still always ready to support his political friends at the polling booth. Though the Conservatives had a large majority in the house, most seats were secured by narrow majorities. In the three divisions of Derbyshire parties were very evenly balanced. 'Forty or fifty influential men would make a great difference. The clergy have now, under the Household and Twelve Pound franchise, more *personal* influence than before. Twenty clergymen going wrong, represents at *least*, on an average, eighty votes.'[83] There was no stint of confirmatory evidence. Thus the rector of South Normanton to Disraeli:

> I cannot tell you the grief it is to me to be compelled thereby to set aside every political tradition of my childhood, and conviction of more mature years, in resigning my post on our 'Local Conservative Committee' at the very moment of victory, and in giving my support to one whom hitherto I have opposed with all the vehemence in my power.[84]

Such signals were of course often concerted and a familiar tactical feature of the game of politics. Even so, when Gorst at the end of 1874 enclosed a letter for Disraeli's notice from an alienated elector in Bath, he was in no doubt that it was indicative of 'a state of feeling on the part of a section of our Party, which has been several times brought to my notice from different quarters during the recess'. No doubt the government, as Gorst tactfully allowed, took on the Public Worship Regulation Bill the 'least disadvantageous course open to us'; but still the result was 'to alienate an important class of our supporters'.

> The High Church party has always seemed to me to occupy on our side a position somewhat analogous to the ultra-dissenters on the other: it has an electoral importance beyond what is due to its mere numbers, and holds opinions, & principles to which party interests are subordinated. There is nothing like an open rupture yet . . . but we must not shut our eyes to the existence of a good deal of sore feeling, which future events may allay or aggravate. If the Archbishop of Canterbury pursues his career of ecclesiastical legislation, there seems to me great danger of the Government being broken up by the High Church Party, as Gladstone's was by the Dissenters.[85]

Here Gorst, the redundant former principal agent, was tactfully giving advice which tactlessly exposed the limitations of Sir William Hart Dyke's appreciation as chief whip of the salient bearings of the case. Certainly, when the Conservative party was next under pressure, in the 1890s, to embark upon a Protestant crusade, its leadership tenaciously declined to undertake it.

3

After the excited flurry of the Public Worship Bill crisis came recessional repose. There seemed nothing difficult or dangerous now in view. In September Derby felt able to assert that 'we are doing very well', and that 'there is absolutely not a cry of any kind that has attracted the least public attention of late'. His opinion that the Conservatives 'ought to be in for 3 or 4 years'[86] seemed, in the circumstances, a curiously modest estimate. (Derby's humour was one of melancholic phlegm: 'Politics are uncertain,' he avowed in January 1875, 'but never since I entered parliament, now 26 years ago, have I known a state of things such as exists now. . . . Yet who will guarantee that this state of things shall last for twelve months?')[87] Northcote felt able to refer in October to 'cloudless skies', though stipulating deprecatingly that he was 'not over-fond of them'.[88] Disraeli himself adopted the phrase in reporting to Cairns of a conversation with the French ambassador: 'Jarnac whom I saw, as

I passed thro' town, said "You have not got a single internal difficulty." I hope he is a prophet, but I am not an admirer – at least in politics – of cloudless skies.'[89] Salisbury, at Dieppe, was back in perfectly good humour. 'I think M. de Jarnac is right. I do not see at present any elements of trouble at home.'[90] So tranquil seemed the lull that Richmond even had hopes of seeing Disraeli at the Doncaster races.

There was even talk of an autumn visit by the prime minister to Ireland. A curious peace reigned there: the peace of the death of Irish Liberalism. That had produced a kind of eerie political desert stillness. Taylor thought that, 'properly managed', a tour by Disraeli '*would do good*',[91] Cairns hoped it might do good in the direction earlier pressed for by Gladstone. He wished Disraeli to consider 'whether some scheme might not be devised for extending to Ireland, in some shape the sunshine of a Royal presence'. Abercorn would offer all assistance.[92] Disraeli flinched at the fatigues. Derby was forthrightly hostile: 'What are you going to say to the Irish?' The thought of 'what may be said' made Cairns 'uneasy'. It was impossible that Disraeli 'should make a series of speeches to mixed audiences of Protestants and Catholics without saying something that must cause offence'.[93] In any case a relapse in Disraeli's health made the project impossible. Northcote, no doubt with Cairns's notions in mind as well as worries about how to handle the question of coercion legislation, thought this a 'real misfortune'.[94] Disraeli, however, would have had no stomach for resuming Gladstone's lost battle with the queen to persuade her to extend the sunshine of a royal presence to Ireland. It is doubtful also whether there was much substance in Taylor's hopes for benefits to the Conservative party's Irish interests. In a larger view, however, there is no doubt that it was a misfortune that a Conservative prime minister should not have been able to extend to Ireland the courtesy of a visit. And there were dangers in keeping Ireland too much out of sight and out of mind. What seemed peace could turn out to be a lull. Perhaps it was the greater misfortune that the possibility of a visit by Disraeli never thereafter took shape. Some sense of Ireland within a few years' time on the brink of agrarian catastrophe might have been an illuminating component of Disraeli's political awareness. Cabinets in November were informed by the Dublin Castle authorities that the Coercion Acts could be dispensed with: 'they have succeeded so completely that they have destroyed the evidence for their own necessity.'[95]

At the end of 1874, however, Disraeli's political awareness was shaped rather by a sense almost of complacent insouciance. He looked forward to the prospect of 'an active, but serene session'.[96] Northcote, reporting Salisbury in 'great force' at his hideous Dieppe villa, confirmed to Cairns his earlier opinion that 'we have materials enough for a good Session'. Cross was at work on the problem of housing for the working classes. Merchant shipping would be attended to; friendly societies likewise. As regards the revenue, he felt 'very cheerful'. 'I have had a cheerful note from Disraeli, giving a good account of himself, which Corry also confirms. He says we must begin cabinets next month, and he is beginning to consider questions for discussion.'[97] Disraeli prepared the way in his November speech at the Guildhall, in which he affirmed the reality of the Conservative working man and the government's interest in the social improvement of the people. He prepared the queen by reporting on the cabinet discussion of legislation for the 'Improvement of the Dwellings of the People', and other measures to complete the code of sanitary legislation. Salisbury's attempt to include some aggressive work for the Church on the endowed schools question was foiled by Hardy's reluctance to support. Derby, distrustful of Salisbury's churchly zeal and convinced that the issue 'may break up the cabinet', could exclaim in relief: 'Thank God, we have got rid of the only rock a-head!'[98]

One undercurrent of anxiety, however, persisted. Disraeli was quite seriously ill at the end of November. 'Reports are current', recorded Derby, 'as to his not being able to go on long: a prospect which for many reasons I do not like to contemplate.'[99] Such was the apprehension of possible crisis that Salisbury got it into his head that there was 'in some quarters a project for making the D. of Richmond the next Premier, when Disraeli's health compels him to resign': an event which Salisbury evidently considered as 'not far distant'. Salisbury protested to Derby against this, 'says it must not be allowed, that the Duke is unfit for the post, that his appointment would justify the title of the "stupid party" as applied to us'; and that in the event of a vacancy Derby must assert his claim. (A great part of Salisbury's aversion to Richmond was because of Richmond's being 'entirely under the influence of Cairns', and especially of Cairns's partiality for 'low' ecclesiastical preferments.) Derby responded in a non-committal fashion, mainly with diversionary remarks on the weakness of any alternative lead to Disraeli in the House of Commons ('I did not enlarge on this, but it is impossible not to see that Hardy, with abundant fluency and rhetorical power, wants judgment, and that Northcote, whose judgment and sound sense can be relied on, is too heavy a speaker to be an effective chief').[100]

Notes and References

1 P. Smith, *Disraelian Conservatism and Social Reform* (1967) 272, n.1.
2 Derby Diary, 9 July 77.
3 Lord Chilston, *W.H. Smith* (1965), 94. Gilbert and Sullivan took up the point in *HMS Pinafore*.
4 R. Nevill (ed.), *Leaves from the Note-books of Lady Dorothy Nevill* (1907), 75.
5 Derby Diary, 4 March 1875.
6 *Ibid.*, 15 March 1872. Derby was commenting on the essays on France by Reeve, editor of the *Edinburgh Review*.
7 Kebbel recorded his pride in the 'intimacy' which Disraeli 'allowed and encouraged'; and his pride also in the 'encomium' he received at the hands of Rowton (Corry) that their 'dear friend' specified Kebbel as 'one who understood him', when 'there were not many such at that time.' T.E. Kebbel, *Lord Beaconsfield and Other Tory Memories* (1907), 66, 70.
8 *Ibid.*, 65–6. See also Buckle, i, 1057 on Disraeli's 'aristocratic fibre'.
9 Kebbel, *Lord Beaconsfield and Other Tory Memories*, 43–3.
10 R. Stewart, *The Foundation of the Conservative Party 1830–1867* (1978), 294.
11 Disraeli to Cairns, 16 Oct. 1874; PRO, Cairns 30/51/1.
12 Buckle, ii, 626. Pakington was shunted to the Lords as Lord Hampton.
13 Cecil, *Salisbury*, ii, 42–3
14 *Ibid.*, 44.
15 *Ibid*, 44–6.
16 *Ibid*, 48–9.
17 Derby Diary, 9 and 11 Feb. 1874.
18 See R. Blake, *Disraeli* (1966), 539.
19 R.A. Cross, *A Political History* (privately printed 1903), 23.
20 Hardy, *Diary*, 196.
21 Buckle, ii, 1421.
22 Derby Diary, 17 Feb. 1874. This was a reference to the stockjobber and company promoter Albert Gottheimer, who called himself Baron Grant.
23 *Ibid.*, 21 April 1875.
24 Derby Diary, 9 July 1877.
25 Buckle, ii, 634–5.
26 Derby Diary, 30 Jan. 1878; 1 Feb. 1878.
27 Blake, *Disraeli*, 657. See also Buckle, ii, 1152. Northumberland was one

of the few cabinet ministers not included in the *Dictionary of National Biography*.

28 Kebbel, *Lord Beaconsfield and Other Tory Memories*, 66.
29 *Ibid.*, 170.
30 *Ibid.*, 167–8.
31 *Ibid.*
32 'Two Conservatives', 'The state of the opposition', *Fortnightly Review*, Nov. 1882, 669, 673. The authors were Gorst and Randolph Churchill.
33 Derby Diary, 9 July 1877.
34 Gorst to Beaconsfield, 3 March 1877; HP, B/XXI/G/258.
35 Dyke to Disraeli, 8 Dec. [1874]; HP, B/XXI/D/463.
36 E.J. Feuchtwanger, *Disraeli, Democracy and the Tory Party* (Oxford 1968), 132.
37 H. Gorst, *The Fourth Party* (1906), 34.
38 Gorst to Disraeli, 26 Feb. 1874; HP, B/XXV/G/250.
39 Gorst to Beaconsfield, 4 April 1878, HP, B/XXV/G/259.
40 Gorst to Corry, 19 Feb. 1874; HP, B/XXV/G/249.
41 Dyke to Disraeli, 8 Dec. [1874]; HP, B/XXV/D/463.
42 Cross, *Political History*, 25.
43 Feuchtwanger, *Disraeli, Democracy and the Tory Party*, 213–14.
44 Gorst to Disraeli, 19 Jan. 1874; HP, B/XXI/G/247.
45 Northcote to Disraeli, 22 March 1874; Bl, Iddesleigh 50016, 178.
46 Salisbury to Northcote, 25 March, 1874. BL, Iddesleigh 50019, 25.
47 Derby to Northcote, 24 April, 1874; BL, Iddesleigh 50022, 103.
48 Memo, 13 May 1874; HP, B/XII/E/111.
49 Northcote to Disraeli, 3 June 1874; BL, Iddesleigh 50016, 228.
50 *QR*, Oct. 1873, 574.
51 Buckle, ii, 673; J.P. Parry, *Democracy and Religion. Gladstone and the Liberal Party 1867–1875* (1986), 412.
52 Northcote to Disraeli, 9 April 74; BL, Iddesleigh 50016, 209. Disraeli to Northcote, 9 April 1874; BL, Iddesleigh 50016, 211. Derby to Northcote, 24 April and 11 June 1874; BL, Iddesleigh 50016, 103, 105.
53 For the issue generally see G. I. T. Machin, *Politics and the Churches in Great Britain, 1869–1921* (Oxford 1987), 70–86.
54 Ellicott to Disraeli, 24 Jan. 1874; HP, B/XII/F/la.
55 Parry, *Democracy and Religion*, 416.
56 See below, 167.
57 Ellicott to Disraeli, 24 Jan. 1874; HP, B/XII/F/la.
58 Buckle, ii, 655–6.
59 Derby Diary, 12 Oct. 1873.
60 Gorst to Disraeli, 16 Dec. 1874; HP, B/XII/F/81a.
61 Derby to Disraeli, 25 March 1874; HP, B/XII/F/21a.
62 Cairns to Disraeli, 25 March 1874; HP, B/XII/F/34.
63 Salisbury to Disraeli, n.d. HP, B/XX/Ce/175, 177.
64 Cairns to Disraeli, 12 May 1874; HP, B/XII/F/25.
65 Salisbury to Disraeli [Feb. 1874]; HP, B/XX/Ce/171.
66 *PD*, ccxxi, 78, 80.
67 Kebbel, *Lord Beaconsfield and Other Tory memories*, 51–2.
68 Feuchtwanger, *Disraeli, Democracy and the Tory Party*, 61.
69 *Ibid.*, 99–100.

70 Tait to Disraeli, 8 July 1874; HP, B/XII/F/16. The queen was censored from the text in R.T. Davidson and W. Benham, *Life of Archibald Campbell Tait, Archbishop of Canterbury* (1891), ii, 212.
71 Buckle, ii, 664.
72 Derby Diary, 11 July 1874.
73 *PD*, ccxxi, 78–80.
74 See above, 40, 50.
75 *PD*, ccxxi, 1358–9.
76 Hardy, *Diary*, 217.
77 Carnarvon to Northcote, 14 Aug. 1874; BL, Iddesleigh 50022, 198.
78 Hardy, *Diary*, 217.
79 See above, 53.
80 R. Bayne to Disraeli, 6 Aug. 1874; HP, B/XX/F/73.
81 Wolff to Disraeli, 28 June 1874; HP, B/XII/F/51a.
82 Wolff to Disraeli, 11 July 1874; HP, B/XII/F/62.
83 Feuchtwanger, *Disraeli, Democracy and the Tory Party*, 100.
84 Massey to Disraeli, 1 Aug. 1874; HP, B/XII/F/68.
85 Gorst to Disraeli, 16 Dec. 1874; HP, B/XII/F/81a. See also Derby Diary, 14 Nov. 1874.
86 Buckle, ii, 687.
87 Derby Diary, 28 Jan. 1875.
88 Northcote to Disraeli, 14 Oct. 1874; BL, Iddesleigh 50016, 254.
89 Disraeli to Cairns, 16 Oct. 1874; PRO, Cairns 30/51/1.
90 Salisbury to Disraeli, 13 Oct. 1874; HP, B/XX/Ce/267.
91 Taylor to Corry, 24 July [1874]; HP, B/XII/J/1.
92 Cairns to Disraeli, 24 Aug. 1874; HP, B/XXI/Ca/123.
93 Buckle, ii, 686; Derby Diary, 15, 22 Sept. 1874.
94 Northcote to Disraeli, 9 Oct. 1874; BL, Iddesleigh 50016, 251.
95 Derby Diary, 17 Nov. 1874.
96 Buckle, ii, 702.
97 Northcote to Cairns, 14 Oct. 1874; PRO, Cairns 30/51/5.
98 Buckle, ii, 700–1; Derby Diary, 22 Sept. 1874.
99 *Ibid.*, 28 Nov. 1874.
100 *Ibid.*, 2 Dec. 1874. 'Stupid party' refers to J.S. Mill's famous dictum that the Conservatives were 'by the law of their existence the stupidest party' *Considerations on Representative Government* (1861), 138.

Chapter 9

'More than one useful measure of domestic reform'

Suet pudding and ambrosia

1

The great irony of the Conservative social reform programme was that it was later depicted in Conservative propaganda as the work of an heroic era, whereas in its day it was intended to convey precisely the opposite effect. Disraeli's government saw it as a kind of political bromide, a salutary contrast to Gladstone's alarms and excursions. Conservative party managers of the 1890s transformed what Thomas Salt, Conservative MP for Stafford, called in 1875 'suet pudding legislation', 'flat, insipid, dull', if 'very wise and very wholesome',[1] into political nectar and ambrosia. Alexander Macdonald, former president of the National Miners' Association, chairman of the Trades Union Council's Parliamentary Committee, and in 1874 one of the first Labour MPs, declared in January 1879: 'the Conservative party has done more for the working classes in five years than the Liberals have in fifty. You have gained more from Conservatives in matters affecting working men than the Liberals would ever dare have granted.' These became among the most oft-quoted words in the voluminous literature issued over the next 20 years by Conservative Central Office and the National Union.[2] Cross made his mark at the Home Office in 1874 and 'gained much credit', according to his patron, Derby, 'by carrying his Factories Bill through without amendments, though much pressed on both sides.'[3]

By the 1880s and the 1890s the question of the relationship between politics and the modern state and modern society had become what it was not in the 1870s: serious. The Conservative party nurtured itself felicitously on these ambrosial secretions. *Conservative Legislation for the Working-classes*[4] of 1891 evoked a bright image of Lord Beaconsfield foremost in legislation 'which has humanised the toil of the people', commencing with the Factories Act of 1874. 'The Conservative party and the working class', Chapter 3 of the *Campaign Guide* for 1892, emphasised particularly the role of the Employers and Workmen and the Conspiracy and Protection of Property Acts of 1875 in its retrospect. *Freedom for Working Men*[5] of 1896 insisted that it was 'largely due to the Conservative Party that Trade Unionism owes its very existence'. *The Rights of Labour, A Word to Working Men*,[6] also of 1896, quoted another grateful Labour leader, George Howell, describing the trade union legislation of 1875 as the 'charter of industrial freedom'. Joseph Chamberlain, by this time a leader of the Liberal Unionists, in a speech at Sunderland in 1891, represented the Conservative social reform legislation as being on a par with the Liberal legislative achievement.

> If you look back to our recent political history you will find that, while it has been the great glory of the Liberal party to remove privileges, imposts, limitations of every kind, and to leave the individual free to create the best of his talents and opportunities, *to the Conservative party belongs the credit for almost all the social legislation of our time.*[7]

Never did a political party make, unwittingly, a more profitable investment for the future in half a dozen items of low-key legislation.

That they were going to be low-key was determined, among other things, by Northcote's concern to stake out limits and make sure there would be no serious financial implications, particularly in the areas of housing and public health. In the recess he had been glad to hear that Cross was working on a Dwellings Bill, 'but I fancy he will find his task a hard one. It will lead us into problems which I don't expect to see solved in a single year.' He wanted to see that question and the sanitary question so brought into relation with their financial implications 'as may enable us to use them as forces for establishing an improved system of local finance and local administration'.[8] For Northcote they were merely means to more important ends. He reported to Disraeli in March 1875 that the revenue fingers were excellent, and that he could offer estimates of £75,550,000, which 'will be accepted as moderate'. His main reservation was that the Conservative government must not become tainted as having simply inherited Gladstone's surplus and simply spent it. Northcote was anxious to keep the income tax at 2d for the next three years, 'unaltered and unalterable except in the case of a real emergency. This will give a character and consistency to our financial policy. We ought to show that we know what we are about.'[9] Obviously, this was not going to be the financial basis for legislating Scott Russell's New Social Alliance into being. It was, rather, the financial basis for Lord Rayleigh's assertion, in proposing the address in answer to the Queen's Speech in the Lords at the opening of the 1875 session, that the first business of a minister was 'not to introduce "blazing" measures, but to give tranquillity to the nation'.[10] When in October 1874 Cross had proposed doing something big about settling the government of London (if only to pre-empt the Liberals with their centralising and anti-City ideas), Disraeli would have none of it: 'We came in on the principle of not harassing the country.' It was to remain consistently the Conservative point of view that, in Derby's formula, creating a 'vast municipality' would be 'politically dangerous'; and that the different parts of London had no community of interest.[11]

2

Business in 1874 had been largely improvised. In 1875 it was to be considered and deliberate. Cross's bill for 'the sanitary reconstruction of towns' was 'carefully discussed clause by clause' in cabinet.[12] Cross at the Home Office and Northcote at the Exchequer both embodied this character of efficient deliberation, and both established their reputations in 1875. Cross's reputation remained politically and historically buoyant because the materials he was dealing with came to take on an aggravated and to a great extent mythic significance with the passing of time. This was not the fortune of Northcote. Yet it is important to note that when the *Quarterly Review* surveyed 'The Conservative government' in October 1875, with much attention to social, labour, and sanitary legislative achievements, and to Cross's part in them, it nevertheless had no doubt that 'beyond any question the most important result of the session to the Conservative party has been the development of Sir Stafford Northcote', with special reference to his disposal of Gladstone's assault on his budget.[13] The judgement of the Commons was clear, Northcote 'had the best of the wrangle'; which was held to mark his emancipation from Gladstone's tutelage.[14] Gladstone had in any case abdicated his leadership of the Liberal party at the beginning of the year, and his seeming eclipse enhanced Northcote's stature more than that of any other of Disraeli's front-bench Commons colleagues.

Cross indeed rather went out of his way to deprecate his legislative programme. 'I should be wrong,' he remarked of his Artisans' and Labourers' Dwellings Improvement Bill, 'if I did not once more caution the House not to imagine we are doing a magnificent and showy work.'[15] The modest idea behind this bill 'for facilitating the improvement of the dwellings of the working classes' was to enable local authorities to demolish fever and plague spots in London and other big cities. Derby, himself a trustee of the Peabody workmen's dwellings scheme, recorded of a cabinet on 14 November 1874 that 'nearly all our time was occupied with Cross's scheme for improved dwellings in London'. Precedents were cited in Edinburgh and Glasgow. 'All the cabinet agreed in the principle of his bill.' Cross planned to house 15,000 people on 36 acres in Battersea comfortably and without overcrowding. 'In fact the model houses save space. They will hold easily 1000 persons to the acre: the worst back-slums in London seldom lodge more than 400 to the acre.'[16]

Cross emphasised heavily that his starting point was that it was decidedly not the duty of government to provide any class of citizens with necessities of life, in this case healthy and habitable dwellings. Such state provision or state encouragement of such provision would create social dependency, an undoubted evil.[17] The unmagnificent and cautious provisions of the act, especially the restricted extent of compensation awardable to property owners, meant that the measure had little impact other than in the hands of Joseph Chamberlain, then beginning to make his mark in Birmingham as the exponent of 'gas and water socialism'. It was designedly without any coercive or compulsory aspect. It is, nonetheless, characteristic of the historical fortunes of Cross's demure act that, together with the Public Health Act of 1875, it is enshrined as a 'fundamental source' in *English Historical Documents* (Vol. 12), prefaced by an almost obligatory quotation of Alexander Macdonald's tribute to the social conscience of the Conservative party.[18]

Likewise enshrined is Cross's Conspiracy and Protection of Property Act of 1875.[19] This was a more dramatic affair. In the first place it was politically polemical, in that it set out to nullify the restrictions placed by Gladstone's government through the Criminal Law Amendment Act on the Trade Union Act of 1871, with respect especially to the legality of picketing. In the second place, Cross pushed the legislation through in defiance of the majority recommendations of the royal commission on laws relating to trade unionism and against a doubting majority in cabinet. In the words of George Howell, Cross 'pulled off a political *coup* which astounded the trade union world'.[20] Despite intense lobbying by the Federation of Employers Cross gave the trade unions the picketing rights and legal immunities which they argued for as indispensable for the effective representation of the labour cause. Cross, well briefed by such as Callender in Lancashire, put it to his colleagues that legislation restricted to the provisions recommended by the commission would 'cause the artisans to feel severely disappointed in the government'.[21] This was almost certainly the consideration which galvanised the otherwise torpid Disraeli into crucial endorsement of Cross's line. Salisbury and Carnarvon were hostile but accepted the measures as 'unavoidable'. Disraeli doubted whether there would be time to go ahead with them in the 1875 session; but Cross would brook no delay.[22] Howell and the other trade union chiefs found Cross 'not only conciliatory, but sympathetic'.[23]

This conciliation and sympathy seemed all the more manifest in Cross's Employers and Workmen Act, which replaced the old master and servant legislation under which breaches of contract had been civil matters in the case of masters but criminal matters in the case of servants (on the pragmatically old-fashioned presumption that only masters might be mulcted). The very nomenclature of the new Conservative legislation reflected a public mood which the otherwise evanescent New Social Alliance debate had helped to create. Howell remarked that 'one of the many odd things connected with the Labour legislation of 1875 was the sudden conversion of the newspaper and journalistic press. Instead of denunciation there was general commendation'.[24] There was little resistance and much support from Liberals. Disraeli saw the easy passage of both the Friendly Societies Bill and Artisans' Dwellings Bill as 'important, because they indicate a policy round which the country can rally'.[25]

Yet from the Conservative party's point of view it was another comment by Howell which was more aptly to the point: 'Mr. Cross has dished the Whigs once again.'[26] Disraeli, who tended to doze during cabinet discussion of Cross's proposed measures,[27] now discovered their momentous bearings. From being the materials of lowering political bromide they became the exciting inspiration of Disraeli's latest fantasies. To the queen he reported their being hailed as 'a complete and satisfactory solution of the greatest questions of the day; the relations between Capital and Labor'.[28] He assured Lady Bradford similarly of the inexpressible importance of this achievement, with added emphasis on the role of measures 'that root and consolidate a party'.[29] To Lady Chesterfield he insisted that the Trade Union Act 'will gain and retain for the Tories the lasting affection of the working classes'.[30]

In fact, the Conservative party spent the rest of the nineteenth century desperately trying to stimulate the affection of the working classes, with at best modest success, and eventually, at the turn of the century, comprehensive disaster. It hardly needs to be added that the Conservative party, far from having 'settled the long and vexatious contest between Capital and Labor', in Disraeli's comforting fantasy, expended enormous energies thereafter in some respects mitigating and in other respects exacerbating the vexatiousness of that contest. Conservative rhetoric was at odds with social and electoral reality. The National Union conference at Brighton in June 1875 boldly proclaimed the reality of a democratic Conservatism, insisting that the great expansion of the numbers of affiliated societies which had 'contributed so largely to the triumphant success of the Conservative Party at the last General Election' was composed 'almost entirely of the artisan class', appearing to be the 'real refutation' of the 'statement so often made by Radical speakers', that 'the Conservative working man was a fiction'.[31] The Conservative working man was never a fiction; and his real existence in material numbers was crucially indispensable to the plot of what Salisbury was later to describe wonderingly as the 'very strange history' of 'recent times'. But, equally, the Conservative party was never the object of the affection of anything like a majority of politically conscious working men. 'Dishing the Whigs' did as much good for Cross in 1880 as it had done for Disraeli in 1868. The more cynical view, that Conservative trade union legislation in 1875 simply removed the major obstacle to a natural *rapprochement* between the Labour movement and the Liberal party, is undoubtedly cogent.

Still, it remained important for the Conservative party to be able to point out that the 8th Trades Union Congress in Glasgow in October 1875 carried a vote of thanks to Cross amid virtually unanimous applause. And it became even more important that Howell could preface his *Handy-book of the Labour Laws* in 1876: 'I regard these Acts as a great boon to the industrial classes – as, in fact, the charter of their social and industrial freedom, the full value of which is not yet understood or appreciated.'[32] As with W.H. Smith, Cross's reputation burgeoned famously as a totemic image of middle-class Conservatism. Though not exactly, like Smith, a new kind of Conservative, Cross was certainly a new kind of Conservative secretary of state. Clayden's characterisation of him, speaking 'in a loud hard voice, without variety of intonation, in a manner something like that of a Chairman of Quarter Sessions charging a jury of tenant farmers',[33] best captures the quality of his relationship to the industrial democracy. Cross later recalled Smith looking at the volume of statutes for 1875, 'priding himself that it was the biggest volume that had been turned out for many a year, and much of the legislation was of a very useful character'.[34] Friendly societies were encouraged; adulteration of food and drugs discouraged.

Cross was indefatigable. When, in November 1875, Disraeli wearily threw out hints that there had been quite enough of cabinets preparatory for the 1876 session, Cross was relentless in his persistence. (Derby could not resist a sententious reflection: 'D. is unequalled in his judgment as to what line the public will expect us to take on a difficult question: and his skill is also conspicuous in getting out of an embarrassment: but he dislikes detail, is easily bored by it, and cares little about the preparation of bills while the session is still distant.')[35] There would in the next year or two be measures to discourage pollution of rivers, and two further refinements of factory legislation. By 1877, indeed, the Conservative cabinet could accommodate without tremor Sclater-Booth's proposals for elective county financial boards. Carnarvon was the only resister. Hardy was in favour; others took the view that it could not be opposed. Salisbury, strongly hostile two years previously, was now quite amenable. Bulking large in Smith's volume was the great consolidatory Public Health Act, providing the code which became the basis of English health policy for the next 60 years.[36] This consummation was the life's work of Sir Charles Adderley, at this point very unhappily situated at the Board of Trade, wrestling unavailingly with the merchant shipping question, which bristled necessarily with the kind of difficulties by which Cross's blandly permissive and unprohibitory measures were happily untroubled.

Difficulties: shipping, tenant farmers, education

As Northcote had put it to Cairns in January 1875, 'Adderley is a charming fellow, and willing to work, but he really has no head for the kind of business with which he has to deal.' And George Cavendish-Bentinck was 'rather worse than useless to him' as undersecretary. The shipowners were 'getting at Adderley' and leading him 'altogether astray'.[37] Northcote anxiously watched for signs of an assault from Samuel Plimsoll, 'advanced' Liberal MP for Derby, well known as the scourge of shipowners allegedly sending out unseaworthy ships with a view to collecting insurance money at the expense of drowned seamen. Northcote warned Disraeli in April that the situation with regard to merchant shipping was dangerous. 'Our shipowners hate it; and they distrust Adderley. Plimsoll and his followers mean to trip us up if possible; and he has a great many friends in our own ranks.' Northcote wanted Adderley kept away from the closing stages of the debate.[38] Disraeli found the whole business wearisome. 'I thought Disraeli ill and feeble', Derby noted of a cabinet discussion of merchant shipping: 'he seems at times half-asleep, and it costs him an effort to speak.'[39] Prominent among the friends of Plimsoll in the Conservative ranks was Gorst. When in July the cabinet decided to abandon the bill for the session, Plimsoll created his famous scene in the Commons, which obliged the government to resuscitate a temporary version of the bill. 'You will have to steer between seeming to Plimsollise too much and to Plimsollise too little', Northcote warned Disraeli. 'Great care will be needed not to make an enemy of him.'[40] In the end, in spite of Adderley's continued debility, the matter was scrambled through. Plimsoll got his famous loadline, soon generally dubbed 'Plimsoll line'. The Plimsoll scandal exposed major deficiencies in the upper reaches of the Conservative administration. Northcote so wanted to be rid of Adderley that he offered to step down and take over the Board of Trade and reconstitute it as a Ministry of Commerce.[41] The Plimsoll scandal also proved to be an indicator that the easy days of Conservative domestic reform were over.

Too many other pressures were crowding in. There was, for example, the Agricultural Holdings Bill. This was designed ostensibly as a rural counterpart to the measures of urban social amelioration. Clare Read, a Norfolk MP since 1865, had been appointed to minor office by Disraeli to 'enchant the farmers'; instead, Read set about trying to enchant the government in the interests of his fellow disaffected tenant farmers. The pragmatic purpose of the Agricultural Holdings Bill was to close a chink in Conservatism's agricultural armour; in the candid words of one Scottish Conservative, to 'forever shut the mouths of that class of Radicals who have made themselves notorious in denouncing the Conservatives as being the stern opponents of the Tenant-farmers' interests'.[42] Traditional Conservative partisanship thus took pains to cover one of its potentially vulnerable flanks in the county constituencies. But not without difficulty. Many Conservative county members thought it the thin edge of an anti-landlord wedge, inspired by landlord defeat and appeasement in Ireland. Disraeli, dismayed at their resistance, tried to persuade the cabinet to drop the measure. His colleagues, however, were in fear of a tenants' agitation during the recess. After Disraeli gave way it was agreed to call a pacificatory party meeting. The Conservative cabinet was ready to offend the Plimsollites but not the tenant farmers. Even so, Read resigned in December 1875. Northcote reported nervously from Burghley: 'I do not find that there is much feeling in that part of the world about Clare Read, or local taxation; but I hear from various quarters that there is dissatisfaction; and two or three friends who have been at the Chamber of Agriculture speak of the feeling as serious.' Northcote wished 'we could do something to allay it'; and was anxious for 'a fair consideration' of Sclater-Booth's proposals on rating.[43] Derby drew a rather more sombre moral from the tale of the Agricultural Holdings Bill:

the evidence of a violent and reactionary temper on the part of our supporters is a bad omen for the future. Should Disraeli, who to a certain extent is able to control the H. of C. abandon his post, I do not think I can go on with the rest of the party, either as leader or follower.[44]

Traditional county considerations were also awkwardly near the nub of the government's principal domestic initiative of the 1876 session, Sandon's Elementary Schools Bill. Presented ostensibly as a reinforcement to the 1870 act, it was also a conveyance for Sandon's insistence that the country 'must not become possessed with the notion that it is the policy of the Conservative party to grudge and restrict the education of the people'.[45] Derby noted of Sandon: 'he is very strong for compulsory schooling. I did not at first see why: but he is against school boards, and thinks that if more children can be forced into the existing schools, they can be kept up as at present on the voluntary system, to the great content of the local clergy. Hence his zeal.'[46] The great problem for Sandon was how to encourage the education of the people and at the same time both discourage the expansion of board schools in rural areas and also not impair the interest of rural employers of labour. Tensions within the Conservative party on these issues were reflected in tensions between Sandon and his nominal chief, Richmond. Sandon would brook no delay with his bill, and threatened to resign. 'He is really the most touchy suspicious man I ever saw', Richmond told Cairns, 'and seems to have a great opinion of his own importance. He seems to ignore me altogether in the matter of the Bill, but this I do not care for.'[47] Derby groaned at the prospect of incited religious sectarianism. His fears of 1874 were now about to be realised: 'the fire is lighted now, and will not be easily put out.'[48]

Sandon's social reforming premiss was that of 2,300,000 children available to attend elementary schools, only 1,850,000 were in fact forthcoming; and of those a mere 200,000 were in 'upper standards'. How to get in the missing 450,000? And how to keep more children longer at school? Compulsion of some kind and degree was the obvious answer. Sandon was prone to move in that direction, in the teeth of the well-advertised Conservative doctrine that social reforms must be founded on permissiveness and non-compulsion. In this way Sandon's problem was akin to Adderley's. Nor did Sandon abandon compulsion without a struggle. Dyke reported nervously to Disraeli: 'I have been getting some information with reference to the feeling about Compulsory Education in the rural Districts, & I am sure that the greatest caution is required, and that unless the enthusiasm of the vice-president be moderated, he will make havoc of our County seats.'[49] Sandon's enthusiasm was sharply moderated by an adverse vote in the Commons: the 'country party' had fired a menacing shot across his bow. Disraeli reported this chastening with satisfaction to the queen, though apologising for the unimpressive numbers of the majority, attributable to 'casual and social causes; primarily Ascot races, always perilous to the Tories'.[50]

Thus rebuffed, Sandon perforce confined himself to the tactic of expanding restrictions on employment of children not in possession of a certificate of primary education. Sandon tried to balance the annoyance this caused to Conservative county interests by his second tactic, which was to devise means whereby children might by various oblique compulsions be pressed away from country board schools into church or denominational voluntary schools. Sandon's view was that board schools in big cities were no problem. They were politically harmless and educationally necessary. But board schools in small communities had a pernicious political effect as affording a platform and notoriety for Dissenting ministers.[51] To strengthen Sandon's hand in this work of justice and enlightenment Albert Pell, Conservative MP for Leicestershire, backed by other advocates of the Church's cause such as Beresford Hope and Lord Henry Scott, offered a saliently efficacious clause to the bill providing for the dissolution of School Boards superfluous to genuine educational needs which had 'originated from merely party motives.'

Pell's clause provoked intense Liberal outrage and resistance. Disraeli, as ever, found it difficult to identify with the higher ecclesiastical temper, and seemed ready to throw Pell's clause over in order to expedite progress. There was what Disraeli called 'a strong cabinet'. Derby noted: 'Hardy & Salisbury want one, or both, of two things: that voluntary schools may in some shape receive help out of the rates, so as to put them on an equal footing with schoolboard schools: and that children may be compelled to attend them in the same way as they are where schoolboards exist.' Derby opposed both these proposals, 'Cross supporting me, & Disraeli, though he said little, taking the same side'.[52] But the *parti prêtre* would not be denied. Salisbury impressed upon Disraeli that to abandon Pell's clause 'would be a very grave error indeed'. The act of 1870 professed to hold an even balance between voluntary and board schools; but while it allowed a voluntary parish to come under a board, it did not allow a board to come under a voluntary system. Because of temporary local problems this would mean ultimately that all schools would come under boards.

> Now the unpopularity of Boards is increasing every day – especially among country gentlemen & the county clergy. If it can be said that having a large majority . . . for the clause, you perpetuated school boards in parishes where they were unnecessary, either to save a day, or to avoid offending the Opposition, I think you will profoundly offend the largest & most important section of your party in the Constituencies & in the House of Commons. This is no 'sacerdotal' movement. . . . We are getting to a critical time in the life of the Ministry. Some accidental circumstance, in a time of excitement may cause you to be hard-pressed in the spring. Ecclesiastically-minded persons are proverbially unforgiving . . . or what is still worse, unsympathetic & doubtful support from the denominational school party all over the country, on a dissolution.

Opponents of the bill, Salisbury warned, would not be grateful for the concession. 'The party, especially the large section of it interested in this matter stood by you successfully in the Empress question[53] & they deserve not to be abandoned.'[54] Thus disarmed and propped up, Disraeli showed a stiff front; and, with the desertion from the Liberal ranks of the Roman Catholic Home Rulers and squabbles among other factions, Sandon's bill with Pell's clause passed triumphantly up to a sympathetic House of Lords. Derby could not repress a certain wry satisfaction in noting in December 1876 that the elections for the London School Board had resulted in a 'decisive success for the supporters of school-board schools, as against the denominational party: in other words, the parsons have been beaten'.[55] Still, in the country parishes ecclesiastically minded persons did not repine. Something had been done for the education of the people; a little more had been done for the benefit of the Church; which was about how the Conservative party wanted such things to be in 1876.

Notes and References

1. P. Smith, *Disraelian Conservatism and Social Reform* (1967), 203.
2. See, for example, CCO, June 1989, no. 57: *Labour Interests and Conservatives*.
3. Derby Diary, 24 June 74.
4. NUCCA *Tracts and leaflets*: CCO, 1891, no. 29.
5. CCO, Oct. 1896, no. 13.
6. CCO, Oct. 1896, no. 12.
7. *Campaign Guide* (1892), 210.
8. Northcote to Disraeli, 14 Oct. 1874. BL, Iddesleigh 50016, 254.
9. Northcote to Disraeli, 31 March 1875; BL, Iddesleigh 50017, 16.
10. *AR*, 1875, 7.
11. Smith, 198; Derby Diary, 12 Nov. 1874.
12. *Ibid.*, 13 Jan. 1875.
13. *QR*, Oct. 1875, 555.
14. Derby Diary, 7 May 1875.
15. *PD*, ccxxii, 110.
16. Derby Diary, 14 Nov. 74.
17. *PD*, ccxxii, 100.
18. *English Historical Documents, 1874-1914*, ed. W.D. Hancock, Pt 2, (1977), 613–16.
19. *Ibid.*, 659–60.
20. E.M. Leventhal, *Respectable Radical. George Howell and Victorian Working-class Politics* (1971), 179–80.
21. Smith, 245.
22. Derby Diary, 30 May 1875; 7 July 1875.
23. G. Howell, *Labour Legislation, Labour Movements and Labour Leaders* (1902), 368.
24. *Ibid.*, 370.
25. Buckle, ii, 714. See also E.J. Feuchtwanger, *Disraeli, Democracy and the Tory Party* (1968), 75–6.
26. Howell, *Labour Legislation*, 369.
27. Derby Diary, 30 May 1875: 'Both at this and the last Cabinet, D. has appeared much exhausted: and today fell asleep and remained so for some minutes: which I never saw him do before. The work is too heavy for a man of 70.'
28. Buckle, ii, 712.
29. *Ibid.*
30. *Ibid.*

31 NUCCA, minutes of conference, Banqueting Room, Royal Pavilion, Brighton, 19 June 1875.
32 Leventhal, *Respectable Radical*, 385.
33 Clayden, 48.
34 R.A. Cross, *A Political History* (1903), 32.
35 Derby Diary, 6 Nov. 1875.
36 *English Historical Documents, 1874-1914* Pt. 2, 607.
37 Northcote to Cairns, 10 Jan. 1875; PRO, Cairns 30/51/5.
38 Northcote to Disraeli, 2 April 1875; BL, Iddesleigh 50017, 21.
39 Derby Diary, 10 July 1875.
40 Northcote to Disraeli, 26 July 1875; BL, Iddesleigh 50017, 42.
41 Northcote to Disraeli, 22 Sept. 1875; BL, Iddesleigh 50017, 60.
42 Highet to Cunningham, 25 June 1875; HP, B/XX/Cr/26a.
43 Northcote to Disraeli, 24 Dec. 1875; BL, Iddesleigh 50017, 143. For Scottish aspects of this problem see B.L. Crapster, 'Scotland and the Conservative Party in 1876,' *Journal of Modern History* (1957), 359.
44 Derby Diary, 6 March 1875.
45 Smith, 256.
46 Derby Diary, 10 Feb. 1875.
47 Richmond to Cairns, 5 June 1876; PRO, Cairns 30/51/3.
48 Derby Diary, 24 July 1874.
49 Dyke to Disraeli, 1 Jan. [1876]; HP, B/XXI/D/467.
50 Buckle, ii, 720.
51 Smith, 249.
52 Derby Diary, 17 Nov. 1875.
53 See below, 273, 278.
54 Salisbury to Disraeli, 22 July 1876; HP, B/XX/Ce/80. See Disraeli's comments to the queen on this letter, Buckle, ii, 824.
55 Derby Diary, 2 Dec. 1876.

Chapter 10

Places, honours, careers

The laws of patronage

1

A political party in a constitution of responsible government within parliamentary sovereignty is painstakingly attentive to the arts of gaining and exercising power, enjoying place, and distributing patronage to induce or reward services to those ends. Patronage was at least as important as policy to governments and parties in the nineteenth century. When the Conservative government entered its first extensive period of office in the later nineteenth century it contended with three interlocking problems in its distribution of favours. The first was simply that the long drought of office had created a large thirst at the fount of honour. Not many Conservatives would have agreed with Disraeli's opinion in 1872 that after office in 1866–8 the party was in no immediate need of the tonic of patronage. The second was that the reforms of the Peelites and their greatest surviving exponent, Gladstone, had reduced the scope of political patronage, especially in the Civil Service of the Crown. The third was that, compared with the earlier times of Pitt or the later times of Lloyd George, the high Victorian epoch cultivated a restrictive jealousy with respect to the granting of honours. Salisbury put the problem in his piece on 'The position of parties'. Patronage had, he argued, increased in importance since the eighteenth century and ministers were now much more dependent upon it precisely because then 'the business was done much more corruptly and offensively than it is now'. But once done, it was done; cash down, obligations discharged, minister free. 'But he cannot pay in ready money now, and therefore he remains in debt. He pays in places, honours, and careers, given as opportunity arises, and consequently deferred, as regards the large majority of those who, at any one time, think they have claims.' Salisbury's experience of office had taught him that the 'moral pressure of such claims upon a leader is enormous; and modern statesmen are not made to resist pressure'.[1]

Modern statesmen differed considerably in their manner of coping with those pressures. Derby, like Salisbury, was prone to be squeamish. He and Salisbury were agreed that the increasingly canvassed notion of state purchase of railways was objectionable on both financial and constitutional grounds; but beyond that, as 'creating in various forms an enormous patronage'.[2] What was moral agony to Salisbury was often expedient amenity to Disraeli. When Salisbury sent his recommendations as secretary for India to Disraeli in 1876 he told Corry: 'Now I can say with a clear conscience that I have sent them all before the Prime Minister: & of course if his obduracy of heart, or dullness of perception is blind to their obvious & transcendent merits, it clearly is not my fault. If Jack Cade came on earth now he would proclaim that the two-volumed Debrett should have seven volumes.'[3] Disraeli dealt robustly with patronage. This was because he found anything savouring of deliberate high mindedness repellent. 'Prig' was always one of his more damning verdicts. Patronage was the mortar which bound a party. 'Nothing is more ruinous to political connection than the fear of justly rewarding your friends . . . and qualified adherents. It is not becoming in any Minister to decry party who has risen by party. We should always remember that if we were not partisans we should not be Ministers.'[4]

It was also because Disraeli set out to undermine the new restrictiveness imposed by Gladstone's Order in Council of 1870. Disraeli 'had become convinced that the cult of examinations had been carried far enough and that the Prime Minister and the Patronage Secretary must consolidate their position at the Treasury lest they should become Treasury ministers only in name.'[5] He adopted an aggressively old-fashioned view of the candidly partisan claims on places. It always annoyed him that ambassadors had come to be considered permanent officials. He wanted embassies to revert to being places susceptible to political patronage.[6] He impressed upon the chairman of the Board of Inland Revenue that appointments in his office 'should be considered not as official promotions but as political prizes'.[7] He instructed the permanent secretary at the Treasury that the first lord must be consulted in future about all patronage in his gift, and took care personally to make appointments specifically in order to preclude any attempt by Treasury officers to usurp, as he saw it, his prerogative. Dyke as patronage secretary took similar steps to guard and extend his claims against any Gladstonian tendencies among the permanent Treasury officers.

Disraeli remained true to his doctrine of 1858: patronage was 'the outward and visible sign of an inward and spiritual grace, and that is Power'.[8] In no respect was Disraeli's attachment to aristocratic government more manifest than in his traditional attitude to the distribution of official favour. 'I want a man of the world and of breeding, culture and station to be Chief of the Civil Service Commission', so that if any 'absurd or pedantic schemes of qualification' were put before him he might 'integrate and modify them and infuse a necessary element of common sense'.[9] This was the occasion of the creation of that £2,000 per annum place as a bolt-hole for Adderley. Eventually, however, it did the same service for the erstwhile Pakington, now Lord Hampton. This was widely denounced as a job, and Hampton later complained to Northcote that his appointment should be subject to 'annual attacks'. Though he placed himself in Northcote's hands, Hampton confessed that 'it would not be convenient to me in these times of Agricultural difficulty, to be deprived of the office'.[10] Nor was Disraeli the only minister to counter-attack pedantic schemes of qualification. Cross informed Cairns:

> The Treasury have agreed to my proposition to take the appointment of sub-inspectors of factories out of the order placing them under Competitive Examination. I have therefore great pleasure in offering an appointment to your nephew about whom you wrote very highly some time ago.[11]

The law of patronage permeated all levels of the administration. All political heads of government departments exercised patronage autonomously and guarded their prerogative with a hedge of political etiquette. 'I never interfere with the patronage of my colleagues,' as Disraeli remarked to Cairns; 'but there are exceptions in all things.'[12] Very few ministers at the top could be regarded purely as dispensers of it as against being dispensed to. In the case of Disraeli's cabinet, Cairns by weight, Derby by heredity, Northcote by assiduity, and Salisbury by menace could be thought of as the inner group of ultimate dispensers. Cross was naive in this respect when he asserted that 'there was no shadow of a cabinet within a cabinet'.[13] This left some people ostensibly at the top in what proved in fact to be an ambiguous position. Hardy was the prime example of a minister supposedly dispensing patronage who turned out to be dispensed to. Very few outside the uppermost level of official ministers could presume to dispensing stature. Abergavenny was perhaps one such. Montagu Corry was in an inevitably singular position. Abergavenny used to refer to him not entirely jocularly as 'Prime Minister No.2 – the Great Monty',[14] and would refer to visiting 'both P.M.s' when calling at 10 Downing Street.[15] Corry's necessarily sensitive and influential relationship to Disraeli became the subject of sour comment. The 'Two Conservatives' of 1882 (Gorst and Churchill) remarked that Lord Beaconsfield's patronage, ecclesiastical and civil, 'whether to places or honours', was 'apparently administered by some Gil Blas or Figaro behind the scenes, who guarded all the approaches to his chief's confidence with sordid assiduity'.[16]

2

Places at the top level of the administration were its head's greatest and most immediate concern. Adderley's collapse of 1875 caused perturbations which Disraeli could not readily resolve. He wanted to avoid the scandal and discredit that Adderley's summary dismissal would have brought upon the government, especially in the context of the Plimsoll agitation. He was prone also to detect conspiracies against Adderley among the permanent officers of the board, which provoked a sharp and hot defence of them from Northcote.[17] Conflicting claims in the projected reshuffle were not reconcilable. Cairns had warned Disraeli: 'I strongly suspect from what I hear indirectly that Hardy is *very* tired of the War Office, & will be most anxious for a change to some other Department.'[18] Disraeli insisted that he had no wish to move Hardy: that would have provoked trouble from the queen. He was more concerned to promote Beach from the Irish Office. But how to replace him? To Cairns:

> Both Sclater-Booth, & Fred Stanley, are capital men of business, & are excellent at their present posts. But Booth is a boor & F. Stanley a stick – at least at speaking, & an Irish Secty should have the gift of the gab. He shd be a gentleman too, & rather a fine one. In this respect F.S. wd have done, particularly as he has a charming wife.
>
> Could I venture on offering the Irish Sectp to Chaplin? He is a first-rate speaker, very rich, a capital rider, & altoger. still horsey, wh. the Irish like, tho' he has dispersed & parted with his stud. Wd. the preferment be too great for a start? He wd. not take office, nor shd I wish him, unless he represented a Department in the Commons.

There were many possibilities; but in any feasible case, 'there would be nothing for Adderley, & I don't see how anything is to be found for him. What are we to do?'[19]

Enthusiasm for Chaplin was entirely lacking. Disraeli's next inspiration was that George Hamilton might go to the Irish Office. This was judged impossible in view of Hamilton's father's being lord-lieutenant. Hardy (whom Disraeli invited Cairns to consult if he wished) thought Stanley's 'deficiencies' in speaking would be 'a great disqualification'. Hardy doubted if Sclater-Booth would accept the Irish Office without the cabinet, and was not sure 'he would be a good man to deal with Irish MPs'. Rumours that Taylor would give up the duchy of Lancaster and go to the Lords Hardy interpreted as preparing a way 'to break Adderley's fall'. But Taylor, it appeared, declined to cooperate.[20] Northcote's offer to step down and take over the Board of Trade was rejected by Disraeli as a 'monstrous proposition'. Northcote was, Disraeli insisted, and ever had been, 'my right hand, my most trusty counsellor; and I look to your filling a higher post than that which you admirably discharge'.[21]

Breaking Adderley's fall involved elaborate projects of departmental reconstruction and displays of mollifying official etiquette. Disraeli reported to Cairns:

> I have broken to Adderley the business, & have told him, that the Queen has decided on the reconstruction of the Board of Trade, & making it a cabinet office: that I shd wish to place him in a position not inferior in official rank to that wh. he now occupies, but I have nothing immediately to offer him & that my difficulty is this, that no time should be unnecessarily lost in appointing the new President of the B of T in order that he may prepare for the severe labors, wh. await him. Of course, A. does not like this, & it is a very painful duty for me.[22]

Northcote contributed the notion of replacing Adderley with Stephen Cave, then paymaster-general. But Cave insisted on a cabinet seat.[23] Northcote confessed to Cairns in despair: 'It seems that we have no real alternative but to leave the Office at present in Adderley's hands.'[24] The upshot was that Adderley was spared the chairmanship of the Civil Service Commission and clung on at the Board of Trade until flung out by the shocks of 1878. All that Disraeli achieved was to find a soft billet for 'little George Bentinck' as judge advocate-general.

The next major perturbation in the cabinet orbits arose out of a crisis in Disraeli's health, his initial idea of retirement, then his staying on with translation to the Lords as earl of Beaconsfield. After a levee early in March 1876 Disraeli raised with Derby the question of his removing to the upper house, discoursing on his old fears about the Commons' leadership getting into confusion. Disraeli circulated his cabinet colleagues in July 1876 with the stark choice imposed by his doctors: retirement or the Lords. Cairns had already hinted to Hardy that the question of the leadership of the Commons would soon arise, one way or another.[25] The queen was unhappy at the thought of Disraeli's retiring, and pressed strongly for a move to the less exacting upper house. Partly this was because Disraeli suited her, both politically and personally. (Hardy told Cairns that she had shown him some of Disraeli's letters to her, 'which are of the most soothing & sympathetic character. They amused me very much.')[26] But partly it was also because she had good reason to fear that she might be confronted with the distasteful prospect of asking Derby to take over the government. Derby was not a soothing and sympathetic person, and his conduct of the Foreign Office in the current crisis of the Eastern Question was little to her taste. As it later transpired, it was Disraeli's intention initially to recommend Derby as his successor and Hardy as leader of the Commons.[27] He never actually did so; and Derby both 'utterly scouted' the idea of leadership and stated that he would not serve under anyone but Disraeli.[28] Derby was simply being realistic. By now he had used up his credit with his former partisans. Even Cairns stressed Derby's 'unfitness'.[29]

This was certainly also Salisbury's view. He gave no hint at this point of any pleasure or relief at the prospect of Disraeli's retiring. When he told Disraeli that retirement 'at this juncture' would be 'a most serious blow to the Ministry & the party' there is no doubt that Salisbury meant what he said. It was not merely that 18 months had inured him to 'slavery'. His explanation made quite clear what he thought of Derby's performance at the Foreign Office.

> Foreign affairs are the absorbing topic of the day. It is quite evident, from the quiescence of parliament & the Country on the subject, that very general confidence is felt in the present conduct of our foreign policy: & in the shaping of that policy, the largest share is generally, & justly, attributed to you.

In view of the storm which was about to break upon the government over the 'Bulgarian atrocities', this was an unprescient judgement. But for its present purpose it was apt enough. If Disraeli were to withdraw, 'the most essential element is that public confidence would be taken away'. It was a 'choice of evils'. Disraeli would find the Lords the 'dullest assembly in the world'. But if there were no other alternative, it was 'infinitely better' that Disraeli should go to the Lords than that he should retire.[30]

For Richmond the matter was rather more personally poignant, as Disraeli's going to the Lords would mean Richmond's surrendering the Conservative leadership there. However, as he reported to his keeper Cairns, he responded to Disraeli's circular 'in the terms we had agreed on and said no one would welcome him more sincerely or cordially than I should, and that I considered it not only the best but the *only* arrangement that I considered was at all practicable and likely to keep all parties together'.[31] Disraeli accordingly became earl of Beaconsfield at the end of the 1876 session. Malmesbury took the occasion to resign the privy seal to allow Disraeli to assume that office 'as an appendage to the Premiership as it wd give him what his office wants namely high social precedence & a sufficient income'.[32]

Richmond's eclipse in the Lords was as nothing to Hardy's eclipse in the Commons. This was the most important consequence for the Conservative party of Disraeli's move to the Lords. Hardy recorded an interview with Disraeli at the War Office on 11 July. He told Hardy of his desire to retire with Derby as leader of the party and Hardy as leader in the Commons. 'Nothing passed in any way to settle it & Disraeli only in passing mentioned his view on wh. I said nothing as without fixing anything he spoke of Beach for the Cabinet.'[33] But before long it became clear that moves were afoot in the background to block Hardy. Cairns made a point of suggesting to Hardy that his work at the War Office 'was very heavy & said that if I gave it up I should break up the Government (in which I do not at all agree)'; which Hardy was in no doubt was 'meant to convey to me the opinion that the lead of the House would be too trying in conjunction with it. My impression was that Disraeli who had been with him had talked of this and that he has other designs to be made smooth to me that way.' Hardy's problem was that he could not 'make up my mind as to what I wish. What I think due to me, what will be best for the party.'[34] This inability to act decisively would cost Hardy dear, and possibly the party dearer. Richmond reported to Cairns on 16 July: 'a long conversation with Hardy yesterday. He entered very fully into the whole subject about which you and I had some conversation. I think he will offer no objection for the arrangement but he did not seem altogether satisfied. I fancy it will all come right in the end.'[35]

Hardy himself had more talk with Disraeli on the 15th. 'H.M. however would not hear of my leaving the W.O. . . . (This is D's report. What does he wish himself?)' By the time Hardy had had his conversation with Richmond it was not strange that he should comment : 'I wonder if they *want* me to decline the task to wh. I am assumed to have a right?'[36] In the painful end Disraeli came out with it at the beginning of August: the queen 'expressed herself very strongly as to her personal wish' that Hardy should not leave the War Office. Northcote was 'in more frequent communication with the members'. Disraeli regretted that his 'original purpose has not been practicable'.[37] Hardy did not fight. He conceded that 'Northcote's office and qualifications' pointed him out to Disraeli. Derby noted: 'There appears, contrary to expectation, to have been no difficulty in persuading Hardy to acquiesce in the lead of the House being given to Northcote.'[38] All Hardy could do was not to disguise from Disraeli 'a certain pang of disappointment at this practical limit to my career'. He would probably at no distant time ask to be relieved of the War Office and go to the Lords.[39]

To some extent Hardy had helped to dig his own political grave by his immensely ingratiating relationship with the queen. He was a victim of his own implicating monarchist enthusiasm. There were other counts against him. He exasperated the whips by his unwillingness to keep late hours in the Commons.[40] He was feared for his rashness and temper, especially on Church questions. Derby found him, for that, and for other reasons, uncongenial. Derby had used his special relationship with Disraeli to block Hardy from the Home Office in 1874. Now he used it to help keep Hardy out of the Commons leadership in 1876. At the point of his own eclipse in the Conservative party, he was still able to exercise leverage on the party's leader. Derby resented Hardy's characteristically unconcealed contempt for his conduct of foreign policy. Northcote, on the other hand, was rather prone to sympathise with Derby's soft tendencies.

There were positive counts in Northcote's favour. He was assiduous where Hardy was impatient. Disraeli took care to flatter him as his 'right hand' as he had earlier done to Hardy. Disraeli's comments on Northcote sum up the matter: 'There never was such an indefatigable worker as the Chanr of the Exr'; 'he is the best of my colleagues for that sort of work. He can put his hand to anything'; 'He is quite "a little busy bee".'[41] Northcote had been impressive in handling Gladstone in 1875 over the budget. In any case, the abdicated Gladstone seemed politically a spent force. Hartington now led the Liberals in the Commons, and no one doubted Northcote's capacity to keep the upper hand over that undevious Whig. Northcote, even as a little busy bee, seemed a safe enough bet in August 1876. It was then not easily foreseeable that by the time the foreign policy crisis was over in 1878 Northcote's reputation in the Conservative party would be compromised very seriously; nor that by 1880 Gladstone would storm back to the Liberal leadership. Looking back in 1892, Hardy noted: 'I am far from disputing the wisdom of selecting Northcote for the post . . . but it changed my position altogether. . . . How often has the Queen, how often others regretted that I was not the chosen man, but I doubt whether my temper or health would have stood the strain.'[42] Certainly, Northcote's did not.

In many ways Derby's case remained the most problematic. His standing in the party certainly suffered slippage during the foreign policy turmoils of 1876. Yet there was no evident compromising of his standing as party chief in Lancashire. In ruminating in January 1877 on 'a matter which is often in my thoughts', Derby could still see himself in the running.

> When Ld Beaconsfield retires, as from age & infirmity he is likely to do in a year or two, what is to be my course of action? If not offered the vacant post, I should not hesitate, for no one is bound to serve under a junior, & in official life both Richmond & Salisbury are my juniors. But if it should be offered, the reasons for & against accepting are fairly balanced.

Against were considerations of 'being tied to the life of a political leader', with dreary obligations, flattering of followers, coping with the queen, and concern with ecclesiastical affairs. On the other hand, there were the considerations of the honour to the family and of keeping up political interests. On the whole Derby thought the 'balance of advantages is clearly in favour of retiring'. Again, in March 1877, worries about his wife's health made Derby 'seriously consider whether this being so I can go on with official business'. He recalled the 'weariness & disgust of official business' which often came over his father. 'The *parti prêtre* would exult at getting rid of me, the Conservatives as a body would probably regret my withdrawal, but I have read & seen enough to know that no politician is long missed.'[43]

3

Malmesbury's retirement created a cabinet vacancy which Disraeli was delighted to fill with Sir Michael Hicks Beach in February 1877. This gave the Irish Office an official lift which Disraeli did not relish; but that could not, for the time being, be helped. An opportunity to remedy this came in July 1877 with the sudden death of Ward Hunt. 'I hope B. will be very careful as to whom he selects to fill the vacancy', Richmond told Cairns. 'I always fancy that M. Corry is not a very good adviser in these matters, and in these times the Admiralty requires a real good man at the head.'[44] Disraeli offered the Admiralty to Sandon, who declined. Disraeli then summoned Smith from the Treasury, recommending him to the queen as 'purely a man of the middle class and the appointment would no doubt be popular'. The queen feared that it might '*not please* the Navy in which Service so many of the *highest rank* serve, & who claim to be equal to the Army – if a man of the Middle Class is placed above them in that very high Post'; and suggested instead Manners or Beach.[45]

Disraeli got round her by linking Smith to Cross, by now a favourite of the queen's; 'a character similar to Mr. Cross – in mind, manner, energy, but more weighty & with much more repose'; who had 'entirely gained the confidence of the House as Mr. Cross has'. He also insisted that Smith was not socially inferior to either Childers or Goschen in the previous government, as well as being far richer. He clinched his case by pointing to the need to have a 'City or Borough member in the Cabinet'.[46] Even so, Derby's comment a few days later that Disraeli had 'carried his party as to Smith'[47] is indicative of a widespread sense of anomaly. Richmond's point about the Admiralty needing a strong hand was also material. Disraeli had come to respect Smith as a painstaking man of business.[48] But Richmond's point really was that he hoped and expected to get the Admiralty himself. 'The arrangement you mention', he confessed in some dismay to Cairns, 'had not occurred to me, but I dare say it will suit, and I should make no objection to W.H.S.'[49] The great consolation for Richmond was that at least the detestable Sandon did not get it.

> I am certain he is much better in the Cabinet than Sandon. I have formed a very high opinion of W.H.S. since we have been in Office. Lady Bradford told me on Friday morning that she had heard from the P.M. who had told her that he thought W.H.S. would be the new First Lord, but that he had not quite decided.
>
> I quite concur that he ought to be in H[ouse of] C[ommons].[50]

This opened up the prospect of Sandon's going to the Irish Office to release Beach. Richmond rejoiced. 'I do not know how my Lieutnt's very decided low Church views will suit the R.C.s in Ireland. He will not be regretted in the Dep.'[51] But even by the end of 1877 Beach still remained unreleased. There were family reasons which made it impossible for Sandon to live in Ireland. Sandon had made so many refusals that he wanted a public announcement so that his constituents could be reassured that he had not been passed over.[52] It took the high crisis of Eastern affairs and the cataclysmic resignations of Carnarvon in January 1878 and Derby in March to resolve matters. Hicks Beach replaced Carnarvon at the Colonial Office (with James Lowther promoted to the Irish Office, no longer represented in cabinet). Salisbury replaced Derby at the Foreign Office. The hapless Hardy was translated to the India Office, stipulating for a peerage (he became Viscount Cranbrook). Frederick Stanley replaced his elder brother as the family presence in the cabinet by taking over the War Office. Adderley was at last dropped from the Board of Trade, consigned to the Lords as Lord Norton; and Sandon replaced him. It was a measure of the gravity of the situation that Sandon did not stipulate for the cabinet immediately. As Northcote explained, Sandon would take the Board of Trade without the cabinet on a temporary basis; he did not want to leave the government at this juncture: 'this is not a moment even to seem to quit the Government.' 'The real thing at the bottom of his mind is of course the Cabinet. But he fully admits the propriety of the present arrangement, and he is most anxious not to be supposed to have a grievance.'[53]

The 'present arrangement' was Disraeli's rather doctrinaire insistence on the parity of the Lords in the cabinet. He resigned the privy seal to allow Northumberland in to this end, to general amazement. When Hardy shortly afterwards became Cranbrook a Commons' place in cabinet became available for Sandon. This was the cabinet which took the Conservative government through to its end in 1880.

4

Places and careers at the subcabinet or subpolicy-making level of the administration touched so widely and deeply upon the personnel of a party as to make this stratum in purely and practical party terms much the more important. Few men were disappointed at not achieving cabinet status; and they were harmless as far as party morale was concerned. The mass of unavoidable disgruntlement at the lower reaches of the patronage system was always a matter of lively concern to party managers. Places at Court, as Derby remarked, 'seem to give more trouble than others, as everyone feels himself qualified for them'.[54] Disraeli talked of 'an earldom for Skelmersdale, he having been active and unselfish, and it being difficult to find anything else'. As it turned out, the captaincy of the Yeoman of the Guard was duly found; but Skelmersdale eventually, in 1880, was rewarded with the earldom of Lathom as well. It was, moreover, in these reaches that the classic technique of bestowing patronage had to be most deftly exercised: of which the cardinal rule was that patronage bestowed too soon is patronage wasted. Keeping people waiting and keeping them hungry is the best way of fuelling the energies of partisanship.

Lord Henry Lennox, a rare case of genuinely deluded cabinet pretension, was a running sore in the administration with his fond persistence in asserting the Board of Works' freedom from Northcote's control at the Treasury. Disraeli, exasperated, excised Lennox as a colleague in 1876, despite pleas in mitigation from Lennox's brother Richmond. Even Richmond was disconcerted at Lennox's assertion that a message had been received from the prime minister through Sir Philip Rose that Lennox was to get 'the next best place' that fell vacant, and that his resignation – 'a sacrifice to save the Gov. last Session' – had led Disraeli to consider 'in consequence of the services he had rendered to the Party' that the 'heads of the Party ought to pay his debts'. Richmond could only conclude, as he told Cairns, that 'Henry must have been dreaming or Rose imposing upon him.'[55] There was always great reluctance at this level of administration to make a public exposure. As Cairns put it to Northcote apropos of Lennox: 'I don't enter on his merits or demerits: but these esclandres do infinite harm, as it seems to me, to a Govt., raise much ill-will, & lead people to suspect that there is more of the same sort of thing behind.'[56] Having been disappointed at Taylor's unwillingness to exchange the duchy of Lancaster for a peerage, and thus free the duchy as a slot for Noel, Disraeli was at least able to accommodate Noel in Lennox's vacant place.

This intermediate stratum of placements was the scene also of the difficulties created by Selwin-Ibbetson, an Essex MP and Cross's undersecretary at the Home Office, who made a profession of claiming mortal illness but refusing to retire. He was eased out of the Home Office in 1878 to make way for one of the brightest of Disraeli's new generation of young men, Matthew White Ridley. Another such was Edward Stanhope, who succeeded George Hamilton at the India Office in 1878 when Hamilton was promoted to succeed Sandon in charge of education. These were the aristocratic successes who made up for the failures of Pembroke and George Cavendish-Bentinck. Derby tended not to be impressed at the quality of the material available for promotion to the cabinet. When Richmond in 1875 complained at Hunt's laxness at the Admiralty, Derby pointed out that replacing him would not be easy. 'It is one of the weak points of our Cabinet, that we have scarcely any competent men outside to fill vacancies if they should occur.' He had no high opinion of his own undersecretary, Bourke ('does what he can, with tact & skill in general, but he is not forcible nor eloquent'); not much more of Hamilton ('succeeds in every speech that he makes, but appears to want ambition'). Derby's brother Frederick 'dislikes putting himself forward'; 'of the rest there is nothing to be said. They do their work decently, earn their pay, & that is all.'[57]

5

There were extensive areas of party patronage confined largely within their own specialised professional demarcations. The law provided places ranging from prestigious and lucrative judgeships to comfortable commissionerships to petty official or municipal solicitorships. The attorney-general, Sir Richard Baggallay, had been denied the vice-chancellorship in 1868 because his Hereford seat was too vulnerable to risk at re-election. Now Disraeli could promote him to a lord justiceship of appeal 'in high spirits'; for Sir Richard's new seat was Mid-Surrey, 'a large & formerly very democratic constituency', but now to the south of the metropolis what Middlesex was to the north, copious with smug middle-class villas. The Liberals in 1875 could find no one to contest Sir Richard's replacement.

Nor was the party neglectful of loyal and serviceable connections: not the least of Hardinge Giffard's claims to the solicitor-generalship in 1875 was his father's devoted editorship of the *Standard* over many embattled years. H.C. Lopes, QC, MP for Launceston in 1868 and Frome in 1874, was another telling example at the more exalted level of the profession. He applied to his fellow West Countryman Northcote in 1876 for the solicitor-generalship. 'I believe most people feel I have been unfairly passed over on several occasions.' Lopes had been nine years in the Commons incurring great expenses, 'now holding this seat at my own cost, and through my own property'. He had led the Western Circuit for eight years; and had a large family to provide for. So: if not the solicitor-generalship, then at least a vacant judgeship.[58] Cairns was in a position to provide handsomely for Lopes with a lord justiceship of appeal in November 1876. William Charley, MP for Salford, was well rewarded for his early organisational work in Lancashire with the common serjeantship of the City in 1878, and by a knighthood on his defeat at Salford in 1880.

Expenses and costs could indeed be insupportable burdens. Northcote pleaded with Disraeli for a charity commissionership to rescue William

Forsyth, QC, MP for Marylebone, who 'found himself unable to afford Parliamentary life'. It was held to be vital that a vacancy on the Charity Commission must be filled by 'a really good Chancery lawyer'; but also it was held 'desirable, if possible, to get a political friend'. 'Is Marten (M.P. for Cambridge) fit?' Northcote asked Cairns. 'He is a very useful supporter.'[59] (Marten, like Charley, had been one of Raikes's helpers in the early days of the National Union.) In the same healthy spirit of party Gathorne Hardy was much gratified by Cairns's obliging transfer of a Norfolk judge wanted for the party in Oxford, where he could be a political asset: 'He is the invaluable person at a University Election knowing everybody's address & his residence near Oxford would be a very great advantage.'[60] Some claims were felt to have little purchase. Dyke advised Disraeli about an application for a commissionership in America from a baronetical barrister: 'Sir Herbert Croft late member for Herefordshire – he urges it on the ground chiefly, that he has been managing a Rose show in the West of England: an insufficient reason enough.'[61]

Ireland was its own intense world as far as patronage was concerned. Wilson Patten never quite lost the scars of his brief experience as chief secretary. Derby noted him 'rather nervous about an appointment he has made, and which he thinks will be attacked by the Irish'. Patten reported that 'the corruption he found exceeded all that he had expected, or could have believed, though prepared for a good deal'. No person was ever recommended on grounds of merit; 'everything was and is treated as a matter or bargain and jobbing.' Altogether Patten 'seems to have been thoroughly disgusted with his post, as from the first he expected to be.'[62] An Irish privy-councillorship was the modest object of desire of Charles Frewen in return for services to the party in County Cork, which he begged to remind Disraeli had cost his family several thousand pounds.[63] It was always assumed that English appointments to Irish offices required a certain bonhomous stamp of personality and character. When by the end of 1875 Abercorn signalled that he was ready to quit Dublin, Beauchamp was mentioned as a possible successor. Derby, ever ready to put obstacles in the way of the *parti prêtre*, was clear that 'his ritualism would be unpopular with the Protestants, and his pedantic stiff ways peculiarly objectionable to the Irish.'[64] There was the other side of the question also to bear in mind: what Irish ways might be peculiarly objectionable to English ministers. When Henry Lennox applied to Stanley for help in getting Mayo's place in 1868, Stanley doubted his 'temper, which dealings with Irish members would be likely to try very severely'.[65] This, among other things, was again held against Lennox in 1874.

The colonies and India equally offered vast scope for due recognition of partisan merit. The range from great to petty places was of dizzying declivity. At the very top was the governor-generalship of India, a place of special import at this time because of the queen's impending assumption of the imperial title. Northbrook, appointed by the Liberal government, was at odds with Salisbury, especially over Salisbury's zeal for the interests of the

Lancashire textile industry; and decided to retire early. This put Disraeli and Salisbury in a difficulty. Lord Powis declined the offer of India. So did Lord John Manners. So did Lord Carnarvon. Disraeli was then at a loss. Salisbury, in despair at the 'barrenness of the Tory land', could only suggest names that seemed to him 'just tolerable'. Derby was clear that Buckingham would not be equal to it. Napier was reckless in finance. Lyons would refuse. Bartle Frere? Dufferin? The queen mentioned Dufferin; who was held to be disqualified as being a Whig who had accepted appointments from Gladstone. But the queen's real hope was that India might be the means of ridding herself of Derby. As Salisbury remarked to Disraeli, the 'appearance of Derby's name is a charming touch of nature. It reveals a world of untold suffering – and desperate hope.'[66]

Meanwhile, Salisbury had the governorship of Madras at his disposal. Hobart had 'left us a "peck of troubles" at Madras', as he told Disraeli; and with Burmese war impending. Disraeli wanted to dump Loftus, the ambassador at St. Petersburg ('a mere Polonius'), there; but Salisbury objected to his age. 'At present.', he reported to Disraeli, 'I have offered the place to Lytton – who is young able & has great hereditary claims upon the party: and who as far as I have seen & heard has done efficiently all he has been entrusted with.'[67] Lytton was an obscure diplomatist at that time obscurely minister at Lisbon; better known in the guise of 'Owen Meredith', exponent of a Polish mystical poetic tradition. Derby registered 'surprise': he thought Lytton 'quite fit for the place, as far as brains go: but he has weak health, no great love for business, and is much devoted to his wife and children'.[68] Salisbury defended his offer on the grounds of the need to have a man of rank for the position, 'and one accustomed to the conciliatory habits of diplomacy'. When Lytton refused, Derby suggested another of his diplomatists, Layard. Even Madras might have been considered excessive for one of Lytton's modest qualifications. But Salisbury was in a weak position to resist when Disraeli proceeded to convert the Madras offer into the empire of India. It became a Disraelian gesture by one romantic literary man to the son of an old romantic literary friend. Hardy's response reflected a general public astonishment: 'I see with surprise Lord Lytton named for Govr. Genl. vice Northbrook. I had no idea that his claims or merits were so high.'[69] Lytton might well refuse Madras on the grounds of delicate health. But as Derby cheerfully pointed out, it would be quite something to die as viceroy. He proved to be an appointment which gave Salisbury keener cause to lament the barrenness of Tory land and so singular a case of great hereditary claims upon the party.

Madras was filled by the duke of Buckingham, who could not be fitted back into the cabinet in 1874. But this was not before a bid had been launched by Lord Bath, earlier thwarted for a Household appointment. Abergavenny told Corry: 'Last night I was smoking a pipe with Bath & five others when he said "that would be the place for me" meaning Madras. Henry Thynne thinks he was in earnest.' Abergavenny thought that Disraeli might like to know.[70] Derby protested strongly: 'though rather sharp, he has no habits of business, no experience of any kind, strong prejudices of rank and class which make him unpopular at home, and an amount of personal conceit which is offensive.'[71] He was also, of course, of the *parti prêtre*. Bath remained unemployed. The fate of Loftus illustrates the uses to which the colonial dimension of external patronage could be put. As long as Derby was at the Foreign Office Loftus was safe in St. Petersburg; but Salisbury came to share Disraeli's desire to be rid of him. They were even willing to replace him with Dufferin. But Salisbury tempered this desire with mercy. Negotiations had been entered into with the Colonial Office.

> Turning out Loftus to starve – given his condition of debt it would be little else – would be a very harsh measure . . . it would create a great deal of observation: & even scandal: which would not be lessened by the fact that Loftus is a Tory & Dufferin a Whig. On the other hand Loftus must be got rid of: while it is very material that he should be got rid of in a natural way. Under these circumstances New South Wales is a godsend.[72]

Being sent out by the secretary of state for the colonies to govern New South Wales could be in such circumstances a kind of classic doom of patronage. Patronage could on occasion rescue deserving candidates from such dooms. The chairman of the Conservative Registration Committee at Par in Cornwall asked Northcote for the favour of a commissionership in lunacy for Nicholas Kendall, late MP for East Cornwall. Northcote put the case to Disraeli that Kendall was 'a most active and consistent supporter, and has suffered much as you probably know in fighting our contests in East Cornwall'. There was a feeling that he should not return to Gibraltar but stay 'where he can be so useful to the Conservative party in this division'. Northcote urged that 'any kindness that could be shown to poor Kendall would be much appreciated in Cornwall, and would, I am sure, help our party there'.[73] Non-partisan appointments were on occasion unavoidable. Preferment of Lord Lorne, Whig MP for Argyllshire and son of the duke of Argyll, to the governor-generalship of Canada in 1878 is readily accounted for by the detail that the marchioness of Lorne was Her Royal Highness the Princess Louise, daughter of the queen.

6

Clerical preferment was another professionally demarcated world of political patronage. It had a special importance for the Conservative party because of the historical intimacy of Toryism and the Church of England. Clerical influence as an electoral factor was never discounted. The great distinction as far as government was concerned in this area was that patronage was confined to the first lord of the Treasury as making recommendations regarding the prelatical patronage of the Crown, to the lord chancellor, and (to a relatively minor degree) the chancellor of the duchy of Lancaster. Bishops and deans and chapters themselves exercised most of the patronage to livings in the Church, together with the universities and colleges of Oxford and Cambridge and some of the greater public schools. The other important dimension of clerical patronage, amounting to something like a quarter of the Church's benefices, was that of livings in the gift of private patrons. There were over 5,000 such patrons, overwhelmingly owners of landed estates. The average well established peer would have half a dozen or so livings in his gift. A rather grand English duke like Northumberland disposed exclusively of 23 livings. Salisbury had 7 in his gift. The average private patron was likely to be a squire with one or two benefices to give. Disraeli himself had but one, the vicarage of Hughenden, at £280 per annum. Thus clerical patronage had two practical aspects from a Conservative party managerial viewpoint. High dignities in the Church were important as patronage not only in themselves, but for the patronage they exercised in turn. And clerical patronage was important in county constituencies because of the nexus of parson and squire. It was a grievance among the Scottish gentry that such patronage was abolished in the Kirk in a feeble attempt by the Conservative government to appease Scottish popular sentiment. At one point in 1874 disaffection in the party in the Lords was explained to Disraeli as a consequence of abolition being 'disliked by some Scotch lords'.[74]

It was not easy for outsiders to gain the ear of ministers officially competent in Church patronage. Dartmouth, a peer with nine livings in his gift, felt he had cause to complain to Corry about the curt and barren responses he had had to his clerical recommendations.[75] On the other hand, Bath thanked Cairns for making an appointment at Upton Lovell which was gratifying to 'Personal and Political friends' interested in the parish, which had for many years been neglected.[76] Cairns as lord chancellor was the prime distributor of the government's lesser clerical patronage; and no doubt applications to him from cabinet colleagues tended not to be curtly received. In pressing the claims of 'an old & valued friend of mine', an old-fashioned High churchman, Salisbury carefully added that he was aware that Cairns administered 'this patronage wholly apart from personal considerations'.[77] From Hardy there was 'an early supporter at Leominster' asking for a lord chancellor's living for his son.[78] From Northcote there was the case of the second master at Blundell's School, Tiverton, in need of a chancellor's living of not less than '£5 – 600 to keep a large family'.[79]

At the altitude of bishoprics and deaneries Disraeli was more circumspect with his patronage than in his earlier spell of office. Undoubtedly, Salisbury's presence had a sobering effect, reinforced by Carnarvon and then Sandon's 'earnest though moderate' churchmanship. 'Nothing gives me more trouble than the Episcopacy', complained the prime minister. 'There are so many parties, so many "schools of thought" in the Church.'[80] In the case of Archdeacon Trollope of Stow, for example, Disraeli was advised that he 'belonged to the Old High Church Party & may be a somewhat too uncompromising defender of the rights of the Church'; indeed, an advocate of 'no surrender' on the burials question.[81] The great count against Dean Johnson of Wells, as conveyed by the 'decidedly unfavourable' Lord Bath, was that, quite apart from being 'unequal to his position', he had damned himself by being secretary to the Reform Commission at Oxford. 'In Politics he was opposed to us, as a Churchman he has no claim; his only ground of appeal is ad misericordiam, and although I shall not be sorry to see him removed from Wells, he ought not to have anything more important conferred upon him.'[82]

Cairns and Salisbury clashed over the claims of Farrar, master of Marlborough. Cairns thought he would make a good bishop for the new see of Truro; Salisbury, who had been looking into his writings with a view to the bishopric of Calcutta, thought him too theologically loose in the 'Essays & Reviews' manner. Salisbury warned Disraeli that there would be a 'considerable outcry if he was made a Bishop; certainly more outcry than the man is worth'. Moreover, it was Salisbury's opinion that, 'though the Archbishop cannot be expected to agree in that view, schoolmaster Bishops are always a doubtful experiment'. No doubt a man 'somewhat of Farrer's colour' was desirable for Truro. 'They are all Wesleyans there: & a High Churchman of any kind would be out of place.'[83] It was Hardy who slipped between Cairns and Salisbury to secure Truro for Edward Benson, High 'but not extreme in his Church views'.[84] Benson proved so little out of place as to make the reputation which led to his succeeding Tait at Canterbury.

Cairns and Salisbury, however, were always ready to return to the fray. It was part of the function of patronage to keep the grievance-laden schools of thought in the Church as near to a state of discontented equilibrium as feasible. Cairns to Disraeli: 'Dr. Benson's promotion seems to give the Crown a Canonry. As Dr. B. would probably be ranked in the non-Evangelical school you may perhaps think it right to look in the Evangelical school for a Canon; & such an appointment wd. certainly be well received.' The suffragan bishop of Guildford had recommended that Canon Garbett of Christ Church, Oxford, was 'facile princeps among the Evangelical clergy', and deserving of a 'real' canonry.[85] Salisbury had a style of advocacy which Disraeli doubtless relished: 'As for Rochester I do *not* advise Setterton. He is quite a mediocrity. Have you thought of Maclagan of Kensington? A man who contrives to combine the good word of the Queen, the Archbishop, the Bishop of London, & the High Churchmen, must be something of a genius.'[86] Maclagan later got Lichfield. Lady Salisbury helped to deflect Disraeli's nomination of the Evangelical J.C. Ryle to the deanery of Salisbury by encouraging his immediate promotion to the new bishopric of Liverpool, the last gasp of the ministry's clerical patronage. 'Do make a rather high Church & *gentleman* Dean of Salisbury. It is an old fashioned &

exclusive place & Dr. Ryle would do better among the epiciers of Liverpool than there. His appointment lost us votes there.'[87] The calculation was that Ryle would gain votes in Lancashire. Disraeli assured the Queen: 'Lord Sandon says his seat at Liverpool depends on the appointment being made by your present advisers.'[88]

The question of clerical influence on voters was never far from party managerial minds. Disraeli was advised in 1879 apropos of the bishopric of Durham of reports from Skene about 'the politics of Canon Lightfoot and Canon Westcott. They are both Conservatives. The former has always been so: the latter has become so since the last General Election, on which occasion he used his influence to help the Liberal Party.'[89] Lightfoot was duly preferred, one of the great scholarly ornaments of the bench. Disraeli's promotions at this epoch were creditable as well as being politically generally astute. Salisbury's report that he had been 'quite besieged by recommendations for Stubbs'[90] contributed decisively to the canonry at St. Paul's for the Oxford medieval historian.

At the lower levels of the strata in which politics and religion mixed less elegantly, the case of the *John Bull* newspaper, and its proprietor, the Rev E.A. Fitzroy, is illustrative of certain clerical manners of the 1870s. *John Bull* was a Saturday five-penny paper devoted to 'Constitutional Toryism', 'battling bravely for the old orthodoxy of Church and state', claiming to be the 'favourite organ of the gentlemen of England'. The Queen in 1876 found it 'so ultra and extreme in its religious views' as to prevent her 'taking it in any longer, the last 3 years'.[91] Her view was evidently prevalent; and Fitzroy needed a clerical safety-line to rescue him as his paper headed for wreckage on the rocks of tolerant moderation. He appealed to Northcote: 'I have spent the best years of my life in the endeavour according to my abilities to serve the Conservative & Church party, from which I have received but little encouragement. I have sunk £6000 in the paper & the last year has been the least successful of all!' The clerical journalist would have to sell up, despite support from Lord Rosslyn, Lord John Manners, and the lord chancellor. Could the Conservative and Church party provide him with a living? If it was thought that he was 'merely a political parson', he could cite references from several bishops; and the Dean of Lichfield assured Northcote that Fitzroy's 'claims to preferment are not merely political', being 'quite free from any extremes of doctrine or of ritual'. Northcote was able to assure Disraeli that Fitzroy had done 'good party work'.[92] Whether the party was able to do anything for Fitzroy in return is not clear. Certainly, he is not listed in subsequent registers of the beneficed clergy. Rather as with the case of Archdeacon Trollope, it can be assumed that the failure of Fitzroy's *John Bull* reflected the disintegration of the 'Old High Church Party' school of uncompromising assertion of ecclesiastical prerogative from which the Conservative party, in the aftermath of its defeat over the Irish Church, was extricating itself.

7

It was in the lower depths of secular and often petty patronage where the loaves and fishes were most voraciously competed for and where deficiencies of supply were most keenly complained of. Gorst assumed an almost emblematic role as a kind of shop steward of the deprived Conservative classes. Deprivation was the more keenly felt when discreet exchange of patronage at the highest levels of the party occasionally came into view. Thus W.S. Northcote, eldest son of the chancellor of the Exchequer, became in 1877 a commissioner of the Inland Revenue (alongside Keith-Falconer). Northcote was very grateful to Disraeli for this favour, which he could assure the prime minister was bestowed upon a 'worthy recipient'.[93] In his turn, Northcote had taken pains to interest Disraeli in the question of a place in the Department of Woods and Forests for Gathorne Hardy's younger son Alfred.[94] Nor was Cross's complaisance in the matter of the factory subinspectorship for Cairns's nephew likely to have passed unnoticed.[95] Cairns in turn took trouble with his ecclesiastical patronage to gratify Gathorne Hardy in the matters of a clerical brother-in-law and a clerical nephew.

Disraeli's cavalier robustness with patronage could occasionally rebound against him. Derby disapproved the appointment to the chief charity commissionership in 1875 of Sir S. Fitzgerald, MP for Horsham, long suspected of corruption. Disraeli defended his patronage:

> He says with some truth that the reports against him have never taken any public shape, nor have they prevented his being returned without opposition for a borough in which party feeling usually runs high: that he (F.) has been 30 years an active member of the party, has held a high Indian appointment, and cannot well be ignored without some assignable reason. Perhaps he is right, and the choice may have been inevitable, but it is unlucky.

When in 1877 the government was defeated in the Commons over a case of patronage in the Stationery Office being given to the son of Disraeli's vicar at Hughenden as a 'job', Derby blamed the vote on the impression created by the places given to Hampton (as chief Civil Service commissioner) and Fitzgerald: 'the first being too old for new work, & the latter suspected of corruption. These selections did harm at the time, & have not been forgotten.'[96]

Gorst's appeal to Disraeli on behalf of Balls, chairman of the Conservative Association in Cambridge borough, was typical of his efforts. 'If I may be so bold as to make a suggestion, I should say he would make quite as efficient a Poor Law Inspector as some recently appointed.' Gorst confessed furthermore that he could not see how, in these days (August 1874), 'when everyone is supposed to seek his own interest & passion & enthusiasm have ceased to be political forces, we are to keep a political party together, unless those who have made sacrifices for the cause while it was in adversity are to share in the advantages of success'.[97] Disraeli commented to Corry: 'I have answered, at length the enclosed insolent epistle from Gorst, & have snubbed him, but with dignity.'[98]

Unabashed, Gorst turned his sights on Smith, as one likely to be more sympathetic, on this occasion in the matter of Gorst's brother, T.W. Gorst, who sought legal preferment.

> I am by this time so accustomed to the refusal of every request I make of the Conservative Government, whether on political or personal grounds, that I am neither surprised nor mortified at the announcement that the promise made to us on my brother's behalf is not to be fulfilled. My own attachment to the cause is I hope of a character that cannot be affected by anything the leaders of the party may do: but on political grounds I greatly deplore the forgetfulness which all the members of the Government exhibit of those men, to whose exertions they largely owe their present positions. Most people in these days hold political opinions of a slight & easily modified character: and I cannot see how we are to keep our party together, unless those who have worked & made sacrifices for the party in days of adversity are to have some share of the advantages which attend success. I admire the few, who set before themselves the consciousness of helping a good cause as their only motive for political activity: but I greatly doubt whether, if there had been no motive but this at work during the last four years, our friends would be now enjoying the sweets of office.[99]

Hart Dyke was Gorst's next target. Gorst cited alleged patronage of 'personal friends of the ministers & our political opponents' which had excited 'general discontent' among the party's 'most faithful adherents'.

> I call these things to your notice because the present conduct of the leaders is bad for the interests of the party. There has long been a very prevalent idea that the Radical party does reward its adherents & the Tory party does not. I have heard this as long as I have had anything to do with politics: & what is now going on is likely to confirm & not destroy this notion.
>
> *Liberavi animam meam* . . . I have not mentioned my brother T.W. Gorst's case, because though in point, it is, or may be thought to be, partly personal.[100]

T.W. Gorst was a candidate for the clerkship of parliaments: which particular preferment happened at that moment to be a microcosm of the world of patronage. Northcote pushed for Sir J.R. Mowbray. To Corry:

> Of course I need not remind you of his party claims. Durham was a difficult seat to hold, and Oxford was a great seat to win. He has taken his disappointment in not having office very well, and, though he can hardly be called a popular man, there are a good many of his friends who would be pleased to see him provided for.[101]

Disraeli, however, had the idea of offering it to Corry: 'the best post in my gift, both in matter of dignity, agreeable duties, & income.'[102] Corry declined, as he had declined earlier offers from Disraeli. He was unwilling to 'sacrifice his present invisible position as private Secretary'. Gorst pressed for his brother, enlisting Dyke's support as one 'well acquainted both with his services to the Conservative Party and his personal qualifications'. Gorst would be most grateful 'for any consideration that could be shown to him by the Conservative Party'.[103] Taylor then weighed in on behalf of Spofforth, who declared the clerkship to be the object of his ambition. 'Mr. Spofforth worked with me in the service of the "Party" so long', and had so honourably tried to persuade Corry to accept it, that Taylor felt his cause must be pleaded.[104]

Disraeli, however, eventually promoted the deputy clerk of parliaments, Sir William Rose.[105] Mowbray was consoled later with a baronetcy. T.W. Gorst got a solicitorship in the Woods, Forests and Land Revenues Office. Spofforth got a taxing mastership in Chancery. And the deputy clerkship vacated by Sir William went to Ralph Disraeli, brother of the prime minister.

Gorst's own case remained meanwhile in a most unhappy state. He was convinced of the bad faith of the managers in failing to find a parliamentary seat for him: 'I think that any claim to the consideration of the Party should have been recognised and not ignored.'[106] Cairns did his best to pacify him. Dyke 'dissected' with him his grievances about patronage.[107] In November 1875 Disraeli offered Gorst the parliamentary secretaryship at the Local Government Board, in place of C.S. Read, who, as an advocate of the interests of tenant farmers against landlords, had offended Richmond. Gorst declined the offer 'so kindly made' with thanks. The president of the board, Sclater-Booth, was in the Commons; and Gorst felt that this would deprive the post of any real consequence.[108] Then in March 1877 Dyke decided that the question of the party's principal agentship, officially suspended in effect since 1874, needed to be restored to a regular footing. W.B. Skene was appointed, like Spofforth, as a salaried officer. This marked Gorst's first break with the party management; on which occasion he addressed to Disraeli a swingeing denunciation of the whole system of the whips 'managing elections at the Treasury' instead of letting Central Office do its job properly.[109] When soon after it was rumoured that Smith's successor as financial secretary at the Treasury, Stanley, was to be promoted, Gorst asked Disraeli that he be considered for the place.

> You were good enough some years ago to encourage me to hope that the work I was then able to do for the Conservative party would entitle me at a future time to employment in the Public Service. I am the only person engaged in the party management in 1874 to whom our accession to office has brought no political advancement as yet.[110]

Disraeli, of course, had an obvious answer to Gorst on that score. But it was not so obvious that he had an answer to a memorandum from Dyke which in effect echoed Gorst's earlier complaint about the party's management of patronage.

> A growing feeling of dissatisfaction, with regard to the distribution of Patronage, amongst our supporters in & out of parliament induced me in December last to endeavour to test its extent & reality. A confidential meeting takes place annually

in London, consisting of the Chairman and Secretaries of Local Conservative Associations in the English Counties & Boroughs. The meeting therefore is comprised of men who are voluntarily sacrificing both time & money in the service of the Party – paid agents being with few exceptions excluded. At a meeting comprising upwards of 50 of these gentlemen in Decbr last I purposely invited a discussion upon the Distribution of Patronage.

A very strong and unanimous opinion was openly expressed, that the mode in which Government Patronage is at present dispensed, is causing the greatest danger & injury to the interests of the Party. It was argued, that in the Lower Ranks of the Public Service, where merit is supposed to be the sole ground of advancement, partiality is shown to Radicals – those who examine & judge the merits of Public Servants of this Class are mostly Radicals, and take care to favour their own Partizans. Doubtless the Parliamentary Chiefs of Departments are informed & believe that this is not the case. But the Public Servants themselves who enjoy some opportunity of judging the merits of their fellows, assert as a fact that, the profession of Conservative opinions is an obstacle to advancement in the Public Service. It was urged that many individuals who rendered conspicuous services to the Party when in opposition have been completely ignored & in some cases treated with indifference.

It was again & again stated by influential local leaders from Yorkshire Lancashire & other Counties, that they did not complain of a Liberal if a better Candidate for an appointment being considered, & a Conservative rejected; but of a constant giving of place to a Liberal inferior in every capacity to another Candidate a Conservative.

Complaints of this kind are easily urged I am aware, & a feeling of discontent engendered, when a Political Party having had a small share of Power for many years, at length has considerable patronage to distribute. Making every allowance of this kind, I venture to say that no one really anxious for the future of the Party could have heard the discussion referred to without the gravest alarm – & when the additional fact remains, that daily and increasing complaints are made by our supporters in parliament more especially with regard to the Political action of the permanent Officials in every Department, I can not too strongly urge careful & immediate attention to a danger which if not checked must prove fatal to the very existence of the Party.[111]

Honours: lieutenancies and great Court orders

1

Honours in the gift of ministers had less substance than places but not less purchase in a political society aristocratic in its tone, with a monarchy at its apex. Here the materials of patronage were lord-lieutenancies of counties (a kind of combined place and honour); the exclusive Court orders of chivalry: Garter, Thistle, and St. Patrick; peerages and steps in the peerage; privy-councillorships; baronetcies; and an assorted range of knighthoods, some of them available from lesser orders of chivalry not entirely reserved for the supposedly non-political 'official' servants of the Crown.

Lord-lieutenancies held pride of place because they were indicative of high aristocratic status and acknowledged local 'popularity', which was the current cant for willingness to disburse money in good causes, directly or indirectly political. They were also endowed with considerable secondary county patronage in the form of such things as deputy-lieutenantships, magistracies and commissions in the yeomanry and militia. Between 1874 and 1880 Disraeli conferred 39 lieutenancies (the 'initiative' with Irish lieutenancies, as with Irish places and honours, lay with the Irish lord-lieutenant).

Party criteria were strictly applied. Lord Bath, having failed to get Madras, made a bid in 1878 for the lieutenantship of Wiltshire. But his renegade behaviour over the Eastern Question had been much resented in the Conservative party. Abergavenny made no bones about it to Corry ('Private & confidential save & except P.M.No.1'): 'Bath deserves not Wiltshire & ought not to have it, unless he can be made to eat "humble pie." Were I the Great Chief I think I should offer it to Pembroke who has a much larger stake in the County & is 10000 times a better & more popular fellow.'[112] Pembroke's youth and the fleetingness of his War Office career were perhaps held against him; Lord Radnor was in the end preferred. Very often there were no problems: Beauchamp for Worcestershire in 1876; Bradford for Shropshire in 1875; Headfort for Meath in 1876; Powis for Montgomery in 1877; Sir Joseph Bailey, Bart., MP for Herefordshire, for Breconshire in 1875; Northumberland for Northumberland in 1877; Richmond for Banff in 1879: such were characteristic instances. But occasionally even an undoubted grandee had to stoop to soliciting. Athole wrote to his fellow Scottish duke Richmond concerning the lieutenancy of Perthshire, disputed between Lord Mansfield and himself. Mansfield was already, Athole pointed out, a lieutenant (Clackmannan, 1852). 'He is 72 and therefore for the good of the Conservative cause I think his appointment would be rather a mistake. As far as rental in the county goes mine is double his.' Athole felt that his Thistle (1868) and deputy-lieutenancy (1875) still left a gap. 'Ld Beaconsfield seems of late to have ignored my existence and never even asks me to his Parliamentary dinners.'[113] Athole did not stoop in vain.

In Scotland and Wales scarcity value played its part. 'Conservative landlords are scarce in Ross-shire,' as was pointed out on behalf of the veteran pre-1832 MP for Cromarty, Duncan Davidson of Tulloch, by his cousin and brother-in-law; who added details of Davidson's 'services on behalf of the Conservatives, since you told me that information on that point might be useful'.[114] It was. Arthur Walsh, MP for Radnorshire, informed Disraeli in 1875 that his father Lord Ormathwaite was resigning the lieutenancy of Radnorshire, and ventured to submit his own claims to the office. 'There is no [other] peer resident in Radnorshire, and *on our side* in politics I do not know of any county gentlemen who would be considered eligible for the office.' Walsh, in view of his likely succession to the peerage, had been looking for someone to take on the parliamentary seat for the county, but could not find anyone

> who would be able either to bear the expense of the contest or unite the party in his support. I am also perfectly certain that nothing would be more unpopular than to create any non-resident in the County Lord Lieutenant. In making this application to you I do not wish to rest on what little service I have been able to render the party. I have given a full and cordial support to you because I believed that a liberal radical policy was mischievous to the country, and because I believed that you were the only man capable of successfully opposing that policy.[115]

Walsh succeeded to both the peerage and the lieutenancy in 1875.

The case of Kincardinshire in 1876 illustrates many of the inward saliences of the genre. The issue was between Sir Thomas Gladstone, Bart., of Fasque (W.E. Gladstone's eldest brother) and Lord Inverurie, heir to the earldom of Kintore (the Keith-Falconer peerage). Gladstone, as Major Keith-Falconer pointed out to Abergavenny, was 'an old man by no means popular & a great screw & has done nothing that I know of for the party'. Gladstone could not in the course of nature hold the office very long 'but he would probably outlive the Govt. in which case the next presentation might revert to the Rads-Irish'.[116] A count against Inverurie was that he was but a recent convert from the predominantly Whig politics of his family. Moreover, his father Lord Kintore was already, by grace of the Liberal party, lieutenant in Aberdeenshire. But the person who had 'converted Lord Inverurie from the error of his ways & thinks he is the right man' was no less than Lord Abergavenny himself: who had groomed the young Scot and taught him well that 'the Carlton was a *pleasanter* place than Brooks'.[117] Cairns was brought in to adjudicate between the claims. No doubt Lord Inverurie's abandoning the 'traditional politics of his family' and becoming a Conservative gave him a claim to Lord Beaconsfield's consideration.

> No doubt his father's property in Kincardineshire stands at the top, & there is a precedent in Scotland for making Father & Son Lds. Lieut^{t}.: (tho' in Lord Fife's case both are of the same politics). . . . But I am bound to say – I have said it to his uncle, Major K. Falconer – that I cannot see that it is likely Sir J. Gladstone can be passed over. He is not very popular; & I should think has always done more harm than good to the party: but he has always been earnest & consistent, & it wd have an ugly appearance if he were set aside.[118]

Cairns's argument held sway; and Sir John's lieutenancy became the one gleam of success in an otherwise long and disastrous Conservative political career.

Cumberland and Westmorland in 1875 also offer insights into the arts of managing lieutenancies. Gerard Noel reported to Disraeli that there was no one except Lord Lonsdale with sufficient property or position to enable his holding two lieutenancies. For Westmorland alone the candidates might be Lonsdale, the Hon. W. Lowther, Lord Bective (the two county MPs), or Sir

Richard Musgrave, the unsuccessful Conservative candidate for the eastern division of Cumberland in 1874.

> Lonsdale is not of age till next October & for *other reasons* I could not recommend the appointment. William Lowther has no property or residences in either county & would be looked upon as a stop gap. Such an arrangement *might* be made but it would hardly be satisfactory to the County.
>
> Bective has a large property but is unpopular and this recent messy law suit has considerably affected his position. I think no fear need be entertained about his being able to do any political mischief were he passed over.
>
> With regard to Sir R. Musgrave, he is most popular, has considerable property in both Counties, & though Eden Hall is in Cumberland it is on the banks of the river which divides the Counties. He has fought two battles, & his appointment would give general satisfaction.

The latest of Musgrave's unavailing contests for East Cumberland had been in the April 1876 by-election. Clearly, he deserved well of the party; and it is possible that his appointment as lord-lieutenant aided in his ultimate capture of the seat in 1880, against the prevailing trend.

Noel proceeded with a review of the Cumberland candidates. Eliminating Lonsdale and Lowther, Lords Leconfield and Muncaster and Sir Robert Graham, 10th baronet, of Esk, were *prima facie* candidates.

> Leconfield is not known in either County and never takes any part in Cumberland politics. He is most unpopular, and though he has a large stake in the County the chief part is derived from minerals which interest is adverse to us. Through his apathy and unpopularity we lost Cockermouth, his appointment would give real displeasure.

Graham was not known in the county and in any case did not seek the honour. Muncaster, an Irish peer and MP for West Cumberland, was on the other hand willing and eligible. 'Muncaster has an income of £23,000 a year, though part of this is in Lancashire and part of Yorkshire, but he has over 11,000 acres in Cumberland is very popular and his family has been known in the County since the Conquest.' Muncaster had to be Disraeli's choice.

It was, nonetheless, of the essence of the decorum deeply invested in the code of creating lords-lieutenant that there should still persist an 'ugly appearance' in the setting aside of the Lowthers of Lonsdale. Noel felt obliged to make an oblique apology: 'Of course, I should be too happy to see Lonsdale Lord Lieutenant for one, or even both Counties, as this distinction has been held so long in the family, but I am unable conscientiously to offer you other advice than I have done.'[119]

2

Garters, Thistles, and Patricks were important for very much the same reasons as lord-lieutenancies. They were outward and visible (and very decorative) signs of the inward and invisible grace of being well born in the world of society and well regarded in the world of politics. English Garters were more esteemed than Scottish Thistles; which in turn looked down upon Irish Patricks, an order created to cater for unslakeable Irish chivalric appetites as recently as 1783.[120] Yet, though it might seem a long view down from a Garter stall at Windsor to a Patrick stall at Dublin, the view upwards from the lesser equestrian orders would tend to group them more nearly within an exclusive aristocratic ethos. Apart from royalties both home and foreign, there were but 25 Garters, 16 Thistles, and 22 Patricks. The great practical distinction between them was that whereas noble Garters were very rarely openly canvassed for, ancient and noble Thistles and illustrious Patricks were begged for by Scottish and Irish peers respectively with unabashed persistence.

The arts, manners, and decorum involved in making the offer of a Garter are well exemplified in the case of the duke of Norfolk in 1878. The 28-year-old duke was both the premier peer of England and the premier Roman Catholic layman, with hereditary attachments to Whig politics. What Disraeli had in mind was the expediency of capitalising, after a decent interval, on Gladstone's explosively offensive *Vatican Decrees* outburst of 1874. Accepting an honour in such circumstances was tantamount to declaring a political allegiance. Norfolk was a member of the Council of the Catholic Union of Great Britain, and the recipient of Newman's riposte to Gladstone. Norfolk, however, felt that the interval was not yet decent enough.

> I have always thought that I should some day join the Conservative Party and it is easy to see at this time that questions may come up at any moment which would make me feel it to be my duty to do so at once.
>
> Were I to do this however I should be breaking from the traditions of my family and I think that anyone so acting ought to take care that his motives be not misunderstood as mine would probably be if I became a supporter of Her Majesty's Government within a short time of my accepting the Garter.[121]

It was Salisbury who eventually received Norfolk into both the Conservative party and into the order. Opportuneness was of the essence of the code. The queen offered Disraeli himself a Garter at the height of the war crisis early in 1878; but in such circumstances he felt obliged to decline.

When Derby declined a Garter on his resignation in 1878 he signalled that his political allegiance was cancelled. Had he accepted it he could not, in decency, have moved across, as he did, to the Liberals. Quite logically, he accepted a Garter from Gladstone in 1884. Disraeli gave Garters to two of his ducal colleagues, Richmond and Marlborough. The Queen insisted that he accept one himself on his triumphant return from Berlin in 1878; Disraeli in turn stipulating that Salisbury also should be so honoured; and stipulating further and covertly through Corry with Lady Salisbury that if Salisbury declined, he must too. This was enough to melt even Salisbury's cynicism.[122]

Thistles were much livelier affairs. Disraeli characteristically took his earliest opportunity to honour young 'Lothair', the 3rd marquess of Bute. His Lords' whip, Colville, an exigent contender in 1874, was eminently right and proper as deserving well of the party. The more usual mode of application is illustrated in the case of Lord Dunmore, in 1875, who approached Colonel Taylor.

> I hate asking for things, but I believe one never gets things if one dont so I am going to ask you to put in a good word for me to Mr. Disraeli for this vacant 'Thistle'. . . . I have served my party faithfully for 15 years . . . In the election before last Mr. Baillie of Red Castle only got in for the County of Inverness by a narrow majority. We had no polling place in the Hebrides, but our votes carried the election & it cost us over £500 to get our votes carried down to the poll. *We* won Invernessshire . . . In this last election in Stirlingshire I have no hesitation in saying that I carried the member in – not only by giving £1000 to the election expenses without which example on my part the Whig candidate would have had a W[alk]. O[ver]. but I made the excuse of a wet harvest to let my tenants off 10 per cent of their rents which was a pretty good sum out of my pocket. Well it had the desired effect . . . Since then I have worked v. hard at the Board of Trade without a salary & have conducted all the business of that department in the House of Lords. . . . I have a large property in Scotland & will undertake to say that I have worked harder for the Conservative Party than any other Peer in Scotland.[123]

Taylor passed this on to Corry, to whom Dunmore addressed an extra appeal: 'With Lord Kinnaird's death there is a Thistle vacancy. Put in a good word for a *pal* who has *worked* for it. Charlie D.'[124] Even this failed to move Disraeli, who evidently felt that Dunmore's lordship in waiting and the lord-lieutenancy of Stirlingshire were adequate acknowledgement.

Lord Lothian suggested perhaps the advantages of a more deviously modest application. He wrote to Corry:

> There is now a vacant 'Thistle' at the disposal of the Prime Minister, and I take this opportunity of writing to say, that although I do not in any way wish to *ask* for the honour, as probably there may be many others, who have more claims, yet I should be very much obliged if you could, as you may think best, let Mr. Disraeli know that I should be very much gratified if he could sooner or later bear me in mind.[125]

Though Lothian presented his case more on ancestral than overtly political grounds, he gained his end. Lord Orkney, however, did not, in his offer to settle for a Thistle instead of a U.K. peerage.

It was possible for a person below the rank of a peer to get a Thistle, as witness the instance of Sir William Stirling-Maxwell, 9th baronet, in 1876. The distinctive charm of the great Court orders was always, as Lord Melbourne had memorably put it, that there was 'no damned nonsense of merit' about them. But a non-peer's claims would have to be buttressed by very exceptional marks of merit: in Stirling-Maxwell's case, long service as a Scottish county MP combined with the highest reputation as a man of letters and 'virtuoso'.

Rival claims in 1878 between Seafield and Fife were adjudicated by Abergavenny's advice to Corry that 'unless the T is promised it had better be given to Seafield'. Fife was going to be punished for his niggardliness to party funds. 'The Lord Lieut^{y} old "Duffy" doubtless would like & as he would the T – but he is the d– – –l to screw I know & never would "part" for party purposes.'[126] Duffy Fife was consoled in 1879 with the lieutenancy of Elginshire; but had to wait long for Seafield's departure before securing his 'T'.

A certain degree of polite blackmail was not absent in cases where grandees felt there was an invidious gap between their political purchase and their party's gratitude. Thus Colville to Corry in 1879:

> This is for <u>your</u> most private ear. And you must excuse me – but I should be inclined to think that if Montrose does not get the Thistle – he will go over to the other side & he has considerable influence in *two* Scotch counties that at *present* return Conservatives.
>
> I do not know him so my motives are perfectly pure.[127]

The 5th duke of Montrose was installed as a knight of the Thistle in 1879. Disraeli 'grieved' at not being able to give it to Rosslyn: 'but', as Hardy commented, 'political before friendly considerations.'[128]

Patricks, like Irish lieutenancies, had to surmount the initial hurdles of the lord-lieutenant and his chief secretary. The mores were much as with Thistles. Apart from the prince of Wales, Disraeli disposed of three Patricks in 1868 (including one for Mayo), and four in his second term of office. Lord Waterford, preening himself as the premier marquess of Ireland, was much put out in 1868 when his application was denied in favour of Lord Erne. However, Lord Farnham's atrocious death in a railway disaster providentially cleared the way. As Corry remarked to Disraeli: 'What a catastrophe on the L & NWR! and how strange that, almost at the moment you were reading Waterford's letter, another green ribbon should have fallen in!'[129] Waterford was gratified in due course with a lieutenancy as well. Lord Courtown's perhaps injudicious disclaimer in his application in 1874 that '*Personally*' I am indifferent to decorations',[130] invited the obvious response of being taken at face value; which it apparently was. Lord Limerick's application failed also in 1874. But Portarlington's complaint in 1878 that, despite being an Irish representative peer, he was always being passed over, led to his claim being successfully pushed by Hicks Beach.[131]

Peerages

1

Peerages, steps in peerages, and U.K. peerages for Scottish and Irish peers, were the stock in trade at the upper end of party political patronage in honours. The great distinction between lieutenancies and exclusive orders on the one hand and peerages on the other was that, while a general criterion of appropriate social eligibility obtained, peerages varied enormously in their status and consequence. At the bottom end of the range a political peerage promoted from the House of Commons was as likely to be a consolation for failure as a mark of success. This was the case with the baronies of Winmarleigh (Wilson-Patten), Hampton (Pakington), and Norton (Adderley). Lamington (Cochrane-Baillie) was a sentimental accolade for political hackdom. Gathorne Hardy's viscountcy of Cranbrook in 1878 was as signal a mark of defeat as this political epoch provided. As against this, for a long-serving MP, retired or defeated, a peerage could signify an honourable ambition ultimately attained. This was the case with Ardilaun (Guinness), Alington (Sturt), Ormsby-Gore (Harlech), Tollemache, Trevor (Hill), and Haldon (Palk). Disraeli's own earldom of Beaconsfield in 1876 was of course *hors concours* as far as patronage was concerned.

Disraeli habitually consulted Derby, who cultivated a broodingly critical, scholarly expertise over his own order.

> Talk of peers: he is much pressed, says he must make some: thinks of Tollemache, Gerard Sturt, Ormsby Gore, & perhaps Gerard . . . all of old family, & large territorial wealth: in every way fit: except that Gerard is *bête* by nature, & that his son is a bad sort of fool . . . He is prepared to make Ld. Edwin Hill a peer, for which there appears no adequate reason: and Cochrane, which is absurd.

Derby had to admit that Sturt 'had received from my father a sort of half-promise'; and recognising the party services of the heir to an existing peerage, as in the case of Grey de Wilton defeated at Bath in 1874, 'cannot be objected to'.[132]

Certain promotions within the peerage were decidedly marks of sharing something of the inward and invisible grace which is political power and which radiated from the Beaconsfield peerage. Abergavenny's marquessate in 1876 was one such (though Derby, from his own peculiar Stanley viewpoint, was sniffy on the ground that it was 'odd that he should wish to be, as it is no great promotion for the head of a very old family already an earl').[133] Cairns's earldom in 1878 was another. These were power-brokers, and rare instances. By contrast, the extra dukedom (Gordon) for Richmond was almost a satire on the system. There were rewards for signal services of different kinds. Sondes was promoted to an earldom for the work he did in saving the Kent constituencies from electoral rout in 1880. Lytton got an earldom in 1880 for having put swagger back into the government of India. The ultimate range of the Beaconsfield radiation was attained in the Rowton peerage for Corry in 1880. There was the occasional gleam of non-partisan generosity. Salisbury argued for Northbrook's receiving an earldom rather than a viscountcy on his leaving India. Salisbury took the view that with regard to rewarding service in India and overseas with places and concomitant honours, party considerations should not prevail; it was expedient, in fact, to lean rather in the contrary direction to avoid any paralysis of administration.[134] But when Disraeli offered a peerage to Lord Odo Russell, ambassador at Berlin at the time of the congress in 1878, his brother the duke of Bedford refused to endow it on the grounds of the impropriety of a Whig's accepting an honour from a Tory prime minister.

Disraeli was not lavish with peerages. When it came to resignation honours in 1880 he was able to point out to the queen that whereas in five years Gladstone had advised 37 creations, he had, so far, advised in six years only 15.[135] His criteria for applications remained as he had expressed them at the time of Andrew Montagu's refusal in 1868: 'vast possessions, noble lineage, and devotion to the Conservative party.' As with Garters, a positive and unabashed application for a dukedom would be likely to be marked down, as in the case of Lord Shrewsbury in 1874, as indicative of 'excessive conceit'.[136]

The more modestly baronial Ormsby-Gore application of 1874 can stand as a classic model of a parliamentary family's claim. W. R. Ormsby-Gore, MP for Leitrim, wrote to Disraeli on behalf of his brother, MP for North Shropshire:

> Through the parliamentary services of our family; the fact of his representing in his own person, as heir at law, two extinct peerages; as possessing a territorial stake in the County befitting the dignity of a Peer; and by personal character.
>
> I think, taking them all combined, that there is no one, who has as good claims to be considered by the head of the Conservative party.
>
> Since the year 1837, between my father, my brother, and myself, we have always furnished two County Members to the ranks of our party, excepting an interval when my father only sat, caused by my losing my Election in 1852 through the mistake of an Agent.[137]

The Harlech barony, accordingly created in 1876, was founded on the 'beneficial interest' of landed property in two English, four Welsh, and five Irish counties.

An application from outside the House of Commons would put heavier stress on devotion to the Conservative cause in constituencies. Charles Abney-Hastings, of Donington Park, Leicestershire, set out in 1876 an exemplary case. After the New Year's honours he reproached Disraeli: 'I cannot but believe that some new Peers have been made & that I still remain Mr. Hastings.' He was in the position of being able to quote a virtual promissory note by Disraeli of 1868: '"If you can return two members for South Derbyshire, give a good majority for N. Leicestershire & do as you have done before at Dover, you will indeed have rendered transcendent services to the Cause"'.

> These transcendent services we rendered; and we did many smaller, tho' we said little about them. . . .
>
> As regards position, I say nothing, you know it.

As for wealth I am the owner of over 20000 acres in North Ayrshire, South Derbyshire & North Leicestershire; I have besides the Moira Collieries in N. Leicestershire, the Gresley Collieries in South Derbyshire, which give me a large income & from the mass of men & tradesmen employed, considerable influence.[138]

The matter of 'position' added the kind of cogency to this application which Disraeli was prone to acknowledge. The peerage of Donington he bestowed on Abney-Hastings in 1880 masked the more substantial fact that Lord Donington was married to the co-heiress of the Hastings marquessate, who was a Scottish countess and four times an English baroness in her own right.

This kind of penchant for the feudal graces could lead to dispute between Disraeli and those of his colleagues with sterner criteria for the utility of patronage. Cairns had no sympathy, for example, for Mortimer Sackville-West's application in 1874 as the inheritor of the Knole estate to revive a Sackville peerage. 'But I don't see', he protested to Disraeli, 'that he has any special claims, political or otherwise. He is, no doubt, a Conservative, but he has not done, and cannot do, anything for the party, & a peerage for him is just one the less to give to someone with higher claims.' Disraeli, however, was under pressures of which Derby was aware, though equally disapproving.

This is not a wise proceeding, as it rewards no public service, & pleases nobody: M. West being half crazy, and not having a friend in the world. But it seems the Queen thought herself bound by some promise to the old Ld & L'y Delawarr, that a second title should be created for the family: & the Buckhurst barony having merged in the earldom, she has replaced it by a new one.[139]

Doubtless Cairns fumed also over the case of the barony of Gerard, which Disraeli created in 1876 on grounds, it seems, purely of the illustrious pedigree of a 13th baronet.

There was certainly no stint of disappointed claimants. There was always the criterion of presentability; which might include eccentricity or even degrees of witlessness; but which excluded a case recorded by Derby of a Lancashire MP:

Saw Major Starkie, M.P. of Huntroyde, at his request: he came to tell me that he had refused an offer of a baronetcy from Disraeli, not thinking it worth his acceptance: he wanted a peerage: and asked my support to obtain one. He is a large landowner, rich, active in the service of his party, and has political influence: but rather stupid & loutish. As he stood holding his hat & turning it between his hands, shifting from one leg to the other, & asking me to say a word for him, I could not think him exactly of the stuff from which peers should be made: but peers are made from the same sort of material.[140]

Nor did the feudal graces always work. Probably disappointment was guaranteed by the gambit chosen for his application by R. Neville Grenville,

MP for Mid-Somerset, who wanted an extinct family peerage revived, or a privy-councillorship as second best. It was, he was sure, 'owing to our mid-Somerset majority in 1868 (1500) that your six staunch supporters in this County walked over in 1874'. 'As an old Peelite who has never wavered in his allegiance to the Conservative Party, I have seen all those who changed their politics, – I believe to a man, – promoted to every dignity & honour, as the enclosed list imperfectly shows.'[141] Neville Grenville listed 21 'Peelites and their Whig rewards', ranging from Gladstone ('Twice Premier') to Lord Alfred Hervey ('Receiver General'), replete with Garters, lieutenancies, peerages, cabinet places, colonial governorships, and every variety of lucrative office.[142] Disraeli's brilliant tactic was to respond to this with scholarly addenda, making the list even more scandalously dripping with Whig bribery. This inspired riposte nonplussed Neville Grenville and forced him back upon the theme of demonstrating how 'richly baited the man-trap was which caught so many', but 'against which I was proof'.[143] Disraeli was only too ready to grant him that further proof of self-denying virtue. Neville Grenville in disgust took the Chiltern Hundreds in 1878. Disgust was also the lot of the Kekewiches of Devonshire, in spite of Trehawke Kekewich's best efforts on behalf of his father through the good offices of Northcote. The material point here was that Northcote's offices were far from good: 'I do not, however, imagine that more can come of it.'[144] (The 'state' of Kekewich's 'affairs' had been 'very publicly talked about' in 1868.) It may be surmised that the Haldon peerage for the retired Devonshire MP, Palk, in 1880, was insult added to Kekewich injury. Sir Edmund Lechmere of Worcestershire acknowledged failure sadly ('After 30 years of faithful service to the cause, in and out of the House, and four Contested Elections, I ventured to urge my claim'); and could but hope for justice when Lord Beaconsfield again took office.[145]

A petition to Disraeli from 'Landowners and Inhabitants of the County of Derby' introduced the theme of a local grievance at patronage deprivation. In drawing the prime minister's attention 'to the services rendered to the County, to the Conservative Party, and to the Country at large' by William Mundy, former MP for South Derbyshire, the petitioners also drew attention to the fact that 'this County has not received any addition to its titled aristocracy from the ranks of the Conservatives during the present century, whilst more than one peerage, and other honours, have been conferred upon Derbyshire Whigs'. It was now 'generally felt that some recognition of the Conservative Landed Interest would materially strengthen the party, and recompense them for the struggles they have successfully made to secure a fair share of the County Representation.' Since the dissolution of 1868 there had been 'no less than six hotly contested elections in the County, five of which resulted in the return of Conservatives; and there has also been one Conservative walk-over.'[146] Even so, Disraeli was not prepared to assuage this ache of deprivation by ennobling an MP who had been defeated as far back as 1865.

Claims could be made on grounds of the familial *dignitas* of a senatorial *gens*. Sir Edmund Beckett, 5th baronet, of the Leeds banking family, asked for a peerage as the 'only possible recognition of the political services of our family' in the West Riding of Yorkshire only incidentally on behalf of the parliamentary role of his two brothers. He put this case to Corry:

> From the time when my father managed your father's election in 1826 till now it may be said that my people have been the chief managers of the Conservative party in this county and riding. Five of our family have had 16 contests since the first Reform Bill. There has never been a Conservative success in the West Riding unless one of my family have been victorious; I suppose it is certain that nobody but William Denison could have won Retford in 1876. I doubt if any other family could say all this, and add to it that their exertions have never been in any way recognised – or at any rate in any public way. . . . If I alone were concerned of course I have no personal claim, having devoted myself more to other things than politics. But I am not, especially as I have no children. But there are plenty of precedents both in old & modern times of dignities being granted to a man with remainder to the heirs male of the body of his father. Of course you know that a peerage is not likely to suffer starvation in our family.[147]

Despite having the imprimatur of Abergavenny, this claim was not allowed until Salisbury's time, in 1886, with the Grimthorpe peerage. There were, in any case, rival claims as to Conservative managerial chiefdom in the West Riding.[148]

The duchess of Northumberland's recommendation in 1878 on behalf of the Shirleys was of Irish consequence. Evelyn Shirley's 'exertions for the Conservative party have been great & difficult & expensive', she pointed out. 'His father & he have fought *many* contests both in Warwickshire & in Co. Monaghan; and in '74 he brought in his Son, beating a Home Ruler.' In 1868 he 'rescued the seat from Lord Dartrey'. 'The Shirley tenants *will* vote for a Shirley, but for *no other Conservative*, & their 500 tenants turn the Election.'

> Mr. Shirley has made his ward, Ld Ferrers a Conservative – (the head of the Family) – they *were* Whigs. Mr. Shirley has always been a resident landlord and a good Churchman.
>
> Ld Dartrey, his near neighbour, was largely rewarded by the Liberal Governments – an English Peerage, Ribbon of St. Patrick, Earldom, Ld Lieutenancy etc. etc.[149]

Shirley was indeed a greater landlord in County Monaghan than Lord Dartrey. But in 1880 his son was beaten in Monaghan 'by a combination of the Roman Catholic Priests and the Presbyterian Ministers, to which I must add the desertion of Lord Bath'.[150] His hopes that the claim would not be forgotten (seconded again by the duchess) were unavailing: he died a commoner still in 1882. Lord Bath had a kind of revenge.

Disraeli had a kind of revenge on Colonel Taylor, whose unwillingness to exchange the duchy of Lancaster for a peerage in 1875 inconvenienced dispositions regarding Gerard Noel. Taylor's complaint at being passed over for a peerage in 1880 was briskly dealt with by Disraeli:

> But you never resigned your office, but have enjoyed it more than six years: a capital office with no mean salary, little work, and the dignity of the Privy Council.
>
> Ultimately, I had to bestow on Gerard Noel a first-class office, disappointing many of my supporters, and not obtaining, either in his case or your own, any strength and assistance in debate.
>
> And yet you now tell me that your services to the party have never been recognized![151]

2

Promotions within the peerage and peerages of the United Kingdom for peers of Scotland or Ireland had their distinct niches in the repertoire of patronage. Without a subsidiary title of Great Britain or the United Kingdom political peers of Scotland or Ireland had to undergo the fatigue of election among their fellows to get a seat in the Lords. Cairns in 1874 very strongly recommended the earl of Dalhousie for an 'English peerage'. He had £60,000 a year from property (and therefore electoral influence); he occupied an unrivalled position in the county of Brechin; his son was equerry to the duke of Edinburgh; 'and with their aid, the whole political aspect of things in this county may be changed.' It was no doubt perfectly natural to have made Lord Strathmore lord-lieutenant; but it would be an error not to give an English peerage to Dalhousie, and it would be 'expedient to make an early offer'.[152] An early offer of the barony of Ramsay of Glenmark was duly made in 1875; but there was not the slightest change in the political aspect of things in the county.[153] Derby likewise recommended, successfully, the claims of the earl of Home. It was certainly expedient in 1880 to give a United Kingdom peerage to the Irish Viscount Barrington, MP for Eye and vice-chamberlain, extremely influential along with Corry in the inner recesses of Disraeli's private office; if only to release an official patronage seat in the Commons for disposal.

Lord Redesdale submitted his application for an earldom on grounds of his services to the party as chairman of committees in the Lords. Disraeli asked Derby's advice.

> In this Ld. R. magnifies his own services, tells a story of how he nearly got an earldom in 1842 and again in 1852 (but which only proves that he tried to get one and failed), & especially claims honors on the ground of his successful resistance to the Lord Chancellor's Appellate Jurisdiction Bill.

Balancing Redesdale's 'laborious habits & honesty in dealing with private bills', against his 'obstinacy & ill manners & the many enemies he has made', Derby had no strong objection, providing the heirless Redesdale's request for a special remainder was refused.[154] Redesdale became an inexpensively heirless earl in 1877.

Lord Tredegar thought he could fairly put in a claim for a promotion to Disraeli on the grounds that he had, in 1874, 'fought three *hard* contests' on his behalf, 'viz., the County of Brecon, the Boros of Brecon and Newport Mon., all three of which seats are now occupied by warm *Conservatives*. My *two* eldest sons represent *County* constituencies – which I believe is scarcely the case with any other Peer.'[155] Tredegar unquestionably had the acreage and the income to justify a viscountcy or even an earldom; but probably the death of the 2nd baron soon after, in 1875, put the matter out of immediate consideration. Certainly, Sherborne's claim for promotion would not have been judged anywhere near comparable.[156] On the other hand, the 3rd Lord Wharncliffe became in 1876 the 1st earl on the strength of this claim advanced through Corry in 1874:

> I want you to bring under Mr. Disraeli's notice a claim which I think the Wortley family have to some degree upon the party from long, & steady support of it except during the brief space when my uncle was Solicitor Genl. to Palmerston, thro' Gladstone's evil counsels – and the increased influence which we possess in the two divisions of the West Riding by the exertions of the family, and by more ample means than formerly. In the North Riding Feversham was raised to an Earldom,[157] & altho' he may own more land than I do, yet in point of family connection with Yorkshire there can be no comparison. . . .
>
> P.S. We have been the mainstay of the party in all the elections, since I succeeded.[158]

Wharncliffe added a rider next day: 'None of the other Conservative magnates here do anything, and the Wortleys are the heads of the party in South Yorkshire.'[159] As with the case of Sondes in Kent, an earldom would not have been thought excessive for such a position.

Privy-councillorships

The 'dignity of the Privy Council', as Disraeli had acidly remarked to Taylor, was an article of patronage which covered a wide variety of party circumstances. It was Noel's honour on retiring as chief whip, but as it carried then no place with it, it was a painfully empty distinction. It carried the style of 'right honourable' and certain procedural privileges in the House of Commons. It was an essential attribute for ministers dealing with confidential affairs; but otherwise it was a magnificent braided uniform. In the case of Hubbard's candidacy for the City of London in 1874 it was employed very effectively as a simple bribe.[160] It could be asked for as second best to a higher claim. Its possession could equally mark the rise of youthful success or the dignified decline of ageing hacks.

Raikes, who was trying his best to be a youthful success, felt that the limbo of being chairman of committees deserved some 'legitimate recognition'.[161] It took two more increasingly desperate applications and the fall of the government for Raikes, still exiled in his political outer darkness, to gain his prize. Northcote had to put in some urgent advocacy. As leader of the Commons he was in a good position to insist that it had been 'well earned', and he was sure it would impress Raikes's constituents, and 'could be of material assistance to him in an arduous contest'. Were Raikes not to get it he would have nothing to show for twelve years' service.[162] The category of declining hack is well represented in the case of Sir G. Graham Montgomery, MP since 1852 for Peebles and Selkirkshire. He justified his claim on the grounds that no Scottish Conservative member had received the honour since the equally ageing hack Sir James Fergusson in 1868; and on 'my past services in office and in maintaining successfully for so many years a seat for the party. My father represented Peebleshire for 30 years before the Reform Act of '32 and since then by his exertions & mine the county has been kept from the enemy.'[163] Montgomery lost both his seat and any last hope of the privy-councillorship in 1880.

Salisbury obtained the honour for one of his Indian Council members retiring in 1876. 'You have been so liberal to me in the matter of departmental rewards', he disarmingly assured Disraeli, 'that I have some scruple about pressing any more upon you. Nor do I know what rule you guide yourself by in the distribution of this particular honour.' The nub of Salisbury's review of Sir Henry Montgomery's excellent record of public service over 54 years was: 'He is a strong Tory.'[164] Party lines could be breached. Northcote suggested, unavailingly, that a privy-councillorship might induce Hugh Childers to go to India to look after the finances. Disraeli was very ready to reward the old Radical, Roebuck, with a privy-councillorship for his support during the Eastern Question crisis in 1877–8. Pointing out to Lady Bradford that Hume was neglected by Liberal governments, Disraeli was glad to have consoled Roebuck's last, sad year: 'I was more generous.' The rule by which Disraeli guided himself in the distribution of privy-councillorships was not, however, liberal enough to encompass the application of Sir Henry Drummond Wolff; in spite of the pathos of Wolff's declaration apropos of the elections in 1880 that 'this great catastrophe probably takes from me my last chance & I suppose no one is more stranded and snuffed out by fate.' Salisbury had said to Disraeli of Wolff in 1879: 'Your estimate of him is I think correct: unfortunately in our profession most of the good horses have bad mouths.'[165] Wolff would bounce back.

Baronetcies and Knighthoods

1

Party political patronage virtually monopolised lieutenancies and their decorative appendages, peerages, and provided the majority of privy-councillorships. Baronetcies and knighthoods were an entirely different matter. Patronage managers had a more or less minority share of them. The majority, particularly knighthoods, were bestowed on grounds of meritorious official service (which included the government legal officers), or even, and increasingly, for meritorious achievements in such spheres as science, medicine, and the arts. As stock in trade, honours at the lower end of the market in political patronage were more numerous but in many ways more problematical than at the upper end.

In the decade 1875–84 48 baronetcies and 448 knighthoods were bestowed, compared with 36 peerages.[166] Baronetcies were thus still, relative to peerages, restricted by an only marginally more relaxed version of the criteria of eligibility applicable to hereditary honours. These proportions remained fairly constant through the inflation of honours which built up towards the end of the century. New baronetcies and knighthoods in 1875–84 were about a third of those created in 1895–1904; peerages inflated rather more slowly, rising only to 52 creations in the later decade. The great inflation of lesser honours, particularly for 'political services', came with the twentieth century.

Baronetcies were readily applicable to party patronage, but since they were not much more readily available than peerages they were not an easy resource for the managers. Among the first which could be found in 1874 was one for Philip Rose, well-deserving as a martyr for the party. The other problem with them was a problem of esteem: their prestige relative even to a barony was far less than comparative numbers might suggest. Disraeli blamed Whig and Liberal patronage for diluting the order with 'civic baronetcies' as mayoral honours, and determined to restore their traditional 'honourable and territorial' character. He advised the queen in 1878 to knight the lord mayor of London rather than to give him a baronetcy deliberately to check the 'unreasonable ambition' of such municipal dignitaries in assuming a 'vested interest' in the superior honour. At the same time Disraeli recommended a wider distribution of civic knighthoods.[167] Given the electoral revolution in the metropolis and many of the other great cities, the Conservative party would be naturally attentive to the City. Northcote, for example, fussed about the fact that no cabinet minister from the Lords was due to attend the Lord Mayor's Dinner in 1877. He warned Disraeli: 'We have reason to fear that the Lord Mayor will be deeply offended, and that it may lead to our losing his support in the City at some future pinch.'[168] Disraeli took the point: two years later he reported to Lady Bradford that he was obliged to accept the lord mayor's invitation for 6 August: 'a horror, but it is demanded by party interests, wh. no one can resist.'[169]

Lancashire was naturally another area which engaged the careful attention of the party managers. The question arose in 1874 of an honour for A. Barclay Walker, a brewer, and mayor of Liverpool. Sentiment in the city expected a baronetcy. Sandon's advice to Corry was, 'in strict confidence, I hardly think that socially this will do'. On the other hand, 'our party in Town, which they say led the Conservative re-action, are most anxious about it, and he is a very popular man.' Walker had donated between £20,000 and £30,000 for the city's art gallery; he had received His Royal Highness the duke of Edinburgh. Cross, moreover, advocated the higher honour. So did Taylor. Corry reported to Disraeli: 'Taylor much regrets the mode in which Walker's name was lately brought to your notice, as he considers him a person generally worthy of distinction.' Sandon wavered between defending the social purity of the baronetical order and offending the rude sentiments of Liverpool Toryism.

> I am still very worried as to the Baronetcy – & perhaps before you take any definite opinion I had better see the leaders of the Party personally at Liverpool.
>
> It is of course very important that we should do nothing as a Government to shake the Liverpool feeling. . . . No doubt this Mayor is a great popular & Conservative favourite.[170]

In the end, aristocratic prejudice against civic baronetcies prevailed, and Walker was gazetted at the close of his second mayoralty in 1877 as a knight. Salisbury, who cared little for baronetical territorial integrity, created Walker a baronet in 1886. Derby was disturbed to learn in 1875 that Albert Grant, the shady financier, had purchased the *Echo*, a Liberal half-penny paper, and was to turn it into a Conservative organ. Grant had recently made himself a conspicuous public benefactor by handing Leicester Square over to the people of London. Derby uneasily foresaw that 'the position which Albert Grant is making for himself and us will be difficult. He has done too many dirty acts to be whitewashed: and too many that are useful to be neglected. Probably some day he will ask for a baronetcy.'[171]

The classic employment of baronetcies as a patronage resource remained that of catering for the upper squirearchy, whether in or out of the House of Commons. The 'knights of the shires' in the Commons were usually baronets. Of Disraeli's replenishments to the species Sir Walter Barttelot, MP for West Sussex, or Sir John Hardy, MP for South Warwickshire (and brother of Lord Cranbrook), or Sir John Scourfield, MP for Pembrokeshire, or Sir John Mowbray, MP for Oxford University, were typical. Sir John Leslie, MP for County Monaghan, was an example of an Irish subspecies. Some who represented small boroughs were hardly to be distinguished from the type: Sir John Walrond of Tiverton, or Sir Thomas Meyrick of Pembroke Boroughs. Outside the Commons Sir Gerald Codrington of Gloucestershire or Sir Peter Fitzgerald of Valentia, knight of Kerry, represented territorial squirearchy, with 5,000 and 8,000 acres respectively. There were variations on the theme. Sir John Heathcoat Amory, the other MP for Tiverton, owned 5,000 acres of Devonshire; but his family fortune came from Tiverton lace-making. Sir Henry Peek, MP for Mid-Surrey, owned no county land: he was a biscuit manufacturer and a great City merchant, and represented the Conservative party's consciousness of its new debts both to suburbia and the City.

Debts to Lancashire were also redeemed in the baronetcies for Callender, MP for Manchester and Disraeli's host in 1872 (though he died before the honour could be bestowed), Sir Gilbert Greenall, MP for Warrington, and Sir Edward Bates, the Liverpool shipowner and MP for Plymouth. Callender's honour was remarkable, in that he had previously declined nomination for a county division on the grounds of social ineligibility. The baronetcy for Sir George Elliot, Durham coal-owner and wire ropemaker, MP for North Durham, also reflected attention by the managers to an area of patronage not entirely traditional and territorial. Derby, always an advocate of middle-class Conservatism, noted in 1874: 'Disraeli has made 4 new baronets: Kelk the contractor: Elliot, a great coal-owner of the north: Peek the biscuit manufacturer, member for Surrey: and Rose the election agent. The last of these is thought a job, & blamed: the other three are unobjectionable, being millionaires, respectable, & warm supporters.'[172] The New York *Herald Tribune* went so far as to see Disraeli as unable to 'afford to irritate the plutocrats, shippers, merchants, and others who are the backbone of the Conservative party'.[173] The backbone of the Conservative party was still, in the 1870s, territorial; but it would become increasingly less so in the following decades.

Baronetcies seem also to have been the honour most subject to rumours of corrupt inducement. There were reports in 1874 of a tout professing to represent persons connected with the government who promised baronetcies secure on receipt of £20,000. Derby discounted this as a 'mere swindling trick', being certain that 'in the Cabinet there is no man who would sell his influence: in the inferior posts there are one or two of whom I should be less sure, but they have none to sell.' In another instance, the mayor of Liverpool reported being approached by a tout purporting to come from the Foreign Office, offering to procure him a baronetcy if £40,000 were transferred to a friend of the Prince of Wales. The prince was, no doubt, as Derby commented, 'in great straits for money, & his friends are not scrupulous, but I cannot think that he would be mixed up in a transaction of this kind'.[174]

2

Baronetcies were at least a homogeneous category. Knighthoods were heterogeneous as a category and complex as materials of patronage. The gap of esteem between the red ribbon of a grand cross of the Bath and a simple knight bachelorship, six steps down in precedence as it then was, was far greater than the gap above a grand cross of the Bath to the exalted sphere of Garters, Thistles, and even Patricks.

There was a problematic grey area of demarcation between the white of official knighthoods and the black of political knighthoods. What, after all, is not to some degree, in the end, 'political'? Salisbury's recommendation for an ambassador illuminates this intermediate area: 'Sir Augustus Paget is very anxious also for the red ribbon. If you have one to give him, I think he ought to have it – because he is the only ambassador without it & is the only Tory Ambassador.'[175] In pointing out to Disraeli in 1874 that the last two presidents of the Royal Society had been knight commanders of the Bath, Derby, with Carnarvon and Richmond in support, noted that there was 'a wish among scientific men that the same thing should be done for the present president – Dr. Hooker, whom you well know . . . as I have been appealed to, I cannot refuse to say I think it would be a good thing to do, in the interests of the Government'.[176] A KCB, however could not by 1877 be found for Hooker: as Salisbury remarked apropos of a disgruntled recipient of a knight commandership of St. Michael and St. George, 'KCBs are not to be had'.[177] Hooker's botanical researches in India allowed ministers to get around the dearth of KCBs by supplying a knight commandership of the Star of India.

Derby, himself genuinely concerned in intellectual affairs, consistently pressed upon Disraeli the consideration that the party should 'advantageously deal' with honours for men of science and letters as a much-needed boost for its intellectual prestige. In 1874 he recommended especially Tennyson and Carlyle. To Derby's dismay Tennyson refused a baronetcy 'in a letter which D. describes as "impertinent", at the same time referring to a promise which he alleges was given to him, that his eldest son should be made a baronet in his place'. Derby could but reflect that 'D is sensitive, and Tennyson is credited with extreme vanity'.[178] When Disraeli offered Thomas Carlyle a grand cross of the Bath ('A Government should recognise Intellect. It elevates & sustains the tone of a nation'),[179] it is not to be thought that he regarded the reactionary sage as an appropriate recipient of the Conservative party's political patronage. Yet he was certainly not unaware of the kind of political credit implicit in such a transaction pointed to by Derby in the case of Hooker and others, even were Carlyle to refuse (which he did). Among men of science Derby pressed also for recognition of Darwin and Richard Owen, mentioning for later consideration Huxley, Tyndall, Stokes, and William Thomson. 'I advised that a pension should be offered to Darwin, and either a baronetcy, or, better, a K.C.B.' Though in general amenable, Disraeli was nervous about Darwin; he 'rather shrinks from making the offer to Darwin singly', and stipulated that the prophet of evolution could only be honoured in tandem with his great literary enemy, Carlyle.[180]

Simple party-political knight bachelorships were a rarity at this time. Sir William Wyatt's party affiliation was perfectly clearly exhibited in his deputy-lieutenantship for Middlesex in 1867; but his honour in 1876 was for his work in asylums. Sir Henry Taylor became a notable Conservative MP; but his honour in 1877 was firmly founded in his railways inspectorate for the Board of Trade. No doubt Salisbury took a special pleasure in knighting the hammer of John Stuart Mill, James Fitzjames Stephen; but Stephen was a legal member of the viceroy's council as well as being, tenuously, a Liberal. Sir Edmund Currie deserved well of the Conservative party for his services on the London School Board; but he was honoured for his hospital work. One of the few overtly political knighthoods given in gratitude was that of Sir Algernon Borthwick, proprietor of the *Morning Post*, in 1880. Another instance was W.T. Charley, MP for Salford, a great figure in Lancashire Conservatism and Protestantism, whose serjeantship in the City was already considered to be a sufficiently scandalous job. Civic knighthoods were the most conspicuous generic aspect of Conservative patronage. The species is well exhibited in the case of Ireland: Sir William Miller, mayor of Londonderry; Sir George Owens, lord mayor of Dublin; Sir George Penrose, mayor of Cork; Sir John Preston, mayor of Belfast.

Political knights, other than lawyers, were rare in the House of Commons. Sir James Fergusson's honours were of the Colonial Office; Sir Henry Drummond Wolff's of the Foreign Office; Sir James Hogg's of the Board of Works. A curiously hybrid equestrian class existed, however, of ministerial Conservatives whose honours were somehow associated with their departmental work rather than their Conservative politics. Sir Henry Holland at the Colonial Office was one such; but the grand exemplar was Sir Stafford Northcote, Bart., GCB. Northcote's red ribbon as a grand cross of the Bath seemed to speak for the equivocal relationship in his career between the official servant of the Crown and the political servant of the party.

This was not the case with Cross's GCB in 1880. That simply reflected the fact that there was a class of ministerial Conservatives grateful for an honour which someone like Salisbury would never have dreamed of accepting. Cranbrook's grand commandership of the Star of India was merely a decorative appendage of political defeat. The one apparent oddity was the GCB accepted by Manners. Even as the heir to a dukedom Manners could not at that time have expected a Garter, since his brother, Rutland, already had one. Manners would get his in due course.

Notes and References

1 *QR*, Oct. 72, 579.
2 Derby Diary, 20 June 1872.
3 Salisbury to Corry, 12 May 1876; HP, B/XX/Ce/74.
4 R. Blake, *Disraeli* (1966), 389.
5 H. J. Hanham, 'Political patronage at the Treasury, 1870–1912', *Historical Journal* (1960), 76. Patronage secretary = chief whip when in office as political undersecretary at the Treasury.
6 Derby Diary, 9 Aug. 1876.
7 Hanham, 'Political patronage at the Treasury.'
8 Blake, *Disraeli*, 683.
9 *Ibid*; 682–3.
10 Hampton to Northcote, 23 April 1879; BL, Iddesleigh 50022, 273.
11 Cross to Cairns, 3 Aug. 1874; PRO, Cairns 30/51/12.
12 Disraeli to Cairns, 13 Jan. 1875; PRO, Cairns 30/51/1. The exception in this case was Spofforth.
13 R.A. Cross, *A Political History* (1903), 23.
14 Abergavenny to Disraeli, 11 July 1876; HP, B/XXI/A/55.
15 Abergavenny to Corry, n.d. HP, C/vii/65.
16 *Fortnightly Review*, Nov. 1882, 672.
17 Northcote to Disraeli, 3 Aug. 1875; BL, Iddesleigh 50017, 53.
18 Cairns to Disraeli, 20 July 1875; HP, B/XX/Ca/137.
19 Disraeli to Cairns, 6 Aug. 1875; PRO, Cairns 30/51/1.
20 Hardy to Cairns, 5 Sept. 1875; PRO, Cairns 30/51/7.
21 Buckle, ii, 735.
22 Disraeli to Cairns, 1 Sept. 1875; PRO, Cairns 30/51/1.
23 Northcote to Disraeli, 22 Sept. 1875; BL, Iddesleigh 50017, 60.
24 Northcote to Cairns, 1 Nov. 1875; PRO, Cairns 30/51/5.
25 Hardy, *Diary*, 279.
26 Hardy to Cairns, 5 Sept. 1875; PRO Cairns 30/51/7.
27 Hardy, *Diary*, 281–2.
28 *Ibid*.
29 *Ibid*.
30 Salisbury to Disraeli, 27 July 1876; HP, B/XX/Ce/81. Buckle, ii, 833–4.
31 Richmond to Cairns, 27 July 1876; PRO, Cairns 30/51/3.
32 Malmesbury to Cairns, 16 Aug. 1876; PRO Cairns 30/51/20. Neither the prime ministership nor the first lordship of the Treasury then had official precedence. Disraeli's precedence had strictly been that of a mere

privy-councillor. Beaconsfield will, however, remain Disraeli in this text to avoid chronological confusion.

33 Hardy, *Diary*, 281.
34 *Ibid*, 282.
35 Richmond to Cairns, 16 July 1876. PRO, Cairns 30/51/3.
36 Hardy, *Diary*, 283; M. Swartz, *The Politics of British Foreign Policy in the Era of Disraeli and Gladstone* (1985), 37.
37 A.E. Gathorne-Hardy, *Gathorne Hardy, First Earl of Cranbrook* (1910), ii, 7–8.
38 Derby Diary, 12 Aug. 1876.
39 Gathorne-Hardy, *Cranbrook*, ii, 7–8.
40 For examples of Hardy's incorrigibility, see his *Diary*, 161, 164, 205, 279.
41 Buckle, ii, 741, 743.
42 Hardy, *Diary*, xxi.
43 Derby Diary, 21 Jan., 30 March 1877. Swartz (*Politics of British Foreign Policy*, 55) marks a quarrel in cabinet in March as ending Derby's chances of succeeding Disraeli.
44 Richmond to Cairns, 30 July 1877; PRO, Cairns 30/51/4.
45 Lord Chilston, *W.H. Smith* (1965), 94.
46 *Ibid.*
47 Derby Diary, 7 Aug. 1877. Derby further commented apropos of the equal division in the cabinet between peers and commoners: 'It does not seem too much to add one to the non-titled class, especially as he replaces Hunt, who is only a small squire of no great local importance.'
48 See Lord G. Hamilton, *Parliamentary Reminiscences and Reflections, 1868 to 1885* (1917), 77.
49 Richmond to Cairns, 1 Aug. 1877; PRO, Cairns 30/51/4.
50 Richmond to Cairns, 5 Aug. 1877; PRO, Cairns 30/51/4.
51 Richmond to Cairns, 1 Aug. 1877; PRO, Cairns 30/51/4.
52 Northcote to Beaconsfield, 9 Feb. 1878; BL, Iddesleigh 50018, 75.
53 Northcote to Beaconsfield, 1 April 1878; BL, Iddesleigh 50018, 81.
54 Derby Diary, 11 Feb. 1874; Skelmersdale's aunt was Derby's mother.
55 Richmond to Cairns, 26 Oct. 1876; PRO, Cairns 30/51/3.
56 Cairns to Northcote, 19 Jan. 1875; BL, Iddesleigh 50021, 109.
57 Derby Diary, 24 Nov. 1875, 13 Aug. 1876.
58 Northcote to Cairns, 4 Oct. 1876, encl. Lopes to Northcote, 1 Oct. 1876; PRO, Cairns 30/51/5.
59 Northcote to Beaconsfield, 23 Jan. 1879; BL, Iddesleigh 50018, 136. Northcote to Cairns, 14 Dec. 1878; PRO, Cairns 30/51/5.
60 Hardy to Cairns, 18 Feb. 1874; PRO, Cairns 30/51/7.
61 Dyke to Disraeli, 16 Dec. [1874]; HP, B/xxi/D/464.
62 Derby Diary, 17 Feb. 1869.
63 C. Frewen to Disraeli, 25 Nov. 1868; HP, B/c/VI/75.
64 Derby Diary, 13 Dec. 1875.
65 J. Vincent (ed.), *Disraeli, Derby and the Conservative Party. Journals and Memoirs of Edward Henry, Lord Stanley*, (Hassocks, 1978) 336.
66 Buckle, ii, 776–7.
67 Salisbury to Disraeli, 30 April 1875; HP, B/XX/Ce/42.
68 Derby Diary, 29 April, 1 May 1875.

69 Hardy, *Diary*, 257.
70 Abergavenny to Corry, 30 April 1875; HP, B/XXI/A/51.
71 Derby Diary, 1 May 1875.
72 Salisbury to Beaconsfield, 21 Jan. 1879; HP, B/XX/Ce/300.
73 Northcote to Disraeli, 19 Oct. 1874. BL, Iddesleigh 50016, 260. For Salisbury's opinion of the Colonial Service as 'too often recruited from broken down political hacks & people "who have deserved well of the party"', see Swartz, *Politics of British Foreign Policy*, 194–5, n. 96.
74 Derby Diary, 16 June 1874.
75 Dartmouth to Corry, 28 Feb. 1875; HP, C/III/C/120a.
76 Bath to Cairns, 4 Oct. 1874; PRO, Cairns 30/51/19.
77 Salisbury to Cairns, 13 Feb. 1875; PRO, Cairns 30/51/6.
78 Westmorland to Hardy, 23 Aug. 1875; PRO, Cairns 30/51/7.
79 Northcote to Cairns, 28 Oct. 1878; PRO, Cairns 30/51/5.
80 Buckle, ii, 969.
81 E. Turnor to A. Turnor, 23 Oct. 1877; HP, C/III/C/60s.
82 Bath to Corry, 27 April 1874; HP, C,/III/C/117.
83 Cairns to Disraeli, 19 April 1875; HP, B/XX/Ca/151. Salisbury to Beaconsfield, 26 Aug. 1876; HP, B/XX/Ce/82. Tait had been headmaster of Rugby.
84 Richmond to Cairns, 27 Nov. 1876; PRO, Cairns 30/51/3.
85 Cairns to Beaconsfield, 16 Dec. 1876; HP, B/XX/Ca/198.
86 Salisbury to Beaconsfield, 26 Aug. 1876; HP, B/XX/Ce/82.
87 Lady Salisbury to Beaconsfield, 17 April 1880; HP, B/XX/Ce/335.
88 Blake, *Disraeli*, 714.
89 Daly to Beaconsfield, 4 Jan. 1879; HP, B/XXI/D/4.
90 Salisbury to Beaconsfield, 31 Jan. 1879; HP, B/XX/Ce/110.
91 Buckle, ii, 808.
92 Northcote to Disraeli, 7 Jan. 1876; HP, C/III/C/122.
93 Northcote to Beaconsfield, 13 Aug. 1877; BL, Iddesleigh 50018, 51.
94 Northcote to Disraeli, 24 Dec. 1875; BL, Iddesleigh 50017, 143.
95 See above, 225.
96 Derby Diary, 27 Nov. 1875; 18 July 77. For Hampton's complaints, see above, 224–5.
97 Gorst to Disraeli, 31 Aug. 1874; HP, B/XX/D/243.
98 Disraeli to Corry, 4 Sept. 1874; HP, B/XX/D/243.
99 Gorst to Smith, 11 Nov. 1874; HP, B/XXI/D/463d.
100 Gorst to Dyke, 19 Nov. 1874; HP, B/XXI/D/463b.
101 Northcote to Disraeli, 10 Jan. 1875; BL, Iddesleigh 50017, 1.
102 Disraeli to Corry, 9 March 1875; HP, B/XX/D/254.
103 Gorst to Disraeli, 12 March 1875; HP, B/XXI/G/252.
104 Taylor to Disraeli, 12 March 1875; HP, B/XXI/S/441.
105 No relation.
106 Gorst to Disraeli, 7 May 1874; HP, B/XXI/G/251.
107 Feuchtwanger, *Disraeli, Democracy and the Tory Party*, 133–4.
108 Gorst to Disraeli, 20 Nov. 1875; HP, B/XXI/G/254.
109 Feuchtwanger, *Disraeli, Democracy and the Tory Party*, 137–8.
110 Gorst to Beaconsfield, 30 March [1877]; HP, B/XXI/G/257.
111 Dyke to Beaconsfield, 16 Feb. [1878–9]; HP, B/XXI/D/507.
112 Abergavenny to Corry [1878]; HP, C/VII/65.

113 Athole to Richmond, 14 Jan. 1878; HP, C/IV/276.
114 Hall to Daly, 3 Jan. 1878; HP, C/IV/33c.
115 Walsh to Disraeli, 4 April 1875; HP, C/IV/8.
116 Keith-Falconer to Abergavenny, 18 Sept. 1876; HP, B/XXI/A/56a.
117 Abergavenny to Beaconsfield [1876]; HP, B/XXI/A/56. Dyke to Beaconsfield, 25 Sept. [1876]; HP, B/XXI/D/468.
118 Cairns to Beaconsfield, 21 Sept. 1876; HP, B/XX/Ca/190.
119 Noel to Beaconsfield, 28 Aug. [1876]; HP, B/XXI/N/143. The 5th earl, who succeeded in 1876, died in 1882, aged 26.
120 See P. Galloway, *The Most Illustrious Order of St. Patrick, 1783–1983* (Chichester, 1983), an excellent social history of chivalric artifice.
121 Norfolk to Beaconsfield, 12 March 1878; HP, B/XXI/N/157.
122 Cecil, *Salisbury*, ii, 296–7.
123 Dunmore to Taylor, 1 July [1875]; HP, c/VII/29a.
124 Dunmore to Corry, [n.d.]; HP, c/VII/64.
125 Lothian to Corry, 13 Jan. 1875; HP, C/VII/22.
126 Abergavenny to Corry [1878]; HP, c/VII/65.
127 Colville to Corry, 31 April 1879; HP, C/VII/50c.
128 Hardy, *Diary*, 420–1.
129 Corry to Disraeli, 21 Aug. 1868; HP, B/XX/Co/41. Patrick ribbons were in fact blue. Thistle ribbons are green. Corry's misattribution is a tribute to the power of Ireland's association with the colour green.
130 Courtown to Corry [1874]; HP, B/XX/Co/5c.
131 *Ibid.*, 43a.
132 Derby Diary, 13 May, 3 Nov. 1875.
133 *Ibid.*, 28 Dec. 1875.
134 Salisbury to Disraeli, 19 Oct. 1875; HP, B/XX/Ce/60.
135 Buckle, ii, 1399.
136 Derby Diary, 17 Feb. 1874, 11 May 1877.
137 W. R. Ormsby-Gore to Disraeli, 23 April 1874; HP, C/I/b/11b.
138 Abney-Hastings to Disraeli, 12 Jan. 1876; HP, C/I/a/40b.
139 Cairns to Disraeli, 24 Aug. 1874; HP, B/XX/Ca/123. Derby Diary, 10 Oct. 1876. The projected Lord Sackville was Lady Derby's brother.
140 *Ibid.*, 24 Jan. 1876.
141 Neville Grenville to Disraeli, 6 Sept. 1875; HP, C/VI/81a.
142 HP, C/VI/81b.
143 *Ibid.*, 81c, 81e.
144 Northcote to Disraeli, 1 Dec. 1868; BL, Iddesleigh 50016, 67.
145 Lechmere to Rowton, 2 May 1880; HP, C/I/a/66c.
146 HP, C/I/b/38a.
147 Beckett (formerly Beckett-Denison) to Corry, 6 April 1880; HP, B/xxi/A/66c. E. Beckett-Denison designed the 'great clock' at Westminster and 'Big Ben', the bell. He afterwards ravaged the cathedral of St. Alban's. See Peter Ferriday, *Lord Grimthorpe* (1957).
148 See below, 256.
149 Duchess of Northumberland to Beaconsfield, 17 Sept. 1878. HP, C/I/a/67b. 'English' = UK peerage.
150 Shirley to Beaconsfield, 12 April 1880; HP, C/I/a/67b.
151 Beaconsfield to Taylor, 14 April 80; HP, B/XX/T/140.
152 Cairns to Disraeli, 24 Aug. 1874; HP, B/XX/Ca/123.

153 Properly Forfarshire.
154 Derby Diary, 28 Aug. 1876.
155 Tredegar to Disraeli, 19 March 1874; HP, C/I/11e. Major the Hon. G.C. Morgan, MP Brecknockshire; Hon. F.C. Morgan, MP Monmouthshire.
156 Sherborne to Disraeli, 29 March [1874]; HP, C/I/11b.
157 A Conservative peer (Duncombe), promoted in 1868.
158 Wharncliffe to Corry, 21 Feb. 1874. HP, C/I/b/4a; succeeded 1855.
159 Wharncliffe to Corry, 22 Feb. 1874; HP, C/I/b/4b.
160 See above, 176. Northcote to Disraeli, 16th Jan. 1868. BL Iddesleigh 50016, 1.
161 Raikes to Northcote, 12 Aug. 1876; HP C/VI/85a.
162 Northcote to Beaconsfield, 8 March 1880; HP, C, VI/85g.
163 Montgomery to Disraeli, 4 March 1874; HP, C,VI/77. Graham Montgomery had been an unacceptably pessimistic Scottish whip.
164 Salisbury to Beaconsfield, 10 Oct. 1876. HP, C/VI/86.
165 Buckle, ii, 1374. Wolff to Salisbury, 16 April 1880; HP, C/VI/102. Salisbury to Beaconsfield, 11 Sept. 1879; HP/XX/Ce/308.
166 H. J. Hanham, 'The sale of honours in late Victorian England', *Victorian Studies* (1960), 277.
167 Buckle, ii, 1261.
168 Northcote to Beaconsfield, 26 July 1877; BL, Iddesleigh 50018, 44.
169 Buckle, ii, 1318.
170 Corry to Disraeli, 29 Oct. 1874; HP, B/XX/Co/103. Sandon to Corry, 26 Oct. 1874; HP, B/XX/Co/103a.
171 Derby Diary, 27 June 1875. The system of honours remained proof against any ambitions Baron Gottheimer might have entertained.
172 Derby Diary, 1 May 74.
173 Feuchtwanger, *Disraeli, Democracy and the Tory Party*, 77. Bates had been Plimsoll's target in the famous scandal in the Commons in July 1875.
174 Derby Diary, 20 Nov. 1874, 25 Sept. 1876.
175 Salisbury to Disraeli, 10 April 1880; HP, B/XX/Ce/141.
176 Derby to Disraeli, 27 April 1874; HP, C/VIII/9b. Derby Diary, 23 April 1874.
177 Salisbury to Northcote, 27 Sept. 1879; BL, Iddesleigh 50019, 181.
178 Derby Diary, 13 May 1875.
179 Disraeli to Carlyle, 27 Dec. 1874; HP, C/VIII/13aa (draft).
180 Derby Diary, 18 Aug., 10 Sept. 1875.

Chapter 11

Maintaining the empire of England

Re-equipping the party with a foreign policy

1

When in February 1874 the Conservative party arrived in office and in power, precipitately and unexpectedly, it had no working tradition of distinctly Conservative foreign policy ready to hand. Under Derby and Malmesbury the Conservatism of Conservative foreign policy had consisted of shreds and patches of the counter-revolutionary principles of 1849. The coming of Stanley in the 1860s had deprived the party even on such meagre consistency as that provided. Drastic events in America and Europe had obliterated almost all the familiar landmarks and bearings. Of all the major political forces in the country, the Conservatives alone were without an inherited set of received values which offered a sense that guidance was available. The ex-Canningite Palmerston had appropriated – or misappropriated – the Canningite tradition and taken it over to the Whigs. The Peelite tradition of Aberdeen, Castlereagh's disciple, had been taken over to the Liberals by Gladstone, where it consorted uneasily with the native Liberal tradition of Cobden. In consequence, Conservative views about foreign policy became little more than a rag-bag of prejudices left over from these grand exportations: futile aristocratic evocation of memories of Pitt and Grenville; and, in practice, patriotic preference that hegemonic Whig-Liberal governments should conduct policies of a Palmerstonian rather than an Aberdonian-Cobdenite cast.

Disraeli was as representative a Conservative in these prejudices as any. Though he criticised Palmerston, he was in no doubt that he supported, as he put it in 1854, the 'British' politics of Palmerston and Russell as against the 'Russian' politics of Aberdeen. In 1853 Gladstone had made a declaration in effect in almost precisely the opposite terms: it is not too much to say that, as things turned out, the great conflict between Disraeli and Gladstone over foreign policy in the 1870s was in essence a logical and consistent fulfilment of their respective positions in the 1850s. Gladstone's urging in 1858 the unity and independence of Romania on the grounds that the best barrier against any Russian drive to Constantinople would be the 'breasts of free men' became a signal premonitory exemplar of the doctrine he was again to urge in 1876 over Bulgaria. The government to which he pleaded that cause in 1858 was the government of Lord Derby and Disraeli. That government rejected Gladstone's plea to act with France and Russia to save Romania from being strangled at birth by Austria and Turkey. Disraeli, speaking in the Commons on behalf of Derby and Malmesbury, echoed Palmerston's argument that the Crimean War had been fought to maintain the independence and integrity of the Ottoman Empire; and that it would be absurd to set about undermining that independence and integrity in the aftermath of victory.[1] Romania was indeed created in spite of British policy in the 1850s; the question facing a Conservative government in the 1870s was whether or not an analagous problem might be responded to in a different way.

Given his life's ambition to re-establish Toryism on a national foundation, it was necessary for Disraeli to begin re-equipping the Conservative party with something to fill the large gaps where the materials of its old foreign policy used to be. In 1872 he offered some ideas and some slogans. On the one side he reached back to the 1850s: 'British' ('national') politics, but not turbulently or aggressively so. On the other side he looked to contemporary trends in sentiment and opinion. For domestic policy there was the New Social Alliance. For foreign policy there was empire. Neither was to be taken all that seriously. They would be the politics of gesture rather than substance. The one would be a policy of tame gestures after Gladstone's domestic heroism; the other would be a policy of heroic gestures after Gladstone's 'little England' tameness. The substantial thing was that Disraeli envisaged future Conservative foreign policy in the terms he had indicated in 1871:[2] to restore the 'equilibrium' of Europe which had been destroyed by the 'German revolution', and to remove the disabilities thereby imposed upon Britain as a power. Disraeli's analysis of the problems was excellent. But there is no evidence that he ever gave serious thought as to how British policy would set about achieving this purpose. The great problem for Disraeli here was that whereas in domestic affairs he had colleagues who could provide the required policy and do the necessary work, in foreign affairs it was a matter of what foreigners might do and what Lord Derby would be willing or could be persuaded to do about it. That was, as things proved, a most awkward conjunction.

In his earlier period as foreign secretary, 1866–8, Stanley (as Derby then was) had directed British policy away from European commitments and interventions as far as he could. This was a sensible enough policy in the aftermath of the fiasco of the last British effort to throw weight about over the Danish duchies question in 1864. It chimed in with the then ascendant Cobdenite isolationism, and Stanley found himself to his embarrassment (as was also the case with Gladstone) receiving the praises of the Manchester School. Derby later denied being a Cobdenite. He told Northcote in 1877:

> I have never thought Cobden an oracle either on foreign or home affairs. He believed three things with all his heart – that the repeal of the corn laws would break the power of the landed aristocracy. That the example of England would

> bring about free trade all over the world. That great wars would never be made again, being incompatible with the idea of an industrial age. On all three points he has been wrong. The landowners are stronger than before – Europe is showing more protectionist tendencies than 20 years ago, and America itself following suit – and all the world is armed to the teeth.[3]

Derby's great problem was that he disliked intervention and commitment and the responsibilities they incurred by temperament rather than by conviction. He was too intelligent to be a Cobdenite on principle, but too diffident and cautious not to be a Cobdenite in practice. This meant that it was ultimately impossible for Derby to defend his isolationist predilections on firm or convincing intellectual grounds. When pressures were on him there were only three things he could do: be stubborn, be shoved, or get out.

In manoeuvring for his own interests in 1866 to get Stanley into the Foreign Office, despite the misgivings of Stanley's father and the queen, Disraeli pickled a rod for his own back. Disraeli and Derby in 1874 were to make the worst possible combination of prime minister and foreign secretary. Disraeli knew there was a great problem but did not think it through. When things came to the point, he relied instead on solving matters by applying what he thought of as the 'traditionary policy of England', trusting that all would come well of it. Conducting foreign policy on the basis of seeing what happens was anathema to Derby; but he was helpless to propose a positive and plausible alternative. Balfour later wrote a memorandum of his uncle Salisbury's comments on this disastrous partnership.

> Discussed with Lord S. admissibility of writing some account of the late Govt especially in relation to the secret history of their foreign policy. He again imparted . . . that the part played by Dizzy was entirely misunderstood out of doors. As a politician he was exceedingly short sighted though very clear sighted. He neither could nor would look far ahead, or attempt to balance remote possibilities: though he rapidly detected the difficulties of the immediate situation and found the easiest if not the best solution for them. As the head of a cabinet his fault was want of firmness. The chiefs of departments got their way too much – the cabinet as a whole got it too little – and this necessarily followed from having at the head of affairs a statesman whose only final political principle was that the party must on no account be broken up and who shrank therefore from exercising coercion on any of his subordinates. . . . But with a man like him at the head of affairs who *could* not look far a-head, and with a man like Derby at the Foreign Office who *would* not look far a-head, we naturally drifted. Lord Derby indeed would never have consented to fix on any determined line of policy which would or might end in serious and decided action: and Dizzy shrank to the last from insisting on anything to which Lord Derby would have refused his assent.[4]

The essential undertaking which Disraeli made to the Conservative party in 1872 about the future conduct of foreign and imperial policy was that it would be characterised by national as against cosmopolitan values, by 'firmness and decision', and by making it evident to other powers that they misapprehended the situation if they supposed that Britain was a power in decline or decay.

There is no doubt that the surge of electoral support for Conservatives in the constituencies in 1874 owed much to sentiment dismayed at what seemed an unrelieved period of setbacks and rebuffs in foreign affairs and hopeful of a new era of restored national pride in British greatness. It was quite clear that this is what the Conservative government in 1874 would have to set about doing; and it is equally clear that it had not the slightest notion of how to set about it.

The keenest mind which had applied itself to questions of foreign policy in that government was Salisbury's. In a classic series of pieces in the *Quarterly Review* in 1863 and 1864,[5] the secretary of state for India had provided a brilliantly comprehensive exposition of how not to conduct foreign policy. Implicitly, Salisbury recommended that policy be always free of sentimental humbug, that it define vital interests clearly, that it have an intelligently realistic view of how best to defend those interests, and that it eschew all forms of blustering moralism and all threats which it is unwilling to back up by force. This would have been an invaluable text for the Conservative party in 1874 but for one unfortunate fact: it amounted to a devastating indictment of Palmerston and Palmerstonism; which were precisely the watchwords of the new public mood and the codewords of the revived Conservative national values. What Salisbury demonstrated was that the bankruptcy of the 'Western' dimension of Palmerstonism had been exposed in the Danish duchies case; from 1875 he would be trying to convince Disraeli that Turkish financial bankruptcy aptly symbolised the bankruptcy of the 'Eastern' dimension of Palmerstonism. Salisbury would be condemned for four long years to witness a bankrupt tradition being inconsistently applied to British foreign policy before getting his chance to get a grip on it.

When Borthwick of the *Morning Post* promised Disraeli through Spofforth that if he adopted 'a Palmerstonian policy' he would be prime minister for life,[6] Borthwick spoke as an admitted partisan of the former Whig chief and by Palmerstonism he clearly meant something more comprehensive simply than foreign policy. Still, the fact remained that Borthwick, not to mention the innumerable sleek denizens of smug villas as depicted by Frederic Harrison, did assume that a 'national' vocation in foreign affairs would necessarily and inevitably link back to the most famous exponent of the 'national' policy in recent times. It was, in fact, by no means necessary or inevitable that this should be the case; and the Conservative party suffered great harm from its being allowed to happen by default. There were perfectly adequate alternative modes available for conducting a 'national' policy, and Disraeli was greatly at fault for not thinking the problem through, or listening to someone like Salisbury who was willing to think it through.

Disraeli allowed himself to drift into a Palmerstonian mode mainly as a matter of habit. He had settled his ideas about these matters in the 1850s. Rethinking them would be disturbing. He had a ready-made 'national' tradition to hand, which, embellished with new 'imperial' touches, could easily be converted to Conservative guise. The great problem about Disraeli as an exponent of foreign policy was that the prescience of his analysis of the 'German revolution' in western Europe was not matched by any disposition to rethink the question of eastern Europe and the Near East in the same perceptively intelligent manner. By May 1875 he told Derby: 'My own impression is that we shd. construct some concerted movement to preserve the peace of Europe, like Pam did when he baffled France and expelled the Egyptians from Syria.'[7] Again: 'I believe, since Pam, we have never been so energetic, and in a year's time we shall be more.'[8] By 1876 Salisbury was urging upon Disraeli golden words of wisdom: 'It is clear enough that the traditional Palmerstonian policy is at an end.'[9] Disraeli would not heed his advice.

Salisbury offered implicitly in his critique of Palmerston (and Russell) in the 1860s a model of a possible alternative Conservative foreign policy. In his critique of Derby and Beaconsfield he offered an explicit alternative. By May 1877 he despaired of being listened to. 'It seems to me', he told Carnarvon, 'we must give up all hope of any *positive* action on the foreign policy. We may prevent evil, but we can do no more. The result will be an emasculate, purposeless vacillation, which will be very discreditable. But perhaps it is what suits the nation best.'[10] As he put it to Lytton:

> The commonest error in politics is sticking to the carcasses of dead policies. When a mast falls overboard, you do not try to save a rope here and a spar there, in memory of their former utility; you cut away the hamper altogether. And it should be the same with a policy. But it is not so. We cling to the shred of an old policy after it has been torn to pieces; and to the shadow of the shred after the rag itself has been torn away.
>
> And therefore it is that we are now in perplexity.[11]

Even though he disapproved of the traditional Palmerstonian policy, Salisbury would have acquiesced in it and supported it had it been prosecuted vigorously and consistently as the product of a 'settled plan'.[12] He was always of the view that in foreign affairs the choice of a policy was as a rule less important than the methods used to pursue it.[13] A bad policy intelligently pursued was always likely to conduce to better results than a good policy unintelligently pursued.

2

This 'perplexity' of 1877 lay unimagined in the future when Lord Derby returned to the Foreign Office in 1874. Derby got a fright in 1875 over the war scare caused by Bismarck's threatening attitude to France. But the Russians were very ready to take the lead in warning Bismarck off, and Derby was spared any obligation to take up Disraeli's suggestion of constructing 'some concerted movement to preserve the peace of Europe' on the model of Palmerston in 1840. Once that blew over there seemed little reason to carry on being 'energetic', in Disraeli's phrase at the time.

Disraeli's great hope was that somehow Bismarck's *Dreikaiserbund* (Three Emperors' League) which ruled the European roost might be subverted. The supine Derby resolutely declined to be energetic in that cause. What of the empire? At the Colonial Office Carnarvon contemplated the prospects in South Africa of the kind of great work of construction by which the Dominion of Canada had been created during his earlier spell of office. Derby noted in April 1875 that Carnarvon's South African plan was 'sharply criticized, and I think that no member of Cabinet quite likes it'. Derby agreed with Disraeli that Carnarvon was 'inclined to be too hasty in his action, and wholly under the influence of Froude', one of the more expansive intellectual prophets of Anglo-Saxon empire-building: 'though', Derby added, 'up to this time all has gone well.'[14] In the India Office Salisbury was concerned with such mundane things as discouraging Indian efforts to build up their own cotton textile industry by means of a protective cotton duty. This was the policy of the Whig governor-general, Northbrook. Tory Lancashire took it in bad part, which soon had Conservative ministers scurrying. Salisbury remarked to Disraeli that the Indian tariffs had 'created come commotion in the Northern towns'.

> I had promised them that as soon as there was financial elbow room the cotton duty should be dealt with: & they were rather disaffected at finding [Northbrook] moving in the opposite direction. Of course, in spite of his legislation, I must keep my word. But to do it civilly, & in as workmanlike way as possible, we have resolved . . . to send out Sir Louis Mallett . . . to set the tariff right in the sense desired by Lancashire.[15]

While Mallett civilly throttled the Indian cotton industry, Salisbury was startled to discover that Disraeli was ready to humour the queen in her long-cherished desire for an Indian imperial title. 'I knew nothing about the "Empress of India",' he told Disraeli in December 1875. 'What *does* the Queen mean?'[16] Salisbury did his best to head it off: 'Will she not be satisfied with the fact that she is already called Empress in formal documents in India?'[17] But if it must be done, certainly Lytton was a better governor-general to do it than Northbrook.

Given tranquil international times and appropriate opportunities, Disraeli might well have tried at something along the lines of 'reconstructing the Colonial Empire' he had sketched in 1872. But by the time in 1876 when he declared that it was the government's paramount duty 'to maintain the Empire of England',[18] he was talking of empire in quite a different sense and in increasingly untranquil international times.

Trouble came upon the Conservative government out of the East. Throughout the latter part of 1875 the Ottoman Empire began to sag badly and then looked like being near collapse. It was unable to suppress revolts of Christian subject peoples in Bosnia and the Herzegovina; and in October declared itself bankrupt. The powers, concerned at instability in the Balkans and at the larger instability of a possible Turkish collapse, began to stir. Bismarck's

Dreikaiserbund took it upon itself to give the necessary lead to Europe. Disraeli strongly resented this, and began to cast about for ways of baffling them, putting pressure on Derby accordingly.

That things should have happened in this way and from this direction was trebly unfortunate. In the first place Crimean memories were inevitably aroused. This had the effect of reviving the credit of Palmerston's 'Crimean system', still substantially in place in international law, and still very much in place in the hearts and minds of the British foreign and diplomatic services. At the centre of this system remained the cardinal doctrine that it was a capital British interest to preserve and uphold the independence and integrity of the Ottoman Empire. Any indications of public opinion repudiating the Crimean War as a mistake did not appear until too late, in the late summer and autumn of 1876. The second unfortunate circumstance arising out of this was that Derby quite specifically disbelieved in the Crimean system. In a speech in 1864 which was often and embarrassingly reproduced in the 1870s,[19] the then Stanley declared that the question of the breaking up of the Turkish Empire was only one of time, probably not a very long time. The Turks had played their part in history, but their day was now over. Stanley could not understand, 'except it be from the influence of old diplomatic traditions, the determination of the elder statesmen to stand by the Turkish rule'. Stanley thought that Britain was in danger of making enemies of races which would very soon become in eastern Europe dominant races; Britain was keeping back 'countries by whose improvement we, as the great traders of the world, should be the great gainers: and that we are doing this for no earthly advantage, either present or prospective'.

It did not take long for the influence of the old diplomatic traditions and the determination of the elder statesmen to stand by the Turkish rule to impose themselves on Stanley in 1866–8, particularly in the case of the Cretan insurrection against the Turks. Derby now faced the dismal prospect of the same pressures on a much larger scale as the situation of the Ottoman Empire deteriorated with increasing instability over the winter of 1875–6 and questions proposed themselves urgently as to what the British government proposed to do about it. Occasionally, Derby broke out into candid reminiscence of this 1864 doctrine; as when he told Disraeli in January 1876: 'It is too late to stand on the dignity and independence of the Sultan; a Sovereign who can neither keep the peace at home, nor pay his debts, must expect to submit to some disagreeable consequences.'[20]

The third unfortunate circumstance bearing on the responses of British policy to the Eastern Question at this early stage was that in November 1875 Disraeli pulled off what had every appearance of being a brilliant coup by purchasing a 44 per cent holding of shares in the Suez Canal Company for £4 million from the sultan's tributary, and equally bankrupt, vassal, the khedive of Egypt. It was a financial transaction (and a good investment) concerning a Paris-based company; but under Disraeli's management it became a chapter on international *haute politique* from one of his own novels. Northcote's objections to the flavour given to the event perfectly expressed the effect Disraeli wished to produce. Northcote wanted a 'frank declaration of our intentions in the matter of the Canal so as to keep ourselves right in the eyes of Europe'.

> Our policy, or our proceedings, with regard to the Canal has not been such as to gain us much credit for magnanimity. We opposed it in its origin; we refused to help Lesseps in his difficulties; we have used it when it succeeded; we have fought the battle of our Shipowners very stiffly; and now we avail ourselves of our influence with Egypt to get a quiet slice of what promises to be a good thing. Suspicion will be excited that we mean quietly to buy ourselves into a preponderating position, and then turn the whole thing into an English property. I don't like it.[21]

This truly Gladstonian outburst was seconded in effect by Derby: 'I have always expressed my opinion that the best arrangement for all the world would be the placing of the Canal under an International Commission, like that of the Danube; and I think so still.'[22] Nor could Derby repress a sense of dismay at some wider implications.

> So far as I can make out, the purchase is universally popular, I might say even more, it seems to have created a feeling of something like enthusiasm, far in excess of the real importance of the transaction. It is a complete political success: yet the very fact of its being so causes me some uneasiness: for it shows the intense desire abroad that pervades the public mind, the impatience created by long diplomatic inactivity, and the strength of a feeling which might under certain circumstances, take the form of a cry for war.[23]

The 'national' public responded to Disraeli's initiative indeed in such a spirit. As Disraeli put it to the queen: 'It is vital to your Majesty's authority and power at this critical moment, that the Canal should belong to England, and I was so decided and absolute with Lord Derby on this head, that he ultimately adopted my views . . .'.[24] Disraeli succeeded in conveying an impression that a great stroke had been struck for British power and authority in the world and that somehow the canal now 'belonged' as an attribute of that power and authority. The *Punch* cartoon depicting Disraeli as 'Moses in Egypt', holding the 'Key to India' in his hand and exchanging winks with the Sphinx, faithfully hit off the mood of this kind of grateful response. The queen was especially concerned to interpret the coup as a 'blow at Bismarck', and his 'insolent declarations that England has ceased to be a political power'.[25] Even Salisbury had to admit: 'It seems to me impossible to rate too highly the importance of that decision, as a declaration of policy.'[26]

The success of the Suez coup boosted confidence and discouraged any likelihood of serious questioning of the validity of received traditions of British Eastern policy. Disraeli, clutching the key to India in his hand, was in fine fettle when Bismarck launched his next 'insolent declarations'.

These, known in diplomatic parlance as the Andrassy Note and the Berlin Memorandum, concocted by the three imperial powers in December 1875 and May 1876 respectively, tried to convince the Turks that they must concede reforms to settle with their disaffected Serb peoples if they wished to avoid Europe's intervening to settle things for them. The French and Italians cordially acceded. Disraeli's instinct was for outright veto. Apart from the hurt to British dignity, with Britain being treated as a mere secondary consenting party on the same level as the French and the Italians, the cardinal 'Crimean' principle of non-intervention in Turkey's internal affairs was being grossly breached. The reforms, moreover, reeked of Home Rule and tenant right ('fancy autonomy for Bosnia, with a mixed population: autonomy for Ireland would be less absurd'). He was persuaded to accede to Europe outwardly in the first case, the better to collude with the Turks to stultify the reforms. But over the Berlin Memorandum he led Derby and his cabinet into a defiant refusal. For good measure, the Mediterranean fleet was ordered to Besika Bay outside the Dardanelles, where twice before (in 1849 and 1853) it had been sent at the instance of Palmerston, to signal to the Turks that they had Britain in support.

This was the first decisive act of British assertiveness in Europe since the days of Palmerston. The public in general gratefully received it as such. Disraeli thought this 'policy of determination' had brought Bismarck's 'tripartite confederacy' to an end. 'It was an unnatural alliance, and never would have occurred had England maintained, of late years, her just position in public affairs.' Her Majesty, he thought, would be restored 'to her due and natural influence in the government of the world'.[27] 'Something', he was able to say by early July, 'like the old days of our authority appear to have returned.'[28]

It all looked very well. Where the Whigs were content and where Gladstone practically alone complained that Britain had broken the concert, the Conservative party could rejoice in this validation of its 'national' credentials. The problem was, however, as Salisbury was later to observe, that Disraeli did not have, and Derby would not have, any substantial prospective notions of what to do with this 'authority'. Disraeli had confided to Corry in April: 'Turkish & Egyptian affairs get worse every day . . . we have plenty of troubles ahead, but perhaps they will vanish when encountered.'[29] That sums up the *modus operandi* of Disraeli's Eastern policy as aptly as anything he said.

His great difficulty was that Turkish affairs continued to deteriorate, and he never got beyond the response to them represented in his veto of the Berlin Memorandum: that there must be no coercion of Turkey; and that Russia was 'at the bottom of the whole affair'. His mind imbued with these two fundamental preconceptions, for almost the next two years Disraeli pushed and shoved Derby through a long series of encounters with worsening affairs which did not vanish on being encountered. And it must always be remembered, apropos of Disraeli's notions of affairs and how they vanish on encounter, that, for example, he would account for the war by Serbia upon Turkey in 1876 as the work of the 'Secret Societies of Europe'. In December 1877, at the beginning of one of the very worst affairs of the series, Salisbury put it to the Northcote in terms accurately applicable to the problem at any time after the affair of the Berlin Memorandum or before the affair of the Congress of Berlin:

> An active policy is only possible under one of two conditions – that you shall help the Turks, or coerce them. I have no objection to the latter policy: or to a combination of the two. With the former alone, I cannot be content. But, as you know, neither the Queen nor the Prime Minister will have anything to do with the latter.[30]

Disraeli could not conduct an 'active policy' as here defined because he could never carry his cabinet far enough away from coercing the Turks and near enough to helping them. The remarkable thing is that throughout all this the Conservative party was 'staunch'. It was the Conservative cabinet which was fracturable. The danger for Disraeli was that the breaking of his cabinet could have serious repercussions on the party.

3

The Conservative party hardly came into the matter until the government began to get into trouble towards the end of the 1876 session over the affair of the Turkish massacres in what later became Bulgaria. Bulgarian patriots had tried to foment insurrection in the spring of 1876 in emulation of their fellow Serb Christians. The Turks loosed Circassian irregulars planted among the Bulgars on to them; and these Bashibazouks brutally massacred many thousands of Christians. Reports began to trickle in to the British press, notably the Liberal *Daily News*, during June. They went largely unnoticed. They were not confirmed by consular or diplomatic sources. The pace of other events crowded them out. The Serbian principality declared war on its Ottoman suzerain in aid of its brethren in Bosnia. Pan-slav sentiment in Russia led thousands of volunteers to aid the Serbs. Disraeli denounced to Corry 'the party intriguing for a European war' manipulating the Serbian crisis.[31] Two Turkish sultans were meanwhile deposed and murdered amid turmoil and growing Muslim excitement. The Turks, victorious over the Serbs, refused Europe's demands for an armistice. All this, however, would not protect the Conservative government from extreme embarrassment and vulnerability were it to emerge that in vetoing European intervention and in bolstering the Turks by sending the fleet to Besika Bay it was in effect making the British state and the British people accomplices to gross and extensive atrocities inflicted by Muslims on oppressed Christian peoples struggling to be free.

Disraeli's last session in the Commons was exhausting. There was a great deal of Liberal resistance to the new Indian imperial title for the queen. It savoured of autocracy, and might be contagious. Old-fashioned Tories and Whigs who had no quarrel with autocracy in India, and who indeed thought a dose of it nearer home would do no harm, still found its flamboyance and its 'un-English' resonances distasteful. Disraeli would have preferred to wait for a less fraught time, but the queen would not be denied. She even went to the lengths of disarming Disraeli by opening the session in person. The title issue led to a bad-tempered Commons' row which ended the innocent phase of the government's foreign and imperial policy. Derby recorded a conversation with Cross: he 'thinks our troubles are over for the time, but I can see from his way of talking that he considers Disraeli to have lost the confidence of the House.'[32] Disraeli was vexed at a blunder by Dyke in his handling of a sudden vote of censure. Disraeli had presented the empress of India title as bearing 'the semblance of deep and organised policy: connected, as it will be, with other things'. This was precisely what was urged against it: it seemed to connect only too deeply Suez with Besika Bay.

Already Salisbury was remarking to Lytton of 'the new British province of Egypt'.[33] Salisbury was left with the cynical intellectual pleasures of settling with Lytton about the details of the new viceroy's proposed 'show' in India. As Salisbury put it to Disraeli, it 'must be so adjusted that it shall be gaudy enough to impress the orientals, yet not enough to give hold for ridicule here: a difficult point to hit.' Salisbury approved of Lytton's strategy of using the occasion to rally the Indian aristocracy to the Raj.

> My general opinion is favourable. I think his principle is sound – that of classes in India, the aristocracy is the only one over whom we can hope to establish any moral influence. The masses are no use – the literary class, which we have unwisely warmed into life before its time, is of its nature *frondeur*. Whether the aristocracy are very powerful may be doubted: & any popularity we may establish with them is not much to lean upon in a moment of trial. But it is good as far as it goes: & their goodwill, & co-operation, if we can obtain it, will at all events serve to hide to the eyes of our own people & perhaps, of the growing literary class in India, the nakedness of the sword on which we really rely.[34]

It would not be long before Salisbury transferred his consideration of the nakedness of power and the capacities of native elites from India to the Near East. What was emerging from the chaos of events in European Turkey was the notion that there must be a conference of the powers at Constantinople to persuade the Turks to agree to pacificatory arrangements. The British government, by now in no position to pretend that the Turks were capable of resolving their problems without the aid of 'Europe', would send a first-class plenipotentiary. The logic of the situation pointed cogently to the secretary of state for India. He commanded wide public confidence. His appreciation of the problems was acute. He told Mallett in January 1876:

> The time will come when something must be done. A government of some kind must be found for all these wretchedly oppressed multitudes. It cannot be left as

> a no-man's-land. But the division of that kind of jetsam is particularly difficult. If the Powers quarrel over it, the calamities of a gigantic war must be undergone. If they agree, people call it partition and denounce it as immoral.[35]

But by the time Salisbury went to Constantinople in December 1876 the Conservative government had undergone the trial of the greatest and most furious storm of public agitation and protest on a question of foreign policy ever to erupt in the country. And when he left for Constantinople the loudest good wishes ringing in his ears were those of the National Conference on the Eastern Question, a massive demonstration designed to articulate the force and energy of that storm of protest and its counter-demands for an Eastern policy repudiating that of the government of which Salisbury was a member.

The cyclone out of Bulgaria

1

The government began to grow aware of public unease about news from Bulgaria at the end of June. In the absence of any guidance to the contrary from Elliot, the ambassador at Constantinople, there seemed no particular reason to take alarm either at the reports themselves or at the public reaction to them. Elliot provided reassurance. His dispatch of 8 June informed Derby that while the employment of Circassians and bashibazouks had 'led to the atrocities which were to be expected', reports of extensive massacres could be discounted as Russian propaganda.[36] Ministers were unwise to entrust confidence in Elliot in this matter. He was known to be wholly Russophobe and imbued with the deepest convictions of Palmerstonian orthodoxy. Salisbury reminded Carnarvon in September 1876, when the storm had broken, that he had been 'preaching' for the past two years, privately and in cabinet, against Elliot's 'stupidity and caprices'.[37] Salisbury made a scathing indictment to Disraeli on 29 August of Elliot's 'stupidity' as a prelude to one of his efforts to promote a revision of policy.[38] Derby admitted that it was a 'reasonable criticism' that Elliot 'ought to have known more of what was passing, and known it sooner, than he appears to have done: and to this there is no quite satisfactory answer.'[39] Nevertheless, Disraeli and Derby incautiously allowed Elliot to remain their only source of information. Elliott incautiously in turn relied on Turkish assurances; and did not send any member of his own staff to make an independent investigation. This was not done until Derby, prodded by Carnarvon in cabinet, instructed him to do so. Questions in the Commons elicited from Disraeli a fantastic rigmarole about Bulgaria being invaded by 'strangers', who caused peaceful Circassian settlers to defend themselves, no doubt ferociously. By 7 July, in the Lords, Derby conceded that he was aware of 'strong public feeling' and announced that he had telegraphed Elliot urgently for information.

By now ministers were conscious that the matter had become an embarrassment, but could look forward to scrambling through to the approaching end of the session. Derby judged that the 'anti-Turkish cry' being got up by the opposition 'may very possibly come too late'.[40] Disraeli allowed himself to be soothed by Foreign Office assurances which endorsed Elliot. He made unfortunate remarks which seemed flippant and which raised untimely laughter: this would be held against him. Hardy recorded on 18 July that Disraeli 'made a very good statement on the Bulgarian atrocities & no debate ensued'.[41] On 31 July he came out with his famous reference to the exaggerations of 'coffee-house babble'.[42] As even Salisbury remarked, it was quite evident, 'from the quiescence of Parliament & the Country on the subject, that a very general confidence is felt in the present conduct of our foreign policy'.[43] Whigs and moderate Liberals were supportive. Gladstone clearly had no stomach for challenging the 'national' consensus. His earlier reactions gave no hint of awareness that an issue of foreign policy could possibly have the government on the run. At the time of the Turkish bankruptcy he was quite confident that Disraeli would handle the problems 'rationally'.[44] He was very critical of the Suez arrangements; but he had gone out of his way to applaud the solidarity with the European concert of the government's seeming adhesion to the Andrassy Note, cutting across Whig complaints in the process. He accordingly denounced the vetoing of the Berlin Memorandum. But when in debate on 31 July he had a great opportunity to open up the question of the atrocities, he conspicuously did not do so. Gladstone criticised the anti-'European' character of the government's policy, but concluded with the hope that even yet the Crimean War had not been fought in vain.

It was not that Gladstone was not looking out for opportunities to strike back with a vengeance at Disraeli and the Conservatives. On the contrary, while he used his abdicated status to please himself regarding what he attended to in the Commons, he took every available chance to do damage to the government except, precisely, the one chance that proved, eventually, the most magnificently damaging of all. This was largely because hard experience had taught Gladstone that there never was – and it seemed never would be – any political benefit to be had out of challenging the 'national' foreign policy. Gladstone had made no serious effort to equip his Liberal government with a post-Palmerstonian foreign policy. There seemed to be no large public demand for it then, and Gladstone would have agreed completely with Salisbury's analysis that there was clearly no large public demand for it now. No more than Disraeli did Gladstone foresee the 'clearing storm which was about the break'.[45] Like Disraeli, he assumed that the end of the session would be the end of the matter. He left Disraeli free in his last speech in the Commons to round off the session on 11 August with a bravura and wholly unapologetic re-assertion of the government's Eastern policy, deprecating atrocity-mongering, repudiating notions of a special British relationship with the Turks or any degree of complicity in alleged massacres, and insisting that above all it was the government's duty to maintain the empire of England.

Conservative ministers sighed with relief. An awkward little passage had been scrambled through. The end of the session did not come a day too soon. Reports began coming in which made it clear that rumours of widespread massacres and gross barbarities were all too true. It seemed that something like 15,000 to 20,000 Bulgarians had been massacred. The new Lord Beaconsfield bitterly reproached ambassadors and the Foreign Office for bad briefings. Demonstrations were beginning to erupt everywhere, stimulated by the *Daily News* reports of a young and 'sensational' American journalist, sparing no detail of horror and rapine. Hardy was soon complaining that the 'Bulgarian horrors are being made political capital of. Gladstone alone of men of mark has basely lent himself to the movement.'[46] Indeed, sudden inspiration had come upon Gladstone that, in spite of all, a great new force and energy of public feeling against the 'Crimean' policy existed, and might be conjured into capital political being and effectiveness. He set aside his notes on the theological problem of eternal damnation and started to think of a pamphlet that would emulate in public impact his *Letter to the Earl of Aberdeen* in 1851 on the Neapolitan atrocities. As he put it in candid terms (which his biographer Morley later squeamishly censored), he suddenly realised that 'the game was afoot and the question yet alive'; he perceived that the 'iron was hot and that the time to strike had arrived'.[47] On 29 August he told the dismayed Granville: 'Good ends can rarely be attained in politics without passion: and there is now, the first time for a good many years, a virtuous passion.'[48]

Conservative ministers were now thoroughly alarmed. Derby telegraphed Elliot that the 'universal feeling of indignation' in England against the Turks had reached such a pitch that in the extreme case of Russia's going to war against Turkey the British government would find it 'practically impossible to interfere'.[49] Hardy wrote to Cairns 'because I know that you generally are more consulted on foreign affairs than others of the Cabinet'.

> The Eastern matter is so serious that I did not like to remain in total darkness & wrote to Derby for some information. . . . The stir about the atrocities is I think real and is penetrating deep. My information is that in any negotiations they must be recognised and repetition if possible provided against. Derby is I fear not enough alive to things but I hope our Chief who generally feels the public pulse will not be unmindful of it on this occasion. Horrible as war is at its best the accounts of what took place exceed as they become more authentic what was first reported.[50]

Cairns in turn wrote to Disraeli:

> The very strong feeling which occupies me is that now that mediation has been set on foot we should use absolute pressure – in fact everything short of compulsion – to make the Porte[51] come into liberal & *un*vindictive terms of peace: & also that, in some way or other, we should recognise and place on record our disgust at what now too truly appear to have been the almost incredible barbarities practised

> in Bulgaria. Now that the truth on the subject is known – (& we may well be excused for withholding our belief as long as a doubt could be entertained) – there is no kind of condemnation as to the past, & no form of stipulation as to the future, wh. this feeling in the country would consider too strong. . . . We are, I think, at the most critical point in our foreign policy which we have yet seen.[52]

Disraeli now echoed Salisbury's denunciations of Elliot: 'he has nearly destroyed a strong and popular government.'[53]

Carnarvon's connections with the High Church party made him uncomfortably aware that the Conservative government was going to be paid back with interest for the Public Worship Regulation Act. (Beauchamp assured Cairns that he was always 'desirous of checking the attack of the High Church Radicals upon the Conservative Party'.)[54] Carnarvon warned Disraeli that 'public feeling' about the atrocities was 'very strong', that it existed 'in classes which we cannot afford to overlook', and that it would grow unless some means of checking it were found. 'If indeed it runs its course much further, it will, I fear, become ungovernable and will either drive us into some precipitate and undignified course or will end in a serious catastrophe.' Some 'decided action' to reassure the public mind, urged Carnarvon, was essential. Northcote and Salisbury wrote urgently in the same vein.[55] The Conservative government was confronting the sudden outburst of the deepest moral energies of the Victorian age. It was a question at this point of how much longer Disraeli and Derby could hold out in their stiffly resistant line.

2

Then, on 6 September, came Gladstone's pamphlet, *Bulgarian Horrors and the Question of the East.* Moderate in content, but violent in rhetoric, it caught the passion of the hour, sold in sensational numbers, and gave the multifarious public protests a unifying text and a charismatic leader. In one sense it made the government's situation more dire, in that it stoked and fanned the heat of the agitation. In another, and ultimately more important sense, it had a steadying effect on the Conservative party and the Conservative government because, unavoidably, it helped to shift the question on to more openly partisan lines. And in this respect the Conservative party proved to be much more coherent in opinion and less fissile in structure than the Liberal party.

Many Conservatives joined in the initial expressions of shock and outrage at what the Turks had done in Bulgaria. Bourke at the Foreign Office received daily batches of letters from MPs conveying their constituents' indignation.[56] Opinion among Conservatives was quite often conformable with the views of such a sceptic about Palmerstonian traditions as Salisbury. Although the Conservative governments of Derby and Disraeli took the Crimean system on board after the war, the Conservative party bore no responsibility for the Crimean War. Disraeli's steady opinion, then and later, was that it was a supremely unnecessary war, caused by Aberdeen's weak and appeasing approach to the Russians, 'drift', and lack of decisiveness. Had Derby taken office in 1855 his most likely policy would have been to offer the Russians an honourable compromise settlement. Many an 'old Tory' had no more quarrel with the czardom than with rule by the naked sword in India; and found no fault with Carlyle's fulminations in 1876 against the 'abominable Turk'. Very few Conservatives, however, persisted as 'atrocitarians', and these were usually irreconcilable High Church zealots such as Lord Bath. The influence of the Anglo-Catholic divine, H. P. Liddon, was intense among this group. One rare instance of persistent Conservative agitation, that of the future MP, Ellis Ashmead Bartlett, indicates a revealing degree of youthful emotional instability (he was overwhelmed in St. Paul's by one of Liddon's sermons). But by 1878 Bartlett would be as violently Russophobe as he was Turcophobe in 1876.[57]

Gladstone's intervention certainly had the effect of setting the whole question of Eastern policy in a very different light. Partly it was the primitive Tory instinct expressed in Disraeli's own aphorism, 'Damn your principles! Stick to your party.' Partly also it was that Gladstone's style and tone manifested in salient high relief a certain kind of public moralism with which Conservatives were instinctively uncomfortable: in Gladstone's own formula, the politics of 'virtuous passion'. This had doctrinal implications with respect to state policy which quickly established themselves at the core of the intellectual debate as to the meaning and significance of the atrocities agitation. In the name of their self-proclaimed virtue the leaders of agitation who now found in Gladstone their long-awaited messiah were insisting that the classic problem of the vexed relationship between policy and morality must be transcended by an instant moral absolutism of simple right and simple wrong. The 'Nonconformist conscience' rallied instinctively and in a sense nobly to this absolutism. Liddon was among its more influential exponents. He identified the issue at the bottom of the protest movement as being the conviction that patriotism is 'the feeling which we have about our relatives'.

> We wish our relatives to be good men in the first instance, and then successful men, if success is compatible with goodness. I cannot understand how many excellent people fail to feel thus about their country too; it would seem to me that exactly in the proportion in which we realise the fact that a nation is only a very overgrown family . . . will be our anxiety that this country should act as a good man would act; and that patriotism consists in wishing this.[58]

The average Conservative mentality would have no difficulty in distrusting such facile anthropomorphic moralism. Nothing of it was in fact in Gladstone's *Bulgarian Horrors*. Gladstone was far too much of an old hand in statecraft so to indulge himself. His art was to disguise the quite modest character of his practical recommendations (much as they had been back in July) with famously blazing verbiage. The point was that Gladstone seemed to be offering a refreshing new kind of public morality. He repeated the technique in a speech at Blackheath a few days later, when he affirmed solemnly his conviction that the agitation sprang, pure and undefiled by party or political motives, from the simple, undesigning conscience of the masses. Where the average Conservative mentality would have its greatest problem in this matter was in confronting the kind of deliberately brutal *raison d'état* offered by Sir Henry Elliot, no doubt with salutary intent, in his notorious dispatch to Derby of 4 September:

> To the accusation of being a blind partisan of the Turks, I will only answer that my conduct here has never been guided by any sentimental affection for them but by a firm determination to uphold the interests of Great Britain to the utmost of my power, and that those interests are deeply engaged in preventing the disruption of the Turkish Empire is a conviction which I share in common with the most eminent statesmen who have directed our foreign policy, but which appears now to be abandoned by shallow politicians or persons who have allowed their feelings of revolted humanity to make them forget the capital interests involved in the question.
>
> We may, and must, feel indignant at the needless and monstrous severity with which the Bulgarian insurrection was put down, but the necessity which exists for England to prevent changes from occurring here which would be most detrimental to ourselves, is not affected by the question whether it was 10,000 or 20,000 persons who perished in the suppression.[59]

These virulently Palmerstonian words, along with Gladstone's rhetoric about 'bag and baggage', became the most oft quoted in the propaganda of the 'atrocitarians'.[60] Many Conservatives, having to choose between Liddon and Elliot, would gulp Elliot; many others would feel that Elliot's words were tendentious and question-begging. They had much to do with Salisbury's opinions about Elliot's 'stupidity'. They had more to do with Salisbury's continuing efforts to convince his chief that Palmerstonism was a bankrupt policy.

The greatest obstacle in the way of his doing that was now, quite simply, Gladstone. It was Gladstone who rallied the Conservative ranks. In his distress about the 'very wicked, & unprincipled though for the time telling' agitation, Cross could 'conceive nothing more reckless than Mr. Gladstone's conduct'.[61] It was Gladstone who provoked Derby to add his echo of Disraeli's opinion: 'We have nothing to unsay or undo and we must not make things look as if we had.'[62] Disraeli explained to Salisbury: 'Our great object, wh. Derby & myself have had during what Ld Overstone calls "a frantic ebullition of public excitement," has never been to admit that we have changed our policy, & that we have adopted the views of the Opposition. This greatly irritates them.'[63] Derby addressed delegations; 'calm & clear,' as Hardy described him to Cairns, 'but cold & too much addressed to the reasonable world only.'[64] Disraeli assured Cairns: 'I think from the tone of the Press, that Derby has quenched the agitation.'[65] Carnarvon was inclined to hope that a 'slight reaction' against the 'political cyclone' was taking place, caused by the 'extreme violence of Gladstone & from some of the Liberals'.[66] Carnarvon supported Cairns in his advice to Disraeli that an unseasonable cabinet should be called.

Ministers were nervous about the impending Buckinghamshire by-election for Disraeli's former seat. A contest in normal times would not have been thought of. (Corry to 'My loved Chief': 'In the name of Heavens! . . . Surely the thing is a ridiculous forlorn hope . . . is it not?')[67] Carnarvon knew that Disraeli regarded him as an 'alarmist'; but he was satisfied that 'the feeling has gone deeper and further than is supposed – and I shall not be surprised if the Buckinghamshire Election shows signs of this. I know that there has been *shakings* amongst a certain number of our ordinary supporters there.'[68]

Cairns turned his formidable pressure upon Disraeli. 'I wish I could see some daylight in the East.' Derby's speech was good, as far as it went; 'but it was in my judgment too negative & too destitute in sentiment or suggestion for the present gale of public opinion.' But what was to be done? 'Lowe & Gladstone are atrocious in suggesting what they know they could not attempt were they in our place; but the public don't see this; & I fear the result is to paralyse us at Constant^{l}., & and make Russia the Mistress of the situation.' Cairns wanted a cabinet '*whether or not*' they were to take some decided step. 'Things are utterly changed since we last met. Hardy is "uncomfortable", "dissatisfied" at not knowing what is going on.' Cairns's 'own idea' was that 'we should agree on a definite object: such as forcing (with the other powers) Turkey to make a liberal peace . . . & then a Conference with a view to the Powers who now guarantee Turkey, guaranteeing a system of autonomous, but Tributary, states'.[69] Disraeli had no intention of calling a cabinet to dismantle the Ottoman Empire; and took trouble to convince Cairns that Derby was showing 'an energy & fertility of resource, & fixity of purpose in the matter for wh. I never previously before gave him credit'.[70] Cairns could only respond that while he could not recall that the basis of Derby's policy had ever been before the cabinet, he had to agree that 'it seems to me now . . . to be wise & adequate'.[71] The Turks would be made to settle an armistice with the Serbs. Britain would participate in a conference of the powers.

But not before Disraeli, in a speech at Aylesbury before the Buckinghamshire poll, declared comprehensive defiance of and contempt for everything the agitation over the Bulgarian atrocities stood for, not sparing Gladstone on either head. He rather ruined the shock effect with rodomontade about the sinister role of the 'Secret Societies of Europe', which provoked scathing comment from newspapers otherwise inclined to be supportive. Had Buckinghamshire been lost, the disaster would have been complete. There were serious grounds for anxiety, as Carnarvon suggested. Smith excused himself from supporting the Conservative candidate on the grounds that he was embarrassed at his lack of information. 'In the present excited state of the public mind one might easily say too little to satisfy one's friends and too much for difficult work in which the Foreign Office is engaged.'[72] Abergavenny reported: 'A telegram has just informed me that Buckinghamshire is safe by a majority of 187. I need hardly say how rejoiced I am – for altho' I never could bring myself to think it was possible to lose, still one rather funked when one was told that Carrington had offered to lay £100 down, his brother would win & tht Lord Granville has done ditto.' Abergavenny fully agreed with Disraeli's comments about the 'Jesuitical Tree Cutter': 'His hatred & jealousy of you breathes thro' every speech.' Abergavenny further rejoiced that the 'insane violence' of feeling in the country was subsiding and a reaction coming.[73]

The matter of the growing intensity of personal feeling between the leader of the Conservative party and the former leader of the Liberal party had by now taken on an enhanced importance of its own among the factors of the political equation. Disraeli usually defined it in terms of Gladstone's 'vindictiveness'. Abergavenny sympathised:

> I have no doubt you are quite right. You always are. I only hope & trust you will live to see the Old Man go to the 'Happy Hunting Grounds' & will be still Prime Minister when the event occurs. The conclusion of peace has greatly strengthened the Government & Gladstone is undone. Did you see the Arch Knave has been felling one of the large trees at Raby – one probably planted by a Nevill 400 years ago.[74]

From the party point of view the great thing was that the Buckinghamshire seat was held. As Cross put it, the '*small* majority will have no weight as compared with victory'.[75] Disraeli put it to Cairns: 'we carried our County, but it was too near a thing to be pleasant. A defeat, however, would have been intolerable.'[76] Dyke put the whips' view.

> The Bucks election was too near to be pleasant, but considering the country at the time was suffering from the 'rabies Bulgarica' & other influences brought to bear I think it is well that we won. I have many letters from my supporters in the House just now and although the professional funker who dreads Fawcett & still has a lingering belief in Gladstone takes a gloomy view the tone generally is excellent. There was a capital meeting at Maidstone a few days ago. . . . Gorst wrote to me from London on Saturday & expressed an opinion that the agitation was subsiding but that your speech at Aylesbury was not strong enough against the Porte. I thought it excellent because of its boldness, just at a time when courage of all things was required. To my mind Gladstone never tried harder in his lifetime to damage an old opponent than with his Pamphlet first & then his Speech . . . attacking Turkey & then his letter full of misrepresentations & falsehoods as to our Policy.[77]

Holding Buckinghamshire meant that the party, though shaken, was sound. Though, as Taylor put it to Corry, 'the mischief of the agitation rests with Gladstone – d him!',[78] it remained mischief rather than structural damage. And there were grounds for thinking that the cyclone, or tornado, had spent itself.

Barrington wrote to Disraeli on 8 October: 'I congratulate you on the gradual return of Englishmen to sanity.'[79] The turning tide was most clearly signalled in the press. Once Derby had been seen to secure an armistice and a conference both the *Telegraph* and *The Times* came across to the Conservative government. Derby noted: 'The "Times" as usual, has been most conspicuous in the suddenness of its change. The "Telegraph", "Pall Mall", "Standard", & "Post", are more or less on the Turkish or moderate side.'[80] These proved to be the two of the most valuable legacies given inadvertently by Gladstone and the agitation to the Conservative party. The agitation's impact opened up fault-lines in the sectarian and intellectual as well as the political strata of British public life which, after the immediate shock and outrage had dissipated, revealed more substantial damage to Liberalism rather than Conservatism.

In the Church the 'High Radical' party's zeal for Greek Orthodoxy found but faint echoes in the Protestant bulk. Apart from a few mavericks the Bench of Bishops accepted the logic that the state Church should uphold the state. Disraeli's assertions about the unpopularity of the High Church at last hit their political mark. The rancorous atrocitarian, the historian E. A. Freeman, disgusted at the Church's refusal to endorse the extreme High Church programme of restoring Constantinople to the Greeks, announced that he was now prepared to purchase liberated Hagia Sophia at the price of disendowed Canterbury. The zeal of the Nonconformists for Gladstone's policy of virtuous passion and their identification of their cause with that of the Eastern Christians as the 'Nonconformists of Turkey' was far from grateful to the Jewish interest, more impressed with their own historical memories of Muslim tolerance and Greek Christian anti-Semitism. (This was material for the Levy-Lawsons of the *Telegraph*.) There was a considerable amount of 'Jewish plot' anti-Semitism among atrocitarians, generally directed at Disraeli: a kind of counter-fantasy to his own secret societies. Liberal churchmen of the 'philosophic' school found the zealously simplistic political moralism of the Anglo-Catholics and the Nonconformists all too reminiscent of theological obduracy. Roman Catholicism both in Britain and Ireland had no love for the Gladstone of *Vatican Decrees* or for the Russophile and Orthodox implications of Gladstone's line. Irish Home Rulers contributed their own obvious twist of identifying British oppression of the Irish with Turkish oppression of Bulgarians; and pointed to Gladstone's compassion for the Bulgarians as yet another example of hypocritical English philanthropy increasing as the square of the distance.

The debate set off in the intellectual dimension of British public life was the most famous of the effects of the agitation's impact. There were resonances of the earlier and much less extended controversy provoked by the suppression of the alleged negro insurrection in Jamaica in the 1860s. The fault-line which widened decisively in 1876 was the line dividing the Liberal intelligentsia. This line had long been discernible: the rival texts could well be defined as Mill's *On Liberty* of 1859 and Arnold's *Culture and Anarchy* of 1867. Dispute about political morality and state policy in 1876 and afterwards jolted this fault-line into an uncloseable fissure. The great intellect of Liberalism, by far the most prestigious and influential body of public and social thinking and the secular glory of Liberal politics, had lost its old sense of solidarity and united purpose. A school of Liberal intellects now began to emerge that reacted against what seemed to them to be Gladstone's demagogy and populism. Arnold's tough-minded evocation of the authority of right reason in the state and Fitzjames Stephen's excoriation of Mill's tender-minded libertarian sentimentality seemed all the more apropos in a context of excited crowds emanating virtuous passion. The Bulgarian agitation was the baptism of fire of Liberal imperialism. All this would have immensely advantageous implications for what Mill had contemptuously dubbed 'the stupidest party'.

Other political advantages were more immediately apparent in the cool aftermath of agitation. The Radical schools of Liberalism largely resisted the moral lures of Gladstone's appeal. The Cobdenite isolationists stood firm with John Bright against any interference in foreigners' quarrels. More important, the school of Russophobe Radicals tended markedly to cleave to Disraeli's policy, led by the great Newcastle figure of Joseph Cowen and the veteran John Roebuck. Some younger Radicals, like Joseph Chamberlain, hoped to use Gladstone against the Whigs. Others, like Dilke, were not so sure. Above all, the Whigs were not amused. The Palmerstonian duumvirate of Granville in the Lords and Hartington in the Commons did not enjoy being upstaged and hustled by Gladstone. Whigs had an instinctive distaste for 'forcing the Executive in foreign policy'. They looked with a wry face at swarming Dissenters, pulpiteering Ritualists, and tub-thumping professors. They did not like the look of the way Gladstone seemed to be going. The practical advantage of all this from Disraeli's point of view was that when at the beginning of the 1877 session Gladstone wanted the Liberal party in effect to resume the agitation in parliament, it simply refused.

3

That crucial advantage of confronting a fractured Liberal party while retaining a substantially sound Conservative party was the enabling circumstance which allowed Disraeli to persist indefatigably with his method of encounters. He often tacked and jibbed, but always returned to the bearing set with the rejection of the Berlin Memorandum. It was of the essence of his method, as Salisbury pointed out, that he formulated no settled plan nor balanced any remote contingencies. These would have been vulnerable to rational resistance. Cabinet colleagues were never able to grasp anything as tangible as a policy. In this respect Derby's sullen negativism could be exploited as a tactical resource.

Already, in the aftermath of the Bucks election, Salisbury made yet another bid to shift the bearings. He tried to exploit the narrow majority. 'The Bucks election shows that the agitation has not been without effect on our party. It is clear enough that the traditional Palmerstonian policy is at an end.' What Derby had offered was good enough for an 'emergency'; but much more, Salisbury insisted, would be required for any permanent arrangement. Salisbury went on to outline a comprehensive project for a 'Protector of Christians' to be nominated by the concert and appointed by the Turks, with adequate powers, who would in turn nominate Christian governors for provinces and make subsidiary arrangements for autonomous provincial councils.[81] Derby blanched at this 'large and new' scheme. 'It amounts to a new constitution for the Turkish empire.' Disraeli himself would not countenance it. It would look 'contemptible' as a concession to public agitation. He assured Salisbury that a 'great reaction' would soon set in; which was true but not quite to Salisbury's point.

On this flood of reaction Disraeli floated himself free. As Conservative confidence revived, atrocitarian leaders who had once been bogeys became figures of fun. Back in September Hardy had expostulated against the 'malignant calumny' of 'violent men like Freeman who impute wilful connivance'. Hardy could only hope that Freeman's historical works were more objective.[82] Now, in October, Barrington reported to Beaconsfield:

> Of course you have heard of the party which is to assemble at Longleat on the 14th prox°: the Gladstone family, Liddon, Williams (the ritualistic parson of Ringwood), Mr. Dickenson, of whom great things are expected in the Slavophile line, & that monstrous Freeman, whose manners in society are such very American ones, that he is said to be 'quite a caution'. Really Bath must be gone quite mad.[83]

It was not quite so funny when news got about that Carnarvon's house parties at Highclere were not all that different in composition and tone.

If the Conservative party preserved soundness of body, the Conservative cabinet decidedly did not. To the receptive Carnarvon Northcote plaintively pointed out that he would be in no position as leader of the Commons to state the government's case since he had no idea what it was. 'But at present we seem to be living from hand to mouth, with no true conception of our own, or any other Power's policy.' The strains were beginning to tell. Northcote was clear that 'no injury which could be inflicted on "British interests" by Russian aggrandisement' would be 'so great as the injury we should suffer, from an indefinite prolongation of the Eastern crisis'. Perhaps the Russians now were playing the historical role which the Turks played when they destroyed the 'old Eastern Empire'. Yet a threat by the Russians to Constantinople would be a 'signal for a serious war'. What hopes could there be for the conference? 'If one cook has so much difficulty in making that kind of broth, what are we to expect from six?'[84]

Disraeli took the opportunity in his Guildhall speech on 9 November to stir the broth with a flourish. Salisbury's appointment as Britain's first representative at the conference had been announced, to general public satisfaction. The great danger from Disraeli's point of view was that Salisbury might well strike a bargain with the Russians along the lines of his proposals for what amounted to a new constitution for the Turkish Empire. Elliot had been named as the second representative, as insurance against any such project. As reinsurance Disraeli took an opportunity to encourage the Turks by baiting the Russians. The czar had announced that if the conference failed to persuade the Turks to reform, Russia was prepared unilaterally to coerce the Turks by war. Disraeli responded in terms clearly meant to warn the Russians off any such venture; explicitly stating that there was no country so well prepared to wage war and sustain war through many campaigns as Britain was. Disraeli was signalling that in no circumstances would a Russian military presence in Constantinople be tolerated. The fortuitous Russian order for the mobilisation of six army corps chimed in with precision for his purposes.

Tempers in cabinet started to fray. Ministers were tending to divide into softliners and hardliners. Derby noted on 24 October his surprise on hearing from Hunt that Disraeli had desired Hunt to order the admiral at Besika Bay to send the fleet up to Constantinople in the event of a Russian vessel passing through the Bosphorous. 'I cannot quite believe that Disraeli would have directed this to be done without consulting me,' Derby commented, 'but he is in an odd excited state, & talks carelessly about the possibility of our being at war, and the steps to be taken, before people who repeat & probably exaggerate all his utterances.' Derby could foresee the 'possibility, or at least, the chance of a breach between us: not that as yet we have differed materially in regard to anything that has been done, but that our points of view & objects are different.'

> To the Premier the main thing is to please and surprise the public by bold strokes and unexpected moves: he would rather run serious national risks than hear his policy called feeble or commonplace: to me, the first object is to keep England out of trouble, so long as it can be done consistently with honor and good faith. We have agreed in resisting the agitation got up by Gladstone: but if war with Russia becomes popular, as it may, we are not unlikely to be on different sides.[85]

If the affair of the atrocities' agitation exhibited the staunchness of the party, the affair of the Constantinople conference exhibited the fracturability of the cabinet.

Disraeli now had an excellent Russian threat to use against those of his colleagues who wanted to equip Salisbury with instructions to join in a European coercion of Turkey. Those in favour were Cairns, Salisbury himself, Carnarvon, Northcote, and Richmond. Against Beaconsfield and Derby and their supporters Cairns insisted: 'Such a restriction on Lord Salisbury's authority I could not bring myself to agree to.'[86] Within a week things had got to the point where Cairns was agreeing that 'any break in our harmonious action wd be disastrous to us as a party: &, in a crisis like the present, might be equally so to the country.' But he remained opposed to tying Salisbury's hands; with reasons conspicuous for their prescience. The powers would need to retain the option of threatening to impose 'collective action' on the Turks, 'so that there may not again arise an idea that Russia must act alone because no one else will do anything'.[87] In the end Salisbury was empowered with coercive instructions which, however, excluded any form of military occupation in which Russians would be included: a fudge. Balfour later recorded:

> When Lord S. was going to Constple for the conference he constantly urged on his colleagues that it was little use his going unless it was previously decided exactly what should be done in the event of the Turks refusing the propositions of the Powers. 'Oh! but they won't refuse' was the only answer he could ever get; and with that he had to be content.[88]

Salisbury set off for Constantinople on 20 November, in hopes of doing something 'for all these wretchedly oppressed multitudes'; but oppressed himself with a sense of futility ('sea-sickness, much French and failure'). Salisbury was aware that Lady Derby, his former stepmother, was telling Shuvalov, the Russian ambassador, everything Derby was telling her about cabinet discussions; and Shuvalov in turn was passing on the invaluable intelligence to Ignatiev at Constantinople. Salisbury arranged with Carnarvon a special cypher code by which they could exchange confidentially information respectively from the conference and the cabinet. More: among Carnarvon's house guests at Highclere had been Liddon; and Liddon it was whom the Gladstone group deputed to address a 'moral appeal' to Salisbury by means of Lady Salisbury.[89] This was by way of being preliminary to Gladstone's own individual moral appeal to Salisbury, which took the form of a piece in the *Contemporary Review*, 'The Hellenic factor in the Eastern question'. It was entirely oblique, because Gladstone did not want to embarrass Salisbury; and ostensibly it was a plea that the case of the Greeks and their claims should not be forgotten at the conference. Substantially, Gladstone composed it as a parable of British statesmanship. He offered the brilliant example of 'the Canning policy'. Gladstone's parable told of how Canning, having rescued British policy from the dire influence of Castlereagh and the Holy Alliance, rescued Czar Nicholas from the 'debasing influence of Metternich'; of how the czar responded to Canning's 'far-sighted appeal', and how this clinched success for the restoration of Greek freedom; of how Byron's lofty part and martyrdom may be supposed to have been among the encouragements to the 'bold policy of Canning'; and, above all, of how it was to be hoped that their example might 'yet supply a guiding light to some British statesman'.[90]

It is doubtful whether the example of Canning would much have impressed Salisbury as a model of Conservative statesmanship. After all, the liberation of Greece had been followed by a period of Russian domination of Turkey which Canning's disciple Palmerston had great difficulty in redressing. It was with precisely this point in mind that Disraeli, in his notes on the cabinet of 22 December which decided to refuse Salisbury powers to sanction coercion, added: 'Mr. Canning's experiences and its consequences.'[91] It is possible that this was directly prompted by Gladstone's article.

A much larger guiding light was also offered to Salisbury by the most distinguished public demonstration ever assembled to urge a cause in British foreign policy. This was the National Conference on the Eastern Question, which sat in two sessions in St. James's Hall, Piccadilly, on 8 December. Its purpose, in Gladstone's words, was to cut Salisbury 'adrift from the Guildhall speech'.[92] The conference of the powers at Constantinople was due to gather on 14 December. The conference at St. James's Hall, called to the 'high and glorious mission' of vindicating the 'principles of humanity' and blotting out the legacy of the 'fatal Crimean War', addressed itself to reparation for the Bulgarians, disarming of the Muslim population, autonomous government for Christian peoples in Turkey, and fruitful cooperation with Russia. Granville and Hartington tried to persuade Gladstone that he would embarrass Salisbury by taking part. He asserted, on the contrary, that his purpose would be to buttress Salisbury's position.[93]

Granville and Hartington, however, were nearer the truth: Salisbury's position needed buttressing not at Constantinople, but in Disraeli's cabinet. A gathering which, in effect, reaffirmed the principles and reassembled the groups and interests of the autumn agitation, undermined rather than buttressed Carnarvon and Salisbury's other supporters in cabinet. Gladstone's ostentatious links with Shuvalov, the Russian ambassador, and Madame Novikov, whom the queen described as a 'Russian female spy, about wh. there is much gossip',[94] caused scandal. Disraeli, in his notice of 'this organised attempt to revive agitation', expatiated on the insolence of this 'intolerable assembly'; and was able to draw attention to the facts that of 89 MPs among the 710 conveners, 88 were Liberals and one only (Lord Robert Montagu) a Conservative; and an eccentric one at that. Of 23 peers only three (Bath, Shaftesbury, and Seaton) were Conservative. Disraeli was in a position to dwell with gratification on the 'very favourable' parliamentary situation of the government despite all the agitators could do. 'It is not merely, that our own men are unanimously staunch, but the whole of the Irish party has been instructed to support the Government.'[95] Derby remarked on the conspicuous absence of 'deserters from our side', 'a foolish letter from the foolish Bath being the only approach to an exception'. He calculated that 'in parliament, we may lose the support of a few high churchmen: but the Catholics are not hostile: they will be neutral, if not friendly: and to our own large majority we ought to add a section of pro-Turkish or anti-Russian Liberals, more than enough to balance any defections.'[96] On top of Conservative staunchness, Disraeli cheerfully calculated the 'decided anti-Russian section' of the Liberals as 'not less than sixty'; and Derby took further comfort from the quite 'remarkable' 'absence & silence of the Whig chiefs', apart from those with close Gladstonian links such as Argyll and Westminster.[97] Nor was it immaterial that the queen and the Court were indiscreetly partisan for Disraeli. Softline ministers could find themselves in highly intimidating situations. The Conservative press, which by now, for all intents and purposes, included *The Times* and the

Telegraph, was as staunch as the parliamentary party. In short, Disraeli's position was impregnable. Carnarvon was quite helpless to use his cyphers with Salisbury to any effect.

At Constantinople Salisbury got on excellently with the chief Russian representative, Ignatiev. Left to themselves, they would have had no difficulty in agreeing on arrangements for the benefit of the wretchedly oppressed multitudes. Salisbury's great problem (other than the Turks themselves) was Elliot, whom Disraeli and Derby insisted on retaining. Salisbury's pleas that Elliot be removed offended Disraeli. He used the party to warn Derby: 'If Elliot is recalled, or even returned, and it gets about . . . that he has been returned or recalled thro' Ignatieff, the ministry will be turned out, the first night of the session, by their own men. Have, care! We are treading on very dangerous ground.'[98] Derby recorded on 18 December:

> My expectation was that the Cabinet today would press for some kind of coercion to be exercised against Turkey, in the event of a refusal of the proposals of the Conference: and on this point I was prepared for a rupture: but to my surprise the general feeling was with me, & I shall have no excuse for retiring as I had hoped.

Carnarvon was the only dissentient.[99] Salisbury was refused permission to join in a plan of European coercion in the face of Turkish intransigence. The Turks had reason to believe that Elliot represented the British decision-makers who really counted. Elliot believed the Russian threat of war was a bluff. Disraeli and Derby ignored Carnarvon. ('The Prime Minister does not like my "ideas" on this subject and Derby does not answer when he disagrees with a letter!')[100] The Turks accordingly held out and the conference broke up in failure in January, leaving the Russians in a state of some perplexity. Salisbury returned home, expecting a chilling reception in the party. He was, to his puzzlement, warmly received.[101] It was as if the only people who had taken his role in Constantinople seriously were the earnest conveners of the National Conference on the Eastern Question. The Conservative party was so unruffled on the issue of coercing the Turks that it took no offence that its plenipotentiary had done his best to be a traitor to its cause. Chill was reserved entirely for Carnarvon. Salisbury, embodying British good will, had failed splendidly.

Salisbury made a final effort to get Disraeli to accept a revised Russian scheme. The Russians were indeed not in a state of good military organisation. This was a last bid to convince the Turks that they must yield short of war. Salisbury recommended it as representing an 'extraordinary diplomatic defeat'.[102] If the Turks refused this last chance the Russians must go to war: with probable disastrous consequences for the Turks and for the interests of their British patrons. The Turks thought the Russians were cracking. (Northcote, with sour memories of the *Alabama* treaty, thought the Turks 'cute enough to be Yankees'.)[103] For the first time there was something of a serious fracas in cabinet. Carnarvon made reference to an 'extraordinary address which

Disraeli made us on the disturbances of the unanimity of the Cabinet and which was obviously addressed against Salisbury & myself'. Carnarvon complained bitterly also about Derby's leaking cabinet confidentialities to the virulently Russophobe *Pall Mall Gazette* (not to mention 'Derby's intemperate conduct even in the ordinary relations of daily life'). Carnarvon urged upon Northcote the serious risk to the continued existence of the government involved in such leaks, unprecedented in his experience.[104] Salisbury got his way over this last offer to the Turks – who complacently rejected it. Russia thereupon had no option but to declare war on Turkey on 24 April as executor on behalf of Europe. Cairns's prescient analysis of 23 November was now fulfilled.

Questions of war and peace

1

War was a dismaying outcome for the Conservative government. Salisbury's warning could come true: Russia might well swiftly defeat the Turks and impose triumphantly the Constantinople terms which the British government had prevented Europe's imposing peacefully: British isolation and humiliation would be complete; British interests at Constantinople and the straits would be at the discretion of an armed and victorious Russia. Liddon and Freeman and their friends dreamed of the spectacle of Alexander II handing back Hagia Sophia to the keeping of the Greek Orthodox patriarch and redressing the tragic historic wrong of 1453.

The government and the Conservative party avoided this catastrophe, through no merit of their own. They were saved from it by the Turks, who fought stubbornly and delayed Russian victory until the end of 1877. In some ways this new situation was very awkward for the government. Ministers had, through rescuing and upholding the Turks against 'Europe', created an entirely new and unnecessary problem for themselves. They had to decide what to do in the event of Russian victory. What definition of British interests would they be prepared to go to war to defend?

In another way, however, the new situation of war made things easier for the government. The great issue of Eastern policy seemed now set in clearer terms; not so much indirectly through the Turks, but directly in confrontation with the Russians. On the whole, the Conservative party preferred the emphasis of confronting Russians to the emphasis of bolstering Turks. Disraeli knew that, as party leader, he could continue to prosecute radically confrontational encounters with the Russians, involving if necessary the clear and immediate contingency of war, without risk of breaking the Conservative party. His problem was that he was equally aware that he could not prosecute such encounters without serious risk of breaking the Conservative cabinet.

Concurrently, Disraeli worried that if the government failed to take a tough line it would lose public confidence. In May he despondently assured Derby that 'we shall either be turned out in the present parliament, or be obliged to dissolve at an unfavourable moment: inasmuch as when the Russians begin to threaten Constantinople there will be an outburst of popular indignation, and we shall be blamed for having allowed matters to come to this pass.' Derby observed him in July 'uneasy and excited', insisting that if the Russians got to Constantinople 'there would be an outbreak of popular feeling against us, the bulk of the Conservatives would desert us, the Whigs would join, and Gladstone and his friends would say "if our advice had been taken, all this might have been averted." The ministry would be upset, and that with ignominy.' Disraeli wanted the cabinet to declare Russian entry to Constantinople a *casus belli*. He expected that would mean losing Salisbury and Carnarvon, but was confident they were expendable. Derby had to agree that Salisbury was not generally popular with the party. He was less impressed, however, with Disraeli's extolling Manners as the potential restorer of cabinet fortitude: ('!!'). Disraeli was possessed with the idea that a violent anti-Russian agitation was about to break out, and carry all before it; claiming 'good intelligence' from numerous 'agents'.[105]

Through 1877 the underlying plot was the same, but the ministerial actors shifted parts. Salisbury withdrew to the side. 'Of our foreign policy I say nothing', he told Lytton in May. It filled him with sadness and apprehension. 'The system of never making a plan before the next move is bearing its natural fruits. I trust we may avoid any great disaster.'[106] The logic of his thinking now was that the hopelessness of Turkey as a going concern pointed to the need to defend British interests 'in a more direct way by some territorial arrangement . . . a *pied à terre*'. But British policy was 'to float lazily down stream, occasionally putting out a diplomatic boat hook to avoid collisions'.[107] By October 1877 Disraeli could amuse Lady Derby at a Woburn house party with details of the 'six parties in cabinet': for war at any price were Hardy, Manners, and Beach. For war if the Russians entered Constantinople: Cross, Smith, and Cairns. For war if the Russians refused to *leave* Constantinople: Salisbury. For leading Christian service in St. Sophia: Carnarvon. For peace at any price: Derby. Disraeli counted himself and the queen as the party for reconciling the other parties. Derby himself added Richmond to the party of his keeper, Cairns; and supposed that Northcote was omitted as being a ditherer.[108]

Northcote, indeed, elated as chancellor of the Exchequer with excellent financial prospects, and as leader of the house with Liberal debility, took over where Salisbury had given up. He buzzed about like a veritable little busy bee. 'We ought not to allow the matter simply to drift,' he noted in April. 'We ought to have a policy.' Again: 'I feel how important it is that we should be united. But we shall run great risk of disunion if we do not take full counsel together before anything is done or decided or which commits us to a line of policy which cannot be changed without discredit.'[109] To Cairns he was replete with ideas about Egyptian finances and French and Russian pressures therein. He busied himself in Paris, conferring with Lyons and Decazes on the virtues of concerted action. And to Derby he was full of ideas about the most drastic contingencies, going more than one better than Salisbury. What if Russia were to take Constantinople and dictate to the Turks? In that case Northcote would like Britain 'on many grounds' to assume 'temporary charge of the Canal'. 'It would never be believed that we only took it in trust, and it would be said that we were giving the signal for a scramble.' But if Russia *did* become a great Mediterranean power, 'we seem bound by the law of self-preservation to assure ourselves of Egypt'.[110] This was seconded by Salisbury, who breezily declared that the Russians in Constantinople would not matter all that much and scandalised Derby by cheerfully adding: 'and that we ought to seize Egypt. Against that idea I protested.'[111] That kind of talk Disraeli regarded as defeatist. There was no question of the Russians being allowed to take Constantinople.

But Derby in any case was beyond hope. War and the pressures this entailed as to possible British mediation or intervention were to him an utter disaster. This was the point at which, in logic and credit, he ought to have resigned. His further year at the Foreign Office was painful farce. It became more painful when Disraeli and the queen learned of Lady Derby's indiscretions with Shuvalov. At one time there was a bizarre phase when Lady Derby's intrigues led to counter-intrigues through Corry (Disraeli's 'wife') intriguing with Mongelas at the Austrian embassy as well as counter counter-intrigues between Shuvalov to Disraeli via Borthwick of the *Morning Post*.[112] On 20 June there was agreement to ask parliament for a vote of credit, with a view mainly to stiffening Austrian resolve.

For others war threatened dangers but equally offered prospects of change for the better. Disraeli (and the queen) could hope for Turkish victory; and indeed Turkish successes, as Corry reported to Cairns, did wonders for the prime minister's bronchitis. ('If the 3 Pashas keep on giving the Russians blows, in turn, as of late, he will soon be more than himself again. He is in high spirits today at Osman's last affair.')[113] Russian defeat at Plevna in August 1877 eased critical pressures in cabinet. Salisbury could hope that critical pressures of war might transmute British policy from encounters into plans. As for Derby, Balfour in 1880 commented on his eventual resignation in March 1878:

> Why Lord Derby resigned is obvious enough. Why he did not resign long before is the only problem which requires solution. I suppose it was too great an effort ever to form a decision which would for ever relieve him from the necessity of deciding anything again. The scenes in cabinet towards the end of his official connection with it, must have been highly curious. The issues of peace and war trembling in the balance. Lord Derby between overwork, alcohol, and responsibility, in a

condition of utter moral prostration, doing as little as possible and doing that little under compulsion. As the Ld Chancellor [Cairns] told me the other day, 'During his last year of office all that Derby did was done at the point of the bayonet.' I believe during that period the Chancellor wrote many of his critical dispatches for him and, so to speak, put the pen in his hand and made him sign![114]

One component of the solution of the problem of Derby's delay in getting out was the greatness of Derby's reputation as the king-pin of Lancashire Conservatism and Lancashire's reputation in turn as the palladium of the Conservative 'reaction'. This, as well as the consideration of long personal friendship and obligation to the house of Stanley, always made Disraeli chary of commanding Derby too absolutely. As Hardy noted: 'His name affects the country who do not know his indecision & timidity.'[115]

British neutrality was based on a 'charter' of definitions of essential interests comprising the security of Egypt and the canal, the status quo as to the straits of the Bosphorus and Dardanelles, and Constantinople's not passing into other hands. After a cabinet on 5 October 'with much difference of opinion', Hardy recorded: 'Derby asked me quietly whether the Cabinet or the Turkish Empire wd. last longer as each seems shaky.'[116] Derby noted on 28 July a 'very rowdy & disorderly' cabinet. 'I left this Cabinet with more uneasy & unpleasant sensations than I have yet experienced in these transactions: the war fever is clearly getting hold of my colleagues, & they have the excuse that it prevails strongly in the party generally, & in H. of C.' Derby was especially disturbed to observe that 'even Salisbury' was 'in part gained over'; and reflected how strange it would be, 'after all that has passed, if I were the sole seceder on a question of war or peace'. On 31 July there was a 'very stiff fight', with only Carnarvon in support: 'the sharpest struggle I ever had in any political question', with Manners and Beach violent for action.[117] Derby was rescued for the moment by Turkish victory at Plevna. Disraeli often found himself between reluctant colleagues and the furiously warlike queen. Richmond reported to Cairns that 'Lady Bradford told me she heard from the P.M. . . . that he had left a dismayed Cabinet to go to an angry Court!!, but he hoped his usual lucky star would carry him through.' The prince of Wales, 'energetic in his views', wanted an occupation of Gallipoli: 'it was no use having a majority if we did not use it.' Richmond pointed out in extenuation 'how very awkward our situation was'.[118] The queen was reluctant to have ministers in attendance at Balmoral other than those 'likely to give her support', as Hardy told Cairns; 'although Carnarvon was the only one from whom she expected none.'[119] (Richmond reported to Cairns: 'Hardy told me that Twitters was much disturbed at not being summoned to Balmoral and begged him to find out the reason. He is quite welcome to have my turn.')[120] The queen's hopes revived that if Lytton's health collapsed in India Derby might yet be shunted out there. (Hardy had to point out to her 'how strong Derby was in public opinion especially in the North though perhaps on grounds which would not bear examination'.)[121]

The lull following Plevna gave Derby a chance to recover his composure. The cabinet, he thought, might think itself lucky. 'We have passed through 4 sessions, without one serious check or defeat, without open discontent in the party, with a majority in the H. of C. certainly not lessened since we began, & on the whole in as strong & safe a position as any ministry can well expect.' Derby judged the 'present balance' on foreign policy about right: small war and peace parties; mass support for the government's policy of 'strict but conditional' neutrality. By the beginning of October, though anxious about coming cabinets, Derby was satisfied from all he heard that 'the absence of agitation, or alarm, in the public mind is due to the conviction that we do not meditate intervention of a kind likely to engage us in war. If things were otherwise, the whole middle class would be up in arms.' Disraeli and the queen wanted action; and Derby could foresee 'some rather sharp discussions & not impossible that disruption will follow.' But he also judged his own position to be quite strong. 'My position is so far peculiar, that I can probably stop whatever I disapprove of. The difficulty of replacing me at F.O. would be great just now, & the alarm caused by the resignation of the minister whose department is principally concerned would injure my colleagues more than the abandonment of any scheme.'[122] Derby should have recalled his observation back in July of the disturbing shift in Salisbury's stance.

The 'much difference of opinion' in the cabinet of 5 October was a consequence of Disraeli's attempt to capitalise on the recent Turkish successes. His scheme was to offer terms of mediation calculated to be acceptable to the Turks but not to the Russians. Upon a Russian refusal, Britain would abandon neutrality. As Carnarvon put it, 'It is idle to deny that what is proposed is a threat to Russia and an encouragement to Turkey.'[123] Derby, Salisbury, and Northcote equally would have none of it. Derby could even remark that the 'extraordinary calm of the present autumn in England, I mean the political calm, is worth notice'.[124] It was soon to end abruptly with Russian victory at Kars. Relaxation allowed by Plevna was now cancelled. In Europe also the Turks were near collapse. As the Russians advanced towards Adrianople excited Russophobe crowds marched in the West End. Pro-neutrality and pro-war mobs rioted in Trafalgar Square. Disraeli made another attempt, urging the summoning of parliament, a vote of credit for armaments, and an undertaking to mediate. Derby, supported by Salisbury, refused his consent, intimating resignation. Talking with Disraeli on 27 November, Derby could see that it was clear that 'we are not agreed, & may be more widely divided before long. In truth, I begin to have great doubts whether we can get through the winter together.' It was quite clear to Salisbury that a December parliament would lead to a war to uphold Turkey. The 'infernal newspapers, who dog our footsteps, pretending to belong to us, & howling for blood, will from the very first moment place the most belligerent interpretation on the summons of Parliament.' It would put the cabinet on 'the steep slope which leads to war': 'It will be a Crimean war: only postponed until our allies have been half-destroyed.'[125]

Even with a radically modified and even-handed mediation plan, with naval back-up at Constantinople and a Gallipoli base, as proposed by Northcote, Salisbury foresaw daunting political dangers. Derby's resignation would be certain.

> I shall have to ask myself how, with such a policy laid down, affairs are likely to be conducted in a Cabinet, in which the Queen's & the Prime Minister's wishes are no longer balanced by Derby's well-known aversion for war. His resignation will create, at such a juncture, the utmost consternation. Not only will it unite all sections of the Opposition, & throw into discouragement the non-warlike portion of our own party: but it will divide the nation into two camps – those who are for aiding the Turks & those who are for leaving them to their fate. The latter will attack furiously, by every weapon which popular agitation or Parliamentary forms can furnish: the fight will become intensely bitter.

In the heat of the fight with the opposition all 'half opinions, all nice distinctions will be crushed out'; the cabinet 'will surrender itself to the war party; & any advocate of peace will not be in a pleasant position'.[126]

On New Year's Day Derby ruminated on the mystery of Disraeli. The queen's warlike zeal was making great difficulties for her prime minister. 'He, I think, does not desire a war, but he fears above all things the reproach of a weak or commonplace policy.' In Derby's analysis, Disraeli combined 'great acuteness to see what is most convenient for the moment' with 'apparent indifference to what is to come of it in the long run'. 'We have a divided Cabinet, no continental allies, & a public which expects it does not exactly know what, & wishes to have the results of victory without the sacrifices of war.'[127] On 3 January there was a scene in cabinet when Disraeli censured Carnarvon in 'unusually peremptory terms'. Derby dissuaded Carnarvon from resigning. On 9 January there was keen dispute on the draft of the Queen's Speech; and Derby carried his point against the cabinet majority on the 12th.

2

Parliament met on 17 January 1878. The Russians entered Adrianople on the 20th. The question of defining precisely what the cabinet's stipulations as to the British interest in Constantinople actually meant presented itself urgently. Was a temporary Russian occupation ruled out? The Russians refuted such a notion as militarily absurd. At the other extreme, Cross, amid the hardline section of the cabinet, inclined to the doctrine that even a Russian 'approach' to Constantinople was unacceptable. It was at this point that Salisbury began to execute his crucial lateral shift. He could either go out with Derby or make himself available to take Derby's place, and then do what he could to neutralise Disraeli's war-disease by homeopathic methods. By now Derby could discern the shape of things to come. On 18 January he noted that Salisbury's 'cordial defence' of the majority policy 'is under the circs. very important'. By 21 January it had become dismayingly clear just how important: 'Salisbury is quite gone round, & is hot for Austrian alliance, of which last summer he used to talk with marked contempt.' On 23 January the fleet was ordered through the straits to Constantinople and notice was given for a vote of credit. Derby and Carnarvon offered their resignations. Disraeli asked his chief whip two questions, the second of which must take its place as a classic in the annals of political tendentiousness. Dyke responded on 23 January:

> Of the two alternatives – 'that of taking immediate action possibly resulting in War' – and 'that of allowing Russia to advance to a position from whence she can dictate her terms regardless of those Interests which the Cabinet has pledged itself to preserve' – in my opinion if the first be adopted 'that of taking immediate action' you will find that you have in the House of Commons with a few exceptions a united Party at your back – also a very considerable support from our opponents, resulting in a majority I believe more than double the actual number upon which we usually rely. We shall have some agitation & meetings & much obstruction, but we have passed through such difficulties before, & gathered strength rather than weakness from them.
>
> The following I quote from much information I have gathered of a like nature. Mr. Cowen MP for Newcastle states that he knows well none of the Meetings lately held express Public opinion – they are got up by non conformists chiefly & others entirely to embarrass the Government, & he says openly they are unworthy of any attention.
>
> Mr. Mundella lately held a meeting at Sheffield & he did not even dare summon it by Ticket, but was obliged to pack it, by personal canvass carried on by his Political friends.
>
> Much more evidence I have from Sir Charles Dilke & others.
>
> Should however the second alternative be adopted I can see nothing but disaster in the Future – a Divided Party in the House of Commons – hostile motions from Members sitting behind Ministers & a feeling of disgust among our supporters in the country generally which must prove disastrous at every Election.
>
> The honest and abiding opinion of this country apart from agitation and the only opinion worth estimating at such a time as this is always in some months in process of formation & we must not be deceived because we hear little today of bitter feeling or outspoken complaint. The feeling of the House of Commons amongst our supporters is intense & is largely shared by all the younger members of your Government. This is the tenth year since I first became connected with the management of your Party & I claim a right to speak plainly – although the position is a grave one and even perilous – one thing only can injure the Tory Party of the Future – namely if ever it can be hinted either in Public or Private that in a great national emergency, of two courses open – its Leaders forsook the brave one & preferred the timid.[128]

There is no doubt that Dyke was a better judge than Salisbury of the likelihood of all sections of the Liberals being united.

Disraeli hardly needed to elicit advice from Dyke to take the brave course. But Turkish acceptance of armistice terms and a halt of the Russian advance enabled the order to the admiral to be countermanded and Derby was pressed into withdrawing his resignation. Disraeli was perfectly content to see the last of Carnarvon. Dyke could continue to reassure Disraeli on the parliamentary front:

> All the news I have for you so far is good, & if all I hear is true we shall have a larger majority than I expected. The abstention from voting on the other side, threatens to be considerable at present & we shall have some voting with us. I hear of no defaulters on our side at present, but assume that Forsyth & Hubbard will not support us. Northcote made a capital statement (a trifle too explanatory) but sound & straightforward, & the front Bench opposite are evidently puzzled and divided.[129]

The Russians, impatient with Turkish shuffling, resumed their advance. On 6 February the Liberals withdrew their opposition to the vote of credit. 'The Opposition seems thoroughly broken up', reported Dyke. 'The Liberal Party has put its clock back ten years, & that is the only healthy sign in the situation.'[130] Even so, there was a close shave in the Perthshire by-election following the death of Sir William Stirling-Maxwell. The duke of Athole reported a close-run majority of 184 for his cousin, Colonel Drummond Moray. 'We never had any doubt about it in the County – what may be described as the "war scare" was rather against him during the last few days otherwise I think he would have had a larger majority.'[131]

'War scares' in Scotland were very different affairs from those in the metropolis. An identifiable new 'music hall' culture now manifested itself. Brash, vulgar, intensely patriotic and chauvinist, it expressed a populism of the suburbs; and in the persons of G. H. Farrell, the 'Great MacDermott', and the song-writer G. W. Hunt, it added the word 'jingo' to the language. It demonstrated a form of social energy which Ellis Ashmead Bartlett, on returning from a visit to the scene of the conflict in 1878 as a convinced Russophobe, discerned as offering potential to be harnessed for political articulation.[132] It represented also a very striking public and popular endorsement of Dyke's advice on behalf of the Tory party of the future: that its leaders must not forsake the brave course and prefer the timid. Derby himself recognised on 27 January that the supplementary vote would have to be braved: 'to withdraw it would create a mutiny in the party, & produce an appearance of vacillation nothing less than ridiculous.' He steeled himself: 'we shall not have a pleasant time in Cabinet, but that can't be helped.'

At San Stefano on the sea of Marmora the Russians were converting the armistice into a treaty. The fleet was again ordered up to Constantinople. There was a question as to whether it would have to force its way through against Turkish resistance. Salisbury, with Northcote, had no doubts that the fleet must go in and if necessary push through. If, after all that had been said, 'the fleet once more returns to Besika Bay, our position will be utterly ridiculous. We shall disgust our friends in the country, & lose all weight in Europe.'[133] All parties and factions hailed or denounced Salisbury's move as a recantation or a betrayal. Salisbury himself insisted that he was expressing the role of the half opinion or nice distinction which zealots tried not to allow.[134] Derby recorded 'wild excited talk' at a cabinet on 14 February, where, in his view, Disraeli 'swaggered' and Manners 'talked extravagantly', sending Derby back to the Foreign Office 'ill-pleased & despondent'. It was worse on the 15th: 'Salisbury talks recklessly, & is all for fighting.' Smith at the Admiralty was informed by the director of transport at the War Office that a 'Division of an Army Corps – without horses, could be embarked in 7 *days* from date of order'. With horses and transports it would take 14 days. An army corps complete could be dispatched in about six weeks: in two or three weeks hence it could be done in four weeks.[135] Derby still could not quite make Disraeli out: 'How far he really wishes for war: how much he leads the Queen, or is led by her: or to what extent his policy is guided by the mere fear of seeming weak, & so of growing unpopular, I cannot decide.'[136]

Early in March the terms of the Treaty of San Stefano became known. In a state of reckless exhaustion, the Russians had succumbed to the temptation to impose a kind of pan-Slav peace. Instead of the provisions agreed at Constantinople by the five powers in January 1877 there was now a huge Bulgaria sprawling across the Balkans between the Black Sea and the Aegean, virtually abolishing Turkey-in-Europe. The Serbs and the Greeks regarded San Stefano as a national disaster of the first magnitude. Of more consequence was the Austro-Hungarian reaction to it as totally unacceptable. The Russians had made a gigantic false step which rescued the British government from its predicament. Reserves were called up and plans discussed to mount an expedition from India to occupy Cyprus and Scanderoon (Alexandretta). Derby resigned; but since the expedition project was secret, he could only resign on the reserves issue, which seemed petty and pointless. He resented this. He felt (with reason) that his late colleagues misrepresented his motives. All of which caused bad blood. In the circumstances Derby's resignation fell flat. Dyke reported to Disraeli success at the Worcester by-election on the day following:

> There is much relief & some joy, here at the resignation. Some of the Rads are trying to make capital & to say that the safe man has gone etc. but they will not *dare* say so in Public. Cowen says it will win us S. Northumberland as a certainty.[137]

Northumberland South, hitherto a county uncontested by agreement, was duly, if very narrowly, carried. The party, as ever, was steady, even in Lancashire.

One manoeuvre to help steady Lancashire was that Derby's brother, Frederick Stanley, was promoted from financial secretary at the Treasury to the War Office; which Hardy (soon to be Cranbrook, to the dismay of 150 Conservative MPs who begged him not to leave the Commons) vacated to replace Salisbury at the India Office. For there was no question as to who would succeed Derby at the Foreign Office. The Foreign Office was a place Salisbury desired, and came to love. In later years he would pine resentfully at his exclusion from it; and would gladly have paid the price of the prime-ministership to keep it. In his last years he was prised out of it only with the greatest difficulty and embarrassment. In Salisbury Disraeli knew he was getting the most formidable of his colleagues into the place most pivotal to his own deepest concerns. But in the new situation created by San Stefano the old problems no longer obtained. New and critical pressures created an atmosphere in which British policy was transmuted from encounters into plans. Salisbury was no less ready than Disraeli to confront the Russians and insist, along with the Austrians, that San Stefano would have to be brought before a full European conference for reconsideration. He had already indicated to Disraeli what he thought were the issues about San Stefano at which Britain should stick. He would be 'disposed to be satisfied with war or negotiations which ended in these results': driving back the 'great Bulgaria' to the Balkans and substituting a tributary Greek province in the south; effective securities for free passage of the straits; two naval stations – 'say Lemnos and Cyprus, with an occupation, at least temporary, of some place like Scanderoon; for the sake of moral effect'; possibly a reduction in the Turkish indemnity to Russia which would give Turkey a reasonable prospect of paying and thus remove a pretext for fresh encroachments. Here was a brave course. Here were the *pieds à terre* to defend British interests 'in a more direct way', as he had earlier stipulated to Lytton. Salisbury made it clear to Disraeli that as foreign secretary he would not be a 'believer in the possibility of setting the Turkish Government on its legs again, as a genuine reliable Power'.[138]

Peace with honour

1

All that remained was to convince the Russians that they could not expect to get away with a unilateral imposition at San Stefano of terms incompatible with earlier European agreements and incompatible with the interests of at least two great powers, not to mention several lesser ones. The Russians were furious at the predicament they had got themselves into; which made them all the more furious with everybody else. Their army was shattered; their economy wrecked. They fenced with stipulations that the Asian aspects of the treaty should be reserved from consideration. The Austrians were prepared to accept this, but it would have made the British policy of *pied à terre* impossible. Movements of Indian troops to Malta underlined Salisbury's cool acceptance of a resolution either by war or negotiation. It was unfortunate that Northcote was not in a position to inform the Commons on the eve of the Easter recess;[139] but it was a successful exercise in the arts of gaining 'moral effect'. It seemed to give reality to the jingo boast, 'we've got the men, we've got the ships, we've got the money too'. Dyke could reassure Disraeli that all was well in hand in the Commons. 'We are gaining more votes by degrees & I can now confidently rely upon a majority of more than one hundred.' Liberalism was as fissile as ever. 'Cowen was very severe, and made the Front Opposition Bench look very uncomfortable indeed.'[140]

Bismarck, embarrassed at the quarrel between two of his partners in the *Dreikaiserbund*, offered his services to the Russians at Berlin as an 'honest broker'. The Berlin meeting would be a full-scale European congress. Disraeli decided that he would attend the glittering occasion personally to mingle with the other makers of the world's destiny. Salisbury was glad to have someone to take the limelight and leave him freer to settle things in the background. 'What with deafness, ignorance of French, and Bismarck's extraordinary mode of speech,' as Salisbury reported to Lady Salisbury, 'Beaconsfield has the dimmest idea of what is going on – understands everything crossways – and imagines a perpetual conspiracy.'[141] On the Russian side, Shuvalov sustained the vain and senile Gorchakov. Bismarck's brokerage was to cajole the Russians into settling with the Austrians and the British. 'Big Bulgaria' was trisected. The northern province became a tributary Bulgarian state. A middle region became an autonomous Bulgarian province, Eastern Roumelia. The southern part was restored to full Turkish sovereignty, and Turkey-in-Europe given reality. Andrassy for Austria got the provinces of Bosnia and the Herzegovina and Novibazar to occupy; which, as a Hungarian, he decidedly did want, but which it was essential to prevent Serbia from getting. The Romanians and Serbs got some patches of territory. The Greeks got promises of territory. All that the Russians got for their trouble was Kars in Asia, the small corner of Bessarabia on the Danube they had lost in 1856, and the moral satisfaction of freeing two Bulgarian provinces and seeing Serbia and Romania gain full sovereignty. All that Bismarck got for his honest brokerage was the bitter reproaches of the Russians.

Disraeli and Salisbury departed with Corry and Balfour in tow from Berlin in July bearing, in Disraeli's resonant phrase, 'peace with honour'. They had achieved essentially what they had set out to do in the matter of Bulgaria. The spectre of a Russian satellite state sprawling over Macedonia and on to the Aegean Sea was removed. A decent provision for Bulgarian freedom without too much offence to Serbs and Greeks was arguably attained. Free passage of the straits was not insisted on. The cabinet preferred the 1841 status quo which forbade the passage of ships of war when the sultan was at peace, and which left it to the sultan to suit himself when at war. Salisbury considered the 1841 rule disadvantageous to Britain as the greatest sea power; and would in due course announce a revised British understanding of the rule to take into account the possibility of a weak sultan being under pressure from a foreign power. The only problem Salisbury had at Berlin was 'in meeting the extravagant nonsense talked at home about Batoum'. This was an absurd issue got up under jingo excitement, which held that if this Black Sea port were taken by Russia from Turkey somehow the security of the straits would be dangerously compromised. Salisbury noted that Disraeli at Berlin was 'of course much disgusted at the Jingo outbreak in England'. Corry was told by Dyke that 'Fred our head man from Bristol was with me yesterday arranging about a Candidate etc. – he interrupted me quite suddenly with – "mind no giving up of Batoum, or it is no use your sending a Candidate to Bristol." I think this should be mentioned as showing how firmly the idea has got hold of the Public mind'.[142]

Northcote, left in charge, got into what Salisbury described as a 'considerable tremor – being frightened out of his life by the Jingo manifestations at home'. Evidently, there had been 'some violent revulsion of feeling in our party'. Salisbury's belief was that it was a 'silly season' manifestation: 'the hot weather'. The Batoum nonsense was patched up with a formula making it a free port, essentially commercial. Disraeli, greatly enjoying the gallant junketings with a large proportion of the *Almanach de Gotha*, dismissed his drab colleagues back in England: 'They are all middle-class men', he insisted; 'and I have always observed that middle-class men are afraid of responsibility.' When Salisbury got him to admit that Northcote at least was not middle-class, Disraeli still held that 'he had been early made a bureaucrat and had never lost the feeling'.[143] Northcote was, nevertheless, able to point out that at Bristol Sir Ivor Guest, Bart., failed by a large margin to gain the Liberal seat; and that Dyke's hopes for two more 'Radical seats' were equally unrealised.[144] Northcote, of course, was also in the position of having to find the money. He fended off the worst consequences by making sure that the taxpayers of India bore a due share of imperial burdens. But even so, the income tax was up a penny in 1877 and would be up a further penny to 5d in 1878. All the high hopes of March and April 1877 of a surplus which would allow the rate to be held without recourse to other taxation were no more.

2

The great thing with which Disraeli and Salisbury were going to return to London was a secret convention with Turkey, negotiated as a subsidiary affair to the Berlin negotiations by Layard, the new ambassador at Constantinople. This provided for a 'defensive alliance' between Britain and Turkey in Asia. Britain would support Turkey by force of arms should the Russians attempt any further penetrations into Turkey-in-Asia. In return the Turks undertook to introduce necessary reforms for the protection of Christian and other subjects of the Porte in those Asian territories; and 'to enable England to make necessary provision for executing her engagement', the Turks assigned the island of Cyprus to be 'occupied and administered by England'.[145] This was to be the *pied à terre* and the naval station.

A copy of the dispatch in which the Anglo-Turkish Convention was proposed to Layard '& its purpose defended' was sent by Salisbury to Northcote on 6 June. Salisbury diverted himself and tried to cheer Northcote up by composing a comic calendar of the events of the congress and Liberal reactions thereto: 'Mr. Gladstone makes a speech four hours long on the selfishness of England & the purity of Russian motives.' 'Daily News conclusively proves that the idea of taking Cyprus could only have occurred to the Semitic instincts of the Prime Minister.'[146]

Salisbury told Northcote to keep the convention 'dark till Beaconsfield comes home', as 'the jingoes require to be calmed in their own language, & he is the only one among us who speaks it fluently'.[147] Barrington wrote to Disraeli on 24 June after a visit to Windsor:

> The jubilant faces of Cairns, Cross & Northcote, with whom I went down, clearly showed that the rumours . . . of a great advance being made in the negotiations were not only true, but that even better news was in store. Northcote read me a h.page in yr letter to him describing yr long session with Bismarck, & its satisfactory issue.

Dyke reported to Disraeli on 25 June on party morale:

> The news yesterday from Berlin, has acted like magic, in this Country, & altho' some few Radicals, try to sneer at what you have done, the whole effect is marvellous, & I hear today from all parts that the feeling of relief is intense, & that you have astounded all those who doubted the effect of the Congress. This I hear from the outer sphere of Politics – within here, our friends are jubilant at your success.
>
> I am bothered every day as to a Dissolution, & Adam[148] tells me the same: however I let them gossip & spend their money too in preparing if they like, on the other side. . . . We all look forward intensely to your return, & if with the result I anticipate, we shall be lively enough, for some time.[149]

On 3 July Salisbury warned Northcote about the Anglo-Turkish Convention: 'our torpedo must explode now in a very few days.'[150]

It exploded with great execution. Cyprus was now part of the British Empire. Dyke dilated to Disraeli on the great enthusiasm in the party.

> Gladstone is rabid, and looks as if he must tear something or somebody in pieces or expire with rage. My impression is that they are utterly confounded at present, but the old story will be repeated. Harcourt will frame a Resolution & Gladstone & others will bully Hartington into a contest which he hates. It seems to me that you have placed us in a glorious position & your return will be a triumph. . . . We had an excellent Meeting of the Party yesterday, & I never knew a better spirit shewn or more anxiety to pull together. . . . Northcote is going on as well as possible.[151]

Disraeli and Salisbury arrived back in London on 16 July amid cheering throngs. Disraeli made his 'peace with honour' claim from a window at 10 Downing St. Disraeli and Salisbury accepted Garters, but Disraeli declined a dukedom or marquessate.

Appropriately stately speeches were made in parliament presenting and justifying the Treaty of Berlin. Derby rather marred the éclat of the occasion by insisting on presenting his side of the case of his resignation. Northcote congratulated Disraeli on 'a great speech, which gave much satisfaction. What a business Derby's was!'[152] In the Commons Gladstone was denunciatory, but Hartington made no attempt to repudiate the treaty. There was much talk of the government's capitalising on the public mood of elation by dissolving the Commons. Dyke advised Disraeli against:

> Many Liberals say that they wish the Government a good majority so as to take away any excuse for a Dissolution. . . . Derby is most severely condemned, and has hung himself Politically instead of Physically as you once suggested. . . . I am more than ever certain as regards not dissolving – it would be like throwing up a rubber at Whist whilst holding nothing but good cards. You may reduce the Army & especially the Navy expenditure to a great extent the coming year – you have forestalled ship-building expenditure for some years & Smith tells me he quite sees his way to a large reduction. This will all help a future Budget.[153]

With income tax now at the highest rate since 1871–2, Dyke was nervous about 'our friends out of doors'.

The seal was set by the Conservative party on the foreign policy triumph of its government by a congratulatory banquet honouring Disraeli and Salisbury, given by the Conservative members of both Houses of Parliament at the Duke of Wellington's Riding School at Knightsbridge on 27 July, the duke of Buccleuch, KT, presiding. It would, said the *Standard*, long be remembered 'as one of the most interesting incidents in our recent party history'.[154] It was the occasion of Disraeli's famous rebuke to Gladstone ('a sophistical rhetorician, inebriated with the exuberance of his own verbosity') for having stigmatised the Anglo-Turkish Convention as an 'insane covenant', and an 'act of duplicity.' This was the 'sensation' of the banquet. Disraeli's more sober point was to draw from the Crimean War and the recent Russo-Turkish War the moral that neither would have been necessary had the voice of England been so 'clear and decided as to exercise a due share in the guidance of European opinion'. Salisbury extolled the 'civilising mission' transferred by the convention from India to Asia Minor. He also denounced the partisanship of Liberal speakers and writers who had attempted to obstruct the Conservative government's striving 'to pick up the broken thread of England's old Imperial traditions'.

Notes and References

1 See R. T. Shannon, *Gladstone* (1982), i, 292, 353–4.
2 See above, 102.
3 Derby to Northcote, 26 Feb. 1877; BL, Iddesleigh 50022, 131.
4 Memorandum by A. J. Balfour, Hatfield, 8 May 1880; BL, Balfour 49688, 24–5.
5 'Poland', *QR*, April 1863; 'The Danish duchies', *QR*, Jan. 1864; 'The foreign policy of England', *QR*, April 1864.
6 See above, 178.
7 Buckle, ii, 762.
8 *Ibid*, 764.
9 R. T. Shannon, *Gladstone and the Bulgarian Agitation, 1876* (1963), 131; Cecil, *Salisbury*, ii, 85.
10 *Ibid*., 141.
11 *Ibid*., 145.
12 *Ibid*.
13 *Ibid*., 136.
14 Derby Diary, 28 April and 10 Sept. 1875.
15 Salisbury to Disraeli, 19 Oct. 1875; HP, B/XX/Ce/60.
16 Salisbury to Disraeli, 13 Dec. 1875; HP, B/XX/Ce/63.
17 Salisbury to Disraeli, 12 Jan. 1876; HP, B/XX/Ce/69.
18 In his last speech in the House of Commons, 11 Aug. 1876; *PD*, ccxxxi, 1146.
19 See, for example, M. MacColl, *Three Years of the Eastern Question (1878)*, 38.
20 Lord Newton, *Lord Lyons* (1913), ii, 95.
21 Northcote to Disraeli, 26 Nov. 1875; BL, Iddesleigh 50017, 129.
22 Derby to Lyons, 27 Nov. 1875. Newton, *Lyons*, ii, 92. Northcote also preferred an international commission to be set up as trustees to hold the shares rather than the government. Northcote to Disraeli 24 Nov. 1875; BL, Iddesleigh 50017, 121.
23 Derby Diary, 29 Nov. 1875.
24 Buckle, ii, 783.
25 *Ibid*., 790.
26 Salisbury to Disraeli, 26 Nov. 1875; HP, B/XX/Ce/203.
27 Buckle, ii, 903.
28 *Ibid*., 909.
29 Disraeli to Corry, 20 April 1876; HP, B/XX/D/269.
30 Salisbury to Northcote, 15 Dec. 1877; BL, Iddesleigh 50019, 53.
31 Disraeli to Corry, 28 Aug. 1876; HP, B/XX/D/273.

32 Derby Diary, 11 April 1876.
33 Cecil, *Salisbury*, ii, 83.
34 Salisbury to Disraeli, 7 June 1876; HP, B/XX/Ce/77. For Salisbury's administration generally in India, see E.D. Steele, 'Salisbury at the India Office', in Lord Blake and H. Cecil (eds), *Salisbury. The Man and His Policies* (1987).
35 Cecil, *Salisbury*, ii, 80.
36 Shannon, *Gladstone and the Bulgarian Agitation*, 39.
37 *Ibid.*, 19.
38 *Ibid.*, 122.
39 Derby Diary, 10 Sept. 1876.
40 *Ibid*, 10 July 1876.
41 Hardy, *Diary*, 283.
42 *PD*, ccxxxi, 203. Shannon, *Gladstone and the Bulgarian Agitation*, 44–5.
43 See above, 227.
44 Shannon, *Gladstone and the Bulgarian Agitation*, 92.
45 *Ibid.*, 59.
46 Hardy, *Diary*, 289.
47 Shannon, *Gladstone and the Bulgarian Agitation*, 100.
48 *Ibid.*, 106–7.
49 *Ibid.*, 68.
50 Hardy to Cairns, 29 Aug. 1876; PRO, Cairns 30/51/7.
51 'Sublime Porte': Ottoman ministry for foreign affairs.
52 Cairns to Beaconsfield, 31 Aug. 1876. HP, B/XX/Ca/186.
53 Disraeli to Derby, 2 Sept. 1876. R. Millman, *Britain and the Eastern Question 1875–1878* (Oxford 1979), 518.
54 Beauchamp to Cairns, 17 Sept. 1876; PRO, Cairns 30/51/19.
55 Shannon, *Gladstone and the Bulgarian Agitation*, 122.
56 Millman, *Britain and the Eastern Question*, 166–7.
57 See Shannon, *Gladstone and the Bulgarian Agitation*, 61–3; and below, 301, 348–9.
58 J. O. Johnston, *Life and Letters of Henry Parry Liddon* (1904), 228.
59 *Accounts and Papers. State Papers, Turkey*, xc (1877), no. 221.
60 See, for example, E. A. Freeman, *The Ottoman Power in Europe* (1877), 251.
61 Cross to Beaconsfield, 13 Sept. 1876; HP, B/XX/Cr/59.
62 Derby to Beaconsfield, 8 Sept. 1876; Shannon, *Gladstone and the Bulgarian Agitation*, 122.
63 *Ibid.*, 130.
64 Hardy to Cairns, 14 Sept. 1876; PRO, Cairns 30/51/7.
65 Beaconsfield to Cairns, 12 Sept. 1876; PRO, Cairns 30/51/1.
66 Carnarvon to Cairns, 13 Sept. 1876; PRO, Cairns 30/51/8.
67 Corry to Beaconsfield, 27 Aug. 1876; HP, B/XX/Co/14.
68 Carnarvon to Cairns, 15 Sept. 1876; PRO, Cairns 30/51/8.
69 Cairns to Beaconsfield, 16 Sept. 1876; HP, B/XX/Ca/188.
70 Beaconsfield to Cairns, 23 Sept. 1876; PRO, Cairns 30/51/1.
71 Cairns to Beaconsfield, 25 Sept. 1876; HP, B/XX/Ca/192.
72 Smith to Beaconsfield, 8 Sept. 1876; HP, B/XXI/s/306.
73 Abergavenny to Beaconsfield [1876]; HP, B/XX/A/56.
74 Abergavenny to Beaconsfield, 27 Sept. 1876; HP, B/XX/A/57. Gladstone was six years younger than Beaconsfield.

75 Cross to Beaconsfield, 25 Sept. 1876; HP, B/XX/Cr/61.
76 Beaconsfield to Cairns, 23 Sept. 1876; PRO, Cairns 30/51/1.
77 Dyke to Beaconsfield, 25 Sept. [1876]; HP, B/XXI/D/468.
78 Taylor to Corry, 10 Oct. 1876; HP, B/XX/T/137.
79 Barrington to Beaconsfield, 8 Oct. 1876; HP, B/XX/Ba/41.
80 Derby Diary, 28 Sept. 1876.
81 Shannon, *Gladstone and the Bulgarian Agitation*, 131.
82 Hardy to Cairns, 14 Sept. 1876; PRO, Cairns 30/51/7.
83 Barrington to Beaconsfield, 20 Oct. 1876; HP, B/XX/Ba/44.
84 Northcote to Carnarvon, 27 Oct. 1876; BL, Iddesleigh 50022, 203.
85 Derby Diary, 24 Oct. 1876.
86 Cairns to Beaconsfield, 16 Nov. 1876; HP, B/XX/Ca/193.
87 Cairns to Beaconsfield, 23 Nov. 1876; HP, B/XX/Ca/196.
88 Balfour memo, 8 May 1880; BL, Balfour 49688, 24–5.
89 Shannon, *Gladstone and the Bulgarian Agitation*, 254.
90 R. T. Shannon, 'Gladstone and British Balkan policy', in R. Melville and H. J. Shröder (eds), *Der Berliner Kongress von 1878* (Wiesbaden, 1982), 176.
91 Blake, *Disraeli*, 615.
92 Shannon, *Gladstone and the Bulgarian Agitation*, 255.
93 *Ibid*., 258.
94 Hardy, *Diary*, 300–1.
95 Shannon, *Gladstone and the Bulgarian Agitation*, 260.
96 Derby Diary, 9 Dec. 1876.
97 Shannon, *Gladstone and the Bulgarian Agitation*, 260.
98 Millman, *Britain and the Eastern Question*, 223.
99 Derby Diary, 28 and 22 Dec. 1876.
100 Carnarvon to Northcote, 16 Jan. 1877; BL. Iddesleigh 50022, 207.
101 Cecil, *Salisbury*, ii, 126–7.
102 Salisbury to Beaconsfield, 12 March 1877; HP, B/XX/Ce/202.
103 Northcote to Cairns, 29 March 1877; PRO, Cairns 30/51/5.
104 Carnarvon to Northcote, 30 March 1877; BL, Iddesleigh 50022, 209.
105 Derby Diary, 23 May and 12 July 1877. Derby commented on the last point: 'I thought, but I did not remind him, that he had been equally certain in 1868, & quite mistaken.'
106 Cecil, *Salisbury*, ii, 135.
107 Millman, *Britain and the Eastern Question*, 255. Manners offered his resignation in July 1877. Swartz, *Politics of British Foreign Policy*, 184, n. 85. On Cross see F.J. Dwyer, 'R.A. Cross and the Eastern crisis of 1875–8,' *Slavonic and East European Review* (1961).
108 Derby Diary, 21 Oct. 1877.
109 Northcote to Beaconsfield, 21 April 1877; BL, Iddesleigh 50018, 22 (draft), 26.
110 Northcote to Derby, 26 May 1877; BL, Iddesleigh 50022, 144.
111 Derby Diary, 16 June 77.
112 Millman, *Britain and the Eastern Question*, 205.
113 Corry to Cairns, 2 Sept. 1877; PRO, Cairns 30/51/12.
114 Balfour memo, 8 May 1880; BL, Balfour 49688, 24–5. It is material to comment that nothing in Derby's voluminous and informative diaries betrays anything in the nature of 'utter moral prostration' of this Hatfield interpretation.

115 Hardy, *Diary*, 352.
116 *Ibid.*, 340.
117 Derby Diary, 28 and 31 July 1877.
118 Richmond to Cairns, 1 Aug. 1877; PRO, Cairns 30/51/4.
119 Hardy to Cairns, 6 Sept. 1877; PRO, Cairns 30/51/7.
120 Richmond to Cairns, 10 Sept. 1877; PRO, Cairns 30/51/4.
121 Hardy to Cairns, 6 Sept. 1877; PRO, Cairns 30/51/7.
122 Derby Diary, 11 Aug., 2 Oct. 1877.
123 Carnarvon to Northcote, 15 Dec. 1877; BL, Iddesleigh 50022, 227.
124 Derby Diary, 4 Nov. 1877.
125 Salisbury to Northcote, 15 Dec. 1877; BL, Iddesleigh 50019, 55.
126 Salisbury to Northcote, 18 Dec. 1877; BL, Iddesleigh 50019, 61.
127 Derby Diary, 1 Jan. 1878.
128 Dyke to Beaconsfield, 23 Jan. [1878]; HP, B/XXI/D/471. This letter was read to the cabinet on 23 January. Swartz, *Politics of British Foreign Policy*, 157–8.
129 Dyke to Beaconsfield, 28 Jan. [1878]; HP, B/XXI/D/472. W. Forsyth was MP for Marylebone (see above, 233–4); Hubbard was one of the City members.
130 Dyke to Beaconsfield, 7 Feb. [1878]; HP, B/XXI/D/473.
131 Athole to Beaconsfield, 4 Feb. 1878; HP, C/IV/27c.
132 See H. Cunningham, 'The Conservative party and patriotism', in R. Colls and P. Dodd (eds), *Englishness. Politics and Culture, 1880–1920* (1986), 284–5.
133 Salisbury to Beaconsfield, 10 Feb. 1878; HP, B/XX/Ce/232.
134 See Cecil, *Salisbury*, 197–202.
135 W. R. Meads to Smith, 16 Feb. 1878; HP, B/XXI/s/314.
136 Derby Diary, 24 Feb. 1878.
137 Dyke to Beaconsfield, 28 March [1878]; HP, B/XXI/D/474.
138 Cecil, *Salisbury*, ii, 213–14.
139 P. J. Durrans, 'A two-edged sword: the Liberal attack on Disraelian imperialism', *Journal of Imperial and Commonwealth History* (1981–2), 268–9.
140 Dyke to Beaconsfield, 23 May 1878; HP, B/XXI/D/477.
141 Cecil, *Salisbury*, ii, 287.
142 Dyke to Corry, 28 June [1878]; HP, B/XXI/D/479.
143 Cecil, *Salisbury*, ii, 286–7.
144 Middlesborough and Argyllshire.
145 T. E. Holland, *The European Concert in the Eastern Question* (1885), 354. Swartz, *Politics of British Foreign Policy*, 94–7.
146 Salisbury to Northcote, 6 June 1878; BL, Iddesleigh 50019, 74.
147 Salisbury to Northcote, 23 June 1878; BL, Iddesleigh 50019, 79.
148 Liberal whip.
149 Dyke to Beaconsfield, 25 June [1878]; HP, B/XX/D/478.
150 Salisbury to Northcote, 3 July 78. BL, Iddesleigh 50019, 87.
151 Dyke to Beaconsfield, 9 July [1878]; HP, B/XX/D/480. For the elaborate preparations of triumphal reception (Henry Lennox impresario) see Swartz, *Politics of British Foreign Policy*, 97–9.
152 Northcote to Beaconsfield, 19 July 1878; BL, Iddesleigh 50018, 97.
153 Dyke to Beaconsfield, 19 July [1878]; HP, B/XX/D/481.
154 *AR*, 1878, 96.

Part IV

The Undoing of Disraelian Conservatism, 1878–81

Chapter 12

At home: 'a complication of disastrous influences'

To dissolve or not to dissolve

Was Disraeli well advised by Dyke not to dissolve parliament in 1878 and go to the country after his return in triumph from Berlin? In view of what happened in 1880, it was, then and since, a question much canvassed. There has been a general disposition to assume that a great opportunity was missed. Kebbel was sure that had Disraeli appealed to the constituencies in 1878, 'he would certainly have died Prime Minister'.[1] Alfred Austin, the journalist and poet, thought Disraeli's decision a 'tactical blunder'.[2] The cabinet considered the matter on 10 August, and decided against.[3] The best guess of modern political research is that an election in 1878 would have left the Conservatives very much as they would have been had they taken office and dissolved parliament in 1873: probably a majority over the Liberals, but not over Liberals and Home Rulers combined.[4]

Dyke's formal advice on the matter was conveyed to Disraeli on 26 August. The obvious argument in favour of dissolution was, of course, the feeling of 'great gratitude' in the constituencies and 'much popularity' evident over the peace and settlement of the Eastern Question. Dyke was in no doubt 'that a considerable gain may be expected at the Polling Booths'. His reasoning offers a compendium of Conservative managerial thinking at this moment; and suggests particularly the influence of Northcote's anxiety as to getting the finances back in order.

> This being the close of the fifth Session of the parliament it may be urged, that a good chance should not be lost of gaining such a majority as may secure a fresh lease of Power for some years, & that if the Dissolution be deferred, difficulties may arise & the Foreign Policy of the Government, may cause Taxation which will press heavily on the people, obliterate our present triumph & bring disaster.
>
> From a Party point of view therefore it may be asked – why not make an appeal to the country, which will have the effect of placing again, a strong Conservative Government in power for some years.
>
> Against Dissolution the first reason which naturally occurs to me, is not unimportant – namely, the intense disgust it would excite amongst your supporters in the House of Commons, who have for five years, never failed us on a Division of importance. The next that of Taxation & Trade – after the immediate success of the moment has passed away – the pressure of taxation will begin to be considered, &

should we dissolve this Autumn, our opponents will, not only make much capital, out of our Expenditure but will point to every species of unknown Taxation in the future with reference to our Eastern policy; & here you will afford them an unlimited field of attack without the reply which, time & good Administration alone can give.

But the gravest reason appears to me, to be the want of precedent, or reasonable excuse for such a course. After a majority of 143 in favour of a Policy, which has been attacked & criticized for many months, you will be told that you are simply gambling with the situation, & that you have initiated a new Policy, bold in its conception & opening out a vast field for English enterprise, but that you dare not yourselves face results, & considering only the triumph of the moment, you hand over the future with all its doubts & difficulties to successors you cannot name.

The present Government may produce two more Financial schemes, & I believe they may show if they elect to wait, such a Balance Sheet in 1880 as can command the support of the Country.

The Birmingham School led by Mr. Chamberlain are promoting daily more & more discord in the ranks of our opponents, & I hear of Divisions increasing in every Constituency – such Divisions I believe will not be healed for many years.

In Ireland our position is certainly an improving one – there is more loyalty, less discontent, owing to greater prosperity, and a respite from agitation, owing to the practical disruption of the Home Rule Party – from information I possess, I believe we should lose seats in Ireland upon a Dissolution at this moment.

The present state of Trade also would render this a most unfortunate time for a Dissolution – a popular feeling obtains in many of the Manufacturing Towns, that a Conservative Government invariably causes bad Trade.

There appears now to be a more favourable prospect, & should this continue, it may fairly be urged that this has been brought about by the success of our Foreign Policy & we shall gain full credit for such a result. On the whole I think the reasons against a Dissolution strongly preponderate.[5]

With hindsight, this memorandum reads as a particularly poignant specimen of the vanity of human wishes. Every argument here as to trade and taxation and the advantages of waiting on favourable prospects was, as things turned out, an argument for going to the constituencies as quickly as possible to escape the worst consequences of the onset of what was soon to be identified as the Great Depression.

Moreover, the date of Dyke's memorandum, 26 August, was also the date of the poll for the by-election at Newcastle-under-Lyme. Sir Edmund Buckley, Bart, (a Disraeli creation in 1868), who topped the poll ahead of the Liberal MP in 1874, had retired. The seat was lost by a decisive margin. Dyke reported in some consternation:

I was much surprised at our Newcastle defeat, & naturally so, when our opponents there met 3 days before the Poll was taken, & decided by a large majority, that it was hopeless to fight. I hear from those who were engaged in the struggle on our side, that the Irish Vote turned the Election, coupled with the strong feeling as to the badness of Trade (all ascribed by agitators to the Government). Sir

> Charles Russell, whose brother-in-law was our Candidate, wrote to me that he was quite astounded, how little the Eastern Question influenced the Electors & that Financial considerations completely swamped it. Cross writes to me today – 'Our future depends upon our Estimates, & I hope the Treasury are alive to it.' I do not think this affects us in the South of England, but in the North to a great extent. . . . The opposition are very quiet this Autumn, a curious sign after the end of our Fifth Session. I still think our Prospects good, if we devote ourselves to the production of a sound Financial scheme in 1880.[6]

Newcastle was a disturbing case, but if anything it confirmed Dyke's arguments for caution.

Nor did it dent the general sense of confidence in the Conservative party's overall standing in the country. The party 'out of doors' seemed in sound shape and good spirits. In August 1878 Disraeli and Salisbury received a thousand delegates from Conservative associations at the Foreign Office, as part of the celebrations for Berlin. Disraeli harangued them with references to the organisation and discipline of the Macedonian phalanx, the Roman legion, and Cromwell's Ironsides. Salisbury dilated on the need for the party to place confidence and trust in its leaders. There seemed to be no apparent indications either of deterioration in the party's organisation or discipline on the one hand or in its confidence or trust in the leaders on the other. Corry wrote to Disraeli from Arthur Balfour's 'forest' in Scotland in September, supplying an instance which possibly helps to explain the curious quietness of the Liberals that autumn. He recounted an earlier party at Glen Quioch at which the former Liberal solicitor-general, Vernon Harcourt, was 'the male "piece de resistance," & full of attack and fence and knowing far more about Berlin and the future than the Prime Minister does, I am sure. *Every* thing has been done wrong! but, strange to say, he and Bass[7] agree in naming 1886 as the date of the return to power of the great Liberal party: two dissolutions hence!'[8]

Nothing in by-elections early in 1879 seemed to hint at any hidden current running against the Conservatives. Dyke managed two important divisions in Cambridgeshire and Norfolk. It was possible in the first case to avoid a contest; but for North Norfolk he predicted a 'real tough fight', and a 'near thing'. In the event, Edward Birkbeck saw off Sir Thomas Fowell Buxton with a Conservative majority of 500, cheering Cranbrook much ('a great victory, a real majority'). Dyke further reported:

> I have a good account from Winn, of the feeling in the North as to our Foreign Policy. He has been attending some large Registration Meetings lately, & he says the general tone, of opinion is most favourable, towards our Policy, but the Rads work the distress cry, without intermission: & we are going to get Lecturers & speakers to do down, and counteract this as much as possible.[9]

The 'distress cry' at commercial and agricultural depression was indeed a worry; but the orthodox view was that by January 1879 the country had come through the worst of it.

Domestic inactivity

1

In 1883, looking back at the Conservative government of the late 1870s, St. John Brodrick, MP for West Surrey, referred to the 'domestic inactivity of 1878 and 1879', caused not only by a 'spirited foreign policy' but more by the 'fatality which linked together parliamentary obstruction and foreign war'. Dilke and Chamberlain, he added darkly, could 'throw much light' on this episode.[10] No doubt Charles Stuart Parnell, emerging leader of the radical wing of the Irish Home Rule party, could also have contributed illuminatingly. Decidedly a malaise had come upon the government's domestic fortunes. The *Annual Register*, for all that its Liberal bias needs to be discounted, could plausibly describe 1877 as the 'lazy session', 'one of singular barrenness'. Derby put the matter simply in August 1877: 'As to home politics, there have simply been none.'[11]

Partly this malaise can be accounted for by reasons inward to the government. Getting rid of Adderley in 1878 was no doubt an advantage, but much damage had been done. Selwin-Ibbetson continued as an embarrassment in not offering to resign: in Dyke's opinion an obstinacy scandalously unfair to Disraeli.[12] Derby's replacement by Salisbury was an enormous improvement; but its public impact was confined largely to the House of Lords, where it was least needed. Hardy's leaving the Commons was widely perceived as a serious loss. Northumberland's appointment to the cabinet to replace Carnarvon in the Lords' contingent (itself a rather pointless fad of Disraeli's) was a grotesque waste of an opportunity to recruit vigorous younger talent. Hardy thought it 'a strange choice surely'; and observed Northumberland's first appearance in cabinet: 'He appears rather deaf & slow & will not I fear add strength to our deliberations.'[13] Hardy, transmuted to Cranbrook at the India Office, in any case himself added little strength to the government. Disaffected and rather sulky, he was slipshod in his handling of Lytton, who soon became aware that in losing Salisbury he had gained scope for adventures. Hicks Beach at the Colonial Office proved disappointing. For a man toughened in Ireland and with a reputation for irascibility – he 'thought angrily' – 'Black Michael' surprisingly soon and confessedly lost all control over the other great 'prancing proconsul' of that era, Bartle Frere in South Africa. In Ireland itself, sliding into critical economic depression and near-famine in parts, Lowther could make little impression. Dyke's assessment in August 1878 of the hopes for 'greater prosperity' was the last possible point of such innocent prognostications. Northcote, uninspiring at the best of times, was in no position to offer financial relief. Above all, Disraeli himself in the aftermath of Berlin was now exhausted, incapable of energetic initiative, reduced increasingly to stoic impassivity, waiting for a fortunate turn of events.

The malaise also had outward causes other than the distractions of foreign affairs. Parliamentary obstruction by Irish MPs became systematic and sapping to morale in 1877. Even in 1876 Hardy had been incensed at having to spend a 'long afternoon listening to Irish rubbish'; and identified the 'Irish ruffians Parnell & Biggar' as the great culprits.[14] Isaac Butt, the courtly leader of the Home Rule party, was striving at this time to establish his party's status as an entity distinct from the Liberals; the third party in the Commons. He agreed wholeheartedly with Hardy as to the ruffianliness of Parnell and Biggar. By the beginning of 1877 Hicks Beach informed Northcote of a scheme to collude with Butt to crush Parnell's and Biggar's obstructive tactics and rebellion against Butt's authority. Success would probably, in Beach's judgement, postpone the break-up of the Home Rule party, but Beach was 'by no means sure that this would be an evil'.

> Their humbug has a good deal to do with keeping Ireland quiet – and, from a party point of view, it must be remembered that we have already derived no little advantage from Butt's sympathies being Tory rather than Whig.
>
> It is, of course, a serious thing to shut the mouth of any M.P. But if his own party even tacitly assents, I think it may be safely done. . . . I think we have good cards, if we choose to play them: and I hope we shall.[15]

But by July 1877 the speaker, Brand, was complaining to Northcote of a 'growing tendency to abuse the forms of the house for the purposes of wilful obstruction'; and rejoiced that Northcote was to take the matter in hand.[16] Far from gagging Parnell in 1877, Butt's leadership of the Home Rule party was destroyed. Parnell replaced him and the 'New Departure' was in train.

Northcote's weakness as a leader was also exposed. Derby had already commented at the opening of the session: 'Northcote was needlessly apologetic, possibly nervous of his new position.'[17] Barrington reported to Disraeli of annoying events in the Commons, including a small revolt. 'Hardy spoke strongly & well, but our able & good-intentioned Ch. of the Exchequer is rather a feeble advocate.' Barrington agreed with *The Times* that this would not have happened were Disraeli still in the Commons.[18] It was no doubt this kind of contrast between Hardy and Northcote which led Taylor to tell Hardy apropos of his going to the Lords: '*All* our friends are loud in their lamentations that our strongest man in debate is about to leave us when most needed.'[19] Disraeli appeared in the Peers' Gallery in the Commons for the first time to witness a debate at the end of July: 'he watched the scene with an air of curious wonder.' It is unlikely that Disraeli was readily convinced by Northcote's assurances that adjustments to procedural rules against 'our friends the Obstructives' would do the trick.[20] But these were still innocent days.

It was also dubiously consoling to Conservatives to learn that Chamberlain was planning to do to the Whig leadership of his party what Parnell was doing to Butt. Barrington told Disraeli in May 1877 that Chamberlain was reported to have said: 'We want to put an end to that gigantic imposture, so-called the Liberal Party.'[21] Chamberlain was concocting his grand scheme for a National Liberal Federation, partly as an answer to the Conservative National Union, but more immediately as a weapon out of doors with which to break the Whig grip on the Liberal party. His cause was boosted tremendously when Gladstone agreed, to the dismay of the Whig chiefs, to speak at the inauguration of the federation at Birmingham at the end of May. The Whigs were being paid back for their lukewarmness over the Bulgarians. Chamberlain was no more put down in the Commons than Parnell was. Northcote noted that 'there was a significant cheer for Chamberlain below the Gangway when he got up to put a question tonight. He has not succumbed.'[22] Chamberlains's contribution to what was in effect the virtual collapse of the government's domestic policy in 1877 was not important; but in the circumstances it did not need to be.

2

Nor was the 1878 session any more impressive on the domestic side. Richmond was yet once more obliged to withdraw a Burials Bill, designed to pacify Nonconformist consciences. No doubt it was soothing for Balfour to have the benefit of Uncle Robert's reminiscences: 'A very good Bill – if men's minds were in a temper to take good Bills. I used, in my hot youth, to spend time in designing similarly perfect schemes for the settlement of the Church Rate Controversy. Hubbard & I used steadily to introduce bills which steadily came to nothing. May yours have a more auspicious ending!'[23] The government got into deep embarrassment with the agricultural interest on the question of financial relief for compulsory slaughter in the Cattle Bill, at a time, moreover, when Chaplin was calling for a royal commission on agricultural depression. Northcote was in difficulties about an amendment from Ritchie. 'It is difficult to refuse this', he told Disraeli; 'and not only our Hermons and Tennants, but even our Pells and Barttelots, support it. At the same time, H. Chaplin, C.S. Read, and others are strongly against any modification.'[24] Grievances of tenant farmers, exacerbated by Irish precedents, nagged away at the party like a toothache. Derby had rejoiced in 1874 at 'the complete defeat of the agitation for trades-unionism and higher wages among the agricultural peasantry in England. The farmers held their own everywhere.'[25] But relief on that front allowed the farmers to turn to the offensive against their landlords. These scuffles in the domestic background of party and government hardly signified one way or the other in the heady times of San Stefano and Berlin. But those times were now over.

So little were 'our friends the Obstructives' cowed that by January 1879 Northcote feared for the government's sessional programme, 'not only on the part of the Home Rulers'. His own special problem of finance was entangled with so many foreign and colonial questions. Here was the essence of Brodrick's analysis of the fatality linking parliamentary obstruction and foreign war. Disraeli's health was not the least of his government's problems. Northcote could only hope that Disraeli had 'taken the turn', and 'meant to be prudent, and to be all right for the coming Campaign'.[26] But what campaign?

Lowther had plans to succeed where Gladstone had failed in 1873, and provide Irish Roman Catholics with a university. For Northcote 'the real question is, whether we can face the University scheme at all'. Dyke's report had to be waited for, and the 'feelings of our Irish friends' on such questions as keeping public money out of the hands of the priests and defending the Protestantism of Trinity College, Dublin, accommodated.[27] Lowther eventually got his university; but in the days of Parnell's 'New Departure' and Davitt's Land League the notion of fostering an educated Catholic gentry elite to provide steadying social and political leadership was almost poignantly irrelevant.

The problems of Stanley's Army Discipline and Regulation Bill project themselves as a kind of parable of Conservative domestic debility in 1879. It was an urgent matter, for it was designed to replace the Mutiny Act. It was vulnerable, therefore, as to time; and it was doubly vulnerable because the military and naval establishments insisted on retaining the 'cat' as an encouragement to discipline. This was a lively public issue; and one Irish MP threatened the House of Commons with a muster of 500,000 anti-flogging Londoners in Hyde Park. Parnell led an Irish assault on the bill, with useful assistance from Chamberlain and Dilke. Northcote was overborne in a scandalous scene in the House on 3 July. Stanley was determined to carry his measure, so Salisbury gathered, 'at all hazards'; and though he did 'not care about flogging, he will resign rather than abandon it now'. What reached Salisbury 'from *other* sources', he warned Disraeli,

> makes me think that any attempt to give up this bill, or any substantial part of it, will split the party in two. The disgust with what was done on Thursday night was very strong. It will give an impression of lamentable weakness. If we show that we cannot lead this docile House of Commons, the Country is not likely to trust us with a new one.
>
> I understand that Northcote has been talking of giving up the bill. Nothing could be more deplorable than such a resolution.[28]

It was possible for Northcote to push through Stanley's bill. But it was not possible for Northcote to avoid the fatality of the costs of Afghan and Zulu wars. Northcote wanted an alternative to a renewed increase in income tax; and asked the cabinet to sanction a big increase in the duties on tea. The response was a horrified refusal. Tea was a working-class staple in times of distress; tea, as Disraeli explained to the queen, was 'the basis of the great Temperance movement'. Northcote was stiff, but could not carry the day. He was forced to have recourse to Exchequer Bonds to cover his retreat. 'I do not want to raise any controversy as to the views expressed at the Cabinet today,' he told Disraeli on 29 July, 'further than to say that they were extremely unsatisfactory to me, and that I feel my position seriously shaken.'[29] Disraeli was ready to pass at least half the deficit on 'to posterity'. As he informed the queen, 'Mr. Pitt would not have hesitated to bequeath the whole of it in that direction'.

But alas! there are no longer Mr. Pitts, but a leader of the House of Commons, who, tho' one of the most amiable and gifted of men, thinks more of an austere smile from Mr. Gladstone, or a word of approval from Mr. Childers than the applause and confidence of a great historic party, and a Prime Minister, who, it seems to me, can do nothing in his troubles, but fly to a too gracious Sovereign, and whimper over his own incompetence.[30]

What a great historic party would have thought of such whimpering would no doubt have been candidly expressed by Mr. Pitt. Meanwhile, Northcote at least had the satisfaction of being awkward about a much canvassed dissolution of parliament after the 1879 session. 'I wish to add', he told Disraeli frostily, 'that I feel myself placed in a very difficult position with regard to a dissolution. I have throughout the Session held language with regard to the distribution of Seats, the passing of an amended Corrupt Practices Act, and other matters which would be cast in my teeth if a dissolution where to be decided on before the House meets again.'[31] That decision was not made before the 1874 parliament met for the last time in February 1880. Ministers could not quite nerve themselves to make the jump in 1879. Gladstone was so sure of it that he launched his first Midlothian campaign in the autumn. But Disraeli waited on for the tide of fortune to turn.

Party management and public opinion

1

Party managements do not in their nature turn electoral tides; but arguably they can help on the flow and may a little stem the ebb. There were good grounds for supposing that by 1879 the Conservative party was at an ebb in the constituencies. The ultimate result, by constituencies, in 1880, seemed to confirm this kind of tidal interpretation. The other explanatory mode that came into vogue after 1880, seeing it in sequence after 1868 and 1874, was the swing of the pendulum effect. But, as Salisbury was one of the first to point out after 1880, the ebbing tide of Conservative votes was small in relation to the sea of voters; and that the turnover of constituencies which made the vast difference between the parties in the House of Commons was caused, in Great Britain, by less than 2,000 electors.

Nevertheless, 'want of suitable organisation' was immediately at the head of Northcote's list of reasons for 'our great defeat'; which cleared the way for his assertion a little later that the Liberal party won because of its superior organisation and not because of any 'real revulsion of feeling' against Conservatism.[32] For Cranbrook disaster came suddenly, 'out of a clear sky'. Salisbury's reaction was one of puzzlement. 'Some stray bits of gossip & comment', he told Disraeli, '. . . seem to indicate a certain amount of discontent with our electioneering organization. But I suppose that is natural after so great a disaster. Still it is puzzling that our authorities should have had no glimmer of the electoral condition, which appears to have been well known to our opponents.'[33] What struck most attentive people without any specially partisan axes to grind in 1880 was the pattern which seemed to be emerging in the second Reform Act epoch in which organisation or no organisation, general elections abruptly and decisively dismissed governments: something quite new and portentous. Kebbel expressed this feeling in 1880:

> That the government of this country, whether Liberal or Conservative, should be at the mercy of a popular opinion, working, as it were, underground, invisible, inscrutable, and throwing up no indications whatever to mark the course it is taking – that it should be possible both for political parties and for the general public to remain to the last in total ignorance of the intentions of that great lower class which can turn elections at its will – is not only so remote from the commonsense of politics, but so manifestly inconsistent with the maintenance of any dignified or regular system of government, that it is not necessary for a man to be on the losing side to make him anxious about our political future.[34]

Analysis of the 1880 elections would be, in fact, important in the emergence of a more sophisticated awareness of concepts such as the floating voter and the primacy of public opinion over questions of organisation as explanatory factors. Indeed, as early as 1878, W. Fraser Rae, examining the phenomenon of the 'Birmingham Caucus', produced a splendid jumble of panic about the Radicalism of Chamberlain's new organisation with extremely acute scepticism about what he regarded as the obsessive overestimation among politicians of the role of party organisation. Rae denied bluntly that the Conservative success in 1874 could be attributed, as it commonly was, to 'the perfection of that party's political organization'. It was, Rae was quite convinced, public opinion and not organisation – public opinion quite independent of party and its apparatus – which turned elections. The Liberal party, he pointed out, was quite unorganised in 1868. Rae drew attention to the key role of a

> floating mass composed of electors who, having no settled convictions, are easily roused to frenzy, for or against a particular course, are ready at one time to declare that the government has gone too far, and at another that it must be made to move on. This mass is impressionable as wax and unstable as water. When Liberals and Conservatives succeed in 'organizing' it, they will have learned the art of making ropes out of sand.[35]

That was published in *Nineteenth Century* in May 1878. Rae offered the fundamental concept of later twentieth-century psephological analysis. Any party whip in 1878 would have acknowledged the cogency of Rae's argument. In the Newcastle-under-Lyme by-election of August 1878 Dyke was confronted with the fact of a seemingly secure seat (Conservatives had either monopolised or shared the borough since 1832) lost to Liberals without hope or organisation, and no candidate three days before the poll.[36]

It is possible, therefore, to share Rae's sceptical view about organisational decline as a crucially symptomatic indication of Conservative debility in the years leading up to 1880. The two kinds of pressure which, nevertheless, insisted that, in the first place, there *was* decline in the quality of Conservative organisation, and that, in the second place, this was decisive in accounting for the 1880 result, dominated the field at the time and long after. This was mainly because politicians as a type are reluctant to accept that they operate in an electorally random and ideologically irrational world. All Conservative politicians agreed more or less with Northcote in 1880. They did the perfectly logical thing in consequence and recalled Gorst to service. In 1880 Smith sent Northcote the letter Gorst had written to Disraeli in 1877 on his demission, predicting that by the time of the next general election Conservative organisation 'will be as inferior to that of our opponents as it had been superior in 1874'.[37] Northcote returned 'Gorst's curious, and as you say, prophetic letter'.[38] A few weeks later Northcote and Smith asked Gorst to return to Central Office and win the next general election for them.

Gorst himself was the second source of pressure contributing to the buoyancy of the organisational imperative. The quantity of complaint and grievance from Gorst in these years, by its sheer mass, accrued to itself a kind of self-validating plausibility. Gorst's great line of complaint was about organisational structure. He wanted to emancipate Central Office and the principal-agentship from the control of the whips. 'You must put a stop', he told Disraeli in 1877, 'to that which has been the chief cause of all the mischief that has occurred – the system which Sir W. Dyke has been required to follow of managing elections at the Treasury.' Central Office had been reduced to a mere post office. 'Our organisation in 1877 is greatly inferior to what it was in 1874; and the attempt to renovate and improve it has not come a day too soon.'[39] Underlying Gorst's purely technical opinions about organisational structure was a deep current of feeling – and on occasion of strong emotion – about what he regarded as the corruption of the traditional Conservative managerial class, or clique. Gorst saw this electorally, in the way they were habituated to bribery and sharp practices generally; and in terms of patronage, which he accused them of trying to reserve to their own kind, to the detriment of loyal activists outside the 'ring' or the inner circle patronised by the 'Old Identity', or the 'Old Gang'. This grievance was at the heart of the 'insolent epistle' for which Gorst had been snubbed by Disraeli in 1874, when Gorst had wondered how they were to 'keep a political party together, unless those who have made sacrifices for the cause while it was in adversity are to share in the advantages of success'.[40]

These deeper concerns of Gorst's went, of course, far beyond questions of organisation; and indeed those questions can to some extent be discounted as pretexts. Gorst was demanding the impossible: a social revolution in Conservative management, by which the principal agent and the party 'out of doors' would take precedence above the chief whip and the parliamentary party. Gorst got into the National Union by mistake and into the principal-agentship by accident. Still, those positions were all he had, and to make his way he had to exploit them for all, and more than all, they were worth. The strongest urge possessing Gorst, in fact, was a high-minded bourgeois instinct to purify politics of old-style corruption. That ultimately he should be flanked in this quest on the one side by Lord Randolph Churchill and on the other by Sir Henry Drummond Wolff was one of the more richly comic ironies of the time. In any event what is notable is that Gorst did not last long enough in the 1880s either to win or to lose the next general election. And what he did have to say in 1881 possibly has some bearing on that fact, both for that time and for previous times. 'Political activity', he confessed ruefully to Smith, 'seems to me to depend on causes too wide & deep to be controlled. A gardener might as well try to stimulate the rising of sap in the spring.'[41]

2

It is, therefore, with some reference back to Rae's insights in 1878 and forward to Gorst's subsequent insights in 1881 that the performance of the Conservative party's electoral managers in the later 1870s is perhaps most usefully observed.

William Baillie Skene, Gorst's successor as principal agent in 1877, intersected so briefly and ingloriously the atmosphere of politics as to constitute the very type of the evanescent shooting star in public life. Gorst might have invented him to serve Gorst's purposes. An Harrovian and an Oxford man (Corpus and All Souls), Skene owned several thousand acres of Fifeshire and Kinrossshire. He was a gentleman with a big house at Strathmiglo without 'crotchets' who could get on with Lord Abergavenny and Sir William Hart Dyke, Bart. (Skene's wife was a daughter of Dean Liddell of Christ Church, Oxford: Skene was thus 'Alice in Wonderland's' brother-in-law). He damned himself utterly in the eyes of history by confessing to Corry before the election in 1880: 'I cannot tell you how much I long to get out of my present position wh I feel I was an idiot to have assumed. I do hope you will be able to find me something more congenial & which I shall be better fitted to undertake with credit & satisfaction to myself & others.'[42] These words might of course betoken actual as well as confessed incompetence. But it does not follow necessarily from Skene's dissatisfaction with himself that he was doing a bad job. His words might just as well betoken high intelligence and a perceptive awareness of the realities of political life and party fortunes compatible with the earlier insights of Rae and the later insights of Gorst. Possibly he found life at Central Office too disturbingly reminiscent of life as depicted by his sister-in-law's friend 'Lewis Carroll'. There are no complaints on record before 1880 that Skene was incompetent and that the party was therefore heading for disaster. No doubt Skene was relieved to get out and devote the rest of his career to managing the estates of his father-in-law's college.

When Gorst left the party's service at Central Office in 1877, trusting that 'one part of the new arrangement may be to separate entirely and for ever the electoral management of the Party from the Government Department of the Treasury', he recommended that the management of Central Office should be given to an 'independent' MP who had the confidence of the government, and whom Gorst would be ready to assist with the benefit of his experience. He suggested the Hon. R.E.S. Plunkett, member for West Gloucestershire, who had 'great abilities and plenty of leisure'.[43] The party managers had not the slightest intention of introducing the complication of having a sitting MP as principal agent; especially one of 'independent' virtues. It was doubtless the entire absence of any parliamentary ambitions which recommended Skene to them. Their recalling Gorst in 1880 was the desperate act of men who saw themselves between the devil and the deep blue sea. The notion of an 'independent' MP not only principal agent of the party but joint secretary of the National Union would be even more unwelcome to the party managers. In consequence of the arrangements which Gorst himself made when he brought the National Union into Central Office, the principal-agentship annexed a secretaryship of the union as a matter both of sensible policy and obvious convenience. It is a measure either of Gorst's deviousness or his honest incomprehension of what the party chiefs thought of as elementary management principles not only that he recommended an MP as his successor; but also that when it was proposed that Skene replace Gorst as secretary of the National Union, Gorst added it to his dossier of grievances and saw it as further evidence of conspiracy. Northcote had much ado smoothing him down, pointing out apologetically that the National Union had worked 'so much in connection with the party agency, and there is so much difficulty in keeping them distinct, while they remain under the same roof and employ the same staff of clerks, that it seems to be very desirable to maintain the connection which you yourself established by making the same person party agent and secretary to the union'.[44] Lord Claud Hamilton's offending resolution in the council for the union conference at Nottingham was withdrawn. Gorst eventually resigned as secretary in November 1877, thanked for his 'great zeal and ability' as secretary and 'adviser to the Conservative Party'.

The burden of Gorst's electoral advice to the Conservative party in these years was the fragility of its hold in the boroughs. He made out of losses in the municipal elections in 1874 a psephological theory purporting to demonstrate that the 'political re-action in the English Boroughs which brought us into power' could well be a 'mere temporary movement of revulsion induced by the unpopularity of the late Government' unless the managers took care to build up in each borough a 'permanent Tory faction'. 'I do not dissent from your view', he told Disraeli,

> that the mass of the people is, or may be made, Tory. But masses cannot move without leaders; and in English Boroughs we are grievously deficient in Tory leaders. Those of the higher classes in Boroughs who take part in politics have

> everything to lose and nothing to gain by attaching themselves to the Tory party; and we therefore find wealth, influence, ability and all local political forces arrayed against us.

Gorst had been in hopes that 'the power and patronage which the possession of office has given us' might have been used to help create in boroughs the necessary 'permanent Tory factions'.

> The Radicals during their long tenure of power sedulously pursued such a policy, and have (I think as a consequence) a staff of Borough leaders immeasurably stronger than ours. But I think your colleagues (who are none of them Borough members themselves) either fail to see the necessity for such a policy or despair of maintaining permanently our position in the Boroughs. At any rate little has been done to strengthen or consolidate our friends in the Boroughs and much to alienate and discourage them.[45]

Dyke was sceptical about the extent to which municipal elections could be interpreted as reliable indicators of long-term parliamentary electoral trends.[46] It is noteworthy that at a conference of Conservative agents in December 1875 at which the municipal elections were discussed, Gorst accepted in his report to Dyke that he did not believe that the municipal election losses suggested the loss of a general election. The party agents were clear that recent losses were not attributable to 'any general failure of confidence in the party leaders', but to 'increased activity of the Radicals', 'and "the rascally apathy" of the upper classes of the Conservative party, who will neither themselves discharge the duties of the Municipal Officers, nor take the slightest trouble to secure the return of candidates of their own party'. Some 'very strong remarks' were made by agents 'as to the importance of the leaders of the Conservative party taking a more active part in Conservative demonstrations'; and a desire was 'especially expressed that some Conservative movement should be made in the towns of Birmingham and Sheffield, and the attendance of one or more of the prominent party leaders should be secured'.[47]

This kind of activist grievance was no doubt received by the party managers in good part. Dyke forwarded Gorst's report on the party agents' conference to Disraeli with additional material on the issues of school board elections and the need for financial relief to voluntary schools to succour them against the 'destructive competition' of rate-aided schools,[48] which the party chiefs would have taken in very good part indeed. There was nothing, moreover, in the by-election record in these years to sustain Gorst's diagnoses of decay. In 61 by-elections since 1874, the government had a net loss of four seats by March 1877, and a net loss of seven seats by the end of the parliament. This was a notably good performance for a party in office; and there was nothing remotely like the haemorrhage of Liberal losses in the previous parliament. Hardy noted the loss of an Oldham seat in March 1877 as a 'severe blow to us, possibly our decadence is beginning'. But 'troubles were soothed' by a victory at Salford in April.[49] Barrington congratulated Disraeli on Salford: 'H. James admits it was the greatest "facer" the Liberal party had received for many a day.'[50] Derby's complaint at the new 'marked preference of constituencies for local candidates, generally middle-aged men who have made money, & want a seat for social rather than political reasons',[51] registered precisely, in fact, a new kind of managerial success. Local monied influence and interest was ever what the party had wanted. Abergavenny reported to Disraeli in November 1877 that Dyke had had a 'long day with Skene – going over some of the Boroughs. That from all he hears he is of opinion that we are "in a much stronger position than we were this time last year" & that "some of the municipal returns are wonderful"'.[52] It is not wonderful to find Abergavenny back at the centre of things once more, now that Gorst was out and Skene was in.

Apparent indicators also seemed to suggest that the Liberal party remained as fissile as ever. Waiting for the Whigs and 'moderates' to have their fill of Gladstone, Chamberlain, and Parnell was, and would be for some time to come, a standard feature of the Conservative parliamentary repertoire. Dyke could present Disraeli in October 1878 a set of returns of Commons' divisions for the first five years of his government which Dyke held to be 'very instructive, as showing the support you have received from the opposition during that period'. Of a total of 929 divisions 390 had been majorities of more than 100; 123 at more than 80; and 132 of more than 60. These, in Dyke's view, 'tell their own tale & I think will surprise all those who talk of a mere mechanical Party majority which commenced at 50 in 1874'. The parliamentary Liberal party was decidedly not a threat to the Conservative government. There was also the question of parties 'out of doors'. Dyke could report 'good accounts of Registration everywhere, but much will depend upon Finance, & the energy of our supporters in tackling our opponents & refuting their false views of the Political situation'.[53]

What the party chiefs and managers did not take in good part from Gorst at this time was the kind of advice he was giving the Conservative party at National Union conferences. It was one thing for Gorst to write privately to Disraeli letters recommending drastically what in effect would be the subordination of the whips' office at the House of Commons and the office of the patronage secretary at the Treasury to Conservative Central Office in St. Stephen's Chambers, Westminster Bridge Road. That particular sort of insolence could be quietly snubbed by being ignored. Gorst's departure from Central Office in 1877 was no doubt a matter of personal relief for the inner elite of party managers who formed what was at this time variously called the Committee, the Political Committee, the Central Committee, or the Confidential Council.[54] But it was quite another thing for Gorst to make of the National Union a platform for his subversive preachings. Already, at the tenth conference at Manchester in 1876, Abergavenny presiding and Lord Claud Hamilton in the chair, Gorst engaged in bruising dispute with Raikes about candidates for the council. Gorst accused Raikes of fostering the causes of establishment notables mainly notable for their frequent absence. Gorst lost.[55] Gorst collided with Raikes again at the 1877 conference at Southsea, Gorst's farewell appearance as joint honorary secretary. Gorst opposed setting up a 'general consultative committee' to refer questions of 'importance and difficulty' to the executive on the ground that it would be a barrier against direct access to the leaders.[56]

In the fullness of time and the ripening of spleen, Gorst would, by 1882, elevate these scuffles into evidences of an 'aristocratic' betrayal of the party. Like most good conspiracy theories, it was true in parts, but compromised ultimately by the 'thirteenth chime' effect. Gorst would have it as follows:

> Between 1868 and 1874 Conservative associations on the Lancashire model grew up in every part of England. They universally complained that they were not patronised by the aristocratic members of the party. It was fortunate that they were not. There was no temptation to waste time and energy in organising demonstrations to which no great man would come. They were thus driven to devote themselves to registration and the machinery necessary for an election contest. The victory of 1874, which was totally unexpected by the aristocratic section of the party, was the result. As soon as success was achieved, the men who had stood aloof since 1868 rushed in to share the spoils. . . . Social influence became predominant; it pervaded the whole organisation of the party, with disastrous results. . . . In legislation the interests of the boroughs were subordinated to those of the counties. . . . The Conservative associations, as a natural consequence of these things, steadily declined; their numbers increased, but their vitality was gone. Those by whom the work prior to 1874 was silently performed gradually withdrew to make way for noisier partisans.

It followed that the defeat of 1880 'astonished the aristocratic section as much as the victory of 1874. It was no surprise to those acquainted with the temper of that vast section of the party whose voice never reached their leaders' ears'.[57]

Setting aside the larger controverted issue of the role of party organisation as opposed to 'public opinion' in deciding elections, the strength of Gorst's case lies in the undoubted fact that, from a patronage viewpoint, the Conservative party was virtually a pure system of aristocratic jobbery. How Gorst could have expected it to be otherwise is a measure of the poverty of his imagination. Nor was his lurid picture of promotions and jobs being given to friends, relatives, and adherents of the 'aristocratic section' while the 'real workers for the party' were treated with 'disdain and contempt' helpful to his case. The related, and more important, strength of Gorst's argument is that he drew attention to the profoundly true fact that there was, and would increasingly be, a structural tension within the Conservative party between a traditional 'aristocratic' set of social and political values and a new set of social and political values to which Gorst could not at that time put a convenient label. 'Tory Democracy' as a phrase was not yet helpfully in vogue; and it was inexpedient to use 'middle class' or 'bourgeois' as hostile witnesses such as Frederic Harrison freely did, since they precisely denied the validity of what

Gorst asserted were 'those popular principles in politics' of 'the mass of the people' which Disraeli allegedly taught him, and which the 'party managers' were allegedly betraying.

The cause he was urging Gorst himself betrayed by asking people to believe that in the later 1870s the party managers were conducting a kind of reign of terror: 'independence of political thought was visited with the severest punishment'; to 'doubt the stability of the new Conservative Government, and to point out the decay of the new Conservative associations under the patronage by which they were stifled, was flat heresy'; the 'members of the Ministry desired their followers to speak unto them smooth things and to prophesy deceits'. Gorst pleaded his case that legislation for counties and landowners crowded out legislation for the boroughs and 'the people at large' by citing the abandonment of the Merchant Shipping Bill in favour of the Agricultural Holdings Bill and by simply neglecting to mention Cross or any of the labour and trade union measures.[58]

Gorst was neither so candid, nor so lurid, nor so dishonest in what he was saying openly in the years before 1880. But what he was saying cut close enough to the bones of the matter to give a quite satisfying degree of offence. In Gorst's valediction at the Southsea conference of the National Union in 1877 Rowland Winn, Dyke's assistant whip, found himself listening to this:

> Mr. Gorst . . . spoke of the importance to the Conservative Party of keeping its organisation in perfect order. He drew a distinction between political organisation and party management, the latter of which he characterised as skirmishing while upon the former devolved the real battle. He said that the National Union was increasing in power as was shown by the large number of delegates from distant towns, and he urged that no effort should be spared to improve its organisation, and deprecated the idea which he said had found support in some quarters that the Associations be discouraged. He believed that there was no danger to the Conservative Party from independence of political thought and that no man had less to fear on this account than Lord Beaconsfield. Mr. Gorst concluded by urging the necessity of popularising the Conservative Associations as much as possible.[59]

In this explicit association of the real battlers with the National Union, as contrasted with the mere skirmishers of the whips' office, and (by implication) the traditional style of party management, was the germ of the conflict that was to set the party by its ears in the early 1880s.

Without doubt, however, the most important immediate consequence of the quarrel in 1877 between the managers and Gorst was that the managers were frightened off any sensible consideration of organisational questions or investigation into instances of weakness or defect. If organisational decay was a major, or the major, cause of defeat in 1880, then Gorst ironically bore a large share of the burden of responsibility. By pitching his explicit case so high, and his implicit case so menacingly. Gorst assured in effect that the Conservative party would take no benefit from the current debates and scrutiny provoked by the setting up of the National Liberal Federation; and, more particularly, by the brightest jewel in its organisational crown, the notorious 'Caucus' established as his committee of public safety by that Brummagem Robespierre, Joseph Chamberlain.

By 1880 Lady Salisbury would be crying that 'we must have caucuses'. But when in 1878 Lt Colonel G. Arbuthnot, president of the Hereford Conservative Working Mens' Association and member of the council of the National Union of Conservative and Constitutional Associations, drew to Corry's attention the 'Radical example' of the Liberal Federation, and the 'imperative' need for the Conservative party to take due heed of it, he was met with blankness. Of his elaborate scheme Arbuthnot had reason to suppose, as he later said to Disraeli apropos of Corry, 'probably you never saw it, and he never read it.'[60] Arbuthnot, who held a Conservative seat in a by-election at Hereford in 1878, shared in fact none of Gorst's 'crotchets'. He described to Disraeli his basic philosophy of party management in terms cynical enough to be a model for Salisbury: 'My idea is that the management of a political party, both centrally & locally, should be vested in as few people as possible – provided they have brains & other qualifications – while as many as possible should be induced to believe that they are themselves managers.'[61]

No doubt, however, the superficial impression given by Arbuthnot's 'Outline of a scheme for the consolidation of the Conservative party' of 1 January 1878 was that it smelt too reminiscently of Gorst.

> Our conspicuous success at the General Election of 1874 was no doubt in a large measure attributable to the great stride which we had made in 1868 in organisation by the establishment of Local Associations, but it was not less due to the absence of organisation on the part of our opponents. . . . The question, then, which we have to consider is, whether we are one whit stronger as regards organisation and consolidation than we were in 1874?
>
> I think not. . . . I know that in some a lamentable lethargy has prevailed, and that absolutely nothing has been done to create harmonious working between London and the Provinces.

The setting up of the Liberal Federation made it necessary that at the commencement of the fifth session of the Conservative government 'no steps should be neglected which are calculated to consolidate our Party, so as to derive the full advantage of the numerical superiority which we are confident that we possess in the country'. The Conservatives must be 'up and doing'. The 23 points of Arbuthnot's elaborate scheme had to do in origin with the need he saw to supersede the 'dual system' of the Central Committee in London and the National Union Council, 'between which bodies neither mutual confidence nor friendly feelings appear sufficiently to prevail'. Much of what Arbuthnot recommended about 'Political Territorial Districts' of, say, three average-sized counties and inspectors and organising secretaries in a tightly knit machine became features of the later reorganisations of Akers Douglas and Middleton. But Arbuthnot's notion that the presidents of Conservative 'Alliances' in each 'Territorial District' should be *ex officio* members of the Central Committee would be quite enough in 1878 to ensure that his proposals would be filed into limbo.[62] Arbuthnot sent copies of his scheme to all Conservative associations. The majority of the responses he received were favourable, the remainder doubtful mainly on the grounds of expense. But he also found 'that some misapprehension existed' that his scheme was 'supposed to savour too much of the "Caucus System", and consequently to be of too democratic a character'.

Arbuthnot was not alone in his misgivings about the Conservative dual system of Central Committee at Central Office and the organs of the National Union, and the opportunities for friction between them. W.V. Richards of Exeter, a Devonshire party manager, put the other side of the same coin to Northcote as early as June 1874. Clearly, Richards represented much the same kind of party agent style of thinking as his fellow Exeter activist Joseph Gould. They did not at all follow Gorst in identifying the 'real battlers' with the National Union and the mere 'skirmishers' with whips' management. On the contrary, they saw the National Union as the home of talkers and troublemakers.

Richards particularly had in view the need to put the county organisation on a basis of tightly centralised uniformity capable of dealing ultimately with the coming of the occupier franchise to the counties, which would affect the boundaries of constituencies and throw local organisation into confusion. For Richards the National Union presence in Devonshire represented a dispersion of effort and an encumbering of the ground at a time when Devonshire Conservatism needed firm and decisive management to bring all the localities into line in time to prepare adequately for the coming electoral revolution and confront the Liberals successfully.

> The work may at first sight seem impossible, but with proper manipulation of the sources of influence which Conservatives possess in Landed Proprietors, M.P.s, Associations, Clubs, etc. etc. and the precaution taken to secure the necessary time, it is I am confident possible to establish such uniformity & co-operation throughout the County, as would puzzle our opponents. The end is in itself worth working for, but there could be eventually an immense economy of time, money & anxiety. The cost of fighting Elections is simply enormous.

Northcote did not need to be reminded of that fact. Richards, moreover, foresaw that the 'next General Election will I suspect be the severest struggle we have witnessed for many years'. His lament was that 'the ground however for this kind of work is occupied by the National Union'.[63]

The party managers would no doubt have much preferred Richards's line of subsuming the National Union within a Central Office machine of tightly centralised uniformity to Arbuthnot's line of giving union 'Alliance' bosses places on the Central Committee. But, embarrassed as the managers often were by the frictions caused by the National Union, they would be even more embarrassed by the task of suppressing the union's autonomous existence. Let growling dogs lie, and hope for the best. Dyke's circular to the party from the Carlton Club in early 1878 represents a blandly official 'dual' policy in the matter of fund raising:

> Allow me to draw your attention to the papers relative to the Central Registration Association and the National Union of Conservative and Constitutional Associations which accompany this letter. These associations represent the central organisation of the Conservative party, and are the official medium of communication between the leaders of the party, the local agents and associations throughout the kingdom. The central organisation being directly under my control, I can speak with confidence as to the great political value possessed by the associations, to whose efforts and assistance very many of our past victories in the constituencies are in a manner due. The action of the Central Organisation has been very largely developed during recent years, and its labours have been rewarded with the most signal success; but it is of the utmost consequence that it should be kept in a state of efficiency, and with a view to this I beg to invite you to assist the common cause by a subscription towards the central fund. I should mention that the funds of the Registration Association and the National Union are supplemented from the central fund as occasion arises, and should you prefer to subscribe separately to either, I enclose orders for that purpose. I may add that anything you feel disposed to give will be acknowledged on behalf of the party by yours faithfully, W. Hart Dyke. (Replies to be addressed to Conservative Central Office, St. Stephen's Chambers, Westminster Bridge Rd.)[64]

The party and the Great Depression

1

If the question of alleged organisation deterioration as a telling symptom of Conservative decline in the later 1870s does not admit a ready answer of unequivocal explanatory power, there seems little doubt about the onset of the Great Depression. Gorst's rueful phrases in 1881 about 'causes too wide and deep to be controlled', and the futility of gardeners trying to 'stimulate the rising of sap in the spring', might appear here decidedly more apropos. Until late 1878 it seemed beyond doubt that the great issues of the coming general election would be about foreign policy. But, in the words of the *Annual Register* for 1879, new domestic problems made 'a sudden development of testing consequences'.[65] Depression of trade; rising unemployment; bad harvests combined with heavy importations and falling agricultural prices; increasing incidence of strikes consequent on reduction of wages; withdrawal of capital, bankruptcies; alarms in the money market; ministerial embarrassments at falling revenues: these were the staples of analysis and comment increasingly through 1878 and 1879. The *Bradford Observer* in 1878 registered a general feeling of puzzlement at the apparently mysterious nature of the end of the great Victorian boom era. Its four last annual reports described 'an uninterrupted succession of bad years, and it may thus be inferred that while former panics had simple causes, the present chronic depression must be owing to a complication of disastrous influences'.[66] A wave of strikes made distress manifest, especially in the hard winter of 1878–9. London masons, a great turn-out of Lancashire cotton operatives, with major disturbances in Blackburn and elsewhere, registered the cancellation of most of the trade unions' gratitude for the legislation of 1875.

In 1877 the Conservative managers had been much concerned by the activities of the Agricultural Labourers' Union – 'neither less nor more than a powerful Liberal organisation' as one of the association delegates from Eye described it to the National Union – but by 1878 and 1879 they were more anxious about disaffection among the labourers' employers, the tenant farmers. Always nervous about the dangers of a fault-line opening up between landlords and tenant farmers, Conservative ministers examined the auguries for harvests and cheap importations of foodstuffs with foreboding. Back in 1875 Dyke had rejoiced at the large majority in the Aberdeenshire East by-election: 'the fact of a Tenant Farmers "pet" being beaten in Scotland is worth anything to us just now.'[67] It would be worth even more by 1879, as disaffected tenants built up their resistant lobby, the Farmers' Alliance. In his call in the 1879 session for a royal commission to examine the causes of agricultural depression, Henry Chaplin made abundantly clear how nervous the Conservative party was of the Farmers' Alliance. He also made clear enough his own penchant for a return to measures of agricultural protection against cheap imports. As yet, protectionist sentiment generally in the Conservative party was a relic of a few diehards who remembered the palmy primacy of the agricultural interest before 1846 and a few younger Tories of radical inclination who read and believed the *Foreign Times* and its gloomy predictions of the downward curve of the wholesale price index. Derby noted in January 1877: 'There is much speculation in the press as to the industrial future of England. . . . The balance of trade is enormously against us. Can this state of things go on?' Derby worried at the tendency of capitalists to invest abroad. There were as yet no cries of general distress. Capitalists and manufacturers might talk about ruin, but Derby could not discern any increase in pauperism or in agitation: the working classes seemed 'profoundly quiet & apathetic'.[68] But the cries of ruin were starting to have their effect. 'After 1877, protection was part of England's table talk.'[69] It was certainly an ingredient of the jingo agitation of 1878, in the guise of Lt R.H Armit and his National and Patriotic League for the Protection of British Industries.[70] Comparatively unnoticed in 1879, but soon to be the occasion of much more table talk than the Farmers' Alliance, was the radically militant tenants' organisation set up in Ireland to resist the rising incidence of eviction for non-payment of rent, the Irish Land League.

By November 1877 Derby was detecting indications of industrial working-class distress. 'In a speech made lately at Cardiff, Ld Aberdare describes the state of trade as worse than in the experience of 45 years he has ever known it: & he adds that for want of employment the laborers are in a state of destitution, & many have died from the effects of want.' Derby thought this a 'startling declaration'; but did not observe that it had attracted any notice. By the beginning of 1876 Derby commented that 'for the first time in many years our finance is bad; trade has fallen off, business is slack . . . distress in many districts, especially in those where the coal & iron trade prevail.'[71]

The previous instance of large-scale and widely observed social distress in Britain, the Lancashire cotton operatives' sufferings during the cotton famine at the time of the American Civil War, had given rise to a national subscription, and Cobden even talked of applying to parliament for 'imperial aid'. Gladstone soon put a stop to that, and made sure that relief of Lancashire distress would be a noble monument to the efficacy of voluntary charity. This precedent was possibly in the mind of Frederick Greenwood, editor of the *Pall Mall Gazette*, when he approached Disraeli at the end of 1878. Greenwood preened himself as the person who had tipped off the government in 1875 about the khedive's sale of the Suez Canal shares; now he entertained notions of a corresponding coup in the domestic sphere. He almost succeeded in launching a political stratagem which might have had consequences equally as portentous as those of his claimed Suez initiative; and which, in any case, deserves extended notice.

Greenwood sent to Disraeli in December a memorandum he had composed earlier:

> These suggestions are respectfully submitted to Lord Beaconsfield. They are intended to meet a most serious social difficulty, wh., without some remedy, is likely to prove (in the hands of the opposition) a political danger.
> *Mem.*
> That the distress in the North is very great, & rapidly increasing, & may rapidly take a more or less menacing shape. (The strike riots in Blackburn must not be forgotten nor the fact that the mining population is prone to turbulence.)
> That the distress may be used for political or party purposes.
> That it could easily be so used, & with great effect, if the opposition were to do what I suggest might be done in a far wider, more beneficial & more striking way by the Government.
> That Ministers might advantageously set afoot a great National Subscription, & support it, by these means: – By a subscription from every member of the Cabinet. By similar subscriptions from members of the Royal Family. By appeal to Lords and Commons for the same. *And* by procuring the services of certain Official persons of high administrative faculty to receive (as a private Committee) these funds, & supervise their distribution. – Invitation to be made to opposition leaders, as Mr. Goschen & Mr. Forster, to act on the Committee. This to be done at once. What a Ministry can do, extra officially, in association, that ex-ministers can do in concert, & may do.
>
> The whole thing to be started, perhaps, by a speech from some great minister, emphatically dissociating the plan from the idea of state aid: these means taken because state aid is all but impossible: no reason why state ministers should not associate themselves for the national good, outside their departments.
>
> F. Greenwood Oct. 20 1878

Stated briefly, baldly, & all together, these suggestions look romantic. (They are *meant* to be striking, carried into effect.) But if one detail followed another, at short intervals, there would be a look of growth about them wh. would counteract the romantic impression.[72]

Disraeli's initial reaction was quite positive. Possibly it was the romanticism and the promise of striking effects which appealed to him. He sent off immediately to Cairns, Salisbury, and Northcote:

I fear much that the enemy contemplate making the public distress a party cry, & the effect of such a step in the country as well as the Government, might be serious.

The distress, especially in the North, is great, but its worst characteristic is, that it is not partial, so, as in former instances, London cannot help Lancashire, or the West or South of England the North.

Whatever the opposition suggest, the Government might do with more effect. We could originate a great national subscription, with the Sovereign or the Heir apparent at the head, followed by the Cabinet, & an appeal to members of both Houses.

State Aid is out of the question, but that is no reason why statesmen, & especially responsible statesmen, shd not act.

There shd be a Committee formed of public men most eminent for the faculty of administration. Some of the 'soi-disant' moderate chiefs of the opposition (Goschen, Forster and Co.) shd be invited to be members.

There might, perhaps, be County meetings, as the affair developes.

How to set it afloat? A speech from myself, or any leading Minister? Or I might write a letter having previously received the sanction & aid of the Sovereign etc.

These are suggestions not dogmas. I am sorry to disturb your Xmas, but your opinion weighs always much with me, & I shd like to be guided by it.[73]

Cairns replied encouragingly:

The distress is obviously very great & very general; and, I fear, likely to be worse before it is better. It may be difficult to say, as to some places, where it exists, what exactly it proceeds from, and how long it may be expected to last. It is also difficult to see how a fund adequate to afford relief all over the country can be obtained: & how, if obtained, it can be administered without doing more harm than good. These however are all difficulties wh must be met as best they can. But I quite agree with what I take to be the inclination of your mind, namely, that something shd be originated by the Govent. It is clear that something will be originated by somebody, & that very shortly: & in a matter of such national importance & magnitude I think it wd. be much to be deprecated that it shd fall into individual, & possibly, objectionable hands. If our political enemies were to take it up as a cry & inaugurate a large movement, we could hardly refuse to aid: or if we did, we shd. incur much odium: & if we did aid, still they wd have all the credit.

The course wh. seems to me likely to be most effective wd be a circular letter from you (after sanction &c. of H.M., & I suppose also of the Cabinet or those of its members who are accessible) to the Ld Lieuts of Counties & Mayors of Corporate Towns, referring to the character & features of the distress: the necessity for a general exertion to supplement legal relief: explaining that a great Central Committee wd be invited to act & inaugurate a National Subscription: & that subsequently, & after full preparation, the holding of County &c meetings, & the formation of local Committees (both to obtain subscriptions, &, in distressed districts, to administer relief) wd be desirable. Subscribers shd be allowed, where they desire to do so, to appropriate their subscriptions to particular districts. The formation of the Central Committee will of course be the great difficulty, & I shd say it shd be made sufficiently comprehensive.

I don't see any other way in wch the thing cd be set on foot with sufficient rapidity. A speech requires an occasion to justify it, & there may not be one at hand. The great thing wd be to get an efficient secretary & organiser for the movement.[74]

Cairns's encouragement was powerfully seconded by Salisbury:

The considerations you raise in your letter have been a good deal in my thoughts the last two or three days. I think you are right & that a general subscription in some measure originated by us would be in every sense expedient. The mode of doing it is a matter of some difficulty. A county meeting is open to many objections. It will cause delay: it will be difficult to summon, especially at this time of year & in this weather: & the selection of the County may be invidious. Lancashire is perhaps the chief, but by no means the only sufferer. And in Lancashire Derby's position will produce not inconsiderable difficulties.

A letter would be better; & for similar reasons it can only be addressed to the Lord Mayor of London & by you. In practical workings, the money when collected may be transmitted to local Committees to distribute. Perhaps you might set one up in Lancashire. But the presiding agency must be in London.

The Queen should head it with as large a subscription as she can conveniently give, & of course the Royal Family & Cabinet should follow suit.

I think that a letter from you to the Lord Mayor sent to the papers as soon as possible would do great good in all ways.[75]

Salisbury followed up the next day, with further supportive suggestions:

Would you like me to write to the other members of the Cabinet? . . . I think the first announcement should be simply your letter & the Queen's subscription: accompanied perhaps by Prince Hal's, – if he can afford it. I think this ought to come after, & be printed in ordinary subscription lists – or we may seem like the sons of Levi to be taking too much upon ourselves.

It would be very desirable she should give £2,000. If she only gives £1,000 many people may not like to give as much as she does – & you may lose a certain number of the highest rate of subscribers.[76]

Had Disraeli set out thus resolutely, with Cairns and Salisbury backing him, there is little doubt that the project could have been pushed through cabinet.

It was Northcote who introduced a negative and sceptical note. 'I do not know how far the distress extends, or whether County meetings would succeed. For what particular districts are we to collect? And who is to distribute the funds? . . . Then I don't understand how we are to act as a Government in the matter, except in the collection of information.' Northcote suggested careful inquiries into the extent and localities of distress and, if sufficient facts were assembled to act upon them, to ask the prince of Wales to head a committee including opposition people. 'We should, of course, take care to get some of the leaders of the Press to join us – Walter, Greenwood, Lawson, etc and we should have the great Lord Mayor, and some of the Mayors of the principal towns acting on local subcommittees.' But Northcote felt strongly that 'we ought not to move unless we are in a position to show that there is something exceptional in the circumstances'; as it would be unwise to 'hoist the flag of distress' when there is no 'visible calamity' such as the cotton famine, a convulsion of nature, or a bread or meat famine.

> We have bad trade, and our workmen themselves aggravate the misfortune by their disputes with the employers of labour. We want peace, and confidence, and then we may hope for a return of better times. If there are deeper causes at work we must take care not to encourage the idea that they are to be met by national subscriptions. Think of the danger of having a Relief Committee sitting *en permanence*; yet that is what it might easily come to if the movement were started without great care.[77]

This was enough to knock the stuffing out of Disraeli's initial responsiveness. He lacked the energy to fight Northcote's bureaucratic conventional wisdom, even with Cairns and Salisbury at his side. Disraeli was not convinced; simply overborne. Salisbury replied on Christmas Day: 'Neither am I convinced – but I suppose there is nothing to be done. Starving is starving all the same – whether it comes from a special or a general cause.'[78] And on further thoughts, Salisbury felt he ought to persist:

> My feeling is still distinctly that Cairns is right & Northcote wrong. The only substantial argument used by Northcote is that we may have a *coup manqué*, if people should not subscribe in sufficient numbers. Even assuming that this happens, I doubt whether there is ground for any fear. The reproach will not be a serious one – it will merely be that H.M. was more charitable than her subjects: & that H.M. Ministers followed her example. I never remember to have heard or read that the reproach of being too desirous of relieving distress injured any man or body of men in the eyes of the people. On the other hand, Cairns' apprehension is substantial. If the distress should go on, & become more acute, it will be very easy for some opposition men – like Harcourt or Gladstone – to come forward with a backing of rich Whig Dukes – & to say that they had waited on the idea that perhaps H.M. Govt. would take the lead, but that as there was no sign of any such action, they thought the time had come etc. – etc. – etc.[79]

Even these encouragements with menaces could not emancipate Disraeli from Northcote's official fear of precedent. In his correspondence, Disraeli often echoed the phrases of the previous letter which had impressed itself upon his mind. In this case, in a kind of *texte justicatif* to his Egeria, Lady

Bradford, the hand is the hand of Disraeli, but the mind, as well as the voice, is the mind and voice of Northcote. That Disraeli should have allowed the 'little busy bee' so to disarm him is perhaps the most telling omen of his personal debility in the last days of 1878.

> You are right in supposing that the business wh. now takes up so much of my time, is the general distress; but it is the most difficult to deal with. There are so many plans, so many schemes, and so many reasons why there shd be neither plans nor schemes.
>
> What I fear is that the opposition, who will stick at nothing, may take up the theme for party purposes. If we then don't support them, we shall be stigmatised as unpatriotic: if we do, they will carry all the glory.
>
> And yet – what is the cause of the distress? And, if permanent, is there to be a permanent Committee of Relief? And the property of the nation to support the numbers of unemployed labor? Worse than socialism.
>
> To hoist the flag of distress, when there has been no visible calamity to account for it, like a cotton famine, no bread and meat famine, no convulsion of nature, is difficult and may not be wise.
>
> There are 1,000 other things to be said (on both sides) – but after all starvation has no answer. You will see, however, how difficult is my present position with constant correspondence (and no Secs.) of equal and contradictory character – impossibility of calling a cabinet, for that, at Xmas, wd frighten the world – and everybody agreeing with nobody, but throwing the respony. on my shoulders.[80]

The tone here is somewhat reminiscent of the 'whimperings' to the queen about Northcote's financial unhelpfulness and of a prime minister's 'incompetence' and his being able to do nothing for himself in his troubles.[81]

2

This episode invites reflections. Did Disraeli allow himself, against his own judgement and instinct, to be deflected from a project which might have redounded immensely to the credit and possibly the benefit of the Conservative party? As Salisbury's comments suggest, questions as to the actual efficacy of the measures of relief were secondary. As with the social legislation of the early years of the ministry, what counted primarily was the gesture and the impression, the 'image'. In an age of popular politics, what governments seem to do is at least as important as what they actually do. Nothing better calculated to have boosted the sagging myth of Tory Democracy in the boroughs could have been devised. Perhaps this very point, given Disraeli's consistent disparagement of the National Union, is what helped to give him pause. His concoction of the bogey of socialism was purely and gratuitously exculpatory *post facto*. Nothing in Greenwood's proposal, or in Cairns's and Salisbury's endorsements of it, challenged the 'principles of economic truth', or transgressed the bounds sternly set against state provision of relief by Gladstone in the 1860s. Notions later advanced to explain this episode, that Conservatism had no intellectuals or that Disraeli lacked an 'economic brains-trust engaged in policy formulation'[82], misapply political nonsense characteristic of the 1960s, to the 1870s, which possessed quite enough of their own nonsense.

There was no stint of 'official' *textes justificatifs*. Northcote was quick to alert Cross at the Home Office. 'Cross has sent me a large bundle of reports as to the distress in the large towns', he told Disraeli '– the general tenour being that things are bad, but that local effort is sufficient.' The new bank failure in Cornwall was a 'nuisance, and will hit the miners very hard. They were down already'. He reported the queen 'much interested in the question of distress, and has asked me to send the reports which Cross has received, and which are valuable'. The new session was at hand. 'We must try to give a general account of our position and prospects. It cannot be very cheerful; but I do not think it need be depressingly gloomy.'[83] Dyke rallied to the official line, primed by Northcote. 'I am hearing from many quarters that the distress in the country is by no means universal & is being much exaggerated for Party purposes. The late Revenue Returns strongly confirm this view.'[84] Cross, at Liverpool, added his bit: 'Here I hear of nothing but the great revival of Trade.'[85] Greenwood capitulated and made the best of it. 'From what you say', he wrote to Disraeli in the course of accepting an invitation to visit for the following day, 'about the distress I was quite prepared. To me, too, it seems that the prospects brightened immediately after Christmas, instead of darkening, as so many of us feared: doubtless, more harm than good would have been done by the course contemplated.'[86]

3

Prospects did not long remain bright. The Year 1879 which, in the annals of Conservatism, might have been enlivened by the adventure of a government-inspired national subscription to alleviate social distress, was instead notable for the unrelieved pressures of depression on the body of the party. Of the several fissures which made their appearance in the structural fault-lines none was to become of more moment than that dividing the free-traders from the paleo- and neo-protectionists. The cry was for 'reciprocity', for a policy whereby Britain would abandon unilateral free trade with protected economies and adopt a system of retaliatory duties. Andrew Montagu represented a disposition in the party hoping to exploit the beginnings of a stir for industrial reciprocity for an eventual return to agricultural protection. He wrote to Disraeli in February 1879:

> Indubitably the Agricultural interest is suffering very severely, but is not the only & isolated case of suffering as there seems general & grievous depression in every other branch of industry and business throughout our kingdoms.
>
> I fear the introduction of any direct & specific legislative measure for the protection of home agricultural produce would tend to disturb that moderate

> spirit of contentment which fortunately prevails amongst the 'masses' and might imperil the growth of Conservatism or even an ebb in its tide.
>
> The 'reciprocity cry' in Towns may possibly some day give the Agriculturists a chance of 'getting in a word edgeways,' but altho' I see difficulties (& possible disadvantages) which would beset the carrying out of a reciprocity system, yet I for one look favourably upon any clamour or rigorous onslaught made upon non-reciprocity for I think it may be a means of modifying the undoubted disposition of Foreign Governments to (excuse the vulgarism) 'grab all and give nothing' in their commercial treaties.[87]

Disraeli had to balance the nightmare vision of the Conservative party yet again denounced as the party of dear bread with the kind of nightmare vision presented to him by Corry's report of an encounter with the veteran Anti-Corn Law Leaguer, Ashworth, hale and hearty at 85, and with free trade fanaticism undimmed: 'He won't hear of a cry for Protection, by whatever name "except perhaps in Sheffield, which perhaps has always been *bad*. . . ." "Free Trade is to blame for nothing of what is doing – all will come right." I was glad to hear that was his opinion, – "But how," I asked! "Oh, to begin with, by a reduction to a large extent of wages all round!!"'[88]

If Disraeli was not up to taking the risk of a national relief subscription, he was certainly not up to giving any leads in the direction of questioning what had become the received economic orthodoxy. Even Manners, the most susceptible of his colleagues to the ideals of the old tariff, had to admit the brute electoral fact that the old tariff and the new franchise were incompatible. 'We must remember', he told a deputation of West Indian proprietors and merchants, sniffing at the first wafts of neo-protectionism in the air in 1878, 'that in this country the interest of the consumer is stronger than the interest of the producer.'[89] Disraeli himself insisted, in a debate in the Lords in April 1879 on Bateman's motion for a parliamentary inquiry into the expediency of maintaining an unmodified free trade policy, that investigation of all the principal industries of the country gave no grounds for tracing depression to 'our great commercial changes' – 'except, I admit, in the case of land.' Disraeli preferred to believe that there was 'a change for the better in the condition of the industrial world.'[90] In this he reflected the conventional wisdom of the cyclical interpretation of his principal 'commercial' colleague, W.H. Smith, who pronounced that the 'history of the years previous to 1875 was one of inflation and excitement, and had been succeeded, as all inflation and excitement must be, by loss, misfortune, and trouble'.[91] Northcote, for the government, accepted Chaplin's demands for a royal commission on agricultural depression. It would have been most inexpedient for the Conservative party to snub the agricultural interest, already seething with strange and disturbing political symptoms. Without echoing the scandalised denunciations by the Liberal opposition of Chaplin's 'most radical and revolutionary ideas', 'somewhat Protectionist, or, at all events Reciprocitarian', Northcote assured the Commons that such an inquiry would only strengthen the position of the doctrines of free trade, being 'as I believe them heartily to be, the doctrines of truth'.[92]

4

In 1874 Disraeli deliberately relegated Ireland to its obscure recess at the back of the political stage whence Gladstone had dramatically removed and spotlighted it in 1868. Only for a few accidental months in Disraeli's administration from 1874 to 1880 was the Irish chief secretary a member of the cabinet. Yet events were happening in Ireland which, by the time Disraeli came to compose his election manifesto in 1880, would make Ireland his first and greatest concern. Depressed agricultural prices which were a problem in England were a disaster in Ireland. It is estimated that something like a third of the population in the south and west were in a condition of distress. Incidence of agrarian outrages, pauperism, and evictions mounted relentlessly.

Hardy recorded in November 1879 'grave difficulties' in Irish affairs. Lowther, the chief secretary, gave a generally sad account but made it clear that 'very pressing distress limited and local'.[93] Northcote had been in Ireland in October, and reported to Disraeli from Abbotstown, north Dublin, in characteristically measured terms:

> There is a certain amount of anxiety here as to the prospects of the winter. The distress is, I should think, very much exaggerated: but there will be a hard time among the small holders in the West; and there is agitation among the shopkeepers and money-lenders to whom these poor fellows are in debt, and who think their chances of getting paid depend upon plundering the landlords or doing the Exchequer out of some public money.

Northcote foresaw pressures for money either in relief, public works, or direct aid. The lord-lieutenant, the duke of Marlborough, was inclined to such loose notions. 'Mr. Bourke, the Under Secretary, presses for some shiploads of coal to be sent to Galway and distributed to the poor people who have been unable to save their turf; and I think the Duke is rather bitten with the idea; but it will not be safe to open the door to this kind of waste.' Northcote was sceptical also about the duke's scheme to extend the operation of the land purchase clauses of the 1870 Land Act.[94] To Cairns, at the same time, Northcote was more briskly categorical: 'I have had a great many measures suggested for the relief or prevention of distress; but I don't much incline to any of them, nor do I believe the distress to be as great as it is called.'[95]

Northcote was of that numerous Conservative school which tended to be impatient with the Irish. He was impatient too with the English who wanted somehow to be of help. Confronted with the charitable banking heiress Lady Burdett-Coutts's scheme to advance £250,000 for the purchase of seed for Ireland and relief of debt to local money-lenders, the chancellor of the Exchequer was nonplussed. As he put it to Disraeli: 'I don't see how we are to avail ourselves of this noble offer; nor how we are to decline it altogether.'[96] Hardy was another deprecator of well-meaning philanthropy. He considered the lord-lieutenant 'most lax in his proposals for pauperising further the country'. What cure was there for Irish ills? 'Lord Dillon's 3900 tenants under £4 rental each! all paupers in fact, dividing & sub-dividing. We should go no further than preventing deaths by famine in the interests of the people themselves.'[97] A cabinet on 7 November had two Irish agriculture commissioners before it 'and they gave a most lamentable account of the distress on the West Coast. Short crops, no fuel, deep indebtedness to shopkeepers. Farms of 3 or 4 acres which cannot support a family.' Hardy could only repeat his refrain: 'What prospect for such a country?' In his view indebtedness had increased 'since the Land Act of evil memory', as it seemed to provide some security for borrowing at a time when agricultural prospects looked more hopeful. Hardy foresaw 'sore trouble to be firm in nonpauperising while we prevent starvation. Beach & I are to meet Lowther and consult.'[98] The great problem for a firm non-pauperising and prevention of starvation policy was that native Irish capacity for reactive and resistant policies of their own was now more formidable than at any time since the great days of O'Connell and the Repeal movement. In Parnell's New Departure and Davitt's Land League was a combination of unprecedented potential for mobilising Irish political and agrarian energies. Their kind of Home Rule 'humbug' was not in the least going to keep Ireland 'quiet', as Hicks Beach had planned at the beginning of 1877.

There were observers of the Irish scene at this time who were ready to press upon Conservative leaders the idea that something far more radical would have to be essayed than either firm minimalism or extended distress relief. A friend of Corry's sent him a letter from General C.E. 'chinese' Gordon in Glengarrif in 1880 on conditions in the south-western parts of County Cork, 'of a nature to startle the ignorant or apathetic'. Gordon was overwhelmed by the spectacle of the state of misery of the Bantry Irish: 'a state, to which the Bulgarians, the inhabitants of Asia Minor, the Indian peoples and Chinese compare in a tenfold more favourable light.' Gordon's answer to Hardy's hard questions about what cure there could be for Irish ills or what prospect for such a country was apocalyptic in its simplicity: buy up the landlords for £40 million. As Gordon pointed out, the British government had found £20 million to enfranchise the West Indian slaves.[99]

It would take the Conservative party less than five years to come to the beginnings of such a policy; and it would be the agrarian foundation of Conservative Irish policy for the rest of the century. Meanwhile, in 1879, for such brief time as they retained responsibility in the matter, Conservatives divided themselves between hardline minimalists and softline ameliorists. Among the latter, for example, was Cross, who applied to the Irish case much the same kind of empiricism as he had applied to Labour and social questions in his early days at the Home Office. On 31 December 1879 he made clear to Disraeli what his line would be in forthcoming cabinet discussions. He accepted Lowther's advice that there was exaggeration in much of the information about distress that the government was getting from Conservative Irish MPs such as Captain King-Harman of County Sligo. But it remained undisputed that 'in certain districts a good deal of distress will be found to prevail during the winter'. Cross did not take the view he had taken as home secretary of distress in England, that 'local effort' would suffice. Cross decidedly backed the lord-lieutenant's proposal in the 'present emergency' to use part of the 'Church Surplus', set aside from the disendowment of 1869 and yielding something over £300,000 per annum, reserved for relief of 'unavoidable calamities and suffering not provided for by the poor-law', such as asylums, institutes for the deaf, dumb and blind, and kindred objects. Cross particularly had in mind the granting of 'loans to Landowners upon Liberal and advantageous terms' to stem the incidence of evictions, and for construction work on such vital items of infrastructure as harbours, roads, piers 'unfettered by conditions of local contributions', with an appeal to parliament for a Bill of Indemnity. Cross 'very much' leaned towards taking this course, providing there be no ultimate loss to the surplus fund.[100] Cabinets on 3 and 8 January accepted the lord-lieutenant's programme for Irish relief measures, Cross being 'much satisfied' at the decision to divert the Church surplus for the purpose. The chief secretary and the chancellor of the Exchequer exchanged views on the 'liberal and advantageous' rate of interest.[101]

Notes and References

1 T.E. Kebbel, *Lord Beaconsfield and Other Tory Memories* (1907) 55–6.
2 A. Austin, *Autobiography* (1911), ii, 118.
3 R. Blake, *Disraeli* (1966), 655.
4 Hanham, 228.
5 Dyke to Beaconsfield, 26 Aug. 1878; HP, B/XXI/D/484.
6 Dyke to Beaconsfield, 8 Sept. [1878]; HP, B/XXI/D/485.
7 Probably M.A. Bass, Liberal MP for East Staffordshire.
8 Corry to Beaconsfield, 16 Sept. 1878; HP, B/XX/CO/124.
9 Dyke to Beaconsfield, 11 Jan. [1879]; HP B/XXI/D/490.
10 'Functions of a Conservative opposition', *Nineteenth Century* (1883), 161.
11 *AR*, 1877, 3; Derby Diary, 11 Aug. 1877.
12 Dyke to Disraeli, 5 Jan. [1879]; HP, B/XXI/D/488.
13 Hardy, *Diary*, 353–4.
14 *Ibid.*, 272–3.
15 Beach to Northcote, 1 Jan. 1877; BL, Iddesleigh 50021, 227.
16 Brand to Northcote, 25 July 1877. BL, Iddesleigh 50021, 167.
17 Derby Diary, 8 Feb. 1877.
18 Barrington to Beaconsfield, 17 July 1877; HP, B/XX/Ba/49.
19 Hardy, *Diary*, 61.
20 Northcote to Beaconsfield, 4 Sept. 1877; BL, Iddesleigh 50018, 52.
21 Barrington to Beaconsfield, 4 May 1877; HP, B/XX/Ba/46.
22 Northcote to Beaconsfield, 10 July 1877. BL, Iddesleigh 50018, 159.
23 Salisbury to Balfour, 19 March 1878; BL, Balfour 49688, 9.
24 Northcote to Beaconsfield, 2 July 1878; BL, Iddesleigh 50018, 95.
25 Derby Diary, 25 Sept. 1874.
26 Northcote to Beaconsfield, 9 Jan. 1879; BL, Iddesleigh 50018, 129.
27 Northcote to Beaconsfield, 4 Feb. 1879; BL, Iddesleigh 50018, 138.
28 Salisbury to Beaconsfield, 5 July 1879; HP, B/XX/Ce/120.
29 Northcote to Beaconsfield, 29 July 1879; BL, Iddesleigh 50018, 163.
30 Buckle, ii, 1320.
31 Northcote to Beaconsfield, 29 July 1879; BL, Iddesleigh 50018, 163.
32 See below, 381–2.
33 See below, 378–9.
34 T.E. Kebbel, 'A Conservative view of the elections', *Nineteenth Century* (1880), 908–9.
35 W.F. Rae, 'Political clubs and party organisation', *Nineteenth Century* (1878), 908–9, 929–32.
36 See above, 315–16.

37 See above, 242.
38 See below, 397.
39 Gorst to Beaconsfield, 3 March 1877; HP, B/XXI/G/258; E.J. Feuchtwanger, *Disraeli, Democracy and the Tory Party* (Oxford 1968), 137–8.
40 See above, 240.
41 Feuchtwanger, *Disraeli, Democracy and the Tory Party*, 152.
42 Skene to Corry, 16 Feb. [1880]; HP, B/XXI/S/281. Skene was forwarding to Lord Beaconsfield his official recommendation as to dissolution of parliament. In his nervousness he wrote 1881 instead of 1880. See below, 367.
43 Gorst to Beaconsfield, 3 March 1877. HP, B/XXI/G/258.
44 Northcote to Gorst, 7 July 1877; P. Cohen, *Disraeli's Child. A History of the Conservative and Unionist Party Organisation* (1964), i, 51–2.
45 Gorst to Disraeli, 2 Dec. 1874; HP, B/XXI/D/463a. See also Gorst to Disraeli, 10 Nov. 1875; HP B/XXI/G/253; 22 Nov. 1875, HP, B/XXI/G/255.
46 Dyke to Disraeli, 8 Dec. [1874]. *Ibid.*, 463. HP, B/XXI/G/463.
47 Gorst to Dyke, 21 Dec. 1875. *Ibid.*, D/466a. HP, B/XXI/0/466a.
48 Dyke to Disraeli, 23 Dec. [1875]. *Ibid.*, 466. HP, B/XXI/D/466.
49 Hardy, *Diary*, 309, 317.
50 Barrington to Beaconsfield, 20 April 1877., HP, B/XX/Ba/45. Sir Henry James had been Liberal solicitor and attorney-general 1873–4. M. Swartz, *The Politics of British Foreign Policy in the Era of Disraeli and Gladstone* (1985), 155–6, for Corry's report to Beaconsfield, giving David Plunket's assessment that Lancashire's gratitude for Cross's appointment principally carried the poll.
51 Derby Diary, 21 July 1877.
52 Abergavenny to Beaconsfield, 29 Nov. 1877; HP, B/XXI/A/58.
53 Dyke to Beaconsfield, 20 Oct. [1878]; HP, B/XXI/D/506.
54 Noel to Corry, 27 March 1880; HP, B/XII/K/12a; Corry to Noel, 27 March 1880; HP, B/XXI/K/126; Hardy, *Diary*, 442.
55 Cohen, *Disraeli's Child*, i, 39.
56 *Ibid.*, 40.
57 'Two Conservatives', 'The state of the opposition. I. Conservative disorganisation', *Fortnightly Review* (1882), 669–70.
58 *Ibid.*
59 NUCCA, minutes, 11th annual conference, Southsea, 30 June 77.
60 Arbuthnot to Beaconsfield, 4 June 1880; HP, B/XX1/A/199b.
61 *Ibid.* Salisbury's later formulation was: 'it may be said that the best form of government (setting aside the question of morality) is one where the masses have little power, and seem to have a greal deal' (Cecil, *Salisbury*, iii, 297).
62 Arbuthnot to Beaconsfield, 4 June 1880; HP, B/XX1/A/199a.
63 Richards to Northcote, 15 June 1874; encl. Northcote to Disraeli, 16 June 1874; BL, Iddesleigh 50016, 231.
64 Quoted by Rae, 'Political clubs and party organisation', 920.
65 *AR*, 1879, 1.
66 *Ibid.*, 249–50.
67 Dyke to Disraeli, 23 Dec. [1875]; HP, B/XXI/D/466.

68 Derby Diary, 17 Jan. 1877.
69 H. Cunningham, 'The Conservative party and patriotism', in R. Colls and P. Dodd (eds), *Englishness. Politics and Culture* 1880–1920 (1986), 287.
70 B.H. Brown, *The Tariff Reform Movement in Great Britain, 1881–1895* (New York 1943), 8–9.
71 Derby Diary, 17 Nov. 1877, 1 Jan. 1878.
72 HP, 8/XX/A/99.
73 Beaconsfield to Cairns, 23 Dec. 1878; PRO, Cairns 30/51/1.
74 Cairns to Beaconsfield, 24 Dec. 1878; HP, B/XX/Ca/241.
75 Salisbury to Beaconsfield, 23 Dec. 1878; HP, B/XX/Ce/105.
76 Salisbury to Beaconsfield, 24 Dec. 1878; HP, HP, B/XX/Ce/106.
77 Northcote to Beaconsfield, 23 Dec. 1878; BL, Iddesleigh 50018, 121.
78 Salisbury to Beaconsfield, 25 Dec. 1878; HP, B/XX/Ce/107.
79 Salisbury to Beaconsfield, 27 Dec. 1878; HP, B/XX/Ce/108.
80 Buckle, ii, 1275–6.
81 See above, 321.
82 See P. Smith, *Disraelian Conservatism and Social Reform* (1967) 300–1.
83 Northcote to Beaconsfield, 7 and 14 Jan. 1879; BL, Iddesleigh 50018, 127, 134.
84 Dyke to Beaconsfield, 5 Jan. [1879]; HP, B/XXI/D/488.
85 Cross to Beaconsfield, 7 Jan. 79; HP, B/XX/Cr/89.
86 Greenwood to Beaconsfield, 21 Jan. [1879]; HP, B/XX/A/100.
87 Montagu to Beaconsfield, 3 Feb. 1879; HP, B/XXI/M/426.
88 Corry to Beaconsfield, 17 Sept. 1879; HP, B/XX/Co/128.
89 Smith, *Disraelian Conservatism*, 303.
90 *PD*, ccxlv, 1393, 1396.
91 *Ibid.*, 1013–14.
92 *Ibid.*, ccxlvii, 1524, 1526, 1535.
93 Hardy, *Diary*, 427.
94 Northcote to Beaconsfield, 12 Oct. 1879; BL, Iddesleigh 50018, 171.
95 Northcote to Cairns, 12 Oct. 1879; PRO, Cairns 39/51/5.
96 Northcote to Beaconsfield, 9 Feb. 1880; BL, Iddesleigh *ibid.*, 179.
97 Hardy, *Diary*, 427.
98 *Ibid.*
99 J.C. Cowell to Rowton, 22 Nov. 1880, encl. Gordon to Cowell, 17 Nov. 80; HP, B/XXI/G/190.
100 Cross to Beaconsfield, 31 Dec. 1879; HP, B/XX/Cr/88.
101 Cross to Beaconsfield, 7 Jan. 1880; HP, B/XX/Cr/89.

Chapter 13

Abroad: 'certainly the world is out of joint'

Free scope for men in the field

Had the Conservative government been able to close its external account at the high point of the summer of 1878 it might have weathered the hard domestic times of 1878 and 1879. But this was not to be. Something of the same concatenation of disastrous influences infected the government from outside. The most painful infections came out of the imperial frontier theatres of north-west India and northern South Africa. The marked contrast between the two sets of disastrous influences was that whereas the government's response to domestic complications was cautiously orthodox in England and cautiously unorthodox in Ireland, it was extraordinarily reckless and adventurous in the policies it permitted its agents to apply to the complications of imperial frontiers.

In Calcutta Lytton, dizzy from his fairy-tale exaltation from Lisbon, nurtured grand strategic and geopolitical schemes. It was the beginning of the classic, Kiplingesque, phase of the 'Great Game'. Lytton had looked forward to playing a leading part in a Russian war in 1878. He thought a good opportunity had been missed by the home government. It did not take Derby long to conclude that Lytton was a little touched.[1] Salisbury's line with Lytton was to keep him in humour but to keep him under restraint. Disraeli wanted Salisbury to hold Lytton on a longer rein. Lytton inherited a problem which the government of India had long been pondering: how to fix a frontier in the north-west which would best suit interior India and would best promote a workable and stable buffer region against Russian encroachment. (The parlance for this was 'scientific' frontier.) There were arguments for consolidating interior lines and setting the buffer region correspondingly nearer. There was no chance that Lytton would be other than for a 'forward' policy in both lines. By 1877 Disraeli had convinced himself that Lytton had been specifically chosen 'for this very kind of business'; 'we wanted a man of ambition, imagination, some vanity, and much will – and we have got him.'[2] Salisbury was always sardonic about Lytton, remembering that in sober fact he was fourth choice in a rather dim field. The *limes* of India was the only strictly imperial issue in which Disraeli seriously interested himself. It was the only theatre of the outer world in which it could be said that the Conservative party, by proxy, undertook responsibility for a coherent policy of imperial design. Everything else was questions of 'encounters'.

Cranbrook's line on succeeding Salisbury in 1878 was to humour Disraeli by letting Lytton have his way. This way was a war to force the Afghans to replace Russian with British tutelage. Northcote groaned at the prospect of the expense. 'I own I don't like the turn of affairs in India,' he told Cairns, who liked it as little. 'Who is to pay for this expedition? If it is to be an Imperial charge ought not parliament to meet?'[3] Salisbury was even more forthright to Northcote:

> I don't like the Afghan affair – because Lytton has so flagrantly disobeyed the orders sent him. This argues the intention of conducting operations – according to his fancy – & that of those about him – not according to our views. It will, therefore, be directed so as to achieve the most brilliant results – lose the greatest number of men – & spend the largest amount of money. I am urging Beaconsfield & Cranbrook to be satisfied with taking – & keeping Candahar as a material guarantee.[4]

Manners supported Disraeli and Cranbrook on the ground that the men in the field needed to have 'free scope'. Did our experience in two years of European problems, he asked Cairns, give confidence in cabinet control? 'Can any of us look back to those Councils with satisfaction as to the past or hope for the future?'[5] By October Lytton had his war, which went well.[6] At his Guildhall speech in November Disraeli asserted defiantly Britain's empire-building vocation and her unimpaired strength and power. 'The party is what is called on its legs again', he exulted to Lady Bradford, 'and jingoism triumphant!'[7] The short parliamentary session called in December to provide grants for the war displayed the parliamentary part in sound heart. Even Cairns found himself echoing the prevalent military mood: 'I congratulate you on your great battle & victory,' he wrote to Northcote, 'the significance of which is immense.'[8] Disraeli congratulated the Queen on 'a brilliant and enduring success' for her arms.[9]

It was on the strength of the brilliant Afghan campaign in the autumn of 1878 that Ellis Ashmead Bartlett, fresh from his earlier 'jingo' manifestations, launched his project for a 'Patriotic Association' for the 'defence of the honour and interests of England, and the maintenance intact of the British Empire'. His scheme was to harness the more respectable elements of the jingo enthusiasm to an institutional form by means of which their energies could be controlled and directed. The association, in turn, would mobilise the masses through propaganda and agitation. Bartlett approached Disraeli, pointing out that although the proposed association would be officially non-partisan, it would act as a conduit for imperially minded Whigs and Liberals. There would, moreover, be no question but that, in practice, the association would 'throw all the weight we might have, and all the enthusiasm that may with judicious treatment be invoked in favour of Lord Beaconsfield at the General Election'. Bartlett stressed, rightly, how much of an 'immense advantage' it was to the Conservative party 'to have the "Imperial" feeling in the nation on its side'. Bartlett undertook to cleanse his association of all potentially embarrassing links with the protectionist lobbyists who had been among his 'rather strange co-workers' in the earlier, headier Hyde Park mob days. Bartlett's brother (who married Lady Burdett-Coutts) assured Corry: 'We are extremely anxious not to identify the Association with any doubtful connections.' By 1880, Bartlett had an impressive cluster of peers, including the Whig duke of Sutherland, to adorn his association. Bartlett projected in the service of this cause a penny weekly, *England*, aimed at a working-class and lower middle-class readership. The first issue appeared in March 1880.[10] By that time, Disraeli had arranged for Bartlett to be nominated for the borough of Eye, vacated for the purpose by Lord Barrington.

From the other quarter of imperial complications, however, there were disturbing developments. In September 1878 Disraeli wrote to Lady Bradford: 'I am not in a state of consternation about Afgh^{n}, and if anything annoys me more than another, it is our Cape affairs, where every day brings forward a new blunder of Twitters.'[11] Lord Carnarvon had indeed in 1877 extended the government's responsibility deep into the interior of southern Africa by annexing the Afrikaner republic of the Transvaal in 1877. Disraeli was persuaded that there were good reasons for this: the Afrikaners were bankrupt, they had no trade, they were threatened on all sides by Zulu and other warlike peoples. Carnarvon's larger motives were to combine the precedent set by his creation of the Canadian federation in 1867 with the recent annexation by consent of the Fiji Islands as an example of empire's civilising vocation. Carnarvon appointed an eminent Indian administrator, Sir Bartle Frere, as governor of Cape Colony and high commissioner in South Africa, with a view to his being the first governor-general of a new South African federation. Frere was dizzied by coming from India to South Africa in something of the same way that Lytton was in coming from Lisbon to India. Great new possibilities and temptations offered themselves in the matter of a civilising vocation in South Africa which had not been on offer in India.

Annexing the Transvaal was intended to rescue the Afrikaners and to be a policy of peace. But the Zulus, who had had every intention of disposing of the Afrikaners, had no intention equally of being run by the British; and Frere soon had a war on his hands. Beach, Carnarvon's successor in 1878, found it difficult to restrain the masterful Frere's desire for an all-out war to establish the dominance of white civilisation once and for all. 'But I cannot really control him without a telegraph,' as Beach explained to a dismayed Disraeli. ('I don't know that I could with one.')[12] Disraeli had no interest in South Africa, and simply wanted it not to be a problem. It was doubly vexing that Carnarvon was free with critical comment. 'What annoys me more than all in today's papers', Corry told Disraeli on 23 September, 'is the coincident appearance of the speech by that accursed little Twitters.'[13] Nevertheless, when Frere ignored the cabinet's desire to stave off yet another war in January 1879, Beach consoled himself with the hope of a 'short and successful' war, 'like the Afghan campaign'.[14]

What Beach got, on 22 January, at Isandhlwana, was the shock of a British column's being wiped out. The government, the party, and the jingo public, were stunned. Nothing like it was known in most living memories; nothing, in fact, to match it was known since the 'signal catastrophe' of 1842 in Afghanistan. Reinforcements, and Sir Garnet Wolseley, were rushed out. Salisbury wanted to get rid of Frere and replace him with Napier, the conqueror of Abyssinia, then governor of Gibraltar; arguing that efforts to defend Frere would risk a breakdown in the Commons.[15] But Frere was a hero of the 'forward' party and the jingoes, and Disraeli was stuck with him. The party in both houses stood firm in supporting the government's refusal to recall Frere. Salisbury's later analysis of the problems of these complications stressed again the effects of Disraeli's shrinking from 'exercising coercion on any of his subordinates' within a political context bereft of any coherent overall policy of imperial design.

> Thus it became possible that the Transvaal should be annexed – not indeed against the will of the cabinet but – entirely without its knowledge. Lord Carnarvon wished to do it. Lord Beaconsfield was persuaded that it was an excellent thing to do: i.e. the responsible head of the department told him, and he believed, that it was an excellent thing to do – and it was done. Again, Bartle Frere should have been recalled as soon as the news of his *ultimatum* reached England. We should then have escaped in appearance, as well as in reality, the responsibility for the Zulu War. So thought the majority of the cabinet: so thought Dizzy himself. But the Queen was strongly opposed to it, and Hicks Beach was strongly opposed to it: and the Prime Minister was unable to resist his sovereign and the Colonial Secretary together. Again it was decided in cabinet that the invasion of Afghanistan should take place only through one pass. Lytton objected. Because Lytton did Hardy did. Because Hardy did Dizzy did: – for was not Hardy at the head of the India Office? and so the plan was altered.[16]

Salisbury at the Foreign Office

1

At the Foreign Office Salisbury grappled with his own departmental problems. After the scandal of Derby's miserable denouement there, it was important for the party's steadiness and morale that a grip be taken and be seen to be taken on foreign policy. Salisbury never underestimated the importance of big effects and broad impressions. The Congress of Berlin made him a buoyant party property. He saw his role as sustaining buoyancy while dismantling Disraeli's atavistic Palmerstonism within his department and while attempting, in cabinet, to help stem the worst consequences of Indian and colonial misadventures. Salisbury's standing in the party was enhanced not only by his succeeding Derby at the Foreign Office. It was enhanced by his resolute support for the sending of the fleet to Constantinople. Although a consistent critic of Disraeli's Eastern policy, or lack of policy, Salisbury nonetheless contrived to gain party credit from the Eastern Question.

Of all the matters for which he was responsible at the Foreign Office Salisbury was well aware that Egypt bulked largest in the view of the Conservative party. This became the hub around which most of his thinking and attention revolved. On the larger scale he had to concern himself with getting back on terms with the Russians, and easing them out of Bulgaria (Dufferin was appointed to St. Petersburg for that). He had to assess the implications of Bismarck's new course and the move to alliance with Austria-Hungary. There were endless problems in getting the Turks to fulfil their obligations to the Greeks and others under the Berlin treaty and to honour their promises of reforms under the Anglo-Turkish Convention ('I am afraid Layard's exquisite temper is giving way').[17] All these were affairs of consequence, but they had little bearing on opinion and therefore were not of primary political or party concern. But ever since the Suez shares purchase Egypt had been very much such a concern. Conservatives did not accept the justice of Gladstone's accusation that, in an age of 'forward' empire, the purchase of the canal shares together with, in 1877, the effective supervision of Egyptian finances in the interests of her creditors, would mean ultimately the logic of territorial acquisition, and Egypt's becoming 'the almost certain egg of a North African empire'. At the same time they accepted that the importance of Egypt as a British interest gave such an accusation a certain inherent plausibility. But as long as the Ottoman Empire was a going concern and as long as the khedival regime in Cairo was a going concern, there would be no interest or advantage for Britain in any kind of North African empire.

Egypt was officially Salisbury's responsibility at the Foreign Office because its khedive was a tributary vassal of the Ottoman sultan. Egypt's status and position was in practice profoundly ambiguous, and its status and position in British policy and Conservative thinking and sentiment was also profoundly ambiguous. As secretary for India, Salisbury had provocatively referred in September 1876 to 'the new British province of Egypt'. That was a telling measure in practice of Salisbury's insistent doctrine at that time that the Palmerstonian tradition was at an end. Northcote had taken that point perfectly in his representations to Derby in May 1877 that should the Ottoman Empire crumble, 'we seem bound by the law of self-preservation to assure ourselves of Egypt'. This was as yet a minority strain of Conservative thinking. Disraeli never shared it because he never accepted its premiss. Vociferous advocacy of British occupation of Egypt at this time tended to come from the group of Liberals around Edward Dicey, editor of the *Observer*, who, like Fitzjames Stephen, looked upon the existence of a Conservative government in 'these days' as a 'fortunate anomaly'.[18]

The Anglo-Turkish Convention represented a Disraelian policy with which Salisbury could collaborate. It was Disraelian in that it marked out the Turkish heartland, Asia Minor, as the ground of Britain's Near Eastern stance in support of Turkey. Salisbury collaborated because it provided Cyprus as a *pied à terre* and because it gave Britain a remedial voice in Turkish affairs; and above all because it expressed a confident new outlook in British policy. Salisbury encouraged Arthur Balfour to address the issue in the Commons on the theme that by the convention Britain had 'in the face of Europe made a strong declaration of *Policy*'.[19] Beside this, the embarrassing circumstance that Cyprus turned out to be useless for its designated purpose counted for little. In any case, Salisbury did not expect any effective Turkish realities behind the strong declaration of British policy. He took a wry view of Turkish reform promises and grand schemes for a rail link between Scanderoon and Baghdad:

> we shall get the promises of the reforms, which will not be kept: we shall set to work on the railway: we shall get or claim the right to defend the railway, & then we shall carry out with a strong hand what had been promised. All this may happen *if* the railway becomes a reality. But can anything be a reality in the hands of the Duke of Sutherland, Sir Arnold Kemball, & a list of Directors as long as your arm?[20]

And would France be content with so small a share in this 'great scheme' for Asia Minor? ('I prefer the policy, if it be practicable, of giving her Tunis to gnaw at.')[21]

The French, however, had no intention of taking a small share in arranging the affairs of Egypt. Their vulnerable financial houses held the largest share of the Egyptian debt and the firmest resolve to see it paid. Salisbury's policy was to exploit systematically this French financial preoccupation. For British support on the debt question Salisbury exacted from the French political concessions. As he put it, 'the only motive that would reconcile France to our supremacy would be the belief that, without our intervention, the interest would not be paid, and that with it, it would be'.[22] Salisbury carefully kept a clear distance from the British bondholders. He was even less disposed to take up their cause 'out of pure gaiety of heart' than he had that of the Turkish debt bondholders at Berlin.[23] Salisbury's concern for wretchedly oppressed masses was as genuine in the case of the Egyptians as elsewhere in the East; but it was tempered in the short run at least by the need to exact enough from Egyptian taxpayers to keep the French bondholders content. The climax to this policy of bribing the French by squeezing the Egyptians hard for money came in August 1877 with the appointment of Rivers Wilson as co-minister of finance with the highly Anglophile Nubar Pasha. Salisbury exulted: 'all will follow – deputies, increased influence'; 'English predominance in Egypt' would ineluctably be set in train.[24] Salisbury's instructions to Rivers Wilson were appropriate to a proconsul. They anticipated the later policies of Evelyn Baring and

Alfred Milner and the making of Egypt a showpiece of enlightened British imperialism.

2

Salisbury's ingenious policy was ruined by Egyptian unwillingness to be wrung for it. Something like 85 per cent of the Egyptian revenue was expatriated to service the debt. Nationalist reaction to European domination built up, especially among unpaid army officers. Salisbury was more worried that French impatience with Egyptian attempts to wriggle out of the Anglo-French financial grip would lead them to drastic measures. He feared they were 'going too far & too fast' in their notions of deposing the khedive. He joked uneasily with Northcote that the French should wait until 'some storm occurs in France' to divert public attention, 'when it can be done in safety'. 'After all – the acquisitions of most governments won't bear close scrutiny.'[25] In the end, it was a combination of a last desperate wriggle by Khedive Ismail in 1879 and an associated insurrection of the Egyptian army that wrecked Salisbury's plans. Prince Hassan, Ismail's brother, apologised profusely to Rivers Wilson; but Rivers Wilson and Nubar were not reinstated in the finance ministry. Led by the French, 'Europe' arranged that Ismail be dethroned by the sultan and replaced as khedive by his more malleable son, Tewfik. A new Anglo-French dual control of Egyptian finances was set up, not overtly and provocatively a part of the official Egyptian government, but covertly behind the scenes. In this arrangement the French insisted on parity. Salisbury tried to be philosophical about his failure:

> When you have got a neighbour and faithful ally who is bent on meddling in a country in which you are deeply interested – you have three courses open to you. You may renounce – or monopolise – or share. Renouncing would have been to place the French across our road to India. Monopolising would have been very near to the risk of war. So we resolved to share.[26]

All this new entanglement at a time when old entanglements in South Africa and Afghanistan were not going happily caused many Conservatives dismay and anxiety. There was embarrassment about Britain's role as creditors' bailiff. Northcote had more cause than most. Salisbury had to steer him gently away from 'too drastic' disentanglement. 'We cannot cut the tow rope so clean as that.' Britain must keep 'abreast of France' in any hold on the administration of Egypt. 'The position is an anxious one – because it is ambiguous, & hard to explain publicly. But the Khedive is going straight on to ruin & we cannot afford to be out of the way when the crash comes.' Britain had a stake in the Egyptian revenue, in the payment of the tribute, and in the Suez Canal shares. 'But above all these "entanglements" is the apprehension, which forced us to accept them, that if we stand aside France will become as dominant there as she is in Tunis.'[27] Indeed, Salisbury was extremely anxious in June 1879 that the deposition of the khedive would give the French an opportunity to intervene by force. Britain would be helpless to intervene jointly, as Salisbury pointed out to Northcote: 'all our force is locked up. Pa! that Bartle Frere! I should like to construct for him a gibbet twice the height of Hassan's.'[28]

Luckily the French made no such move. Salisbury advised Northcote as to how to present the Anglo-French condominium in Egypt to the House of Commons. French policy, as expounded by Waddington, the French premier, consistently pressed the cause of the French financial institutions with an interest in the Egyptian debt.

> Waddington has confessed to a bondholders' policy – & you will be charged tomorrow night with having the same. You may with perfect truth energetically repudiate such a charge. We have had no thought of bondholders. What we have dreaded is anarchy. . . . We don't want Egypt to become another Turkey. . . . If without speaking plain you can hint that the very fact of France taking a bondholders' interest forced us to take a political interest, you will touch the kernel of the case.[29]

Northcote had no trouble with the Commons. In the midst of tribulations in South Africa and Afghanistan, Egypt was thankfully a quiet imperial backwater. Salisbury had not managed to pull off the subtle coup of British supremacy with French consent; but he had established a British interest in Egypt which, if a second best, was still second to none. Salisbury congratulated Northcote on indications of public confidence: 'It shows that your speech has told: & that a little butter will go a long way.'[30]

South Africa and Afghanistan

1

On 9 April 1879 Cranbrook recorded in his diary: 'Certainly the world is out of joint.' A cabinet on the previous day had confronted a list of eight critical imperial problems, headed by 'Frere & S. Africa', and descending through such items as 'Malet on Turkish imbecility' to 'Khedive's dethronement proposed' and 'treaty with Yakoob', the newly installed ruler of Afghanistan.[31]

Lord Chelmsford, in command in South Africa until Wolseley arrived, adopted a strategy of extreme caution after the shock of Isandhlwana to make up for the rashness which had provoked the disaster. There were Conservative murmurings of impatience. Andrew Montagu passed word on to Corry: 'I think you ought to know how strong & *increasing* is the feeling of utter distrust in Ld Chelmsford's command.'[32] Disraeli was so incensed at what he considered Chelmsford's discreditable dilatoriness that he later refused the queen's express desire that he receive Chelmsford at Hughenden. Then, to add a symbolically macabre touch, came the death in a futile skirmish of the prince imperial of France, the so-styled Napoleon IV, a royal favourite. Chelmsford managed to scramble through a campaign and put down Zulu resistance by July 1879. But the damage and scandal left British South African policy hopelessly compromised. The Cape government had never liked Carnarvon's plans to subordinate it to a great South Africa. The Dutch Afrikaner Boers feared that in Bartle Frere's grand vision of South Africa there would be but little place for them and little chance of realising their own ambitions of a free and pure Afrikaner state.

Worse was soon to come in Afghanistan. A rising in Kabul led to the massacre of Sir Louis Cavagnari and the British mission imposed on the Afghans by Lytton, who planned to dismember the country. Salisbury condoled with Disraeli on 11 September on '*the* catastrophe'.[33] Cranbrook visited the stricken prime minister at Hughenden: 'The Chief is well but feels deeply this new trial.'[34] Cranbrook reported on the catastrophe to Cairns:

> Beaconsfield was well but this dreadful business had made him low and he expressed a sense of all things being adverse which is natural and very depressing. Indeed as I said to him The stars in their courses fight against us – and if we survive our accumulated troubles what can destroy us hereafter?[35]

The Conservative government was confronted with the prospect of a second campaign in Afghanistan to restore the situation. As Northcote noted, 'I am afraid we have a troublesome business before us in Affghanistan.' It was going to be as difficult to prop up the puppet emir, Yakub, as it would be to annex the country.[36] Lytton had entirely failed to find the way in fixing a buffer between complete non-intervention and taking on the whole management of Afghanistan. Salisbury in 1876 had offered Persia as a model of this required flexibility of policy.[37] He was now, as an old India hand, in a position to offer, amid the wreckage, further advice on the strategic disposal of Herat:

> The question – shall we lean on the Persian or the Affghan leg is still perplexing. The Persian Shah is frightened of Russia, no doubt: & is therefore inclined to betray us. But the Affghan Amir (if not a traitor) is so weak that his good dispositions, supposing them to exist, are perfectly useless. To which then shall we confide Herat? The Shah may sell it: the Amir will certainly lose it. We have a certain hold on both, i.e. we can do both a certain amount of harm. But that species of influence though it may overcome ill will, or self-interest, is perfectly useless with impotence. I lean therefore to the view that the Shah will serve us better in Herat than the Amir. We may frighten the Shah, & so manage him: but it is perfectly idle to attempt to manage the Amir: for when managed he can do nothing.
>
> If he retains any kind of value, I should be inclined to transport him to Candahar – & leave the Caboolees to cook in their own gravy.[38]

The wreckage, however, was never sufficiently cleared to permit this 'scientific' arrangement.

Corry did his best to comfort Disraeli. Corry had already been advised by Skene that a dissolution of Parliament in the autumn of 1879 might be the best chance for the government. Skene feared there was little or no chance of 'prosperous times coming back in time to help us, and the Protectionist agit[n].

is a very awkward one, is daily gaining strength and in spring there will be the Bill to pay for the Zulu war'. Skene had well-founded misgivings about the possibility that Afghanistan might 'also efface our successful European policy'. He thought it 'not impossible that before spring great complications may occur'. Skene's judgement was that the Conservative party in July 1879 did not stand 'nearly so well as we did last Autumn when I think our real chance of a great victory was missed – but I should imagine we may hold our own now & no one can say how we shall stand in the future especially if the harvest is a failure as seems probable'.[39]

That was before the catastrophe in Afghanistan. But even so, Corry, by way of soothing assurances to 'my beloved Chief' that 'you had no alternative to your policy, and that its execution was purely an Indian matter', now offered a plan to snatch victory from the jaws of disaster.

> I assume, now, that it is going to be a great War. . . . Nothing can look worse! But the war will be popular; and the opposition are sure to be unwise. May not one good out of evil be an opportunity for going to the country, before the bad harvest and the impending reduction of wages tell their tale?[40]

Dyke, however, was offering different advice,[41] and parliament remained undissolved. In any case, Corry's expectations of a popular war postulated a campaign as brief, decisive, and glorious as the 1878 adventure. The second Afghan campaign, however, dragged on, with mixed fortunes, throughout the autumn and winter of 1879–80; and Afghanistan was not to be pacified in the lifetime of the Conservative government.

Cranbrook reported to Cairns from Balmoral at the beginning of October:

> The Chief talked of a cabinet soon. . . . He says the opposition will concentrate their attack on Zululand – but . . . if S. Africa is at peace they will not be regarded. Affghanistan affords a better field for them. . . . They are carrying on the Campaign with vigour and fortune seems to be against us. Personally I have no dread of being out but as you said cannot be indifferent to our successors and fear that they will pay for their places to the public detriment.[42]

Cranbrook mused at Balmoral, wondering if it would be his last visit there. 'No use speculating but our opponents are moving every force against us & there have been misfortunes which will be construed as misdoings naturally enough. Speeches are multiplying.'[43]

2

Given that the party leadership had decided against dissolving parliament in autumn 1879, Disraeli had no great lead to give in the season of speeches 'out of doors'. At the Guildhall in 1878 he had spoken amid triumphant jingoism with the party 'on its legs again'. In 1879 he was on the defensive. One of the main Liberal lines of attack, led by Gladstone, was that empire abroad was a threat to freedom at home. Gladstone had made much of the horror of Indian troops, untrammelled by the Mutiny Act, being brought so near as Malta; evoking memories of the 'epoch of Charles I'.[44] Disraeli insisted at the Guildhall in November that the citizens of London were not ashamed of their empire and would not be beguiled into believing that in maintaining it they might forfeit their liberties. Disraeli professed to recall that 'one of the greatest of the Romans' described his politics as *Imperium et Libertas*; which 'would not make a bad programme for a British Ministry'.[45] The grammar was questionable; and no one ever discovered who the great Roman was.[46] But in any case it was the profession of a tired man and a party leader with no more bolts to shoot. He could offer only hope for trade and patience for agriculture.

The case was far different with Gladstone. Galvanised by a misconception that dissolution of parliament was imminent, the abdicated Liberal leader, after careful consultation with the Liberal whip, decided to abandon his Greenwich seat and select a conspicuous Conservative-held but vulnerable county constituency in which to set up a comprehensive challenge to and indictment of Disraeli and the Conservative government's record in power. The selected target was Midlothian, or Edinburghshire, won for the Conservatives in 1874 by Lord Dalkeith, heir to the duke of Buccleuch. Gladstone's electioneering technique was a refinement of the pattern he had established in Lancashire in 1868 whereby he toured the constituency making a series of speeches on major specific issues at different places, addressed ostensibly to the constituency, but in practice to the electorate at large. Cranbrook recorded on 27 November: 'Gladstone has begun his electioneering, an enormous speech without novelty and disgracefully bitter.'[47] Novelty was the last thing Gladstone felt in need of. He framed his indictment from the materials familiar in his usage since his intervention over the Bulgarian atrocities in 1876, and well diffused since in speech and print. Against Disraeli and all his works Gladstone was in a state of moral rage. He declared at a meeting in Oxford in January 1878 that for the past 18 months he had 'played the part of an agitator', with the purpose 'day and night, week by week, month by month, to counterwork as well as I could what I believe to be the purpose of Lord Beaconsfield'.[48] To Disraeli this declaration exposed a 'vindictive fiend' behind the fallen mask of a pious Christian. Disraeli was getting a more intense dose of the moral ban to which Palmerston had been subjected in the later 1850s. The difference was that whereas circumstances in 1859 obliged Gladstone to suspend his hunting of Palmerston, nothing in 1879 stood in the way of his tracking his quarry to the kill.

The hunting image was apt; Gladstone chose it himself. His loyal biographer, Morley, discreetly suppressed Gladstone's choice. Disraeli's equally loyal biographer, Buckle, unaware of Morley's discretion, ironically adopted the same image independently: Gladstone the relentlessly stalking hunter.[49] Gladstone identified his quarry as 'Beaconsfieldism', a composite of moral delinquencies in politics, with reference especially to foreign and imperial policy. His 'pilgrimage of passion' (in Disraeli's disgusted phrase) to Midlothian was an appeal directly to what he had convinced himself was a sense of righteousness abiding in the masses, over the heads of the Whigs and moderates who had thwarted his quest against Disraeli in parliament. Although misconceived in relation to the anticipated dissolution, Gladstone's Midlothian campaign, largely for that very reason, fortuitously took on a commanding stature as a dramatic public event. Amid an unprecedented season of recessional oratory, Gladstone's almost gladiatorial challenge at Midlothian exacerbated the adversarial strain in politics. Gladstone dominated the arguments of the parliamentary recess. And his arguments against Conservative foreign and imperial policy hit the harder in the immediate aftermath of what could be given the colour of a bondholder's annexation of Egypt and in the midst of the wreckage of the government's Afghan policy. Gladstone framed a moral indictment of Disraeli's imposition upon his government of a comprehensive and sinister imperial design, encompassing deep Suez plots, Indian Caesarism, virtual complicity in atrocities, unholy alliance with Metternichian Austria, and consistent suppression of the freedom of small struggling peoples, whether in Europe, North Africa, South Africa, or Central Asia.

Gladstone's arguments had a plausibility all too perversely flattering to the struggling Conservative government. Gladstone's accusation that there must be a plot behind so elaborate a play took to itself a natural demagogic authority. To Gladstone in 1880 the 'downfall of Beaconsfieldism' seemed 'like the vanishing of some vast magnificent castle in an Italian romance'. He thought the 'gradual unravelling of the tangled knots of the foreign and Indian policy' would 'indeed be a task for skilled and strong hands'.[50] Derby's comment in 1875 on the Suez coup was perhaps more apropos:

> It shows also what guess-work the management of English administration is. . . . I have often said that an English Cabinet is probably the only body of men in the world which is compelled to guess at its employers' wishes, under penalty of abuse and failure if it guesses wrong.[51]

As Salisbury pointed out, the notion of Disraeli, ascendant in cabinet, imposing consistent policies of design on submissive colleagues, was grotesquely the opposite of the actual case. Manners's question to Cairns in October 1878 about the sad record of attempts at 'cabinet control'[52] made the same point from a different angle. Manners's assumption that 'free scope' for men in the field could not do worse than the muddled compromises of twelve ill-informed men in Whitehall seemed unanswerable at that moment of apparently grand proconsular achievements; but it was to be proved comprehensively false.

The fact was that the foreign and imperial policies of the Conservative government were largely characterised by both these kinds of debility. Prosaic reality, embedded in the voluminous archives of the responsible participants, reveals a picture of confused and conflicting and usually unreconciled aims and attitudes. 'Together', concludes one recent scholarly investigator, 'they constitute a body of evidence overwhelming in its corroboration of the failure of the government as a whole to develop a coherent strategy with respect to the conduct of external affairs.' Liberal accusations that Disraelian imperialism posed a threat to British democracy were wide of the mark. 'British democracy posed a threat to the Empire rather than the reverse.'[53]

Notes and References

1 Derby Diary, 7 Oct. 1877.
2 Buckle, ii, 1251.
3 Northcote to Cairns, 26 Sept. 1878; PRO, Cairns 30/51/5.
4 Salisbury to Northcote, 27 Sept. 1878; BL, Iddesleigh 50019, 12.
5 Manners to Cairns, 11 Oct. 1878; PRO, Cairns 30/51/13.
6 See J. L. Duthie, 'Lord Lytton and the second Afghan war: a psychohistorical study', *Victorian Studies* (1983–4), and M. Cowling, 'Lytton, the cabinet, and the Russians', *English Historical Review* (1961).
7 Buckle, ii, 1265.
8 Cairns to Northcote, 14 Dec. 1878; BL, Iddesleigh 50021, 132.
9 Buckle, ii, 1277.
10 See H. Cunningham, 'Jingoism in 1877–78', *Victorian Studies* (1971); and 'The Conservative party and patriotism', in R. Colls and P. Dodd (eds), *Englishness. Politics and Culture, 1880–1920* (1986), 287.
11 Buckle, ii, 1291.
12 *Ibid.*, 1295.
13 Corry to Beaconsfield, 23 Sept. 1878; HP, B/XX/Co/125.
14 Buckle, ii, 1291.
15 Salisbury to Beaconsfield, 11 March 1879; HP, B/XX/Ce/112.
16 Balfour memo., 10 May 1880; BL, Balfour 49688, 24–5.
17 Salisbury to Beaconsfield, 2 Jan. 1880; HP, B/XX/Ce/132.
18 R.T. Shannon, *Gladstone and the Bulgarian Agitation, 1876* (1963), 214–15.
19 Balfour to Salisbury, 1 Aug. 1878; BL, Balfour 49688, 11–12.
20 Salisbury to Northcote, 5 Aug. 1878; BL, Iddesleigh 50019, 99.
21 Salisbury to Northcote, 27 Aug. 1878; BL, Iddesleigh 50019, 113.
22 R. A. Atkins, 'The Conservatives and Egypt, 1875–1880', *Journal of Imperial and Commonwealth History* (1973–4), 197.
23 Salisbury to Northcote, 20 June 1878; BL, Iddesleigh 50019, 76.
24 Atkins, 'The Conservatives and Egypt', 197.
25 Salisbury to Northcote, 3 July 1878; BL, Iddesleigh 50019, 87.
26 Cecil, *Salisbury*, ii, 331–2.
27 Salisbury to Northcote, 11 May 1879; BL, Iddesleigh 50019, 148.
28 Salisbury to Northcote, 13 June 1879; BL, Iddesleigh 50019, 155.
29 Salisbury to Northcote, 10 Aug. 1879; BL, Iddesleigh 50019, 119.
30 Salisbury to Northcote, 29 Aug. 1879; BL, Iddesleigh 50019, 173.
31 Hardy, *Diary*, 406.
32 Montagu to Corry, 17 March 1879; HP, B/XXI/M/427.
33 Salisbury to Beaconsfield, 11 Sept. 1879; HP, B/XXI/Ce/308.

34 Hardy, *Diary*, 420.
35 Cranbrook to Cairns, 12 Sept. 1879; PRO, Cairns 30/51/7.
36 Northcote to Cairns, 12 Sept. 1879; PRO, Cairns 30/51/5.
37 Salisbury to Disraeli, 10 Jan. 1876; HP, B/XX/Ce/68.
38 Salisbury to Northcote, 24 Sept. 1879; BL, Iddesleigh 50019, 176.
39 Skene to Corry, 16 July 1879; HP, B/XXI/S/280.
40 Corry to Beaconsfield, 17 Sept. 1879; HP, B/XX/Co/128.
41 See below, 362–3.
42 Cranbrook to Cairns, 1 Oct. 1879; PRO, Cairns 30/51/7.
43 Hardy, *Diary*, 424.
44 W. E. Gladstone, 'Liberty in the East and West', *Nineteenth Century* (1878), 1155, 1163, 1168.
45 Buckle, ii, 1367.
46 For materials bearing on the mystery consult HP, B/XII/J.
47 Hardy, *Diary*, 428.
48 *The Times*, 31 Jan. 1878, 10.
49 R.T. Shannon, 'Gladstone and British Balkan policy', in R. Melville and H.J. Schröder (eds.), *Der Berliner Kongress von 1878* (Wiesbaden, 1982), 166.
50 Morley, *Gladstone*, ii, 223.
51 Derby Diary, 29 Nov. 75.
52 See above, 348.
53 P.J.Durrans, 'A two-edged sword: the Liberal attack on Disraelian imperialism', *Journal of Imperial and Commonwealth History* (1981–2), 274–5, 279.

Chapter 14

The election of 1880: Toryism disestablished

Augurs and entrails

1

Amid the tribulations of cabinet resistance to Northcote's taxation plans in July 1879, Disraeli received this advice from his chief whip:

> As the sixth Session of the present parliament is now closing, I wish to place shortly before you my views as to the Political Situation. During the past few months I have had ample information from Agents, Chairmen of Election Committees and others as to our prospects and position. The opinion I can form from all Reports which have reached me, is to the following effect. That in the South, East & West of England your Government is more popular, at this moment, than at any period during the past three years – that in the North bad Trade will tell against us but not to any serious extent – that in Scotland although we shall lose a few seats, our party is organising in a manner we have never before attempted. In Ireland the split in the Home Rule Party has so far altered our position that our estimate of loss is reduced almost to a minimum. After a most careful review of the Position, by our Political Committee I have a strong opinion that we need not fear an appeal to the Constituencies. The all important question for your cabinet to consider is how & when this appeal should be made. In deciding this, I would humbly suggest, that you should consider your position as a whole & not from a Financial point of view alone. You have to estimate the strength you possess in having solved some of the most difficult problems in Foreign Affairs, & in having landed the Country through difficulties which might have destroyed many Governments, & place it fairly in the balance against the odium which you may incur from having to ask the Country to pay for the success you have achieved.
>
> Then at once arises the question as to how you propose to deal with Finance, & on your conduct of that depends to my mind your future success. You can not it seems to me separate without danger, your Estimate of the Financial position, from that of your general position, & your ultimate decision as to the date of Dissolution assuming that a debt must be incurred involving taxation next year.
>
> I place before you two alternatives.
>
> To meet parliament next Session & state Taxation direct or indirect is necessary. The other to dissolve parliament next February. In the second case you will be told that having pursued an ambitious & disturbing Policy you dare not ask the country to pay the Bill – that your postponement of liabilities is most immoral & you will be subject to every kind of violent declamation.

> If on the other hand you dissolve after Taxes have been actually imposed you have an argument against you which is simply invincible. I would humbly venture to suggest therefore that if Taxation be inevitable, as little Financial information as possible should be given to our opponents before the close of this Session. If the bill for the Zulu war be less than our opponents prophesy we shall be the gainers. At the very worst we shall be fighting with only this incubus upon our shoulders – a possible debt and Taxation to a limited amount accruing from a war, commenced without the sanction of your Government.
>
> I have only to say further that I have the greatest confidence in the efforts now being made, for the forthcoming Registration.[1]

In recommending this prudently evasive stratagem, Dyke reckoned without Northcote's ultimatum of 29 July that he felt honour bound to meet parliament in a new session before dissolution, quite apart from financial considerations. Given that Northcote felt his position as chancellor of the Exchequer 'seriously shaken' in any case, his colleagues were not prepared to defy him as to the extra session; and so it was arranged eventually that the government would meet parliament in the new year, and confront the 'invincible argument'.

In such circumstances Dyke felt his own position somewhat compromised. Corry reported to Disraeli in September 1879 from the Scottish highlands:

> Dyke was at Auchnashelloch [*chez* Ivor Guest]: anxious of course, but not really shaken in his confidence as to the future. His opinion is in favour of an early dissolution – as soon even as January – when the new Registers will come into force. He would insist on waiting till then; rather on account of the extraordinary care which, this year, we have given to registration, than on the strength of returns, which can not yet be satisfactorily made.
>
> I wish I could share all his view as to the result!

Both Corry and Dyke felt reassured that Disraeli's recent speech at the annual Buckinghamshire agricultural gathering at Aylesbury would 'keep the Landlords and Farmers together – for the present'.[2]

It was at this time that Adam, the Liberal whip, was estimating a Liberal majority of 50; and after Gladstone's Midlothian campaign in November–December, 'Adam's figures became so optimistic that Granville declined to believe them.'[3] Adam certainly would not have agreed with Disraeli that Gladstone's premature excursion to Midlothian was a mere waste of powder and shot. There was an attempt at a Conservative counter-attack. Balfour conferred with Dalkeith (MP for Midlothian) and Graham Montgomery (former Scottish whip) in Edinburgh, and it was agreed to urge Disraeli to send up 'a cabinet Minister to hold a meeting here or in Glasgow, as a kind of reply to W.E.G. and for the purpose of encouraging the growth of that very tender plant – Scotch Conservatism.' A 'big gun' was essential, because otherwise *The Scotsman* 'declines to publish adequate reports of Conservative speeches and meetings'. Lord George Hamilton gallantly went up to give battle to the ogre. Salisbury congratulated Northcote: 'You have smashed up Gladstone pretty handsomely on the financial question. He must have lost his head, to expose himself to such wholesale fictions.'[4] It is doubtful whether, in the atmosphere created by Gladstone of a holy drama of political morality, details about finance, fictional or not, were much to the point.

Nor, in general, was the Conservative party outgunned in the great recessional speaking campaign. Granville, at the opening of the 1880 session, remarked that 'in 1879 the majority of the cabinet have done more of what is vulgarly known as "stumping the country" than any previous Administration has done during all the Recesses of any one parliament'.[5] This campaign reflected a special sense of urgency. The 1874 parliament was by now an unusually old one. As Liberals gained confidence, they began to press that it had become unreasonably so. Within the limits of the Septennial Act, it was open to Disraeli to carry on to the beginning of 1881; but that would have given ammunition to Radicals already demanding five-year parliaments. Among Disraeli's colleagues, Cairns certainly preferred waiting until the autumn of 1880 before dissolving;[6] but, especially after the hesitations of late 1879, there was a sense that the mounting pressures of expectation doomed the 1880 session to curtailment. To this sense of urgency Conservatives added their concern not to allow Liberals free play in exploiting the problems of trade and agricultural depression. Disraeli was acutely anxious about the subversion of the Farmers' Alliance and what he called 'Cockney agitators' stirring up tenant farmers against landlords.[7] One motive for dissolving as early as possible in 1880, as he explained to Salisbury, was to get in ahead of an incipient rural revolt.[8] Salisbury's contribution on the theme of depression was one of the earlier of what later became known as his 'blazing indiscretions'. At Manchester, famed as the capital of free trade, in October, he discoursed on the advantages offered by tariffs in providing the means wherewith to negotiate equitable commercial reciprocity. This was not to be the last occasion on which he disconcerted his political friends on that particular topic.

2

By the end of 1879 each by-election took on something of the character of a ritual Roman sacrifice, with augurs picking over entrails and looking anxiously at the flight patterns of birds in the skies overhead. By-election tidings from Scotland were not of an encouraging cast. Richmond was in hopes that Elgin and Nairn (Morayshire) could be taken from the Liberals. But so demoralising was the Conservative defeat that the Liberal was unopposed at the general election. As Lord Dalkeith put it, appealing for help in the form of some senior cabinet minister at Midlothian, 'I am sorry to say that half Scotland forms its opinions after reading the Scotsman.' Scottish popular Conservatism was in any case stronger in the west of Scotland than the east.[9]

Dyke's health collapsed just when Roebuck's death led to speculation about a possible Conservative capture of the veteran Radical's Sheffield seat. Both Roebuck and Sheffield, famed for its armour and weaponry, had been conspicuously friendly to the government's anti-Russian foreign policy. Lady Salisbury put to Disraeli Sheffield's electoral ritual as offering auguries ominous or auspicious: 'We are all wondering how Sheffield has gone. *If* we win the elections are safe – but I fear we shall not.'[10] Still, in such a seat even a good Conservative showing would be encouraging. No Conservative had sat for the city since 1832. No Conservative challenged in 1874. But, as the free trade veteran Ashworth pointed out, Sheffield was 'always *bad*'. C.B. Stuart Wortley came close enough in January 1880 (13,584 to 14,062) to claim moral victory. He reported to Disraeli that the main issue in the contest was 'undoubtedly the electoral approval or not of the *foreign policy* of yr Ldship's administration'. 'Besides scoring so many Liberal votes, we polled those of some out & – out radicals.' The duke of Norfolk's agent joined the Conservative committee (the duke had extensive Sheffield interests) and secured the votes of English Roman Catholics. However, 'the great efforts made by a certain Home Rule MP (assisted by Mr. Mundella) . . . are supposed to have persuaded the Irish Catholics & all . . . worth 1200 votes.'[11] Wharncliffe, Stuart Wortley's cousin, added more detail, stressing that the vote was 'largely gratifying', there being a majority for the Conservatives of 'pure Sheffield voters', beaten only by 'some secret understanding between the Radicals & Home Rulers'. 'I know that the other party regard it as virtually a defeat, and our people are elated.'[12]

On the whole, Sheffield could be interpreted as an auspicious augury. Conservatism, moreover, was to benefit further from the Norfolk interest. Disraeli was much gratified to be asked by the duke of Norfolk to bless his brother-in-law Lord Edmund Talbot's candidacy at Burnley.[13] Both were immediately invited to Hughenden (to no avail, as it happened; Peter Rylands held the seat for the Liberals). Conservatism also seemed likely to benefit at large from the English Roman Catholic shift away from Gladstone, who compounded the offence of the *Vatican Decrees* by advising the Italian people on how to bring the Church to heel on the example of the Scottish Free Church and the principles set out in his Irish Disestablishment Act. Disraeli, astonished, recounted in December 1879 that 'Manning, after 10 years' & more non-acquaintance, called on me . . . and sate with me a long time. He is a fervent supporter!!!'[14] The Roman Catholic Church, as Gladstone observed with disgust, was as Russophobe and Austrophile as any jingo. Salisbury, furthermore, reported 'feelers' from the Vatican about gaining more accurate sources of information about British politics. The Curia, it appeared, was 'anxious to detach R.C. priests from Parnell'; and Salisbury was in no doubt that 'we shd encourage any such initiative'.[15]

It was a measure of the critical urgency of the time that Disraeli kept his cabinet in London over Christmas and New Year. (Richmond, deprived of his hunting and shooting, grumbled to Cairns: 'The P.M. has no turn for sporting and thinks every one must be delighted to be in London.')[16] Richmond also noticed that 'Northcote seems so very nervous'.[17] This was hardly surprising. He was about to raid the sinking fund and raise probate duty. There were plans to improve London's water supply and adjust various parliamentary constituencies in a manner calculated to ingratiate the Conservative party with their electors. An Electoral Practices Bill would renew the Ballot Act and incidentally allow borough candidates in England and Wales the same freedom in the hiring of transport of electors to the polls presently enjoyed by county candidates. This in effect signalled Conservative confidence that, if the elections came down to the spending of money, Conservatism would have the advantage.

For Northcote, however, the 'gravest problem' was putting into effective form the plans for relief of Irish distress: disposing, as he put it to Cairns, the 'plunder' of the Irish Church surplus. He was anxious that the matter had to be thought through carefully and all 'crude schemes' which would discredit the Conservative government avoided. There was a great danger that the mishandling of the issue would expose the government to accusations of being 'unstatesmanlike', and give the opposition a chance for the 'credit of superior skill' in holding out hopes for something better, 'and go to the country on some tempting programme, which, whether ultimately fulfilled or not, will serve for the moment of the Elections'.[18]

These qualms were needless. Since the point of the Irish relief bill was to channel the plunder with statesmanlike care into the responsible hands of improving landlords and keep it out of the irresponsible hands of clamouring exigents, it came down, electorally, to a bill for conserving the Conservative landlord vote and influence – which, by 1880, no longer counted in Ireland anyway. Disraeli made clear at the opening of the session his opinion that the great issue in Ireland, and indeed the great issue of British politics, was the peril of Irish Home Rule and the dismemberment of the United Kingdom. It soon emerged that the session was going to be a sham. Cross (who at one time had wanted to tackle the government of London, the last and yawning gap in municipal reform), made a shambles of the London water bill, and wanted to abandon it. Finance did not take fire; Liberals simply wanted to speed through the routine necessities and clear the way for dissolution. The Irish Home Rulers were conspicuously ungrateful for the relief bill. The only thing to emerge of any note was the elections bill, which was pushed through in record time and which was to be sternly denounced by history as 'the only piece of reactionary electoral legislation of the century'.[19] Since the 'Cabs Bill' was in effect an incitement so spend money at elections, and since the 1880 elections were the most expensive and corrupt elections of the nineteenth century, and since the Conservative party lost heavily by them, Northcote's ingenious little ploy can only be accounted either as a self-inflicted injury by the Conservative party, or simply a waste of time as well as money – probably the latter.

Augurs picking over by-election entrails now dominated the political scene. A Liverpool by-election in February (Sandon as general of the Conservative forces) led to what Cranbrook allowed to be a 'very adequate majority of over 2000' against a Liberal Home Ruler. 'One wd of course have liked a crushing majority but it is enough.' It was enough to encourage Conservatives to a 'general bias' now 'to an early election & if it is pushed for by our opponents they will be gratified I expect soon'. Cranbrook had 'always doubted whether we could keep things going this session'.[20] A Southwark by-election later in February seemed to offer omens decidedly more auspicious: 'a great triumph for the party', with no necessity for reservations. Although two Liberals split their vote, the promising young barrister Edward Clarke still achieved not only the lead but a small plurality. At a cabinet on 14 February the question of dissolution was discussed. There was unanimous agreement to wait further, unless some unexpected crisis should develop out of Irish obstruction or finance; while, as Cranbrook put it, 'these Elections arm us for any course we like'.

3

Thus armed, the party 'wire pullers' offered their advice as to the course advocated at Central Office. Skene conferred with Corry and sent 'rough notes' of their discussion, adding remarks about the impertinence of a novice like himself offering 'any suggestions . . . to so consummate a master of parliamentary tactics as the Prime Minister', and further self-deprecatory comments about his unworthiness which Corry would not have taken too tragically.[21] 'Considerations wh. lead to the conclusion that an early dissolution would be advisable', dated 16 February, listed these points: on foreign policy and Home Rule the Conservative party now had the support of many moderate Liberals, and this would be important in many boroughs as the recent by-elections appeared to demonstrate – 'many moderate Liberals of high courage &c. gave their support to the Govt.' in Liverpool and Southwark; this parliament had been longer than average, and there was the danger of a feeling that the government was 'afraid to appeal to the Country'. The 'revival of trade was now an accomplished fact', and the home trade was not likely to experience a further considerable revival until after a good harvest 'wh. it is hardly safe to predict', and since it would be a long time before the revival was reflected in improved customs and excise returns, it could not help current budget problems. There might be a reverse of fortunes in Afghanistan, with public opinion 'in a very sensitive condition', and if a dissolution were delayed 'we might be forced to dissolve under more unfavourable circumstances'. The Liberal party would no doubt, in consequence of their recent defeats, 'redouble their efforts to perfect their organisation'. The business of the session was being conducted under circumstances which made it 'impossible to carry any measure of importance'. Members of parliament would from this time to the eventual elections be subject to 'continual demands on their resources & a speedy dissolution would be a great saving of expense'. And, finally, it was desirable that in the event of European complications the government should be able to claim that it had the confidence of the country.

Skene's consequent advice as to electoral prospects was modestly congruent with that of Dyke (still laid up with illness):

> With regard to the prospects of the Party in case of a dissolution it is very difficult to give a reliable opinion, but I should be inclined to predict that we should lose 6 or 7 seats in Scotland, 5 or 6 in Ireland and say 5 on balance in England wh. would still leave us a working majority wh. would probably be increased after the Election were the verdict of the country in our favour.
>
> Even were the Seats Bill not carried before the Election we wd. have a substantial advantage in those constituencies to wh. we propose giving an additional member were our proposals known.[22]

Corry does not seem to have been convinced by Skene's estimate. 'I wish I could share all his views as to the result!' had been his comment on Dyke's confident pronouncements in Scotland in the autumn. It is clear from the consternation he was soon to cause at Central Office that Corry was alone among the Conservative managers in taking a sardonic view of prospects.

Cranbrook noted on 19 February that Northcote 'seems to apprehend a state of things wh. must in all probability bring this parliament to a close. I fancy all wish for it.'[23] Northcote and Cross were finding the session unmanageable and pointless. Salisbury's health gave way. Disraeli shifted the cabinet to Salisbury's sick-bed. On 6 March Cranbrook recorded 'a momentous cabinet (Dissolution) in Arlington St', where Salisbury looked 'worn & worried'. Dissolution of the 1874 parliament was announced two days later. Cairns would have preferred an autumn dissolution, 'with a chance of a good harvest & revived trade; but our Ho. of Commons friends were too restless to be restrained'.[24] Disraeli issued his manifesto in the form of a letter to the lord-lieutenant of Ireland, the duke of Marlborough. He denounced those who challenged 'the expediency of the imperial character of this realm' and insisted that peace depended upon the 'presence, not to say the ascendancy, of England in the councils of Europe'. But Disraeli's main thrust was to reiterate his warning of the beginning of the session about the dangers of attacks on the union between Britain and Ireland, and to trust that 'all men of light and leading' would resist that destructive doctrine.[25] This was too prescient for the time. Disraeli ignored what were felt to be pressing and immediate problems of trade and agriculture, and made the party vulnerable to attack for evasiveness. Disraeli had made such a point of relegating Ireland at the beginning of his ministry; this apparently sudden shift puzzled many as seeming to have no central bearing on affairs. Cranbrook could not suppress misgivings: 'I can say personally that I could welcome release but I really dread the predominance of Radicalism & Whiggism is no more. I expect that we shall have much "moderate" support.' The session was to last only to 19 March to see the budget through. By 10 March: 'The war begins. . . . Our Whips Dyke & Winn whom I met yesterday are cheerful but who can tell?'

In conversation with Hartington, Cranbrook observed a distinct absence of hopefulness on the part of the Whig chief. The Whigs looked certain losers whichever way things went. It was by now tolerably clear that in the event of Liberal victory Granville and Hartington would have to stand aside to make way for Gladstone's return to the leadership. Conservative electioneering made much of this 'threat', probably to its own detriment. But to most Conservatives the contingency of Gladstone's resuming his old ascendancy seemed comfortingly remote. The main London papers were unanimous in their confidence: the *Morning Post*, the *Telegraph*, the *Standard*, all prophesied decisive Conservative success. *The Times*, despite efforts by Delane's successor, Chenery, to edge it away from too robust commitment to the Conservatives, still lamented the collapse of the two-party system that would follow from a likely Liberal defeat.[26]

'Infernal luck and no mistake'

1

The die being cast, Central Office girded for the expensive fray. Dyke, in his official capacity as parliamentary or patronage secretary at the Treasury, controlled the secret service fund of £10,000 per annum which provided the bedrock of party finance when in office. Skelmersdale, Colville's successor as Lords' whip, immediately began his appointed task of circularising peers for subscriptions to the party election fund, known as the Carlton Fund (though in practice it was administered entirely at Central Office). His letter to Salisbury of 15 March mentioned that he had as yet not been very successful: 'The Duke of Portland came forward well with £6,000. Duke of Northumberland with £2,000, Ld Egerton £1,000, Ld Wilton & Ld Penrhyn £500 each. Others have not answered me yet.'[27] Skelmersdale's moneybags carrier was the Lords' serjeant-at-arms, Colonel the Hon. Wellington ('Pat') Talbot. The key fact about Talbot was that he was son-in-law to the late earl of Derby. Now, as he later put it disarmingly to one of the numerous parliamentary commissions of inquiry into electoral corruption to which he gave evidence, he 'merely accidentally and casually took office for six weeks'[28] at Central Office as treasurer of the Carlton Fund, and disburser of election expenses to needy Conservative candidates. 'I can hardly call it a committee', he later testified, 'but I was one of a number of gentlemen who did administer funds during the elections, and I was the treasurer of that fund.' Talbot's disbursements remain largely clouded in mystery since, as he explained to a surprised panel of commissioners, he destroyed all his records.[29] What is certain is that unprecedented sums of electioneering money passed through Talbot's hands in an election unprecedented for its expense. Large sums were passed to the Conservative party from the Church Defence Institution (whose executive committee planned to raise £100,000),[30] the Orange Order, and the Licensed Victuallers' Association.

Noel returned to Central Office from the Board of Works to help his old comrades. Dyke was not really up to heavy work. Noel brought with him his secretary at the board, George Russell. On 29 March Russell informed Cranbrook that 'he had nothing but that which is encouraging to report', and that 'our failure to secure a substantial majority would be contrary to *reasonable* expectation'. This made Cranbrook feel that, as he later explained to Cairns, 'the misgivings wh. I could not but entertain seem somewhat unreasonable'.[31] By the time Cranbrook wrote that to Cairns, on 6 April, he had reason to know from the early borough results that his misgivings were well founded.

Corry also had misgivings. Salisbury, retired to Biarritz to recuperate, offered Disraeli the conveniences and comforts of Hatfield as a field headquarters. Corry later noted: 'Lord B was at Hatfield at this time. The Committee greatly objected to the discouraging news wh. I felt it my duty to take down to him there every evening.'[32] Noel wrote to Corry on 27 March from Central Office:

> I wish I had been here this afternoon and seen you.
>
> I really cannot see why you are to be so down about the prospect of the elections. The accounts we receive are I think very fairly good – and if we may be guided by the elections of the last six months there ought to be no cause to fear now. I am sure it does a great deal of harm to come and be doleful *here*. You have now frightened Pat Talbot and if it gets about that this is the result of the Chief's opinion from Hatfield it will be most mischievous.

Noel had examined the case in point of Dorsetshire, and taken advice from the retired former Dorset MP Ker Seymer. 'His information and every one else's is quite opposed to what you heard from Gerard Sturt'; and Noel indignantly refused to allow that because one man wrote alarmingly to Lord Beaconsfield that great damage be carelessly caused at large.[33] Possibly Sturt (Lord Alington) had reported to Disraeli much as Edward Stanhope reported to Salisbury: that Dorset was 'without any attempt at organisation whatever'.[34] But, since there had been but one contest since 1832 for Dorsetshire in a general election (1857), and since there was to be no contest once again in 1880, the matter hardly warranted much in the way of organisation and anything in the way of recrimination. Two Conservatives and one Liberal were effortlessly returned yet again to Westminster, despite all adjurations from central party offices that all seats must be contested.

Corry, stung, responded to Noel's rebuke (his syntax slightly awry) from Hatfield:

Remember *he* has sure sources of no special information apart from your Cee.

Letters such as Alington's he takes at their face value – nor do I send such on to you as the least expressing Lord B's views.

My own belief is that Lord B. during the last few days considers prospects certainly better. That too is my opinion quantum valeat.

But whatever he may say or think, I can't conceive that the confidential Council would for a moment let the outer world perceive them to be depressed. The bare suggestion is alarming!

I shall hope to see you on Tuesday. The time of Lord B's stay here is quite uncertain.

He is very comfortable & well. . . . I am very pleased that you refute franchement to me.

The Cee. at St. S[tephen's] C[hambers]. is the depository of all information in the matter of elections. To it alone the Leader of the party naturally resorts if he has doubts or desires explanations on particular points. In so doing, he (or his ambassador) must by his very enquiry, suggest the existence of dangers. But a question asked in a spirit of caution & criticism must not be taken for despondency. . . . Bear in mind that only too many people say we shall lose 20 seats in Ireland & Scotland, &, then, show me our increased majority in England wh is to save us. That I say is a perfectly fair proposition, and one not necessarily implying despondency: and of a like nature were we to ask questions about Yorkshire, Norfolk, Suffolk, Notts (shire and Borough) Wilton Shaftesbury Dorchester and or threatened losses.

When a man goes to his doctor or his lawyer he does not dwell on his indisputable titles or his physical excellences, but presents his weak points for consideration or advice . . . If then, I say, 'My Chief can't see how this that or the other is going to be achieved', I am merely asking to be shown the way.[35]

Noel's edginess reflected in fact Corry's misgivings. Central Office was nervous, despite receiving reassurances from David Plunket, MP for Dublin University, that '7 seats will be the extent of our losses in Ireland'. Even so, Plunket reported problems:

It is lamentable the way in which that stupid old Dowager Claude[sic] Hamilton refuses on some question of personal feeling to coalesce with Macartney in Tyrone Co! Whatever he does, he cannot prevent Macartney being at the head of the poll; & he *may* peril his own seat by keeping himself apart. Could you get the Chief to put the screw on the Dowager immediately by direct communication, so as to induce him to work heartily with Macartney?[36]

Lord Claud did not upset Macartney; but failed himself to recapture the seat he had lost in 1874.

Talbot reported to Disraeli at the end of March: 'Taylor has come over from Ireland in pretty good spirits. He is going to fight 42 seats, he says at the worst, we shall lose 7 seats but he hopes not to lose more than 6.'[37] Central Office pressed Taylor 'to run men in between the two sects of H.Rs', as there seemed to be 'an opening there if judiciously made use of'.[38] Unfortunately, it was the trend in such three-way encounters for the

Conservative to come bottom: as was the case with Captain King-Harman in Sligo County. Plunket told Corry:

> I enclose a list I made out today after going carefully through all our latest accounts from the different Constituencies with Taylor & Gibson – & I still make out a loss of 7, and believe I am right, but Taylor & Gibson seem to think it will not be worse than 5 or 6.

Plunket and Gibson were at least uncontestedly safe for the university, and telegraphed the glad tidings to Hatfield as the first members of the new parliament. 'Taylor goes over tonight to vote in London. He does not expect a fight in Dublin County, and we are in any case perfectly safe there.'

That proved in fact to be about the limit of Conservative safety in Ireland outside Ulster. Sir Arthur Guinness lost his Dublin city seat to a Home Ruler, despite Plunket's estimate that he would be safe with a 300 majority. One of his four '*off* chance of winning' seats, Leitrim County, was in fact won; several of his 'in considerable danger of losing' category were held (in Fermanagh, Antrim, and Belfast); and even in Down two 'almost certain losses' were held. Plunket's 'even chances of winning' category had mixed but mainly negative fortunes.[39] The net Conservative loss in Ireland proved to be 14 seats, leaving the party with only 23, of which a mere 5 were outside Ulster. The patterns of 1868 and 1874 were now manifestly being fulfilled with a remorseless electoral logic. Southern Irish Conservatism had 'already entered a new political world. Landlords had finally lost all electoral power.' The Irish Conservative vote was being 'picked to its irreducible and ineffective Protestant bone'.[40]

In Scotland, Conservatism did not have even an Ulster redoubt. Talbot reported: 'Our Scotch agent writes this morning "Lochiel seems quite confident. Our friend from Elgin Burghs writes very cheerfully".'[41] Cameron of Lochiel indeed held Invernessshire; but the Liberals held Elgin Burghs with an overwhelming majority. The case of Ross and Cromarty perhaps told most poignantly the Conservative tale in Scotland in 1880. The duchess of Sutherland wrote apologetically to Disraeli: 'I am anxious to tell you that I have . . . let my Tenantry know that I expect them to give their votes according to the principles always held by my house. . . . But, Alas! the young Conservative candidate, the son of the Lord Lieutenant of Rossshire (Davidson of Julland) has – wisely it seems from the circumstances – thought it best to retire.'[42] There had in fact been no Conservative challenge for this seat since 1852; so the retirement was in itself not anomalous. But in an overall context in which, as in Ireland, Conservatives lost twice as many seats as the party managers predicted – from 20 reduced to 7 in Scotland – the collapse of a Conservative challenge in Ross and Cromarty testified to delusory ambitions as much as traditional realities.

Charles Dalrymple, MP for Buteshire, held his seat only with the greatest difficulty, scrambling through in a second election in July 1880; and this in spite of his promoting, as Liberals alleged, a Scottish Election Fund to finance Conservative candidates throughout Scotland even in burghs where they had no chance in order to divert Liberal money and attention away from county seats.[43] All eyes, however, in Scotland, were on Midlothian, and Gladstone's challenge, backed by the Rosebery fortune and influence, to the Buccleuch interest. Talbot reported a telegram from Dalkeith on 30 March 'that he is *safe*. God grant he may be.'[44] With desperate and unconscious irony, Louisa Dalkeith wrote to Corry on 2 April: 'Amidst all these sad telegrams one is thankful for any ray of comfort & therefore I write to tell you that I consider our prospects here most satisfactory, & that we feel very confident of victory on Monday.'[45]

Wales added to the tale a loss of 9 of the 11 Conservative seats of 1874. Central Office had deluded itself that there were 'fair prospects in Flint & Denbigh Boros',[46] which there were not. The signal case in that catastrophe was the defeat of Sir Watkin Williams-Wynn in Montgomeryshire by Stuart Rendel. The Williams-Wynn dynasty had held the seat with only one by-election contest since time out of mind. This defeat of a great traditional landlord ranked emblematically with the 1868 defeat of the ironmasters at Merthyr. Rendel (for all that he was Eton, Oxford, and an armaments tycoon) represented a new kind of nationalist Welshness; and, specifically, he was for Church disestablishment in Wales. Wynn's desperation was marked by his lavish expenditure: his agent returned £13,053 9s ld, of which £5,828 was for conveyances alone. This was the highest individual return in 1880.[47]

As Corry had put it to Noel: 'only too many people say we shall lose 20 seats in Ireland & Scotland, &, then, show me our increased majority in England wh. is to save us.' In fact, Conservatives lost 36 seats outside England, counting 72 votes in a Commons' division. Where English compensation was to come from was not readily apparent. 'Monty has been here today', wrote Talbot at Central Office to Disraeli on 30 March,

> and has asked us to write you an account of how matters are progressing. Our accounts for the last 3 or 4 days have been generally good. We have cheering accounts from Southwark, Lambeth, the City & Westminster. I have just seen Mark Catley the candidate for the first of these Metropolitan Const^cies^ and he says he has 800 more promises than they had at the last election and speaks with much confidence as to his own and other elections.

Catley's confidence notwithstanding, Edward Clarke and Catley were ousted at Southwark. Lambeth remained stubbornly Liberal; but it was cheering and important that Conservatives held their ground in both Westminster and the City. Middlesex was yet again a Conservative triumph: George Hamilton and his partner polled nearly 2 : 1 against the Liberals. Mid-Surrey, pointed to back in 1871 by Derby as the hope of 'middle-class reaction' to Conservatism, stood staunch with its two members, along with the two other Surrey divisions. These victories were crucial for the survival of metropolitan

Conservatism; and therefore for the ultimate fulfilment of Salisbury's 'very strange history'.

Talbot further reported: 'Mr. Bates (Plymouth) has written to us to back him up to a £1000 at 2 to 1.' That would have been a good bet; but still the second seat was lost. 'From Birmingham we get good accounts & hope to get in the minority member.' Chamberlain's 'caucus' was proof against such naive plans; and the military hero of the jingoes, Major Fred Burnaby, failed to breach the Radical ramparts. 'At Sunderland our man is making a good fight and throughout Durham the accounts are very encouraging.' The results were very discouraging. 'We do not expect to get Wortley in for Sheffield.' In the perversity of life, Stuart Wortley did in fact capture the second Sheffield seat he had narrowly missed at the recent by-election: a victory which opened the way for very prosperous times for Conservatism in Sheffield for the rest of the century. 'In Yorkshire the accounts have not been very satisfactory but today they are somewhat better. Legard will probably pull Scarboro out of the fire where the prodigal son has been received with open arms.' The prodigal son ended up at the bottom of the poll; and there were to be grievous losses in the Ridings. 'Bristol they say will very probably return Sir Ivor Guest who is very popular there.' Guest was not popular enough to come better than third. 'We have this moment had an indifferent account from the Isle of Wight Newport where they say our friends will not work in the way of holding meetings.' There was to be no Conservative gain at Newport. 'From Brighton we hear that we shall probably keep both seats.' Both seats were lost.

Prognostications for English counties were likely to be better founded. 'Harry Thynne just come in from Wiltshire says things look as well in that part of the Country as one can expect.' Residual and resilient Conservative county strength here stoutly defended all four divisions; and the Hon. Sidney Herbert beat off the challenge to his family's Wilton seat. 'In Bedfordshire Gilpin has retired, and Col. Stuart replaces him with a good chance of success as I hear from Sir Montagu Borgoigne.' Stuart failed to hold Gilpin's seat; and for the first time since 1832 no Conservative shared Bedfordshire with the Woburn influence of the Whig house of Russell. This loss in Bedfordshire was ominous for Conservatism in its traditional county strongholds.

In the early days, however, what Central Office thought it principally had to grapple with were the sad borough returns. Talbot put the point to Disraeli:

> What we must fear are the smaller boro's where gold may prevail, but I do not think on the whole we shall lose on them. It is in my view quite possible that in the large Constituencies the Jingo cry may be of more use than we imagine but no one can really tell till the event comes off.

Talbot hoped, in conclusion, that 'this account will not make you more sanguine than I *dare* to be myself'.[48]

By 1 April the early borough returns made their impact. 'The news is not good', recorded Cranbrook. 'Yesterday the Libs. gained 25 seats to our nine a large proportion out of the number of contests. It looks to me as if the dangerous condition of almost a tie might result.'[49] Gerard Noel at Central Office tried to rally Corry:

> I think Shaftesbury very shaky but Lady Westminster is down there canvassing herself and I don't at all give it up. Poole we ought to win and I hear Warton is making an excellent fight at Bridport.
>
> Julian Goldsmid told me yesterday we should win both seats in Marylebone.
>
> So please cheer up and if we are beat we can lament afterwards – but I assure you the faces round this table vary very much after your communications and there are plenty of people outside who watch here to see how the cat jumps.[50]

Noel's instances were mixed in fortune: Shaftesbury proved too shaky to be held, despite the indomitable dowager; and the Marylebone seat was also lost. But Poole and Bridport were both gains. There were not, however, many such.

By 3 April the Liberals had made a net gain of 50 seats. These were mainly Conservative borough losses, and could for the most part be philosophically borne. No Conservative had sat for Reading since 1852, and reports from George Russell of great enthusiasm and expectations of getting a Conservative in there would lead only to moderate disappointment in the result. Manners's hopes of taking both Grantham seats were more cruelly disappointed: the Conservative lost the one seat regained in 1874. The Lancashire industrial boroughs engaged much more Conservative anxiety. There was the homeland of the Conservative 'reaction' and there was the native habitat of popular Toryism. Lord Derby declared for the Liberals, which was inevitably hurtful and introduced a note of bitterness.[51] The 1880 results were damaging and distressing, but enough was held, as with the metropolitan constituencies, to preserve a critical core. There were no Conservative gains; and Conservatives held their seats in Birkenhead, Blackburn, Liverpool, and Preston. Hugh Birley saved his seat at Manchester, but he was third in the poll. W.H. Houldsworth, the rising genius of Manchester Tory Democracy, failed in his first bid, and would have to wait for a by-election in 1883 on Birley's death. Conservative borough losses in Lancashire were quite enough to give Lord Derby satisfaction for his trouble: Ashton, Bolton, Clitheroe, one of the Manchester seats, Oldham (a seat had already been lost in a by-election in 1877), two seats at Stalybridge, and Warrington.

On top of that borough devastation, Conservatives lost four of their eight Lancashire county divisions: two in the north-east and two in the south-east. These losses were painful enough in the way they added insult to Conservative borough injury in Lancashire; but they were much more painful as indications of endemic electoral infection in the Conservative heartland counties. This would not have surprised Disraeli. Cranbrook noted on 20 March Disraeli's being 'cheerful about our prospects but had his doubts about counties which surprised me. He often has means of judging which others have not.'[52] But it did surprise, for example, Manners. Manners was aware in the southern division of Leicestershire that Heygate would have a keen contest because 'there the farmers are discontented and bent on what they call "Ratal Reform"'; and Heygate was duly dismissed. But Manners was not aware of anything like an epidemic of such discontent. In reporting to Disraeli 'from the scene of action' at Belvoir Castle, Grantham, Manners judged the 'farmers in good temper, in better spirits than could be expected, and, politically, sound'. He concluded: 'Altogether in this part of the Midlands I think we shall not lose, and may possibly gain one or two seats. Agricultural prospects are good, and not one farm on this great estate is now vacant.'[53] Newark was indeed gained. But one miserable borough weighed nothing in Conservative east Midlands scales against prime county divisions lost not only in Leicestershire, but also in Lincolnshire, two in Derbyshire, one in Huntingdonshire, one in Northamptonshire, and one in Nottinghamshire.

If the 1874 election was famed for Conservative borough gains, the 1880 election was famed for Conservative county losses. Yorkshire West Riding contributed to clean losses of two-seat divisions in the east and south to match the Lancashire bloodletting. East Worcestershire also distinguished itself by exchanging two Conservatives for two Liberals. Then came the tale of other English county seats lost: 18 in all, including pairs of Derbyshire and Staffordshire. The Conservative party had to absorb the shock of losing a grand total of 29 English county seats, with only 1 gain in Norfolk to offset. Add to that 2 Irish county losses, 9 Scottish (including, crowningly, Midlothian), and 5 Welsh, and Central Office was looking at something along the lines of an electoral *Jacquerie*. The agricultural virus could infect small country boroughs. Cranbrook was bitter about Rye, where his son Stewart Hardy failed to hold the seat he had first won in 1868 by eight votes. 'Stewart had a majority of 152 promises *from those who voted* but he always distrusted the Agricultural labourers and they probably betrayed him. Of the better class at Rye,' Cranbrook assured Cairns, 'he really had every one on his side.'[54] County wounds were not the less painful for being inflicted by excruciatingly insignificant majorities. Abergavenny uttered a cry of agony to Corry:

> Fancy losing 5 County Seats
> 52 votes
> We have the most infernal luck and no mistake.[55]

2

Deep diagnostic analysis of this agrarian distemper would later propose that 'the late Government, in their anxiety to pass social reforms which would influence the towns, somewhat shook the loyalty of the agricultural classes'.

Moreover, it seemed that, 'in the prostration caused by bad seasons, the large subsidies from the exchequer to the local rates were almost forgotten'. Landlords both in England and Scotland 'saw little cause for satisfaction in the Agricultural Holdings Act, the voluntary character of which had not made it even a stopgap to Liberal demands, yet English and Scotch farmers grumbled that so little was done to define tenant–right.' It appeared also that certain sections of the clergy were influenced by the same feeling, while Ritualists and their sympathisers bitterly resented the Public Worship Act. As for the boroughs:

> Substantial measures of social reform like the Artisans' Dwellings and Friendly Societies Bills may have influenced the boroughs. But it is doubtful whether they gained the Conservatives half as many votes as were lost under the influence of the placard, largely circulated from the Liberal headquarters, of a British soldier being flogged by a Zulu.[56]

In the immediate shock of events responses were more expressive of surprise and dismay. It is true that, as far back as January 1876, Derby had confided to himself that it was 'not probable that the Cabinet will survive the next general election'; but such intensity of phlegm was Derby's quirky humour.[57] As the clear Liberal majority over the Conservatives mounted to near 100, with Irish Home Rulers something between 60 and 70, Cranbrook found it 'amazing how we could have held out with the hidden current against us'.[58] He told Cairns on 6 April:

> My impression . . . was strong that we held many Boroughs by accident and that our losses would be serious. Never however did I imagine that such a complete crumbling away of our position was possible. Our first defeats have no doubt entailed many others and as the ruin has gone on what would otherwise have been stable has been dragged down. My telegram this morning gives the sickening but not unexpected news of Gladstone's victory in Midlothian. That I admit is gall to me for I dislike seeing personal malignity so gratified. . . . I think we had better on the whole meet parliament and let us hear why we are to be ejected and perhaps we may get some explanation why & where the national hostility to us has concealed itself so long. Much money was available and has been freely spent against us.[59]

Richmond was equally taken aback. 'I was never very sanguine about the result of the Elections, but I confess I did not expect so disastrous a state of affairs.' He could, however, console himself with affairs in Sussex: 'Chichester Election is satisfactory, it shows I still have influence there, and that it has been well looked after. I wish other Boroughs had been similarly cared for – we have *not* a single *liberal* member returned in West Sussex.'[60] Cairns was in no doubt that 'our most Gracious Mistress' would be 'disconcerted by this new element of confusion'; and indeed the queen, Cranbrook gathered, was 'amazed' at the Conservative collapse, 'as she had assurances from the Liberals that we must succeed'. Cranbrook was told that 'she shed many tears on Sunday afternoon', 4 April.[61] One common expression of bewilderment in such circumstances, mass dementia in the electorate, was not lacking among Conservatives in 1880: 'The country seems to have gone completely mad', Richmond told Cairns; extrapolating that 'one dreads to think what may happen with such a madman as Gladstone in the government'. Lady Salisbury solaced Disraeli: 'I feel sure that the madness of the people will soon subside.'[62]

There were initial essays in explanation. Robert Bourke, undersecretary at the Foreign Office, who managed to hold the second seat at Lynn, involuntarily parting company with his former colleague for the borough, Lord Claud Hamilton,[63] assured Disraeli from Scotland that

> amid the general devastation which has fallen upon the party, it may be some consolation to you to know, that every Liberal member of parliament, whom I have met (I have seen over a dozen) thinks that the foreign policy has had nothing in the world to do with the disaster. I dined at the club in Edinboro' last night, and met several victorious members, and they all agreed about this. Bad harvests and depression in trade, has done the business.
>
> The low mass of voters have thought, that any change may bring them better times. At King's Lynn this idea was very prevalent, but Claud Hamilton lost his seat owing to local and personal reasons of a most temporary character.
>
> I worked hard for him, and endangered my own seat, to get him votes, but in vain.
>
> I came down here to vote for Dalkeith and Elcho. I have little hope about either, although the friends of each are sanguine.[64]

(Lord Elcho in fact held Haddingtonshire by 44 votes; and, furthermore, when he succeeded his father as earl of Wemyss in 1883, he successfully handed it on to *his* son and heir in turn. 'Sound' politics in Haddingtonshire, however, ended abruptly in 1885.)

Cairns was not inclined to be greatly surprised; for, as he told Disraeli, 'notwithstanding the very confident expectations & calculations of our managers I had an instinctive feeling that a ballot is pretty sure to be fatal to a Governmt. that has been six years in office, unless under very favourable circumstances'.[65] Salisbury, however, thought there was more of a problem to it than that. He wrote to Disraeli from Biarritz:

> The elections have been a puzzle to me – & I have seen no cause which satisfactorily accounts for so sudden a change. I suppose bad harvests & bad trade have done the most. I suppose a sick man who makes no progress is apt to change his doctor, though the doctor may not be at fault: & the mass of borough voters know that they are pinched – & nothing more. I have not gone into the statistics – but I suspect this election will finally dispose of any interest the Conservative party are inclined to take in the existence of the small boroughs. The question will soon come before us: as County franchise will be one of their first subjects of legislation.
>
> Some stray bits of gossip & comment reach to me here: and seem to indicate a certain amount of discontent with our electioneering organization. But I suppose that is natural after so great a disaster. Still it is puzzling that our authorities should have had no glimmer of the election condition, which appears to have been well known to our opponents. I do not know that it would have helped us much to

have known our evil case earlier. Perhaps we might have gained something by concentrating our efforts & our money on fewer contests.[66]

To Arthur Balfour (who saw off a challenge handsomely at Hertford) Salisbury was equally puzzled three days later but more inclined to foreboding:

> The hurricane that has swept us away is so strange & new a phenomenon that we shall not for some time understand its real meaning. I doubt if so much enthusiasm & such a general unity of action proceeds from any sentimental opinion – or from a new academic judgment. It seems to have to be inspired by some definite desire for change: & means business. It may disappear as rapidly as it came: or it may be the beginning of a serious war of classes. Gladstone is doing all he can to give it the latter meaning.[67]

Disraeli himself, solitary at Hatfield amid a swarm of young Cecils, met the joyless tidings with his accustomed parchment mask of impassivity. He returned to London on 6 April. 'A very dreary business,' as he told Cairns, 'the intermediate stage between power & obscurity; everybody asking what it is difficult, or impossible, to grant. . . . The moment our colleagues' fate on the Hustings is decided, I shall summon the Cabinet to consider our course.'[68] Disraeli could only characterise the vast discomfiture as being 'without an adequate cause'. He told Salisbury: '"Hard Times," as far as I can collect, has been our foe and certainly the alleged cause of our fall.' He defended himself against Cairns's argument for a later dissolution on the ground that more time 'would only have aggravated the mal-disposition of the towns and would probably have landed us at the same time with an insurrection of our old and natural friends, the farmers', who were, as he alleged, 'preparing for it in all directions with their Clubs and Councils, and Candidates'.[69] Cairns offered words of balm:

> Each day seems to make the gloom of the present & the prospect of the future more dark. It is not however by any means the first time you have gone through these deep waters, & you have never allowed yourself to be depressed by adversity, any more than you have allowed yourself to be unduly elated by the long career of power & honour which is about to close.[70]

The problem which had first arisen in 1868, and then again in 1874, now once more arose: after an election result of such unequivocal decisiveness, was there any point in the government's staying on to meet the new parliament and asking for its decision? The situation in 1880 seemed to confirm the pattern suggested in 1874 after initiation in 1868 of governments being summarily condemned by electorates without any hope of appeal. (Lady Salisbury put the point in an inimitably aristocratic style by candidly confronting the fact that by Reform in 1867 the electorate consisted predominantly of what, after all, were the 'servant classes'. 'The moral of the story seems to be that the English voter like the English footman likes "a change" & that therefore at each general election there will probably always be a transfer of power from one side to the other.')[71] That apparent pattern posed in itself an obvious question: did it mean that Conservatives were in the same boat as Liberals? And, if so, was Conservatism thereby acquitted of any presumption that the verdict of the electorate in 1880 necesarily condemned Disraeli's case that by management and generalship power could be retained for the class of birth and property in an age of extended political privilege for the popular constituencies?

Most of Disraeli's colleagues agreed at first with Cranbrook's indignant notion of demanding 'some explanation' from the new parliament. 'Let us see the combined forces in their first action, and then, will not Radical & Home Rulers overpower the Hartington party.'[72] Richmond hoped 'we shall meet parliament and compel the opposition to frame an Indictment agst us. It is really lamentable when such men as Labouchere and Bradlaugh can find constituencies to return them.'[73]

Balfour reported to Salisbury a long conversation with 'Dizzy' on the question of a cabinet to decide the government's course as to meeting parliament or resigning forthwith. Disraeli 'without doubt' was in favour of resignation without further ado. 'Had the Liberals only been in a majority by the help of the Home Rulers it would have been different. In that case a Liberal victory on the address would have thrown discredit on the Liberal cause: and it would have been "madness" not to compel the other side to show their true position.' But what would be gained now? 'Shall we succeed in converting the country to our policy by a parliamentary discussion? Such an opinion is all d – d nonsense. The beaten party is always in the wrong'; and debate would cause confrontation between Commons and Lords, a confrontation which the Lords could not win. 'The H. of L. would "ask to be kicked".'

> Dizzy then, by a natural transition, began to discuss the future policy of the party. He did not take a despairing view of the case, though he said we shall never return to power in his time. Much will depend he thought on the management of the H. of Lords. On the one hand we must not allow our majority there to get dispirited. On the other hand no conflict must be permitted between the two houses except some substantial gain can be obtained thereby.

Next session, Disraeli continued, the Liberals would bring in a bill 'to equalize the County and the Borough Franchise'. If they combined 'such a measure with an extensive plan of redistribution their difficulties will be almost insuperable'. If they did *not* combine it with any such plan the Lords, while assenting to the principle of franchise equalisation, would be able to insist that franchise extension was unacceptable without redistribution of constituencies.

> The old method of coercing the House of Lords is no longer practicable. Formerly in case of a difference between the two Houses the radicals used to dissolve. 'Now (said Dizzy) they will be in such a damned fright of being turned out that they will not dare to do it.' More especially will this be the case if the subject of controversy be the redistribution of seats – a question in which all the small boroughs will of a certainty be opposed to any change.
>
> For his own part (he said) he would not desert a sinking ship: – though what he will desire will be to . . . retire to his favourite pursuits (whatever they may

> be) and see for the first time his country place in the spring and summer. To continue to take an active part in politics would involve a great sacrifice on his part – but a sacrifice he was prepared to make for the sake of the party.
>
> The old man was in an entertainingly communicative humour and kept throwing out these & other remarks as he walked up and down his room in Downing Street.[74]

Apart from being in an 'entertainingly communicative humour', Disraeli had thrown out remarks apropos of the county occupier franchise in relation to constituency redistribution which, as connected with Salisbury's remarks (which would have reached Disraeli that day) on the inutility of the Conservative party's having any further interest in the existence of small boroughs, provided the Conservative party with its most important task and duty in the coming parliament. The only error in Disraeli's assessment (shared by Salisbury) was to assume that the Liberals would press forward with the county franchise in their first session. In fact it was not to be until 1884 that they nerved themselves to that test.

But such far-sighted visions seemed little to the purpose amid the rubble in April 1880. Salisbury agreed that there was no advantage to be had in meeting parliament. It would 'only have the effect of making our defeat seem larger than it is'; for several members whom Conservatives might eventually find on their side would think it prudent to vote against the government on a motion of no confidence. 'The size of the majority against us is portentous: but if it was to be a large majority at all, the great size is not an evil. Our great hope is in Gladstone's arrogance: & late events are of a nature to feed it. Moreover many of our friends want frightening.'[75]

Apart from the 'Hard Times' diagnosis, inquests in the party, as the dust cleared, tended to point accusingly to organisational weakness. Northcote listed the four material causes of defeat as, first, 'want of suitable organisation, and some overconfidence and apathy', second, the bad times and a desire for change in hopes of better luck, third, the unscrupulous assertions of opponents, and, fourth, their very large expenditure of money.[76]

As for the very large expenditure of money, Northcote was simply a case of the pot calling the kettle black. He himself had after all been instrumental in helping on the merry chase with his 'Cabs' Act in the first 1880 session. The experience of both parties in 1880 on the question of expenditure was so painful that for the first time it was clear that there would be parliamentary collaboration to put serious and effective restrictions on constituency spending. Talbot's evidence before various electoral corruption commissions gives no countenance whatever for insinuations by such as Cranbrook and Northcote that the Conservative party was more bribed against than bribing. Chester was a particularly gross case, leading to the voiding of the poll and the suspension of the writ for the borough.[77] The unfortunate Raikes lost his seat, and had to look about until Preston became available in 1882. Canterbury was another gross case, leading also to disfranchisement. Of that scandal Cranbrook's son, the Hon. E.A. Gathorne Hardy, was a victim; and proved not to be as lucky as Raikes in getting back to the Commons. Cranbrook had cause to lament to Cairns the 'idiotic folly of unauthorised persons'.[78]

For Conservative politicians the alibi provided by Liberal corruption in 1880 was never more than a supporting item of circumstantial evidence attaching to the broader exculpation offered by management failure. 'We must notice', Northcote commented, 'that there had never been an election where we lost so many seats by such small majorities.'[79] This seemed to reinforce the point about organisation. Conservatives wishing to be in the convenient position of being able in effect to blame the messengers for the message were greatly aided at this juncture by Joseph Chamberlain. The Birmingham 'caucus' machine and its offshoots were aimed as much at Whig enemies within the Liberal party as Tory enemies without, and Chamberlain was accorded no accolades of gratitude for his organisation by the Liberal party in 1880. Chamberlain himself wrote to *The Times* claiming that the caucus had been successful in 60 of the 67 boroughs where it was established.[80] That was precisely the kind of claim the National Union made in 1874, and amounts to little more than an electoral non sequitur or a banal example of the adage that nothing, in politics as elsewhere, succeeds like success. But it enabled Lady Salisbury to add to her 'madness of the people' and her 'English footman likes "a change"' explanations by piping up with: 'by all accounts the organisation has been deplorable. We must have "Caucuses".'[81] It also enabled Gorst (who held his Chatham seat narrowly) to confuse matters with a new variation on his old theme by declaring unctuously at the National Union conference in 1880 that it was 'not fair' to say that in recent years 'the Conservative organisation went to pieces'; he was glad of the opportunity to state publicly that it was not fair to say that their organisation had gone 'to utter ruin', or that their defeat was mainly attributable to defective organisation. 'It was, however, right to say that their organisation had not greatly improved, and that as compared with the organisation of their opponents they were certainly left far behind.'[82]

Certain specific criticisms of Conservative organisation in 1880 were undoubtedly much to the point. A.F. Egerton, one of the defeated Conservatives in the south-eastern Lancashire division, drew W.H. Smith's attention to the weakness that party canvassers were ignoring the 'miles of new streets just outside of Manchester and other boroughs'. Egerton shrewdly guessed that when the borough and county franchises were assimilated, 'these suburban voters may very possibly strengthen instead of weaken the Conservative Party, as they are a very different class from the workingmen householders in the county'.[83] The weight of evidence, however, tends to validate Rae's insistence on the primacy of 'opinion' as against the kind of alibi desired by politicians such as Northcote or the kind of 'crotchet' being urged by Gorst. Perhaps Lady Salisbury was making a better point when she asserted that 'I do not think that our side has talked enough'.[84] St. John Brodrick, a successful candidate for one of the Surrey seats, judged that Conservatives relied too much on 'indiscriminate abuse of Mr. Gladstone, or by laudation of his predecessors', while Liberal promises were being 'showered on all classes'. 'The complaint of some of the reporters who attended a candidate for a metropolitan constituency throughout his contest that they never heard a word from him on Conservative policy, to vary the glorification of Lord Beaconsfield and of himself as a fit candidate points it own moral.'[85]

Disraeli's refusal to recriminate in 1880 accords with the findings of later scholarship. There is a psephological view: as with the Liberals in 1874, Conservative managers in 1880 failed to keep pace with the increase of the electorate, reflected in the continued rise in the absolute numbers of the Conservative vote. 'This rise shows that neglect of the Conservative party organisation can have been of only limited importance.'[86] There is a view about the special importance of combining in a political programme material benefits to ordinary voters with a special altruistic appeal to activists and party enthusiasts, and the way in which the 1880 election was a landmark in offering materials for this kind of 'general theory of electoral behaviour'.[87] Disraeli knew nothing of these matters, but made his opinion plain by giving Dyke a privy-councillorship.

'Everybody asking what it is difficult, or impossible, to grant' was of the essence of Disraeli's last days in office. Cranbrook found the Carlton on 20 April 'fuller than ever of defeated candidates & friends to be condoled with'. At a last cabinet on 22 April 'we discussed the future & Smith & Salisbury undertook to meet Dyke & others and consult as to our strategy to redeem our position which the Chief viewed without despondency'. The queen made no secret of her regret at parting with her Conservative ministers (she was taken aback at Gladstone's explanation of why he was taking on the Exchequer as well as the premiership: 'I have no one fit for it but *Northcote* & I can't offer it to him.')[88] Disraeli was as sparing as ever with resignation peerages. (Salisbury wrote: 'I send you a couple of applications for Peerages. You must have a voluminous collection of that kind of literature.')[89] Apart from party acknowledgements, Disraeli was scrupulous to repay what he saw as profoundly important personal debts. One was an old debt, to the Cavendish-Bentinck family who had set him up in the party and made possible his career. The eccentric duke of Portland had refused a Garter. Equal to this occasion, Disraeli, in his own eccentric way, ceremoniously conferred on Arthur Cavendish-Bentinck's widow, the duke's stepmother, the barony of Bolsover.[90] On Montagu Corry he conferred the barony of Rowton, endowed by an aunt in Shropshire. The healing of an old quarrel was marked when Lady Salisbury interceded successfully for a privy-councillorship for Beresford-Hope, reminding Disraeli how very hard he had worked for the party of late, and of how his wife was Salisbury's only living sister.[91] For Northcote there was a pension: 'the calls upon me in the country as a County Member and in London as a political leader are very much beyond my private means.' Northcote had no 'foolish scruple' in applying, though he did 'feel a delicacy' about his claim being possibly to the detriment of Lord John Manners, 'whose service in the party has been longer than mine'. Northcote concluded: 'If I do not look back too much, it is because I venture still to look forward to a renewal of my service under you when the Nation comes to its senses.'[92]

Notes and References

1. Dyke to Beaconsfield, 28 July [1879]; HP, B/XXI/D/491.
2. Corry to Beaconsfield, 28 Sept. 1879; HP, B/XX/Co/129.
3. T. Lloyd, *The General Election of 1880* (Oxford 1968), 14–15.
4. Balfour to Salisbury, 12 Dec. 1879. R. Harcourt Williams (ed), *Salisbury – Balfour Correspondence, 1869–1892* (Hertfordshire Record Office 1988), 33–4. Salisbury to Northcote, 25 Dec. 1879; BL, Iddesleigh 50019, 190.
5. *PD*, ccl, 22.
6. See below, 368.
7. Buckle, ii, 1371–2.
8. Lloyd, *Election of 1880*, 150.
9. Dalkeith to Beaconsfield, 15 Dec. 1879; HP, B/XXI/D1. See also B.L. Crapster, 'Scotland and the Conservative Party in 1876', *Journal of Modern History* (1957), for vain efforts to build on the successes of 1874.
10. Lady Salisbury to Beaconsfield, 22 Dec. [1879]; HP, B/XX/Ce/328.
11. Stuart Wortley to Beaconsfield, 1 Jan. 1880; HP, B/XII/K/66.
12. Wharncliffe to Beaconsfield, 26 Dec. 1879; HP, B/XX/K/6a.
13. Norfolk to Beaconsfield, 10 Dec. 1879; HP, B/XXI/N/162.
14. Buckle, ii, 1275.
15. Salisbury to Beaconsfield, 2 Jan. 1880; HP, B/XX/Ce/132.
16. Richmond to Cairns, 5 Jan. 1880; PRO, Cairns 30/51/4.
17. Richmond to Cairns, 19 Jan. 1880; PRO, Cairns 30/51/4.
18. Northcote to Cairns, 13 Jan. 1880; PRO, Cairns 30/51/5.
19. C. O'Leary, *The Elimination of Corrupt Practices in British Elections, 1868–1911* (Oxford, 1962), 118.
20. Hardy, *Diary*, 435.
21. See above, 324.
22. Skene to Corry, 16 Feb. 1880; HP, B/XXI/S/281a.
23. Hardy, *Diary*, 437.
24. Cairns to Beaconsfield, 3 April 1880; HP, B/XX/Ca/261.
25. Buckle, ii, 1386–88.
26. Lloyd, *Election of 1880*, 97–99; R. Blake, *Disraeli* (1966), 710.
27. Hanham, 374.
28. *Parliamentary Papers*, 1881, xliv, 484.
29. *Ibid.*, xl, 760–1.
30. HP. B/xxI/F/85 (Alfred T. Lee. Sec.)
31. Cranbrook to Cairns, 6 April 1880; PRO, Cairns 30/51/7.
32. Note by Corry on Noel to Corry, 27 March 1880; HP, B/XII/K/12a.

33 Noel to Corry, *ibid.* Gerard Sturt, former Dorsetshire MP, had been created Lord Alington in 1876.
34 M. Pugh, *The Tories and the People 1880–1935* (1985), 100.
35 Corry to Noel [n.d.]; HP, B/XII/K/126.
36 Plunket to Corry, 27 March 1880; HP, B/XII/K/11.
37 Talbot to Beaconsfield, 31 March [1880]; HP, B/XII/K/17.
38 Plunket to Corry, 30 March 1880; HP, B/XII/K/15.
39 Talbot to Beaconsfield, 30 March 1880; HP, B/XII/K/16.
40 T.K. Hoppen, *Elections, Politics, and Society in Ireland 1832–1885* (Oxford, 1984), 329.
41 Talbot to Beaconsfield, 31 March [1880]; HP, B/XII/K/17.
42 Duchess of Sutherland to Beaconsfield [1880]; HP, B/XII/K/23.
43 O'Leary, *Elimination*, 122.
44 Talbot to Beaconsfield, 30 March 1880; HP, B/XII/K/16.
45 Lady Dalkeith to Beaconsfield, 2 April 1880; HP, B/XII/K/19.
46 Talbot to Beaconsfield, 30 March 1880; HP, B/XII/K/16.
47 O'Leary, *Elimination*, 156.
48 Talbot to Beaconsfield, 30 March 1880; HP, B/XII/K/16.
49 Hardy, *Diary*, 442.
50 Noel to Corry [1880], HP, B/XXI/K/12a.
51 For Cranbrook's comments to Cross on the 'pitiful sneak at Knowsley' see M. Swartz, *Politics of British Foreign Policy in the Era of Disraeli and Gladstone* (1985), 200, n. 104.
52 Hardy, *Diary*, 441.
53 Manners to Disraeli [28 March] 1880; HP, B/XXII/K/22.
54 Cranbrook to Cairns, 6 April 1880; PRO, Cairns 30/51/7.
55 Abergavenny to Corry [2 April 1880]; HP, B/XXI/A/68.
56 St. J. Brodrick, 'Functions of a Conservative opposition', *Nineteenth Century* (1881), 161–2.
57 Derby Diary, 2 Jan. 1876.
58 Hardy, *Diary*, 445.
59 Cranbrook to Cairns, 6 April 1880; PRO, Cairns 30/51/7.
60 Richmond to Cairns, 3 April 80; PRO, Cairns 30/51/4.
61 Hardy, *Diary*, 446.
62 Richmond to Cairns, 16 and 17 April 1880; PRO, Cairns 30/51/4. Lady Salisbury to Beaconsfield, 17 April 1880; HP, B/XX/Ce/335.
63 Younger kin to the 'Dowager' Claud of County Tyrone.
64 Bourke to Beaconsfield, 4 April 1880; HP, B/XII/K/20.
65 Cairns to Beaconsfield, 3 April 1880; HP, B/XX/Ca/261.
66 Salisbury to Beaconsfield, 7 April 1880; HP, B/XX/Ce/139.
67 Salisbury to Balfour, 10 April 1880; BL, Balfour 49688, 22–3.
68 Beaconsfield to Cairns, 6 April 1880; PRO, Cairns 30/51/1.
69 Blake, *Disraeli*, 719.
70 Cairns to Beaconsfield, 7 April 1880; HP, B/XX/Ca/262.
71 Lady Salisbury to Beaconsfield, 4 April 1880; HP, B/XX/Ce/333.
72 Hardy, *Diary*, 443.
73 Richmond to Cairns, 3 April 1880; PRO, Cairns 30/51/4.
74 Balfour to Salisbury, 8 April 1880; BL, Balfour 49688, 18–21.
75 Salisbury to Beaconsfield, 11 April 1880; HP, B/XX/Ce/140.
76 A. Lang, *Life . . . of Sir Stafford Northcote, First Earl of Iddesleigh* (1890), 313.

77 O'Leary, *Elimination*, 137.
78 Cranbrook to Cairns, 6 April 1880; PRO, Cairns 30/51/7.
79 Lang, *Iddesleigh*, 318–19. Lloyd, *Election of 1880*, 136, estimated that a shift of 4,054 votes would have cost the Liberals all of the 72 marginal seats.
80 O'Leary, *Elimination*, 129.
81 Lady Salisbury to Beaconsfield, 17 April 1880; HP, B/XX/Ce/335.
82 Minutes, NUCCA, St. James's Hall, London, July 1880.
83 Foster, 'Tory Democracy and political elitism', in A. Cosgrove and J.L. McGuire (eds), *Parliament and Community* (Belfast 1983), 171, n.27 (Egerton to Smith, 9 April 1880).
84 Lady Salisbury to Beaconsfield, 17 April 1880; HP, B/XX/Ce/335.
85 'Function of a Conservative opposition'. *Nineteenth Century* (1883), 161.
86 J.P.D. Dunbabin, 'Parliamentary elections in Great Britain, 1868–1900: a psephological note'. *English Historical Review* (1966), 88, n.2.
87 Lloyd, *Election of 1880*, 1–2.
88 Hardy, *Diary*, 446–8.
89 Salisbury to Beaconsfield, 14 April 1880; HP, B/XX/Ce/142.
90 Blake, *Disraeli*, 705–6.
91 Lady Salisbury to Beaconsfield, 14 April 1880; HP, B/XX/Ce/334.
92 Northcote to Beaconsfield, 13 April 1880; BL, Iddesleigh 50018, 186.

Chapter 15

Disraeli's last year, 1880–1

'Still placing at their service all the advice he could afford'

1

It was predictable that in the aftermath of stunningly unexpected defeat there would be in the Conservative party an inquest into management and a great deal of disaffection in the party both within and 'out of doors' directed at the managerial establishment. It was also predictable that the inquest and the disaffection would be largely at cross-purposes. The inquest would be conducted by the managerial establishment for the purposes of improving organisational performance, the better to sustain the continued existence and power of the managerial establishment. Party disaffection would express itself in varieties of complaints and grievances, most of which could be collected under a tag called 'Tory Democracy', the gist being that the party must be run in a rather different way by rather different people.

So long as Disraeli lived and retained his ascendancy as leader of the party, the energies of the various interests and factions competing for advantage and influence in the post-1880 dispensation would be decently united and restrained. Once Disraeli died, in April 1881, the knives would be out.

In the rather brutal mêlée which characterised the internal politics of the Conservative party in this period, five material factors, interests, or categories may be identified and defined. These were to make up the party equation of forces and energies which resolved themselves in a series of crises of conflict between 1884 and 1887. However, they all took root and form in Disraeli's time and, for good or ill, constituted his legacy to his party. There was no question of their being problems for Conservatism subsequent to his departure and detached from his leadership. They were bone of his Conservative bone and flesh of his Conservative flesh.

The first was the managerial establishment itself, representing the actual Disraelian party (as opposed to the mythic one) and the traditional aristocratic and territorial values of that party. It identified itself as the responsible leadership embodying executive experience and parliamentary wisdom, proven worth, and trusty guardianship of the party's abiding political treasure. These were men created and promoted by Disraeli. In the current shorthand of public life they came to be identified under the label 'Central

Committee'. This designation (among others) hitherto had simply meant the elite of party managers who conducted business at Central Office. Because of a misapprehension that Disraeli in 1880 created an entirely new kind of body for the purposes of a grand inquest, the title Central Committee took on a special and enhanced significance as representing the promoters and defenders of the party *in statu quo*.

A second factor in the equation had its roots in the traditional establishment, but ramified far beyond it. This was the rivalry between Northcote and Salisbury for the party leadership in the event of Disraeli's abdication or death. One reason, indeed, why Disraeli could not abdicate was that such an act would have brought that question to a head awkwardly and unseasonably. Northcote would have been the prime contender and, in the circumstances, the only contender. His formal qualifications were unrivalled. He had first held high office in 1859. He was a member of Derby's cabinet in 1866 and a secretary of state in 1867. As chancellor of the Exchequer he had held his own against Gladstone. Above all, since 1876 he had led the party in the House of Commons. The counts against him were that he was essentially a fussy bureaucrat who learned his politics in the era of party coalitions, convergence, and consensus in the 1850s, and who would be entirely out of his natural element in a political epoch of polarised conflict, which the 1880s clearly promised to be. Further, he had not been an impressive leader when confronted with the kind of unpleasantly combative politics represented by the new personalities of Parnell or Chamberlain, or the old but revived personality of Gladstone. He had no physical presence; nothing in the way of an aura. Further yet, Northcote gained no credit in the party for his consistently intelligent and sensible and cautious moderation in matters of foreign policy. Even so, there still would have been such a feeling of obligation, desire to avoid an 'ugly appearance' of things, and sense of the gentlemanly decencies of political manners in the parliamentary party that had Disraeli, one way or another, gone quickly in 1880, Northcote would almost certainly have been recognised as his successor.

Salisbury was twelve years Northcote's junior; but he became a member of parliament two years before Northcote and a privy-councillor on the same day as Northcote in 1866. He did not become Conservative leader in the House of Lords until Disraeli's death in 1881. But he had been much canvassed for that role following the old Derby's death in 1869 and the new Derby's passing back that cup. Richmond as leader up to 1876 was simply a walking reminder that the great powers or talents of the party in the Lords were for one reason or another disabled. The great counts against Salisbury were his reputation for wildly reactionary domestic and Irish attitudes and his behaviour between 1867 and 1874. But all that was now quite a long time back and there were the 1880s to confront. Were it a question simply of polarised adversarial politics then the case for Salisbury as party leader was strong. He was rather a grim pessimist about worldly things in general, and on the surface of a profound High Anglican faith his turn for cynicism made it quite agreeable for him to say hard things which he thought were true. He had a fine presence and shared much of Disraeli's glory for Berlin. He had all the normal human vanities of political ambition. Given Northcote's formal precedence as to the succession it was awkward for Salisbury to make any signals of his own ambitions for it. There is no doubt, however, that by 1880 Salisbury would have been Disraeli's own preferred candidate. There is no doubt, equally, that Salisbury took the view, quite dispassionately, that he would make a better leader for the party as a whole than Northcote. Possibly a majority of Conservatives would have agreed with Salisbury on that point in 1880; certainly a majority by 1881. It was for that reason that on Disraeli's death it was agreed to place the party leadership for the time being in suspension rather than offer it to Northcote.

The rivalry of Northcote and Salisbury was never covertly acknowledged before Disraeli's death and never overtly acknowledged by the two men afterwards. In a sense it was unnecessary for Northcote to assert his ambition. He had reason to believe that the queen would call on him to form a Conservative government as Disraeli's heir and such things were widely known and understood. It would have been extremely bad form on Salisbury's part, within the conventions of the mores, to have said or done anything to call this understanding in doubt, even though he was well, and increasingly, aware of party sentiment slipping away from Northcote. All he could do was wait and see.

One of the great political questions bearing upon the Northcote–Salisbury rivalry was the problem of what to do about the Whigs. It was a commonplace of Conservative doctrine that under the pressures created by the Radicals, the Irish, the Whigs themselves, and with Gladstone now adding his own special intensities, the Liberal party must fracture and break apart. The understanding was that the logic of such a situation would be that most, if not all, Whigs would want to move across to their fellow aristocrats and territorialists in the Conservative party. The Conservative party was thus faced with the problem, in the meantime, of whether to adopt postures of attractiveness and allurement to the Whigs as a means of helping them across and helping along the crumbling of Liberal cohesion, or whether to adopt a sterner view that the Whigs, having made their bed, must lie in it, and suffer, and learn from, the punishments deserved for their hereditary arrogance and delusions. It was a question, in the first case, in practical terms, of adapting the Conservative party in one sense for the convenience of the Whigs, but in another, wider sense for the benefit of the Conservative party itself. The postulate was that it was most improbable that another 1874 would happen for quite a while and that therefore it needed all the help it could get to entrench itself effectively; and that such help was only to be expected on reasonable terms. It was well appreciated that if Conservatives accepted that argument their most appropriate leader would be Northcote.

The counter-argument attaching itself to Salisbury was that the Conservative party ought not to adapt itself for Whig convenience, but should preserve its integrity, wait on events without any attempt to anticipate them, and accept any Whig refugees entirely on Conservative terms. There was no dispute about the improbability of being rescued in the near future by any fortunate event such as a second 1874; and no dispute about the need for effective political entrenchment to hold Gladstone, Radicalism, and the Irish at bay. The counter-argument had to do with traditional Conservatism's having enough confidence in itself to hold on and fulfil its task from within its own resources.

These were the terms of what it was assumed would be the great argument about the future of the Conservative party within the party's managerial establishment and the body of the party more or less loyal to that establishment. In fact, that argument impinged upon and became entangled with other arguments coming from within the party, having to do with rather different interests and views about its future.

Thus the third major component of the Conservative mélange in the early 1880s was the National Union. There was an argument about the need for the Union to realise itself as an autonomous body representative of popular Conservatism, and thereby to emancipate itself from being merely Central Office's propaganda agency. But necessarily such an argument could not help having a bearing on the wider issue of the location and legitimacy of ultimate authority in the party. This possibility – the 'Frankenstein's creature' model – had been recognised from the start, and had never ceased to be a feature of the managerial establishment's jaundiced view of the union. Disraeli's address at the 1872 conference at the Crystal Palace was to be the one and only time he permitted himself to be received by the union. That 'true union' argument, however, was never very strong in itself. It was much more often a part of arguments used by other interests for their own purposes. The main importance of the National Union was that it provided the field of battle for those other forces. Issues ostensibly about the nature of the National Union were actually about getting or keeping control of the union. Still, there was a class of Conservatives, mainly provincial association activists, who were dissatisfied with the existing character of the union as a 'nondescript body', 'not in any way representing or professing to represent' the constituencies in which they worked for the Conservative cause. They wanted, in the words of Henry Howorth of Eccles, a 'properly representative body with proper consultative functions', either by converting the existing union, 'which is a mere sham institution packed with co-optative members' into a reality, or 'by ignoring it altogether and starting *de novo*'.[1] They would be disposed also to recall some of the features of Colonel Arbuthnot's scheme of 1878 to consolidate the party organisation in such a way as to overcome the frictions within the 'dual system' by creating harmonious relations between London and the provinces.[2]

The interest in possession of the union, and intent on keeping possession, was naturally the managerial establishment. They had made sure that one of their men should be joint honorary secretary, to keep a sharp eye on things: first Keith-Falconer, then Colonel Neville. In the early 1880s two new forces emerged, each of which saw in a challenge to establishment control of the union a natural and inevitable means of asserting their views, sometimes in alliance, sometimes in conflict, about the future of the party.

The first was closely related to the kind of provincial Conservatism 'out of doors' represented by Henry Howorth. These were groups of regional notables who now constituted a new party elite in the great cities. Their leading lights were William Houldsworth of Manchester, Arthur Forwood of Liverpool, Albert Rollit of London, and Frederick Dixon-Hartland of London and Middlesex. It was Forwood's article, 'Democratic Toryism', in the *Contemporary Review* of February 1883, which first gave wide currency and notoriety to the concept. Forwood, shipowner and later MP for Ormskirk, advocated a 'wide redistribution of power' and proclaimed his readiness 'to support popular demands for reforms of all kinds'. He wrote the article in response to accusations by the *Standard* that he was promoting war between the classes. Forwood certainly promoted a kind of class war within the Conservative party, in which he wanted a 'wide redistribution of power' away from the aristocratic and territorial interest and toward the commercial and industrial business interest. This widely noticed 'new development of Conservatism'[3] represented an entirely different kind of popular Conservatism from the gaggle of working men's representatives who formed the National Union in 1867. The prototype local party bosses of the early 1880s were a confident, undeferential generation, very conscious of the fact that their political bases in the great cities were the areas of the highest growth rate of Conservative voters.[4] Salisbury, who drew the moral from the 1880 elections that Conservatism could forget the smaller boroughs, was not likely to have overlooked this psephological phenomenon: he was certainly in 1882 very much aware of 'our chief supporter in Liverpool, a Mr. Forwood, who may very possibly be in parliament before long'.[5]

The second new force was much less serious than the local notables, but caused much more havoc. This was the celebrated 'Fourth Party' in the House of Commons, led by Lord Randolph Churchill, with Gorst and Drummond Wolff as rank and file, and Salisbury's nephew Arthur Balfour somewhat tenuously attached in its earlier days. Churchill, MP for the Marlborough family borough of Woodstock, was an aristocratic buccaneer with demagogic talents who planned to go far and fast in the Conservative party on the strength of allegedly Disraelian doctrines of Tory Democracy and at the expense of the existing Conservative front bench in the Commons led by Northcote. Gorst hoped that in Churchill he had found a Conservative of impeccable establishment credentials and brilliant front-bench potential who would lead a campaign to destroy the power of the 'Old Identity', the 'Old

Gang', in the party for the benefit of the principles of popular Conservatism (whatever they may have been) to which Gorst was faithful and to which Gorst believed Churchill was faithful. Wolff, half *frondeur* and half *farceur*, was a cavalier of much frustrated and misconceived ambition, who shared also a great deal of Gorst's turn for paranoia. In its initial stage the Fourth Party was little more than a pro-Salisbury clique determined to do anything to spoil Northcote's chances for the party leadership. They excelled at guerrilla warfare in the Commons and Churchill learned to be a first-rate platform orator in the country. He became, rather in the manner of Gladstone in the early 1860s, the focus of a mass of popular political excitement. Ironically, Wolff's idea of a Primrose League in memory of Disraeli became a much more genuine and successful expression of popular Conservative sentiment than the National Union, mainly because, by definition, it ruled out all directive party ambitions.

2

By the end of the 1880 parliament in 1885 most of these forces, by a complex supervention of conflict, collaboration, and betrayal, had resolved themselves in a new party dispensation. The essence of the matter was that the old force with the greatest power, Salisbury, did a deal with the new force with the greatest power, Churchill, in the arena of the National Union and by the mediation of various factions of the local notables within the union, aided by Arthur Balfour. The price paid by Salisbury was the offering up for sacrifice of the Central Committee and the official managerial apparatus represented by Dyke's successor as chief whip, Rowland Winn. It was left to the queen to administer the logical subplot accessory to this act by passing over Northcote in 1885 when Gladstone resigned and asking Salisbury to be prime minister and (as in 1868) *ipso facto* leader of the Conservative party.

Apart from the benefit of thus stepping over the politically dead body of Northcote, Salisbury was the beneficiary of Churchill's offering up his equivalent to the Central Committee, that is to say Gorst and his crotchets (as well as those of the Tory Democratic successor to Gorst as principal agent, G.C.T Bartley) and his undertaking to domesticate Tory Democracy and to be 'conformable' by abandoning his own leadership ambitions and serving Salisbury in return for Northcote's exile and a major cabinet place.

The National Union enjoyed a high moment as arena of conflict and its resolution; but the local notables' factions could never unite to make a reality out of Churchill's ostensible commitment to and patronage of its ideals. Without Churchill they had no leader. For all that the local notables became MPs they never transcended the localism of their notability. Salisbury made them baronets. The next generation, led by Forwood's successor at Liverpool, Archibald Salvidge, was not much bothered to enter parliament. Salvidge was content to be boss of Liverpool and have the Merseyside Conservative MPs tremble at his displeasure. The National Union settled down to being the arena of the notable hacks such as Ashmead Bartlett and Howard Vincent, competing with the Primrose League in loyalty and devotion.

In place of the incompatible teams of Winn and Gorst and then Winn and Bartley at Central Office was a new and highly compatible team of Aretas Akers-Douglas as chief whip and Richard Middleton as principal agent. Known as the 'Kent gang' because of their provenance in that county under the patronage of Hart Dyke and Abergavenny, they set new standards of managerial competence quite untinged by delusions as to what management in itself could achieve and untinctured by notions of using the managerial apparatus as a weapon of doctrinal warfare in the party. Middleton presided with polite relentlessness over the task of making sure that the National Union was kept safe for the likes of Ashmead Bartlett.

Victims were suitably paid off. Northcote was given formal precedence as first lord of the Treasury and then an earldom (Iddesleigh). Gorst was so disgusted that at one point he almost took a high court judgeship; but in the end settled for the solicitor-generalship (with accessory knighthood), which he could have got in any case from the 'Old Gang'. Wolff got a privy-councillorship and the beginnings of a moderately grand diplomatic career. Rowland Winn was created Lord St. Oswald. Bartley was helped into an Islington constituency. The balm of patronage consoled Dyke with the Irish chief secretaryship and rewarded Balfour with the presidency of the Local Government Board. Abergavenny got his Garter.

What did these wins and losses add up to for the Conservative party? It won efficient steadiness with Salisbury's leadership and the new management team. It lost an historic opportunity to take into itself an infusion of new energies. Too much of the old territorial ballast was left in the body of the party. This was not at all because the old managerial establishment defended itself too well. It was because the new forces were fated to look for leadership in regional factions without a central coherence and in a parliamentary faction consisting of two flawed subordinates and a brilliantly flawed principal.

In the shadow of defeat

1

But, at the start of it all, there was still Benjamin Disraeli, earl of Beaconsfield, leading the Conservative party and the Conservative peers, let alone Northcote leading the Commons' Conservatives. Disraeli's line was that had the government survived the election in 1880 he would soon have sought repose; but that he could not abandon his leadership in the hour of defeat and would remain at the party's disposal. Given growing doubts about Northcote as leader, the party was very ready to fall in with this proceeding. Northcote began to busy himself with reforming the organisation. 'I gave Smith a paper on the subject of the party organisation,' he recorded in his diary on 1 May 1880, 'and Barrington lent me some good remarks on the defects of our party organisation in Scotland.' By 1882, Northcote was eloquent at the inaugural conference of the National Union of Conservative Associations for Scotland at Glasgow on the 'wide spreading' branches of the Birmingham caucus.[6] It was Northcote's notion in 1880 to have 'a small committee of parliamentary leaders, who should keep themselves in constant communication with the managers of the Central Association'.[7] Skene clearly was going to go. Where to find a new principal agent? Gorst was not the first thought of. Alfred Austin, journalist from Mudford's *Standard* and poet, and defeated candidate for Dewsbury, was mentioned. 'There is an idea', Taylor told the new Lord Rowton, 'that he may be utilised in the place of *Skene*.'[8] To do him justice, Austin himself commented after being elected to the Carlton Club: 'But when Colonel Taylor, the most agreeable of men, asked me, on behalf of the Party Whips and the Conservative Central Office, if I would assume the management of the latter, I felt that the demoralisation of defeat could no further go!'[9]

Austin at this moment was more concerned about being excluded from the grand meeting *chez* Lord Ellesmere at Bridgewater House of Conservative peers and MPs and ex-MPs to be rallied by Disraeli and given their bearings and orders of battle for the coming session of the new parliament. Much like Gorst before him, Austin resented the likelihood of *The Times* being included while the *Standard* was not. Taylor pacified him with assurances that all the press would be strictly excluded. Some 500 peers and MPs past and present attended at Barry's palace off Cleveland Row, overlooking the Green Park, on 19 May. Rowton pictured the event for the queen's eyes as a 'conspicuous success', with the picture gallery 'full beyond expectation'. Lord Beaconsfield's observations were met with 'deep attention and constant applause'.

> Enjoining strict confidence, as to all that might be said there, he compared the position of the party with the far worse one wh. it occupied after the election of 1832, pointing the moral to be drawn from Lord Grey's early fall & citing other precedents and reasons for not taking an exaggerated view of the present defeat.
>
> He adverted to 2 principal causes. First, the state of general social distress, comm^{l} and agricultural, which really arose from natural causes, and not as was alleged by travelling agitators from neglect of beneficial legis^{n}., by Y.M.s late Govt. This he proved very successfully by dwelling on their many good social measures in redress of real grievances.
>
> The second cause he described as the 'new foreign political organization' of the Liberal party – a system demanding most minute criticism and consideration wh. duly had been undertaken by a small Cee. of his late colleagues, with the Right Hon. W.H. Smith, as Chairman.

> As to the future, his advice, mainly addressed to the Com. was to watch especially the party of revol^{n}. – perhaps 100 in number – and to support the Govt. with all their force, when resisting, as they must at first, any violent proposals. Such a course would infallibly win for the party the respect and confidence of the country.

The policy of Conservatism was to maintain the empire and preserve the constitution.

> The Empire was especially in risk of being threatened in the regions of the Med^{n}. where it was of supreme importance that England should have such a stronghold as Cyprus could easily be made to afford – a remark which was received with strong assent. The Empire moreover depended much on the maintenance of the tie with the Colonies – a tie wh. he believed to be at the moment a growing one, in proof of wh. he cited, amid great applause the offer of Canada when war seemed probable lately to furnish Y.M. with a contingent of 10,000 troops.
>
> As to the Constitution, he would not criticize the probable domestic action of the party in power as to particular measures. But there could be no doubt that the first step toward any organic change, must be a revolution in the tenure of land – in other words the pulling down of the aristocracy wh. was the *first* object of the revoly. party.

That would be the key note by which all their proposed measures must be examined. Disraeli concluded by announcing his willingness to carry on as leader and 'still place at their service all the advice he could afford'. He sat down 'after speaking for an hour & forty minutes and was cheered long and loudly'. Lord Carnarvon expressed a wish to act with the party in its 'moment of trouble' whatever may have been the case two years ago, adding 'warm approval' of what Lord Beaconsfield had said. After more expressions of approval Sir Stafford Northcote ended proceedings by stating the 'complete confidence' of the late ministers in Lord Beaconsfield.[10]

The 'small committee of parliamentary leaders' recommended by Northcote to keep themselves in 'constant communication with the managers of the Central Association' consisted initially of Smith as chairman, Edward Stanhope, formerly undersecretary at the India Office, and Lord Percy, chairman of the National Union. Another National Union figure, Raikes, was called to the fore: 'your assistance', Smith assured him, 'will be most valuable when we come to consider . . . the recommendations we should make for the constitution of a Central Office.'[11] Not the least of Raikes's merits was that he was chairman of the Church Defence Institution. One problem was Dyke's persistent illness. He was loth to resign in the aftermath of defeat. 'It is very difficult to make a new arrangement,' Northcote complained. Abergavenny was for decided action by July: 'Dyke is no better poor fellow & I feel thoroughly convinced that he ought to be made to retire & his place filled up as soon as possible.'[12] Northcote recommended to Disraeli that Dyke's assistant, Rowland Winn, should succeed as chief whip. Dyke, however, resisted; and it was not until December that the way was cleared.

Cairns reported seeing Dyke at Goodwood: 'He & Lady Emily both say that he will not go on as Whip, on the score of health. So I think there need be no delicacy in approaching him on that footing.'[13] In January 1881 Winn took over, with Lord Henry Thynne and Lord Crichton as assistants.

2

The question of Skene's successor seemed more amenable to settlement. That Alfred Austin had been thought of is testimony to a desperate sense among the managers of the inevitability of Gorst. Gorst's 'prophetic letter' of 1877 predicting doom was exchanged between Northcote and Smith on 15 May in a mood of glum resignation to an ineluctable logic of things. Dyke would be a difficulty. Having Gorst back with all his crotchets seemingly endorsed by disaster would have been a charmless prospect. Dyke's feelings must not be hurt; but Northcote was clear that 'he certainly cannot manage the whole business himself'. As for Gorst: 'I fancy we shall be obliged to make some experimental arrangement in the first instance, and not commit ourselves to any one until we have tried him.'[14] Northcote reported to Disraeli on 7 July:

> Gorst has been talking over his position with Smith and myself. He is ready to take a great share in the Out-door management, and to conform himself to our wishes indoors, on the understanding that if we come in again he shall have an offer either of a Law officership (in case he has by that time attained professional eminence enough to justify it,) or an Under-Secretaryship with a Chief in the House of Lords. I don't think this unreasonable; and Smith and I have both told him that we thought his services, if loyally rendered, would give him a claim to such promotion.[15]

As with his initial appointment in 1870, Gorst was not to be a salaried officer (though he later changed his mind about this, in a manner characteristically causing maximum friction).

Smith sent to Disraeli on 4 August a 'sketch of the proposed constitution of the Central Office'. Edward Stanhope concurred and was quite ready to act as vice-chairman of the committee, otherwise consisting of the chief whip, Gorst, and Raikes. 'Gorst also is satisfied and is ready to do his best: and Rowland Winn puts no obstacle in the way.' There was one more vacancy to fill. 'We think it better not to name the fifth man yet as it is desirable to get some shrewd politician to help us who is not in parliament and does not desire to enter it.'[16] Gorst was to be charged with the primary responsibility of securing candidates for seats, but, while free to initiate proposals as to financial assistance where necessary, would not be at liberty to promise money. It would be for the whip to have discretion as to money, but no contributions were to be made without consulting Gorst; and the agent, for his part, would keep the whip and other members of the Central Committee informed as to all proposals and arrangements as to candidates. It would be the committee's duty to ascertain the state of the party's organisation in every constituency, to make visitations to stimulate local exertions, and to see to the provision of experienced local agents. A secretary should be appointed to the committee to handle confidential business passing between the committee and constituencies and candidates, but it was 'not desirable that he should have the position or the authority of Agent'.[17] It was unofficially agreed, as of old, that Gorst should confine himself to the boroughs. Stanhope (second son of the 5th Earl Stanhope) would look after the counties. The Hon. Fitzroy Stewart was appointed secretary to the committee. Gorst assured Northcote that he liked 'our new man at St. Stephen's Chambers very much. He is vivacious and industrious and pleases everyone who comes into contact with him.' Stewart and the existing Central Office clerk, Rowe, worked together 'with diligence & energy'.

It did not take long for the old tensions to break through this new surface. Raikes complained of Gorst's aiming at 'absolute autocracy' in the National Union, and set out to defend the union's autonomy. The union had plans to make an appeal for its own funds. For his part, Gorst found Winn no improvement on Dyke. He promised Smith that he would do his best to 'menager' Winn and his protégé Shaw, inspector of Registration Associations and 'travelling agent'. Gorst's objection to Shaw, as he explained to Smith, was that Shaw was 'prone to corrupt practices, which accounts for his being in much request among corrupt constituencies'. To Winn's charges that 'I won't fight corruption with corruption', Gorst was proud to 'plead guilty'. Gorst's hope was the the government would push through new legislation to restrict electoral expenditure; 'and if Harry Thynne and his friends will have corrupt practices on our side we must have them locally not fostered and organised from headquarters by Mr. Shaw or anyone else.' Gorst professed to be 'quite in favour of treating Winn and the old identity with consideration, but they can hardly expect us to take their modus operandi as our model or accept Dyke's judgment of character as infallible'.[18] *Vanity Fair*, a fashionable society paper run by Gibson Bowles, who backed Lord Randolph Churchill as the coming new Disraeli, carried inspired pieces on Conservative organisation in May and October 1880 'which bore the imprint of Gorst'. They denounced the 'superannuated oligarchy', the 'paternalistic electoral machinery, indolence and class bias of the Old Gang, their obsession with the landed interest at the expense of the democracy'. Caucus would have to be met with caucus, democracy addressed on its own ground, and in its own language; and great issues of the future such as property and redistribution of wealth squarely faced.[19]

Dyke, now rather a passenger on this new party wagon, professed in November to 'find some good work being done, & hope to devote one day a week during the winter to it'.[20] Still, by the beginning of 1881 the new machinery was sufficiently in place for Gorst to send at Smith's request a 'Memorandum by JEG to the Chief' on the 'Ordinary work' and 'Special work' of Conservative Central Office since August 1880. Under ordinary work were listed procedures as to registration, elections, organisation, meetings, publications, press ('A weekly publication, called the "Editor's Handy Sheet", issued to provide material for political articles to the Conservative Provincial Press. Political telegrams sent from the Lobby to several provincial papers.'), parliamentary statistics, correspondence, interviews, visits. Under special work: 'The Hon. Fitzroy Stewart (our new Secretary) has read up the correspondence of the last six years respecting each constituency. He has seen a great number of candidates for parliament. . . . A great deal of his time has been taken up by interviews with persons who have schemes for starting every description of newspaper, and who persist in explaining them to somebody who represents the Party.' Further: 'The National Union which broke out into discord with the Party Managers after the General Election has been brought into concord.' A committee on county organisation had been formed by the Hon. E. Stanhope. There was a Committee on Ireland and a committee to consider the Corrupt Practices Bill. Mr. Dawson, an Oxford BA, had been employed under the supervision of Stanhope to make an 'Index of Political Events of the last 10 years for reference'.[21]

Gorst helped to bring the National Union from discord into concord with his smooth words at the 1880 conference defending the party managers against accusations of culpability for the 'utter ruin' of the party's organisation. He was also willing to help Smith to stop the union from appealing independently for funds. His argument had to do with the efficiency of disparate appeals for money from within the party; but it was also clear that, so long as he was at Central Office, he would brook no brothers near his throne. It was also clear, as early as September 1880, that the stipulation Northcote thought he had Gorst's agreement to that Gorst would 'conform himself to our wishes indoors', was fraying badly. Gorst made no nice distinctions about the way he behaved to the 'old identity' as principal agent and as parliamentary backbencher. To Smith he made the following declaration, well deserving of Disraeli's old epithet of 'insolent:'

> There is a regular intrigue going on on the part of Bourke and others against Lord Randolph Churchill, Wolff and myself. They tried to detach Balfour from us but failed. We mean to stick together and we shall be loyal to Northcote if he is loyal to us. But self-preservation is the first law of politics as well as of nature, and contingencies may happen which will end in your being obliged to take the place of leader in the Commons whether you like it or not.[22]

3

Northcote's first session as leader of the Conservative opposition in the Commons was indeed not a fortunate one. Northcote faithfully set about implementing Disraeli's deliberate and formal advice to the party at

Bridgewater House 'to support the Government with all their force', excepting only 'violent proposals'. That this line of approach also faithfully reflected Northcote's own personal predispositions only magnified the offence he caused in the eyes of members of his own party who would increasingly promote a cult of Disraeli as a weapon against Disraeli's most faithful lieutenant. Disraeli's advice to the Conservative party, and Northcote's implementation of it in the Commons, was founded on fundamental misreadings of the situation. Conservatives tended, naturally enough, to exaggerate the power and influence of Radicalism in the Liberal party and on the Liberal government; and they tended, accordingly, to premature anticipations of Whig defection. Northcote recorded a conversation with Disraeli on 12 July:

> He said reflection only made him feel more sure that we ought to handle the Whigs carefully, making them seem to take the initiative & supporting them rather than taking it ourselves & putting them in the distasteful position of having to desert their own party & join the Tories. The Whigs ought to come out & assert their *raison d'être* as upholders of the landed interest.

The recent resignation of Lord Lansdowne from the Indian undersecretaryship over Irish policy gave Disraeli great hopes that the 'history of 1834 was repeating itself, & we ought to avoid the mess made of the "Derby dilly" secession, when Stanley & Graham joined the Conservatives too late'. Disraeli said of the present crisis, 'a Government with a large majority may do almost anything with impunity in its first session'. The errors of the Liberal government might be condoned or forgotten, 'but Lansdowne's resignation remains'. That was the 'great fact we have to look to, & it will produce a great & lasting effect'.[23]

There was no stint of other signals as to Whig uneasiness. Chamberlain was no longer at the gate: he was in the cabinet. To most Whigs this was a sign that the world was very evil and the times waxing late. Snippets were eagerly picked up and relayed by Conservatives. Lady Salisbury reported to Disraeli as early as 14 April: 'Thank goodness the troubles of the Liberals are already beginning. I have heard from Lord E. Fitzmaurice & dear Lady Taunton. They are both very uneasy.' Later: 'I saw Ld. Hartington at Ascot. He said "You will soon be back again. I always thought it would be bad but it is much worse than I thought it would be. We have such a lot of cantankerous loons"!!!'[24] Harcourt's defeat at the Oxford by-election on taking office was much rejoiced at as an auspicious event. There was, it seemed to Lady Salisbury, repentance among the High Churchmen. 'There are clearly signs of a split among clerical supporters of the A[rch]. V[illain].! Canon Liddon voted for us in the City & is gone to Oxford to vote against Sr. W. H[arcourt] & he is the leader of the High Church men.' Lady Salisbury echoed the queen's opinion: 'Depend upon it the Great Lady is right. It will not last long.' And the 'real comfort' of Harcourt's defeat was that it caused as much rejoicing at Brooks's and the

Reform as at the Carlton.[25] Northcote ruminated upon its importance 'as a proof of the temporary and local character of the causes which led to our great defeat'.[26] In truth, the importance of the Oxford by-election was much more likely to have been the fact that Central Office invested, as a party morale builder, an unprecedented £3,000 in a dead set against Harcourt.[27]

In this comforting atmosphere Northcote nursed a vision of a 'Conservative cave' being formed among the Liberals, 'with perhaps Goschen at its centre'. Northcote envisaged that 'we may often join hands with them', and 'perhaps ultimately bring some of them to take part in a Conservative Cabinet'. Northcote allowed that this was a vision somewhat in the same spirit as the Roman purchaser's bid for the fields occupied by the Carthaginian army. 'Still, it is necessary to lay our foundations properly.'[28] In at least one respect Northcote envisaged accurately. Goschen was indeed to be the first Whig to join a Conservative cabinet, in place of the resigned Churchill in January 1887.

That ultimate outcome was prefigured in the way the 1880 session contradicted all rational prognostications. Despite Disraeli, it had little to do with analogies of 1834. Despite Northcote, it had little to do with Conservative caves among Liberals. Despite Chamberlain, it had little to do with Radical Nonconformist schemes for the Church and education. Despite Gladstone, for that matter, it had little to do with what he insisted was the one overriding mission which justified his temporarily supplanting Granville, the moral imperative of reversing the spirit and practice of Lord Beaconsfield's foreign policy. It had to do, first and foremost, with transmission through Parnell and his augmented and more coherent Home Rule party to the Commons of the full impact of the crisis in Ireland. That in itself was enough to derail Gladstone's assumptions about the nature and duration of his strictly delimited responsibilities in his recurrence to the Liberal leadership. This was not a fulfilment of Disraeli's lurid words to the duke of Marlborough. They were not written in expectation of Parnellite Home Rule triumph in Ireland. Nor did Ireland figure in the Bridgewater House meeting. The Conservative party was no better prepared than the Liberal party to cope with the Irish impact. It had always been the Liberal intention not to renew the Irish Peace Preservation Act, on the grounds that Irish disaffection, like social distress in Britain, was only to be expected as a natural and inevitable concomitant of Tory Rule. This, in turn, gave a handle to disaffected Conservatives in the House of Commons, notably Lord Randolph Churchill. Lord Randolph, exiled from London society after having tried to blackmail the princess of Wales, had acted as his father's private secretary at Viceregal Lodge in Dublin; and was genuinely knowledgeable about Irish affairs in a way very few Conservatives were. The Fourth Party would always be known for its unconventionally Conservative view of Irish matters.

But even more apt for the purposes of Conservative disaffection in baiting its official leadership were the opportunities for diversion and obfuscation provided by the Bradlaugh affair. This absurd imbroglio arose from the desire of Charles Bradlaugh, elected for the borough of Northampton, to make his point as a professed atheist by making his oath as a member of the Commons by affirmation rather than by the conventional mode of swearing on the bible. This was, in the atmosphere of the time, a provocative request; but affirmation was perfectly feasible, and it was only the way in which his case was entangled with other cases which prevented Bradlaugh from taking his seat. Wolff and Gorst seized the opportunity to use Bradlaugh to embarrass Northcote; and soon drew in Churchill and Balfour. There is no need to doubt that Churchill's Christian outrage was genuine enough. There was never any doubt that Northcote's front-bench authority among the Conservatives was Churchill's substantial target. Gladstone was not in control of all of his party amid this Christian excitement. Northcote was very little in control of any part of his. 'Our friends are (some of them) keen to make a long and adjourned debate out of it,' reported Northcote to Disraeli, 'and try to get up excitement in the country. I think we must take care that we do not overshoot the mark, though I am for giving fair scope to the discussion.'[29] Churchill openly mocked Northcote's 'not overshooting the mark' and 'fair scope' on 24 May; and from that moment Northcote's unnerved failure to assert himself lost him the greater part of his moral authority over his own benches.

The readiness of the two leaders to agree on a sensible resolution came to naught in a Commons which insisted on tying itself into knots by denying Bradlaugh the right either to affirm or to swear. Gladstone, disgusted, took a loftily detached attitude to these antics. Northcote, equally disgusted, was perforce obliged, however, to abet the antics of his most irresponsible followers. He put the best face he could on this virtual state of captivity in his account to Disraeli: 'You will see that we are making history, and that we are in a very peculiar position owing to Gladstone's abnegation of his functions as leader, in consequence of which I have had to act as if I were sitting in my old place.'[30] Northcote's weakness for surrogacy to Gladstone was indeed the charge most insistently urged against him by his critics in the Conservative party; and thus artlessly to boast of it as a cloak for his predicament was to compound both his offence and his humiliation. By now, what was becoming identified as the Fourth Party ostentatiously ignored Northcote (whom they contemptuously nicknamed 'the Goat', apparently because of the shape of his beard) and made a point of asking for their orders from Salisbury.

Disraeli, as leader of the party, had to take cognisance of this problem. He was scrupulous in giving all formal consideration to Northcote. In conversations with Northcote on 11 and 12 July he made a point of speaking 'strongly on Gladstone's vindictiveness, an element never to be left out of sight in calculating the course of events'. It was 'a great fault in the leader of a party'. He 'reverted again to Gladstone's vindictiveness,' Northcote recorded, '& said Cardinal Manning had once told him that he knew Gladstone well &

that he thought him the most revengeful man he ever knew.' Disraeli 'talked over the state of the House, & asked me many questions, as to the progress of Harcourt, Chamberlain, Dilke, James, Herschell etc., & also as to our own bench.' He lamented the likelihood of Sandon's soon succeeding to his father's peerage, '& Smith's inferiority in speaking, which was much to be lamented as he was so valuable in many respects'. He was 'much disappointed in Beach, whom he had expected to see taking a leading part in debate'. Disraeli added: '"When you come to form a Ministry, you will have to leave out several old Colleagues," & amongst them he instanced John Manners.' Northcote 'stood up for him, & said he was often of much use'; and wondered whether the chief had ever heard about the Burghley gathering of 1872 when Northcote and Manners were the only two who 'stood up against the absurd notion of deposing him'.[31] Perhaps a little wistfully, Northcote inquired 'whether Randolph Churchill was forgiven yet in high quarters' (over his insolence to the princess of Wales). Disraeli told him that Churchill was 'all right as far as the Queen was concerned, but that the Prince of Wales had not yet made it up with him'. Nothing would help Churchill into favour again, Disraeli assured Northcote, 'so much as success in Parliament: the Prince is always taken by success'. Disraeli rather tactlessly capped this less than tactful remark by asking Northcote to post on a letter to Drummond Wolff.[32]

On 25 August Disraeli made a 'much-talked-of visit' to the Peers' Gallery in the Commons 'to see the Fourth Party'.[33] He tried to give them sympathetic yet sound advice. 'I fully appreciate your feelings and those of your friends,' he told Wolff; 'but you must stick to Northcote. He represents the respectability of the party. I wholly sympathise with you all, because I never was respectable myself.' Disraeli offered emollient good offices and mediation if necessary. 'Don't on any account break with Northcote; but defer to him as often as you can. Whenever it becomes too difficult you can come to me and I will try to arrange matters. Meanwhile I will speak to him.'[34]

Whether or not as a consequence of Disraeli's speaking to Northcote, the Conservative leader in the Commons decided that it was time to extinguish the contumacious faction. In the course of inviting Gorst to 'a little talk with you about our organisation and our general prospects', and the need for 'both courage and care in the conduct of the Party next Session', Northcote 'inclined to think that the "Fourth Party" has done enough for its fame, and that it will be the wiser course for its members now quietly to take their places in the main body, where they will have work enough and to spare'. There could not, Northcote allowed, 'be too much freedom of discussion among ourselves out of the House, but any appearance of dissension in the House' was 'carefully to be avoided'.[35] Gorst responded by ignoring Northcote's command to come to heel and by dilating on matters of organisation, especially his hope of forcing the government to pass a strong Corrupt Practices Act next session. He insisted:

> Our little association, to which enemies to sow dissension among us have given the name of the 'Fourth Party', will I am sure prove one of your best instruments of political warfare. Each of us feels stronger for the support and wiser for the counsels of his fellows; and we are all determined to back you up loyally in fighting the battle of the Conservative cause against the combination of Whigs and Radicals who oppose us.[36]

This deliberate coupling of Whig and Radical was tantamount to enhancing defiance with truculent insult. 'The Goat has been at it again', Gorst told Balfour. 'Under cover of a friendly letter about organisation . . . he has coolly proposed the dissolution of the Fourth Party and that its members should "quietly" (fancy Randolph & Wolff doing anything quietly) take their places in the main body.' Did not Balfour think 'these repeated attempts upon individual political virtue' were 'most disreputable'? Gorst often fancied that 'the Goat' had his eye upon 'a possible coalition with the Whigs. In some quarters this has been spoken of as the next political combination. This would account for his hostility to us; a leader who really meant fighting would have welcomed our association – at least until by experience he had proved that we were incapable of being managed or led.'[37] Gorst was now quite unabashedly linking his official role as principal agent of the party with the freelance role of the Fourth Party. From the point of view of Northcote and Smith this was both brazen professional malversation as well as rank treachery. Gorst must have known that his outrageous threat to Smith, that Smith might well have to take the Commons' leadership over from Northcote whether he liked it or not, would certainly get back to Northcote. As Rowton put it, 'the fourth party are shaking their spears'.[38]

In such a strained atmosphere Disraeli renewed his efforts at pacification. He even went so far as to invite Gorst to Hughenden in November 1880 in a special effort to mollify him and encourage a modicum of decorum and conformability. 'Lord B.', Gorst reported to Churchill, 'was in his talk anything but Goaty: he generally expressed great confidence in us, thought we had a brilliant future before us, and promised to help and advise us as much as he could.' Disraeli advised them to stop flirting with the government on Ireland. He defended Northcote from imputations of thinking of coalition or being inclined to Derby; and in particular loyally scouted Wolff's particular animus against Northcote's proclivities toward Derby in the late cabinet. Disraeli tried to hit on a formula reconciling the correct degree of insistence on respect and attention to Northcote with an allowed degree of being not *'too scrupulous'* about obedience. 'An open rupture between us would, however, be most disastrous; but Lord B. thinks if we are courteous and firm Northcote will make no open rupture, and will not throw us over.'[39]

Disraeli reported back to Northcote that he had seen Gorst, and had confidence in his future conduct; and would continue to assist Northcote, 'as much as I possibly can, in looking after the Fourth Party'.[40] Disraeli shared with the Fourth Party a cavalier view of the more roundhead of his colleagues. He tended to see the high-spirited group through a sentimental haze of memories of Young England.[41] With Gorst, he tried to humour a humourless man; though he judged that Gorst was 'the only really dangerous Fourth Party member', confessing himself 'quite unable even to guess at the motives which guide him'.[42] And with Churchill, he was prone, in spite of himself, to be too indulgently receptive to Churchill's own cultivation of the analogy of Northcote as a second Peel. Disraeli was not sufficiently aware of the fact that there were in the party serious and dedicated enemies of Northcote's leadership, such as Raikes and Edward Clarke, who thought they had good reason to have a low opinion of Churchill's character and motives.

Disraeli's last stand: 'we can but die like gentlemen'

1

As Disraeli remarked, a government with a large majority might do almost anything with impunity in its first session. A 'discreet' management of Conservative opposition did not, however, seem wanting in feasibility on the strength of the programme declared by the new ministers at the end of April. Foreign policy took Gladstonian priority. There was something for all the Liberal sections. The Nonconformists were to get a Burials Bill. The tenant farmers were to be appeased on the ground game issue. The trade unions were to have employers' liability. The Irish were offered a package: distress relief, borough franchise registration, and non-renewal of coercive legal powers for the Irish executive. When the Conservative parliamentary leaders met on 29 May to consider their responses they felt no sense of dire urgency. They decided not to oppose the second reading of the Employers' Liability Bill and to leave it to the late law officers to point out defects and propose amendments. They would be tougher on burials: Disraeli was to ask the bishop of Lincoln to move rejection and to send out a strong whip, and to propose amendments in committee. It was too early to decide on the ground game question. The key thing was to be consistent in policy as between the two Houses.[43]

Foreign policy proved not to be an area in which the Bridgewater House doctrines on empire were threatened by the new government. Gladstone and Granville made no move to repudiate formally the Anglo-Turkish Convention, but decided instead to use a strict adherence to the public law of the Berlin treaty as a foundation upon which to reconstruct the European concert and as a fulcrum by which to lever the Turks into concessions to the Greeks and Montenegrins. Salisbury carefully monitored Gladstone's apology for his insults against Austria at Midlothian.[44] Liberal withdrawal from Lytton's forward position in Afghanistan was resolutely conducted under cover of the brilliant military exploits by Roberts. Withdrawal from

Frere's forward position in South Africa was irresolutely bungled, provoking the 'first Boer war' and Colley's military disaster at Majuba Hill. This hurt the government, vulnerable to revived memories of Liberalism's reputation for recessiveness in the external dimensions of policy. But, like all else, this particular case of Liberal recessiveness was soon subsumed in the much more immediately momentous and uncomfortably closer-to-home case of Liberalism's reputation for rank appeasement in face of aggressions by the Irish. This in turn came to call into question Disraeli's assumption as to the impunity of governments with large majorities in their first session.

The crisis of the session arose out of a clause originally in the Irish Relief of Distress Bill. This emerged in the hands of the new chief secretary, Forster, as the Irish Compensation for Disturbance Bill. It was introduced as a temporary emergency measure; and its purpose was to discourage landlords from evicting by providing a mechanism whereby in certain areas under certain conditions evicted tenants might apply to be awarded compensation from their former landlords. This short bill occupied most of the session not otherwise taken up by Parnellite obstruction or Fourth Party spoils and stratagems. It was naturally denounced by Conservatives, led initially by Chaplin and Plunket, as being a monstrous imposition upon landlords, as threatening the principle of property, and as representing confiscatory politics. Churchill described it as the 'first step in a social war'.[45] The most effective Conservative arguments, put forward by George Hamilton, challenged the accuracy of the statistics used to justify the measure. Salisbury commented to Balfour on what seemed to him 'a very puzzling state of things':

> Why has Gladstone never taken the trouble to make the most obvious preparations for such a bill? It would not have taken long to have his statistics properly prepared – or to ascertain what it was his Whig supporters on the one side, or Parnell on the other, could really be induced to accept. Both in this matter, & in the foreign policy, there are marks of hurry which in so old a man are inexplicable. I suppose, he still cherishes his belief in an early hermitic retreat from this wicked world – & is feverishly anxious to annihilate all his enemies before he takes it.
>
> The vacillations of the Cabinet are the ordinary indication of divided opinion – & that seems a sufficient explanation.
>
> I am inclined to believe the bill will get through your House – though it seems to be generally agreed that it has no chance in ours.[46]

It was much less easy for Northcote in the Commons to adopt this measured, detached view. There the Irish impact was direct; and Gladstone's 'argument from terror' told. The Irish, too, were shaking their spears. Northcote was pleased to 'see the signs of discontent on the other side'. Gladstone's speech he thought 'one of his least happy performances'. and the manner 'in which he used the argument from terror gave great offence'. Hussey Vivian, the Liberal member for Swansea District, 'even, made a protest against it'.

> But one is tempted to ask, where is the good of their disgust? The Duke of Bedford is reported to have said the other day that he hated the Irish Land Bill, – 'but there

is no use standing up against Gladstone.' And so it seems likely to be for some time. They will swear in their beards, but they will eat any amount of leek.

Northcote added a further point, for Disraeli's benefit, of even more lowering portent: 'There is no doubt that a great many, even of our own men, had fears at the bottom of their hearts which held them back a little, and they would have felt very uneasy if we had won and if Gladstone had precipitated a crisis and gone out into the street.'[47]

Nevertheless, there remained a Conservative disposition to see the matter as a great and promising test case for the Whigs. Rowton assured Disraeli that feeling upon the bill among the Whigs increased rather than diminished. 'They reckon that some 30 or 40 Whigs will vote with us. This, of course, won't be enough; but the Cee. further count on many Whig abstainers from the Division.' The clerk of the Commons, Sir Erskine May, was reported as expressing a private opinion 'that the measure will not leave the Commons'.[48] Disraeli could not share this sense of promise. He declared 'no faith whatever' in Whig defection on a bill which was 'the most dangerous thing' that had happened in his time. The Whigs might be indignant, but they were pusillanimous: Spencer 'weaker than water'; Granville 'with not an acre'; Kimberley 'not much'; Argyll 'will only kick for Scotland'; Westminster 'a creature of the A.V.'; 'and, I fear we know the length of Hartn's foot. Alas! Alas!'[49] In the event, Northcote reported that the division on the second reading was 'disappointing'.

I think 20 of the Whigs voted with us, and a good many abstained; but our own men were sadly slack. Even Fred Stanley thought it more important to attend a Grand Jury in Lancashire than to be at his post in the House of Commons! . . . Randolph Churchill made an excellent speech.[50]

Disraeli concluded that he really thought that the country was going to the dogs; but resolved to fight the Irish bill in the Lords 'on its principle, and we must be fools and cowards if we do not win'.[51] He had a dismayed awareness of what Kebbel was to describe as the redolence of prophetic power in his speech of March 1873 outlining the deeper and higher reach and range of the important questions which must soon engage the attention of the country with the closing of the 'fiscal period' of politics.[52] But also evident is a new determination that the Conservative party and the House of Lords would not be overborne on this issue as they were overborne in 1869.

Rowton declared himself to Disraeli as being 'quite satisfied with the tone of all as to the course you propose, and with the assurances of personal co-operation in the Lobby'. Lord Longford was quite sure that a new clause, 'virtually extending Ulster Tenant Right throughout Ireland', would be 'an aggravation of the iniquity of the Bill'.[53] The following day, 9 July, Landsdowne announced his resignation from the government. Here at last was something startling, and possibly significant, from the Whigs. Disraeli conceded that 'people generally don't know that he is a young man. Many will think it is his grandfather. Anyhow it is a great name, &, as a fact, he is a devilish clever fellow, who ought to be in the Cabinet.'[54] Ever eager to improve the shining hour, Rowton reported from the Lords rumours that the duke of Argyll was to resign – 'and this, in spite of his being in his place, at this moment.'

> The feeling certainly grows against the Bill, and our people express renewed hope of killing it in the Commons if Northcote will speak out. I am much satisfied with the look out, and find our Peers resolute, in spite of Bath's efforts to make a cave.[55]

As to the rejection of the bill in the Lords there was no doubt. 'Waterford's Whig contingent is more violent in language than ever: denying the possibility of any compromise.' A rather concessionary speech by Spencer at the Cobden Club merely revealed that 'a seat in that dreary room at 10 Downing St. has made him forget that he is a landed proprietor and an Englishman. It will only strengthen the Whig secession.'[56]

The Conservative party was in turmoil between Disraeli's bravery in the Lords and Northcote's fears about possible consequences in 'the street'. It was a bold course to defy a government so strong in the Commons in its first session. Parnell withdrew Irish countenance for Forster because of a Whig amendment giving tenants the option of selling to landlords. Richmond saw resistance to Forster 'not solely upon Irish grounds, but as involving a principle dangerous to the whole Kingdom', made the more feasible by 'the fact, that as now altered the bill does not please the Irish Home Rulers representing the tenants' and on the other side Lansdowne's resigning because as a landlord he objected. 'The more evidence we have about Ireland,' concluded Richmond, lately returned thence with his commission on agricultural depression, 'the more perplexed I am to know what can be done.' Everything, as he informed Cairns, 'seems so different to what one is accustomed to in England or Scotland. Emigration if it could be carried out on a large scale would I have no doubt be an excellent thing.'[57] This dismal conclusion perhaps exposed severe limitations of Conservative political imagination. It certainly exposed contradiction between such a perception of the Irish case and the core of the Conservative argument that (in the words of a doubting Liberal, Rylands, as relayed by Northcote), though a 'very small measure', it contained a 'great principle' and that it was 'absurd to regard it as a local or temporary measure'.[58]

By now Disraeli had worked himself up into a conviction that Forster's measure 'is to lead to other measures'. He assured Cairns: 'Gladstone is resolved to destroy the aristocracy: were he younger, the Crown wd be in equal peril – from one, whom Manning described as the most vindictive of men.'[59] Northcote could not summon up the nerve to 'speak out' in the Commons to kill the Compensation Bill. It would be up to the Lords. Disraeli, whom Richmond recently complained of as never being seen about apart from the 'occasional division', now querulously demanded attendance and attention. 'Affairs here are most critical', he insisted to Cairns, '& I go up to town, to stay, & try to guide a ship in a very stormy sea.' There was much pressure upon him from a committee of peers and members of parliament earnestly requesting a strong Conservative showing in the Lords for the second reading, especially a weight of legal authority 'equal to Selborne & O'Hagan' (the 'government talk very big of what O'Hagan & Selborne will do for them, that their speeches will be unanswerable'). Whig allies would be 'numerous'. Salisbury reported himself 'quite well' enough to be in at the kill. If Cairns were absent, fretted Disraeli, 'we have neither a lawyer, nor an Irishman, on our bench!!'[60] In the event, Disraeli was able to acclaim Cairns's speech as 'overwhelming': and the Lords dealt summarily with the Compensation for Disturbance Bill on 3 August. Forster reacted in the Commons with what Northcote described as an 'outrageous speech', which 'seemed to appal Hartington and some others, and I hear that the Whig Peers were greatly discomposed by it'.[61]

That was indeed bold, if probably misguided as to specifically Irish exigencies and even more misguided as to Gladstone's alleged resolve to destroy the aristocracy of the three kingdoms. (Rowton fed Disraeli with intelligence such as: 'Gorst tells me that Sir H. James tells him, very privately, that Gladstone is touched, in the head. And I hear less definite whispers to the same effect.')[62] Gladstone exacted immediate revenge by insisting on an extended session to make up for Bradlaugh and Fourth Party nonsense. Northcote, now confronting bills for ground game, burials and employers' liability, contemplated with dismay a further series of brave acts in the Lords; and saw it as his duty to present the case for circumspection and the longer view. On employers' liability Disraeli insisted that 'the situation is very grave' ('many of our friends in H. of Lords are deeply interested in mines') and that Cairns did not 'understand what is taking place'.[63] Disraeli was apt to talk of 'other most important questions, that are on the tapis, & may arise': possibly 'some important communication on the state of Ireland is at hand'. There was 'a week of some anxiety & considerable excitement. I found the troops very disorderly, but I hope I restored discipline.' He feared that he would not be able to maintain his amendment to employers' liability, 'but the Game Bill . . . has turned out well'.[64]

Amid these febrile scenes of anxiety and excitement Northcote had his own notions about discipline. After assuring Disraeli that Cross and Smith were 'fully in possession of my views as to the course which it would be wise for our friends to take in the H. of Lords', Northcote proceeded:

> I wish to express very strongly my sense of the importance of *husbanding* the influence of the Peers.
>
> We have a most dangerous House of Commons, led by a very dangerous Ministry.
>
> It is not impossible that they may next year bring forward measures which

will outrun the feeling of the country. It will be for the House of Lords to afford a rallying point around which the Conservatism of the nation may make a stand. It is important that they should not have weakened their influence before the time comes.

They have greatly raised that influence by their rejection of the Irish Compensation bill. They may fairly stand on the limitation of the operation of the Employers' Liability bill so as to obtain for it a fuller consideration. But I hope they will not make the mistake of throwing out the Ground Game bill, and so at once aggravating the difficulties which their friends in the House of Commons are feeling with reference to their relations with their farmer constituents, and giving colour to the impression that they are more anxious to secure the rights of sporting than they ought to be.[65]

'Rights of sporting' touched very sensitive territorial susceptibilities. Richmond confessed himself 'very much at a loss as to what we ought to do'. Harcourt's 'Hares and Rabbits' Bill was 'a very bad bill, and by no means wanted'.[66] For Disraeli, giving tenants the right to destroy noxious ground game was yet 'another attempt to divert and separate the farmers from the gentlemen'; and 'much the most devilish of the A. V.'s schemes'.[67] Four leading Whigs had given notice of opposition in the Commons to the 'Rabbits Bill' 'on the "Freedom of Contract" ground', as Northcote reported.[68] He was in any case afraid that Conservatives in the Commons would split on the question. 'The majority are for supporting the men from Brookes' . . . but Pell and Read will be satisfied with nothing that involves a vote against the 2nd Reading.'[69] Northcote's advice was followed in the Lords. 'The Carlton', as Rowton described on 20 August, 'is divided about Hares and Rabbits. The cooler heads are for passing the Bill. wh. I feel pretty sure will get thro' Committee here tonight.'[70] Conservative benches in any case were conspicuously thinned by the decamping of peers for the shooting season. In fact, all the Liberals achieved with this manoeuvre was to remove a cause of ill-feeling between gentlemen and farmers in much the way Conservative trade union legislation in the previous parliament had improved relations between Liberal employers and workmen. (Gladstone's abolition of the malt tax in his 1880 budget similarly gained little gratitude and served much the same unintended result.) The Lords dealt circumspectly, likewise, with Chamberlain's Employers' Liability Bill. There was pressure from Conservative MPs such as Edward Clarke[71] for effective legislation in the area of employers' negligence; though the principle of proving negligence was retained.

2

Conservative defiance of Gladstone's government in 1880 was the striking fact of that session. It was a fact, however, which exposed Northcote's position as the exponent of the 'husbanding' of defiance to further vulnerability. The essential soundness of his advice availed little against the manner of his giving it and, even more, the manner of his practising it. Gladstone would punish the Lords and the Conservative party with a menacing Irish Land Bill in the coming session. Salisbury, retired to the charms of his chalet at Puys, heard reports from Balfour near the end of the 1880 session. Discounting predisposition and partiality, both report and response reflected accurately enough a growing sense of unease in the party about its Commons' leadership of Northcote flanked by Cross and Smith (the two latter dubbed wickedly by Churchill 'Marshall and Snelgrove'). 'I am very sorry to hear your account of the state of affairs on our front bench in the H. of C.', replied Salisbury. 'But I see no remedy.' Salisbury feared that the 'efficacy of our party' would decay; '& that we shall not recover the confidence of the country.' For it was, he held, 'the central figures of a party in the Commons to which constituencies are wont to look, if their confidence is asked for that party'. All that could be done meanwhile was to 'have patience & make up our minds to wait for some time'.[72]

Meanwhile, there seemed no good reason to decline a pressing invitation from Lord Randolph to speak at Woodstock. 'I have promised to attend a dinner at Hackney', explained Salisbury to Balfour, and therefore would have 'had my say upon general politics; but if I can be of any use at Woodstock I shall be very glad.' Salisbury was studious to establish his *bona fides* apropos of Northcote.

> I am disposed with you to doubt that Northcote expects any coalition with the Whigs as a party. He may hope by adopting a moderate attitude to lure over Whig rank & file to become Tories: & this, if Gladstone becomes violent, is not an unlikely occurrence.
>
> I think his tactics, so far, are wise. The leader, even of a diminished party, must behave as the arbitrator between its various sections: & if he has fair ground for hoping to attract a new section, they must come within the scope of the arbitration. But that arbitration involves no censure or slight on any one of the sections, who are not in the least forced to adopt the same attitude.
>
> If there is any feeling in his mind against the fourth party (which I have no ground for believing) it is probably due to the great impudence with which Wolff talks about him. I have no doubt Wolff's language gets round to his ears, & he thinks it represents the feelings of all Wolff's friends.[73]

Northcote certainly had reason to think it represented the feelings of at least Gorst; whose own contribution to Churchill's autumn season of political demonstrations at Woodstock was a comprehensive attack on his chief in the Commons.

The autumnal pre-sessional atmosphere was now heavy with forebodings about Gladstone's revenge for the loss of the Irish compensation measure. 'I hope this time,' Salisbury told Disraeli. 'the Whig resistance will be something more than a Brookes's pout. All the Whigs I have heard, or heard of are getting very savage.' A big new Irish land bill would indeed test their nerve. It was also a little embarrassing that Mudford was taking an unsympathetic line on Irish landlords. 'What has happened to the "Standard"?' Salisbury asked Disraeli. 'Has Dilke bought it?'[74] Disraeli was in truth near to reaching the end of any notions of continuing as leader in 1881. A 'disagreeable correspondence' with the duke of Beaufort led him to confess to Rowton: 'I feel convinced by it, that it will be utterly vain for me to lead the House of Lords in the coming Session, where must be, necessarily, much compromise & management.' The class represented by the duke 'are not only highly prejudiced, but so inconsistent, that it is impossible to deal with them'.[75] At the end of October he '"resumed the pen" as Grub St. used to say' after three weeks' illness and 'much suffering' with 'volcanic eruptions' and 'disturbances of nature in the shape of very distressing asthma'. In low spirits (possibly suffering from authorial depression – he had recently completed *Endymion*), he confided to Cairns: 'I am not a political pessimist or a disappointed politician, for I think we have had a fair chance & share of serving our Sov. & country, – but with nearly 50 years experience of public affairs, I confess I look on the present with anxiety – not to say gloom.'[76]

Bad reports from Cranbrook on Disraeli's health led Richmond to raise the issue with Cairns that 'we ought to be prepared for Beaconsfield retiring from public life'. Disraeli himself made it clear that *Endymion*, for which Rowton negotiated a £10,000 advance, 'will facilitate my retirement from political life'.[77] Richmond considered that 'Salisbury was the person we must look to'. Richmond told Cranbrook that he had 'had some conversation with Salisbury, most confidential, upon the matter, and that I fancied he would not be unwilling to undertake the office.' The peers were 'rather odd to deal with and whenever anything is done, it must be done cautiously'.[78] Richmond confined himself to the question of the Conservative leadership in the Lords. But Cranbrook was looking far beyond that. He saw Salisbury on 24 October and discussed future arrangements.

> I found that Beaconsfield had urged his succession and it seems to me the natural & inevitable. He is willing to place himself at the disposal of the party if Northcote's feelings are respected. It is obvious that with all his admirable qualities Northcote has not obtained that sort of confidence from the party wh alone could justify his obtaining the Chiefship. A cave exists & will grow. Even Holland complained to me of his weakness. He is often right when they think him wrong but he has the appearance of yielding wh. displeases.[79]

When Salisbury spoke at Woodstock on 30 November on the theme that Liberal impolicy had created two competing governments in Ireland, he was hailed openly by Churchill as the heir to Disraeli's leadership. Salisbury made no demur; he referred to Northcote as leader of the Commons 'but went no further'.[80]

Before departing 'incontinently' from Blenheim to Nice, Salisbury left Disraeli with a few thoughts which would not much have lightened his despondency. The Irish landlord 'has got his tail between his legs; & is disposed to capitulate'. The spirit which dictated the Orange 'invasion' of Mayo in support of Lord Erne's beleaguered agent, Captain Boycott, was 'a mere flash'. Even the Ulster landlords were losing heart. 'It is very inexpedient', insisted Salisbury, 'that they should be allowed to give way. Both for the sake of the party, & their own sake, they should hold their pretensions as high as possible.' It was indeed 'very desirable now that many of them should proceed to eviction, which will bring about a collision, & force the Government either to act or confess its incapacity.' This was very much in Salisbury's best ruthless style. (None of his own 20,202 acres, it might be remarked, was in Ireland.) He matched it by discounting the Whig factor. 'I think the movement among the Whigs towards us is growing in strength, though not rapidly.' And Salisbury in any case doubted its 'affecting at present either those who have office or hope for it'. He had heard of symptoms indicating instability in Argyll, Brassey, and Evelyn Ashley among office-holders; but 'all depends on the course of events in Ireland.'

This hard line doctrinally emphasised Salisbury's distance from Northcotism. Salisbury proceeded delicately to transform doctrinal distance into what amounted, in the circumstances of the questions about the party leadership, to infinity:

> There is no real danger of Randolph Churchill's breaking away. But he must be watched & humoured – for he is not a man who calculates consequences, when his temper is moved. There must have been something unsound in Northcote's plan of dealing with him – for it is evident that his feelings towards N. are very sore. The chief grievance I gather to be that Northcote lets him & his friends imagine he intends to support them in some move or other; & then when the debate come on, he announces for the first time that he is unable to agree with them. This gives bitter offence – much greater than would be caused by a private intimation that he could not support them.
>
> Gorst appears hearty enough: but there evidently has been some grievance as to his treatment several years ago: but that I think does not influence him at present. Percy holds the same sort of tone about Northcote that Churchill does – so that the trouble does not arise entirely from the latter's idiosyncracy.[81]

3

Northcote himself, meanwhile, contemplated a 'most anxious Session', full of problems about law and order in Ireland, Parnell's trial for inciting lawlessness, tenant right questions; and offered pre-sessional dinner to the peers as well as his own commoners, since Disraeli's new house at Seamore Place was not yet ready. His own notions about Ireland could hardly have been more in contrast to Salisbury's advocacy of collision-course evictions. An article by a Miss O'Brien in the *Nineteenth Century* inspired Northcote with ideas of government land purchase and resale in small lots: 'Let a public Commission be intrusted with moderate funds, out of Church surplus or a Parliamentary grant, to purchase suitable plots of land at a fair price, and to resell them in small allotments, taking care to reserve a proportion for labourers' cottages and gardens.' Assisted emigration would be far too unpopular to be taken up. A 'Settlers at Home' policy on the basis of amending the Land Act would be much better, if only to be 'useful as a safety valve'.[82] Cairns was not inclined to believe that Gladstone could be diverted from anything less than a bid now to achieve what he had failed to achieve in 1870. He did not see that 'any Land Bill' would be a great difficulty for the Liberals. 'I think there will be a strong feeling among Irish Landlords to accept any Bill, not altogether unreasonably, rather than let the relations of Landlord & Tenant continue as they are.'[83]

Disraeli set aside Northcote's busy expedients and Cairns's Irish despondency: he was much possessed of Salisbury's defiant thinking. 'If Honesty is the best policy, Cowardice is certainly the worst.' He thought landlords 'ought not to have diminished their utmost legal pretensions. If some evictions had produced outrages, they, & their consequences, wd. have prevented the insufferable reign of terror wh. now prevails – & seems established.'[84] Cairns confirmed that the state of Ireland 'becomes daily more alarming, & the lawlessness more chronic & confirmed': as indeed both Forster and Parnell had earlier predicted as believers in Gladstone's 'argument from terror'. '*Our* great difficulty', in Cairns's view,

> will be in knowing how to deal with the Government proposals as to the land when they come to be made. We shall have the Ulster Landlords –, strong supporters of ours; & generally erring on the side not of cowardice but of rashness – looking at the subject through the light of tht wh is so unintelligible to the minds of Englishmen, & especially of English landlords, the Custom of Ulster Tenant right, & great caution will be needed to prevent any appearances of dissension on our part, or of (what wd be even more dangerous) – our *party* setting itself to weaken the Ulster Custom.[85]

It was now known that the 'Three F's' associated with Ulster custom – free sale, fair rent, fixity of tenure – would be recommended to the government (to Gladstone's incredulity) by the Bessborough Commission; and Cairns was annoyed by Northcote's and Lowther's 'discounting the question'. At Bristol Northcote had mocked them as Fraud, Force, and Folly. 'Their joke', Cairns was pained to say, 'is not a good one, & does infinite harm in Ulster.'[86]

Nor was Disraeli in any joking mood. 'Affairs are critical: some expect a disruption before the meeting of parliament', he informed Cairns. 'I do not, but the opinion is entertained by persons of authority.' Under such circumstances of a possible crumbling of the government's support, it was 'of the utmost importance that we shd be discreet. Let us have no pilot balloons from the Conservative camp.' 'Our friends' were 'too fond of these essays & airing their remedial theories. Every act is noted, & word is watched, by the enemy.' Disraeli was concerned particularly to keep Richmond quiet. 'You will find him very much changed in these matters', he warned Cairns, '& projecting a report founded, as I collect, on what, in barbaric tongue, are called "the three Fs".'[87] Disraeli had in mind elaborate plans to avoid a frontal attack at the beginning of the session, 'with the Irish operating in the rear, & looking like allies'. The tactic must be to manoeuvre so as to have 'the moderate Whigs, secretly or openly, on our side, & the Irish with Gladstone against us'. Meanwhile, a frontal attack in the Lords, where there were 'no Irish rebels to confuse the issue', would begin the session by inflicting a defeat on the government without coming into collision with the Commons. The Land Bill could not reach the Lords until May or June.[88]

All such careful preparations, however, would be wasted if the Whigs did, indeed, merely 'pout'; or if the Irish landlords failed to live up to Salisbury's requirement that for the sake of the Conservative party as much as for their own sake they should hold their pretensions as high as possible. Northcote reported disquieting news as to the great differences of opinion 'among some of our friends as to the line we are to take on the Irish measures'. 'The Fourth Party are for no compromise.' They denounced the 'frightened landowners' of whom they considered Gibson and Plunket to be the representatives. Gibson and Plunket were indeed ready to accept and support a 'fairly satisfactory' bill.[89] Gorst, in one of his forays as principal agent, offered intelligence from Lancashire and Yorkshire that while the government's Irish policy had produced 'much dissatisfaction among educated people even of their own party', this discontent had 'not gone very deep into the population'. There seemed no strong popular excitement about Irish affairs at all; 'still less any marked revulsion of feeling against Gladstone.' In any case the Ulster landlords seem 'ready to jump at any compromise the government might offer'.[90] From Nice (whence he was determined not to return until it was climatically safe, citing in mitigation the precedent of Cairns's staying the whole spring of 1870 at Menton) Salisbury sadly gathered that Ulster 'has surrendered to the three Fs: & with Ulster doubtless will go Gibson Cairns & Richmond – & a good number of our Peers. . . . Bad for us, & bad for them!' They thus 'sacrificed every vestige of principle, on which they can fight for proprietary rights; & we are left with the choice of giving in, or else of being Hibernia Hiberniores.'[91]

By the new year the extent of the debilitating allurement of the 'Three Fs' was only too apparent. The Ulster party, Salisbury agreed with Disraeli, had 'sold the pass' on the question of compulsory arbitration as to rents: Belmore, Castlereagh, Lifford, Close, Portarlington, 'probably Abercorn & his sons', Gibson, Clarke; '& in the end I suspect by Cairns & Richmond'. Nevertheless, Salisbury agreed that 'we must resist any departure from sound principle: though we may be beaten in the attempt'. Salisbury could not see his way 'to accepting any system of compulsory arbitration rents'. 'Our only hope is in the extravagant demands of the Irish. I earnestly hope that they will reject any land bill that the Whigs can be pressured to pass.' Salisbury gloomily predicted 'many damaging admissions from Conservative outsiders in both Houses'.[92] Balfour recorded a conversation with Disraeli on 28 January:

> He is very gloomy about the Irish Land Bill. He anticipates that the Govs proposal will embody the 3 F's or something equivalent, that the Irish landlords will on the whole support such a solution of the question, & that the H. of L. will not resist any measure wh. the Irish landlords are prepared to accept. I hazarded the observation that I hoped the party would adhere to the plain principle of property & freedom of contract. Upon which he said – 'we shall, but we shall be beaten. I do not for my part,' he went on, 'mean to give an inch: we can but die like gentlemen.'[93]

Epilogue 1881: 'What is it that lies before us?'

Irish land would be the one substantial measure for the 1881 session. Gladstone presented it as a further development of the principles of 1870 to meet the wants of landlord and tenant. There was also to be county government reform in Ireland, with a view to extending the formation of habits of local self-government; which was susceptible to Conservative forebodings of a drift into legislative separation. Disraeli could point to the pertinence of his letter to the duke of Marlborough of March 1880; but he could not hope for much in the way of serious Conservative defiance in the manner of the previous session. Salibury's obstinate unwillingness to quit the Riviera exacerbated Disraeli's gloom. Balfour reported back to Nice:

> I went to see Dizzy yesterday afternoon. He grumbled a good deal at your absence: though I could not make out that he really had any strong and definite reasons for wishing you to come back. The alleged reasons which most nearly answered to this description were (1) that he contemplated passing a censure in the H. of Lords on the proposed action of the Govt. in abandoning Candahar; and that he should like to have your assistance and advice in doing so and (2) that he thought that Greek affairs demanded your presence here . . . the impression left on my mind was that Ld. B. was more influenced by the personal desire of confidential intercourse with you, resulting in part from the contempt with which he regards a large number of his late colleagues.

Disraeli was sure that there was 'a serious danger of Fenian outrages in this country – "ending perhaps in massacre"'. He had received confidential information from sources to which the government also had access 'that a serious conspiracy of some kind was on foot'; and he also learned 'with dismay' that unlike his own government in 1867, the present administration had no informer in the ranks of the enemy.[94]

Possibly ministers were suitably alarmed at this menace; certainly, they were by now alarmed at the deterioration of public order in Ireland. They decided to strike with efficacious precision at the fomentors of disorder. Forster announced special and stringent measures to secure life and property in Ireland. This jolted politics in the Commons into new shapes. The Parnellite Irish offered furious resistance. Their arts of parliamentary obstruction brought business to a stop. One notorious sitting lasted an unprecedented 41½ hours. Conservatives were willing enough to assist Forster in the matter of suppressing Irish agrarian crime. However, they found themselves in a quandary when Speaker Brand, after consultation with Gladstone, produced a scheme for a summary system of '*Clôture*' to restrict debate and defeat Irish obstruction. The House was now, as Brand pointed out to Northcote on 19 January, 'through the activity of this Party, paralyzed'.[95] And there was no doubt that the longer the measures were delayed in Westminster the less efficacious they would be in Ireland; as Davitt well appreciated. On the other hand, interference with hallowed parliamentary custom was a sad and serious thing which gave pause. The Fourth Party, skilled obstructors themselves, were against. To Salisbury it was 'the old story – Gladstone is master of the country but cannot manage the House of Commons. His great quality is eloquent indistinctiveness of expression. It deceives the electoral gull easily: but of course it breaks down when the draughtsman has to translate it into clauses.' Salisbury hoped that the party would 'not go too far' in accepting closure. He wanted a distinction drawn between parliamentary functions necessary for the working of the executive machine 'and those which, having no object but to change laws under which we are living quite tolerably, can be suspended certainly without serious injury, & often with great advantage'. Salisbury would limit closure to a first category restricted to supply, mutiny, continuance bills, and measures declared by the Crown to be necessary for the maintenance of the public peace. 'It is not our interest to grease the wheels of *all* legislation: on the contrary, it may do all the Conservative classes in the country infinite harm.'[96] Salisbury pressed the point also upon Disraeli of a 'press of democratic legislation thrown upon the House of Lords which would strain our powers of resistance' if closure were allowed for ordinary bills.[97] Disraeli was uneasy: 'the business is too vast & grave to settle in this off-hand manner.'[98] He told Balfour that he had 'given Northcote advice "of so pressing a kind that he hoped it would be taken as an instruction" to the effect that no assurance of any kind of support was to be given to the Govt. in the meanwhile.'[99]

Gladstone's proposal of a flat-rate two-thirds majority was considered by a meeting of Disraeli, the Commons' members of the late cabinet, Beresford-Hope, Walpole, Chaplin, and – a sign of the times – Randolph Churchill. Only Walpole and Manners were for agreement. 'On the whole however it was decided that the scheme was inadmissible & N. was requested to communicate the fact to W.E.G. without making any definite proposal himself. W.E.G. expressed', Balfour was informed, 'great disappointment.'[100] A party meeting was arranged for 3 February in the face of what Northcote regarded as Gladstone's 'astounding' bid to ram the new rules of debate through by an unlimited sitting. In the event Speaker Brand intervened and closed the sitting on his own authority. Northcote marched indignantly out of the chamber, followed by most of the Conservatives present. Brand proposed new rules as to 'urgency' agreed by Gladstone, which Northcote amended as to details and mode of operation. Balfour complained that 'our Parliamentary system has been revolutionised'.[101] The 'urgency' rules remained at the discretion of the speaker: an 'arbitrary initiative he was loth to exercise'.[102] Forster got his bill through (it passed the Lords and became law in three days flat) after a paroxysm of Irish defiance: in scandalous and disquieting scenes of clamour and tumult, first Dillon, then Parnell (not to be outdone), and in sequence practically the entire body of the Parnellite Irish was removed from the chamber.

Amid the distressing turbulence Northcote kept in view the larger themes. A party meeting of Commons' members on 3 February at Disraeli's new house in Curzon Street approved the amendments which were successfully attached to the speaker's new rules. Northcote pleaded to the chief:

> I hope you will say some general words of encouragement to our party, who are standing together most manfully, and are exercising great forbearance toward the Government in the interest of law and order – at the same time they should be warned that the time may soon come when they will have to exercise other qualities and to guard the Constitution against the supporters of the Govt. if not against the Govt. themselves.
>
> While supporting the measures for Law and Order, we must be most careful not to commit ourselves prematurely about the Land Bill.[103]

As Sir Herbert Maxwell recalled, it was a scene very different from that of the Bridgewater House meeting. Instead of that noble 'vast saloon' with its sober colourings and mellowed gilding, now there was 'the newly-upholstered drawing-room, tricked out with blue and gold, and gaudily carpeted. Beaconsfield stood upon a high stool placed at an angle between the front and back rooms – a lean, dark, feeble figure, against a tinselly background.' It was thus 'that the rank and file of the Conservative party – in great measure his own creation – were to look upon Benjamin Disraeli for the last time. Few of those present ever saw him again.'[104] No doubt Disraeli encouraged and warned in due course. He was sharply critical, however, of Northcote's proposed response to a further initiative by Gladstone on the rules of debate question. Northcote wanted a party meeting at the Carlton to approve the tactic of giving Gladstone assurance of general support in the case of such a 'national emergency as makes it absolutely necessary to lay aside every consideration of an ordinary character'. Disraeli could not approve of Northcote's amendment: 'It does not seem to me to hit the nail on the head; to be any security against future unconstitutional acts; & to be rather a panegyric than a protest.'[105] Northcote was satisfyingly stiffer against Gladstone's next attempt to put pressure on the Conservatives in the Commons.[106]

By the time Gladstone introduced the Irish Land Bill on 7 April Disraeli was sinking. He made his last appearance in the Lords on 15 March, to support a vote of condolence on the assassination of the Emperor Alexander II of Russia. Northcote transferred negotiations on questions of concerted action on the Land Bill to Salisbury. 'We ought to act in concert, and to understand whether you are calling for trumps or not.' It was a bill 'rooted and grounded in injustice'. But, 'of course, we might accept it as a framework on which to mend, and darn, and cut out, and sew in: but the difficulty of making a good job will be very great.' How to resist the 'first introduction of dangerous principles of a highly infectious character'? It was certain that it would not content the Home Rulers, who saw it merely as a step to subsequent agitation. A 'bad moral lesson' had been given to Ireland '(and England too)' by the success of the Land League terror. 'I hope', concluded Northcote, 'the Chief is really making progress. One cannot feel sure against a relapse at any moment; but I am veering round to a hopeful view again.'[107] Smith was pressing amendments beneficial to tenants but hostile to any transfer of a large share of property from owner to occupier without fair compensation. But Northcote could see 'economical objections to the measure' even so: 'it is likely to drive capital out of Ireland: it will encourage shiftless, shambling habits: it will set a premium upon agitation: it will probably do more harm than good to the labourers etc. etc.' Northcote would be 'sorry to give the enemy occasion to say that we were resisting a measure of general advantage because it would be inconvenient to a small body of landowners'.

Northcote's great worry was about the steadiness of 'our House of Commons party' if it came to a fight on the second reading in that House: 'I am not sure our Ulster members will stand by us if we do: while, on the other hand, I think a good many of our English members will be disgusted if we don't.'[108] Salisbury deprecated such fears; and recommended that concert would be most effective on the strength of determined resistance in the Commons rather than the Lords. 'I fear the return of the East wind will be dangerous for the Chief.'[109] Richmond rejoiced at Disraeli's powers of resistance. 'The party will be spared the very invidious task of selecting a leader out of that list of Eminent Statesmen that appeared in the Times the other day!!'[110] *The Times* of 11 April had tipped Richmond as a likely compromise leader under whom the two strong men, Cairns and Salisbury, could agree to serve. Northcote was ostentatiously not mentioned.

Salisbury was right about the east wind. Disraeli died at Curzon Street on 19 April. Rowton, Barrington, and Rose were with him at the last. The queen had been sending bunches of cheering primroses from Windsor and Osborne. Gladstone's offer of a public funeral was declined with thanks. One of the two wreaths sent by the queen to the funeral at Hughenden on 26 April was of primroses, with the dedication: 'His favourite flowers, from Osborne, a tribute of affection from Queen Victoria.' Among the mourners were all his old colleagues save Cranbrook, away in Italy. Derby attended. Abergavenny was there. Gladstone was prevented by business. Salisbury wrote to Raikes of the 'very striking sight', 'inexpressibly sad'. It seemed 'like the passing away of an epoch. What is it that lies before us?'[111]

Notes and References

1 J. Cornford, 'The transformation of Conservatism in the late nineteenth century', *Victorian Studies* (1963), 51.
2 See above, 330–1.
3 *AR*, 1882, 181.
4 A. Frisby, 'Has Conservatism increased in England since the last Reform Bill?' *Fortnightly Review* (1881), 829: 'taking a comprehensive view of the whole of the constituencies which were contested by Liberals and Tories in both 1868 and 1880, the percentage of Tory voters has increased from 44.3 to 45.9 and . . . this growth is due entirely to the rapid advance of Tory principles among the very large constituencies'.
5 Salisbury to Cairns, 17 April 1882; PRO, Cairns 30/51/6.
6 *AR*, 1882, 161 (4 Oct.) 8.
7 A. Lang, *Life of . . . Sir Stafford Northcote, First Earl of Iddesleigh* (1890), 315.
8 Taylor to Rowton, 12 May 1880; HP, B/XI/J/65.
9 A. Austin, *Autobiography* (1911), ii, 132.
10 Rowton to queen. 19 May 1880 (draft); HP, B/XII/J/103b.
11 H. St. J. Raikes, *Life and Letters of H.C. Raikes* (1898), 157–8.
12 Lang. *Iddesleigh*, 321; Abergavenny to Beaconsfield, 7 July 1880; HP, B/XXI/A/64.
13 Cairns to Beaconsfield, 18 Dec. 1880; HP, B/XX/Ca275. Winn, MP for North Lincolnshire, had applied for a peerage in 1880. His seat was Nostell Priory, Wakefield.
14 Lord Chilston, *W.H. Smith* (1965), 161.
15 Northcote to Beaconsfield, 7 July 1880; BL, Iddesleigh 50018, 213.
16 Smith to Beaconsfield, 4 Aug. 1880. HP, B/XXI/S/337.
17 P. Cohen, *Disraeli's Child. A History of the Conservative and Unionist Party Organisation* (1964) i, 52–3; E.J. Feuchtwanger, *Disraeli, Democracy and the Tory Party* (Oxford, 1968), 145, 148–9.
18 Feuchtwanger, *Disraeli, Democracy and the Tory Party*, 147.
19 R.F. Foster, *Lord Randolph Churchill* (Oxford, 1981), 77; 'Tory Democracy and political elitism', 12.
20 Dyke to Beaconsfield, 1 Nov. [1880]; HP, B/XXI/D/492.
21 Gorst to Beaconsfield, 24 Feb. [1881]; *HP*, B/XXI/G/264; Feuchtwanger, *Disraeli, Democracy and the Tory Party*, 150–1.
22 *Ibid.*, 147.
23 HP, B/XX/Ce/175/6. Extract from Northcote's diary in Rowton's hand.
24 Lady Salisbury to Beaconsfield, 14 April and 15 June [1880] HP, B/XX/Ce/334, 339.

25 Lady Salisbury to Beaconsfield, 29 April and 12 May [80]. HP, B/XX/Ce/336, 337.
26 Lang, *Iddesleigh*, 317.
27 W.B. Gwyn, *Democracy and the Cost of Politics in Britain* (1962), 112.
28 Lang, *Iddesleigh*, 314.
29 Northcote to Beaconsfield, 22 May 1880; BL, Iddesleigh 50018, 189.
30 Northcote to Beaconsfield, 23 June 1880; BL, Iddesleigh 50018, 201. For a conspectus survey which treats Northcote more tenderly than is customary, see B. Coleman, *Conservatism and the Conservative Party in Nineteenth-Century Britain* (1988).
31 See above, 112.
32 HP, B/XX/Ce/175/76.
33 Buckle, ii, 1460.
34 W.S. Churchill, *Lord Randolph Churchill* (1907), 127–8.
35 Northcote to Gorst, 11 Sept. 1880; BL, Balfour 49791, 1.
36 Feuchtwanger, *Disraeli, Democracy and the Tory Party*, 148–9.
37 Gorst to Balfour, 15 Sept. 1880; BL, Balfour 49791, 5.
38 Rowton to Beaconsfield, 25 Oct. 1880; HP, B/XX/Co/150.
39 Churchill, *Randolph Churchill*, 126–7.
40 Buckle, ii, 1461.
41 So also John Manners: R. Faber, *Young England* (1987), 258.
42 Foster, *Randolph Churchill*, 70.
43 Richmond to Cairns, 29 May 1880; PRO, Cairns 30/51/4.
44 See Salisbury to Balfour, 18 March 1880; BL, Balfour 49688, 13–17. Salisbury to Northcote, 20 March 1880; BL, Iddesleigh 50020, 1.
45 *AR*, 1880, 82.
46 Salisbury to Balfour, 16 June 1880; BL, Balfour 49688, 27.
47 Northcote to Beaconsfield, 2 July 1880; BL, Iddesleigh 50018, 208.
48 Rowton to Beaconsfield, 3 July 1880; HP, B/XX/Co/133.
49 Buckle, ii, 1453–4.
50 Northcote to Beaconsfield, 6 July 1880; BL, Iddesleigh 50018, 210.
51 Buckle, ii, 1454.
52 See above, 153–4.
53 Rowton to Beaconsfield, 8 July 1880; HP, B/XX/Co/136.
54 *HP*, B/XX/Ce/175 and 176.
55 Rowton to Beaconsfield, 9 July 1880; *HP*, B/XX/Co/137.
56 Rowton to Beaconsfield, 12 July 1880; *HP*, B/XX/Co/139.
57 Richmond to Cairns, 11 July 1880; PRO, Cairns 30/51/4.
58 Northcote to Beaconsfield, 9 July 1880; BL, Iddesleigh 50018, 215.
59 Beaconsfield to Cairns, 20 July 1880; PRO, Cairns 30/51/1.
60 *Ibid.*
61 Northcote to Beaconsfield, 4 Sept. 1880; BL, Iddesleigh 50018, 228.
62 Rowton to Beaconsfield, 20 Aug. 1880; HP, B/XX/Co/145.
63 Beaconsfield to Cairns, 19 Aug. 1880; PRO, Cairns 30/51/1.
64 Beaconsfield to Cairns, 1 Sept. 1880; PRO, Cairns 30/51/1.
65 Northcote to Beaconsfield, 27 Aug. 1880; BL, Iddesleigh 50018, 224.
66 Richmond to Cairns, 25 Aug. 1880; PRO, Cairns 30/51/4.
67 Buckle, ii, 1453.
68 Northcote to Beaconsfield, 7 June 1880; BL. Iddesleigh 50018, 196.
69 Northcote to Beaconsfield, 12 June 1880; BL, Iddesleigh 50018, 199.

70 Rowton to Beaconsfield, 20 Aug. 1880; HP, B/XX/Co/145.
71 Clarke, defeated at Southwark in April, won a Plymouth seat in June 1880.
72 Salisbury to Balfour, 2 Sept. 1880; BL, Balfour 49688, 29.
73 Salisbury to Balfour 5 Oct. 1880; BL, Balfour 49688, 33.
74 Salisbury to Beaconsfield, 14 Nov. 1880; HP, B/XX/Ce/147.
75 Beaconsfield to Rowton, 14 Sept. 80; HP, B/XX/D/307.
76 Beaconsfield to Cairns, 29 Oct. 1880; PRO, Cairns 30/51/1.
77 Beaconsfield to Cairns, 7 Dec. 1880; PRO, Cairns 30/51/1.
78 Richmond to Cairns, 27 Oct. 1880; PRO, Cairns 30/51/4.
79 Hardy, *Diary*, 460–1.
80 Foster, *Randolph Churchill*, 75.
81 Salisbury to Beaconsfield, 1 Dec. 1880; HP, B/XX/Ce/148.
82 Northcote to Cairns, 18 Dec. 1880; PRO, Cairns 30/51/5.
83 Cairns to Beaconsfield, 3 Dec. 1880; HP, B/XX/Ca/272.
84 Beaconsfield to Cairns, 7 Dec. 1880; PRO, Cairns 30/51/1.
85 Cairns to Beaconsfield, 11 Dec. 1880; HP, B/XX/Ca/273.
86 Cairns to Beaconsfield, 15 Dec. 1880; HP, B/XX/Ca/274.
87 Beaconsfield to Cairns, 12 Dec. 1880; PRO, Cairns 30/51/1.
88 Beaconsfield to Cairns, 16 Dec. 1880; PRO, Cairns 30/51/1.
89 Northcote to Beaconsfield, 18 Dec. 1880; BL, Iddesleigh 50018, 237.
90 Gorst to Beaconsfield, 29 Dec. 1880; HP, B/XXI/G/263.
91 Salisbury to Beaconsfield, 20 Dec. 1880; HP, B/XX/Ce/149.
92 Salisbury to Beaconsfield, 2 Jan. [1881]; HP, B/XX/Ce/131.
93 Balfour to Salisbury, 29 Jan. 1881; BL, Balfour 49688, 41.
94 Balfour to Salisbury, 24 Jan. 1881; BL, Balfour 49688, 41.
95 Brand to Northcote, 19 Jan. 1881; BL, Iddesleigh 50021, 181.
96 Salisbury to Balfour, 15 Jan. 1881; BL, Balfour 49688, 37.
97 Salisbury to Beaconsfield, 2 Feb. 1881; HP, B/XX/Ce/150.
98 Beaconsfield to Northcote [20 Jan. 1881]; BL, Iddesleigh 50018, 248.
99 Balfour to Salisbury, 24 Jan. 1881; BL, Balfour 49688, 41.
100 Balfour to Salisbury, 28 Jan. 1881; BL, Balfour 49688, 41.
101 Balfour to Salisbury, 3 Feb. 81; BL, Balfour 49688, 50.
102 A.L. Lowell, *The Government of England* (New York, 1920), i, 295.
103 Northcote to Beaconsfield, 2 Feb. 1881; BL, Iddesleigh 50019, 254.
104 H. Maxwell, *William Henry Smith* (1893), ii, 48.
105 Northcote to Beaconsfield, 17 Feb. 1881; Beaconsfield to Northcote, 21 Feb. 1881; BL, Iddesleigh 50018, 258, 260.
106 Buckle, ii, 1479.
107 Northcote to Salisbury, 15 April 1881; BL, Iddesleigh 50020, 3.
108 Northcote to Cairns, 16 April, 1881; PRO, Cairns 30/51/5.
109 Salisbury to Northcote, 17 April, 1881; BL, Iddesleigh 50020, 6
110 Richmond to Cairns, 17 April 1881; PRO, Cairns 30/51/4.
111 Buckle, ii, 1491–2.

Index